DECISIVE DECADES

nelson

DECISIVE DECADES

A History of the
Twentieth Century
for Canadians

A. B. Hodgetts
J. D. Burns

Design by Michael van Elsen

Typeset, printed and bound in Canada by The Bryant Press Limited

Typeface: 10/12 pt. Caledonia

Stock: 55 lb. Lithopaque

PUBLISHER'S FOREWORD

The first edition of *Decisive Decades*, published in 1960, was written by A. B. Hodgetts, then senior history master at Trinity College School in Port Hope, Ontario, and now Director of The Canada Studies Foundation. Mr. Hodgetts' fluent writing style and fine interpretive ability made this book an instant success, and its popularity has never waned.

In order to produce the current edition of *Decisive Decades*, Mr. Hodgetts enlisted the help of J. D. Burns, also associated with Trinity College School. Mr. Burns has ably undertaken all revisions and the writing of new material. He has brought the book up to date with a new section on the sixties and the seventies and has skilfully reduced and revised the original text in the light of the present day. As a result the new edition maintains the high standard of the original and extends the scope without increasing the length.

Mr. Burns wishes to acknowledge his gratitude to A. B. Hodgetts for his inspiration and encouragement; to A. C. Scott, Headmaster of Trinity College School for his unfailing co-operation; to Mary Robson for patience and dedication in her editorial role; and to his wife and family for their understanding and forbearance.

TABLE OF CONTENTS

LIST OF MAPS

part 1
rendezvous with destiny

1   DOLDRUM DAYS

A Prelude to Progress

'Anyone who has studied the corrupt methods by which Canadian elections are won will admit that five or six million dollars wisely spent in that country would secure a majority in Parliament pledged to join Canada to our United States of America.'

Here is an insult if ever there was one: Canadian politicians to be bribed, Canadian votes for sale and some arrogant American writer suggesting that a few million dollars could buy this country! Can you imagine the furor if *The New York Times, Life* or some other well-known American publication dared to carry such a statement about Canada today? The very thought is out of the question and yet this insulting editorial did appear in a January 1890 issue of the New York *World*.

There was, of course, a storm of protest in Canada, but it assumed a somewhat strange and most interesting form. The suggestion that our politicians could be bribed aroused but little resentment. Canadian newspapers had been making these same accusations time and again and were to continue doing so for many years. Joseph Pulitzer and the editorial staff of the colourful *World* were let off lightly—Canadians did not expect much friendship from across the border in those days—and Canadian anger was directed against the traitors in their own country!

'So, they plan to buy our fair land,' wrote the editor of the Toronto *Empire* on February 7. 'These plotters are contemplating the wholesale purchase of our electors to return members of Parliament ready to surrender Canada to a foreign power. And for such ideas as this we have only to blame the dastardly traitors from our own country who have, by their secret information and encouragement, invited this insulting attack.'

Annexation: A Debate on Canada's Future

True it was that an agitation had arisen in Canada, for the fifth time in less than one hundred years, to join this country to the United States, and the editor of the *Empire* was probably right in saying that these 'traitors' had put ideas into the minds of our American neighbours. The 'Annexation Movement', as it is called, was revived during the closing decade of the nineteenth century because conditions in Canada were so very discouraging. A great many Canadians thought that the solution to their problems lay in closer trade relations with the prosperous United States. A small but determined group led by Goldwin Smith, a former history professor at Oxford University, and Edward Farrer, editor of the Toronto *Globe*, were prepared to go much further and openly urged that

Canada join the United States. These men were the 'continentalists' of their day
and formed the Continental Union Association to 'reunite the English-speaking
people of North America'. Completely free trade with the United States became
the main issue in the federal election of 1891 and many people freely admitted
that the closer economic ties which they favoured might lead one day to the
political union of the two countries.

After the Civil War the rapid completion of western settlement caused by the
vast immigrant flood from Europe, together with tremendous industrial development, changed the midcontinental United States limits of 'Manifest Destiny' to
a North American and global concept. Consequently many American political
and business leaders were more than willing to assist the Annexation Movement.

The New York branch of the C.U.A. included in its membership leading
statesmen of imperialistic tendencies. They were led by Theodore Roosevelt,
aggressive wielder of 'big stick' diplomacy, John Hay, diplomat of the 'Open
Door' policy in China, and Elihu Root, able jurist whose work on the Platt
Amendment to the Cuban constitution of 1901 turned the country into a U.S.
protectorate. The business magnates were represented by Andrew Carnegie,
steel tycoon, John Jacob Astor, giant of real estate and transportation, and
CharlesTiffany of international jewellery fame. These industrial emperors with
their monopolistic operations and international connections foreshadowed the
vast multinational corporations that are of such concern to Canadians today. Nor
was the press neglected; it was represented by Charles Dana and Joseph
Pulitzer, powerful newspaper owners of the time. The intellectual approach to
continental union was taken by the famous Seth Low of Columbia University.
Canadian politicians, often more interested in campaign funds than in the
reunion of English-speaking people in North America, slipped across the border
to Andrew Carnegie's home or to Dana's offices at the New York *Sun* for secret
meetings.

Annexation of Canada was openly discussed in the cabinet and Senate of the
United States. The Secretary of the Navy estimated that 'four small armies of not
more than 25,000 men could take Canada easily', and Robert Sherman, chairman
of the Senate's Committee on Foreign Relations—which frequently considered
plans to absorb Canada—held that political union had to come or war was
inevitable.

Patriotic Canadians conducted a vigorous counterattack against the Annexa-
tion Movement. Secret agents worked their way into meetings of the Continental
Union Association, bringing back reports and photographed evidence of a
'dangerous conspiracy'. Edward Farrer secretly published a series of pamphlets
advising American officials how a U.S. 'takeover' of Canada might be achieved.
One of the pamphlets was stolen and produced with telling effect against the
Liberals by Sir John A. Macdonald before a political rally in the old Princess
Theatre in Toronto. Large meetings were organized by the Sons of England, the
St. George's Society and the Imperial Federation League with the favourite
orator being Colonel George Denison, the bitter opponent of Goldwin Smith. Sir
John A. Macdonald, the Conservative Prime Minister of Canada, and Oliver

Mowat, the Liberal Premier of Ontario, vied with each other in making patriotic speeches and both coined, at about the same time, the now famous phrase: 'A British subject I was born, a British subject I will die.' The dedication of war memorials, especially at places where American troops had been beaten, suddenly became popular and the War of 1812 was fought all over again in colourful ceremonies at Niagara-on-the-Lake, Chateauguay and Lundy's Lane. Annexationists were dismissed from their jobs, compelled to resign from clubs and fraternal organizations, howled down in tumultuous meetings and frequently driven from halls with surplus local produce.

Contestants on both sides of this intense argument did Canada a great deal of harm. As men so often do when they become too deeply involved in a cause, the leaders of the Annexation Movement and their opponents became angry and unreasonable. In their speeches and writings they helped to create damaging prejudices which were to reappear time and again at critical times in our history.

The groups opposing closer ties with the United States advocated a loyalty primarily to the British Empire rather than to Canada. They seemed to reflect a lack of faith in Canada's future as a truly independent country. To them the United States was an aggressive, greedy nation with a foreign policy hostile to English interests. It was a politically corrupt nation with lawless and violent tendencies.

The groups favouring commercial or political union with the United States saw it as a land of unlimited opportunity and accelerating progress. They were followers of the American dream of settlement, expansion and prosperity. They wanted Canada to share this destiny of success. They saw England as an imperialistic power dedicated to wars of Empire and exploitation. Its leaders were contemptuous of colonial Canadian life and only too willing to sacrifice Canadian interests in the diplomatic game of furthering Empire power.

Thus the annexation controversy helped to develop inaccurate and emotional ideas in Canada about both the British Empire and the United States. It created in the minds of many people a vehement and unthinking loyalty to Britain and an overcritical attitude towards the United States. In others it aroused an extreme distrust of England's policies and an exaggerated impression of American power. These conflicting opinions, as will be seen later, made it much more difficult for this country to develop an independent Canadian outlook on world affairs.

A Loss of Faith

Canada in the early 1890s seemed indeed to be a poor country. The wonderful future predicted by Confederation orators had failed to materialize. The great depression that hit Europe in 1873 had ruined the export trade on which the country depended. Prosperity had not returned and for twenty years Canada had been drifting in economic doldrums, making headway with difficulty. The surplus manpower of the world passed by and those immigrants who did come paused only long enough to find their bearings and then headed for the free lands of the American West. They were joined by so many native-born Canadians that Canada's population figures in this period almost stood still. A meagre 4½ million people, spread out over three thousand miles of broken continent in a thin band of settlements never more than one hundred miles from the border, had found no common interests, no unifying national spirit.

After the first flush of pride following the achievement of Confederation, Canadians had lost faith in their new country, and strong local, religious and racial interests had arisen to divide their loyalties. Manitoba seethed with discontent over the federal government's land and railway policies. Railways that the province wanted to build in competition to the hated Canadian Pacific were not allowed; the government at Ottawa held the province down in size, refused to extend its boundaries and retained control of all the crown lands out West. Manitoba joined with Nova Scotia and New Brunswick to complain about the niggardly money grants that they received from the Dominion government and in these and other disputes encouraged intense provincial feelings. The execution of Louis Riel, the Jesuit Estates argument and D'Alton McCarthy's crusade against the separate schools of Manitoba had placed Orangeman against Catholic, Englishman against Frenchman, and Ontario against Quebec. Grave charges of political corruption in four provinces and in the 'Scandals Sessions' of 1892 in the federal House added to the general feeling of discontent.

The new transcontinental railway from which so much had been expected had become the greedy 'monster' charging monopoly rates to farmers struggling to break even on wheat at forty-three cents a bushel. The Great Lone Land out West had been hit first by August frosts and then by drought. Politicians seeking office—Conservatives trying to oust Oliver Mowat, for long the Premier of Ontario, and Liberals desperate to replace Macdonald at Ottawa—blamed the bad conditions on the party in power, painted a dark picture of Canada and helped to undermine confidence at home and abroad.

Above all else, the main cause for the discouragement and discontent in Canada towards the end of the nineteenth century was the failure of the 'National Policy.' This was the name used to describe the various plans of the federal government to bind the country together—plans which were to create a united and prosperous nation from coast to coast. The first step in implementing the National Policy was taken when the government decided to give a large part of the publicly-owned land in the Northwest Territories to settlers in order to encourage the development of the almost vacant prairies. An Act was passed in 1872 that followed very closely the free land principles of the American Homestead Act and was based on the American system of surveys. This Act gave the federal Department of the Interior power to grant 'homesteads'—that is, free farms of 160 acres each—to settlers in the Northwest Territories. All the even-numbered square-mile sections of each township in the Territories were laid aside for homestead purposes. The next step was taken in connection with railways. The need to open up the free lands of the Canadian West and the promises made to bring British Columbia into the Dominion in 1871 made it necessary to build a transcontinental railway. The building of this line over empty spaces and forbidding mountains could not be undertaken without a large amount of government assistance, and this could be provided, as in the United States, by generous land grants to private railway companies. The government, therefore, decided to reserve most of the odd-numbered sections in the Northwest Territories to promote the construction of railways. Finally, in one of the most momentous elections in our history, the Canadian people in 1878 decided to follow the example of the United States one step further and voted for the Conservative party and its platform of high tariffs. Free home-steads to develop the West, government assistance to railways and the protection of the home market from foreign competition by the use of heavy taxes on imports—these were the cornerstones of the National Policy.

The success of this entire program for national development depended on people—people to open up the West, populate the cities and create the market for goods of all kinds. The Dominion government advertised, sent agents abroad, offered cheap passage across the Atlantic and did everything in its power to persuade people to come to Canada—all to no avail. We simply could not compete with the 'Gilded Age' of prosperity in the United States, and as long as there were free lands left in the American West immigrants would not come to Canada in sufficient numbers to make the National Policy work. Thus the North-west Territories remained almost empty, the great markets failed to develop, Canadian trade and industry languished, and the Liberal party in the election of 1891 appealed to the voters with the billboard question: 'Has the National Policy made you rich?'

Signs of Progress

The failure of the National Policy and the other difficulties of the times must not be taken to mean that Canada was standing still. Although the development of the country seemed exasperatingly slow compared to the swift expansion of the United States, there were many signs of progress throughout the nation. The ordinary Canadian citizen reflecting on the changes he had seen within his lifetime must have been encouraged to hold high hopes for a brighter future.

Early Winnipeg settlers must have glowed with pride and amazement as they recalled the days when their thriving city, with its street railway, arc lights and new telephone exchange, its schools, banks and varied industry was a struggling outpost of nineteen unpainted, frame buildings—the village of Dirty Water, linked to the outside world only by the annual brigade of Red River carts coming up from St. Paul. Well within memory was the arrival of James Hill's first steamboat, the coming of the telegraph and the little railway from Pembina, the end of the Dawson road and finally the miracle of the C.P.R. For some years, a small but steady flow of immigrants had been passing through the city on their way to the Territories. Most of these had come only from Ontario but some were from faraway places, and already the *Free Press*, the *Tribune* and the *Nor'-Wester* were competing for circulation with newspapers in German, Scandina-vian and Icelandic languages. The West was indeed beginning to change.

An automobile was something to stare at in Ashcroft, B.C., in 1907.

Out on the West coast the brand new, glistening *Empress* liners steaming out of Vancouver harbour for China, Japan or Australia stirred the imagination of many old-timers who had seen their Gas Town grow in so short a time to a great railway terminal and the gateway to the Orient. Across the continent, other men watching the activity in a more ancient harbour may have noticed that steam vessels for the first time outnumbered the graceful clipper ships at anchor in Bedford Basin. In Ontario, where the glitter from across the border was more dazzling than elsewhere, there were changes to be seen at every turn. The marching lines of ugly, new cedar poles carrying a maze of telephone and electric wires up the streets were evident signs of progress. So also was the appearance of electric streetcars, water mains and concrete paving on the main streets. In the downtown parts of the larger centres the one-family home with its back garden and little cluster of fruit trees was being replaced by the apartment building, providing bird-like dwellings for the increasing city populations. These and a great many other changes were being made in all parts of the country during the early 1890s, but the rate of change was slow, the pace of life generally was leisurely and Canada was still in the 'horse-and-buggy' days.

2 THE LAST BEST WEST

The Land of Open Doors

Along the banks of the Canadian River in the Oklahoma Territory one of the closing scenes in a long and tragic drama was about to start. This was the finale to the broken treaties, stolen lands and terrible wars that arose from the resistance of the American Indians to the relentless advance of the white man. The spirit of the Indians had been broken in over a thousand full-scale battles and now, in June 1901, the last of their reserves was being thrown open to settlement. Desperate homesteaders, knowing that this was their last chance to own good free lands anywhere in the United States, converged on this spot weeks in advance of the opening day. Arriving by buckboard or covered wagon, on horseback or on foot from the nearest railway, coming from nearby Kansas or distant Montana, they made camp beside the river, waiting for the starting guns and the wild race for land.

A big, glistening white tent stood out above all else along that fifty-mile stretch of river. High on its peak flew the Union Jack and a banner, stretched between two poles across the entrance, carried the words: THE GOVERNMENT OF CANADA: DEPARTMENT OF THE INTERIOR. Day after day, restless impatient men, looking for ways to pass the time, drifted into the tent and talked to the Canadian agents. They inspected the samples of wheat, looked at pictures of the empty prairies with covetous eyes and listened to lecturers assure them that 'the last best west' was not there in Oklahoma but thirteen hundred miles away in the Northwest Territories of Canada.

A little group of weather-beaten men, dressed in overalls and open shirts, loitered outside a real estate office on the dusty main street of Mountain Lake, Minnesota. Schwab and Company, so they learned from the advertisements in all the newspapers, had purchased 125,000 acres of black prairie soil northeast of a place called Weyburn in western Canada. Good land, near the railroad, for only seven dollars an acre! Minnesota land, to be had for the asking not so many years ago, was now worth six or seven times that much. Why not sell out here and start all over again up in Canada? The old homestead, prosperous though it was, could not support more than one family and here was a chance for the children to have a farm of their own. Breaking new sod would be easy compared to the old days when they had nothing but a wooden walking plough. And Canada really wasn't so far away. Just a few hundred miles north—perhaps two or three days by wagon, or overnight on the train.

The photograph and letter shown opposite were sent together to Ottawa in 1902.

Canadian Government Agency,

Office of J. C. Koehn, Agent.

MOUNTAIN LAKE VILLAGE PROPERTY FOR SALE OR RENT.
NORTH DAKOTA AND MINNESOTA FARMS AND WILD LANDS.

TAXES PAID, RENTALS COLLECTED, INVESTMENTS
MADE AND ESTATES SETTLED FOR NON-RESIDENTS.

Mountain Lake, Minn.,   April 21th, 1902,

Department of The Interior,
c/o Mr. Frank Pedley. Superintendent of Immigration,
Ottawa, Canada,

Dear Sir:-

This Picture represents the second solid trainload of
Emigrants leaveing Cottonwood County Minnesota. for Points in Western
Canada, 67 Cars have left mentioned County during the last two months.
and about that many more will follow before November 1th,
the Majority of them settle in the Prince Albert District,

Yours Truly,

J. C. Koehn

CANADIAN GOVERNMENT AGENT

Not only at Mountain Lake, Minnesota, but all across the United States from Wisconsin to the State of Washington, groups of shrewd, successful farmers gathered outside the offices of the land companies. The real estate agencies, the Hudson's Bay Company, the Canadian Pacific Railway and a dozen smaller lines drew an ever-increasing stream of prospective buyers to their doors. The government of Canada displayed advertisements offering a free homestead and giving the location of the nearest agency from which information could be secured. Deluged with inquiries, the agents sent out by the Department of the Interior were constantly writing back to Ottawa for more pamphlets and more magic-lantern slides to show these American, Scandinavian and German farmers of the western United States that Canada was indeed a land of open doors.

The Men in Sheepskin Coats

Far away in eastern Europe about fifty miles from Lemberg, in a miserable mud-walled hut, a man was talking earnestly to a family of poor peasants. The man called himself Vassil Paish, but everyone felt that wasn't his real name. He had been around their village occasionally during the spring, but all they really knew about him was that he spent his time trying to persuade the peasants to emigrate to some strange new country. Naturally the government did not like to see these people leave: the more of them there were the cheaper would be their labour. And now that Europe seemed bent on war, these sturdy men were needed for the army. Thus, encouraging emigration in the old Austro-Hungarian Empire was illegal and Vassil Paish had to work secretly, hiding the fact that he was a sub-agent for a group of steamship companies drawing a small commission from every fare he sold. So carefully concealed were these operations that even Vassil Paish himself did not know that, along with hundreds of others through-out eastern and northern Europe, he was really working for the North Atlantic Trading Company—a company formed in London in 1899, two years previously, for the sole purpose of convincing some of the exploited, surplus population of the continent to seek a new life in western Canada.

How eagerly did these poverty-stricken, illiterate peasants listen to what men like Vassil Paish had to say. Free land! A hundred and sixty acres of free land! It sounded like a fairy tale: no mortgage to the local pahn, no landlords and no oppressive taxes. Here was freedom from an indifferent ruling caste, from an intolerant state church and from the cruelties of compulsory military service. A passage across to this new world, so the agents explained, cost seventy-five dollars. This was the minimum for the month-long trip to Winnipeg, but they would need a little more to buy food and cover their expenses at places like Hamburg where delays were inevitable. Seventy-five dollars, the price of a pair of oxen. They might just make it, if they sold everything and set out for Canada with nothing but the clothes upon their backs.

Canada was somewhat late in throwing out her nets to draw in these immi-grants from Europe. Agents from the United States, Brazil and other countries had been busy for many years and had already started a movement from eastern and southern Europe unique in the annals of history. Long before Canadian agents appeared on the scene, a vast, endless horde, without organization or leaders, dressed alike in drab sheepskin coats, had begun to move at the rate of over a million a year to the New World. This great stream of humanity, springing from the huts of the plains and the hovels of the mountains in Europe, flowed across the Atlantic and found its outlet mainly in the United States. Now a small branch of this ever-increasing stream of immigrants was being diverted to the shores of Canada.

The Balkans about 1900. The distribution of Slavic peoples in and around the Austro-Hungarian Empire not only affected the population and growth of Canada but also was a factor in bringing about the First World War.

The American and British Invasions

The fourth Dominion census figures released in 1901 proved disappointing to the Canadian government and people. The population total of 5,371,000 indicated an increase of only half a million people in a decade—a growth increase no better than that of the depression years of the 1880s. Few Canadians seemed to realize the importance of the core settlements from Europe and the Orient that were being established in the West. Little attention was paid to the development of ethnic groupings in the Eastern cities. The upward flow of immigration from a low of 17,000 in 1896 to 56,000 in 1901 was considered inadequate. And above all, the fact that the rate of immigration exceeded the rate of emigration for the first time since Confederation was virtually ignored. The newcomers may have been arriving slowly but they were staying.

Studying the census figures, the opposition newspapers made an alarming discovery. An 'American Invasion' of Canada had begun; 86,000 had crossed the border in the past three years! Official statistics covering the years 1899–1904 show that immigrants from Great Britain numbered 137,000 and those from the U.S., 159,000. However, the initial effect of the increase in the American move north provided a reason for condemnation of the policies of the Laurier government.

The Toronto *World* warned its readers: 'Americans are pouring into the West by tens of thousands, are buying land through companies and agents in thousands of acres a day, and are preparing to control the factories and trade of the whole region as well as stock of the Canadian Pacific Railway.' Not to be outdone in raising the alarm at the menace from the South, a special correspondent reported back to his British paper: 'If the Motherland and the East will not help the West with money and men then depend upon it, in this part of the Empire, the next generation will sing more "Yankee Doodle" than "God Save The King".'

This flurry of anti-American feeling reached a climax during the first six months of the year 1902 and soon subsided. Most Canadians realized that these experienced farmers from the western States were about the best settlers to be found anywhere. Clifford Sifton, Minister of the Interior, was given credit for being one of the first to believe that they could be attracted to Canada. Businessmen, immigration officials and political leaders in Manitoba and the Territories were quick to point out that almost half these settlers were Canadians returning home, and many more were second-generation Scandinavian or German Americans with no dangerous loyalties to the United States.

Speaking in Montreal that September, Sir William Van Horne, former president of the Canadian Pacific Railway, summed up the accepted viewpoint this way: 'The greater part of them are people from Iowa, Minnesota, Nebraska and others of the better western States who originally bought their lands very cheaply, or took up homesteads which they are now able to sell at very high prices and who are coming to the Canadian North-west to repeat this operation. Let them come: we need them.'

Not only did the Americans come, but their arrival in such large numbers along with the European peasants made people in the eastern provinces and in

Great Britain finally realize the possibilities of the Canadian prairies. The United Kingdom showed very little interest until the 'American Invasion' started and then patriotic orators and journalists began to give the Northwest great publicity. Strengthening the ties of Empire, hostility towards the United States and hard-headed business considerations all entered into a tremendous drive to persuade more people of British origin to migrate to the West. 'We must not sit back any longer,' the *Fortnightly Review* cautioned its readers in England, 'and watch one of the most promising daughter lands being peopled by settlers of alien blood.' The London *Times*, the *Manchester Guardian* and many other British newspapers began to carry feature articles on Canada and reporters were sent across the Atlantic to see this wonderful country for themselves. Political leaders from Canada toured England giving lectures and even casual summer visitors were besieged with requests to speak at official luncheons, garden parties and club meetings. Premier Ross of Ontario assured the large crowds that turned out to hear him that Canada could have a population of 12 million if she received a proper share of British emigrants and she would then 'furnish the food supplies for the Empire and an admirable recruiting ground for army and navy'.

British emigrants, escaping from the overcrowded labour market of England with its low wages and tough competition for employment, had been swelling the population of the United States for many years. Over seventy per cent of the two hundred thousand who annually left the British Isles joined the throngs from Europe, seeking a new life in America. Now, because of the sudden interest stirred up in Britain, the Canadian Department of the Interior was encouraged to believe that a great many of these English, Scottish and Irish people could be enticed away from the United States. Consequently, the Immigration Service in Great Britain was reorganized in the year 1902 and put under the capable supervision of W. T. R. Preston; 350,000 copies of 'Western Canada' were mailed to English farmers and labourers; medals were offered to schoolchildren for the best essays on Canada; wall maps of the Dominion were placed in almost every schoolroom; and in 1904 two motor buses toured the country displaying samples of Canadian produce.

All these activities received full support from the government of Britain, and over a hundred emigration societies which had been placing the poor of the British Isles in the United States were now advised to direct their energies towards Canada. These organizations were eager to co-operate because the United States had begun to tighten up her immigration laws. While the United States was attempting to close its doors, those of Canada were flung wide open, giving access to a country thirty times the size of the United Kingdom and offering to the local taxpayers and charitable societies a chance to settle their destitute people on good Empire soil.

Emigration from Great Britain changed direction very rapidly and by 1905, for the first time in over half a century, more of these people were coming to Canada than to the United States. Although the Irish remained unconvinced, the English and Scots now arrived at the Atlantic ports of Canada in sufficient numbers to more than balance the American settlers crossing the border.

Meanwhile the people of eastern and southern Europe kept on coming by the tens of thousands, in numbers almost as great as those from Britain or the United States. Rising steadily from the ebb of the 1890s, the tide of immigration from all directions was now in full flood, mounting each year to reach an all-time high in 1913 when over 400,000 people surged into Canada.

The 1911 Census
Rudyard Kipling, speaking to a Canadian Club luncheon in Ottawa on October 21, 1907, paid many compliments to 'Our Lady of the Snows' for the great progress she had made since his last visit eighteen years before. During the course of his speech, he said he was certain that, at the next census, Canada would have a population of at least 9 million. In attempting to predict the results of the 1911 census, this distinguished visitor was playing a very popular guessing game. Several among the four hundred guests listening to him, including Sir Wilfrid Laurier and two of his cabinet ministers, already had made their predictions and many other Canadians continued to do so until the actual results were published. Eight million was a cautious estimate—some said 10, even 11 million, while the majority seemed to agree that Kipling's forecast of 9 million people would prove to be just about right.

All these optimistic predictions were a long way off the mark. The 1911 census recorded a population of precisely 7,206,643—a total gain for the ten-year period of only 1,835,318 people. This was a most surprising figure because it showed a total increase in population almost exactly equal to the number of immigrants who had come to Canada since 1901. There should have been, so people said, at least another million native-born Canadians; either the census figures were wrong or the natural increase by births was nil. This little mystery was solved when Canadians finally realized that their border officials counted all the people coming in—even casual seasonal labourers—but completely neglected to count the ones going out. Forty to fifty thousand Canadians annually left the country for the United States, even in these good years, and so the secret of our 'missing million' in 1911 lay hidden in the immigration statistics of the United States.

It was inevitable that the immigration officials in Canada, or in most other countries for that matter, should lose track of some of the millions of people who were on the move in those days. The course of this tremendous migration—the greatest mass movement in the history of the western world—rising to a climax in the early years of the twentieth century, shifting, changing direction, coming and going by never-ending tens of thousands, was almost too complex to record. Peasants and farm hands, clerks, industrial workers and unskilled labourers of every race and tongue pressed into the seaports of Europe and the British Isles. The emigration sheds were filled to overflowing and ocean liners, each one of

Immigrants on the Empress of Britain, *about 1911*

which could carry more steerage passengers than a dozen ships of a bygone age, lay waiting with agents ready to cheat and lie, if need be, to win a share of this rich human cargo. Fast trains carried them across Europe over distances undreamed of not so many years before, and powerful engines hauled crowded colonist cars across North America, covering in a matter of days a journey that had once taken weeks.

Nor was the traffic all one way. Ships steamed into the harbours of the New World, spilled their passengers out among the crowds waiting on the docks, took on a new load and headed back carrying throngs of American tourists and innumerable European and British people—some going home to visit and others, disillusioned, discouraged and lonely, going home to stay. Some immigrants landing at Quebec soon found their way into the United States; other immigrants landing at Boston or New York worked up into Canada and both groups added to the confusion created by Canadian and American citizens restlessly moving back and forth across the border hoping to find a satisfactory life on alien soil.

The importance of this period in Canadian history cannot be overemphasized. Although the census figures did not measure up to expectations, the thirty-four per cent increase in population recorded in Canada from 1901 to 1911 was greater than in any country in the world and had been exceeded only once before in history—by the United States in the years just before and immediately after the Civil War.

This overall increase was not in itself as important as the way the population of Canada shifted its location inside the country during this decade. The number of people living in the Yukon and in Prince Edward Island had declined while the increases recorded by Nova Scotia and New Brunswick were small and unimportant. The population of Ontario and Quebec had increased about seventeen per cent—a figure well below the national average. However, startling changes had taken place in the towns and cities of the two central provinces. The great migration from rural areas to urban centres which began towards the end of the nineteenth century continued to accelerate. Over 1¼ million Canadians moved from country to cities and towns during the period 1901–11, almost one-third of the total population. This shift in residence was most apparent in Ontario where farming had passed its peak and the province had swung to mining, manufacturing and trade. Even traditionally rural Quebec was barely managing to hold its own with the rapidly expanding cities of that province.

Much more important than even these changes in eastern Canada was the growth of the West. The vitality of the country, the bustle and excitement everywhere showed—even the cold census figures showed— beyond any doubt that most of the newcomers and many native-born from the older parts of Canada had settled west of the Great Lakes. Alberta and Saskatchewan were made into full-fledged provinces in 1905; these former parts of the Northwest Territories now contained four times more people, an increase of over 400 per cent in one short, strenuous decade! Brandon, St. Boniface and Winnipeg tripled in size. Farther west, Moose Jaw, Regina, Calgary and Edmonton were six to fifteen times bigger, while Saskatoon, which had barely made the 1901 census lists as

Galician immigrants at Quebec, about 1911

a tiny village of 113 people, was now a city of over 12,000! During this period farm settlement in Manitoba, Saskatchewan, and Alberta almost quadrupled in area from 15 million acres at the beginning of the decade to 58 million at the end. There was a correspondingly amazing increase in the actual crop cultivation of these Western prairie lands from 3 million to 18 million acres between 1901 and 1911—a fantastic addition of crop acreage in ten years. This fresh, rich, prairie soil, once condemned as useless, in 1911 produced 475 million bushels of grain (wheat, oats, barley, flaxseed, mixed grain)—more than 75 per cent of the total Canadian grain crop of that year. After so many years of waiting, after the painfully slow growth of the 1880s and 1890s, the Great Lone Land had been opened up.

Now that the West was settled the success of the National Policy was assured. Land, tariff and transportation plans, which seemed to fail during the nineteenth century, now combined to create a prosperous Canada from coast to coast, a true transcontinental nation. Canada was under full sail, the 'doldrum days' gone and forgotten.

Strangers Within our Gates

At dawn on May 9, 1911, the S.S. *Lake Champlain* tied up alongside one of the piers at Quebec City. A raw northeast wind whipped down from the snow-covered hills across the bleak, inhospitable docks, bringing little encouragement to the immigrants huddled together on the lower decks. There was a full load on board again this time—1,080 steerage passengers; men, women and children from sixteen different countries. Most of them were pitifully poor and ragged, probably lonely, afraid or uncertain, seeing for the first time this new land in which lay all their hopes. There was, however, little time for either memories or dreams. The *Royal George* and the *Lake Nipigon* were due to dock later on that day and all these people had to be put through a medical, customs and immigration inspection and answer a multitude of questions before a new group arrived.

What is your name? Where do you come from? Wie heissen Sie? Woher kommen Sie? Where were you born? Where are you going in Canada? Have you twenty-five dollars? Waar was U geboren? Ik was in Amsterdam geboren. Dove e nato? Sono nato a Milano. Wo wurden Sie geboren? Ich komme aus Stettin. Wat is Uw naam? Waar komt U van daan? Da dove viene?

The immigration officials manning the 'cattle pens'—the long iron-barred passageways leading off the docks—were able to classify most of the new arrivals fairly accurately. Swedes, Norwegians, Danes, Dutch and Finns were easy; so, of course, were the English, Scots and Irish; the Italians, the Greeks, and even the Jews from Romania and Russia could be identified somehow or other. The Germans caused some difficulty because so very few of them came directly from their native land. Prosperous Germany had the strictest emigration laws in Europe and most of the German-speaking people who came to Canada in this period came either from Austria-Hungary or from Russia: thus many Germans were undoubtedly listed as Austrians or Russians. Likewise some Jews were recorded as Poles, Austrians, Russians or Romanians and people from the United States were sometimes hurriedly entered as American when in reality they were second or third generation Europeans from many different countries.

These were minor difficulties compared to the complete confusion caused by 'the men in sheepskin coats'. Here was the largest single group of European immigrants yet no one knew who they really were; they themselves did not seem to know. As they shuffled past the immigration officials they called themselves Galicians, Ruthenians, Bukovinians or Russians and this is the way the Canadian government recorded them. Who were these ignorant, illiterate people, these Galicians?

They were, first of all, the real heroes in the opening of western Canada. They were the ones who took up homesteads miles away from the railroad on rough land that other people would not touch, working it with primitive tools, building a first mud-walled home with nothing but their bare hands. In the off-season, the men tramped across the prairies to find construction work on the railroads, in the lumber and mining camps, saving a few dollars from their miserable wages to buy a bit of farm machinery or a cow. Doing some of the roughest work in Canada under conditions that only the strongest could endure, cheated and exploited more than any other foreign group, they stuck it out to become respected and valuable Canadian citizens.

Galicia, Ruthenia and Bukovina were regions in the old Austro-Hungarian Empire. Before the First World War smashed it to pieces, this sprawling Empire contained over 50 million inhabitants from many different racial groups and was divided into a bewildering number of provinces. When a man claimed to be a Galician, Ruthenian or Bukovinian he was merely stating where he had lived within the Empire and not giving his racial origin. Not until after the First World War were Galicians, Ruthenians, Bukovinians and Little Russians grouped together and called by their correct name, 'Ukrainians'. Then it was seen that these Slavic people had become the fourth largest racial group in Canada, surpassed only by those of British, French or German origin.

The settler's first home on the prairie was of sod, on a frame of poplar or willow. Buffalo bones, worth six dollars a ton, were often the first crop. Later, a frame house would be built nearby, as shown in the picture above.

Yes, strangers were within our gates; strangers from more than thirty-five different countries, from every quarter of the globe, speaking a babel of languages and practising well over a hundred different religions. Before this great migration to Canada started the foreign elements in our population were very small, over ninety per cent of the inhabitants being descendants of the original British or French stock. The only foreign group of any size before 1900 was the German settlement in southwestern Ontario, formed at the end of the eighteenth century by refugees from the Thirteen Colonies.

Now all this was beginning to change. The 1911 census, in addition to showing the movement to the cities of Ontario and Quebec and the great growth of the West, also revealed very clearly the extent to which Canada's foreign population

Settlement in the West. The breaking of sod in the area of light soil and scanty rainfall, known as Palliser's Triangle, led to the dust bowl of the 1930s.

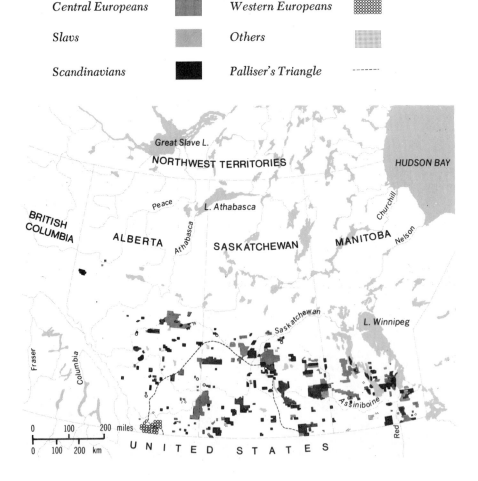

had increased. Almost one person in every five across the whole country was listed as an alien. The ratio of British people in the total population had fallen from sixty to fifty-five per cent, but here again the overall national figures do not tell the whole story. Although all parts of Canada were affected and most of the cities now had their Italian or Jewish quarters, or their Chinatowns, it was in the West that the variety of races was most evident. Seventeen per cent of the total population was foreign, but in Alberta and Saskatchewan it was over forty per cent.

What a strange part of the country the prairies had suddenly become! School-children pledging allegiance in all the tongues of Europe; more foreign-language newspapers than anywhere else in the world; queer place-names like Touecka, Esterhazy, Josephburg and Wapella; Doukhobors running around with too few clothes on; Mormons with too many wives; Mennonites stamping out in anger to seek peace in distant Paraguay; and a bewildering array of national costumes, dances and songs at every fall fair. The Canadian mosaic was starting to form a pattern.

The Sodbusters

A New Star in the Western Sky
During the early summer of 1902, in connection with the coronation of Edward VII, Canada built a huge Arch of Wheat in Whitehall, London, at one of the best points along the route of the Royal procession. Standing over fifty feet high for all to see, it carried the words, CANADA: FUTURE GRANARY OF THE EMPIRE. No idle boast was this, for in the not too distant future Canada was to become the greatest of all the wheat-exporting nations, supplying over half the world's international demand. It was fitting also that the senior colony of the Empire on this occasion should be symbolized by wheat, for this one product was indeed the arch through which Canada passed into the tremendous boom years of the early twentieth century.

Laurier and the Liberal party naturally claimed the credit for these prosperous years and it is true that the coming of much better times coincided almost exactly with the election of the Liberals to office in 1896. In the Dominion elections of 1900, 1904 and 1908, the Liberal party pointed to the soaring statistics of progress —more people and more acres in wheat, more miles of railway track and power lines, more trees cut down, more pulp and paper, more mines opened up and more telephones and bathrooms installed—and successfully carried the voters on the strength of their record. Whatever political party won the 1896 election was fortunate in the hour of its success, for after years of waiting Canada's turn had finally come. By the end of the nineteenth century, developing world conditions now favoured Canada and external factors over which Canadians had little or no control combined to give particular importance to the rich prairie lands of Manitoba and the Northwest Territories.

S. A. Fisher, Canadian Minister of Agriculture, in his annual report for the year 1902 used these words: 'I am happy to congratulate the country on a most prosperous agricultural year. The enormous crop which our North-west produced last year has been exceeded in the present season. Average farm income over and above living expenses is $1,170—a figure, may I emphasize, that is forty per cent greater than the average income of farmers in the United States.' Farmers could have sold more than they produced and prices were good. The great Canadian wheat boom was beginning.

This boom was impossible as long as the United States had free or cheap land available for settlement. Now the free lands had been used up, wheat production in the United States had ceased to expand and attention shifted to the Canadian Northwest. Greedy farming methods, taking everything from the soil and putting nothing back in—wheat mining—had affected the fertility of American soil and the average yield in the wheat-growing states had fallen to a low of fourteen bushels per acre. (By way of comparison, the bumper crops to which Fisher referred were based on average yields of twenty-five bushels per acre.) The teeming cities of the industrialized United States demanded more and more food supplies at a time when food production had levelled off and this meant that there was a declining amount left over for export to other countries.

Another very important wheat-growing country was in difficulty. Russia, with her vast Ukraine area—the 'Bread Basket of Europe'—had suffered several bad crop years in a row. Her disastrous defeat by Japan in the war of 1905 brought unsuccessful revolution and continuing political turmoil which seriously handicapped her export trade. Thus the two largest wheat-producing countries in the world were unable to increase their exports and the field was open for new competitors.

While exports from Russia and the United States were stationary or declining, the demand for wheat continued to expand. World population figures, due to improving medical knowledge, were skyrocketing. In the industrialized nations of western Europe, with the great movement from the country to the mushrooming factory towns and cities the people relied more and more on other nations for their food and raw materials.

Division of labour among the nations, the easy flow of goods and people across national boundary lines, expanding population, industrialization, increasing demand for food and raw materials, rising prices and new methods of transportation combined to form a particularly favourable situation with respect to the one product, wheat, and set the stage for entry of Canada's prairie lands upon the world scene. The time had come, in the eloquent words of Laurier, for 'a new star to arise resplendent in the western sky'.

Number One Northern
A famous English statesman once said that nothing was so uncertain as a figure unless it was a fact. Notwithstanding this uncertainty, here are some facts about the wheat boom in Canada during the early years of the twentieth century. The volume of wheat produced in Canada rose to an all-time, pre-war high of 232

million bushels in 1913 and ninety-five per cent of this crop came from the prairies. In good years and bad the 'sodbusters' on the prairies put more and more land under wheat so that by this record year 11 million acres were devoted to the growing of this one product.

Standing alone, these figures have no meaning. Considering that the United States produced over 650 million bushels of wheat in 1913 and Russia about 800 million bushels, the Canadian crop was not one to shout about. And it dwindles to insignificance in the 1960s when Canada's wheat production over the decade averaged 670 million bushels per annum. Despite the vast increase in world production—9 billion bushels in 1969—Canada remains the third largest wheat-producing country in the world with only the U.S.S.R. and the United States surpassing our annual crop.

The 1913 wheat crop of 232 million bushels, almost all of it from the West, had importance only when compared to a crop of 55 million bushels, most of it grown in Ontario, in the year 1900. An increase in prairie wheat production of over six hundred per cent in a little more than a decade was indeed a source of pride, and when Canadians realized that the 11 million acres on which this crop was grown represented but a small fraction—about six per cent—of the fertile land out West their ambitions really soared. A Manitoba senator, not content with the West as a granary for the Empire, predicted in a moment of extreme enthusiasm that 'within the next decade Canada will be growing four times more wheat than the United States'.

Two hundred and thirty-two million bushels of wheat are given added significance by the fact that, unlike the United States, the small population of Canada could not come close to consuming this large crop by themselves. Seeding requirements and a domestic consumption of about five bushels per capita left well over half the crop available for shipment to other countries. Wheat accounted for more than one-third of our exports and completely dominated Canada's external trade. In contrast to the glutted wheat markets of today, the Canadian crop had a ready sale. Number One Northern, at prices averaging almost exactly a dollar per bushel, brought in a rich reward to the western wheat farmer.

Most of this wheat—in fact fifty per cent of all our exports—was sold to industrial Great Britain. On the other hand, Canada, who once relied on the mother country for most of her imports, began to shift her buying to the markets of the United States. To some extent the government of Canada tried to stop this trend. Tariffs were retained against American goods and trading privileges were given to Britain—all to no avail. American raw materials needed by Canada were so close at hand, her mass-produced articles so cheap and suitable that Britain could no longer compete for the Canadian market. By 1914, two-thirds of all our imports came from the United States. Thus the profits made from wheat and other sales to Great Britain helped to finance imports of coal, iron, machinery and other products from the United States.

However, Canadian exports were not nearly large enough to cover all her imports. There was an 'adverse balance of trade'—not enough money coming in

Harvesting scene near Brandon, Manitoba, in the early 1900s

from our exports to buy what we required. The additional supply of foreign exchange was provided by British funds which were being invested in Canada. It was wheat that first inspired confidence in Canada and persuaded British financiers to invest in land and mortgage companies, banks, railways and other industries.

The golden flow of grain from the terminal elevators at the Lakehead through the St. Lawrence river system to the markets of Europe touched almost every phase of business life and swept Canada into the boom years of the early twentieth century. The prospect of a quick cash crop from wheat attracted settlers to the West. Prairie prosperity based on wheat created a new demand for manufactured goods, stimulated the long-awaited east-west trade and sparked a fresh burst of railway building. These live currents, in turn, reached into the lumber and mining camps, inciting activity in southern British Columbia, northern Ontario and Quebec. All these developments were financed in part by foreign investments that were encouraged by the volume of wheat being exported to England. Finally, these investments helped to pay for the tremendous imports from the United States without which industry could not have progressed. As hydro-electric power, pulp and paper, base metal mining, and manufacturing rose to prominence, Canada developed a better balanced economic life, but the initial momentum for her prosperity in this period came from the West.

The Tares Among the Grain

No one questioned the wisdom of this Canadian emphasis on wheat. Even when a financial crisis hit the country in 1913 and the wild and often crooked speculation in western land came to an inglorious end, a record crop kept the prestige of wheat as high as ever. It is understandable that in those confident days people failed to realize that, by specializing in wheat, Canada was leaving herself open to future years of trouble. During the wheat boom the prairie scene was all 'gold and blue', but wheat is one of the riskiest and most uncertain products in the world.

After a western farmer plants his seed in the spring, he loses control and nature takes over. Wheat needs just the right amount of moisture and coolness during the growing period and then a spell of hot, dry weather long enough to ripen the grain before the frost comes. The cool springs with a rainfall of ten to twenty inches and the dry summers of the prairies are usually ideal for wheat-growing, but nature sometimes plays strange tricks. Spring may be late, there may be too much or too little rain, the ripening period not long or dry enough, and the farmer may lose his crop through disease, drought or frost. Beginning with Sir Charles Saunders' discovery of Marquis wheat, Canadian scientists have produced disease-resistant and faster ripening seed, but even these improvements cannot protect the farmer from the uncertainties of the weather. From one season to the next, he never knows what his crop will be.

During the early years of the twentieth century Canada staked huge sums of money in the production and marketing of this unstable product. Almost $2 billion were invested in farm land, buildings and machinery and a very costly transportation system—elevators, docks, whaleback grain boats and especially railways—was developed to handle the export of wheat. Once made, this tremendous investment could not be adjusted in any way to changing, unpredictable market or weather conditions. Canada had committed herself, regardless of what happened to the wheat crop.

Canadians also stored up trouble by allowing the prairies to be developed—'exploited' would be a better word—without any plan or thought for the future. Like Topsy, the West just grew. The government had no policy except to bring in settlers and grow still more wheat. A kingdom was given away almost at random. A hundred and twenty million acres of land were handed out to private companies and individual homesteaders without any knowledge of the resources they contained or the purpose for which they were best suited. Overambitious little towns and villages in a hurry to grow up borrowed money without restraint or regard for the day of reckoning. The farmers themselves had but one ambition and worked the soil for all it was worth.

A survey taken in 1911 by the Department of Agriculture showed that not one in a dozen used any method of crop rotation or soil conservation. Towards the end of this period, the government did set up a Conservation Commission and a few—a very few—far-sighted men began to call attention to the fact that Canada's resources were not unlimited. Their warnings passed unheeded in the 'progress and prosperity' of the times, and not one recommendation of this Commission was carried out.

Perhaps the most disastrous mistake of all was made in 1908 when the 'dry belt' was opened up to homesteading. This is an area of some 40 million acres in southeastern Alberta and southwestern Saskatchewan where the soil is light and the margin between enough rainfall and drought is very small. It had been reserved for land grants to the railways or used as grazing land by ranchers. When the railways refused to take up any grants in this area the government finally released it for homesteads. The cattlemen were pushed aside by the encroaching farmers and the whole dry belt was occupied very rapidly. Time and hard experience were to prove that of all the land out West the dry belt should never have been broken for wheat. In the years to come this region developed into the dust bowl of Canada, the 'next-year country' where hardships were so great that the government paid people to move out.

Meanwhile the West, oblivious to the future, went rollicking on its 'wild and woolly' way. New subdivisions extended for miles outside each town and city; every other building on Main Street seemed to be a real estate office; corner lots changed hands two or three times a week; and far away in Britain unsuspecting Englishmen bought 'choice sites just outside the town limits'. If men in their haste to make money sometimes cut corners no one seemed to mind. New railway tracks stitched across the country at an average rate of two miles each day and whistle stops grew almost overnight into thriving towns. Every little town had its newspaper and the buoyant spirit of the times was reflected in the pages of advertisements that they carried: real estate and mortgage companies by the dozen offering improved lands, wild lands, good town sites and money to lend; travel agents with excursions, hotel space and guide books for sale; farm equipment ranging from Campbell's original oscillating churn with the figure-of-eight movement to the Monitor kerosene stove, guaranteed not to explode. Eastern Canadian manufacturers tempted the farmer with everything from a sewing machine that made little or no noise or a foot-organ for the village church to Pond's Extract, Peruvian Syrup, Lyman's Universal Pain Remover and a multitude of other patent medicines. Every nook and cranny where a dollar might be made was fully explored. Young clerks with a thousand dollars or so pinned to their shirts rode out to the 'head of steel' setting up new branches for the Traders, the Union, Molson's or some other bank. Three transcontinental railway companies shuttled their busy trains back and forth and the flying sparks from their locomotives sometimes added to the excitement by setting prairie fires. Clumsy steam tractors boiled along the furrows in the rush to grow more wheat and the harvest excursion trains hauled in the hired hands to reap the all-important crop. Somewhere in the middle of it all the rocking chair was becoming standard equipment. Out West in those days people were on the move even when sitting still.

3 THE FLOOD TIDE TO FORTUNE

Bonds of Steel

Sir Wilfrid Laurier,
1896–1911

'The flood tide is upon us that leads to fortune: if we let it pass it may never recur again. If we let it pass, the voyage of our national life, bright as it is today, will be arrested in the shallows. We cannot wait because time will not wait.' With these glowing words Sir Wilfrid Laurier on July 31, 1903, began one of his longest and most eloquent speeches, laying before the House of Commons the plans for a new multi-million-dollar transcontinental railway.

Twenty-two years earlier, in 1881, the same House of Commons had witnessed the longest and most vicious debate in its history over the passage of the Canadian Pacific Railway bill. During that session a clean-shaven, thirty-nine-year-old Laurier, in one of the least vituperative speeches from the Opposition, had advocated a go-slow railway-building policy. But now the times had changed; 'expansion equals progress' was the new political faith. In a country of vast geographical distances, huge areas of unsettled land and sparse population, government and the railway could never be separated. Supporters of railway expansion declared that the prosperity of eastern and western Canada had been achieved by the railways and clamoured for additional mileage to assure continuing good times. Politicians spoke glowingly of the unifying effect of the railways and proclaimed the virtues of a stronger nation drawn together by 'bonds of steel'. Railroad building, wheat, immigrants: these were the permanent triumvirate of the National Dream in the early days of twentieth-century Canada.

People became aware that a railway project was in the air when Charles M. Hays, the American railroader who had been imported to save the crumbling Grand Trunk from bankruptcy, announced in November 1902: 'Our Directors, having observed the wonderful developments of the North-west, have decided to extend their present lines in eastern Canada from North Bay to the Pacific coast. We expect to receive the same assistance in land grants and money as the government has meted out to the Canadian Pacific Railway.' The English shareholders of the Grand Trunk not so many years before had scorned Sir John A. Macdonald's plan for an all-Canadian line. By refusing to build round Lake Superior where they said no railway could ever make money, this company had lost the chance to engineer Canada's first transcontinental and had left the field to the Canadian Pacific. Now the board of directors, encouraged by the growth of the West and possibly by the success of the C.P.R., had decided to tackle the rugged wilderness of spruce forest, muskeg and rock lying between North Bay and the grain fields of the prairies.

There were other railway promoters in 1902 with an eye on the West. In Manitoba, the provincial government for some years had been supporting William Mackenzie and Donald D. Mann in their efforts to give the C.P.R. some healthy competition. Several small lines built by these two men in Manitoba were grouped together in 1899 to form the Canadian Northern Railway Company. Two years later the new company submitted a bid to lease some three hundred and fifty miles of railway owned by the Province of Manitoba. Although their bid was much lower than that of the C.P.R., the Conservative administration of Premier Roblin awarded the lease to them and almost overnight the Canadian Northern became the third largest railway company in Canada. In the same year it obtained authority to expand eastward and no time was lost in purchasing small lines in Quebec, Ontario and the Maritimes. This initial success spurred the transcontinental ambitions of Mackenzie and Mann and they applied to the federal government for permission and financial assistance to extend their lines from coast to coast.

Once these plans became known, a rumour spread that the Canadian Northern with its lines in the West and the Grand Trunk with its holdings mainly in Ontario and Quebec would get together. It is certain that the Grand Trunk attempted to buy out the Canadian Northern, but the negotiations were so secret and later investigations of them so contradictory that it is impossible to decide if valid offers were made and refused. Government attempts to persuade the two companies to co-operate failed, and finally, faced with the popular demand for more railways and the powerful lobbies of financial interests, Laurier agreed to back the transcontinental plans of both the Grand Trunk and the Canadian Northern.

We Cannot Wait

Mackenzie, Mann and their lawyer slipped into Ottawa early in 1903 and made their arrangements with the government without stirring up any political fuss. The bill giving government assistance to the Canadian Northern was passed almost without debate. By this bill the government agreed to guarantee—to the amount of $13,000 per mile—the bonds of the Canadian Northern to build from Grandview in Manitoba to Edmonton. The company also received permission to build eastward from Port Arthur to Ottawa to tie in with its lines in Ontario and Quebec.

The contract between the Canadian government and the Grand Trunk which Laurier presented to parliament at the end of July, 1903, was a much more ambitious scheme than the one Hays had proposed six months earlier. The Grand Trunk's original plan to build westward from North Bay was no sooner submitted than the towns and cities of Quebec and the Maritimes—regardless of whether they already had a railroad—began to clamour for the new line to come their way. The Prime Minister and his colleagues yielded to this pressure and extended the proposed eastern terminal first from North Bay to Quebec City and finally to Moncton.

Since the line was now much longer than the Grand Trunk had bargained for, the government agreed to build the eastern section from Moncton to Winnipeg. This section became known as the National Transcontinental. A new company was formed under the control of the Grand Trunk, called the Grand Trunk Pacific. This new company was to build from Winnipeg to the coast. When the eastern section was finished, it was to be rented from the government by the Grand Trunk Pacific. Thus the National Transcontinental and the Grand Trunk Pacific, operated together, would form a new transcontinental railway indirectly controlled by the Grand Trunk. Finally, the bonds of the Grand Trunk Pacific were to be guaranteed partly by the parent company but mainly by the Canadian government. This government backing was intended to give investors confidence

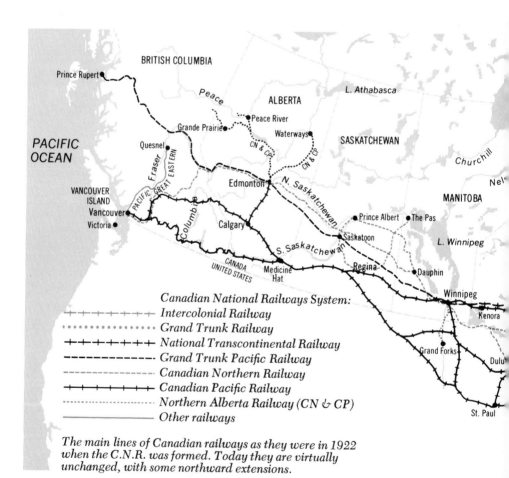

Canadian National Railways System:
+‑+‑+‑+‑+‑+‑+‑+ *Intercolonial Railway*
················· *Grand Trunk Railway*
+++++++++ *National Transcontinental Railway*
‑ ‑ ‑ ‑ ‑ ‑ ‑ ‑ ‑ *Grand Trunk Pacific Railway*
‑‑‑‑‑‑‑‑‑‑‑‑‑ *Canadian Northern Railway*
+‑+‑+‑+‑+‑+‑+ *Canadian Pacific Railway*
················· *Northern Alberta Railway (CN & CP)*
——————————— *Other railways*

The main lines of Canadian railways as they were in 1922 when the C.N.R. was formed. Today they are virtually unchanged, with some northward extensions.

and make it easier for the Grand Trunk Pacific to raise money for the construction of the western part of the railway.

'This is one of the most senseless railway transactions which has ever taken place in this country. It is difficult to understand why the Government should build and own the lean section of this railway and provide a private company with Government credit to build and operate the fat section.' With these angry words A. G. Blair, the Minister of Railways in Laurier's cabinet, handed in his resignation and became one of the leading critics of the government's policy. During the parliamentary debates on this subject, Blair said that the whole plan was premature; the surveys were incomplete and no one knew just where the new line would run; if the government was going to build one half and guarantee the rest, the entire line should be built as a government-owned railway. As a former premier of New Brunswick, Blair spoke with special vigour about the Maritimes. The eastern part of this new line, he said, would take traffic away from the Intercolonial Railway which the government already owned. Why build two

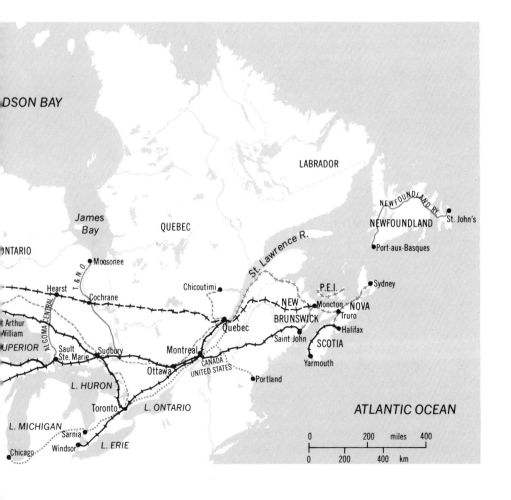

government railways in competition to each other? The better plan would be to extend the Intercolonial from Montreal to some port on Georgian Bay and then use the cheap water route of the upper lakes. In this way, much-needed business from the West would be given to the Intercolonial and the Maritime provinces would prosper.

Government supporters pointed out that the financial arrangements in the contract were very sound, providing against any waste or extravagance; millions of dollars of British capital would be attracted to the project and British interest in Canada would be that much greater. In the words of W. S. Fielding, the Minister of Finance: 'The co-operation of the Grand Trunk Company ensures the efficient and business-like operation of this new railroad and guarantees that the Grand Trunk Pacific will fulfil all its promises to the Government and people of Canada.'

The 1904 Election and the Railways

The National Transcontinental Railway Bill passed both houses of parliament in the fall of 1903, but all the arguments about it were revived within less than a year as the political parties began to campaign for the tenth Dominion election. In the centre of the national stage were the two party leaders. Robert Borden, testing his strength as Conservative leader for the first time, drew large crowds, but his cold, factual speeches failed to arouse great enthusiasm among his listeners. Sir Wilfrid Laurier, his popularity rising with Canadian prosperity, his wonderful, flowing eloquence carrying deep emotional appeal, was greeted with wild acclaim all the way across Canada. The reception given to him in 'Tory Toronto' during this campaign was one of the greatest in the political history of Canada. When towards the end of his speech on that occasion he made his now famous declaration that 'the twentieth century belongs to Canada', the rafters of Massey Hall, so the newspapers said, rang for ten minutes with a standing ovation for the Prime Minister.

The Conservative party made the Grand Trunk contract their main point of attack against the prestige of the Liberal government. Borden, using Blair's arguments, urged full government ownership and stressed that since the main line of the Grand Trunk ran to Portland in Maine, most of the traffic of the new railway might end up going through this American port. On the other hand, the Liberals brushed aside the contract and paraded their list of precisely '100 things done since 1900'. At the top of the list stood the success of Sifton's department in opening up the West, the 107 per cent increase in trade, the work of the new Department of Labour under Sir William Mulock, the completion of the Trent Canal as far as Peterborough, the telegraph to the Yukon, and the $500 head tax on Chinese labourers which was sure to get votes in British Columbia. Adding interest to the usual charges of election bribery were the ballot boxes with false bottoms imported as 'bee-hives' into two Ontario ridings, the purchase of several Liberal newspapers by financial interests opposed to the Grand Trunk contract and the rumour that these interests were going to buy off Liberal candidates in Quebec for $10,000 each. However, when all this smoke had cleared away, it was found on November 3, 1904, that the Liberals had been returned to office with a majority of over sixty seats. The Board of Trade in Portland sent a telegram of congratulations to Laurier. The Grand Trunk contract was now safe, and work on both sections of the new line could begin in earnest.

The Success of the C.P.R.

As the government was thus encouraging the development of two new transcontinental railways, the Canadian Pacific Railway, with a long head start, was racing forward enjoying the prosperous times.

The early success of the C.P.R. was due mainly to the rapid expansion of western settlement. When the company received its charter from the Conservative government in 1881, one of the stipulations was that lines linking British Columbia with eastern Canada be completed within ten years. Construction went on at an amazing speed; the last spike was driven at Craigellachie, B.C., on November 7, 1885, and on June 28, 1886, the first scheduled transcontinental passenger train left Montreal, arriving at Port Moody, on Burrard Inlet twelve miles east of Vancouver, on July 4. This incredible feat of railroad building, uniting Canada from Atlantic to Pacific, had been completed in five years!

Other important factors contributed greatly to the continuing success of the C.P.R. It was built according to American practice, as a first-class railroad capable of carrying all varieties of rolling stock from elegant passenger cars complete with lamp-lit 'diners' and plush-seated 'salons' to the seemingly endless lines of freight that wound through Kicking Horse Pass to the western sea. While the original running equipment was expensive and of a high standard, the operating and maintenance costs were relatively small. Its southerly route, close to the U.S. border and passing through land suitable for the immigrant flood, was well chosen. Much of the credit for this sound beginning belongs to William C. Van Horne, the American-born railroader whose career amazingly parallels that of C. M. Hays of Grand Trunk fame.

The financial structure of the company followed the conservative English model, particularly in one area—a relatively small amount of bonds was issued. This enabled the organization to combat depressed periods of operation without being saddled with the payment of high, fixed interest rates on large bond issues and assuming the possible risks of reorganization. American financiers contributed to the initial investment, French and German financial houses provided capital and, later on, British companies participated. Government assistance was extensive in cash subsidies, vast land grants, monopolistic charters, and stretches of railway track, particularly in B.C. Most important of all, the government did not guarantee the interest payments on bonds issued by the company.

From 1900 the C.P.R. built branch lines across the prairies at the rate of almost three hundred miles each year. It battled the Great Northern Railway, backed by the House of Morgan, for control of lines in southern British Columbia; it tackled big mining interests in Montana for the mineral wealth of the Kootenay and the Klondike; it built a chain of hotels across Canada; it planned and carried out extensive irrigation schemes in the West, particularly near Calgary. In 1903, the

(Above) Arrival of the first transcontinental passenger train at Vancouver, May 23, 1887.
(Right) A track-laying machine on the Grand Trunk Pacific west of Edmonton.

C.P.R. purchased the Beaver line of steamships and moved in to the Atlantic
shipping trade. By 1915 it was ready to take over the Allan line and add those
vessels to its ocean fleet. Its Pacific shipping line had been operating since 1889.

By 1914 the Canadian Pacific, with almost nine thousand miles of railway and
with ocean liners on both the Atlantic and the Pacific, now girdled the globe and
was the largest transportation system in the world. Despite a continuing
expansion program, it had paid all its year-to-year obligations, had savings of over
$30 million and could move into the war years in a sound financial position.

The Railway-building Boom

The years 1903 and 1904 set the stage for the Canadian Northern, the Grand
Trunk, the Grand Trunk Pacific, the National Transcontinental and the Canadian
Pacific to begin the greatest railway-building splurge in Canadian history. In
addition to these big companies, the government of Ontario began to build the
Timiskaming and Northern Ontario in 1903, over fifty smaller companies were
formed and twenty-nine branch lines from American railroads started to reach
across the border 'like fingers grasping for trade'. All these companies began to
blast, grade and level, put down ties and 'lay iron' across the country so fast that
the number of miles of railway increased from 19,500 in 1904 to 30,800 in 1914.
The frantic rush to complete lines already under construction in 1914 carried this

railway-building boom through to the end of the War. An all-time record was set in 1915 when almost 5,000 miles of new line went into operation in a single year, and by 1918 Canada possessed 39,000 miles of railway! By way of comparison, it may be noted that since the First World War railway mileage has increased very slowly, reaching 42,000 miles by 1930 and 43,600 miles in 1969.

In the opening decade of this century, one in every three wage-earners in eastern Canada was working for a railroad or for a company making railway supplies, and railway building became the greatest single factor in the industrialization of Canada. Year after year employment was provided for sixty to eighty thousand men working on the surveys, in the pick-and-shovel gangs or in the brawling, undisciplined camps at the 'head of steel', drawing wages at an average rate of $2.50 per day. (In those days a five-room house could be rented for about $9.00 per month, a ton of coal cost $5.00 or a pair of 'patent calf, fair stitched' boots $2.00, and a dozen eggs, a pound of butter or a yard of good material for a skirt could be had for all of seven cents.)

In addition to gigantic quantities of dynamite, timber, spikes, cement, tools, hardware of all kinds, girders, steel wire and other bridge-building materials, the railway companies placed orders in this ten-year period for almost 2 million tons of rails, 150,000 freight cars and 3,200 locomotives. Creating even more business was the construction by the railway companies of grain elevators, warehouses, docks, lake freighters, round houses and great workshops. Hundreds of stations

—including the C.P.R.'s Windsor Station at Montreal, the Grand Trunk Station at Ottawa and the first big 'union' stations at Toronto and Winnipeg—were built across the country and every little town had its railway depot. Luxurious railway hotels such as the Grand Trunk's Chateau Laurier in Ottawa, the Canadian Pacific's new Chateau Frontenac in Quebec, the Windsor in Montreal, the Alexandra in Winnipeg and the Empress in Victoria were constructed in this period, offering a 'home away from home' for the increasing number of travellers. Altogether, the railway companies in the period 1904–14 poured at least $775 million in wages and $825 million in the purchase of materials into the business life of Canada.

All these figures, however, cannot tell the story of the hot arguments and feverish excitement about railways during this period: towns claiming that the new railway coming in would ruin a residential area, the agricultural fair grounds or a view of the lake. How were level crossings to be protected and who was to pay for this protection? Should the railway tracks be raised above the streets or the streets above the tracks and how high should a railway bridge be above street level? To handle these and dozens of other questions the government created the Board of Railway Commissioners in 1902 and the thousands of cases brought before it give some idea of the growing pains suffered by the railways: angry farmers demanding more elevator space, more freight cars, more loading time and cheaper rates for shipping grain; other groups complaining about the poor service, the irregular schedules and the three-cents-per-mile rate for passengers. Inexperienced engineers, perhaps instructed in a hurry, roared their trains out of control through crowded stations or rolled them off sharp curves, irresponsible conductors let passengers fall off the back platforms, switches failed to work causing head-on collisions and a ten-year accident toll of 5,180 persons killed and 27,200 injured indicates the frantic tempo of the times.

Built with a Lavish Hand

Late in the afternoon of August 29, 1907, a section of the huge cantilever bridge nearing completion at Quebec City crashed in a twisted mass of steel into the St. Lawrence River, causing the loss of sixty lives and damage of over $1½ million. (Investigation later revealed that poor materials had been supplied by an American company and that the supervising engineer had failed in his duties.) The private company building the Quebec bridge was directed by S. N. Parent, formerly Liberal premier of Quebec and at this time a member of parliament and the government commissioner in charge of building the National Transcontinental. This company had received $375,000 in cash grants and the government had guaranteed its bonds. Thus when the bridge collapsed, bringing Parent's company down with it, the government had to take it over and finish the work as a government project. Although no one would have thought so at the time, the failure of this bridge company may be regarded as an omen of what the government would soon be compelled to do with many of the railways.

The railway promoters found it too easy in these prosperous years to raise money. They did not have to be careful because conditions were good, investors had confidence and governments were in a most co-operative mood. Competition drove up the price of labour and materials, the cost of constructing new lines soared far beyond the original estimates, but the railway men could always come back to the government for assistance. The Laurier administration was replaced in 1911 by the Conservatives under Borden and provincial governments changed hands from one party to another, but the lavish aid to railways continued without interruption. By 1914 the municipal, provincial and federal governments had given to the private railway companies $179 million in cash and almost 60 million acres of valuable land, and had guaranteed the capital and interest on bonds amounting to $235 million.

The Canadian Northern and the Grand Trunk Pacific in particular were financed by the sale of government-guaranteed bonds. These companies built up great debts in the form of bonds which carried fixed or compulsory interest payments of many millions of dollars. On the eve of the First World War neither of these two companies had finished laying track on their main or branch lines; terminal warehouses, stations and hotels were still under construction. Between 1913 and 1915 the Canadian Northern completed its transcontinental system. In mid-Canada it linked Port Arthur, Sudbury and Ottawa to the Maritimes. In the West it linked Winnipeg and Edmonton via the Yellowhead Pass to the Pacific. September of 1915 saw the first through train from Quebec City to Vancouver on the Canadian Northern line. By 1914 the Grand Trunk Pacific's westerly route had been finished from Winnipeg to the Pacific, crossing the Rockies at the Yellowhead and turning north to the new port of Prince Rupert. As the war situation curtailed the availability of private finance, the rush to completion of these lines required additional public financing and huge sums were required from government sources.

The government line from Moncton to Winnipeg—the National Trans-continental—had to face the rapidly rising costs of production during the boom years. It had an apparently unlimited supply of easy money coming directly from the rich government treasury, and economy may not have seemed important. There were frequent charges that the management was inefficient and wasteful. In addition, it was said that some contractors were guilty of 'overestimating' their work and charged the government many millions more than they should have. Certainly the unfortunate attitude was held by some that the government had lots of money and if one could cheat a bit it did not matter, but it should be kept in mind that the line was built through some rough, almost unexplored areas and unforeseen engineering difficulties were sure to appear. At any rate, by the time the National Transcontinental was completed at the end of the year 1913, it had cost the country $160 million—almost exactly $100 million more than the original estimate presented to parliament in 1903.

The final blow to the National Transcontinental came in November 1914. The Grand Trunk Pacific, on the verge of bankruptcy, refused to lease the line from Moncton to Winnipeg on the grounds that it was not up to their specifications and would be too costly to operate, and the National Transcontinental became a publicly-owned railroad operated by the federal government.

Within the next three years the Grand Trunk, the Grand Trunk Pacific and the Canadian Northern all plunged into government receivership. The railway boom was over. World War One had stopped the immigrant stream and the golden flow of British and foreign investment. The federal government had to come to the rescue, and in 1922 the Canadian National Railway came into being, combining the 'iron horse' trails of the Intercolonial, the Grand Trunk, the Grand Trunk Pacific and the Canadian Northern.

It is easy enough now, looking back, to see the mistakes made during the pre-war railway-building era. At the beginning of this century the Canadian Pacific may have needed competition and the expansion of the country may have required more railways, but for neither reason were two new transcontinental railroads justifiable. One new, strong company with a good system of branch lines would have been better than two weak ones, and a bad error in judgement seems to have been made when the plans of both the Canadian Northern and the Grand Trunk were not only approved but generously encouraged by the government. Lavish aid meted out to railroad promoters who used other people's money and took few risks themselves seems to have inspired extravagance and waste. The failure to supervise properly some of the construction work and the general unforeseen rise in the price of materials and wages combined to drive the cost of construction far beyond original estimates. All these mistakes are understandable. During years of rapid development people seldom pause to make careful considerations or count the costs. Canadians speaking through their elected representatives in parliament not only supported the government's railway-building policy but urged it on, and Laurier's 'we cannot wait' was only an echo of the confident, rushing spirit of the times.

The Attack on the Forest

Sawdust on the Shore
Our forefathers came into possession of one of the most richly endowed countries in the world. Its great natural wealth seemed inexhaustible. The future, surely, would take care of itself.

Nowhere is this attitude more apparent than in the way we completed the destruction of one of our greatest natural resources—a national asset far more precious than all the silver and all the gold to be mined at Cobalt or Porcupine. Here is the way it was described by the president of the Ontario Lumbermen's Association at their annual meeting in January 1901: 'This vast forest, extending from Lake of the Woods eastward through the Nipigon, Algoma and Georgian

This section of the National Transcontinental north of Lake Superior shows the difficulties and triumphs of the railroad builders. They had to blast through outcrops of the Shield, raise wooden trestle bridges over rivers, pile firm beds of debris across the muskeg, and tunnel through rock.

Bay districts to the Ottawa River, is the most valuable in the world. While it contains excellent spruce for paper and birch for furniture, it is the natural habitat for the most valuable tree of them all—the lordly white pine. In New Brunswick the pine has disappeared, in Quebec forest fires and the work of lumbermen have taken their toll, but in some parts of Quebec and in Ontario there are stands of white pine to last this country for generations.'

This forest of white pine, the finest on the North American continent, had been ruthlessly cut over during the days of the squared timber trade and later, towards the end of the nineteenth century, had supplied millions of board feet of sawn lumber to British and American markets. At the beginning of the twentieth century it still contained great stands of virgin pine, capable of yielding pure white planks two feet or more in width, running knot-clear in lengths unknown to the modern lumber industry. The rapid development of eastern Canada during the early years of this century made these pine forests of Ontario more valuable than ever. Never before or since in our history has so much pine lumber been produced as during the years 1900 to 1914. Production reached an all-time high in 1911 when 1,189 million board feet of white and red pine were cut. Today the lumber industry produces less than 265 million board feet. The tragedy of the lordly white pine is summed up in those depressing statistics.

In the period 1885–1900 when the sawmills in the United States had exhausted the white pine in the states of Michigan, Wisconsin and Minnesota, American lumbermen crossed the Canadian border for new sources of raw material with as little restraint as birds of prey. Early in their history the lumber companies had cut the forests of the New England states and then shifted to the St. Lawrence and the southernmost part of Ontario. Now they directed their attention to the last pine forest left in North America. American companies took out timber permits in Ontario and began to tow huge rafts of pine saw logs across the upper Great Lakes to keep their mills in operation. To get some of the business for themselves, the lumbermen of Ontario persuaded the provincial government in 1898 to prohibit the export of saw logs to the United States. As a result, many American firms moved across the border, mills and all; the busy little tugs still plied the lakes but now they towed barge-loads of lumber instead of the booms of saw logs. Thus the tremendous demand for lumber in both the United States and eastern Canada completed the destruction of the white pine forest.

Even as the president of the Lumbermen was delivering his address in 1901, at the very beginning of this period, the dammed and frozen headwaters of the streams flowing into the North Channel, Georgian Bay and the Ottawa River were being filled with pine saw logs ready for the spring drive. All through the region from the Ottawa River to Georgian Bay, in a broad belt some two hundred miles wide, the winter woods rang to the sound of the axe, the crosscut saw, the lusty shouts of 'Timber!' and the crescendo of crashing trees. Year after year the Mississagi, Magnetawan, Petawawa, Madawaska and other rivers carried down an increasing supply of logs to the shores of Georgian Bay or the waters of the Ottawa. Year in and year out children on their way to school in Thessalon,

A huge load of white pine logs

Sturgeon Falls, Parry Sound, Midland, Pembroke or dozens of other places became accustomed to the high-pitched zinging screech as sawyers directed their logs against the whirling saws. At the end of the period huge, almost unbelievable piles of sawdust rimmed the shores and filled the bays—and the pine forest had helped to build the growing towns and cities of central Canada. In the process, the forest which would 'last this country for generations' was wastefully cut to pieces and by 1914 the great days of the white pine were already numbered.

Even before the end of this period the lumber industry in Ontario, like that in New Brunswick, was beginning to assume a somewhat scruffy appearance. Dozens of the smaller sawmill owners cut their timber limits relentlessly and then closed down, leaving their ramshackle buildings and slab-piles scattered across the country. A great many more hung on, using spruce, hemlock and other inferior woods once so despised by the lumbermen. Some of the romance of lumbering was fast disappearing; the days of Paul Bunyan and Maria Chapdelaine were no more. The cheery, reliable French-Canadian logger was edged out of the bush into the frontier towns by increased mechanization and the highly competitive labour influx of 'Sifton's Sheepskins'. Always a rugged individualist, the mackinawed lumberjack could not become a cog in the wheel of an industrial

(Above) Men lived in shacks aboard this huge raft of timber as it floated down the Ottawa River. It was owned by J. R. Booth and valued at $50,000. (Right) Cookery aboard the raft.

machine seemingly determined to destroy the raw materials that gave it its very existence. From 1900 to 1914, Ontario managed to hold its lead in the lumber trade of Canada, but its pine resources were declining so fast and the province was becoming so rapidly industrialized that it would soon become a lumber-importing region.

Lumber from B.C.

The tremendous growth of settlement in the Canadian West created a great demand for lumber. The treeless prairies needed wood products at almost every turn: wood for every little country elevator, station, or siding warehouse, for each new barn or farmhouse, for town or city homes, factories, schools and hospitals; boxcar-loads of wooden stopes for the coal mines; miles of wooden poles for the extending telephone systems; and railway ties by the million.

At first the young lumber industry of British Columbia found it difficult to compete for this market with American lumber imported duty-free from Wisconsin or Minnesota. The lumbermen worked hard for tariff protection against this competition, but their efforts were thwarted by the prairie provinces, which quite naturally wanted to buy all the materials needed for their rapid

development as cheaply as possible. During the first two or three years of the twentieth century, without the use of any tariff on imported lumber, the tide turned in favour of British Columbia sawmills. The mounting shortage of lumber in the United States, the refusal of British Columbia and Ontario to let their logs across the border to feed American sawmills and the consequent rise in American prices all combined to give the prairie market to British Columbia. This Canadian market, plus a growing export trade to the Orient, Australia and even the United States, raised lumbering in British Columbia to a major industry in the short space of fourteen years. In 1911 our most westerly province produced twenty-seven per cent of the Canadian output of sawn lumber.

Today British Columbia spruce, cedar and the magnificent Douglas fir, represent seventy-five per cent of a total production estimated at over 10 billion board feet. In many parts of eastern Canada the shipments from the Pacific coast have driven local lumber out of the market, and British Columbia is the top producer in the Canadian lumber industry.

'We Are Out of Pulpwood'

President Theodore Roosevelt was exaggerating—as seemed to be his habit—when he told a group of state governors in May 1907 that the United States was out of pulpwood. However, the very fact that a special conference of governors from the timber-producing states had been summoned and that the President

Laurentides Pulp Mill, Grand'Mère, Quebec, about 1901

had used such emphatic words shows that the forest industries of the United States were in difficulty. Over the years an apparently indifferent and in some cases corrupt government had given away or 'sold for peppercorn' over ninety per cent of all the forest area in the United States—to the railways, to the timber barons or to bogus homesteaders working on the side for the lumbermen. The tremendous expansion of the United States had created a demand for lumber of all kinds while the great city newspapers, increasing in size and circulation every year, required more and more pulp and paper. For these reasons, the great privately-owned timber preserves had been ruthlessly exploited and American forests were not only running short on lumber but were also being depleted of pulpwood.

The provincial government in Ontario was as quick to notice this growing shortage of pulpwood as it was to see the plight of the American sawmills. In 1902, the law prohibiting the export of pine logs was extended to include spruce, hemlock and other pulpwood logs. This was done not as a conservation measure but to encourage the development of more pulp-and-paper mills. However, Ontario did not fully control the supply of pulpwood (as she did the supply of pine) and she could not interfere with the other provinces. The only way in which the export of all pulpwood could be prevented was by general federal legislation applying to all provinces. The government at Ottawa, however, was caught in a cross-fire of conflicting interests and concluded that the safest, if not the wisest, policy was to take no action.

As leader of the pulp-and-paper division of the Canadian Manufacturers' Association, American-born match king E. B. Eddy of Hull, Quebec, pressed hard for a federal law to prevent the export of raw pulpwood. Members of parliament from New Brunswick and Quebec tried to prevent any such law. Millions of acres of timber land in these two provinces were owned by the farmers and with the price of pulp logs rising from $4.00 to $7.25 per cord during the early years of the twentieth century they saw a chance to make a lot of money in a hurry. Some lumbermen, including two or three who were senators, also resisted any efforts to control their activities. For these reasons the government hesitated to act and the lumber companies and especially the farmers remained free to cut and export logs to the United States. This they did so thoroughly in some areas that farm woodlots were completely ruined and within a few years they found themselves having to buy their supplies of firewood. Over sixty-five per cent of all the pulpwood exported to the United States during the 1900–1914 period came from the farms of Quebec and the legislation passed in Ontario had very little effect.

The United States was not anxious to see her valuable paper companies migrate to Canada and establish branch plants close to the source of pulpwood. She encouraged the importation of logs or semi-manufactured pulp but placed a very high tax on newsprint made in Canada. As a result of this American legislation and of the lack of restrictions in Canada, the development of a domestic paper industry was somewhat delayed. However, the rising costs of making newsprint in the United States and the increasing supply in Canada of cheap electric power, which is so essential to the pulp-and-paper industry, caused many pulp and some paper mills to develop in this period regardless of the American regulations.

Finally, the shortage of newsprint in the United States became so acute and the pressure from the big influential newspapers so intense that the U.S.A. in 1913 removed most of the tax on newsprint from Canada. By this time also, Quebec and New Brunswick, following the example of Ontario, had passed laws to prevent the export of pulp logs. Therefore, during the two or three years before the outbreak of the First World War the forty-six paper companies which already had been established expanded their production greatly and many new Canadian, English and American firms were formed. In an extremely sudden burst of expansion—too fast to be healthy, as we shall see later—Canada by 1914 had become the world's leading exporter of newsprint, the foundation of what is today our largest industry had been laid, and a new and most important use for our great spruce and hemlock forests had been found.

Canada's Forest Policy

When the federal government purchased Rupert's Land from the Hudson's Bay Company in 1869, it retained control over all the crown lands in the Northwest and these lands were used to encourage railway building and homesteaders. In the older provinces of eastern Canada and in British Columbia, crown lands were left under provincial administration and thus the control of Canada's main forest areas lay in their hands. During the years under consideration in this chapter, the provincial governments allowed these forest resources to be exploited with very little thought for conservation or scientific principles of forest management. Some experts today say that the provinces were not then rich enough to finance a costly program of conservation, that scientific knowledge was lacking and that despite the heavy cutting there was no need for reforestation schemes. They seem to feel that a certain stage of destruction had to be reached before it became worthwhile to renew the forest by any means other than natural growth.

On the other hand it might be said that very large profits were made from the forests and conservation projects could have been supported. Some of the forests of Europe, especially those of Germany and Sweden, had been carefully managed for centuries. Their methods were known and advocated in Canada and could have been adapted to our conditions. The government of Ontario now plants several million white pines annually, but it takes many years for one of these trees to mature and lumber has yet to be cut from any of these reforested areas. The truth of the matter seems to be that most of the ctizens of the different provinces were not interested in conservation and allowed their governments to use the forests almost entirely to raise revenue.

Since each province regulated the fees to be charged for cutting timber on crown lands and since these regulations were changed frequently, there existed by 1914 a bewildering number of different long-term contracts between the lumber companies and the various provinces. In Ontario and Quebec timber limits—that is, the right to cut timber over a certain area of crown land—were usually, but not always, sold by auction to the lumber companies. (There were frequent charges of favouritism in granting these timber limits, and investigation sometimes revealed that choice areas had gone to the lumberman on the right side of the government and not necessarily to the highest bidder.) All provinces charged an annual 'ground rent' of so much per square mile and finally 'stumpage dues' were paid on the number of board feet of lumber cut. In all cases the ground rents and stumpage dues were ridiculously low, even for those days. In British Columbia, for instance, ground rents and stumpage combined allowed the lumber companies to cut Douglas fir for a payment to the government of less than 65 cents per thousand board feet at a time when they were receiving $17.50 or more per thousand at the mill. Since these contracts were on a fixed, long-term basis every increase in the selling price of lumber was an extra windfall for the lumber companies.

The responsibilities of the lumbermen under these generous contracts were very few and in Ontario they were non-existent. Companies operating in Ontario could cut down any size of tree, they could leave great piles of slash in the bush as a fire hazard, they did not have to share in the cost of forest fire-fighting or protect their limits in any way, and they could feed their camps on unlimited quantities of fish and game. In Quebec and British Columbia the lumber companies were compelled to share the cost of forest fire protection; in Quebec young trees less than thirteen inches in diameter could not be cut; only in British Columbia was a start made in clearing up the slash and this was at the government's expense; otherwise the companies in these two provinces were as free as those in Ontario to do as they pleased.

An outstanding Canadian authority on the history of lumbering in North America came to this conclusion: 'The species "lumberman" has been the same on both sides of the border, that is to say he has been primarily interested in making money for himself. In accordance with the spirit of this continent, he has been neither overly scrupulous nor far-sighted in his invasion of the forest.'

During the first decade of the twentieth century as our forest resources became more valuable, one cause of their destruction did arouse all public-spirited Canadians and completely overshadowed all other thoughts about forest conservation. Senator Edwards, when asked in 1907 why the forests were being depleted even though nature was continually replenishing them, replied: 'Because of forest fires; forest fires caused by passage of railways through or near the limits; by camping parties, fishermen and more recently by explorers for minerals; and by the criminal negligence of settlers on the land who have always regarded the forest as an obstacle and an enemy.' If the Senator had added to this list the slash piles left in the woods by his own and other lumber companies this picture of the causes for forest fires would be complete.

Forest fires have always been an important but tragic chapter in our history. During the expansion of the 1900–1914 period they were more frequent and more destructive than ever before and became the nation's major problem in conservation. Nor were their effects confined merely to the destruction of timber. In 1911 the Porcupine fire, a forty-eight-hour disaster, burned 73 people to death as it blazed over 864 square miles. It wiped out South Porcupine, Pottsville, Cochrane and Goldlands, destroyed $3 million worth of gold-mining property, and left 3,000 people homeless. The Matheson fire, a one-week holocaust in 1916, destroyed the town and took a toll of 232 lives. And just fifty years ago the town of Haileybury and the settlements of North Cobalt, Charlton, Heaslip and Thornloe were devastated as flames roared over 2,000 square miles, killing 44 inhabitants, destroying the homes of 7,000, and causing property damage of $7 million.

All the provinces did their best to cope with this gigantic challenge: much more money was spent, the ranger service was greatly expanded, laws were passed to control the railways, and squatters 'with their two-acre potato patches' were chased off the timber limits. However, without the airplane, powerful portable pumps or chemicals of any kind, without adequate telephone service and with the indifference or ignorance of so many people, the task was far beyond them. Year after year in all parts of the country, and especially in Ontario and British Columbia, great fires lifted from their starting points to the tree tops and raced out of control across the forests. They caused more permanent damage to the forests of Canada than all the assaults of the lumbermen.

Of Metals and Men

Before the Cobalt Strike

Alfred La Rose, a blacksmith working on the Timiskaming and Northern Ontario Railway, was on his way home to Hull for a holiday. He had with him three little pieces of rock and $1,500. The rocks came from a patch of ground that he had just staked as a copper mine claim and the money was from his boss, one of the contractors building the railway, for a half interest in the claim. On his way to Hull, La Rose stopped off at the lumbering village of Mattawa and showed his three 'floats' to the owner of the general store, who eventually bought a quarter interest for $3,500. Neither Duncan McMartin, the contractor, nor Noah Timmins, the storekeeper, had any idea that the steps they took to acquire the La Rose mine were the first towards the most spectacular event in the history of Ontario mining, an event which began to reveal the tremendous wealth of the Laurentian Shield and founded the mining fortunes on which later developments of utmost importance to Canada were based.

Before Fred La Rose staked his claim in September 1903, at what was soon to become the town of Cobalt, Ontario was not an important mining province. Mining attention during the last half of the nineteenth century had centred in British Columbia. Gold discoveries in the Fraser River valley lured prospectors from the depleted California fields. The famous Cariboo Road opened up the Kootenays and the towns of Rossland, Nelson and Barkersville sprang up.

The Yukon was the scene of the last great rush when free gold was found in the gravel bars of the turbulent Klondike River in 1896. From all over the world the seekers came, braving the rigours of the treacherous Chilkoot and White passes, in their search for the final Eldorado. Dawson City, numbering ten thousand souls in its short-lived golden age, is now a crumbling ghost town of less than fifteen hundred, revived sporadically by tourist festivals trying to recapture the roaring days of the sourdoughs. By 1903 the little claims along the fabled creeks like Bonanza and Hunker were being bought up by the Guggenheim family and moulded into the Yukon Consolidated Gold Corporation, and placer mining was a thing of the past.

There was, however, one major mining development well under way in Ontario before the Cobalt boom. This was in the Sudbury district where two companies had begun to mine the copper-nickel deposits first revealed in 1883 by dynamite blasts clearing the the roadbed for the C.P.R. One of these was the Canadian Copper Company, an American concern with its smelter at Copper Cliff and its refinery at Orford in New Jersey. This company's first shipment to New Jersey caused great consternation because the ore contained nickel. At the time, nickel had few known uses and no process existed to separate it from the much more desirable copper. By the beginning of the twentieth century Orford scientists had solved the major technical problems and the president of the Canadian Copper Company had convinced the steel-makers—and especially

Shipment of gold dust worth $750,000, Dawson City, Yukon Territory, September 20, 1899

those manufacturing armour plate for the world's increasing navies—that nickel was the best of alloys for hardening their product. Dr. Ludwig Mond, a chemist of German origin working in England, also discovered a method for separating nickel from copper. When the Canadian Copper Company turned down his offer to sell this process, Dr. Mond formed the Mond Nickel Company with a smelter at Coniston and its refinery in Wales. Thus the two companies that were to form eventually the famous International Nickel Company, now supplying over ninety per cent of the world's requirements, had made a good start before 1903.

Twelve Square Miles of Wilderness

'Two years ago the land about Cobalt would not have sold for ten cents an acre. It is rocky and swampy and it would take a quarter section of it to feed a goat. Yet today some of it would bring a hundred dollars a square inch and there is one tract of forty acres, within a stone's throw of where I am writing, that you could not buy for a million dollars in cash.' At the time this account was sent out, in December 1906, by a reporter for the Buffalo *Express*, the Cobalt strike was in full, wild-eyed swing. The area round Kerr and Cobalt Lakes had been staked out in thousands of small, overlapping forty-acre claims, 584 mining companies had been formed to sell $504 million worth of shares to the unsuspecting or grasping public, and enough ore had already been shipped to New York to make this twelve square miles of wilderness the greatest silver-mining camp in the world, producing 'more silver than all the mines in Montana put together'. Cobalt had grown from the marshes to a town of over seven thousand, but was still so raw that one man was killed by dynamite exploded by an eager prospector looking for treasure right on the main street. Gray cyanide slime was dumped ruthlessly into the clear waters close to the town and the name 'Poison Lake' became a grim reality. Unlike most mining booms which seem to occur in far-off places accessible only by packhorse or dogteam, this one lay along the railway tracks and old sourdoughs, amateur prospectors, lawyers and promoters could 'mush to El Dorado by pullman car'. During the summer of 1906 eleven coach-loads of speculators from New York and Toronto were reported to have arrived at Cobalt in one day and the stampede to buy shares in Cobalt silver mines was so great that a special detachment of police was called out for a few days to control the crowds on Wall Street.

After the Cobalt area was solidly staked, prospectors paddled and portaged, during the summer months, out from Haileybury, New Liskeard or Cobalt in every direction, and others during the winter added to the confusion by 'snow-staking' on top of claims already made. In quick succession Larder Lake, Elk Lake and Gowganda flashed across the headlines in spectacular reports, but few good mines were found. In fact very few of the mining companies formed in the whole Cobalt area had any chance of success. Some did strike it rich beyond their wildest dreams; some fizzled out in honest efforts to create producing mines; a great many were nothing more than the fraudulent schemes of dishonest men. In an article about the wildcat companies at Larder Lake in 1907, the Canadian *Northern Miner* summed up the situation with these words: 'The reputation of the mining industry is being ruined by these brokers who continue to sell gold bricks to the people. The money put into this region has passed mainly into the pockets of the promoters and of the newspapers who will play up any company advertising in their pages.'

Only twenty-nine companies of all the ones formed during the Cobalt boom developed producing mines, but those companies (fifteen of which were Canadian and the rest American) made many millions of dollars. The thin, soft silver veins at Cobalt lay right on the surface and the only mining equipment really needed was a pick, a burlap bag and a husky pair of shoulders. Even when the diggings went deeper and expensive machinery and reduction plants were installed, the costs of producing silver remained very low and the profits made were enormous. These mines by 1914 had yielded silver worth $115 million and silver ranked second in the value of Canada's mineral production. Today the world's sources of silver are nearly exhausted. Silver production has fallen to twentieth place in Canada, and in the second half of 1968 the Royal Canadian Mint changed over to pure nickel from silver alloy in the production of Canadian coinage.

Of the $115 million yield in those early years, it is estimated that over sixty-five per cent was profit for shareholders and promoters. This is the importance of the Cobalt strike. It created a few mining men who had the wealth and experience

Cobalt Lake Silver Mine

to finance the exploration of northern Ontario's resources and who could develop other areas just as soon as the prospector's hammer revealed new mineral wealth.

The Golden Pole beyond Description
One day in September 1909, W. S. Edwards, a businessman from Chicago, was persuaded by four prospectors whom he had grub-staked to risk the rough bush country west of the T.N.O. Railway (frequently called the 'Time-no-object Line') and see for himself what they had found. When the party returned to Matheson Junction a week or so later Edwards wired to his partner in Chicago: 'We have discovered the golden pole beyond description.' Immediately Larder Lake, Elk Lake and Gowganda were forgotten, prospectors streamed northwards, and the great Porcupine Lake gold rush was under way. Within two years, five townships were staked out in ten thousand claims. Despite repeated warnings that this was not a poor man's camp as Cobalt was and that if there were millions in the ground it would take millions to get it out, despite all efforts to keep the advertising honest, speculation again ran riot in Porcupine stocks. One famous mine was temporarily devastated by the fire of 1911. West Dome had been organized by Auguste Heinze, a ruthless mining man from Montana who had built the first smelter at Trail. William Van Horne purchased the smelter and other Heinze interests, refinanced the mine and in 1906 organized the Consolidated Mining and Smelting Company, today the largest base-metal mining company in Canada. Associated with Heinze in his Porcupine venture was Sir Henry Pellatt, who was doing very well at the time with two silver mines at Cobalt and other interests across the country. Financial ruin and the loss of Casa Loma—'Pellatt's Folly'—still lay many years ahead.

Three big mining companies were formed before the fire and survived it.
W. S. Edwards, backed by New York men with interests in Cobalt and in the
Canadian Copper Company at Sudbury, formed the Dome Mining Company;
Noah Timmins, Duncan McMartin and their legal adviser, David Dunlap,
bought the claims of Benny Hollinger; and an American group took over the
claims that the unfortunate Sandy McIntyre had sold about the countryside for
a few dollars. By 1914 Hollinger, Dome and McIntyre—outstanding companies
in Canadian mining history—had made the area round the new town of Timmins
into the greatest gold-producing camp in Canada. Before the Porcupine discoveries in 1909, the province of Ontario produced no gold; five years later the
annual production was over $6 million and gold ranked next to silver and nickel
in the rapidly expanding mining industry of the province.

All That Glitters

The history of Canadian mining is one story after another of adventure and
daring development. There is the saga of the prospectors, most of them amateurs
in the old days, travelling by canoe through the forest wilderness; to some it was
a grim necessity in the quest for riches, to others it became a way of life. There
are tales of those who succeeded and of those who, had they but scraped the
moss a few feet farther on or drilled an inch or two deeper, would have found
great wealth. A story could be told of two rival groups of men meeting by chance
on a bitterly cold winter night in 1912 at an abandoned mining claim and of the
partnership formed which indirectly led to the Wright-Hargreaves and Lake-
shore gold mines, the town of Kirkland Lake and the fortunes of William Wright
and Harry Oakes. On the other side is the struggle of the miners to rise above
the almost animal existence of the early mining camps and to secure through
their trade unions a better share of all this wealth. Finally, there is the patient
but equally dramatic work of the scientists finding new processes and new uses
for metal, all helping to roll back the mining frontiers.

By 1914 mineral production in Canada had reached an annual value of $145½
million. This may seem a paltry figure compared to modern-day production
which reached a record high in 1968 of $4,725 million, but compared to the year
1900—even with the Yukon at its height—it represented an increase of over one
hundred per cent. Only since 1945 with the tremendous developments in iron,
uranium and oil has the period 1900–1914 ever been equalled for the rapidity of
growth in mining. In these early years of the twentieth century Ontario rose to
prominence as the mining province, eventually producing almost 50 per cent of
the total mineral wealth of Canada; British Columbia slipped into second
position with 22 per cent and was trailed by Nova Scotia (10 per cent), Quebec
(8 per cent) and Alberta (8 per cent). Ontario's dominant position was secured
almost entirely by the development of silver, gold and nickel which we have been
considering in the preceding pages.

However, the somewhat spectacular growth of Ontario must not be allowed
to obscure the record of progress in other parts of the country. The mines of
British Columbia held their lead in all base metals, especially copper, and yielded

almost as much gold as did those in the Porcupine area. Coal outshone all the more glittering metals and was much the most valuable product of the mining industry during all of this period, yet Ontario had no coal mines. Nova Scotia's rank as third in mining was due to the fact that half the coal in Canada came from within her boundaries. Likewise coal from the Lethbridge and Drumheller areas accounted for almost all the mining in Alberta. Quebec, in those days before Noranda, Chibougamau and Labrador iron, relied on asbestos and cement to give her any standing in the mining industry. Like all other Canadian statistics in this period, those for the production of coal, iron (from imported ores), nickel, copper, precious metals, cement and asbestos soared upwards, bringing additional prosperity.

At first glance, the causes of this rapid development of mining do not seem to fit into any pattern. In particular, the Kootenay district, the Yukon and Cobalt appear to be only happy accidents not connected with western settlement, wheat and railways. Indeed, the Klondike must be regarded as a dramatic accident: it had no specific national causes and it left only a few permanent results. Silver mining at Cobalt, however, would not have started when it did, and might have been delayed many years, but for the T.N.O. Railway. Since this railway was built as a colonization road to extend settlements into the Clay Belt, it may be said that Cobalt does fit into the general pattern of development. Southern British Columbia was opened up for definite reasons, but these were, at first, associated almost entirely with the westward expansion of the United States. Businessmen in the nearby states of Montana and Washington began to mine the Rossland-Trail area for American markets before Canada was in a position to do much about it. Later on, the settlement of the Northwest Territories and the building of railways made the mineral wealth of southern British Columbia important to Canada, and as a result, Canadian companies began to invest in this area. Not only here, but all the way across the country to Nova Scotia, every phase of mining—and especially coal, iron, copper, nickel and cement—was stimulated by the settlement of the West, by wheat, by railways and the general expansion of the Canadian economy that they caused.

4 'MADE IN CANADA'

Business before Politics

When the colourful young Benjamin Disraeli gave his maiden speech in the British House of Commons, he was shouted down in a tumult and could not finish what he had to say. An old friend cautioned him to make his speech on some tarnished and uninteresting subject: 'Wait until something comes up about imports and exports and then address the House on tariff legislation; nothing is so dull as the tariff.' Although Disraeli followed his friend's advice and his speech was dullness itself, it does not necessarily follow that all tariff questions are lacking in interest. The importance of the tariff in the history of Canada's industrial development cannot be overemphasized.

A tariff to protect the Canadian market for Canadian manufacturers was one of the cornerstones of the National Policy. During the general election in 1896 the Liberals promised they would lower the tariff—and so the prices to the consumer of imported goods—and although this was not the main reason for their victory, they did take over the government of Canada on the clear understanding that duties on imports would be lowered. However, they no sooner came into power than the tariff suddenly became much too important to challenge. The rush of immigrants, the settlement of the West, the burst of railway building, the boom in lumbering and mining, all helped to create a rich market for manufactured goods. Taxes on imports were really wanted now by the Canadian factory owners to block out foreign competitors, and increasing tariff protection became the Golden Fleece of Canadian manufacturers during the prosperous early years of the twentieth century. Their efforts to boost the import duties were strenuously resisted by other groups in the country and for over ten years the tariff was one of the most lively issues in Canada. When the Liberals finally listened to the siren song of those who favoured free trade, it brought about their downfall in the elections of 1911.

The Campaign for Higher Tariffs
The campaign for higher tariffs began as soon as imports from the United States began to pour into Canada, and as these imports increased the demand for more protection grew louder and louder. Robert Borden, leader of the Conservative opposition, gave the reason which all high tariff supporters had in mind when he said: 'Our raw materials are being bought by United States manufacturers and Canada is buying back manufactured products which should be made in Canada. We need more protection and a tariff which will keep within this country the money now going to swell the coffers of other lands.' In 1902, when a delegation of industrialists asked W. S. Fielding, the Minister of Finance, for

increased duties on imports they received an evasive reply and were told to 'educate the people to your viewpoint'. This the industrialists set out to do at once and a great drive was started to educate the people to the blessings of the tariff.

The Canadian Manufacturers' Association, which had been formed in 1885 with the main purpose of promoting tariff protection, was reorganized in 1900 and swung into high gear, a powerful organization speaking for all the major industries of the country. Its membership shot up from 342 to over 2,000 in seven years, surely an indication in itself that manufacturing was flourishing. To popularize the 'Made in Canada' idea, *Industrial Canada,* an official publication of the C.M.A., was set up to tub thump for higher tariffs, and a $50,000 fund was raised to promote pro-tariff advertising. The Canadian Industrial League coined the popular slogan, 'Canada for Canadians and business before politics'. In this campaign the people were given to understand that most of what was being imported could be made in Canada and that Canadian industries simply could not survive without the tariff.

All this tariff propaganda was phrased in lofty, patriotic terms. A high tariff, it was said, would make people richer because their money would be spent in Canada; it would develop the cities, give more employment to Canadian workers and keep 'our boys' from going to the United States; it would provide a prosperous urban market for Canadian farmers; it would prevent American manufacturers from exploiting our natural resources and compel American companies to establish branch plants on Canadian soil. Politicians, however, regulated the tariff and the government was besieged with petitions and delegations pressing for increased duties. Finally, in 1905, Fielding in his budget speech promised to set up a tariff commission which would tour the country to see what changes should be made in the existing rates of duty.

The record of Canadian businessmen appearing before this Tariff Commission, which held sittings across Canada during the fall of 1905, makes rather humorous or dismal reading, depending on your point of view. Completely conflicting, selfish interests arose at every one of its twenty-seven sessions. Industry after industry pleaded for higher tariffs to protect its products from foreign competition and in the same breath requested lower duties on everything it used as raw materials. Perhaps the climax was reached when the Ontario Society of Artists demanded a flat ten-dollar tax on every oil painting imported into the country.

The spokesman for one of the many farm groups appearing before Fielding's Commission concluded his remarks with the following neat summary of the attitude towards the tariff held by most of the farm population: 'We took the manufacturers into our arms twenty years ago when they were infants; we bought their protected products when American prices were far lower; we nursed them along until they were big, strong men. Is it possible that now, when they are able to stand alone, the tariff is going to be increased? Their finished product is our raw material and if our prices are to be raised, to use a barnyard phrase, we will kick like steers.'

A barn-raising near Thornloe, Ontario, 1912

Most of the farmers in Ontario and all of them out West kicked against the tariff and in doing so were but continuing an age-old North American argument between agriculture and industry. Farmers claimed that their product was sold in the free, unprotected markets of the world, that a tariff compelled them to buy at higher prices from protected home industries and that every increase in their costs made it more difficult for them to compete in world markets against other countries.

Faced with this hostility from the farmers and unable to see through the welter of conflicting evidence submitted by the industrialists, Fielding and his associates decided not to tinker with the tariff too much. As a result of the Commission's findings some changes were made in 1907, but the basic average rates of duty remained about the same as they had been when the Liberal party came to power in 1896. The Canadian Manufacturers' Association, of course, was extremely disappointed; on its behalf H. Cockshutt, the agricultural implement manufacturer from Brantford, sent a strongly worded statement to the government: 'We had every reason to expect that the new tariff would impose a higher scale of duties. The proposed tariff will not encourage either the establishment of new industries or further the expansion of those already established.' At the Toronto branch meeting of the C.M.A. many uncomplimentary things were said about Fielding's new tariff, and E. Gurney, the stovemaker, declared that the

Association should make the tariff its politics until every industry in Canada received more protection. 'I would make the tariff,' he said, 'as high as Haman's gallows if it would keep the Yankee out.' One cannot help but wonder whether Gurney ever realized that, if his suggestions were carried out fully, Canadian industry might have suffered more or less the same fate as Haman did in the Bible story.

The Champions of Free Trade

On the morning of December 16, 1910, one thousand or so farmers from western Canada—the largest delegation ever to appear before the Canadian government —marched down the streets of Ottawa and overflowed into the House of Commons. No shuffling horde of sheepskins these, but confident, successful farmers dressed in their Sunday-go-to-meeting clothes. Only by their broad faces and foreign accents could the former immigrants be distinguished from the Canadian and American farmers who descended on the parliament buildings that morning. All day and well into the night the Governor General, members of the Senate, Sir Wilfrid Laurier and his cabinet, and the crowded press gallery listened to those representatives of the Grain Growers' Association from the three prairie provinces.

They protested against the terminal elevator and cold storage companies and demanded government ownership of them; they protested against the railways and demanded still lower freight rates; they complained about the high cost of living and blamed the tariff. They attacked the industrialists in no uncertain terms, claiming that the tariff allowed businessmen to build up huge companies and to form 'combines' among themselves by which they controlled prices and soaked the public. All of what the farmers had to say carried a familiar American tone of discontent. Fifteen or twenty years ago many of these men, or their fathers before them, had been members of the Populist party and had used these same terms to attack the growing power of 'big business' in the United States. Now this campaign, with far less justification, was being transferred to Canadian soil. The West, striving to build a civilization from scratch on the prairies and interested in any experiment which might speed up its development, was a natural hotbed for these radical American ideas, and in 1910 the wheat farmers threw the first of their many bombshells into the political arena of Canada.

The cure for all their real and imagined troubles, so the farmers urged, was free trade with the United States. Reciprocity! The old cry and bitter arguments of a bygone age all over again? North-south trade when Canada finally had her own east-west trade and was building railways at the rate of two miles a day to handle more of it? Free trade with the industrialized United States just as Canadian businessmen had found their long-awaited home markets and were expanding their production by leaps and bounds? Free trade for the farmers when eighty per cent of all they produced was now being sold in the thriving cities of their own country and a profitable export market easily handled the remainder? Surely they could not be serious and if they were, who would listen to them?

The Prime Minister of Canada—making the biggest political mistake of his career—listened. But important as the prairie lobby was, other factors influenced Laurier's decision and not the least of these was American in origin.

In 1908, the American presidential election was won by William Taft and the Republican party. One of the appeals made to the electorate had been a promise to revise the tariff structure and this had been considered by many as a declaration of tariff reduction. At this time in the U.S. the protectionist policy was under public criticism. City populations blamed the high tariff for rising costs of living; the muckrakers, the Ralph Naders of the Gilded Age, frequently unearthed tariff favours sold to businessmen by politicians; more and more the tariff was attacked as legislation favouring the privileged few.

Once in power the Republicans did little to change the policy but pressures continued to mount. The 1910 Congressional election saw the Democrats control the House of Representatives and many Republican senators favouring tariff reduction sat in the narrowly divided Senate. U.S. industry was now producing far more than they could sell in their own country and a potential market in prosperous Canada looked good to American businessmen. Taft, responding to internal economic and political influences, expressed interest in a new trade agreement in an interview with the editor of the Toronto *Globe*, and Fielding, a Nova Scotian exponent of free trade, persuaded Laurier to begin discussion.

At first the negotiations attracted little public attention. Canadian statesmen had made Washington pilgrimages many times since Confederation almost begging for free trade. Each time the American government had turned a deaf ear to their proposals and prohibitive tariffs continued to exclude Canadian products from expanding U.S. markets. In desperation Canada hit back with the National Policy of protecting her industry, but Liberals and Conservatives alike would have changed this policy any day, if the U.S.A. had been willing to admit Canadian primary products duty-free across the border.

This time the situation was different. The Americans had taken the initiative; they had come to Canada. This was no cap-in-hand appeal by impoverished Johnny Canuck politicians but sophisticated negotiation by two fast-developing nations. In the frank words of President Taft: 'Free trade gives us an opportunity to increase the supply of our natural resources which, with the wastefulness of children, we have wantonly exhausted. The resources of Canada which will be open to us under this Agreement are now apparently inexhaustible.'

The sweeping trade agreement that had been worked out was presented by Fielding to the House of Commons on January 26, 1911. The correspondent of the Montreal *Herald*, a Liberal newspaper, described the House as aware, within ten minutes, that Fielding's speech was making history. 'The duty-free list of products had swelled and swelled and swelled and as . . . members leaned forward to catch every word, triumph was written on the faces of the Liberals and dismay on the visages of the opposition.'

The opposition benches were indeed stunned; the bargain was much better than anyone expected. The National Policy of protecting Canadian manufacturers remained almost intact, President Taft and his colleagues clearly recognizing the need for Canada to shield her young industries from American competition; the duties were lowered but not removed from a long list of products which, it was felt, would benefit the farmer and the consumer. (These included farm implements, automobiles, plumbing fixtures and building materials, and food products such as meat, tinned fruit, flour and biscuits.) Most important, there was to be complete free trade across the border in all primary products and the majority of Canadian farmers pictured the rich urban markets of the United States opened to them.

As soon as the news of this reciprocity agreement flashed out across the country from Ottawa the industrial, financial and railway interests in Canada took alarm and decided to fight it every step of the way. Railway promoters feared that their long east-west hauls would be ruined; manufacturers, although the proposed changes did not affect most of them, felt that this was the thin edge of the wedge and they would be next; bankers, connected through their loans with both the railways and the manufacturers, gave their full support. Borden and his colleagues, sensing that here at last was an issue that might defeat the government, used every device to obstruct the passage of the bill. The Liberals, instead of using

UNCLE SAM—"I CAN ALMOST HEAR THEM SINGING THE STAR SPANGLED BANNER' IN OTTAWA, BE GOSH."

the closure rules and forcing the bill through, finally accepted the challenge of the opposition. On July 29 parliament was dissolved and the government placed reciprocity before that 'million-headed Caesar', the voters of Canada.

The Election of 1911

The Conservative party, 'down to fighting weight after fifteen years of hungry opposition', waged an intensive, well-organized campaign for the next seven weeks. It was most vigorously supported by the flour-milling and canning companies, the meat packers, the railways, the agricultural implement manufacturers, the cement companies, certain sections of the iron and steel industry and all others whose products were on the free or lower duty list. Robert Meighen, president of the Lake of the Woods Milling Company, J. W. 'Porky' Flavelle, Harry Cockshutt, George Drummond, president of the newly formed Canada Iron Corporation, Sir W. M. Aitken, the young millionaire promoter of the Steel Company of Canada and the Canada Cement Company, Sir William Van Horne, ex-president of the C.P.R., and many other industrialists made no bones about their deep personal interest in defeating the reciprocity agreement. Eighteen prominent Toronto men, all well-known Liberals, broke with Laurier and signed a manifesto protesting against freer trade with the United States. This 'Revolt of the Eighteen'—led by Clifford Sifton and including Sir Edmund Walker, president of the Bank of Commerce, W. D. Matthews of the Dominion Bank, Z. A. Lash, lawyer for the Canadian Northern Railway, John C. Eaton of the T. Eaton Company and E. R. Wood, one of the leading financiers in Canada—was used by the Liberal politicians as further evidence that the 'big interests' were opposed to something that would benefit the mass of the people.

The British Preference, that is, the system of lower duties on British imports which had been introduced by Laurier in 1897–1900, became much more popular with Canadian industrialists—a patriotic move intermingled with the fact that British competition, even with the Preference, was less severe than American competition. Above the selfish clash of obvious economic interests there was a strong and in many cases sincere feeling that national unity and the Empire ties were at stake once more and it was on this issue that the campaign of 1911 was mainly contested.

Supporters of the reciprocity agreement in the United States played right into the hands of the Conservative party in Canada. The more President Taft and others tried to persuade Americans that the bargain was a good one for them, the more suspicious Canadians became of it. Furthermore, the Canadian-American negotiations for free trade revived some of the old hopes for annexation. Beauchamp 'Champ' Clark, Speaker of the House of Representatives, was by no means alone in his thinking when he said: 'I am for reciprocity because I hope to see the day when the American flag will float over every square foot of British North America, clear to the North Pole.' These foolish American sentiments about reciprocity, receiving wide publicity in Canada, lent truth to the Conservative argument that our national independence was in jeopardy and helped to doom the Liberal party.

As September 21 drew closer and Conservative confidence gained with each passing hour, the public was deluged with a tremendous appeal to national sentiment. The faltering voice of Liberal orators, trying to arouse the people with thin, precise arguments about free trade with the United States, had little chance against such appeals as the Conservative candidate in Edmonton used the night before the elections: 'You are given an opportunity to say that the flag under which we stand is good enough for us. The people of this country have felt the touch in this election of a vanished hand and there has stolen into the hearts and minds of us all the echo of a voice long since stilled in death—the still small voice from the sacred shadow of that grave in Kingston. I hear it and the course is clear to me: "A British subject I was born, a British subject I will die." '

In the cold light of the present, many historians and political scientists would say that all this was dangerous political nonsense. But whatever the judgement of our generation may be of the methods used in 1911, the fact remains that the majority of Canadians decided, in the passionate debates of those days, that a vote for Borden was indeed a 'vote for King and Flag and Canada'. Industrialized Ontario and British Columbia voted so solidly for the Conservatives that small Liberal majorities in the other provinces were wiped out and the Laurier regime was ended. Somewhere along the line a prosperous, confident Canada had concluded that the tariff was the price to be paid for national independence.

When the Liberal party came to power in 1896 the average duty paid on imports coming into the country was 30 per cent. Except for the British Preference, which did not stem the growing importance of American products in our markets, these duty rates that the Liberals inherited remained almost unchanged. Efforts to raise these duties and give Canadian industry more protection failed in the years 1905 to 1907. Likewise, efforts to lower the duties and expose a larger part of the Canadian economy to outside competition collapsed before the successful campaign of the Conservatives in 1911. Thus throughout the period 1896–1914, at a crucial time when Canada's home market was expanding so fast, Canadian manufacturers received protection on a very wide range of products. Duties varied from 17½ per cent on agricultural implements to 35 per cent on certain kinds of railway equipment—the average rate of all duties being about 28 per cent. With this protection, the calamities predicted by the Canadian Manufacturers' Association in 1907 did not occur. New industries grew apace, old industries expanded and products 'made in Canada' enjoyed 75 per cent of our sheltered domestic market.

Behind the Tariff Wall

Primary and Secondary Industries

From the very day in 1879 when Sir John A. Macdonald invited Canadian businessmen to set the import duties of the National Policy, the tariff has been a major cause of bribery and industrial trickery, and a source of bitter political argument. This should not be allowed to obscure the basic fact that a very large part of Canadian manufacturing industry could not have developed without tariff protection. Blocking out foreign competitors could not in itself stimulate manufacturing. High duties existed in the nineteenth century but industrial development, as we know, was painfully slow because there were few good markets. The great majority of the 76,000 manufacturing establishments in Canada in 1900 were unimportant small factories, employing fewer than five workers and struggling to survive on a limited local market. The forward surge of manufacturing came only with the upswing of world prosperity, the settlement of the West and the building of railways. The tariff did not cause the great buying spree in this period but it did direct it into Canadian channels. Despite the complex history of manufacturing through two world wars, despite the appearance of new industries and the discovery of new resources, the manufacturing industry of Canada today rests squarely on the foundations laid during the formative early years of this century.

Leading the field were the great natural industries of Canada. These primary industries processed our natural resources and produced mainly for the export market. Some were the traditional older industries—flour milling, lumbering, dairy production and meat packing—and others such as pulp and paper and metal refining were more or less new to the twentieth century. Just as they do today, these primary industries provided the main source of revenue from exports. We have already seen how they helped to finance the imports from the United States and the investments from Great Britain without which the rapid development from 1900 to 1914 would have been impossible. Primary industries grew in response to market conditions in Britain and the United States and tariff protection, although they did receive it, was less important in their development than it was in fostering 'secondary manufacturing'.

Secondary manufacturing is the name given to industries making machinery, agricultural implements, automobiles, electrical appliances and a multitude of other finished products. It is used also to describe such industries as iron and steel and aluminum which process raw materials not available in Canada. Unlike many primary industries, secondary manufacturing is almost entirely for domestic consumption. From the beginning of the twentieth century to the present, these industries have sold well over ninety per cent of all they produced in the Canadian market. Today, secondary manufacturing industries are much more important in many ways than our primary industries: they employ more men, have more capital invested in them and produce about three-quarters of all the

manufactured goods in Canada. They have added a whole new section to our
economy.

In the years before the First World War Canada relied on her basic export
industries and was exposed, therefore, to world conditions beyond her control.
Secondary manufacturing, dependent on domestic markets, has given us greater
stability and independence. This does not mean that Canada, lying cheek by jowl
beside the United States for three thousand miles, is fully independent of
business conditions across the border. Nor does it mean, as will be seen later, that
secondary industries are not hit by world depression just as hard as are primary
industries. It does mean that we are now in a far better position than we were in
the days when all our eggs, so to speak, were in one basket—or all our wheat was
in the one flour bag. For these reasons the rapid progress of secondary manufacturing is one of the most important of all the developments in the 1900–1914
period.

'Big Business' Comes to Canada

In 1894 an ambitious young lawyer from Philadelphia came up to the village
of Sault Ste. Marie with multi-million-dollar ideas in his head. When Francis H.
Clergue arrived at the Sault he found a primitive settlement in a wilderness. Six
years later, due to his promotional efforts, the Sault had the makings of a great
steel industry. Iron being mined locally at the Helen Mine and imported ore
from the Carnegie-owned Mesabi Range southwest of Lake Superior fed the
new blast furnaces and foundries. It had street railways, a ferry line, freight and
passenger steamers and the new Algoma Central Railway; great power canals
and power houses were in full operation. Twenty-five million dollars, so Clergue
said, had been spent on all these various enterprises.

In 1904 the Lake Superior Corporation, controlling all these companies,
tottered in financial chaos and Francis Clergue left Sault Ste. Marie. At a farewell
dinner, he gave a piece of interesting advice to some of his Canadian friends:
'You people up here,' he said, 'are still in the bush. The markets for any of
your products are not really large and yet in every industry dozens of small,
inefficient companies are to be found competing furiously with each other. This
results in loss of profits to all concerned. You cannot turn out great numbers of
low-cost, standardized products unless you build big factories, equipped with
expensive machinery. And you can't afford to do this until a lot of these small
companies are eliminated.'

Possibly Canadian businessmen did not need this advice. By the beginning of
the twentieth century they had begun to scent the advantages of combining or
'merging' small companies into bigger ones and they had before them the shining
example of the United States. The Gilded Age of the American 'Robber Barons'
was in full swing. Giant railway company mergers dominated the transportation
system. In 1890 the formation of two huge monopolistic companies set the
pattern—the American Tobacco complex under the control of James B. Duke
and the global giant of Standard Oil led by John D. Rockefeller. The climax of
the great combines came in 1901, when J. P. Morgan and Andrew Carnegie

A small iron foundry at Midland, Ontario, 1901

created the United States Steel Corporation, the world's first billion-dollar trust. Canadian companies could never hope to equal these American records, but within the limits of our much smaller market they could follow the example of the United States.

Some of the most important Canadian mergers were in the iron and steel industry. This industry was not one of our natural ones and yet it was basic to industrialization. Canada had virtually no iron mines in those days and all ores were imported. The blast furnaces at the Sault and Hamilton relied on iron ore from the Mesabi mines and imported all their coal from the United States also. The Cape Breton industry combined native Nova Scotia coal with iron ore from the Wabana mine on Bell Island, Newfoundland. Under these circumstances it is not surprising that a large part of the imports from the U.S.A. were iron ore, coal and various forms of raw steel. The Canadian government encouraged the industry by a system of 'bounties'—money grants to companies that produced iron and steel in Canada—and by tariff protection to companies using these as raw materials. The demand for locomotives, rails, freight cars, agricultural and mining machinery, nails, wire and many other iron and steel products was great. With this assured demand—much of it coming from generous government contracts—and fully encouraged by bounties and tariffs, the Canadian iron and steel industry expanded its production by over 300 per cent in the early years of the new century and led the secondary manufacturing field from 1900–1930.

A few Canadian businessmen decided to take full advantage of these favourable conditions, and from their efforts arose some of the large iron and steel companies that we know today. Coal and iron companies at Sydney, Nova Scotia, after several years of bitter argument, combined to form the Dominion Steel Corporation; steel works and rolling mills at Montreal and Hamilton joined with the five companies comprising the Canada Bolt and Nut Company to lay the foundations of the Steel Company of Canada; the Pioneer Iron Company at Drummondville, Quebec, amalgamated with several other foundries in the Canada Iron Corporation. Finally, British and Canadian financial interests reorganized some of Clergue's enterprises at Sault Ste. Marie into the now famous Algoma Steel Corporation.

In almost all industries the spirit of merger ran high. Promoters were busy in cement, asbestos, boots and shoes, paints and such flourishing primary industries as flour milling, brewing, canning and meat packing, and lake shipping companies joined the procession. In the years 1909 to 1911 when the stock market was particularly favourable to the sale of new stocks and bonds, some forty amalgamations absorbed 196 separate companies. There have been other more important merger periods in Canadian history, but in the years before the First World War a great many of our large corporations were formed. Some of the companies were carelessly or hastily organized and have been dissolved; others have lost their identity in later mergers, but many of the great names in this early period are familiar to us today.

The most ambitious of all these amalgamations was the Canada Cement Company which combined eleven companies under its control and left only one or two competitors of any size. This enterprise was the handiwork of Sir W. M. Aitken, E. R. Wood and Sir Rodolphe Forget, M.P., whose names reappear many times in this period as promoters of important mergers. American and Canadian interests formed the Amalgamated Asbestos Company which controlled about sixty-five per cent of the national output; C. R. Hosmer manoeuvred eleven companies into National Breweries; and Canadian Canners absorbed close to fifty smaller concerns. Dominion Textiles, Penman's Belding-Corticelli Ltd., Canada Bread, and Sherwin-Williams paints were but a few of the mergers in this period. Ogilvie Flour Mills and the Lake of the Woods Milling Company were faced with the new International Milling and Maple Leaf Milling companies, raising to four the number of giants in this flourishing industry. The increasing flow of traffic on the Great Lakes prompted eleven shipping companies, owning over one hundred ships and extensive docks and warehouses, to unite into the Canada Steamship Lines. Several very important amalgamations were formed to supply natural gas and hydro-electric power to the rapidly growing cities, the most notable being the large Montreal Light, Heat and Power Corporation. In some instances these services were supplied by government-owned agencies. The best known of these was the Ontario Hydro-Electric Power Commission (now Ontario Hydro), organized by the government of Sir James Whitney in 1906 with Adam Beck, a former mayor of London, Ontario, as its first chairman.

About 1908 a number of Canadian newspapers and some of the farm and labour leaders began to make war on these and other mergers. Joseph Atkinson's *Toronto Star* in a February 1909 issue expressed the accepted viewpoint of these critics as follows: 'The government has the power to abolish tariff protection in cases where a merger is formed to eliminate domestic competition. Such companies should be exposed to foreign competition and not be free to jack up prices whenever they feel like it. Most of these combinations injure the public and are for the benefit of a few new-rich millionaires in Montreal and Toronto.' Mergers were also charged with being promoters' schemes to make quick profits. The soaring stock market, so it was said, encouraged the sale of far more shares than the size of many of these new amalgamations warranted. The promoters made money in the stock market at the time a new company was formed, but with so much 'watered stock' the company would probably fail and would have to be reorganized, and the investors would lose out. The failure of some thirty-five mergers since 1900 was used as evidence to support this view.

The fact that few promoters were involved in so many transactions also provoked sharp criticism. It was said that twenty or so financiers held over-lapping positions on the boards of directors of the ninety largest corporations in Canada and that a large amount of wealth had been gathered into a few hands. Among the men mentioned in this connection by the *Toronto Star*, the *Telegram*, the *Grain Growers' Guide* and other publications, the following seemed to appear most frequently: Senator C. A. Cox, Sir R. Forget, W. D. Matthews, Sir Edmund B. Osler, Sir William Van Horne, E. R. Wood, Sir H. Pellatt, Sir W. M. Aitken and Sir Herbert Holt. (The growing number of knights among these financiers also began to cause some adverse criticism.)

There was a good deal of American influence regarding the protest against mergers at this time. The 'trust-busting' tactics of Theodore Roosevelt and Woodrow Wilson and the anti-trust philosophy of the Progressive movement found favour with some Canadians. U.S. government action against Standard Oil and the U.S. Steel Corporation in 1911 was widely acclaimed.

In general, Canadian government action against mergers was slow. As early as 1888 a select committee of the House of Commons had been set up to deal with combines acting in restraint of trade; it censured several associations, among them being manufacturers of coffins and dealers in undertakers' supplies. A Customs Tariff Act in 1897 provided for a decrease of tariff to be used against a combine 'fixing prices'; this control was used once in a ten-year period when, in 1902, the Canadian Press Association appealed and won a case against paper manufacturers. The Combines Investigation Act was introduced by W. L. Mackenzie King in 1910 and provided for public investigation of combine restraints; only one investigation was held, that of the United Shoe Machinery Company in 1914. With the outbreak of the Great War, orders in council were used to deal with the problems.

This attack on mergers and big business was to some extent political. Many of the promoters were members of the Conservative party and all of them were opposed to the reciprocity plan of 1911. Free traders claimed that the tariff allowed these amalgamations to charge exorbitant prices—a point that has not yet been proved, one way or the other. A great deal of the criticism was un-founded, due to misunderstanding the nature of and need for many of these mergers. The majority were straightforward industrial enterprises and not promoters' schemes. Some industries secured dominant positions in their field, but for the most part the Canadian market remained very highly competitive.

An ice-cream parlour in Cobourg, Ontario, about 1910

Only a few men were involved, but any grand financial combination among the competing companies that they represented was out of the question.

Many of these men held their directors' positions not so much because they owned a lot of stock as because their business knowledge and experience would give the public confidence in the companies concerned. The rise to prominence of the financial promoter in this period underlines one important fact. Canadian business, in keeping with the times, was becoming so large that one individual could no longer finance certain types of industry. Companies had to be organized to raise money through the stock market to a greater extent than before and this naturally placed the financiers in a dominant position. The day when the man in the front office not only managed but also owned the company was passing and big businesses owned by many shareholders had come to stay.

Our Ever-vigilant Competitor
American investors played an important part in the development of manufacturing in these years. They were to be found in almost every Canadian industry and seemed particularly willing to gamble on 'riskier' enterprises when other investors hesitated. British finance participated in iron and steel, railways, pulp and paper and other industries but tended to concentrate on municipal, provincial and federal bonds. Thus the British investor helped to finance the

(Above) The pipe shop at Eaton's, Toronto, 1904. (Right) A typical office of the period.

tremendous government spending on public service—roads, street railways, water systems, schools—and that was another very important factor in causing the booming market conditions of 1900–1914.

It was in this period that American companies began to establish branch factories in Canada. Some of these were jumping the tariff wall and others came mainly to be close to resources such as pulpwood and cheap electric power. The Ford Motor Company, Fisher Body and other companies came with the young automotive industry; General Electric, Westinghouse and others with the development of hydro-electric power. The Aluminum Company of America built at Niagara Falls in 1894, moved four years later in search of power to Shawinigan Falls and laid the basis for the Aluminum Company of Canada at Arvida and Kitimat. International Harvester, Procter & Gamble, International Paper, Imperial Oil and many other equally well known companies established themselves in Canada. By 1911 some 225 American corporations had invested over $500 million in branch factories on Canadian soil.

The majority of Canadians wanted these branch factories and they seemed to agree that it was the tariff which compelled them to cross the border. This helps to explain the very strong opposition to reciprocity by such places as Sarnia, Windsor, Niagara Falls, Peterborough and other centres where American com-

panies were beginning to build. One of the main reasons advanced against freer trade with the United States in 1911 was that it would destroy the east-west trade designed by the National Policy to build a strong Canada.

It must be admitted that powerful north-south influences exist today because so many American subsidiaries are located here. American investors now control 97 per cent of the automobile manufacturing industry, 90 per cent of the rubber industry, 90 per cent of the industrial electrical manufacturing industry, 72 per cent of the petroleum refining industry and 72 per cent of the synthetic textile manufacturing industry, to mention only a few. Foreign non-residents of Canada have invested $37 billion in the country and 80 per cent of that amount is from the United States. Many people are critical of this situation, but it should be remembered that in the years before the First World War national policies deliberately encouraged many of these American companies to build in Canada.

The Development of Trade Unions
Canada also imported her labour movement from the United States. During the early years of the twentieth century, eighty per cent of the Canadian unions were branches of their American counterparts. In the beginning they were craft organizations of skilled workers and faced strong opposition from manufacturers based on the judgement that their use of the strike weapon was in 'restraint of trade' and hence any group using it was committing an illegal act. A printer's

strike in Toronto in 1871 ended in the arrest of several union leaders on charges of seditious conspiracy. Strong union representation against this accusation, led chiefly by the Toronto Trades Assembly, and ensuing public support for the union stand, resulted in the government passing an act in 1872 legalizing unions and making some attempt to define strike action and picketing.

The chief problem in the emergence of the Canadian union movement, and a continuing one at the present day, was the formation of a central authority to correlate their activities. An attempt to solve this problem was the formation of the Trades and Labour Congress of Canada in 1886. This Congress was affiliated with the American Federation of Labor (A.F. of L.). However, union progress was very slow and by 1900 there were only 135 'locals' in the entire country with a membership of 9,000 and an annual dues income of less than $1,000.

The Knights of Labour, an American movement coming into Canada in 1881, had limited success. Its appeal to anyone 'working for wages or who had worked for wages' was relatively widespread, and its idealistic concepts of reform were acceptable to the early manufacturers. In Winnipeg it achieved some favourable changes in child labour laws. Popular in Quebec, where it had the tacit approval of the Roman Catholic Church, the influence of its conservative reform program lasted for some time. The increase of more aggressive union tactics and inter-union competition for membership eventually eliminated its effectiveness and by 1908 it was no longer of importance in the Canadian union movement.

More militant unions, again all American in origin, moved into the national scene in the early decades. The Western Federation of Miners was operating at Rossland, B.C., by 1895 and had organized sections of the mining areas in Ontario and Quebec by 1905. A new union philosophy emerged in an increasingly industrialized age; Bob Roadhouse, organizer for the W.F.M., outlined it at a miners' strike in Cobalt in 1907: 'Things aren't like the old days when you knew the boss. These great big companies don't give us a chance. Suppose I walk into Henry Pellatt's office and say, "Look, Henry, I need a raise," what chance have I got? But if I walk in with a strong union behind me and say, "We want a raise," he'll listen.' Listen the industrialists were forced to do as the Canadian trade unions grew in size and strength to balance the growing power and increased size of industry. By 1914 over 150,000 workingmen had decided that in order to bargain more effectively for higher wages and better working conditions they should band together into trade union organizations. Great as this increase was in union strength, 93 per cent of all the workers in Canada were not union members in 1914 and the Canadian trade union movement still had a long way to go.

The very fact that Canadian and American unions were so closely linked and that so many Canadian strikes were directed by the 'foreign labour boss' from the United States resulted in our trade unions being tarred with the same black brush as were those across the border. In this period there were about 1,500 strikes in Canada involving over 10 million working days. Some of these strikes were long and often violent. However, compared to the warfare that scarred labour-management relations for many years in the United States, the Canadian labour movement in the years 1900 to 1914 was generally a credit to both the companies and the unions.

The antagonism towards trade unions in Canada seemed to reach a peak during the years 1906 and 1907. The success of the newly-formed Labour party in the British general election of 1906 encouraged Canadian labour leaders and the number of strikes increased. Those started by the Western Federation of Mines focused attention on the very bad record of this union in the United States. The trial of William Haywood, the notorious treasurer of the Federation, for the alleged murder of Idaho's governor and his acquittal secured by the brilliant criminal lawyer, Clarence Darrow, gave the miners much unfavourable publicity. The coal miners' strike in British Columbia during the bitterly cold winter of 1906–7 caused much hardship and helped to make trade unions unpopular on the snowed-in prairies.

The increasing friction between labour and management resulting from Canada's industrial expansion, persuaded the Dominion government to extend the laws controlling the right to strike. The Industrial Disputes Investigation Act was passed in 1907 making it compulsory for the mines, gas, electric and street railway companies and certain other industries providing essential public services to submit any dispute to an arbitration board. The law did not force either labour or management to accept the decision of this board, but in practice it did settle a great many disputes by conciliation rather than by industrial warfare.

The Industrial Disputes Investigation Act won the immediate support of many Canadian unionists and businessmen and received much favourable recognition in other countries. President C. W. Elliot of Harvard University described it as 'the best piece of industrial legislation to be produced in the last two decades'. This Act was the work of the thirty-one-year-old Deputy Minister of Labour, who had established by this time an enviable reputation in labour matters and seemed to have the esteem of Canadians in many walks of life. In 1908 Laurier persuaded this young civil servant to enter politics as his Minister of Labour. In this capacity, it will be recalled, he introduced the Combines Investigation Act, passed in 1910, which was intended to prevent an abuse of their power by business interests just as the law of 1907 was to prevent an abuse of power by trade unions. While this minister was defeated along with others in Laurier's cabinet in the election of 1911, Canadians would hear a great deal more in the future from William Lyon Mackenzie King.

part 2
the world crisis

5   THE ROAD TO WAR

The Balance of Power

Sarajevo, capital of Bosnia, one of the many provinces of the empire of Austria-Hungary, was outwardly a sleepy little town on the sunny morning of June 28, 1914. To the Slavs of the Balkans it was Vidovdan, an anniversary of mourning, marking the defeat of the Serbian kingdom by the Turks and the enslavement of the Christians in the fourteenth century. To the nationalist Bosnians it was a day to intensify their hatred for the Austrian annexation of their province in 1908.

Archduke Franz Ferdinand, heir to the Austro-Hungarian throne, was visiting the town as Inspector General of the armed forces. He was accompanied by his wife, Archduchess Sophie, a commoner of Czech birth ostracized at the court of the Hapsburgs in Vienna. He knew that in this remote section of the empire she would be treated as royalty and he had arranged this trip on a special day for her —it was their wedding anniversary.

The procession rolled slowly through the silent, crowd-lined streets to the Town Hall; an ill-made bomb was tossed at the cortege, but it missed the royal car and damage was slight. It was 10:00 a.m. The reception with the municipal authorities was not pleasant; the Archduke's reply to the mayor's welcome was terse. The visitors, cancelling the rest of the scheduled visit, drove back along the same route they had travelled, towards the safety of the Governor's palace. Shortly before noon, Gavrilo Princip, a nineteen-year-old Bosnian, jumped on the running board and opened fire with an automatic pistol. The Archduke and his Duchess died on the way to the hospital.

Sarajevo today is the capital of the Yugoslav People's Republic of Bosnia. There is a plaque to mark the spot where the assassination took place. The inscription reads, 'Here Gavrilo Princip was the annunciator of Liberty on the day of Vidovdan, June 28, 1914.'

The murder of Ferdinand had been arranged some weeks before in Belgrade by Colonel D. Dmitrivitch, chief intelligence officer in the Serbian army. Peter Karageorg, King of Serbia in 1914, owed his throne to these murderers and had rewarded Dmitrivitch with a good army commission. His plot to assassinate Ferdinand was known to many Serbian officials; it was the sixth violent attempt by Serbs against leading Austrians in less than two years; its success was hailed in Serbian newspapers as a patriotic act and a great national achievement.

During the First War, the Serbian government decided that Dmitrivitch knew too much. When an attempt to murder him failed, he was condemned on a trumped-up treason charge and shot by a firing squad in 1917. Thus Serbia tried

A scene in Sarajevo on the morning of June 28, 1914, showing the arrest of the man who threw the first bomb. Princip himself was later also arrested and died in prison in 1917.

to hide the fact that Archduke Ferdinand's assassination was a carefully laid plot. The victorious Allies also tried to conceal the true story of the Archduke's murder. Princip, so they said, was an insane youth and not responsible for his actions. Serbia was pictured as an oppressed and innocent little country to whose aid they had so valiantly rushed. The Paris Peace Conference in 1919 officially concluded that 'the crime committed at Sarajevo in Austria-Hungary can involve Serbia in no way. The war was caused as a result of Austria-Hungary's deliberate intention to destroy this brave little country.' However, the full story of the causes of the First World War was eventually revealed by peculiar circumstances which require careful explanation.

Facts on File

The foreign office of any nation keeps records in much the same way as does a business firm. When France, for instance, writes to Russia, a copy of the letter is kept in France and the original goes to Russia. Russia, in replying, files a copy of her letter and the original is sent to France. Likewise copies of all the letters, cablegrams and other documents that pass back and forth between the home office and its ambassadors in other countries are stored carefully in the 'archives' of the government. Documents dealing with any important controversial subject are kept under lock and key in the archives until the event is so far lost in the past that it has interest only for historians.

The incriminating evidence of treachery and double-dealing which most of the nations taking part in the First World War had tucked away in their archives was forced out into the open, years ahead of time, by the Russian Revolution in 1917. The communists, wishing to discredit the Tsarist government, invited historians to come and take a look at the records of Imperial Russia's foreign affairs. These records, of course, contained not only Russian documents but also volumes of correspondence which they had received from other countries. Thus any evidence which, say, Serbia or France might want to hide was partly revealed in the Russian archives. In time, this highly embarrassing situation compelled most countries to open up their archives and the full story of the events leading up to the First World War was made public years before it otherwise would have been.

Nations fighting for their lives cannot tell all the truth; the war must be made popular and the people must be convinced that they are fighting for a wholly just and honourable reason. All news has to be censored to prevent information from reaching the enemy. All debate must be silenced; hatred for the enemy must be whipped up and any suggestion that some justice lies on the opposite side must be stifled; some facts must be distorted and other facts invented; millions must be spent to make the people believe not that which is true but that which will inflame their passions.

Today many disclosures are being made of concealed events that took place during World War Two, for example the manoeuvring of Franklin Delano Roosevelt to involve the U.S. in that war long before Pearl Harbor; the appalling carnage resulting from the Allied fire-bombing of Dresden; and more recently, the political and military intrigue in Viet Nam as revealed by the Pentagon Papers.

As Winston Churchill wrote in 1909, with war clouds beginning to gather: 'A serious antagonism between two nations is not caused by natural hatreds; it is the result of the vicious activity of a comparatively small number of individuals and the complete credulity of the masses.'

Thus there are two broad sources of information about the causes of the First World War. There is the great volume of literature built up in all countries— regardless of which 'side' they were on—by wartime propaganda; and there is the documentary evidence from the archives.

In the next chapters we will be considering Canada's foreign relations in the period 1900–1914. We will see that this country entered the War with practically no knowledge of the tangled events leading up to it. During the War, Canada was subjected to as rigid a censorship as existed anywhere in the world. The law read that 'it shall be an offense to print, publish or publicly express any unfavourable statement, report or opinion concerning the causes of the present war or the motives for which Canada or any allied nation entered into it which may tend to create unrest or unsettle public opinion—under penalty of a maximum fine of

$5,000 or of imprisonment for five years or both.' Under these circumstances, Canadians acquired their ideas about the causes of the War almost exclusively from completely controlled propaganda sources.

After the War, the documentary evidence received very little attention in Canada and was bitterly resisted because it conflicted so sharply with everything the people had been taught to believe during the war years. Furthermore, our school textbooks have tended to brush aside the causes for the First World War as events which did not directly involve Canada. It may safely be said that some of the violent prejudices and misconceptions arising from the War have been retained to this day in the minds of a great many Canadians.

Unless we accept the fatalistic view that war is an inevitable condition of man and that deliberately fostered hatreds are essential for survival, the elimination of the tragedy of war is the major problem of all nations today. In the history of the events leading up to World War One can be found all the dishonest distortions of propaganda and many of the causes of warfare among nations.

The Alliance System

The Great Powers of Europe took the first steps towards war when they began to range themselves in two military alliances against each other. Well before 1914 Europe was divided into two armed, hostile camps—the one called the 'Triple Alliance' (Germany, Austria-Hungary and Italy) and the other, the 'Triple Entente' (France, Russia and Great Britain). These alliances, as they were formed, were announced to the world as friendly, non-aggressive arrangements to promote peace. The archives reveal that whenever any two of the above six nations signed a 'friendly understanding', they also exchanged secret letters containing some kind of selfish, shoddy bargain which had to be hidden from their neighbours. Once one of these bargains had been made, the two countries involved had no hesitation in negotiating secretly against each other in an attempt to make a deal with the opposing camp.

The treaties and understandings which formed the Triple Alliance and the Triple Entente were not signed because any two nations respected each other or shared common ideals. The Great Powers split into rival factions so they could pursue their selfish ambitions more aggressively—ambitions that seem to spring from two basic causes.

In the first place, the map of Europe contained many sore spots dating back to the end of the Napoleonic Wars and the Congress of Vienna (1815). This Congress had completely ignored the aspirations of many racial groups to have their freedom and independence. Many racial problems in central and eastern Europe remained unsolved at the end of the nineteenth century. These problems led to bitter arguments and helped to create the two big alliances.

Secondly, a great deal of the diplomatic scuffling that finally produced the Triple Alliance and the Triple Entente arose from the conflicting ambitions of European nations to build up colonial empires in the backward areas of the world. The struggle for colonies and commercial supremacy, which began in the days of Columbus and Vasco da Gama, was greatly intensified by the industrialization of Europe during the latter half of the nineteenth century. The machine age compelled the industrialized nations to seek out cheap raw materials produced by primitive, native labour; it drove them to Africa, the Near and Middle East, the Orient and even into the remote islands of the Pacific Ocean looking for markets; and it caused them to search the world over for undeveloped regions where surplus funds could be invested in railways, mines and other business ventures at high interest rates. With such ideas in mind, the Great Powers before the First World War combined against one another and made imperialistic bargains to carve out colonies for themselves in every quarter of the globe.

Bismarck and France

The European system of alliances began to develop after the Franco-Prussian War. By the Treaty of Frankfurt (1871), victorious Germany took the valuable provinces of Alsace and Lorraine from France. (These provinces have been exchanged between Teuton and Frank so many times in history that any question of original or lawful ownership is lost in antiquity.) Prince Otto von Bismarck, the German Chancellor, feared that France might try to regain Alsace and Lorraine in a 'war of revenge' and this he set out to prevent by building up alliances that would isolate France. Using all the tricks of secret diplomacy, Bismarck built up a tangled web of agreements against France. As early as 1873, by an understanding known as the League of Three Emperors, he persuaded William I of Germany, Franz Joseph of Austria and Alexander II of Russia to attempt to formulate a common policy on their divergent interests in Europe. The Austro-German alliance of mutual assistance was signed in 1879 and this became a cornerstone of German foreign policy until the final dissolution of the Dual Monarchy in 1918. In 1882 the Triple Alliance of Germany, Austria and Italy was formed. Thus the only hope for France lay in an agreement with England, but the possibility of an Anglo-French treaty in those days was most remote. These were two 'traditional' enemies and their colonial ambitions conflicted at so many points that Bismarck had no worries about an accord between them.

Bismarck's greatest fear was a Franco-Russian alliance which, in the event of war, would compel Germany to fight on two fronts. Therefore, the League of Three Emperors, designed to hold both Austrian and Russian friendship, was a vital part of his policy. Keeping Austria and Russia on friendly terms was a very tricky proposition and only someone with Bismarck's skill and ruthlessness could have managed to do it. These two countries had directly opposed interests in the Balkan peninsula and the German Chancellor kept them together only by a temporary bargain which divided the Balkans into two 'spheres of influence'. When the League finally broke up in 1887 over a dispute between Austria and Russia in the Balkans, Bismarck continued to support Russian ambitions by the very secret Reinsurance Treaty, signed behind Austria's back. This clash of Russian and Austrian aims in the Balkan peninsula plays a very important part in precipitating the First World War and merits some detailed explanation.

Russia had no ice-free ports except those along the coast of the Black Sea and these could be reached only through the narrow, easily-fortified Dardanelles belonging to Turkey. A strong fleet which could retire through the Straits to the safety of the Black Sea at any time of the year would have greatly increased Russian power.

Therefore, the 'historic mission' of Russian statesmen was to gain control of the Dardanelles from Turkey. During the nineteenth century, Russia began to encourage the different racial groups living under Turkish rule in the Balkan peninsula to revolt, hoping to work through them down to Constantinople and the Straits. With Russian help, Serbia and Montenegro (both now in Yugoslavia), Bulgaria and part of modern Romania broke away from Turkey and became independent countries. However, Turkey managed to retain the land round the Dardanelles and so the necessity continued for Russia to stir up and support nationalistic ambitions in the Balkans. In all these efforts to break up the

The diplomatic map of Europe about 1900

Nations of the Triple Alliance

European part of the Sultan's Empire, Russia pretended to be helping 'her little Slavic brothers'. Russia was a Slavic nation and so also was Serbia, but helping the Balkan Slavs was only a smoke screen laid down by the Tsarist government to obscure its real aims. The secret treaties in the archives reveal that Russia negotiated against the little Balkan states whenever she thought her historic mission could be satisfied in some other way.

The nationalistic feeling aroused among the Balkan peoples by Russia threatened the very existence of the Austro-Hungarian Empire. This sprawling Empire contained several different racial groups. Most of the people living inside Austria-Hungary were closely related by race and language to those living just outside the Empire round its borders. There was always the danger that the Italians, Slavs, Romanians or Poles inside the Austro-Hungarian Empire would want to join with the people of their own nationality across the border and form a country of their own. The government of the Dual Monarchy was fully aware that the country might break up and tried to prevent it by suppressing all national feeling not only among its own subjects but also among certain racial groups outside its borders. In particular, Austria-Hungary tried to prevent the further break-up of the Turkish Empire in the Balkans and stop the growth of fanatical little nationalistic states along her southern and eastern frontiers.

The Serbs, once they had gained their independence from Turkey, began an agitation among their fellow-Slavs living in the southern part of the Austro-Hungarian Empire. The aim of this 'Pan-Slav' movement was to tear three provinces away from the Dual Monarchy and create a 'Greater Serbia'. The Serbs also had their eye on the adjacent Turkish province of Bosnia—an ambition that the officials of the Dual Monarchy were equally determined to frustrate because the larger Serbia became, the more attractive it would be to the Slavs in Austria-Hungary. Of all the nationalistic threats to the Austro-Hungarian Empire, this Great Serbian plan was the most dangerous because it was supported most of the time by Russia. This Austro-Russian rivalry in the Balkans made Germany's plan exceedingly difficult and finally ended the isolation of France.

When the aging Bismarck was forced to retire in 1890, his successors in Germany decided that they would no longer try to hold both Austrian and Russian friendship. The Balkan situation, they concluded, was much too complicated and so the Reinsurance Treaty was abandoned. Instead of attempting to balance the conflicting ambitions of Austria and Russia, German statesmen elected to support only Austria. Thus Russia was free to join France and the very situation arose which Bismarck had managed to avoid for twenty years. After negotiations lasting almost three years, France and Russia announced to the world in 1894: 'Our two governments, desirous of contributing to the maintenance of the peace which forms the object of their sincerest aspirations, declare that they will take counsel together upon every question which may threaten the general peace.' Behind closed doors, the peace-loving diplomats, so the archives revealed, made saw-off bargains settling Franco-Russian differences in Turkey, Bulgaria, Romania, Egypt, Tripoli and China to their mutual satisfaction. They also signed seven equally secret military agreements aimed right at the Triple Alliance.

During the age of Bismarck, the German system of treaties prevented the formation of any other strong combination of countries. Although there was much sabre-rattling and innumerable diplomatic deals, the danger of a world war in this period was very slight. The Dual Alliance of 1894 between France and Russia created a 'balance of power' in Europe and the battle-lines at once became more sharply drawn. After this date the Great Powers, reassured by the definite support of their allies, pursued their colonial and nationalistic ambitions more vigorously and the rivalry between them was greatly intensified. It is a tragically ignored lesson of history that one alliance breeds another, that the balance of power is always restored and that a division of the nations into two allied camps seems to be a prelude to war.

The Diplomatic Revolution

The End of Splendid Isolation
Until very late in the nineteenth century, England pursued what her own statesmen were pleased to call the policy of 'Splendid Isolation'. The phrase implied that Britain did not meddle in European politics, that she remained aloof from the shoddy bargaining of the other Great Powers and was free, therefore, to devote her energies to affairs of empire. England in the nineteenth century was indeed busy, building the 'Empire on which the sun never sets' and in the process arousing the jealousy and hostility of almost every nation in the world.

However, 'Splendid Isolation' really meant that England would not commit herself to any long-term treaty, preferring to bargain on a day-to-day basis as the occasion demanded. The British records show that England was as involved as any of the other nations in the diplomatic dealing and secret bargaining that preceded the First World War. In particular, Great Britain was drawn into European affairs by her determination to prevent Russia's advance towards the Dardanelles. After Britain purchased shares in the Suez Canal (1875), her rich trade with India began to flow in greater volume through the Mediterranean Sea instead of round South Africa. Englishmen soon became convinced that a powerful Russia in control of the Straits would be a real threat to this 'life-line' to India. Thus England, Austria-Hungary and Turkey, each for their own reasons, were intent on driving Russia away from the Dardanelles and frequently negotiated with each other for this purpose. Great Britain also dealt with Germany to secure certain colonial aims at the expense of France and Russia. During Bismarck's day, German attention was focused mainly on Europe, and England tended to give Germany a free hand there in exchange for her support in the race for colonies. In spite of some minor Anglo-German disputes, British foreign policy during the nineteenth century inclined towards Germany and Austria-Hungary and was hostile to both France and Russia.

Although the full extent of her unpopularity was not revealed until the Boer War started in 1899, it had become increasingly apparent that England was not trusted and had few friends. The balance of power created by the Dual Alliance made it more difficult to play a lone hand, and foreign diplomats backed up by their allies seemed much tougher to handle. British statesmen decided, therefore, to abandon the chilly policy of isolation and began to look around for friends and entry into one of the alliances. At first, England's preference was for the Triple Alliance. During the early part of the nineteenth century many attempts were made by both German and British diplomats to effect an alliance between the two countries. While it is true that these negotiations were usually at the expense of other nations or involved land belonging to native peoples, there was a consistent effort to arrange an understanding between the two powers. Germany and Britain had been allies in Continental wars since the seventeenth century; the ruling families of both empires were closely related; and cultural affinities between the countries were strong. However, the basic change in German foreign policy, brought about by William II and his advisers to make Germany a world power through colonial and naval expansion, made conflict with Britain almost inevitable. Yet, despite this obstacle, negotiations continued and as late as 1912 Lord Haldane, British Minister of War, held talks with the Kaiser to prepare for a German-British accord.

While these negotiations with Germany were going on, England was also dealing with Russia for an alliance based on a somewhat grandiose scheme to divide parts of China into two large spheres of influence. However, these Anglo-Russian talks collapsed when Russia let the cat out of the bag and told the Germans what England was doing. British diplomats were more successful with Japan and in 1902 an Anglo-Japanese treaty was signed. This agreement was designed to check the colonial ambitions of Russia in Manchuria, Korea and other parts of the Far East.

The growing tension in Europe after 1895 also prompted Great Britain to seek the friendship of the United States. It may be noted here that England's efforts were successful enough to encourage her to work for a definite alliance between the United States, Germany and herself. Although this hope was shattered in December 1899 on the historic American principle of 'friendly relations with all, entangling alliances with none', Anglo-American friendship greatly improved during the early years of the twentieth century. Likewise it will be seen that Great Britain began to take a greater interest in Canada, Australia and her other self-governing colonies and 'our promising daughter lands' received flattering attention in the mother country.

The Entente Cordiale

During the years 1903 and 1904 there occurred one of the most important changes in the entire modern history of British foreign policy—a change so sudden and startling that it is called the 'Diplomatic Revolution'. France and Great Britain, age-old, bitter rivals, came together. Two nations which had fought each other round the globe for colonial mastery; two nations which had been ranged on opposite sides in every major war (except the Crimean War in 1856) during the past three hundred years; two nations which, in 1893 over Siam and in 1898 over the upper Nile River, had been on the very brink of war—these two nations decided to resolve their differences and become friends. Thus was ended the continental friendship with Prussia which from the Seven Years' War to the beginning of the twentieth century had served England's purposes so well. Now, her future lay with France.

The Diplomatic Revolution, a turning point in history, was moulded by a handful of individuals who rose to political prominence in France and England at the very beginning of the twentieth century. These few men—not necessarily great or good men, but men with power—'took history in their two hands' and redirected it to their liking. Foremost among them was Théophile Delcassé, a strongly pro-British, anti-German diplomat who had risen from poverty and obscurity by sheer brilliance and determination to become the Foreign Minister of France. Paul Cambon was the French ambassador to the Court of St. James— a post he held for over twenty years, devoting his exceptional talents to promoting harmonious Anglo-French relations. In England the haughty, Prussian-like Lord Salisbury decided that the dual position of prime minister and foreign secretary was too much for him and in 1900 gave the Foreign Office to the pliable Lord Lansdowne. The death of Queen Victoria, with her pro-German tendencies, paved the way for Edward VII, who soon displayed strong French sympathies and a bitter dislike for his nephew, 'that meddling Willy' of Germany. In turn, William II and von Bulow, the German Chancellor, distrusted Edward VII, 'the arch-intriguer and mischief-maker of Europe'.

Do we assume then that these few personalities alone brought about the Entente Cordiale? Hardly so. More deep-seated reasons were beginning to create a strong British fear of Germany. With other men in power, the outcome might have been different, but the tremendous industrial success of Germany after 1871 and the upward surge of her world trade played right into the hands of the diplomats who desired an Anglo-French understanding. As early as 1897, while negotiations for an alliance with Germany were still under way, the following article appeared in a British periodical, the *Saturday Review*: 'England,' the writer said, 'with her long history of successful aggression, with her marvellous conviction that in pursuing her own interests she is spreading light among nations dwelling in darkness, and Germany, bone of the same bone, blood of the same blood, now compete in every corner of the globe. In the Transvaal, at the Cape, in Central Africa, in India and the East and in the islands of the Southern Sea, the German bagman is struggling with the English pedlar. Where there is a mine to be developed, a railway to be built, a native to be converted from breadfruit to tinned meat, from temperance to trade gin, the German and the Englishman are struggling to be first. Nations have fought for years over the rights to a city. Must they not fight for two hundred and fifty million pounds of commerce?'

However one may wish to answer this frank question, the fact remains that Germany's success in world trade drove England into the arms of France. And when Germany decided that she too would police her sea-lanes and protect her commerce with a powerful navy, the possibility of continuing Anglo-German friendship completely disappeared. German rivalry in manufacturing, in trade and even in merchant shipping might have been tolerated in Great Britain, but the appearance of Germany as a competitor in naval power clinched the Entente Cordiale. This fear of Germany—whipped up by sections of the press, by some political and business leaders and by certain influential officials in the Admiralty and War Office—compelled Great Britain to support France and later Russia and keep their friendship at all costs. These two countries pursued aggressive policies relating to Alsace and Lorraine and the Balkan peninsula which they might not have dared to do without British support. These Franco-Russian ambitions, as we shall see shortly, brought events in the Balkans to a climax and helped to precipitate the First World War.

Unlike the Triple Alliance and the Dual Alliance, the Entente Cordiale, at first, contained no military agreements. As designed by Delcassé and Lansdowne it was simply a colonial understanding, hammered out by months of hard bargaining round the conference table. Of the eight Anglo-French colonial disputes put to rest by the Entente, the most important concerned the British position in Egypt. British control over Egypt began on July 11, 1882, when Admiral Seymour shelled Alexandria and troops were landed to quell a revolt which had broken out against British interference in Egyptian finances. Despite assurances by English statesmen that the troops would leave, the British occupation of Egypt continued. During the last two decades of the nineteenth century, France, with a large interest in the Suez Canal and secret hopes of sharing in the control of Egypt, protested long and vigorously against its continued occupation by British troops. By the Entente Cordiale, Delcassé agreed that France would stop this embarrassing criticism and England was given a free hand in Egypt.

France had acquired her troublesome colony in Algeria and had taken Tunis from under the nose of Italy. Now she was casting a covetous eye towards the rich independent sultanate of Morocco which would nicely round out her North African empire. Great Britain promised to support the ambitions of France in Morocco. By the Entente Declaration of April 8, 1904, both countries announced that they would respect the independence of Egypt and Morocco; secretly, they agreed to destroy the independence of these two countries and reduce them to colonial status. Delcassé safeguarded his Moroccan plans still further by secret treaties with Spain and Italy. Spain was promised a piece of Morocco when the time came and Italy was given a free hand to seize Tripoli (owned by Turkey), provided she would not object to what the French had in mind for Morocco. In all these tangled dealings, Delcassé haughtily and deliberately ignored Germany, which also had interests in Morocco.

As the two Entente nations tried to carry out the bargains they had made with each other, they held diplomatic, military and naval talks to discuss what they would do in the event of war. Beginning with the first Morocco crisis in 1905, the military and naval experts of France and Britain continued to meet until 1912, by which time a definite set of plans had been made for a war against Germany. Sir

Edward Grey, who succeeded Lord Lansdowne as the British Foreign Secretary in 1905, secretly authorized military and naval agreements which committed England to aid France in any war with Germany. France assumed that she could rely on England's help and spoke more boldly in international affairs. Yet it was not until August 1914, when the war in Europe had already started and the British cabinet was debating what course they should follow, that Grey finally had to reveal the full extent of the promises he had made to France. This situation prevented Grey from taking a strong stand during the critical days following the murder of Archduke Franz Ferdinand and seriously hampered the efforts of the British government to hold back France and Russia.

The Triple Entente

France, now friendly with Great Britain through the Entente Cordiale and tied to Russia in the Dual Alliance of 1894, naturally tried to bring her two allies together. However, an understanding of any kind between England and Russia was not easy. England had opposed all Russian attempts to control the Dardanelles and worked with Austria-Hungary during the nineteenth century to frustrate the historic mission of the Tsars. Furthermore, England and Russia had seriously conflicting aims in Persia, Afghanistan, Tibet and the Far East. Next to France, Russia had been the traditional foe of Great Britain in many quarters of the globe.

A combination of events finally enabled these two countries to reach an agreement in 1907. After the Russo-Japanese War (1904–5) a defeated Russia did not seem so powerful to the British in the Far East. More important, a new threat had appeared at Constantinople and the Straits. Industrialized Germany, in her search for markets, began to play for the friendship of Turkey and negotiations were opened up for the construction of a very important railway which would run from Germany through Austria-Hungary and the Balkans to Constantinople and from there through Turkish territory in Asia Minor down to the Persian Gulf. The famous 'Berlin to Bagdad Railway', when completed, would greatly increase Germany's influence at the Dardanelles and throughout Asia Minor. Great Britain decided that German expansion in Turkey was a more serious danger to her interests than the Russian threat to the Dardanelles. Thus Anglo-German rivalry in the Near East, more than any other factor, persuaded the British to seek an agreement with Russia.

Finally, in 1907, a settlement of Anglo-Russian differences in the East was reached. The agreement ignored the Dardanelles, an implication that the ambitions of both countries concerning that vital area had not changed. Interference with Afghanistan, long a territory of conflicting interest, was to end and both sides agreed to cease their power intrigues in Tibet. In a pious pretence at protecting the independence of Persia from Ottoman cruelty, the powers divided that oil-rich country into two spheres of influence and were to control it for many years.

The Anglo-Russian agreement completed the division of Europe into two hostile groups of nations. On the one side was the Triple Alliance of Germany,

Austria-Hungary and Italy formed back in 1882 by Bismarck to isolate France. German and Austrian statesmen knew from the beginning that Italy could not be trusted as a member of this alliance. During the early years of the twentieth century, Italian foreign policy slithered along from one side to the other, inclining more and more towards England and France—especially after both countries promised to support Italian ambitions in Tripoli. When the First World War started, Italy held back to see which way the wind would blow and finally was bribed to come in on the Allied side. However, Turkey and Bulgaria drew closer to Germany and Austria-Hungary and these four nations eventually fought together as the 'Central Powers'.

Ranged against the Central Powers and hemming them in by land and sea was the Triple Entente of France, Russia and Great Britain. To the treaties and understandings which bound these countries together should be added the Anglo-Japanese Alliance of 1902 which France and Russia joined when the tensions from the Russo-Japanese War had subsided. After the outbreak of hostilities in 1914, these four nations were joined eventually by twenty-six others, forming the

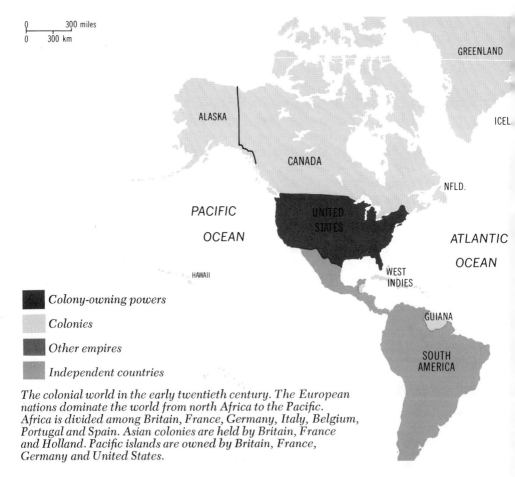

The colonial world in the early twentieth century. The European nations dominate the world from north Africa to the Pacific. Africa is divided among Britain, France, Germany, Italy, Belgium, Portugal and Spain. Asian colonies are held by Britain, France and Holland. Pacific islands are owned by Britain, France, Germany and United States.

group of countries known to history as the Allied and Associated Powers or more simply, the 'Allies'. The nucleus of this victorious wartime combination was fully formed when England and Russia settled their colonial differences and the Triple Entente was created. Thus by 1907, after years of tangled diplomacy, the stage was set for the final, dramatic events which caused the tragic struggle between the Central Powers and the Allies.

The Witches' Cauldron

Colonial Rivalry

As the Great Powers vied with each other to carry out their conflicting nationalistic and imperialistic plans, the rivalry and tension between them naturally became more acute. Starting about the year 1895 colonial clashes occurred with increasing intensity and regularity in Africa, Asia and the distant islands of the Pacific Ocean.

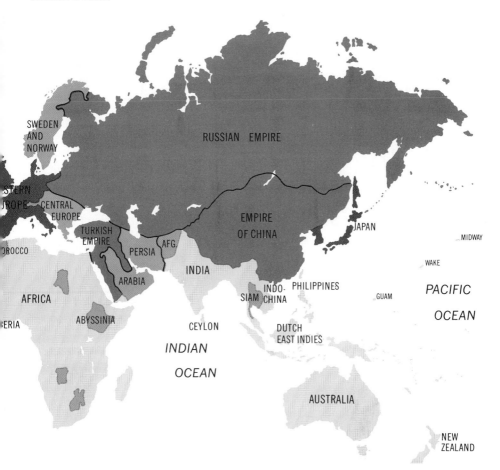

In the Far East, Japan fought China (1895) for the possession of Formosa, Korea and parts of Manchuria. When Japan won easily, the other nations tumbled over each other in a disorderly, five-year scramble for territory which caused the collapse of an independent China. In a final, clumsy protest, the 'Boxers' revolted in 1900, but the Sacred Fists of Righteous Harmony failed to drive the foreigners out and presented yet another excuse for the European nations to squabble for riches in the Orient. During the years 1904–5, the Manchu dynasty sat by helplessly while Russia and Japan waged war across Chinese soil for railway, mining and other 'rights' in Manchuria. But for the fact that England and France were busy with their designs in Egypt and Morocco, the Russo-Japanese War might well have become a European conflict.

Across the vast heartland of Asia, where the Russian border comes near to British possessions in India and the Middle East, rival diplomats schemed with native rulers, plotted internal revolts and tried to build 'buffer states' against each other. Britain and France, already at loggerheads in China and in the jungle borders of Burma and Siam, nearly came to blows miles up the Nile River at a place called Fashoda (1898), an unknown village of mud huts until Lord Kitchener encountered General Marchand raising the Tricolour in the name of France. In other parts of Africa, Portugal, Belgium, France, Italy, Great Britain and Germany made a multitude of diplomatic deals until the only independent native kingdom left in this once dark and unexplored continent was Abyssinia. In the Transvaal and Orange Free State, Great Britain tangled with the Boers, who stood athwart the 'all red route from Cairo to the Cape', and beat them after three years of bitter fighting (1899–1902), to the cheers of her few friends and the boos of her many rivals.

During most of the nineteenth century, the aggressive instincts of the American people were confined to North America. The United States was kept busy fighting Mexico for the southwestern part of the continent, subduing the last of the Indians and breaking open for settlement a virtual empire lying to the west of the Mississippi. All this, they decided, was somehow different from what the other nations were doing and so they called it 'Manifest Destiny' instead of imperialism. However, in the Spanish-American War (1898) the United States caught the spirit of the times and stripped Spain of her overseas possessions in Cuba, Haiti and the Philippines, picking off the Hawaiian Islands in the process.

Coming into the colonial race late, Germany gathered up crumbs in the Pacific Ocean, carved out a share of Africa and China, and swaggered into the decadent empire of the Sultan of Turkey.

The division of the spoils was completed in a splurge of colonial rivalry round the world.

Crises in Morocco

The Great Powers shifted their attention a little closer to home in 1905 when France went after Morocco and the Entente Cordiale swung into action. According to plan, the French began to press for privileges which would have destroyed the Sultan's independence. Germany, already angry because Delcassé had ignored her interests in North Africa and suspicious of what Britain and France were scheming to do, sent the Kaiser off to see the Sultan at Tangier. The German Emperor proclaimed he had come to protect the independence of Morocco and demanded a conference in no uncertain terms. The belligerent Delcassé, determined to stand up to Germany right then and there, refused and for a while war seemed imminent. However, statesmen from several countries, including France itself, recognized the justice of German claims, and urged the French Foreign Minister to submit. As Winston Churchill wrote of these events later: 'The Treaty of Madrid, signed in 1880 by France, Germany and ten other countries, guaranteed the independence of the Sultan and France did not have a good case.' Delcassé finally resigned as minister of foreign affairs and France, under more moderate guidance, agreed to an international conference.

The Conference of Algeciras (1905) fully confirmed the Treaty of Madrid, upheld most of the German claims and denied the right of France to the exclusive domination of Morocco. Although France lost her case at the conference table, she gained immeasurably in other ways. The bitter feelings and harsh diplomatic bargaining arising from this first crisis in Morocco enabled France and Great Britain to cement their newly found friendship. It was at this time that Sir Edward Grey authorized the first Anglo-French military talks.

In 1911, France and Spain took another, and this time successful, stab at Morocco. Native disturbances, in many cases provoked by the unwanted presence of foreigners, had provided France and Spain with opportunities to extend their influence over the Sultan and increase their troops in Moroccan coastal cities, and on April 27 the French dispatched troops inland to the city of Fez on the grounds that a revolt threatened the lives of Europeans living there. Germany denied that any such emergency existed and warned that they would not long tolerate the troops at Fez in violation of the Act of Algeciras. After waiting six weeks for the French to get out, the Germans suddenly steamed 'that busy, little belligerent boat', the *Panther*, into the port of Agadir on the Atlantic coast of Morocco. There she lay at anchor, a symbol of German authority, while excitement in Europe mounted and the German press cried out for German rights.

By this time Germany had given up hope in Morocco, and the real reason for dispatching the gunboat was not to force the troops out of Fez but to force a saw-off bargain with France. In the blunt words of the German Foreign Minister to France: 'You have bought your liberty in Morocco from Spain, England and even Italy; as to us, you have left us aside. On what basis will you now treat with Germany?' The French were quite willing to trade and asked what Germany had in mind. The German Foreign Office then demanded, as compensation for withdrawing all claims to Morocco, the whole of French Congo—a preposterous proposition to which the French would never agree. These confidential discussions were slipped out to the newspapers in France and Britain and the public outburst against Germany rose to threatening extremes. Thus during the summer of 1911, with the French troops in Fez, the *Panther* at Agadir and the contending powers insulting each other, the second crisis in Morocco brought Europe to the very brink of war.

The Kaiser arrives amid colourful ceremony to inspect some of his troops, 1913.

Hard bargaining finally won out and the furor subsided, leaving undercurrents of dangerous discord in Europe. Germany gave up all claims to North Africa and received as her price a piece of French Congo not quite as large in area as Morocco. France and Spain divided the Sultan's lands according to plan. Italy was free to seize Tripoli, which she did in war with Turkey in 1912, and Great Britain consolidated her hold over Egypt. In this complex way the secret deals made by Delcassé at the beginning of the century were fulfilled. Had he bargained with Germany in the first place, the two crises in Morocco would not have occurred and the resulting tension would have been avoided.

All these events helped to create a divided and hostile world. One crisis followed another; tension between nations increased; excited statesmen hurled insults at one another, cheered on by the 'home crowd' and by some completely irresponsible newspapers in every country. The fiery, patriotic oratory of Kaiser William II, demanding 'a place in the sun' for Germany, was matched by David Lloyd George extolling 'the Empire on which the sun never sets'; Delcassé spoke of the glories of 'la belle France' and Theodore Roosevelt bragged in unrestrained language of the 'big stick' he carried to shake at other nations.

German leaders sent their gunboats bristling about the oceans of the world on intimidating missions and found they were outnumbered three to one by French,

British or American ships which showed up at every port where a skirmish seemed imminent. As the tension mounted to fever pitch, the nations spent more and more on armaments until each alliance became an ominous camp and the race for arms was itself a cause for distrust, hatred and war. And when the breaking point came at Sarajevo, the nations camouflaged their selfish aims in glowing, patriotic phrases, while the record of secret treaties, broken bargains and years of plotting lay hidden in the archives.

The Balkans Boil Over

The Balkan peninsula, where 'double, double toil and trouble' was a way of life, began to boil over in 1908 when the Young Turks revolted against their Sultan. The resulting upset conditions in Turkey gave all the European countries that had designs on the Sultan's possessions another chance to satisfy their ambitions. The Austro-Hungarian Empire stepped in first and seized Bosnia, a Balkan province owned by Turkey. Bosnia was inhabited by Slavic people and so Austria, by this action, added over a million Slavs to her already discontented population. Little Serbia, with dreams of becoming Greater Serbia, had been plotting for years for this province and her anger at Austria knew no bounds when the Bosnian prize was taken from her grasp. From this date, Serbian newspapers, Serbian politicians, teachers and students waged a violent campaign against Austria-Hungary. Secret Serbian societies met in cellars, used childish passwords and gang-like vows, practised pistol shooting, fashioned homemade bombs, and smuggled revolutionary leaders and Pan-Slavic pamphlets across the Austrian border in a determined effort to smash the Empire to fragments. Austrian statesmen where only asking for more trouble when they took over the Slavs in Bosnia.

A few months before Austria occupied Bosnia, the Russian Foreign Minister, I. Izvolsky, made a secret agreement against Russia's little Slavic brothers in Serbia. He agreed to let Austria-Hungary steal Bosnia provided the government of the Dual Monarchy would support his efforts to open the Dardanelles to Russian ships in time of war. Acting under this arrangement, Austria promptly took the Slavic province away from Turkey but Russia, once again, was blocked from the Dardanelles by Great Britain. Unable to secure his part of the bargain, Izvolsky proceeded to run round the European capitals demanding a conference to return Bosnia to Turkey! Naturally anxious to hide his double-dealing from Serbia, Izvolsky could not press his case vigorously. Furious with Austria over a situation that his own poor judgement had helped to create, this disappointed diplomat turned right round and decided to support Serbia. He persuaded some of his colleagues that Russia could secure the Straits only by means of a war in the Balkans and that her best interests, therefore, lay in the steadfast encouragement of Serbia's ambitions against Austria.

The trouble caused by Austria's seizure of Bosnia did three things. It stirred up more racial hatred and discord within her own borders; it greatly increased the anti-Austrian movement in Serbia; and it kindled a warmongering faction in Russia which was prepared to back Serbia to the very hilt.

In 1912, the little Balkan countries formed a secret pact to wage war deliberately on Turkey and divide among themselves the remaining portions of the
Sultan's Empire in Europe. While Italy and Turkey were embroiled over Tripoli,
this 'Balkan League' decided that the time had come for military action. Finding
a flimsy excuse, they invaded and easily defeated Turkey. As her share of the
spoils, Serbia was to receive the province of Albania—a rich prize indeed, giving
her much-needed access to the Adriatic Sea. However, some of the Great Powers,
led by Austria-Hungary, protested that the Balkan League had taken the law too
much into their own hands and demanded, as might be guessed, an international
conference. After much diplomatic wrangling and more sabre-rattling, the Great

*The Balkans in 1914. Compare this map with the one on page 21. Bosnia was
annexed by Austria-Hungary in 1908.*

Territories lost by Turkey in the Balkan Wars

Powers met in London and, with complete disregard for Serbia, made Albania into an independent country! This disastrous decision was accepted by Serbia only after a squadron of British, French, German, Italian and Austro-Hungarian warships lay off the Adriatic coast and bullied her into submission. Partly but not entirely because of Austrian interference, Serbian national hopes were crushed once again.

To make up for the loss of Albania, Serbia now demanded that her fellow-conspirators in the Balkan League should split the remaining spoils with her. This demand severed the League and in 1913 the former allies battled each other in a brutal struggle for the other Turkish provinces in Europe. Serbia, who was on the winning side in this Second Balkan War, emerged with such a large share of the booty that Austria-Hungary became greatly alarmed. Now, a Serbia almost double in size and more cocky in victory than ever before threatened her southern Danube frontier and this time Austria could see no way to interfere.

The evidence clearly reveals that in 1913—long before the murder of Archduke Ferdinand provided a more obvious excuse—Austria-Hungary was prepared to declare war for no other reason than to strip Serbia of her newly won territory. Germany held Austria-Hungary back from such a dire course, but after this date a definite war party existed in the Dual Monarchy. Led by the Austrian Foreign Minister, Count von Berchtold, this warmongering group was as determined to exterminate the Pan-Slav movement in Serbia as the Russians under Izvolsky were ready to support it.

In 1912 the foreign policy of France took one of its unpredictable, sharp turns and headed for the Balkan peninsula also. Since Delcassé's resignation over the first Morocco crisis, a succession of French politicians had remained on friendly terms with Germany and Austria-Hungary. Therefore, France paid little attention to her alliance with Russia and from 1906 to 1912 the partnership formed in 1894 lost much of its strength. In January 1912, Raymond Poincaré became Premier of France and immediately the 'unpatriotic', pro-German trend in foreign affairs was reversed. An astute corporation lawyer, as shrewd and ruthless as Bismarck, the new Premier was born in Alsace-Lorraine ten years before the Franco-Prussian War. He retained a childhood hatred for Germany and professed that life was not worth living as long as 'the lost provinces were in German hands'. Poincaré believed that only by a European war, involving Germany on at least two fronts, did France have any chance to regain Alsace and Lorraine. Furthermore—and this is very important—he was one of the few resolute Frenchmen who realized that large-scale European conflict could arise in the Balkan peninsula. To Poincaré, a war in the Balkans meant Alsace-Lorraine, to Izvolsky, Constantinople and the Straits; and so these two men, seeing eye to eye on 'the sore spot of Europe', worked together towards a common goal.

Before Poincaré took office, the people of France were not remotely interested in the problems of Serbia. Their sympathy for the Slavs had to be aroused deliberately and this Izvolsky and Poincaré set out to do by bribing the newspapers of France—some of which have always been willing to sell their freedom for francs. Influenced by this 'jingling persuasion', the press began to give favourable.

publicity to Russia's policy in the Balkans and the gullible French populace swung into line. Russian and French officials exchanged colourful, crowd-pleasing visits while naval guns boomed salutes, bands played and glittering state banquets drew attention to a renewed friendship. French loans helped Russia to finance new railways and armaments—a development perhaps pleasing Poincaré for the additional reason that he had a personal interest in the largest munitions plant which filled many of the Russian orders. The Franco-Russian alliance, by the end of the Second Balkan War, had become the strongest diplomatic partnership in Europe with the possible exception of the one between Germany and Austria-Hungary.

By the end of the year 1913, the trouble in the Balkans was smouldering to a fiery climax. This ferment, poured in on top of all the rivalry for colonies and the fear created by the naval and armament race, had strained the tension in Europe to its utmost limit. Well before June 28, 1914, a few influential statesmen had become convinced that another war in the Balkans was inevitable. They felt that such a rupture probably could not be 'localized' but would spread, because of the alliance system, to all the major powers. Thus they prepared for war, they pledged assistance to their allies and they knew exactly what they would do when the time came. This does not mean that the Great Powers wanted war or wilfully plotted to hasten the day. The diplomats, however, found themselves so trapped in the dark web of hatred and distrust spun round Europe by three decades of selfish international rivalry, that they could not avoid the consequences of the fatal shots fired by Princip.

The Armed Head Rises

On July 23, 1914, almost a month after the murder of the Archduke, Austria-Hungary presented Serbia with ten demands which Berchtold was certain it would not accept. By this date, Count von Berchtold, the Austrian Foreign Minister, egged on by some of the Austrian military leaders, had persuaded the hesitant members of his own government that Serbia, this time, should be punished by war. He had exaggerated and lied to the aging Emperor Franz Joseph and had secured his reluctant consent to a limited war against the Balkan Slavs. And he had tricked Kaiser William II and Bethmann-Hollweg, the German Chancellor, into a promise to back Austria-Hungary no matter what they might do to humiliate Serbia. Pashitch, the Prime Minister of Serbia, had received warm assurances of support, come what may, from Russia. Raymond Poincaré made another official visit to St. Petersburg and in a militant, gay and confident 'campaign mood' had pledged French assistance to the Tsar. By the time Serbia received the ultimatum from Austria-Hungary, therefore, the European alliance system was geared up and ready to go.

A few minutes before the six o'clock deadline on Saturday afternoon, July 25, Pashitch reported to the Austrian embassy in Belgrade with Serbia's written reply. His government agreed to control the anti-Austrian newspapers, to eliminate propaganda against the Dual Monarchy from the schools, to dissolve the secret societies and bring the murderers to justice (although it had just finished helping one of them to escape). The Austrian ambassador did not bother to read any of this. He glanced at Point Six and left the room. Half an hour later, he was on his way home to Vienna and diplomatic relations between Austria-Hungary and Serbia were severed.

Point Six had demanded that representatives from Austria-Hungary should be allowed into Serbia to take part in the investigations dealing with the assassination of Archduke Ferdinand. Considering the degree to which Serbian officials were mixed up in the Black Hand society, which planned the crime at Sarajevo, and considering that Pashitch denied all knowledge of the plot when, in reality, he was aware of it days before it happened, the government of Serbia did not dare accept this part of the ultimatum. Knowing ahead of time that it would be refused by Austria, the Serbs wrote their answer in humble words, hoping to win approval for their side of the quarrel. In this they were successful. The statesmen who did not realize at that time the extent of Serbia's guilt thought their reply was satisfactory. This was true in England where public opinion, at first, was sympathetic to Austria. It was true in Germany where William II, on reading the Serbian reply, said: 'Every reason for war now falls to the ground.' Thus encouraged, Sir Edward Grey, the German Emperor and other diplomats suggested various plans to bring Austria and Serbia together to settle their differences. Berchtold and his associates, however, had made up their stubborn minds. In what must be regarded as a deliberate attempt to prevent any further discussion, Austria-Hungary on July 28 declared war against Serbia.

The Russian Foreign Minister, Sasanov, and the scheming, overeager military leaders in St. Petersburg now decided that a European war could not be avoided. On July 29 they took the step which ended any hope for peace. Committed to aid Serbia and assured of French support, they ordered the mobilization of the vast, clumsy Russian army—not just along the Austro-Hungarian border as the Tsar wanted, but against both Austria and Germany. By this action, the Russians compelled Germany to play an active part: they put the alliance system into operation; and they practically killed the efforts of Sir Edward Grey and other diplomats to isolate the quarrel in the Balkans and prevent a general European conflict. The peace-loving Tsar of all the Russians, poor faltering Nicholas II, signed the mobilization decree, then cancelled it and finally yielded again to the pressure of his advisers. Almost exactly four years later Nicholas, his wife and their five children fell before a Bolshevik firing squad, victims of the Revolution that broke up the Russian Empire during the First World War.

After July 29, frantic, last-minute telegrams flashed back and forth across Europe in a desperate attempt to stop Austria's attack on Serbia and hold back Russia. Weary diplomats worked round the clock, tossing through the sleepless, hot hours of the night waiting for the next telephone call. Jean Jaurès, the socialist leader who had opposed the policies of Poincaré, was assassinated in Paris, a French ambassador collapsed with nervous prostration, a Russian ambassador dropped dead with a heart attack and the statesmen of Europe were at the end of their tether. The military men in France and especially in Germany, seeing the vain efforts of the diplomats and anxious to get the first jump, now took control as they had done in Russia a few days before. On July 31—with Austrian batteries bombing Belgrade, with Russian armies along the Eastern Front and mobilization orders ready in both Germany and France—the German Chancellor, urged on by the impatient Admiral von Tirpitz and General von Moltke, sent a twelve-hour ultimatum demanding that Russia should withdraw her troops. Twenty-four nerve-wracking hours went by without a Russian reply. At 6:00 p.m. on Saturday, August 1, the overwrought German ambassador in St. Petersburg handed Sasanov the declaration of war, burst into tears and stumbled out sobbing: 'I never could have believed that I should leave here under these terrible conditions.'

The lighted fuse now ran towards France. On August 1, a few hours before Germany declared war against Russia, the French Minister of Foreign Affairs and the German ambassador in Paris stood stiffly facing each other across the table. The German repeated his demand that his country must know at once what France intended to do. Although the French government had sent its share of telegrams urging caution, it left no doubt in Russia's mind, at any time, of what its final stand would be. After his visit to St. Petersburg, Poincaré had devoted most of his energies towards enticing a definite promise of aid from Great Britain and assuring Russia of his continued support. Therefore, it was no surprise when the German ambassador to France was informed: 'France will act in accordance with her interests.' Three days later, as the setting sun glowed red across western Europe, Germany declared war on France.

Up to this eleventh hour, the people and the government of Great Britain remained hesitant and undecided. The British had not been aroused by the murder of Archduke Ferdinand and it would have been difficult indeed to persuade them to fight for the Balkan Slavs. Although Sir Edward Grey made the most determined efforts of all the statesmen to prevent a European war, he personally favoured, from the beginning, outright support for France and Russia if it came to a showdown. Despite the Anglo-French naval and military talks that he had authorized, his hands were tied by public opinion, by parliament and by a division within his own cabinet. On August 4, the German General Staff took the step which brought Great Britain wholeheartedly into the war. In accordance with plans made long before, the German army, to defeat France more quickly, invaded Belgium. Now British interests were more obviously at stake.

Sir Edward Grey, with the full approval of the British cabinet, demanded that Germany should stop the invasion and requested that a satisfactory reply should reach London before twelve o'clock that night. The British ambassador in Berlin, calling to receive the German reply, reported that he found Bethmann-Hollweg very excited: 'His Excellency began a harangue which lasted for about twenty minutes. He said that the action about to be taken by His Majesty's Government was terrible to a degree. Just for the sake of Belgian neutrality—just for a scrap of paper—Great Britain was going to make war on a kindred nation who desired nothing better than to be friends with her.' But the 'scrap of paper', as the German knew full well, was a treaty almost one hundred years old by which Great Britain guaranteed Belgian neutrality. The scrap of paper was a vital part of British foreign policy protecting the country that lay across the Channel only a few miles from England. On August 4, as the guns spat fire into the darkness along the Eastern and Western Fronts and in the Balkans, as the clock struck midnight, Great Britain went to war against Germany.

While the Great Powers of Europe blundered into the agony of war during those days of August, secret moves by an aggressive Japan and a faltering Turkey received little attention. Yet the results of these manoeuvrings were to have far-reaching consequences on the future developments in the Far and Near East.

A series of Anglo-Japanese agreements signed between 1902 and 1911 guaranteed that British interests in that area would be protected by the use of Japanese naval power, if necessary. During this crisis period the Japanese Empire saw the opportunity to ostensibly honour its treaty obligations and to further its imperialist aims by seizing German possessions in China, particularly the naval base of Kiaochow in Shantung province. On August 15, a Japanese ultimatum to Germany demanded the withdrawal of all German warships from Japanese and Chinese waters and evacuation of all German bases in China. The Germans refused; and on August 23, war was declared on Germany.

Desperate Turkish statesmen, long dominated by German influence, saw a chance to recover some of their lost Balkan dominions and sought a firm bond with the Triple Alliance. On August 2, a secret treaty was signed and Turkey agreed to enter the war on the side of the Alliance if Russia attacked Germany. German warships entered Turkish waters; on November 3, Russia declared war on Turkey and the following day Britain and France followed suit.

The war moved into its global phase.

6   THE UNGUARDED BORDER

Imperial America

Before the First World War, Canadians were too busy at home to pay much attention to the outside world. Population and immigration figures, wheat fields and timber limits, silver and gold mines, railways, canals, tariffs and politics, babies, bungalows, new telephones and the rising costs of living absorbed their thoughts. The younger generation rushed away from school as soon as the law allowed or the truant officer wasn't looking, and entered life with little more than a smattering of British and Canadian history, a vague geography of North America and the Empire, and a keen desire to share in the material wealth of Canada. In those untroubled days, most Canadians had their minds focused on national progress and household matters, not on the war clouds over Europe.

When it came to foreign affairs, Canada found that her relations with Great Britain and the United States kept her occupied, without worrying about the Balkans or Alsace-Lorraine. Anglo-American questions almost always involved Canada and our statesmen sometimes had the idea that they were but pawns in the large game of world politics being played by the United States and Great Britain. Canada, growing restless under colonial restrictions, caused the mother country many perplexing moments as she exerted her desire for more freedom. Three thousand miles of 'unguarded border' provoked enough feuds to allow both Canada and the United States a little gentle sabre-rattling on their own account. While European diplomats pulled strings in every corner of the globe, Canadian statesmen had their hands full with old and new problems arising from the historic 'North Atlantic Triangle' of Canada, the United States and Great Britain.

It may seem illogical to bring our studies to the very brink of a shooting war, and then direct our attention back to less adventurous events instead of proceeding with the history of the First World War. However, the three-cornered diplomacy between the United States, Canada and Great Britain should be considered against a background of the wider world scene. Only if we keep in mind the rivalry of the Great Powers in Europe, Africa and Asia will we be able to understand fully what follows in the next two chapters.

Twisting the Lion's Tail
Among the countries that disliked Great Britain, the United States stood high on the list until almost the end of the nineteenth century. The old embers of hatred, dating back to July 4, 1776, were being constantly fanned and kept alive by anti-British textbooks, patriotic fiction stories and the Fourth of July 'orator of the day' who annually and perspiringly berated the tyrannical government of George III. Hundreds of thousands of Americans, raised on a textbook history of the War of

Independence in which the dark villain was always Great Britain, sincerely believed that England was an undemocratic, land-grabbing power. They were equally certain that nowhere in the world could life, liberty and happiness be pursued as fully as in the wonderful land of the free, the United States of America. In this swaggering spirit, the Republic posed as the democratic champion of the underdog and frequently took upon itself the criticism of British colonial policy.

This nagging, 'sniffish' attitude towards Great Britain was intensified by the arrival of tens of thousands of Irish immigrants who flocked into the United States, bringing with them their unrelenting hatred for England. Although despised by many people in America—the sons of Erin had to accustom themselves to signs reading 'no Irish need apply' and to the favourite wisecrack that the wheelbarrow was the greatest invention because it taught Irishmen to walk on their hind legs—the Irish Americans held a great deal of political power. After the Civil War, all the presidential elections were fairly close and the large Irish-Catholic vote, concentrated in the key eastern cities, could not be ignored by the political bosses. A sure way to catch this Irish vote was to taunt Great Britain. Every four years, therefore, when the United States prepared to elect a new president, the rival candidates found some excuse for 'twisting the British lion's tail'. Fortunately, British statesmen seemed to understand the situation and came to expect a bit of tail-twisting from time to time.

In 1895, Richard Olney, the Secretary of State in President Cleveland's administration, decided to give the lion's tail a really good twist. Some years before, gold had been discovered in the border area between Venezuela and British Guiana and a dispute arose over the territory boundary. The British regarded the controversy as rather a minor matter to be settled slowly and diplomatically. Not so the government of Venezuela; it appealed twice to the United States to arbitrate the question, but the British rejected both offers. A Washington propaganda agent was then hired by Venezuela to publicize the case and soon the U.S. 'yellow press' portrayed Britain as a bullying land-stealer in South America. Olney, a headline-hunting politician, sent a dispatch to Britain charging violation of the sacred Monroe Doctrine.

Lord Salisbury, the British Prime Minister, denied the charge firmly but politely. However, the United States, caught up in the muscle-flexing nationalism of the time, pressed the issue still further and the unsuspecting British were caught somewhat off guard. Most sensible Americans knew that a war over a mosquito-infested Venezuelan swamp was most unlikely, but there were irresponsible politicians trumpeting warlike threats. A leader of this new, swashbuckling attitude was the young and aggressive Teddy Roosevelt, who proclaimed: 'The clamour of the molly-coddling peace faction has convinced me that this country needs a war.' Surprised by the severity of this anti-British outburst in America, Salisbury backed down gracefully and allowed the United States to draw the Venezuelan boundary line—which they eventually did to the complete satisfaction of the British.

In bowing to Olney's demands, the British government was influenced more by world events than by any fear of the United States. Just before the Venezuela crisis, the balance of power in Europe had been restored by the Franco-Russian alliance and British statesmen had already decided to drop 'Splendid Isolation' and search for friends. While the crisis was at its height, an Englishman by the name of Dr. Jameson had led a raid against the Transvaal, as a preliminary manoeuvre to the Boer War. The German Kaiser took this occasion to insult Great Britain and sent a telegram of congratulations to Paul Kruger, leader of the Boers, when he foiled the Jameson Raid. This famous Kruger telegram reminded Great Britain of her shaky position in Europe and persuaded her to pay more courteous attention to the United States. British statesmen decided that the time had come 'to pat the American eagle on the head'.

Patting the Eagle's Head

Very important changes which occurred in the American way of life during the last decade of the nineteenth century presented Great Britain with several good opportunities to pat the eagle on the head. In the 1890s, as the accumulated result of almost one hundred years of strenuous activity, the Great American West was finally settled and the United States ceased to be primarily an agricultural country. The industrial revolution, which had been gathering momentum since the Civil War, changed the United States into a raw-boned industrial giant, seeking new markets, raw materials and imperial ventures overseas.

The American eagle took its first big flight when it flew at Spain in 1898. Three years before, the natives in Cuba, chafing under a cruel and inefficient Spanish administration, revolted yet again and were suppressed with the same ruthless barbarism as the revolutionaries had themselves used against the Spaniards. One of the techniques used by the revolutionaries had been the deliberate destruction of U.S. property, which had reached an investment value of $50 million, to induce American intervention. United States citizens had been killed in the revolts and repressions and the American people were genuinely horrified at this continuing bloodshed taking place so close to home. While a cynical senator might state that bananas and self-government could not grow in the same country, most Americans held the highly idealistic but dangerous belief that all people were capable of ruling themselves. They were on the side of the colonial underdog and these feelings, coupled with the economic interests, created an atmosphere favourable to expelling the Spaniards from Cuba.

Leading the outcry for direct intervention, and supporting the imperialist policies of politicians like Henry Cabot Lodge, were the newspapers of William Randolph Hearst and Joseph Pulitzer, the presslords of sensational and yellow journalism. The papers vied with each other in concocting atrocity stories, some true, many manufactured for the occasion. The Hearst *Journal* intercepted a letter from the Spanish Minister at Washington in which President McKinley was described as 'weak and a bidder for the admiration of the crowd'; it was front-page news. The American battleship *Maine* blew up in Havana harbour and while a U.S. Navy court of inquiry could not determine the cause, Spain was accused and President McKinley was forced to declare war.

The Easter Parade on Fifth Avenue, New York, in 1905

Although supposedly fighting to liberate Cuba, the United States also went after the Spanish possessions in the Pacific. 'Roughrider' Teddy Roosevelt, at that time Assistant Secretary of the Navy, acting quietly and on his own initiative, dispatched the American Asiatic Squadron under Admiral Dewey to Manila Bay in the Philippines. Here, 'Handy, Yankee Dewey Dandy' blew the assortment of antiques that passed for the Spanish navy out of the water—to the complete surprise of the people back home. In five months it was all over at a cost of 5,500 dead, only 380 of them battle casualties, and an expenditure of $250 million.

The United States suddenly had become an imperial power with overseas possessions in the Caribbean and the Far East. Old-fashioned Americans, alarmed at the prospect of their country actually owning colonies, prevented the government from taking outright control of Cuba, but the Platt Amendment to the new Cuban constitution made that country a U.S. satellite for many years to come. As for Guam, Puerto Rico, the Philippines and Hawaii, the Americans persuaded themselves that they too had a duty to civilize their 'brown brothers' and these areas were made into colonies of the United States.

This bold American venture into the world struggle for markets and raw materials naturally aroused the suspicions of other nations with interests in the Caribbean and the Far East. To the despair of the United States, who naively thought that the sincerity of her motives would never be questioned, all the continental European powers sided with Spain. In fact, hostility towards the United States was so great in France and Germany that the State Department, learning fast, earmarked some good American dollars to 'persuade' the newspapers in those two countries to be more friendly during the Spanish-American War. Shortly after the war, the United States was further embarrassed when the Filipinos broke loose with primitive ferocity in an attempt to gain their freedom from American control. Leader of this attempt was Emilio Aguinaldo, who with his insurrecto army had aided the Americans in the capture of Manila from the Spanish. The rebellion failed and for two years seventy thousand U.S. troops fought a bitter campaign against Filipino guerrillas to crush the revolt. The war caused much public protest in the United States. It is interesting to note that only in 1964, following a term of imprisonment for assisting the Japanese in World War Two, did Aguinaldo swear allegiance to the United States. He was ninety-five years of age.

The American suppression of the Filipino rising was obvious, naked imperialism and the rest of the world derided democratic America for such an extreme departure from her cherished principles. Under these circumstances, the United States was sincerely grateful when England, alone among the Great Powers, stood by her and cheered her progress in both the Spanish-American War and the Philippines. For the first time, the United States began to appreciate the kind of problems Great Britain had had to face in building her Empire and which the Americans, up to this time, had been so ready to criticize. A change in attitude towards Great Britain was clearly revealed when the Boer War broke out in 1899 while American soldiers were still in the Philippine jungles. While sympathy for the Boers was being openly expressed all over Europe, the government of the United States used this occasion to return British friendship and gave the Empire moral support throughout the three-year struggle in South Africa. Thus the policy of patting the eagle's head paid dividends and the United States and Great Britain entered the twentieth century with a better understanding between them than had existed since colonial days.

Cowboy Diplomacy

In Buffalo on September 1, 1901, Leon Czolgosz waited in a reception line to meet the President of the United States touring the country to celebrate his re-election for a second term. William McKinley was proud of his accessibility to the people and his secret service guards were always few. He extended his hand in greeting and Czolgosz, a fervid anarchist, shot him twice. A week later President McKinley died, and the Vice-President, in accordance with American law, was sworn in to replace him. The colourful, cocky and vain Theodore Roosevelt, bursting with energy at only forty-two years of age, full of zeal to clean up corrupt politics, to check the power of 'big business' and to make his own or his country's voice heard in world affairs, was now 'the cowboy in the White House'.

The new President inherited a thorny international problem which involved Great Britain and gave her statesmen another very important opportunity to show their goodwill towards the United States. American empire-building and

Although the Panama Canal was completed in 1914, use of it was limited by constant landslides, many of which occurred at the Gaillard (Culebra) Cut, shown here during construction.

the addition of overseas colonies after the Spanish-American War had accelerated the long-standing ambition of the United States to link the east and west coasts by a water route through the Isthmus of Panama. Unfortunately the shortest distance for this project lay through the Republic of Colombia, a country highly suspicious of U.S. motives. To prevent American interference Colombia in 1879 granted canal-building rights to a French concern including at one time Ferdinand de Lesseps of Suez fame. This company went bankrupt and the New Panama Company, an association far more favourably inclined to listen to American investors, was formed in 1894 despite Colombia's resistance.

Added to the Central American republic's refusal to co-operate was the barrier of the Clayton-Bulwer Treaty of 1850, whereby Britain and the United States had agreed not to gain exclusive control over any canal project in Central America. However, by 1901, Britain, seeking continuing U.S. friendship, consented to renegotiate the 1850 agreement and finally gave the Americans a free hand in the Isthmus. Congress authorized millions of dollars to purchase the New Panama Company's properties and building rights and the canal project seemed to be well on its way. At this point the Republic of Colombia refused to allow the canal-building rights to be transferred.

Roosevelt did not allow this new development to upset his calculations. Not having to worry about England's reactions, he was free to engage in some 'cowboy diplomacy'. In November 1903, a revolt among the natives, said to have been engineered in Washington and financed by J. P. Morgan, broke out in Panama. An American battleship happened to arrive just in time to stop Colombian troops from landing to quell the uprising and so the independent state of Panama suddenly appeared in Central America. Within an hour of hearing the news Roosevelt recognized this convenient new nation and entered into hurried negotiations with it for permission to complete the Panama Canal. In less than two weeks an agreement was signed whereby the United States, for a down payment of $10 million and an annual fee of $250,000, received a strip of land ten miles wide across the isthmus for all time to come. Another great American ambition was fulfilled and the dirt began to fly down in Panama.

The interests of the United States now ranged far afield. 'The Marines have landed and the situation is well in hand' became a byword in dealing with 'the wretched banana republics' and Teddy Roosevelt wielded his 'big stick' so strenuously in the Caribbean that European nations quickly realized that this area was an American preserve. The 'Open Door' policy in the East, particularly in China, became an open corridor for American expansion and, at the conclusion of the Russo-Japanese War in 1905, the oft-derided 'little yellow men' of the Rising Sun sat opposite the bearded autocrats of Holy Mother Russia at a conference table in Portsmouth, Maine, to have their differences adjudicated by Theodore Roosevelt; that settlement won the Nobel Peace Prize for the boisterous President of the United States. American observers watched the wily European diplomats spin their webs of deceit at Algeciras, during the first Morocco crisis. Adding fuel to a long-continuing quarrel that was to culminate on a December day in 1941, the 'Happy Warrior' President quarrelled with Japan over immigration quotas and sent sixteen American battleships around the world to visit Tokyo and 'show the flag'. The fleet's triumphant return in 1909, just in time to usher the 'cowboy' out of the White House, was symbolic of the long road the once-isolated United States had travelled since the Spanish-American War.

Many people in the United States, however, thought that American interests and foreign policy had strayed, like their fleet, much too far from home. Taught to revere the old policy of isolation and to distrust the European nations, they were convinced that the new imperial course was undemocratic and contrary to all American traditions. Roosevelt's 'big stick' diplomacy and his aggressive participation in world affairs aroused more bitter controversy in his own country than in Great Britain or elsewhere. The British government's official pro-American policy was made easier at home because Englishmen of all classes seemed to admire such an uninhibited and colourful personality as Teddy Roosevelt. Many of the working class in England looked to North America as the land of opportunity and to Roosevelt as the lusty champion of the people. Thus the policy of patting the eagle's head had a great deal of popular support while the Roughrider was in the White House.

Dollar and Grape-juice Diplomacy
In 1909, having failed to gain re-election to the presidency, Roosevelt bounced off to hunt big game in Africa, leaving William H. Taft, an amiable, rotund, home-loving man, in charge at the White House. Taft and his advisers decided to withdraw from European entanglements and American foreign policy slipped back towards isolation. Under their administration, the United States concentrated on Central America and the Caribbean islands. American dollars poured into this region in greater volume than ever before, with special attention being paid to Guatemala and Honduras. Taft liked to believe that his 'dollar diplomacy' pleased the Latin-American countries as well as the American businessman, but United States domination was resented bitterly and the dollar proved to be a very poor diplomat.

At the conclusion of Taft's four years in the White House, the people found themselves in the thick of a most interesting presidential election tussle. By that time, the United States was tossing in restless discontent. The machine age had bred teeming, filthy slums and grimy factories where long, weary working hours with miserable wages ground down men, women and children alike. An ever-increasing horde of insecure, city-dwelling, industrial robots waged incessant class warfare, through their trade unions, against the hated owners of industry. The unruffled agricultural society had disappeared in the tumult of modern life. Unable to understand the complexities of a great industrial nation, the electorate seemed powerless to prevent their government from falling into the hands of the giant trusts. Many politicians were bribed by the captains of industry, and 'muckraking' reporters scraped up sordid tales of corruption, extravagance and dishonest legislation purchased for the benefit of the favoured few. Storms of protest reached hurricane proportions in 1912 and neither the Republicans nor the Democrats could ignore the clamour for reform.

Among those who heard and understood the crying need for reform was none other than Theodore Roosevelt—the 'trust-buster' once feared by businessmen— now back from triumphs in Africa and Europe and still 'rarin' to go'. Pressed by a multitude of admirers to run again for president, the Roughrider, with a characteristic yip and kyoodle, proclaimed, 'My hat is in the ring,' and thereby sounded the gong for a real fight within his own Republican party. But the tycoons of finance and industry made sure, when the time came, that William H. Taft was renominated to lead the Republican party. Undaunted, the supporters of Roosevelt gathered together in the Chicago Coliseum and with wild enthusiasm formed their own 'Progressive party'. Meanwhile, the Democrats, searching for a leader to take them to victory after sixteen years of frustration, sweltered through forty-six ballots at their August nominating convention before choosing Woodrow Wilson, a former president of Princeton University and an ardent reformer. Wilson often left his audiences with the impression that 'only the Devil would dare to disagree with him', and campaigned for his 'New Freedom' for the masses with righteous self-confidence. In the resulting three-way contest, the Republican vote was split between Roosevelt and Taft, allowing the austere, granite-faced clergyman's son to slip in as President of the United States.

In his inaugural address, Woodrow Wilson forecast a return to the old ideals of democracy with these words: 'The great Government we loved has been too often made use of for private and selfish purposes. . . . There has been something crude and heartless in our haste to succeed and be great. Our thought has been: "Let every man look out for himself." . . . We have come now to the sober second thought.' The President also promised a second sober look at dollar diplomacy, declaring that his administration 'was not interested in supporting special groups with investments in Latin America or anywhere else'. Appointed as Secretary of State to carry out this anti-imperialistic foreign policy was William Jennings Bryan, a thunderous champion of the people and the only man in American history with the dubious distinction of being three times an unsuccessful candidate for the presidency. Bryan, a staunch teetotaler, added a new, dry touch to life in Washington when he refused to serve alcoholic beverages at state functions— thereby causing some dignitaries, so it was said, to fortify themselves in advance and introducing what his opponents called a period of 'grape-juice diplomacy'.

Even with the best of intentions, Wilson and Bryan found that the imperial course laid out in the days of McKinley, Roosevelt and Taft had to be followed and the new administration actually used more armed intervention to support American investments than any of its predecessors. As one wag said: 'There seemed to be a great deal of grape-shot mixed up in the grape-juice.' The United States continued to crush native revolts, using methods fully as ruthless—especially in the Dominican Republic and Haiti—as those employed by the European nations in Africa, and an embarrassed Wilson was forced to set up military dictatorships in several Latin-American countries. Like the British, the Americans cloaked their imperialism in lofty phrases and pointed out the schools, roads, improved sanitation and other benefits enjoyed by their brown brothers as a result of the law and order established by the United States.

Neither dollar nor grape-juice diplomacy caused any interruption in the pro-American policy that the British government had been following. The era of Taft and Wilson coincided with Austria's seizure of Bosnia, the second Morocco crisis, the Balkan Wars and the final stages of the Anglo-German naval race—all of which made it more necessary than ever before for Great Britain to be careful of American feelings. Anti-British feeling still ran high among the Irish and German groups and the transatlantic courtship was somewhat one-sided because the United States seemed to take it for granted that all nations needed her friendship. However, the policy which began with the Venezuelan border dispute, when the British decided the lion's tail had been twisted long enough, continued to the very eve of the First World War and successfully avoided giving the American eagle any reason to ruffle its feathers.

There was, indeed, only one fly in the ointment: cocky Canada, rollicking along in the flag-waving spirit of the times and revelling in her newly found prosperity, was not at all sure that she wanted to pat the nearby eagle on the head. The Canadian beaver, growing stronger, began to carry a bigger chip on its shoulder at the very time the mother country was most anxious to encourage Anglo-American friendship.

Confident Canada

The Beaver Carries a Chip

In the city of Quebec, on August 23, 1898, five British and five American delegates settled down to unravel all the knotty problems that had been causing trouble between Canada and the United States. The meeting of this Joint High Commission is a landmark in the history of our external relations, because the British delegation for the first time contained a majority of Canadians. Before Confederation, all our foreign affairs were handled for us exclusively by the British government and we could not deal directly with any foreign nation. As one Canadian historian has written: 'Miss Ottawa had a voice but etiquette forbade her speaking to Mr. Washington except through Papa London.'

After 1867, Miss Ottawa, resenting her inferior colonial position, pressed the British government for more freedom in external affairs. As a result, the Colonial Office began to invite representatives from the Canadian government to sit in on discussions involving Canadian interest. This was particularly true of trade negotiations at that time when the Canadian delegate made all the decisions and the British agent merely signed any resulting treaty to make it legal. In more important diplomatic matters, however, Canada was restricted to a minority role until the appointment of the Joint High Commission in 1898. Lord Salisbury's government, anxious to please its North American colony as well as the United States, readily gave in to the soaring spirit of nationalism in Canada.

The Canadian people were unfortunately in no mood to be friendly and co-operative with the United States. As far as they were concerned, there was no reason for suddenly changing their critical and somewhat hostile attitude towards the United States. As the United States grew more prosperous—and possibly more disdainful of a struggling Canada—our chronic jealousy of American success was greatly increased. It did not help matters for Canadians to see the Northwest Territories empty when immigrants by the tens of thousands were flocking into the United States to share in its riches. Also Canada, unlike Great Britain, could neither understand nor tolerate the tail-twisting that went on across the border. During the Venezuela dispute there was a particularly violent outburst of anti-American feeling in Canada—and this, it should be noted, followed soon after the annexation argument. In 1896, the very year in which the Canadian people elected Laurier and the low-tariff Liberal party into power, the Americans elected the high-tariff Republicans under William McKinley. An extremely nationalistic Congress soon passed the Dingley tariff, the highest in American history, and thereby dashed Canada's hopes for better trade relations with the United States.

Against this background of jealousy and anger, it is easy to foresee what Canada's reactions to the Spanish-American War would be. The Canadian people were not aware of the tense European situation that persuaded Lord Salisbury's government to support the United States in this war. As the United

States swaggered on to the world stage, Canadian public opinion was critical of every move.

Despite the unfavourable temper of the times in both Canada and the United States, the Commissioners at Quebec worked together in a frank and friendly spirit. The American delegates, having in mind the encouragement given to their government by Great Britain during the recent war with Spain, were willing to compromise on many points. However, they were hamstrung by public opinion and by the clause in the American Constitution which states that all treaties must be approved by the United States Senate. Whenever their Commissioners showed any inclination to give in to Canada, the American people raised a hubbub about 'pandering to the British'.

Line-fence disputes along a three-thousand-mile boundary had given the United States and Canada ample room for differences of opinion. Twelve of these specific border difficulties, some of them dating back almost to the beginning of the nineteenth century, had been presented for settlement to the Joint High Commission. The Commission failed to solve any of the problems submitted to it and in February 1899, after six months of futile discussion, it was disbanded. Therefore, as Canada moved into the present century, the unguarded frontier was still charged with high-voltage electricity induced by years of friction between the two countries. The old issues had not been settled and new ones were constantly appearing. Thus the British government, attempting to maintain friendly relations with the United States during the years immediately preceding the First World War, was going to have trouble with its unruly colony.

Quarterdeck Methods in Alaska
The Alaskan Panhandle gave Canada her first opportunity in the twentieth century to disturb Anglo-American relations. The exact location of the Alaskan boundary lay hidden in the fuzzy wording of an old treaty signed in 1825 between Russia and Great Britain. Even after the United States purchased Alaska from Russia in 1867, no one seemed to know or care just where the line should be. Canada had suggested many times that a proper survey should be undertaken. However, the issue had remained unsettled until gold was discovered in the Yukon in 1897. As hordes of prospectors began to struggle across the mountain passes of the Panhandle on their way to the Klondike, the ownership of the land through which they travelled suddenly became an urgent question. National pride in both Canada and the United States now made a friendly settlement of the Alaskan boundary impossible.

The Alaskan boundary had been one of the twelve problems submitted to the Joint High Commission in 1898. The American delegates had been willing to compromise with Canada on this point but were prevented from doing so by the angry hue-and-cry raised by their people on the west coast. In Seattle, particularly, the businessmen were doing a roaring business in the Klondike and had no desire to let Canadians share it.

The Laurier government next saw a glimmer of hope when Great Britain and the United States began to discuss the Panama canal zone in 1901. Canada urged

For almost two years, endless lines of prospectors struggled over the three main routes across the mountains to the Klondike. Pictured here is the beginning of the Chilkoot Pass route, the most dangerous of all.

the mother country to bargain for return favours in Alaska and, at first, the Foreign Office agreed. However, the British government changed its mind and told Canada, in diplomatic language, to be quiet about Alaska. In their anxiety to please the United States, the British government thus lost the best chance Canada had for a satisfactory solution to the Alaskan boundary question. The truth of the matter probably was that Great Britain, faced with the loss of prestige and the hostility of European nations resulting from the Boer War, was in no position to drive a hard bargain with the United States.

When the Panama episode was over, the Canadian government appealed to Great Britain to tackle the Alaskan question again. Early in 1903, the Foreign Office accordingly completed an agreement with the United States whereby six impartial judges, three from each side, should be appointed to study the old Anglo-Russian treaty and decide, once and for all, just where the boundary line was meant to be. President Roosevelt shared the common view—one which was not in keeping with the facts—that Canada had trumped up a claim only after gold was found in the Klondike. 'The Canadian case,' he said, 'is an outrage, pure and simple. They have no more right to the land in question than they have to Maine.' To support this claim he appointed the following men to the Alaskan

Tribunal: Senator Henry Cabot Lodge, a fiery, nationalistic tail-twister; ex-Senator George Turner, who hailed from Seattle; and Elihu Root, the Secretary of War, an able, thoroughly respected lawyer but, like his two colleagues, fully committed to the American cause. These were Roosevelt's 'impartial' jurists!

Laurier, solidly backed by public opinion, took the extreme step of protesting to Great Britain and threatening to withdraw entirely from the proposed Tribunal. To forestall such drastic action, the British government immediately ratified the agreement with the United States and then calmly advised Ottawa to accept its decision without causing further trouble. Canada's representatives, however—Sir Louis Jetté, the Lieutenant-Governor of Quebec and A. B. Aylesworth, a lawyer from Toronto—were determined to stand together for Canada's rights. This situation left the sixth member of the Tribunal, Lord Alverstone, Lord Chief Justice of England, in a most unenviable position. However impartial his reasoning, whatever verdict he might give, the Lord Chief Justice was sure to be pilloried by one side or the other.

On October 20, 1903, after a full month of intensive discussion, the news of the Tribunal's decision was flashed from London across the Atlantic. Four to two against Canada; Lord Alverstone had sided with the Americans; Sir Louis Jetté and Aylesworth had angrily refused to sign the award; Canada had lost the Alaskan boundary dispute. Expecting this very thing—almost waiting for it—a great many Canadian newspapers, before they had time to study one word of Lord Alverstone's reasoning, broke out in violent abuse and in screaming head-lines proclaimed the view that Canada had been 'sacrificed on the altar of Anglo-American friendship'. Old Sir Charles Tupper, a former Conservative prime minister of Canada, summed up what must be regarded as the general feeling of the people with these words: 'The whole course of British negotiations with the United States is marked with a line of gravestones under which Canadian rights are buried.'

The anger of Canadians might have been much greater had they known, as we do now, how Roosevelt privately used his 'big stick'. In August, before the Tribunal had commenced its meetings, he dispatched a special agent to inform the British government that, if the decision went against the United States, he would 'ask Congress for permission to run the line as we claim it, . . . without regard for the attitude of England and Canada', and since some American troops had already been sent to the Panhandle the British authorities, including Lord Alverstone, knew that Roosevelt meant business. It was almost impossible for the Lord Chief Justice, serving under this kind of political pressure, to decide in favour of Canada.

The most unfortunate part of the whole Alaskan dispute, from a Canadian point of view, was the selection of the politicians to represent the United States on the Tribunal. Perhaps the Senate, as Roosevelt asserted later, forced his hand and insisted on 'stacking' the Tribunal with safe men. The United States actually did have the better claim, and it is lamentable that Roosevelt should have taken such strong measures to ensure a victory. Had the American government made even a pretence at choosing impartial jurists, Canada probably would have accepted the award without too much complaint. As it was, the Canadian people, convinced they had been cheated, directed their bitter resentment against Lord Alverstone, the United States and Great Britain in about equal doses.

Line-fence Disputes
The pressure along the unguarded border continued. After 1903, the century-old controversy about the rights of American ships fishing inside Canada's three-mile limit bobbed up again along the Atlantic coast, giving the 'sea-going voters' from Senator Lodge's state of Massachusetts another chance for a salty argument with the Maritimes and Newfoundland. Inland, the government of the United States annually dumped twenty million pike and pickerel into its end of Lake Champlain, while at the other end, using nets and ignoring the spawning season, Canadians fished them out. But on Lake Erie an American fleet of sixty or so boats, poaching for pickerel, hauled in a catch worth twelve thousand dollars daily as the *Vigilant* scurried about, firing random but sometimes accurate shots in an attempt to stop them. Out on the Pacific coast, fishermen from south of the border trawled over our halibut grounds and retorted to Canadian complaints by demanding that we should give more protection to the salmon running up the Fraser River to spawn. And out on the wide-open Pacific, despite repeated and very justifiable protests from the United States, marksmen from British Columbia continued to shoot the swimming seals, males and females alike, on their way to breed on the American-owned Pribilof Islands in the Bering Sea.

Relations were not improved by another series of irritating problems connected with the lakes and rivers that formed a part of or crossed the international boundary. Lumber, irrigation and hydro-electric power dams built on one side of the line affected the water levels, the navigation rights, the farming and business interests of residents on the other side. Canadian irrigation schemes on the Milk River in Alberta's dry belt, for instance, interfered with similar places in Montana. Chicago's drainage canal threatened the Upper Lakes level as power installations diverted jointly-owned boundary waters at Niagara and Sault Ste. Marie. And New Brunswick lumbermen, enjoying a new lease on life from pulpwood, protested loud and long against American-built obstructions on the St. John River in Maine.

Contrary to a popular misunderstanding, Canada's attitude towards the United States did not mellow when the two countries began to do more business with each other during the first decade of the twentieth century. In fact, the growing prominence of American interests in almost every phase of Canada's business life seemed to multiply the sources of friction. As we noticed in an earlier chapter, Fielding's Tariff Commission heard many bitter complaints about American competition. The signs of a 'get-rich-quick' outlook were usually attributed, not to native-born characteristics, but to the 'American influence' in Canada. It may be concluded that the Canadian people, inspired by a confident and crowing press, held an exaggerated opinion of their achievements during the boom years, freely criticized the American way of life and were not ready for a peaceful settlement of border difficulties with the United States.

Wiping the Slate Clean

Many of the problems associated with the fisheries, the fur seals and the boundary waters were more explosive and certainly more important than a few ghost towns along the Panhandle coast. Had they been tossed into the political arena, they might have caused uglier disputes than the one over Alaska. That this did not happen is due to the British policy of patting the eagle's head and to the work of a few men who set the world an example in true statesmanship.

At the beginning of 1907, Sir Edward Grey appointed a new ambassador to represent Great Britain in Washington. No better man for the position could have been selected than James Bryce, a thoughtful, scholarly diplomat and one of the most popular British ambassadors ever to be in Washington. The breadth of his knowledge and interests was remarkable not only for his time but for any time. He was able to write monumental works on history, law and politics and at the same time to lead a distinguished, active life and make a host of friends. For almost seven years, Bryce devoted his energies almost exclusively towards improving Canadian-American relations.

Before Taft took over from Roosevelt in the spring of 1909, Bryce was very ably assisted by Elihu Root, another great statesman whose name was unfortunately associated in the minds of Canadians with the Alaskan boundary award. Serving as Secretary of State in Roosevelt's second administration, Root brought to his position the same dignified skill and the same conviction that nations could solve their difficulties by peaceful discussion as did James Bryce. His name more correctly should be linked with the International Court of Justice at the Hague, the Nobel Peace Prize in 1912 and his successful efforts to settle many difficulties between his country and Canada.

Since Canada did not yet control her own foreign affairs, Bryce and Root had to work through both the Colonial Office in England and the Canadian Governor General. From the Colonial Secretary and especially from the Governor General, Earl George Grey, they received many patient hours of co-operation.

Briefly, what Earl Grey, Root and Bryce, with their advisers, tried to do was remove from the tumult of politics as many border problems as possible and set up permanent boards of experts, where needed, to prevent future difficulties. In 1908, for instance, an agreement was signed by Root and Bryce defining Canada's responsibilities for the Fraser River salmon, providing for uniform laws to protect the game and commercial fish in the inland boundary lakes, and creating an International Fish Commission composed of experienced men from both countries. A year later, the Boundary Water Treaty amicably settled most of the existing difficulties and set up a very important permanent Joint High Commission with broad powers to control the use of all the waterways shared by Canada and the United States. Since this Joint High Commission could make and enforce regulations and was composed of Canadian and American representatives only, it is regarded as a great forward step in Canada's freedom to handle her own foreign affairs.

Also in 1909, Root and Bryce persuaded the United States and Canada to submit the long-standing, dangerous Atlantic fisheries dispute to arbitration before a tribunal of impartial jurists at the Hague. This tribunal solved one of the most difficult international problems to the satisfaction of all concerned. Finally, James Bryce and Elihu Root began the discussions which resulted in a treaty to protect the fur seals. In 1911, Canada, Japan and Russia agreed not to hunt seals anywhere in the Bering Sea, provided the United States would share the profits from the male animals which they alone were allowed to kill on the Pribilof Islands.

Without arousing public passions in either country, most of the old issues had been wiped from the slate by 1911. Four short years of amazing achievement were just beginning to soften the harsh memories of the past when reciprocity hit the headlines again in a Canadian general election. The good work of Bryce, Grey and Root was torn down in three months of bitter political warfare over the emotional pocket-book question of tariffs and trade. Whether the newspapers and platform orators who 'used the old loyalty cry' really thought Canada was at a parting of the ways or whether they meant what they said about the United States, is beside the point. The majority of people in Canada did believe what they heard and read. Traditional anti-American prejudices, stirred up from time to time over the previous twenty years, came boiling to the surface again in 1911. Before these feelings could be submerged, Canada proudly went to war by Britain's side while the United States followed a neutral course until April 1917. During these three years, as the war spirit mounted and the casualty lists grew longer, the Canadian people raised an angry, accusing cry against the United States and the discords along the unguarded border reached their most sullen tone since 1814.

7 BRITANNIC ALLIANCE

The Future Course of Empire

During the spring of 1901, the people of Great Britain had been hotly debating reports that the War Office and the British officers on the spot had bungled in the South African War. Many of them agreed with Sir Arthur Conan Doyle, who wrote a good history of the Boer War as well as Sherlock Holmes stories, when he said: 'In the face of their blunders and miscalculations, our professional soldiers have not shown that they were endowed with clear vision or a serious attitude towards their work. The idea that an infantry soldier is a pikeman has never quite departed in our army. We take immense pains to give him the best modern rifle, but instead of teaching him to use it we waste his life in childish exercises on the parade ground.' How else, the people asked, could you explain the fact that almost half a million men, drawn from every part of the Empire, had been required to crush two Boer states possessing a total population of less than four hundred thousand?

Although their capital cities had been occupied and their country annexed by the British government, the stubborn Boers refused to give in. Guerrilla bands—crack shots and expert horsemen—had begun to ride the veldt, taking a devastating toll. Winston Churchill describes with these words the measures Lord Kitchener was forced to take: 'Blockhouses were built along the railway lines; fences were driven across the countryside and more blockhouses were built along the fences. Then, area by area, every man, woman and child was swept into concentration camps. . . . By February, 1902, more than 20,000 of the prisoners had died, mostly of disease. At first the authorities denied that anything was wrong but at length an Englishwoman, Miss Emily Hobhouse, exposed and proclaimed the terrible facts.' Public opinion in Great Britain was thoroughly aroused and the conduct of the Boer War undoubtedly helped to defeat the Unionist government in the general election of 1906.

The Boer War Debates

While Great Britain was engaged in this controversy, an equally vigorous and very important argument about the Boer War was going on in Canada. Neither the causes nor the conduct of the war provoked as much discussion in this country as they did in England. The Canadian people paid little attention to events in South Africa until the first shots were fired in October 1899. Then a sudden outburst of patriotism and loyalty to Britain, more than the merits of the conflict, forced the Laurier administration to issue a call for volunteers. Over seven thousand troops—equipped and transported by Canada but paid while on active duty by Great Britain—eventually fought with distinction in the Boer

War. Never before in our history had the Canadian government sent soldiers overseas, and the decision to do so in the South African War was greeted with strong but mixed feelings across the country. From the ensuing debates arose the whole question of Canada's future place in the Empire and the ideas which finally formed the British Commonwealth of Nations.

To the people in Quebec this was an Anglo-Saxon war for the glory of the British Empire, and it was not surprising that most of the French-Canadian population remained sullen and unenthusiastic. As *La Presse* explained in simple language: 'We French Canadians belong to one country, Canada; Canada is for us the whole world; but the English Canadians have two countries, one here and one across the seas.' The main spokesman for this extreme Nationalist and mainly French-Canadian point of view was Henri Bourassa, the gifted grandson of Louis Joseph Papineau. He and his followers could see no reason why Canada should fight England's 'commercial, selfish and colonial wars'.

From across the provincial boundary the angry Protestant voice of extremists in Ontario growled, 'Traitors!' 'British Canadians,' the Toronto *News* asserted, with a fanaticism equal to any in Quebec, 'will find a way, through the ballot box or otherwise, to rid themselves of the influence of this inferior and disloyal race.' Striking out at Laurier, this group loudly protested that Canada's aid to the Empire had been offered in a niggardly and uncertain spirit. So spoke those who clung to the old 'colonial' belief that the foreign policy and defence of the Empire should remain in the hands of the British government.

Amidst this angry babble of voices could be heard the advocates of yet another opinion—the British Empire League urging a new 'Imperialism'. Believing the day of colonialism to be dead and abhorring the thought of an isolated and almost independent Canada, these men held out for a reorganization of the British Empire. Canada and some of the other colonies should be allowed to take part in shaping the policies they were expected to defend. The time had come to form a council or parliament for the Empire in which all the dominions should help to decide questions of foreign affairs and defence.

Faced with criticism from these conflicting groups and especially from Henri Bourassa, Laurier had to defend and explain the policy of his government many times. On the public platform and in parliament, he repeatedly assured his listeners that sending troops to the Boer War did not establish any hard and fast rules for the future. Lacking any control over England's foreign policy, we were not committed to aid in all her wars. What about a council of Empire, a reorganization along the lines suggested by the Imperialists? No, said Laurier, Empire defences and foreign affairs were Britain's concern; Canada did not want a voice in these matters. To accept any responsibility for policy-making would draw Canada into 'the vortex of European militarism' and this he was not prepared to see. Canada must not commit herself in advance to the defence of any Empire policy; she must wait and decide when the time comes what course to follow. 'I claim for Canada that she shall be at liberty to act or not to act, to interfere or not to interfere, to do just as she pleases.'

As events were to prove later, this middle-of-the-road declaration of policy

Crowds on Yonge Street, looking north from Adelaide Street, Toronto, celebrating the successful siege of Pretoria, June 5, 1900.

was the only one acceptable to the great mass of citizens in all parts of the Dominion. Laurier gave concrete expression to the maturing national desires that were to guide the future course of this country. Here, also, he forecast the British Commonwealth of Nations—no longer an Empire, but a galaxy of independent states bound to the homeland only by the strong, invisible ties of loyalty.

Pomp, Power and Poverty

In June 1902, a few weeks after the resistance of the Boers finally had been broken, the Fourth Colonial Conference began its meetings in London. The premiers from the different parts of the Empire gathered in a spirit of intense loyalty to Britain; the flood tide of racial pride and imperial sentiment was running high. More important still, the colonial secretary and chairman of the Conference was Joseph Chamberlain, a fiery patriot, an advocate of the British Empire League and a man who had been preaching, during his eight years in office, an arrogant but rousing gospel of Anglo-Saxon superiority. Surely, the Imperialists thought, the time was ripe to draw the colonies and the mother country closer together in a common defence and foreign policy.

In his opening address, Chamberlain told the Conference: 'Gentlemen, we do want your aid. We do require your assistance in the administration of the vast

Empire which is yours as well as ours. The weary Titan staggers under the too vast orb of its own fate. . . . If you are prepared at any time to take a share in the burdens of the Empire, we are prepared to give you a voice in the policy of the Empire.' New Zealand, the recently formed Commonwealth of Australia, Natal, Cape Colony and Newfoundland were all prepared to take up Chamberlain's offer. The first four of these states lay exposed, in the Pacific and in Africa, to all the dangers of European colonial rivalry and felt the need for Britain's diplomatic skill and the comforting presence of her sea power. They readily agreed to contribute money for the maintenance of the fleet and the way seemed open to create a policy-making council for the Empire. However, Laurier, sensitive to national feelings back home and never sure in his own mind that Canada needed England's protection, refused to follow the other colonial premiers in this decision. As did many other Canadians in those days, Laurier seemed to feel that the broad Atlantic, and perhaps the American fleet, provided strong enough security. Thus the Colonial Secretary's stirring appeal failed because the Canadian Prime Minister would not commit his country to any general scheme for imperial defence.

Never again would the Imperialists have such a golden opportunity; their hour slipped away unfulfilled in 1902. By the time another Conference was summoned, the whole situation, especially in Great Britain itself, had changed. In the British general election of 1906, the Unionist government, which had been under the leadership first of Lord Salisbury and then, after his illness in 1902, of his nephew Arthur Balfour, came down in resounding defeat.

In keeping with the imperial spirit of the closing years of the nineteenth century, it was natural that the Diamond Jubilee in 1897 should have been made a great state festival, displaying to the world the splendour of the English monarchy. The brilliant marching troops drawn from every corner of the Empire, the rousing martial music of the bands, the princes and potentates of India, the gold and the braid, the cheering crowds in the streets and above all the tumultuous homage paid to Queen Victoria revealed in vivid colours the glory of Great Britain and the wide range of her far-flung Empire. Less than four years later, on January 22, 1901, the announcement by the Prince of Wales that 'my beloved Mother, the Queen, has just passed away,' awakened feelings of sympathy, of sorrow and of imperial sentiment such as the British Empire had never known before.

A few weeks later, Edward VII told parliament that 'in accordance with her late Majesty's wishes' a Royal Tour, planned before she died, would not be postponed. Adding still further to the emotional pitch of Great Britain's subjects beyond the seas, the Duke and Duchess of York, later King George V and Queen Mary, sailed from Portsmouth on a nine-month tour of the Empire—thirty thousand miles around the world to countries owing allegiance to the British crown; escorted into gaily decorated ports by magnificent units of the fleet; more parades and more martial music; children in every clime standing along the Royal route waving British flags; gala banquets, toasts and addresses of welcome all spoken in ringing words of praise for the British Empire. Then, within a year, came the pomp and pageantry of the coronation services for Edward VII, bringing statesmen from the Empire once more to England.

There was, however, a dark and seamy side to these triumphant years. While the Empire glittered in the eyes of the world and the upper and middle classes of England enjoyed their gay, carefree and supremely confident lives, thousands of men, women and children in the British Isles existed under conditions of abject poverty. Unyielding selfish interests, especially in the House of Lords, had rejected Irish Home Rule. As one historian has written: 'It might have been better if the Salisburys, the Chamberlains, the Rudyard Kiplings, and all others who sang the praises of the Empire had paid less attention to carrying the White Man's Burden and more—much more— attention to the Irish peasants and to their own gin-sodden, dejected countrymen in the east-end slums of London.'

Perhaps the most important sign of discontent with these conditions appeared in the year 1900. Some of the British trade unions, no longer expecting favourable labour legislation from either Liberals or Unionists, and finding they gained but little from their strikes, decided to join the Fabian Society. This Society was dedicated to socialism, to the theory that the government, rather than individuals, should own and control the economic resources of the nation. When the trade unions joined with the Fabians and planned to run their own candidates for parliament, the foundations were laid for the British Labour party, whose great influence in recent English history will become more apparent later in this text.

Chamberlain and his friends also had a remedy for the poverty and distress in England. To a country which had had free trade for over fifty years, they proposed to place duties on imports once again. Also, by granting slightly lower rates to colonial imports, trade within the Empire would be increased—Canada might indeed become the granary for England—and the colonies would be held more firmly to the mother country.

In the general election of 1906 the Unionist government was resoundingly defeated. The new Liberal government had no great love for Chamberlain's grand schemes to strengthen the ties between England and her colonies. Great Britain, they believed, should not share all her diplomatic secrets; she should be free to make her own decisions, unfettered by colonial advice. However, in return for this freedom and in keeping with the traditions of their party, the Liberals were more willing to see the colonies in control of their own foreign affairs. It was in this spirit that James Bryce was sent to Washington in 1907 with instructions to consult Canadian officials at all times in his efforts to wipe the slate clean along the unguarded border. Also in 1907 and in the same liberal spirit, the Fifth Colonial Conference was summoned to meet in London.

Sir Wilfrid Laurier came to this Conference confident that Canada, now entering the heyday of her prosperity and fairly bursting with national pride, was almost solidly behind him. The Alaskan boundary award had confirmed his judgement that our line-fence disputes with the United States should not be handled by British diplomats and he was more determined than before to defend the

Part of Queen Victoria's Diamond Jubilee procession. Sir Wilfrid Laurier is in the carriage.

principles of colonial freedom in external affairs. This time he found the task much easier. Imperial sentiment, though strong, was no longer at fever pitch.

Very much in line with the reasoning of Canada's Prime Minister, the Conference passed the following resolution: 'It will be to the advantage of the Empire if a Conference to be called the Imperial Conference is held every four years, at which questions of common interest may be discussed between His Majesty's Government and his Governments of the self-governing Dominions beyond the seas.' As time was to prove, this one simple sentence defined the

H.M.S. Dreadnought, *1907*

future course of the British Empire. There would be a group of self-governing dominions—not colonies—free to follow their own policies, meeting informally and without power, as equals of the mother country. With the unanimous acceptance of this resolution by the Imperial Conference of 1907, the British Commonwealth of Nations began to assume more definite form.

The Naval Question
The Imperial Conference of 1907 also seemed to settle, quietly and for all time, the question of colonial support for the British navy. Laurier refused to agree with any plan for colonial contributions to a common Empire fleet. This time, the delegates from Australia agreed with him. Faced with this opposition, the Conference made no recommendations and it was assumed that the colonies could decide for themselves whether to support the British fleet, build one of their own, or do nothing at all about naval defence.

Then on March 16, 1909, Reginald McKenna, First Lord of the Admiralty, made a speech in the British House of Commons introducing a bill to construct four more Dreadnoughts—a new and costly type of super-battleship. He emphasized the need for this expenditure in as strong terms as possible, hinting that Germany had been hiding the full extent of her naval construction program and that, in reality, she had almost caught up to Great Britain.

Reporters scurried from the Press Gallery, the news spread like wildfire. Britannia no longer ruled the waves! The great 'German naval scare' was on.

In January 1910 Laurier introduced a Naval Service Bill whereby $11 million would be spent on five cruisers and six destroyers to be owned and controlled by Canada. The Bill provided—and this is the punch line—that in case of emergency the Canadian government 'may place the fleet at the disposal of His Majesty for general service in the Royal Navy'.

While Liberals and Conservatives generally supported their respective leaders in the following long and at times very heated debate in parliament, the Naval Service Bill was not fought entirely on party or racial lines. Although the majority of French-speaking members agreed with Laurier and paid glowing tribute to Great Britain, the extreme Nationalists from Quebec attacked the very thought of a Canadian navy, let alone the idea that it should ever be lent to Britain. These extremists were a mixture of Liberals and Conservatives sparked by the fiery Frederick Monk, the French-Canadian lieutenant of the Conservative party in Quebec. In turn, this narrow-minded provincialism was scorned by certain equally violent English-speaking members who criticized all French Canadians in the strongest language. Lasting over three months, this confused debate revealed how difficult it was to find a true unifying national spirit between the extremes of British and French racial pride.

After the Naval Service Bill became law the majority of people in this country seemed to accept the idea of a separate Canadian navy. During the next general election in 1911, as we have already observed, the main issue throughout most of Canada was reciprocity with the United States.

Not so, however, in the province of Quebec where a violent campaign was waged against the Liberal leader and his Naval Service Act. Inflamed by Henri Bourassa, Frederick Monk, and dozens of priests anxious to retain control over their parishioners, the Nationalist movement spread hatred for England and the Empire along the side roads of rural Quebec. From January 1910 until election day over a year and a half later, Laurier, pictured in Ontario as a Roman Catholic French Canadian with, at best, a lukewarm feeling towards England, was denounced in Quebec as an arch-imperialist who had betrayed his country-men to Great Britain. As for the Naval Bill, in the wild language of Henri Bourassa, it would hasten the day when 'draft officers will be scouring the country and compelling young men to enlist, to co-operate with England in the oppression of weak countries and to maintain at the price of their blood the supremacy of the British flag in Asia or Africa'. Reasonable French Canadians tried to point out that the people, through parliament, would control the navy and that service in it was to be completely voluntary. Reason could not prevail against passionate politicians who proclaimed that 'those who disembowelled your fathers on the Plains of Abraham are asking you today to go and get killed for them'. When it was all over, the Nationalists, by breaking the power of the Liberal party in Quebec, had helped to defeat the Laurier government. More important, there remained among the people a legacy of racial hatred too deep to be soon forgotten.

During the summer of 1912, Robert Borden, now Conservative Prime Minister of Canada, paid his first official visit to Great Britain. There, close to the furious armament race and to a continent where the Balkan wars were brewing, the Prime Minister was made to feel the danger of a general European conflict. Private conversations with the new First Lord of the Admiralty, Winston

*Sir Robert Laird Borden,
1911–20*

Churchill, and seeing a review of the magnificent Royal Navy, all confirmed Borden's decision that Canada should give immediate aid to Great Britain.

After his return to Ottawa, therefore, Borden introduced in the next session of parliament a Naval Bill requesting $35 million to buy three Dreadnoughts for the British fleet. After three months of wrangling, the government gagged the opposition by applying the closure rule, and Borden's Naval Bill was forced through an angry House of Commons. Then the Liberal majority in the Senate refused to give assent and thereby settled the navy question once and for all. The Naval Service Act of 1910 remained the law of the land, and the way was clear for a future Royal Canadian Navy, built and manned by Canadians and under control of the Dominion of Canada.

The Ultimate Loyalty

By 1914 Canadians found themselves in a difficult and somewhat confused frame of mind. A great many, thinking of the unbounded prosperity of their country, now spoke in proud terms of a new-found spirit of unity; Canada, they said, had become a nation. Some, however, could not help wondering whether the people were too much concerned with economic progress and material wealth. In wartime, would they be truly loyal and unselfish or would some of them take advantage of their country's distress and exploit it to their own benefit? Some also wondered about the intolerance and lack of understanding between some of the French- and English-speaking Canadians. The unhealthy, over-critical distrust for Great Britain on the one side and the passionate, imperialist zeal for the Empire on the other were equally injurious to Canadian unity and spelled trouble for the future. Then again, others questioned the feelings of their countrymen towards the United States. Although the old feuds had been cleared away, many Canadians had not yet developed a mature, genuinely friendly attitude towards their great neighbour. In other words, on the eve of the First World War, it was not at all certain that Canada had found a unifying national spirit despite her phenomenal progress in other ways.

Nor were Canadians sure of their exact standing in the British Empire. Legally,

the country was still bound to Great Britain; none of the old colonial laws had
been changed. Laurier, Borden and many others had insisted time and again that
when England was at war, no matter where in the world, Canada also was at war.
Yet Canada now had her own army and navy and it was understood that she could
decide for herself whether or not they would be used in Empire wars. In his own
mind almost everyone in Canada seemed to know what the decision would be
when the time came. Never before in history had the people as a whole been
more loyal to Britain. Their nationalist desire for freedom in defence and foreign
affairs had been more than balanced by a stirring series of imperial events
focusing attention on the power and glory of the Empire. Under these circumstances, some Canadians questioned the wisdom of taking so little interest in
world affairs when a major conflict would almost certainly involve their country.
The isolated, 'wait-and-see' attitude was another sign of immaturity and they
hoped to see the day when Canada would play an active and enlightened part in
international events.

As it turned out, Canada went to war in 1914 because of her loyalty to the
British Empire and her confidence in British statesmen. There was no other
reason. In August 1914, Canada did not hate Germany. Only after the War started
and the passions of mankind were stirred to the depths by the life-and-death
struggle in Europe, did many Canadians learn to hate the 'dirty Hun'.

The Weary Titan

Social Turmoil in Britain
It is necessary now to turn back very briefly to conditions in Great Britain during
the years immediately preceding the First World War.

By this time the British budget was strained to breaking point. In the general
election of 1906 over fifty members of the newly organized Labour party had
won seats in the House of Commons. Combining with Lloyd George's radical
wing of the Liberal government, they had forced through parliament many social
reforms, such as the Old Age Pensions Act, all costing the taxpayers more money.
Now, the added expense of the Anglo-German naval race, which Great Britain
could ill afford, made it necessary to find fresh sources of revenue. In 1909, therefore, Lloyd George introduced his famous budget placing heavy new taxes on the
wealthy classes of England. 'A fully-equipped duke,' he had once said, 'costs as
much to keep as two Dreadnoughts and is less necessary.' Fearing the social
results of the new taxes and perhaps worried about their own pocketbooks, the
House of Lords threw out Lloyd George's budget.

Thus the Lords precipitated a crisis such as England had not witnessed in over
seventy-five years. To prove them wrong, Asquith dissolved parliament early in
1910 and appealed to the people. The victorious Liberals returned to the House
of Commons and, amid wild scenes of disorder and anger, passed the Parliament
Bill designed to limit the power of the House of Lords forever. The usually

dignified but now thoroughly aroused Lords refused to sign their own death warrant and the Parliament Bill was defeated. Once again, with tempers flaring and opposing politicians not even on speaking terms, another general election was called—the second in less than a year. In between these two elections, adding to the uncertainty and perhaps indicating the end of a confident era, George V succeeded his father as King. After many more stormy sessions, the new House of Commons again passed the Parliament Bill and once more the Lords fought back. Finally, in the summer of 1911, the King threatened to break the deadlock by swamping the House of Lords with new peers who would support the Asquith government.

Although Labour members sat in parliament, social reform had been painfully slow; unemployment due to international trade rivalry was increasing, and the rising cost of living was making conditions worse than ever. Under these circumstances, the trade union leaders decided to spur the government to greater action by calling a series of massive strikes throughout the British Isles. By the summer of 1911, this social upheaval was coming to a head in long strikes and lockouts, angry public meetings, vicious rioting and desperate countermeasures by the police.

Bills to give the vote to women had been presented regularly to parliament for the past thirty years and, with equal persistence, had been pigeonholed and forgotten. Despairing of such peaceful methods, some of the 'Suffragettes' decided that they could win the right to vote only by attacking the government with any weapon they could lay their hands on and by using every means, foul or fair, to attract attention. Their first big march on parliament had been staged a few weeks before the second general election in 1910 and the police had been given orders by Churchill to keep the women away from an already distraught House of Commons. By the summer of 1911, the 'Militant Suffragettes', led in battle by 'that human flame', Mrs. Emmeline Pankhurst, and directed from the safety of Paris by one of her daughters, had taken the law fully into their own hands.

In the next two years—as the Witches' Cauldron brewed up the Balkan wars and Europe raced pell-mell on its headlong way towards destruction—the British Isles seethed with increasing discontent and social unrest. Industrial disputes became more frequent and more violent. In one month alone, 850,000 men—led by the miners demanding a minimum wage of $2.50 per day for men and $1.00 for boys—were out on strike, tying up essential services in many parts of the country. At the same time, the Militant Suffragette movement reached its most imaginative and ferocious heights. The women threw bricks at the Prime Minister's residence, smashed windows in every fashionable suburb of London, burned churches and government buildings, slashed priceless pictures in the

Mrs. Emmeline Pankhurst under arrest after taking part in another violent demonstration for women's rights. The citizen on the left obviously holds no brief for her claims to equality.

National Gallery, and chained themselves to the railings in Parliament Square
and screamed; one ran in front of the horses at the Derby; and when they went to
jail, they refused to eat although they knew this meant the degrading experience
of forced feeding through a tube.

The Curse of Cromwell

Heaping coals of fire on this troubled scene and reviving all the fierce, deep-
rooted hatreds of the past, the House of Commons now passed a third Home Rule
Bill for Ireland. The Lords rejected it, but by this time the Parliament Act was in
force and their power was no longer absolute; after three years, whether they
liked it or not, Home Rule would become law. The Unionists in opposition—
standing, as their name implied, for the historic Union of Ireland with England
—used the breathing spell provided by the Lords' veto to block the Home Rule
Bill.

In 1912 a feud verging on civil war broke out between the Catholic Irish of the
South, who demanded Home Rule for the whole island, and the Protestant Irish
of Ulster, who were determined to uphold the Union with England. Led by Sir
Edward Carson, the Ulstermen began to drill and arm, smuggled in rifles and
openly declared they would resist the decision of the House of Commons by
force. In this stand they were encouraged to the point of treason by Bonar Law,
the new Unionist party chief. On July 12—a date to stir the blood of all good
Orangemen—he advised Sir Edward Carson in Ulster: 'Whatever steps you may
feel compelled to take, whether they are legal or whether in the long run they
are illegal, you have the whole Unionist party, under my leadership, behind you.'

This situation became so serious and the challenge to law and order so flagrant
that His Majesty's Government early in 1914 dispatched the Third Battle
Squadron to the North of Ireland, threatening their own countrymen in Ulster.
For a few desperate days in March it seemed that the British army would be
used in co-operation with the fleet to subdue the Ulstermen. At the height of this
crisis, amid wild rumours that the King was about to abdicate, the War Office
received the following communiqué from Ireland: 'Officers of the 5th and 16th
Lancers are resigning their commissions today. Fear men will refuse to move.
Brigadier and all officers of Third Cavalry Brigade prefer to accept dismissal if
ordered north of Ulster.' In England, General French and several other high
officers resigned for fear of being sent to fight their friends and for the first time in
well over two hundred years the government of Great Britain could not rely on
the army to carry out its orders. Under these circumstances, Prime Minister
Asquith backed down and began a hopeless search for some other solution to the
melancholy problem of Ireland.

The Lamps Are Going Out

By June 1914 the weary Titan was indeed staggering under the too vast orb of its
own weight. A huge colonial Empire, turbulent and restless, demanded minute
and ever-increasing care and expense. The senior self-governing dominions had
insisted on their freedom and could no longer be relied upon in every emergency.

All efforts to bind the great Empire into one strong English-speaking alliance had failed. In Europe, the shadows of war grew longer with each passing week. And at home, the accumulated problems of many decades had erupted with a violence recently unknown to the serene and peaceful English countryside.

When Princip fired his fatal shots on June 28, Britain paused only briefly, expressed sympathy for the Hapsburg family in Austria, and returned to more pressing affairs at home. As von Berchtold was trying to persuade his Austrian colleagues to punish Serbia with force, British statesmen were meeting at the King's request in a Round Table Conference about Ireland. The Conference failed and the cabinet was considering the next move when the Foreign Secretary interrupted with a copy of the Austrian ultimatum. The First Lord of the Admiralty—the man who had recently dispatched the Third Battle Squadron to Ulster—Winston Churchill, wrote of that moment in these words: 'We were all very tired but gradually, as Sir Edward Grey read and the sentences followed one after another, impressions of a wholly different character began to form in my mind. The parishes of Tyrone and Fermanagh faded back in the mists and squalls of Ireland and a strange light began to fall and glow on the map of Europe.'

Although all thoughts now turned towards the Continent, public opinion in the British Isles remained sorely divided and the British cabinet hesitated, uncertain of its future course. Only when the German army invaded Belgium on August 4 did the contending factions in Great Britain come together.

On Monday, August 3, the day before the Germans crossed the Belgian frontier, Sir Edward Grey and a friend were standing by a window in the Foreign Office. It was getting dark and the lamps were being lit in the courtyard below. Looking down, the British Foreign Secretary quietly said: 'The lamps are going out all over Europe; we shall not see them lit again in our life-time.' The twelve-hour ultimatum had been sent to Germany and they were waiting in the cabinet room for a reply. Midnight in Berlin was eleven o'clock by English time; the last seconds of peace ticked away; the hour struck and Winston Churchill slipped quickly from the room. Moments later the message flashed from the Admiralty Office to the fleet and to British ships on the seas of the world that England was at war.

8   ON THE ALTAR OF MARS

Stalemate on the Western Front

August 1914. The Road to War had reached the point of no return. The jealous rivalries for power and prestige between the alliances, the incessant clash of colonial and trading ambitions, the frenzied outbursts of national pride, the threats and challenges of misguided statesmen, and the insidious influence of constant war-talk among peoples who wanted nothing more than to be left alone—all had produced their final, inevitable and tragic result.

No one foresaw the complete social upheaval the War was to produce. It let loose all the pent-up forces of discontent which finally destroyed the last remnants of the old nineteenth-century world. There were no decisive battles; the nations fought to a deadly stalemate on all fronts, even at sea. The spade, the machine gun and barbed wire transformed military science although it took many tragic months and hundreds of thousands of needless casualties to convince some of the leaders that it was so. To break this deadlock, the combatants soon mobilized, not only an ever-increasing fighting force but also their scientists, industrialists, financiers, their factory workers, their farmers, their women and their propagandists in a total national war effort. For the first time in European history, not just armies but whole nations were locked in a life-and-death struggle. When it was over, the easygoing, comparatively simple life of the past was smashed beyond repair. From the ruins arose a new, turbulent and complex world, a world of change and material progress unparalleled in history, but one which held, from the outset, the seeds of a disastrous depression and a second, perhaps a third, even more deadly war.

A Nightmare for the German Strategists
From the moment war was declared the military and naval advantage lay overwhelmingly on the side of the Allies; the Allied superiority in numbers is clearly indicated in the table below.

Military and Naval Strength in 1914

	Triple Entente	Central Powers
Standing army	2,238,000	1,285,000
Reserves	12,000,000	8,600,000
Battleships	80	52
Cruisers	114	59
Destroyers	310	157
Submarines	115	33

The oft-repeated theory that the German 'juggernaut' was the largest and most devastating force in Europe and that the Allies were fighting partly to rid the world of it was developed during the War; it is one of the many causes for the War manufactured after it started. There were no claims of vast German superiority before 1914, except by some of the fanatic German militarists themselves and a few Entente statesmen trying to frighten the people into supporting a heavier armament program. Each nation, according to its own spokesmen, was armed to the teeth and fully confident of its invincibility. In a pre-war atmosphere poisoned with fear and distrust, Germany was no more diligent—although much more efficient—in her preparations than were the other powers.

The Russian standing army was as large as those of Germany and Austria-Hungary put together. It could be hurled with all its massive weight along the Eastern Front, and it could be reinforced by literally millions of reserves. On the other hand, the forces of the Central Powers had to contend with Russia in the East, France in the West, and Serbia, with an army of half a million men, in the Balkans. In May 1914, a top-ranking French officer—one of their many extremists—described the European situation as follows: 'From whatever aspect Germany's position is studied it will be realized that her future is of the darkest; she is threatened by superior forces on all her frontiers. . . . When the time comes, and it may come soon, when Slavdom wishes to make an end of Germany, our friendship with Russia will serve us well. It will be impossible for Germany to defend the provinces she took from us.' Before the battlefields revealed the pitiful condition of the Tsar's ill-equipped hordes, Russian military leaders were certain that their 'steamroller' would easily crush Germany. The Tsar's Minister of War reflected this confidence in his report for June 1914: 'The reforms of the Russian Army, undertaken in 1906 after our war with Japan, surpass everything that has ever been known. Thanks to these reforms there is in Russia every winter an army of 2,300,000 men. . . . Considering the pace at which we have been building up our field armies, the possibility of a war on two fronts has become the nightmare of German strategists.'

A nightmare indeed, for on the Western Front France in 1914 could and eventually did mobilize a fighting force larger in size than the entire German army. Furthermore, military observers had long regarded the French army as one of the best trained on the Continent, at least equal in quality to that of her powerful adversary. Before the War, the spirit of militarism among the French people became so serious and so obvious that neutral diplomats stationed in Paris wrote to their home offices expressing grave concern. Typical of such comments is the following one written in January 1914 by the Belgian ambassador: 'I have already had the honour of informing you that it is Messrs. Poincaré, Delcassé, Millerand and their friends who have invented and pursued the nationalist, boastful and jingoistic policy whose revival we have witnessed. It is a danger for Europe—and for Belgium. I see in it the greatest peril which threatens the peace of Europe today. . . . French military men, instructed and competent, now say they are certain of victory.'

Earlier in the armament race, the French forces were not numerically as strong as the German. To make up the difference, British and French strategists, shortly after the first Morocco crisis, began to plan a British Expeditionary Force to supplement the French army on the Western Front. Throwing an interesting light on all those who have so foolishly denied the existence of any military understandings between the Entente partners, Lord Haldane, the British Minister of War, has explained: 'In 1906 we first made plans for organizing the Expeditionary Force. Careful calculations made by the French General Staff and our own showed that the addition of a comparatively small but very highly trained Expeditionary Army from Great Britain would offset the German advantage. To these estimates, we added about sixty per cent for greater security.'

Lord Haldane and his associates then proceeded to build the famous British Expeditionary Force, 160,000 strong, 'complete to the last button', the finest and much the largest force ever to be trained in Britain. These were the men, in William II's careless phrase, who formed 'England's contemptible little army'; these were the men whom the people of Great Britain, taking the Kaiser's words and flinging them back, proudly nicknamed 'The Old Contemptibles'.

On the high seas, Britannia and her allies ruled absolutely supreme. According to long-standing plans, as soon as war broke out, the French fleet took care of the Mediterranean, the Japanese policed the Pacific, and over all ruled the mighty Royal Navy, her Grand Fleet, under Admiral Jellicoe, dominating the North Sea and the English Channel, her swift destroyers free to roam the world almost at will. The German fleets were swept into port, the sea-lanes cleared of her commerce, her overseas possessions with one notable exception were conquered, and the coast of Europe was clamped in an impassable blockade—all within the first three months of the War. Never in all history had there been a demonstration of sea power on so gigantic a scale.

The German Plan

Despite the tremendous odds against them, the German High Command was fully confident that when 'der Tag' finally came the Central Powers would be victorious. They, too, had a plan of attack; on its immediate success or failure depended the life of the German and Austro-Hungarian empires. German strategy was based on the belief that two factors would delay the Russian advance on the Eastern Front. The very size of the Tsar's armies, the vastness of the country and the poor transportation facilities would prevent that mighty machine from moving in a hurry. Furthermore, the Eastern Front presented the Russians with a very serious problem. If they marched their troops straight through Russian Poland towards the German frontier, they would be walking into a huge trap; their left flank would be exposed to the Austrians, their right to the Germans in East Prussia. These two bulges or 'salients' would have to be hammered out and the line straightened before Russia could advance—and all this would take more time. Thus the Germans planned to leave the Eastern Front more or less to Austria and throw all their weight against France, knocking her out of the War quickly before Russia had time to start 'rolling'. Later, they would attend to the

Tsar's great armies.

In the West, Germany faced the strong fortifications which France had built along the entire frontier from Belfort to Verdun. Here the German strategists expected a very heavy French attack designed to reconquer Alsace and Lorraine as soon after the outbreak of hostilities as possible. According to a plan developed some years before the war by General Alfred von Schlieffen, the Germans had decided to take a dangerous chance on this part of the Western Front. By pretending to be beaten and by deliberately falling back before the enemy, they would draw the French armies deep into Germany, across mountainous and difficult terrain. Meanwhile the bulk of the German army would drive through Belgium into France. They hoped the Belgians would not resist but they were prepared to blast their way through if need be. Once in France, the German forces would fan out and sweep down in a great arc, to the west of Paris, and come in behind the French armies trapped across the mountains inside Germany. The key to the success of this plan lay in the German left falling back and their right flank being strong enough to drive unchecked through Belgium and France.

It is reported that General Schlieffen's last words before he died in 1913 were, 'If it must come to a fight, make the right wing strong.' Fortunately for France and perhaps for the whole Allied cause, the German High Command disregarded this vital warning. Schlieffen's successor, the nervous, mentally unbalanced General von Moltke, was afraid to take the risks involved in letting the French troops across the border into Lorraine. Under his influence, the German left-wing armies were greatly strengthened—so much so that when the critical time came the French were not only repulsed but the German commanders were encouraged to take the offensive too early. Thus the brilliant strategy designed to crush France in six weeks was doomed to failure before the War began.

The Failure of the Schlieffen Plan

During the invasion of Belgium, the Germans were ruthless in their treatment of the conquered civilians, but they did not crucify their victims, cut the hands off little children, tie priests head down as clappers in the church bells or commit the atrocities which hatred has attributed to them. Coming at the very beginning of the war, the battles in Belgium simply shocked the world more profoundly than many of the later, more dreadful campaigns. Aroused to the first inevitable horrors of modern warfare, imaginations ran riot at every piece of news from Belgium, and Allied propaganda played upon these natural fears, making the invasion a focal point for hatred for the enemy; consequently, the devastation of Belgium and the courageous resistance of that innocent country have remained among the most vivid memories of the First World War. The Germans pulverized the fortified cities of Liège and Namur and then fought a bloody path across southern Belgium to the French border. By mid-August three German armies, right on schedule, were pouring into France like a grey wave ready for the scythe-like sweep towards Paris.

Four hundred and fifty miles away to the southeast, the tradition-drugged High Command of France was doing exactly what General Schlieffen had predicted. Thinking in century-old Napoleonic terms, General Joffre had hurled his cavalry and his 'bayonets' across the border into Lorraine. Not even the fall of Liège awakened him to reality and French troops would have been drawn deeper into Lorraine had it not been for von Moltke's change in German strategy. As it was, an inferior German force finally drove the French back into the shelter of their frontier forts and from there they rallied in the nick of time to meet the main German attack outside the gates of Paris.

Meanwhile, one lone French army and the little British Expeditionary Force alongside it were left to face the Germans advancing from Belgium. The British Expeditionary Force had been dispatched across the Channel for patriotic and sentimental reasons; the best employment of the Force or its safety were second- ary considerations. The war faction in England compelled the British government to rush its army headlong into action. The Old Contemptibles had been trained for this very day; to hold them back, to land them later at the most advantageous spot, would be neither 'honourable' nor 'courageous'. Therefore, during the invasion of Belgium the British Expeditionary Force was hurried across the Channel, arriving at Mons just in time to face a head-on, sledgehammer blow from the vastly superior right wing of the German army.

Against such odds, there was no alternative; on August 23, the French and British armies were ordered to retreat. For the next twelve days, the dusty roads of northern France were clogged with men, gun-carriages, motorcycles, auto- mobiles, horses and ammunition wagons as 300,000 disorganized, dead-tired French and British soldiers fled south through the August heat. Just behind them, equally footsore and weary from their drive through Belgium, marching fourteen hours a day, travelling too fast for their food and ammunition supplies, came 600,000 Germans. Almost a million massed men pushed through countless civil- ians jumbled along the roadsides with their little carts and cattle and household possessions—the first of millions to be uprooted and made homeless by the War.

At this critical moment, the German general commanding the extreme right- wing army made a fatal mistake. Instead of continuing on a sweeping arc to the west of Paris, the Germans wheeled inwards before reaching the city. General Joffre and General Galliéni, the governor of Paris, have since claimed in a somewhat shabby display of personal ambition the credit for seeing the opportunity presented to the Allies by this German change of direction. The important fact is that the French High Command finally realized that if the retreating armies, now being reinforced from the frontier forts, made a stand along the river Marne they could compel the Germans to fight on two sides— along the river itself and in their right flank against troops moving out from Paris. Even before the Germans thus exposed themselves to a counterattack, their High Command, cracking under the shaky hand of von Moltke, had made an even more serious blunder. Intoxicated still further by the heady news of victories in France and afraid of the Russian armies now rolling into East Prussia, von Moltke on August 25 had removed six army corps from the very right wing which his predecessor had warned to keep strong. So it was that, on the sixth day of September, thirteen exhausted German divisions met twice that number of Allied

divisions along the banks of the Marne. If in the long years of the First World
War there was any one decisive turning point it was here, almost at the beginning,
in the First Battle of the Marne. In five days of fierce fighting, the German
advance collapsed, the Schlieffen plan failed, and all hope for a quick victory in
France was lost.

The Race to the Sea

The Allies now pursued the retreating Germans, at a faltering and hesitant pace,
due northward along a wide front. Despite optimistic statements from both
British and French headquarters, the Germans managed to dig themselves in
along the banks of the Aisne River. The power of the machine gun and of a set
defence, however hastily thrown together, was revealed as repeated Allied
attacks failed to budge the Germans. By the end of September, the deadlock
which already existed in front of the frontier forts had spread along the entire
length of the Aisne River. As may be seen from the map, defence had now

triumphed on a long, immovable line reaching from Belfort in the south up through Verdun and from there along the Aisne to its junction with the Oise River, fifty miles to the northeast of Paris.

Both the Allies and the Germans suddenly realized that a large, unprotected area lay between the end of the Aisne Line and the English Channel, and drove their armies northwards into this gap—the Allies trying to outflank and move in behind the Germans and the Germans striving desperately to reach the ports of Dunkirk, Calais and Boulogne. The Germans moved, the Allies covered; the Allies moved and the Germans covered; and so, in October, occurred a series of side-stepping manoeuvres known as 'the race to the sea'. As they struggled forward, other men were left behind digging deep, animal-like burrows into the hard-baked clay, uncoiling the ominous strands of barbed wire, hiding machine guns in the ditches and behind the still green, uncharred hedges, setting up a further extension of the impassable trench lines. On the sand dunes of Nieuport, overlooking the beaches where carefree Belgian bathers had once laughed and played, the grim race to the sea ended. Through a growing forest of iron posts and tangled wire Englishman and German, sixty yards apart, faced each other across a strange, sandy no man's land.

On October 29, the German army, inspired by a personal command from the Kaiser, made one last, superhuman effort to crack the Allied defence and reach the Channel ports. Their most direct route lay straight through from the ancient city of Ypres on the trench line to Calais on the coast. Here, in a little corner of Belgium known as Flanders, in the First Battle of Ypres, occurred the most vicious destruction of life and property the world had ever known. From behind the rain-drenched, sodden trenches, German howitzers and mortars lobbed high explosives and shrapnel shells into the Allied positions until the front lines were churned to mud and the little villages blown to pieces. When they thought no human life survived in the sea of devastation, the Germans came 'over the top', out of the trenches in parade-ground order, singing or screaming as they had been taught to hide their own deep dread, mausers spitting fire as they came and machine guns raking the ground before them. But all life had not been wiped out by the shelling, and grim defenders, firing fifteen rounds to the minute, using their own few machine guns at such point-blank range that they could not miss, mowed the Germans down like grass. As the advancing line was riddled and riddled again, others moved in to fill the gaps until the grey mass of men was surging forward through mud cobbled with the bodies of their fallen comrades. And when the Germans reached the opposing side, the defenders went into them with the bayonet until the dead were piled like sandbags and the trenches flowed with blood.

For two solid weeks, increasing in ferocity with each passing day, thousands upon thousands of soldiers were hurled into this raging inferno. At night, with no time for rest, hungry, haggard men dug in for the fresh onslaught they knew was coming with the dawn, and at night, under cover of darkness, ambulance carts and mangled soldiers staggering out met reinforcements moving in. Finally, reaching beyond the point of human endurance when the dead seemed to out-

In a front-line trench. Pressed against the clammy clay walls, peering through a slit across the desolate wastes of no man's land, a British Tommy keeps guard while his exhausted companions try to sleep.

number the living, the attack weakened and gradually began to subside. On November 18, as the freezing rain turned to the first snow of the year and nature tried to hide the sickening scene under a mantle of white, the fighting came to an end. A thin line of defenders had held their ground against overwhelming odds and the Channel ports were saved. The First Battle of 'Wipers' is a monument over the graves of the Old Contemptibles.

Life in the Trenches
After Ypres, the two great enemy armies were completely deadlocked along a six-hundred-mile front of twisted barbed wire and water-logged trenches that traced their impregnable path across a drab and desolate countryside all the way from Belfort to the English Channel. During the winter of 1914–15, 3 million soldiers guarded this Western Front, leading a queer existence of unbelievable

misery and danger. Like some new subterranean species of nocturnal animal, coming out only at night to move furtively around, they ate and slept below the ground, seldom seeing the sun except when it slanted for a few moments into their dark and narrow burrows. In the front-line trenches men stood against the clammy clay walls peering out through the steel-protected slits in the sandbags, motionless and wet in the bitter cold, staring across the strewn, decaying wastes of no man's land. No sign of human life appeared in that whole unearthly scene and yet other men were peering back, their presence revealed only by the sodden line of sandbags blending into the mud two hundred yards away behind the rusting coils of barbed wire.

When their daily turn in the firing line was ended, the numbed men sloshed back through the half-frozen mud and water of the connecting trenches to their dreary dugouts or to the dripping cellar of a shattered building which someone had once called home. Living on a monotonous fare of bully beef, hard biscuit and plum-and-apple jam, only occasionally daring to light a smudgy fire, perpetually wet and cold, curling up to sleep like the rats which infested every corner, the front-line soldiers somehow managed to carry on. At regular intervals, fresh troops moved up through the pallid, eerie light of the flares and star-shells that rose and fell with restless persistency along the battlefront. Then the mud-caked men who had been holding the line went back into billets—to some still-intact inn or farmhouse a few miles away, always within hearing of the distant rumbling—where they rested for a few precious days before going in again to relieve their comrades.

Attack Regardless of Loss

Poison Gas

How was this gigantic stalemate on the Western Front to be broken? What new weapons or methods of attack might be introduced? Could the trench lines be carried by any assault or were they really impregnable and, if so, should not other fronts be opened up? The grand schemes for quick victory by massed infantry and cavalry attack had failed; what now should be done?

The German answer came on April 22 at the Second Battle of Ypres. The Allies should have been ready for it. Captured German soldiers had warned them what was coming and one prisoner even had a primitive form of gas mask to back up his statements. But the French High Command took no action—despite the fact that the Germans had to wait for a favourable wind—and the commander on the spot was reprimanded for the precautions he attempted. Thus the first gas attack in history caught the Allies completely unprepared. At five-thirty in the afternoon of a beautiful spring day, the cylinders placed along the German lines at thirty-yard intervals began to release their greenish-yellow clouds into the east wind. The deadly, seven-foot bank of chlorine gas drifted across to a section of the Allied lines occupied mainly by Zouaves, coloured troops drafted by France from her

British troops resting in their dugouts a few hundred yards behind the front line. Such scenes were duplicated in the German trenches not far away.

empire in Africa. Unaccustomed to this raw form of western civilization, these unfortunate men, except those who were already suffocated, bolted in utter confusion leaving a four-mile gap wide open to the sea.

According to Sir John French, the British Commander in Chief, this immediate and very serious crisis was saved by the Canadians who had moved into line beside the Zouaves just a few days previously. When the French colonials fled, the Canadian troops spread out to cover the gap. Here, through two days of terrible fighting, withered with shrapnel and machine-gun fire, gassed twice, violently sick and gasping for air through mud-soaked handkerchiefs, they held on until reinforcements arrived. In these forty-eight hours one man in every three was lost from Canada's little force of hastily trained civilians—a grim forerunner of the future.

The staggering losses of the main British army during the Second Battle of Ypres were not due, however, to the gas attack. They were the tragic result of what the war correspondents and some of the High Command praised as the 'Wellington tradition'—a glorious but senseless tradition that 'a gun once lost must be retaken.' Thus inspired, the British soldiers counterattacked to regain useless ground until the commander of the Second British Army protested against the waste. Sir John French, who had always disliked this particular general and who had his own haughty ideas of army discipline, at once sent him home to England.

Fortunately for the Allied cause, the Germans themselves did not expect their attack to be successful. In the cautious manner of the military mind when faced with new ideas, their High Command had decided to try gas as a limited experiment, just to see what might happen, and no follow-up plans had been prepared. Furthermore, the situation on the Eastern Front had become so desperate and so many troops had been withdrawn from France that an all-out sustained offensive at Ypres was impossible. For these reasons the Germans were unable to take full advantage of the initial breakthrough and their attack finally collapsed early in May.

This new weapon would never again be so effective; the Germans had shown their hand too soon and the element of surprise was gone. Gas had failed to solve the deadlock on the Western Front. By using it first, the Germans had only incurred the deeper hatred of the Allies and morally freed them to retaliate without restraint. In this connection it should be noted that Germany was not violating any international law, as so many writers would have us believe. Cruel though the effects of chlorine and other gases were, no rules of war prevented its use. Warfare and human decency seldom go together. Gas was perhaps no more repulsive than burning men alive with flame-throwers as the Germans began to do in 1915.

The Eastern Front

The Germans made no more attacks on the Western Front in 1915. Even before the Second Battle of Ypres they had found it necessary to direct their attention and strength to the Eastern Front. At the beginning of the War, Russia moved faster than anyone expected. We have already seen how von Moltke was forced to draw off troops just before the Battle of the Marne to meet the advancing Russians. Because of the sad condition of the Russian armies and the utter bungling of their field commanders in comparison with the sound strategy of the German generals von Hindenburg and Ludendorff, the Russians were driven from East Prussia with tremendous loss in casualties, prisoners and equipment.

Against Austria-Hungary, however, the Russians had much more success. The Austro-Hungarian army was a hodge-podge of Germans, Magyars and unenthusiastic Slavs—an army which before the end of the War had over a million desertions. By March 1915, it had been driven back to the Carpathian Mountains and the Tsar's hordes were threatening to pour through the passes into the plains of Hungary. It was this situation which forced General Falkenhayn, von Moltke's more skilful successor, to leave holding forces in France and come to the rescue of his ally. Opposed to the combined strength of the Central Powers, Russia for all her huge reserves was no match. The Tsar's government was riddled with almost unbelievable inefficiency, cruelty and corruption; men required for the production of munitions and food were needlessly drafted into the army and the country was desperately short of all war materials. As a result, the uneducated peasant-soldiers in the front lines stood unarmed by the tens of thousands,

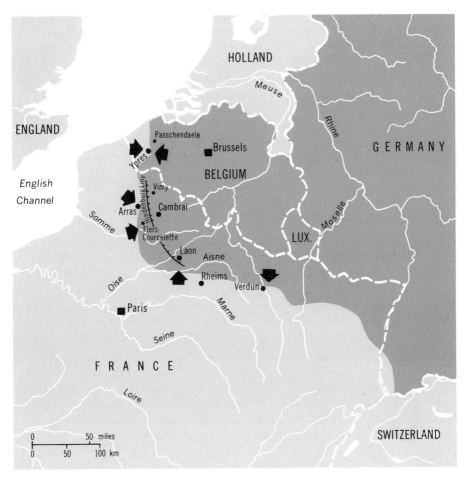

The years of stalemate on the Western Front   *Extent of German advance*

waiting for a comrade to fall so they could take his gun and ammunition belt.

Under these circumstances, the Russians were driven out of Austria-Hungary, fleeing weaponless before the enemy in utter confusion. During the spring and summer they were pushed back some four hundred miles into their own country, losing three-quarters of a million prisoners and countless casualties—manpower being so cheap that the Russian authorities did not even bother to keep records of their dead. Despite their disorganized condition, the Russians managed to dig in and finally hold off the German advance; once again defence, however weak, had triumphed over attack. By October 1915 another great trench line, somewhat similar to the one in France, reached from the Baltic to the Black Sea and the deadlock was extended to the Eastern Front.

During 1914 and most of 1915 the Serbian Front, on which the first shots of the War had been fired, remained more or less inactive. As long as Russia kept

Austria-Hungary busy, Serbia was safe. Why the Allies did not pour aid into the rugged, easily defended mountains of Serbia before it was too late, will be considered shortly; as it was, the Serbians were left to their fate. In October, having driven off the Russians and created a stalemate in the East, the Germans and Austrians, aided by the Bulgarians who joined the Central Powers about this time, knocked Serbia out of the War. By the end of the year 1915, as a result of their campaigns against Russia, the entry of Bulgaria and the defeat of Serbia, the Germans controlled a vast central belt of Europe extending from the Baltic and the North Sea down to the Balkan peninsula, the Dardanelles and thence through Turkey, all the way to the Indian Ocean.

An Ugly New Phrase

Meanwhile, back in France, in the quiet countryside well removed and isolated from the trench lines, the British and the French High Commands made their plans to break the stalemate. Professional soldiers, trained from youth to unquestioned obedience, they remained faithful to the old army traditions—and the age-old methods. If the artillery barrage, the massed infantry attack and the brilliant cavalry charge had won the battles in bygone days they would do so now. Close man-to-man combat, 'charge the enemy with the bayonet and destroy him' as the textbooks said, superior forces massed at the point of attack: such was war. In this way, they decided to crush the tangled mass of barbed wire, the ever-deepening trenches, the machine-gun nests and the dense lines of heavy artillery that faced them in France. A new problem of unprecedented siege warfare was to be solved, they tragically concluded, by applying the old methods. More men in the front lines, more reserves, more civilian and then more conscript armies, more cavalry, but above all more guns and shells—especially high-explosive shells to blow the enemy 'out of their deep holes like rats'—more guns and shells until during six days of 1917, in a rising crescendo of violence, three thousand guns stationed less than thirty feet apart could rain 4½ million shells, over fifty to each square yard of soil, into the opposing trench lines.

Using these brutal and massive tactics, the Allies hurled eleven full-scale offensives at the Western Front during the next three years. All of them were part of one basic strategic idea, to break through and win the war quickly, and for this reason the Allied efforts in France from 1915 to the end of 1917 should be considered almost as a continuous campaign. When one great attack failed another would be designed and undertaken, always in the belief that it would be the last one, until the whole line from south of Verdun to Ypres had been pounded to pieces, fought over and raked with fire not once but several times. Commanders changed—Sir Douglas Haig took over from Sir John French and General Nivelle replaced Joffre—but still the Headquarters of both armies remained obsessed with the idea of all-out attack.

The main battles of 1914 had already shown that in this kind of static siege warfare the great advantage lay with the defence. During the next three years, the casualty lists rising steadily into millions only served to prove again and again that the War could not be won by attacking the Western Front. Despite the almost unbelievable shelling that disembowelled the opposing trenches and the torrent of shrapnel and machine-gun fire that searched out every square foot of the ruins for days before each one of these gigantic campaigns, some defenders always managed to survive. Perhaps it was only a few men huddled together in their trenches or an isolated machine gun manned mechanically by two dazed soldiers. Sometimes a field battery, farther back and still intact, directed its skilful fire into the narrow strip of ground between the two lines: if they blew the remnants in their own front trenches to pieces it did not matter, for the enemy were also killed. At times, it is true, breakthroughs did occur in small dead sectors of the line but they were quickly sealed. More often, at zero hour when the Allied troops came over the top through the fog of fire and gas and smoke hanging over the battlefield, they were cut down in the first advance, falling in tragic, serried ranks.

The fate of each Allied campaign was nearly always decided in the first three or four days. When the expected breakthrough did not come and when the field commanders found that against little pockets of resistance the men could not advance at a uniform pace, the attack deteriorated into a series of costly local battles. These dragged on for weeks and months as the High Command kept hoping that perhaps the next day the German defence would finally crack wide open. It never did, and each successive offensive drive gradually slowed down and ground to a halt, leaving the great trench lines dinted here and there but still basically unchanged. Although Allied Headquarters tried to cover up by magnifying the enemy losses and inaccurately reporting their own, the fact remained that the Germans, always outnumbered in every one of these attacks, inflicted far greater losses on the Allies than they themselves suffered. For three years more, therefore, defence triumphed over attack and the stalemate on the Western Front continued.

Early in 1915, before the Germans released their gas attacks at Ypres, the Allies undertook three winter campaigns—one designed by Sir John French and two by General Joffre—all of which were miserable failures. Joffre began to excuse the staggering French casualties by saying that he was 'nibbling at the enemy', he was wearing the Germans down. 'C'est la guerre d'usure', he assured the war correspondents with his usual bland complacency. Gradually, as four more Allied offensives collapsed before the end of the year, a mean, ugly new phrase crept into the vocabulary of the western world. This had become a 'war of attrition'—a grinding struggle to see which side could hold out longer against death and destruction; the word 'attrition' used to justify the needless waste of life in dismal campaigns which had been planned in the first place to win a sweeping and conclusive victory; a wasteful war of attack waged by the Allies, with time and the resources of the world on their side, against a tightly blockaded foe. Because the Allies finally won, there are some who would have us believe that attrition, meaning death on a vast scale, was the only way. If so, victory came in 1918 not because of brilliant leadership, not because of some superiority in human nature or the justice of the cause, but simply because the Allies had more material and especially more human beings to throw into the raging inferno.

Side Shows

The details of the war of attrition on the Western Front in 1915 may be left to the imagination. Seven Allied campaigns raised the total casualties, dead or wounded, from 800,000 to over 2,500,000 by the end of the year. 'Attack regardless of loss'—and loss was the only result. As soon as the race for the sea ended and the trench lines were formed, many Englishmen began to urge the opening of some other front. Led by Winston Churchill and Lloyd George, they advocated an offensive in the eastern Mediterranean either against the Turks at the Dardanelles or against Austria-Hungary through Greece and Serbia. When he heard of these plans, Sir John French hurried back to England threatening to resign if any men or materials were diverted away from the Western Front for these 'side shows' elsewhere. He was supported in this stand by powerful Conservatives within the Unionist party who seemed to hold the view that the professional soldier was always right. Thus at the very beginning of the year 1915 there developed in England a bitter feud between the 'Easterners' and the 'Westerners' as to where and how the War was to be fought.

It is sad to relate that, although the War brought the British people together in a common effort, it did not unite the top political and military leaders. All the old animosities were carried over into the war years and seriously influenced military decisions—and men's lives. Around the British cabinet and the headquarters of the army and navy swirled a continuous, injurious storm of intrigue and jealousies which unfortunately lasted throughout most of the War. During 1915, for instance, Lord Fisher ignobly resigned as Admiral of the Grand Fleet, in protest against the Dardanelles campaign. And then a group of his Conservative admirers, backed up by influential party newspapers, manoeuvred Churchill out of his position of First Lord of the Admiralty. Political rivalries in England combined with the Allied emphasis on the Western Front doomed to failure the Mediterranean campaigns proposed by the Easterners.

Military authorities seem to agree that a joint naval and military expedition to the Dardanelles in 1915 would have succeeded. As it was, a poorly planned and timidly directed naval campaign in February and a lukewarm attempt by the army in April failed to budge an inferior force of half-starved Turks from the Dardanelles and Gallipoli. Landings were also made at Salonika to bolster Serbia but these were also too little and too late. A fraction of the men and material so futilely wasted on the Western Front might have made the difference. Instead, Turkey retained control of the Dardanelles, providing a vital link between Europe and Asia Minor; Bulgaria was encouraged to join the Central Powers; Serbia was overrun; and for the duration of the War the Allies were unable to ship supplies so badly needed by Russia through the warm-water Straits.

Another result, which plays a very important part in history later on, should be briefly noted here. During the next three years of the War, the British tried to defeat Turkey by sending one army up the Tigris-Euphrates river valley (the Mesopotamia campaign) and another along the Mediterranean coast from Egypt and Suez (the Palestine campaign). In order to encourage revolts among the native people in this whole area, the British made secret, conflicting bargains with both the Arab and Jewish subjects of the Sultan. We shall see that these wartime promises helped to cause many of the difficulties that have plagued the Arab, the Jew and the western world from that day to this—promises that might have been avoided if the Dardanelles expedition had succeeded in the first place.

The War of Attrition

Verdun, 1916
For many days the enemy guns facing the fortified hills surrounding Verdun had been strangely inactive, and French .75's firing their 'morning and evening hates' could provoke no reply. At four-thirty on the morning of February 21, 1916, a German howitzer hidden somewhere in the deep woods along the right bank of the Meuse River threw one fifteen-inch shell into the city of Verdun and then the whole sector became ominously silent again. Three hours later, just at daybreak, fourteen hundred heavy guns released a hurricane bombardment—two million shells in less than nine hours—to announce the war of attrition for 1916 and to commence one of the most brutally famous battles in all military history. Towards nightfall, small groups of German infantry began to advance, feeling their way, testing the effects of their artillery, falling back where necessary and moving forward where no life survived. Occupation of Verdun, however, was not the main German purpose at first. By attacking a point which French pride could not allow to fall and which they would defend to the last man, and by limited advances always threatening to become a full-scale offensive, Falkenhayn hoped to suck French reserves into the narrow, dangerous salient of Verdun and 'bleed France to death' with his merciless artillery fire.

After this opening attack, General Pétain, one of the true soldiers of France, was summoned to headquarters and given his orders in two words: 'Save Verdun.' While thousands of troops and civilians worked night and day to keep open the one road leading to Verdun and motor lorries loaded with supplies climbed in and out of the citadel at fourteen-second intervals, French soldiers from every other section of the Western Front marched eastward, at Pétain's command, in never-ending lines. Soon the Germans lost all sight of their original plan. Just as holding Verdun was a symbol of life for France, so its fall became a moral necessity for Falkenhayn and the prestige of the German army. For the next five months, therefore, massed infantry attacks by both sides ranged back and forth across the hills in a bewildered nightmare of torn trees, shattered villages and tortured ground, amidst a rain of shells and bullets. By the time Falkenhayn finally gave the order to stand solely on the defensive, 800,000 men, over fifty per cent of them French, had given up their lives to the war of attrition.

The Somme, 1916
In May and June, while the Battle of Verdun raged on, Germans entrenched along the ridge of heavily-armed chalk hills overlooking the Allied lines, observed

at their leisure the preparations being made for the Somme attack. Rigid, unimaginative preparations, suggested first by Joffre but, because of Verdun, handed to a British High Command that did not understand, and had never seriously studied, the problems of siege warfare. Nothing new had been added; only more guns—even more than the Germans used at Verdun—and more men directed in the same old way against a great, commanding natural fortress. Yet utmost confidence prevailed in Sir Douglas Haig's Headquarters; the Commander in Chief himself believed that 'every step was taken with Divine help.' A seven-day artillery barrage—not a sudden whirlwind of fire but a long, ponderous bombardment throwing away any remaining secrecy or surprise—would cut the enemy barbed wire to ribbons and clean out his first and second lines. Cavalry were held ready to ride through into open country and the new 'cavalry of the clouds', appearing in force for the first time, would sweep the German Fokkers from the sky. The civilian-soldiers of Britain—the once despised 'army of clerks and shopkeepers'—waiting for their first real baptism of fire were assured that they would be able 'to march across no man's land with rifles at the slope'.

On July 1, in broad daylight, two precious hours after sunrise, the French and British officers blew their whistles and the crowded trenches began to spill out into no man's land. Although repeated raids had already proved the enemy resistance to be still strong and active, the men were ordered to advance shoulder to shoulder in line, one line behind another, along the entire twenty-five-mile front on either side of the Somme River. A race with death—yet each soldier staggered across the shell-pocked ground laden down with 220 rounds of ammunition, 2 bombs, 2 sandbags and a week's rations, while some were further burdened with picks, shovels and boxes containing homing pigeons and telephone equipment. That morning 60,000 soldiers were wounded, captured or killed, many falling in straight rows—the heaviest day's loss ever suffered by a British army. A campaign definitely planned for a big break through the trench lines was now defended, once again, by the British High Command on the grounds that it took a terrible toll of the enemy—attrition, when the German losses, counting the seven-day preliminary bombardment, were less than 25,000!

After this opening attack, the Somme campaign, like all the others, broke up into many local battles which clawed insignificant, piecemeal chunks out of the German lines until the whole front bogged down in the November mud. Thus Delville—a mere pinpoint on the map—devoured 80,000 men in three weeks and is a shrine to the South Africans who suffered so severely there. Similarly, Flers-Courcelette and Ancre Heights became place names sadly familiar to thousands of Canadian homes. At Flers-Courcelette in September, the Canadian troops first participated on the Somme front, their entry coinciding with the first experimental use of tanks in modern warfare. From then until November, when the fighting finally ceased at Ancre Heights, the Canadians were heavily engaged in the Somme battles, raising their casualties, dead or wounded, to 68,000 after two years in France. These losses, combined with even greater ones during the spring of 1917, provoked a very bitter argument in Canada about the question of

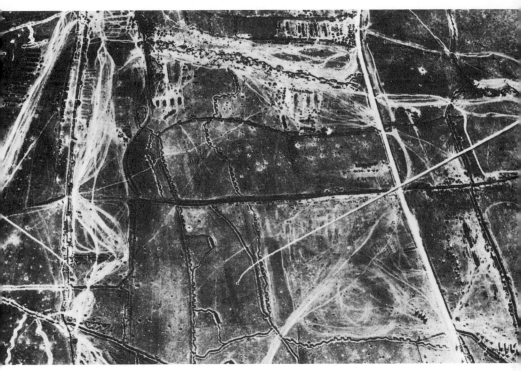

Trenches at Vimy Ridge, 1917, photographed from an observation balloon

compulsory military service to replace the men who had fallen overseas.

By the time the weary survivors settled down in the dirty trenches for their third miserable winter on the Western Front, the Somme had claimed 620,000 Allied soldiers. The German casualties might not have been as high as they were but for the fact that Falkenhayn, before his dismissal at the end of August, issued a soldierly command that 'every inch of lost ground must be regained.' The resulting counterattacks helped the Allied cause and raised German losses to over 400,000—on top of Verdun. Thus the one terrible year, 1916—Verdun and the Somme—had exacted a toll of almost 2 million men. Yet the war of attrition and stalemate had another full year to run!

The Aisne and Arras, 1917

During the last week of February, 1917, General Ludendorff, the new German Chief of Staff, quietly withdrew his armies twenty-five miles back from a large section of the Western Front. The retirement was a master-stroke. It exchanged a long, bulging, war-torn line for a well-situated, much shorter one, which, bristling with every modern defensive device, could be more easily held by the dwindling German armies. In March, the Allies cautiously felt their way forward through a wilderness of mined roads, blown-up villages, polluted wells and scorched farm land until they faced the Germans again along their strong new 'Hindenburg Line'.

Although this German withdrawal altered the whole central part of the trench lines, as even a glance at the map shows, the Allies continued their preparations for a spring offensive without any change whatsoever in their plan of attack. By this time, General Joffre had been replaced—just as he was coming to the conclusion, finally, that direct attacks on the Western Front were too costly—by the popular, 'dashing', French General Nivelle. Despite the fact that his armies were staggering and discouraged after Verdun and the Somme and needed nothing so much as a rest, Nivelle was determined to launch a great offensive drive along the Aisne River. Repeated warnings from the French government and growing misgivings everywhere did not deter him. With 1,200,000 soldiers, however war-weary, and 7,000 guns concentrated on a forty-mile front, he was certain of a breakthrough. This was his chance to win the War in one big battle. 'Laon in twenty-four hours and then pursuit to the Belgian border.'

In connection with this French plan, and purely as a short campaign to attract the Germans away from the Aisne, the British were to attack eastward from the city of Arras. This battle, which opened on April 9, one week before Nivelle's great effort, was the best stroke yet made by the British and clearly showed what careful planning and limited objectives could do. During the first two days, in a letter-perfect assault based on months of detailed preparations, the First British Army, composed mainly of Canadian soldiers, captured Vimy Ridge, a few miles to the north of Arras. Thousands of lives had already been lost in previous attempts to storm this natural fortress, so important because it commanded the great plain of Douai lying to the east. Although the casualties were again exceedingly heavy, the sacrifices were perhaps not in vain because it is probable that the final German offensive in March 1918 might have succeeded had the Allies not held Vimy Ridge. Unfortunately, the Battle of Arras also got out of hand and was continued much longer than had been planned. Splinter engagements, several of them planned on the spur of the moment, dragged on for almost a month, adding another 120,000 casualties to the Allied toll.

The French offensive was launched along the Aisne on April 16 in a blinding snow storm. Never was an attack more confidently undertaken, and never more confidently awaited by the enemy. Nivelle's boastful plans had become almost household gossip in France and his public feuds with cautious politicians and with Sir Douglas Haig had fully alerted the Germans. Prisoners of war—or deserters—had conveniently fallen into enemy hands with detailed plans of the whole campaign. And it was conducted in the same old way with the same dire results. Colonial troops—the coloured cannon-fodder so often used by France—were meant to spearhead one of the main attacks. So numbed with cold they could not even fix their bayonets, these men broke and fled and from then on the campaign became a fiasco. Instead of taking Laon, the French advanced six hundred yards and suffered another 200,000 casualties. Mutiny broke out among the soldiers and the French army—although still numbering over 2 million men —was finished as an attacking force for the rest of the year.

Canadians bringing back a wounded man

Passchendaele, 1917

Now it was Sir Douglas Haig's turn. This overconfident soldier, convinced from the beginning that Sir John French was not qualified to lead the British army, had helped to depose his Commander in Chief in 1915 and had then taken his place! By the spring of 1917, several of his subordinate officers and many political leaders, including Lloyd George, the new Prime Minister, had lost all confidence in Haig's judgement. The Prime Minister, fearing another disastrous Allied attack on the Western Front, wanted to get rid of him but could not do so. The Commander in Chief, by the questionable practice of writing confidential letters to influential friends and even to King George V himself, had built up too strong a following in England to be displaced. With the French now standing solely on the defensive, Haig was at last free to pursue an ambitious scheme which had been in the back of his mind for several months.

Troops and equipment were moved northward from Arras and on July 31, 1917, Sir Douglas Haig began the Third Battle of Ypres—that great offensive in war-torn Flanders designed to pierce the Western Front, capture the German submarine bases thirty miles away on the Belgian coast and finally win the War. Although the United States had declared war on Germany in April, for reasons that will be considered shortly, Haig was not content to wait. He and his staff advisers concluded that the British could win single-handed; the German army, so they said, was exhausted, its morale cracking—a fatal mistake made by British Headquarters not once but several times. The British troops in the front lines knew what they were up against, but the High Command—perhaps from that sense of superiority gained in colonial wars—often underestimated the courage of the German soldier and the skilled way in which he was so frequently led.

The first objective of the Third Battle of Ypres was a little Belgian town called Passchendaele, lying about five miles almost due east of the Allied lines: take it

Passchendaele

and the battle was won. The British had about a month to cover those five miles of low-lying, swampy, reclaimed land. As everyone knew, the weather in Flanders broke at the end of August 'with the regularity of the Indian monsoon' and would so deluge with rain the shell-torn marshes that any further advance would become humanly impossible. Yard by yard, the British soldiers inched towards Passchendaele, through August on into September; the rain did come but still the attack was pressed forward—forward against the most deadly tangle of barbed wire, crisscrossing trenches, concrete pillboxes and machine-gun nests—all through October, fighting under conditions which no words can describe, until November 6, when the troops, in a climax of horror and supreme martyrdom, advanced the final few hundred yards and a riddled Canadian force entered Passchendaele. Honour had been saved and the High Command called a halt at last.

Shortly after the Third Battle of Ypres one of Haig's staff paid his first visit to the battlefront. He was still far short of the real fighting line when he burst into tears, crying: 'Good God, did we really send men to fight in that?' Not only sent them in to fight: 400,000 Allied soldiers lost their lives to gain five useless miles of Flanders mud from which the High Command voluntarily withdrew the following spring.

It is all the more tragic to record that, shortly after the curtain closed on this

sad scene, British tanks broke through the German lines to a depth of more than five miles in one single day. On November 20, at Cambrai, in the first real tank battle in history, 380 of these new monsters rolled across no man's land before a gun had opened fire. The absence of the customary bombardment caught the Germans by complete surprise, the deep trenches of the Hindenburg Line were quickly pierced and by nightfall the Allies had reached the open countryside beyond. The long-expected, big breakthrough seemed to have come at last and for a brief, fleeting moment victory was in sight.

When the project of building an armoured trench-crossing machine was first submitted to the British Engineer-in-Chief in June 1915, he coldly commented: 'Before considering this proposal we should descend from the realm of imagination to solid facts.' A few months later, when the tank demonstrated its prowess before Lord Kitchener, he remarked: 'A pretty mechanical toy: the war will never be won by such machines.' This pessimistic attitude filtered through the High Command to such an extent that, with few exceptions, only the officers in the Tank Corps had any real confidence in the new weapon of offence. Under these circumstances, it is not surprising that the Battle of Cambrai came as a kind of afterthought, late in the year, without adequate reserves. The resources needed to follow up the breakthrough had been sunk in the swamps of Passchendaele and within a few days the Germans were able to regain all the territory they had so quickly lost. The sacrifice, however, had fully revealed the value of a new

A tank crossing the German front line at Vimy

method and recalled the old value of surprise. Nine months later, as we shall see, this object-lesson was applied with tremendous success and the once-despised tank proved to be a determining factor in the final victory. With Cambrai, the year 1917 ended on the Western Front: marked by Passchendaele, the heights of folly had been reached in the War of Attrition.

Breaking the Stalemate

The War at Sea
The chain of events that finally broke the stalemate on the Western Front began at sea. From the beginning of the War, the German High Seas Fleet remained hidden in the Kiel Canal behind an ever-expanding field of mines and the protection of a few very active submarines. As these mines and submarines forced the British Grand Fleet farther and farther north away from the European coast, opportunities were presented to the Germans to make tip-and-run raids across to England and come into occasional contact with units of the British Navy. In each of these resulting engagements the Germans gave a very good account of themselves and the Admiralty records are full of excuses why, when they had the chance, they did not blow the Germans out of the water.

Much the most important of these engagements in the North Sea, and the only full-scale naval action of the War, occurred on May 31, 1916, sixty miles off the coast of Jutland (Denmark). Although the British had some advance warning of what to expect, the German Fleet caught Admiral Beatty's cruiser and battleship squadron offguard and inflicted heavy losses on it before the Grand Fleet, under Admiral Jellicoe, steamed south to the rescue. Greatly outnumbered and holding discretion to be the better part of valour, the German ships, under cover of fog and darkness, slipped home to safety.

One of England's well-known military historians has written: 'In range finding, accuracy of fire and in the skilled and daring leadership of Admirals Scheer and Hipper, the Germans were much superior. Rigid adherence to traditional manoeuvres, failure to plot course accurately and many misinterpreted signals cost the British their opportunity at Jutland to inflict a mortal blow on Germany.' Indeed, if the cruiser action between Hipper and Beatty is used as a basis for judgement, the Battle of Jutland must go down as one of the worst defeats in the annals of the British navy.

However, we must keep in mind that Admiral Jellicoe, old-fashioned and timid though he apparently was, could not risk the loss of his ships. As long as the British navy remained numerically stronger than the German, the enemy fleet was powerless to do any serious damage to the Allies. 'Admiral Jellicoe,' as Churchill once said, 'was the only man who could lose the War in an afternoon.' The purpose of the Royal Navy was to bottle up the German High Seas Fleet and not take chances trying to cripple it in a hit-and-run fight, and the true importance of Jutland lies in the fact that the Germans ran for cover and stayed there for the duration of the War.

The Battle of Jutland also compelled Admiral Scheer to report to the German government: 'Due to the vast superiority of the enemy surface fleet, we can hope for victory only by crushing the economic life of England through U-boat action against England's commerce.' After the German losses at Verdun and the Somme, General Ludendorff also demanded permission to use submarine warfare against commercial ships going to Great Britain. Chancellor Bethmann-Hollweg and other political leaders, knowing full well that U-boat action would bring in the United States, resisted these demands. However, the military and naval chiefs eventually had their way and on February 1, 1917, Germany announced that she was resorting to 'unrestricted submarine warfare'. Thus the Battle of Jutland and the war of attrition at Verdun and the Somme forced Germany to introduce an intensive submarine campaign and this, in turn, provoked President Wilson to declare war against her.

The Periscope Rises

'Peace-loving citizens of this country will now rise up and give a hearty vote of thanks to Columbus for having discovered America.' This was the way the Chicago *Herald* greeted the news in August 1914, and this was the way the vast majority of Americans felt when they heard that the other Big Powers had gone to war. A long history of isolation from Europe, based on geographic location and the traditions of the Monroe Doctrine, found them determined to stay out of this greatest of all 'European entanglements'. Furthermore, 32 million fairly recent immigrants, about one-third of the population, retained many bonds with the land of their birth. The divided loyalties of these 'hyphenated' Americans—especially among the very vocal German and Irish groups—still further emphasized the neutrality of the United States.

Although the Americans wanted nothing to do with the War, the majority undoubtedly sympathized with the Allies from the beginning. The people of the United States—particularly the wealthy and educated classes— could not forget their Anglo-Saxon origins. Also, relations with England had been officially very friendly since the days of the Venezuela crisis. Almost all the members of Wilson's cabinet held these pro-British feelings; the President himself was a strong admirer of English traditions; and Robert Lansing, the Secretary of State, and Walter Page, the American ambassador in London, were strong Anglophiles. Clever propagandists enlisted by the Allies to espouse their cause in the United States played upon these natural sympathies of the American people. Their efforts were made easier by the fact that the Allies controlled the transatlantic cables and all news reaching America passed through the scissors of British censorship.

Another very important situation played right into the hands of the Allies. As the War progressed, the United States began to ship more and more food and materials to Britain and France. When these two countries ran short of funds—England was spending over $30 million a day by 1916—private American firms, including the great banking house of Morgan, with the secret consent of their government, lent them money to continue buying in the United States. By the time the United States entered the War, American bankers had advanced $2½ billion to the Allies compared to a mere $27 million lent to Germany. In this way, the whole economic life of the United States became closely linked with the Allied cause. The American people were sympathetic to Britain and France from the beginning and became more so as the War dragged on. Under these circumstances, if the Germans stepped too far out of line in their behaviour towards neutrals, it was a foregone conclusion that the United States would join the Allies.

The rights of the United States as a neutral trading nation and the whole course of the war at sea led Germany inevitably towards taking her fatal step. In 1914 the United States attempted to protect itself by asking the Allies and the Central Powers to accept the Declaration of London which defined the rights of neutrals trading with belligerent nations. Germany, faced with the prospect of a European blockade, agreed but the Allies refused. If Great Britain had obeyed international law she would have shackled her navy and might have lost the War. Any discussion of international law in wartime is somewhat futile: war is the direct opposite of law and order, and nations fighting for their lives have never obeyed the so-called 'rules of war'. Great Britain, therefore, defined the rules of visit and search to suit herself, added dozens of items (including food) to the contraband list and directed neutral ships into English ports. The North Sea was declared a war zone and so thoroughly mined that overseas commerce could not sail through to Germany. In these ways, Great Britain violated the trading rights of neutrals. Despite angry U.S. protests, Britain would not relax her hold on neutral commerce. She was engaged in a life-and-death struggle and to her, American profits were a minor consideration.

Under these circumstances, the periscope of the German submarine appeared on the scene. Claiming to be acting in self-defence, the Central Powers in February 1915 laid down a war zone round the British Isles in which all enemy shipping would be sunk. At first, the submarines surfaced to see whether they had trapped an enemy or a neutral vessel, but this attempt partially to obey the rules was soon abandoned when they found Allied armed merchantmen flying false neutral flags and enemy warships disguised as commercial carriers. U-boat commanders were given orders, therefore, to sink all ships on sight. This was the difference between the British and the German blockades. Both had the same purpose of starving the other into submission, but the British, with a surface fleet, could direct neutral ships into port without the loss of life: the Germans could not.

Despite these warnings, the United States stood on her rights. Commercial ships continued to carry war materials to the British Isles and American men, women and children embarked on contraband-laden Allied vessels into submarine-infested waters. So it was that on May 7, 1915, the great British ocean liner, the *Lusitania*, was sunk without warning off the Irish coast with the loss of over a thousand lives, including 114 American citizens. Immediately the industrialized eastern part of the United States, already tied by trade and loans to the Allies, wanted to declare war on Germany. But the Middle West, with its strong German population, and the Far West were prepared to suspend judgement and Wilson was unwilling to lead a divided country into war. Such strong protests were sent by the American government that the Germans finally agreed to sink no more passenger ships. During 1916, the submarine commanders were on their best behaviour.

However, following their losses on the Western Front and their experience at the Battle of Jutland, the German High Command were convinced that unrestricted submarine warfare must be renewed. Over the protests of German politicians, Ludendorff announced that 'U-boats will attempt to sink on sight all ships—neutral or enemy, passenger or merchant—in the war zone.' American neutral rights were dashed aside. Up to this time, President Wilson had hoped to bring the two sides together in a negotiated 'peace without victory' and there are many who believe that the whole course of history might have been altered had he succeeded. The German announcement carried away his last hopes and on April 6, 1917, a wildly cheering Congress passed the Declaration of War. 'My message today,' Wilson confided to a friend that evening, 'was a message of death for our young men. How strange it seems to applaud it!'

The Collapse of Russia
The entry of the United States was only a promissory note for the Allies. Completely unready for war, it was not until April 1918, a full year later, that the first American division moved into line on the Western Front. Although the sagging Allied spirit was undoubtedly raised by the American Declaration of War, it is extremely doubtful whether the ordinary British soldier, fighting the Germans, was very much encouraged by the popular slogan: 'The Yanks are Coming.' And in the meantime, as the United States was organizing itself, Russia deserted her Allies. In November 1917, the long-repressed hatred for a corrupt and cruel government and the growing disgust with war exploded in the Bolshevik Revolution. The 'ten days that shook the world' resulted in the Bolsheviks suing for peace; the Eastern Front collapsed and fifty divisions of German soldiers were freed for service against France and Britain. Thus at the beginning of 1918, with over 4 million men at their disposal—a figure showing the futility of the

Allied war of attrition—the Germans began preparations for a great, final, offensive drive on the Western Front. Ludendorff and the other apostles of a complete and crushing victory were confident of success before the Americans could reach France.

Germany's Last Bid

The war of attrition began its final year as a series of gigantic, destructive attacks exceeding in every grim way anything yet witnessed on the Western Front. The German offensive in 1918 was but a vast continuation of the waste and human suffering of earlier battles.

In Germany, the strangling Allied blockade was beginning to tell more and more. The shortage of milk, fats and other essential foods had enormously increased the infant mortality rate and deaths from tuberculosis. A worn and weary nation was out at the elbows, living on dingy, repellent substitutes. Signs of unrest were so apparent that Ludendorff held certain battalions ready for use against his own civilian population. German soldiers now existed on short rations—which may account for the fact that, when they captured Allied supplies of food and whisky, they paused to gorge themselves and thereby helped to upset Ludendorff's great schemes for victory. Farther away, Germany's allies were beginning to crack. Turkey was staggering under pressure from General Allenby's army in Palestine, Bulgaria was tired and ready to quit, and the once-great Austrian Empire, threatened by a now-determined Italian army and by internal revolt, was on the verge of crumbling into pieces.

Even so, the German High Command managed to unleash three assaults against the Western trenches during the spring of 1918, each one of which came within an ace of success. Using at last tactics that almost proved to be the master-key to unlock that great fortified system, the Germans penetrated deep into the Allied lines and thrice came dangerously close to a complete breakthrough into open country. In March, the first of those offensives hit along a tremendous, wide front reaching southward from Vimy Ridge. The German armies, in the biggest advance of the War, drove forward for thirty miles across the old crater-fields of the Somme before the very heavily outnumbered British forces finally closed and held the gap. In April, a second offensive farther north between Vimy Ridge and Ypres broke through for ten miles before it was stopped. The Germans came so close to the Channel ports that preliminary orders were issued for the demolition of Calais and plans were laid to flood the whole country south of Dunkirk—a step which, it is said, would have taken fifty years to repair. At the end of May, a third great attack, this time against the French along the Aisne, drove the lines southward to the banks of the Marne and once again the armies of Germany were forty miles from Paris.

During these critical months, the British and French ceaselessly but in vain tried to persuade the American General John Pershing to hasten his forces to the front. General Foch, the recently appointed Commander in Chief of all the Allied Armies in France bluntly warned Pershing: 'The Americans may arrive to find the British pushed into the sea and the French driven back behind the Loire,

while they try to organize on lost battlefields over the graves of Allied soldiers.'
Disaster was averted by a desperate Allied defence that inflicted over a million
and a half casualties on the advancing Germans. The danger of collapse was over
before the Americans arrived in force; Germany had exhausted her strength.
Ludendorff, through his great attacks, had done to his own armies what eleven
Allied campaigns had failed to do in previous years.

To the Last Quarter-hour
The time had come to break the stalemate on the Western Front. Along its entire
gaunt and devastated length over 3 million soldiers, their number increasing
daily as the Americans poured across the Atlantic, stood ready to hurl the
combined mighty weight of the Allied and Associated Powers against a tottering
Germany. With a folly born of desperation, the Germans launched a fourth
attack, this time towards Paris, but on July 18, in the Second Battle of the Marne,
the last German attack blended into the first great Allied counter-offensive.

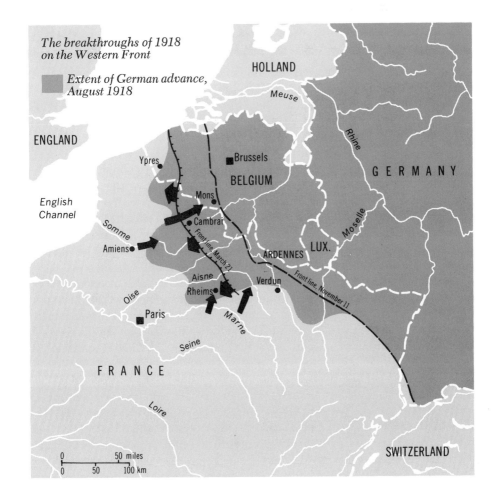

The breakthroughs of 1918
on the Western Front

Extent of German advance,
August 1918

A few weeks later, on August 8, the German lines facing the vital railway centre at Amiens cracked wide open. Here, the Canadian Army Corps carried out another model attack, planned as secretly and as carefully as the one on Vimy Ridge during the previous year. Thirty-eight thousand air photographs, issued to the troops, revealed every detail of the primitive front lines which the exhausted Germans had been unable to strengthen since their spring offensive. Supported by 450 tanks—those once-despised, reeking, boiling-hot machines which the Germans finally admitted were the most terrifying of all weapons used against them—the Canadian forces had a triumphant day. The Germans were driven back eight miles and the cavalry rode through at last while the Canadians and the fast, little whippet tanks played havoc behind the enemy lines. In Ludendorff's words, the Battle of Amiens was 'the Black Day for the German army. It showed beyond all doubt the decline of our fighting power.'

After Amiens, a series of alternating attacks, which thundered up and down the whole front, finally compelled Ludendorff to order a general retreat behind the old Hindenburg Line—thus abandoning almost all the ground he had gained at such ruinous cost during the spring. This withdrawal was completed about mid-September and the stage was set for the greatest of all battles. Foch's final assault on the Hindenburg Line in the west and the Aisne in the south—which began on September 26—was very probably the greatest battle in all history. Despite Foch's order that 'everyone is to attack (Belgians, British, French and Americans) as soon as they can, as strong as they can, for as long as they can', the Allies broke through in only two places—at either end of the Hindenburg fortifications. These two wedges, however, were just enough to force the Germans into a gradual retreat from the Western Front.

During October, as the Germans were driven back against the borders, closer

Canadians passing through Ypres, November 1917

to home, their resistance became stronger and the advance slowed down. By the end of the month, the fall rains once more deluged the land, and it seemed that the German army might hold for another dread winter. But as the war of attrition and stalemate was thus being carried on to the last quarter-hour, other forces, elsewhere, were at work. One by one during October, Bulgaria, Turkey and Austria-Hungary had crumbled out of the War; the gates into Germany from the south were now wide open. The despondent people, seeing no hope and yielding at last to the Allied blockade, rose in revolution. The navy mutinied, Ludendorff cracked under the strain, the Kaiser and the Crown Prince fled to Holland, and a new socialist government took over. With chaos in their streets, starvation in their homes and gloom in their hearts, the Germans could carry on no longer.

On November 11, 1918, as the great guns were silenced in peace, Canadian soldiers celebrated victory in the ruined Belgian town of Mons. The Allies were back where they had started, for it was at Mons that the Old Contemptibles and the Germans first met in combat. During the intervening four years and three months, 65 million men from thirty sovereign nations had been mobilized and forced to take part in the organized destruction of property and human life, the value of which was beyond calculation. Of these men, 35 million were killed or wounded in action while an equal number of civilians, through starvation, disease or revolution, had fallen victims to the War.

The statesmen who gathered to discuss the Peace held a grave responsibility to mankind.

9   CANADA'S BAPTISM OF FIRE

Lest We Forget

During the last week of April, 1915, the people in this country read with glowing pride the day-by-day reports of the Second Battle of Ypres. The Huns had used gas! The French colonial troops had fled! The way to the Channel ports was wide open but the First Canadian Division, so the newspapers said, had closed the gap and saved the day. Men accustomed to civilian life, untrained, undrilled, undisciplined until a few months before—battle-lines composed of lawyers, doctors, college professors and young graduates, businessmen, labourers and clerks, thousands of whom had never handled a rifle until this call came—had been plunged for the first time into the most scientific, bloody and devastating of the world's struggles and had won undying fame. A steady stream of messages— from His Majesty the King, from Sir John French, the Lord Bishop of London, the sister dominions—poured into Ottawa carrying ringing words of praise for Canada's soldiers.

Then, on May 3, the Minister of Militia released the casualty list for publication. Most of the people in Canada knew, in a vague sort of way, that the fighting had been costly but no one expected anything like this. 705 men killed, over 2,000 wounded, 2,600 missing—almost 6,000 Canadians lost in only seven days! And yet, within three weeks, the First Division was back in action. Festubert, Givenchy and other French villages, unknown up to this time, became all too sadly familiar in Canada as the mounting casualty lists recorded a total of 14,500 men dead or wounded by mid-October. One out of every two men sent overseas had been killed or crippled in less than six months of fighting. And this was only the beginning, the very beginning. All the great battles on the Western Front —St. Eloi, Sanctuary Wood, the Somme and Courcelette, Vimy Ridge, Hill 70, Passchendaele and Amiens—had yet to take their fearful toll of Canadian lives.

After the Second Battle of Ypres, as the dread casualty lists followed one another, column after black-bordered column in the newspapers, each one longer than the last, the spirit in Canada gradually changed. The first light-hearted flush of patriotism soon gave way to shocked sorrow. The joyous, rollicking mood of the pre-war days disappeared and a tense, grim determination gripped the people. Stalemate on the Western Front, the war of attrition, normal wastage, to the last quarter-hour and the last platoon—what dreadful phrases these had suddenly become! Anxiety and fear haunted countless homes for, by 1916, one Canadian family in every four had a soldier overseas—and in the towns and cities

The Canadian Memorial on Vimy Ridge

of Ontario and in parts of Manitoba the ratio was even higher. Would their man be next? Would they, too, receive a notice—one of those telegrams from the Minister of Militia that had already carried sorrow to so many families? Would he be invalided home, crippled like the neighbour's boy? Would he, perhaps, never come back? For all these millions of people, the First World War brought long months of gruelling spiritual endurance.

With so many of our citizens wrought up and deeply concerned about their loved ones overseas, it is understandable that sometimes the tension snapped and tempers flared. Families who kept their men at home, however valid the reasons, were bitterly condemned. Peaceful neighbourhoods, lifelong friendships and eventually the whole nation were torn apart by passionate arguments over military service. Anyone who did not do his duty as others saw it was violently assailed for behaviour which, in normal times, might have been overlooked. These angry undercurrents, combined with the ever-increasing casualty lists and the growing feeling that someone must be bungling the job on the Western Front, stirred our nation to its very depths. Never before or since has Canada lived at such a strained emotional pitch. Unlike so many Europeans, the Canadian people were not uprooted and torn from their homes. Few among them had any direct personal experience with the horrors of war. Yet, for a young nation isolated from the fighting front by the Atlantic Ocean, the people of this country brought to the Altar of Mars their full share of sacrifice and sorrow.

Business as Usual

The Wartime Boom

During the War, the world shortage of food became much more serious than the average Canadian could be made to believe. Trying to emphasize this point early in 1917 to a group of housewives in Victoria, a spokesman for the Department of Agriculture described the situation as follows: 'Do you know that last year's grain crop in Europe was about half its normal size: or that ninety million of their food animals have already been slaughtered? Do you realize that over sixty per cent of the fifty million soldiers engaged in the War came from the farms and were food producers before being called to the battlefields? In addition, millions of tons of ships are now being sunk by enemy submarines and most of the ships are carrying foodstuffs. The situation is terribly grave. Our duty is simply this— to produce more and waste nothing.'

Conditions such as these, at the very beginning of the war and becoming progressively worse, naturally offered unlimited opportunities for Canadian agriculture. The most sensational gains were recorded in meat and dairy products. With all Scandinavian supplies cut off by the mine fields and those from Australia restricted by the long, dangerous sea voyage, our dairymen and meat packers enjoyed an assured market and soaring prices such as they had never had before. Cheese exports increased about 300 per cent, pork exports 535 per cent and beef exports rose 75 million pounds annually, a gain of 6,795 per cent.

Wartime developments in the prairie grain-growing, however, were to have the most important, and the saddest, consequences in the future. The sodbusters out West—aided by thousands of Americans who continued to come across the border during the War—picked up where they left off at the end of the Laurier era. Encouraged by the government, urged on by the ceaseless patriotic appeals and the practical voice of Number One Northern climbing to over two dollars a bushel, the wheat farmers put an increasing amount of land under cultivation. By 1918, the wheat acreage of the Dominion had almost doubled and was capable of yielding in a good year about 450 million bushels. During the War, with world markets at their feet, the farmers had few real worries; costs of production, care of equipment and soil conservation were minor considerations compared to a growing savings account at the local bank. But the bonanza could not last. A day of reckoning lay ahead when the peasant soldiers of Europe would return to their farms and the cheap wheat crop of Europe would come pouring back into a world market no long swollen by wartime demands. Special post-war conditions delayed the evil day until 1929, but then the crash came; markets were glutted, wheat prices fell below costs to thirty cents a bushel and the prairie lands were desolate. Perhaps it may be said that the heaviest costs of the War, in the long run, were paid by the Canadian West in the depression years.

During the winter of 1914–15 a number of Canadian companies, convinced that the Allies must be running short of shells, sent agents abroad in search of orders.

There was no reason, they said, why Canada, with its rich mineral resources, could not develop a munitions industry. The results achieved by the Canadian agents, however, were very discouraging. Although the Nova Scotia Steel and Coal Company picked up a small order for empty shell cases and the Canadian Car and Foundry Company, with much more luck, received a Russian contract for 5 million howitzer shells at $17.85 each, the British government paid very little attention to these repeated Canadian offers. Each time the agents visited the War Office they received the surprising and completely unrealistic reply that Great Britain had a good supply of shells on hand, probably enough to last for the duration of the War!

Meanwhile, another first-class row, one of great importance to Canada, was brewing in the British cabinet. This time the storm centred on Lord Kitchener, the Boer War hero so popular with the masses that Prime Minister Asquith had been forced to appoint him Minister of War. The only soldier in British history ever to hold this position, Kitchener distrusted his civilian colleagues—he claimed they told everything to their wives—and refused to discuss the details of this very important department with any other cabinet ministers. Although he occasionally showed flashes of genius, as when he predicted the War would last at least three years, his close associates soon found that this strange, sphinx-like man possessed feet of clay. He maintained that the handful of government arsenals, under War Office control, could make all the shells needed by the British army. Indeed, he could not understand why so much ammunition was being used on the Western Front and had suggested to Sir John French that more care should be exercised by the artillery! Under these circumstances it was not surprising that would-be munitions makers from Canada received a cool welcome at the War Office. They might have been less discouraged had they known that other members of the British cabinet were already waiting for the first opportunity to take the control of munitions away from Lord Kitchener's department.

Their chance came when Sir John French began to blame the failure of his costly campaigns on the shortage of shells. The British had to break off their attack, so he said, just when it was going to succeed, because their ammunition had run out. The resulting quarrel between the War Office and British Headquarters in France—both sides being at fault, for no general should have undertaken an offensive when his army was short of ammunition—broke into the newspaper headlines in April 1915 as England's famous 'Shell Scandal'. This public outcry against War Office inefficiency was all the politicians needed. A new Department of Munitions and Supply was created, with Lloyd George as Minister, and under his dynamic direction England's great industries were geared up for a total, all-out war effort. A Munitions Board, supervised by Joseph Flavelle, a Toronto businessman, was set up in this country to act as a purchasing agent for the British government and through it orders for shells finally began to pour into Canada.

Canadians swung into this new form of business with aggressive energy. The lead, zinc and copper mines of southern British Columbia and the nickel mines at Sudbury now hummed with new activity; the big steel corporations—the Steel Company of Canada, Dominion Steel and Coal, Algoma and Canada Iron, with their twenty-two blast furnaces—turned out rough forgings for the shells; companies experienced in using steel as a basic raw material—Canadian General Electric, Westinghouse, Massey-Harris, Canadian Car and Foundry, the Canadian Pacific Railway and a great many others—finished off the forgings and made a multitude of different parts; a whole new industry sprang up almost overnight to manufacture cordite, gun cotton, TNT, acetone, nitric acid and other supplies needed for high-explosive shells. By the end of 1915, in a few months of outstanding achievement, Canadian industry—which before the War had never made a cartridge case or a fuse—was shipping eight hundred thousand shells a month across the Atlantic.

This feverish pace was maintained; older companies expanded their production and new companies came into existence until fifteen hundred factories, located in ninety Canadian centres, were employing three hundred and fifty thousand men and women in the manufacture of munitions. The following report submitted by the British War Cabinet in 1918 indicates the importance of the Canadian contribution: 'The manufacturing resources of Canada have been mobilized for war production almost as completely as those of the British Isles. Fifteen per cent of the total expenditure of our Ministry of Munitions last year was incurred in Canada. She has manufactured nearly every type of shell from the small 18-pounder to the huge 9.2-inch. All told, she has supplied 60 million shells or roughly one-third of the total used by the British forces during the last three years of the War. In addition, Canada has contributed shell forgings, propellants and explosives, aluminum, nickel, airplane parts, ships, agricultural machinery and timber, besides large quantities of railway materials, including no less than four hundred and fifty miles of rails torn up in Canada and shipped direct to France.' As may well be imagined, a volume of business such as this— combined with orders for many other war materials and the tremendous demand for foodstuffs—created in Canada a wartime boom of unprecedented proportions.

Before the War, Canada exported most of her metal ores to the United States for final processing. It was to be expected that the wartime demand for metals should prompt many Canadian companies to process their own ores. During the 1914–18 period the internationally-known Consolidated Mining and Smelting Corporation, a subsidiary of the C.P.R., built its first base-metal refineries at Trail, and other copper, zinc or lead refineries were established elsewhere in Canada. There was, however, another and most interesting reason for this development. Since the United States remained neutral for three full years of War and was legally free to trade with the enemy, there was always the danger that Canadian mineral resources would find their way, eventually, into German hands. This fear applied with special force to our nickel mines. Canada controlled eighty per cent of the world supply; much of it was refined in the United States and before 1914 about sixty per cent of the total output was purchased by

(Top and bottom) Making ammunition

Germany, mainly by Krupp, one of the biggest munitions companies of the world. Although an army of five thousand British secret service agents was planted in American munitions factories and the supply of nickel was fairly well controlled, the Canadian people were not satisfied. It was under these circumstances that in 1916 Sir Robert Borden requested the International Nickel Company to build their refinery at Port Colborne.

One other, much more important result of Canada's industrial expansion during the War years should be mentioned here. The industries working on war orders and especially all those manufacturing shells belonged to the group which we have defined as 'secondary' industries. As they relied on imported iron and coal, their costs of production were high, therefore they required fairly high tariff protection. Before the War they had produced almost exclusively for the home market. By 1918, these companies had expanded to such an extent that both the number of skilled workers and the capacity to produce manufactured articles in Canada had more than doubled. Furthermore, this rapid development came with no corresponding increase in population and under the most abnormal circumstances—for shells were hardly a standard item of international trade and could be sold in wartime regardless of costs or tariffs. When the War ended, Canadian secondary manufacturing industries were faced, therefore, with the problem of how to employ fully their enormous productive powers within the narrow limits of our small domestic market.

In the post-war period, our factories, mines and skilled labour force were turned for a while to successful peacetime purposes. But here, as with agriculture, very special temporary conditions simply postponed the day of reckoning. During the depression years, the great steel mills were idle, factories and mines were closed and endless lines of patient, hungry and forsaken men stood waiting at the gates. It would be quite wrong to assume that wartime expansion and the eventual overproduction of agricultural and manufactured products were the sole or even the main source of the trouble. They were, however, important factors in causing and prolonging the Great Depression which gripped the country, until the coming of a Second World War—and this alone—lifted Canada into a new era of prosperity.

Financing the War
Before the War, financing the Canadian government was a comparatively simple, straightforward business. The federal authorities spent about $130 million annually, or roughly the amount our present government spends every ten days. Revenue was raised by customs duties on trade and in that pleasant bygone era there was no such thing as income or business profits tax. Governments usually made ends meet and often had money left over at the end of each year. The total national debt—borrowed mainly from Great Britain—was only $541 million and had been incurred for railways, canals, harbours and other valuable public works. The War shattered this beyond recognition. By the time it ended, the Canadian people were burdened with an enormous debt and faced the prospect of paying heavy taxes for many years to come—not for the development of their country

but to cover the costs of four years of organized destruction.

During the War, the Canadian government spent almost $3 billion. Canada raised this huge sum of money mainly by borrowing from her own people through the sale of government bonds. Far too little revenue, in view of swollen incomes and wartime profits, was raised by taxation. Although the Borden administration introduced a business profits tax in 1916 and an income tax in 1917, they were the mildest of measures, for they raised less than $50 million a year. Thus, eighty-five per cent of the total costs of the War were financed by 'Victory Loans'.

Canada launched five of these Victory Loan drives during the War. Accompanied by a flood of patriotic oratory, each one far exceeded its objective. Although this was a truly amazing achievement for a country which had never before borrowed extensively from its own citizens, it did not involve any particular sacrifices. The bonds were gilt-edged securities, carried at least five per cent interest, and were tax-free for ever. Four of every five Victory Loan bonds were purchased, in large blocks, by insurance and trust companies, banks, industrial concerns or individuals with big profits or incomes. In order to ensure the success of the Victory Loans, the government allowed and encouraged high profits, by keeping low interest rates on borrowed money and imposing few direct taxes. As a result of this policy, combined with the growing scarcity of all supplies, prices soared sky-high. Towards the end of the war, half-hearted attempts were made to control this runaway inflation, but they came too late to prevent prices from doubling in less than four years.

It is important to observe that business profits, farm income and some wages managed to increase as prices increased. But there were a great many people in the middle- and low-income class whose earnings fell far behind the rising prices and whose standard of living, therefore, actually declined during the war. These were the only Canadians on the home front who were forced to make personal economic sacrifices. Thus, some of the financial burden of the War was placed on the shoulders of those who could least afford to stand the strain.

The remainder of the financial burden was shifted in its entirety from the war years to the future in the form of a gigantic national debt. This war debt was greatly increased when the government finally decided to stop supporting the Mackenzie-Mann interests and the Grand Trunk Pacific and to take them over, bankrupt, as publicly-owned railroads. This was done, after many tangled lawsuits, between 1917 and 1922 with no loss to either the promoters or the shareholders. The whole cost of these misguided private ventures, amounting to $700 million, was assumed by the Canadian taxpayers. As a result of the War and the failure of these railways, the national debt of the Dominion climbed to over $3 billion! For many years to come, the Canadian people were forced to see one-third of all government revenue being used, not for improvements to benefit the country, but to pay almost $150 million annually in interest charges. In other words, peacetime taxes, raised mainly by methods which hit the mass of the people, were used to transfer wealth into the pockets of wartime bondholders. Here again, however, the real costs of the War for Canada did not become fully apparent until the Great Depression.

Profiteering and Scandals

Within two months of arriving in England to complete their training at Salisbury Plain, the first Canadian contingent of twenty-five thousand men had worn out all their boots. Granted that conditions on Salisbury Plain were appalling and that the boots had been made in a hurry; nevertheless, when the heels pulled off in the mud and the soles wore through in one good route march, it was obvious that someone back home had sold a hundred and eighty thousand pairs of shoddy boots to the Canadian army. In due course, this situation led to a public investigation into the Ames-Holden-McCready and other shoe-manufacturing companies. This was but the first of a very long series of accusations, charges of profiteering, scandals and investigations which marred Canada's record all during the War. This must be recorded to refute those who maintain that the War brought out only the best in human nature.

It is true that the war years revealed many illustrations of high endeavour and complete unselfishness. The wonderful work of the Canadian Red Cross and the multitude of voluntary organizations formed purely to relieve the suffering of others are examples of true dedication. Thousands of women patiently knitted socks, bundled up parcels for the men overseas or visited the homes of grief-stricken families; others took the place of their men in the fields or factories. Government officials and industrialists spent many long extra hours at their desks, directing the war effort with utmost care and honesty. Patriotic farmers laboured from dawn to dark and city workers gave up their holidays to help bring in the crops. Businessmen paid their employees' salaries while on active service and many worked full time for the government without remuneration. The people of Canada contributed over $100 million to war-relief funds and their response when disaster struck Halifax in December 1917 was warm-hearted and generous to the highest degree. It is also important to keep in mind the difference between wartime profits and downright mean profiteering. Many Canadian companies, especially the large corporations formed during the merger period before the War, made very large profits. They often did so, however, simply because their volume of business was so great. A profit of fifty cents per barrel on flour, for instance, may not have been excessive, nor would it add much to the price of bread, but when millions of barrels were sold the total profit was tremendous.

However, it must be admitted that the war years also revealed a story of greed, selfishness and sometimes of complete dishonesty which forms an unpleasant and disgraceful chapter in our history. Many Canadians adopted towards the War the same grasping attitude as they had held in wasting the forests, exploiting the farm land or cheating the government and the people on railroad contracts. Judicial inquiries into the manufacture and sale of almost every kind of wartime product unfolded far too many cases of citizens taking advantage of their country's distress. Meat packers were found to be hoarding urgently needed food in cold storage, often waiting so long for prices to increase that millions of dollars' worth of produce rotted; other companies supplied inferior equipment—which might have cost soldiers' lives—slipping it past government inspectors or bribing them to look the other way; government and consumers were overcharged time

Part of the devastation caused by the explosion of the French ship Mont Blanc *in Halifax harbour, December 6, 1917.*

and again, with exorbitant profits proved in the sale of bread, milk, butter, meat, shells, fuses, clothing and a multitude of other commodities. So bad was the situation in all food products that the Cost of Living Commissioner concluded his Report for 1917 with these words: 'The food purveyors have seen to it that they have been well and sufficiently paid. Their performance has been upon strictly business and not upon patriotic lines. The consumer, who alone has suffered from their swollen profits, is the patriot.'

Many writers have blamed the government for this wartime profiteering, but it seems that the Canadian people as a whole were much more at fault than the political leaders. Although some politicians fell by the wayside and received 'rake-offs' for directing contracts into the hands of their friends, the original trouble in every case stemmed from the business community. Perhaps, considering the weaknesses of human nature, the government should have clamped more controls on our economy. In those days, however, it was the accepted theory that the government should interfere as little as possible in the business life of the country. Sir Robert Borden and his colleagues tried in vain to secure voluntary co-operation. For instance, instead of introducing rationing and price control when food became scarce, they appealed to the people to conserve supplies and help to keep prices down. As a result, responsible citizens planted their little 'war gardens', endured meatless and breadless days and willingly worked with the government. On the other hand, thousands of Canadians hoarded supplies in their basements, wasted good food estimated at $100 million annually, and evaded the few regulations that the government saw fit to impose. It may be concluded that our somewhat grasping national outlook—accustomed to the lavish hand of nature—and not the weakness of government, was responsible for the sordid side of Canada's war effort.

Discords on the Home Front

The Crisis in Manpower

The first wartime session of the Canadian parliament was a deeply emotional occasion marked by stirring oratory, glowing tributes to Great Britain and promises of Canada's unquestioning loyalty. Sir Wilfrid Laurier, in pledging his party's support, said: 'It is our duty to let Great Britain know that all Canadians stand behind the mother country, conscious that she has engaged in this war, not from any selfish motive but to maintain untarnished the honour of her name. . . . The allied nations are fighting for freedom against oppression, for democracy against tyranny, to save civilization from the unbridled lust of conquest and power.' No serious student of history now believes for one moment that the First World War was fought for any such reasons, but Laurier at the time believed what he said and undoubtedly spoke that day for the vast majority of Canadians. In August 1914 Canada seemed to stand more united than ever before in her history.

The veteran Sir George Foster, Borden's Minister of Trade and Commerce, expressed this feeling of unity in these words: 'The last four days of this session have justified parliamentary life for all time to come. A feeling of pure patriotism, love of country and devotion to what the flag means has come to the front, disfigured by no selfish or petty purpose.' Mean and petty things soon reappeared, however, as dollars and patriotism became tangled together. And by the beginning of the year 1917 the stage had been set for the question of manpower and conscription to tear Canadian national unity to pieces. The 'sacred union' of August 1914, between Liberals and Conservatives, Frenchmen and Englishmen, was sundered in two as old racial animosities flamed up once more.

The manpower requirements of the army began to clash with civilian needs on the home front. By this time, 420,000 Canadians had joined the armed forces and four full divisions—over 100,000 men—held front-line positions in France. By December 1916, Canadian casualties had risen to 68,000 dead or wounded— Courcelette in September had taken 27,000 men—and voluntary recruiting methods failed to find the necessary replacements. The situation was aggravated by the fact that our army, under patriotic and military urging, had been made larger than it should have been, considering the size of the country and all the other demands put upon it for food and munitions. Furthermore, the Dominion government—unlike any other Allied country—insisted on keeping this army at full strength all the time. As a result, the Canadian Corps was stronger, in the final days of the War, than any similar British formation and it had been called 'the most powerful, self-contained striking force on any battlefront'. Such an extreme emphasis on the armed forces of the Dominion unquestionably placed a heavy burden on our manpower resources.

It was under these ominous circumstances that Sir Robert Borden, early in 1917, left to attend an Imperial Conference in England and to pay a visit to Canadian soldiers at the front. Apparently, conscription was not yet in his mind.

Crowds gather to watch a detachment of cavalry parade on Yonge Street, Toronto. Among the spectators, peaked caps and bowlers still outnumber the soft fedora that is beginning to become fashionable. Signs along the route advertise a movie for five cents, a ton of coal for seven dollars.

Although a manpower survey had been undertaken in the previous months and many people thought it was a forerunner to compulsory overseas service, the government denied any such intention. Indeed, just before leaving Canada, the Prime Minister had assured the influential French-Canadian Bishop Bruchési that conscription would not be introduced by his administration.

Overseas, something happened to make Borden change his views. Perhaps it was the sense of fear he found in Britain, with the submarine campaign just beginning to reach its climax, or the gloomy predictions of Admiral Jellicoe that the British navy could not control the U-boat menace. Perhaps it was the news of Vimy Ridge—costly victory that it was—which began on Easter Monday while he was still in England. More than likely, however, it was due to his long talks with the Canadian general, Sir Arthur Currie, and Sir Douglas Haig in France. The professional soldier usually underestimates the needs of the home front and exaggerates his own manpower requirements; and he is never convinced that the problem is solved until the civilian authorities introduce conscription. Whatever the reasons, the Prime Minister returned to Canada and announced that he would ask parliament to pass a conscription bill. Compulsory military service overseas—this was the step so many Canadians feared, and it was this which brought the country to the verge of civil war.

Facts and Fiction

Long before Borden made this announcement certain parts of Canada, led once more by overheated newspaper editors in Toronto and Winnipeg, were on the warpath against Quebec. As early as January 12, 1917, the Winnipeg *Free Press*, for instance, had thus assured its readers: 'The failure of the Province of Quebec to participate in the War is the greatest tragedy in Canadian history.' The Toronto *Globe* asserted that French Canadians were cowards, afraid to fight. Miserable accusations, certain to arouse equally violent feeling in Quebec and to drive the people still deeper into their isolated little world along the St. Lawrence.

When the War broke out there were in Canada over one million recent immigrants from the British Isles—'British-born' citizens as the census-takers called them. These men retained strong loyalties to their homeland, of course, and were quick to volunteer for service. Over seventy-five per cent of the first Canadian contingent came from this group of British-born, and up to the end of 1916 they continued to supply about fifty per cent of all recruits. Most of these men had settled in Ontario or the prairie provinces and in the government record of enlistments they were entered to the credit of these provinces. Discount the British-born recruits and it would be found that a great many Anglo-Canadians —that is, English-speaking people born and raised in Canada—had also been reluctant to volunteer for service. Generally speaking, the longer a family, English or French, had been in Canada, the less emotionally involved it was in the War and the less willing to provide recruits for the army. But newspapermen outside Quebec closed their eyes to considerations such as these.

The editors also failed to observe that, according to the 1911 census, there were almost twice as many single men between the ages of twenty and thirty-four in Ontario and out West as there were in Quebec—an old settled community with a long tradition of early marriage and large families. Nor did they record that recruiting in rural Ontario was about as fruitless as in rural Quebec; farmers proved difficult to enlist wherever they lived. Reporters were quick to condemn French Canadians slipping across the border to the United States, but were silent about the English-speaking citizens who quietly left the Maritimes and Ontario. The parish priests alone were condemned for interfering in politics although the Protestant clergy were doing exactly the same thing. Some of the fiercest recruiting speeches and the strongest political support for Borden came from the Anglican clergy. And the Methodists were certainly playing politics when they used the wartime scarcity of grain to secure their long-cherished prohibition laws against intoxicating drink.

Also, there is no doubt that the Minister of Militia failed to endear himself to the people in Quebec. The flamboyant, self-confident General Sir Sam Hughes, was an intolerant, fighting Irish Protestant who failed in every way to understand the 'Canadiens'. He proclaimed once: 'The world has never witnessed such a spectacle as eighty thousand Orangemen from Canada fighting or dying to save Roman Catholics in Belgium.' He placed Protestant clergymen in Quebec as recruiting officers and insisted on the use of English in training French-Canadian soldiers who often did not know the language. He authorized very few purely French-Canadian regiments despite the fact that the Royal Twenty-second, the famous 'Vandoos', raised entirely in Quebec, had a wonderful record at Courcelette and elsewhere. Without detracting from the amazing energy the Minister of Militia displayed in dispatching the first contingent across the Atlantic in such short order, it must be admitted that he was the kind of politician the Canadian people might have been wise not to elect. Sir Robert Borden thought so and dismissed General Hughes in 1916, but not before he had done irreparable damage in Quebec.

We may conclude that the Canadiens were not all as indifferent as their opponents claimed, that many Anglo-Canadians shared some of their views, and that things might have been much better had the government handled this delicate situation with less intolerance and more wisdom. It is true that enthusiasm in Quebec for the War sagged quickly and that, as the call went out for more and more volunteers, French-Canadian enlistments fell behind. But if too little was given by Quebec, altogether too much was expected. The Canadiens were expected to have the same enthusiastic feelings as their English-speaking fellow citizens and to take the same patriotic action in support of Great Britain. Yet the people of Quebec had no deep attachment to England; a conquered race themselves, they tended to support the underdog, as in the Boer War, and often regarded England's colonial conflicts with suspicion. Many of them could not be convinced that the First World War was much different from the others. 'It is the work of maniacs who glorify a horrible butchery in which people slaughter each other without knowing why.' So said Henri Bourassa.

Also, the recruiting orators, English or French, could not persuade the people of Quebec that their freedom in language, law and religion depended on British justice. They refused to believe that, if England were defeated, they might lose this freedom. The Canadiens had been well and perhaps truthfully taught that they owed their freedom not to a generous Britain, but to their own strength and to their eternal vigilance against repeated threats from English-speaking Canada. While many outstanding French-Canadian lawyers, judges and parliamentarians fully appreciated the value of the British connection, the majority in Quebec probably agreed with the Nationalist spokesman who declared: 'We French-speaking Canadians owe nothing to England but forgiveness.' This was, of course, a despicable attitude in the eyes of all good Englishmen, but understandable in a people who had not been steeped in the textbook romance of British history and the glory of the Empire. The pious French-Canadian 'habitant' had been trained, first and foremost, to be devoted to his own race. He was deeply attached to his family, his province and his religion, not to the British Empire. Thus the distant struggle in Europe did not touch his imagination or stir his feelings as profoundly as it did the rest of Canada. The whole long history of Quebec made it inevitable that the introduction of compulsory military service overseas would cause a tragic rupture in Canadian unity.

Political Battle-lines

Sir Robert Borden, cheered on by his Conservative followers, introduced the Military Service Bill into the House of Commons on June 11, 1917. The European situation, he frankly admitted, now compelled him to break the promise which he had given to the country previously. Voluntary recruiting methods had failed to produce the men needed 'to maintain the Canadian army in the field as one of the finest fighting units in the Empire'. In the ensuing debates, it soon became apparent that the conscription issue was going to split the Liberal party. Many English-speaking Liberals rose to support the Prime Minister, to praise him for his courageous stand, while only a few joined the members from Quebec in condemning the government.

Voluntary methods, the opposition claimed, had not failed; General Sir Sam Hughes and his bungling recruiting officers were the ones to blame, not the system. And what about conscripting wealth? Why should a man be forced to give his life or 'disembowel a fellow human' while wartime profiteers enjoyed their gains? All they ever did was make patriotic speeches and buy Victory Bonds. Was it fair or reasonable to expect some men to join up, to endure the dirt and the danger of the trenches for $1.10 a day, while others stayed at home and gathered in 'fat wages running from four to twelve dollars a day'? Conscript wealth also, take away the huge profits, raise the soldiers' pay, limit wages, control prices, make the burdens and sacrifices more equal—then the volunteers would come forward again.

Why should Canada introduce conscription? South Africa and Australia did not have it; they understood their limitations. What was Canada trying to prove by keeping up with the great military powers of Europe? Of course the war effort must continue, but conscription would do more harm than good. 'If this Military Service Bill is passed,' Laurier declared, 'we will face a cleavage which may rend and tear this Canada of ours down to its very roots.'

As if to underline Laurier's warning, the mass meetings in the province of Quebec became larger, more frequent and more violent. Huge crowds of ten to fifteen thousand angry people gathered night after night to hear Nationalist speakers tell them that 'you should go to jail or be shot' before accepting conscription. Caution and common sense were thrown to the wind. 'If you have anything to shoot with don't be afraid to use it. Be resolved to sprinkle the soil of Quebec with your blood instead of reddening the soil of Flanders for the benefit of England.' After listening to such words as these, the meetings broke up and excited crowds moved through the streets, smashing windows, wrecking the offices of conscription newspapers, chanting 'Down with Borden', and finally, after one stormy meeting, dynamiting the country home of Sir Hugh Graham, the publisher of the Conservative *Montreal Star*.

The government met this threat by calling out special police—who usually stood aside, doing nothing, in sympathy with the crowds—and by closing down the most violent of the French-Canadian newspapers. Some extremists in Ontario were prepared to take the law into their own hands. Led by the Grand Master of the Orange Lodge, they urged that 'if the occasion should arise, two hundred and fifty thousand Orangemen, too old for overseas service, could be enlisted in a month to put down the province of Quebec.' More so than many people realize, the Dominion of Canada in June, July and August, 1917, was on the verge of civil war.

Despite these signs of serious resistance, the Military Service Bill was passed in August by a large majority; over twenty English-speaking Liberals voted with the government; and plans were made to issue the first draft call sometime within the next two months. However, this was just the beginning, not the end of the trouble. The Borden administration had to face a general election, not because they wanted to let the people vote on conscription, but because the legal life of parliament had expired. A general election, already overdue, had to be held before the end of the year. The date was finally set for December 17 so that, all during fall, while Canadian and British soldiers were fighting and dying in the mud at Passchendaele, the bitter quarrel over conscription raged on to its climax in Canada.

The Conservatives were on shaky ground. It was by no means certain, at first, that they would win the forthcoming election. Rightly or wrongly, many people blamed the government for the rising cost of living, the profiteering, the scandals and the failure of voluntary recruiting methods. Honourable to the highest degree himself, the Prime Minister suffered from the behaviour of colleagues like Hughes and of a few profiteering Tories. Furthermore, the government decided at this time to pay for the common stock of the Canadian Northern Railway—although it had been declared worthless by a special investigating commission. This step was not popular with a nation already disturbed by the influence of big business in politics. Perhaps because of this growing discontent with their administration, the Conservatives forced through parliament two most undemocratic measures, designed to make sure that they would win the election.

The first of these acts allowed the party in power to manipulate some of the soldiers' vote to their own advantage. Instead of voting for a candidate in his own home riding, a soldier could have his vote applied to any electoral district in Canada—especially one where the government candidate might be defeated. There was little doubt, of course, how the soldier would cast his ballot. Much more important than this, however, was the Wartime Election Act which gave the vote to women; not to all women, as a reward for working in the fields and factories, nor to those who already held the franchise in provincial elections, but only to female relatives of soldiers—women who, more than likely, would support the government and conscription. This Act also took the right to vote away from a great many immigrants who had become naturalized Canadians. Enemy aliens, the Conservatives said. Perhaps so, but it must be admitted that thousands of these people had come to Canada to escape European militarism and undoubtedly would have voted against conscription. As one historian has written: 'In no other country in the world which claimed to be democratic had such a measure ever (or since!) been enacted into law.'

These two somewhat disreputable election acts, combined with the emotional appeal of conscription in the English-speaking parts of Canada, should have been enough to assure the Conservatives of victory. To make doubly certain, Borden —assisted by Sir Clifford Sifton, that mastermind of all previous Liberal revolts— set out to create a coalition between the Conservatives and those Liberals who favoured conscription. Several weeks of intensive bargaining—dozens of local meetings, interviews with rival editors, telegrams back and forth across the country, politicians scurrying in and out of Ottawa—were required before a majority of English-speaking Liberals swung over to the idea of a coalition. By mid-October, however, Borden was able to form a 'Union government' of ten Liberal and thirteen Conservative cabinet ministers supported by almost all the members of parliament except those from Quebec. The battle-lines were now more sharply drawn than ever before. 'At last,' the Toronto *News* exclaimed, 'we can show those sluggards from Quebec who is boss in Canada.'

The Election of 1917

The next two months witnessed the most virulent and probably the most disgrace- ful scenes in the whole course of Canadian history. With unlimited funds, with practically every English-language newspaper, with high-powered speakers and writers, with all but one provincial government and almost the entire Protestant clergy behind them, the Unionists set out with a vengeance to show Quebec who was indeed the boss in Canada. No claim of patriotism can justify the campaign of vile abuse and falsehood which so many Unionists waged against all those who disagreed with them. No reason can be found—not even by those who somehow managed to convince themselves that the Allies would lose the War if Canada did not have conscription—to excuse the passionate appeals they made to jealousy, self-interest, and racial, religious and class prejudice.

Each wild statement made by the extremists in Quebec was paraded in all its gory details and attributed to Laurier. The once-revered Liberal leader was denounced by former friends, who must have known they were lying, as a traitor to his country. 'A vote for Laurier is a vote for the Kaiser.' Laurier was trying 'to open doors to office with a key stained by the blood of our boys in Flanders'. So the great billboards across the country proclaimed to the people. The Nationalists were condemned in unrestrained language by the very Conservative party who, in the previous election, had employed Bourassa's influence to get into power. Workers were stirred to anger and resentment—the penalties were to be paid later—by vote-seeking demagogues who denounced all rich men alike, set class against class and promised impossible reforms to control 'the money-grabbing violators of our fair democracy'. Clergymen preached blood-and-thunder sermons instead of tolerance and Christian understanding. Speaking with all the authority of their high office yet often revealing a glaring lack of knowledge about national and world affairs, abusing the priests in Quebec for doing no more and frequently much less than they themselves were doing, the Protestant clergy

A Solid Quebec Will Vote to Rule All Canada Only a Solid Ontario Can Defeat Them

TOO LATE!

Citizens' Union Committee

A poster used in Ontario for the federal election in 1917

yielded to the popular passions of the moment and became fervent champions of the Unionist cause.

Although the tide was running with them, the Unionists took one final important step to assure themselves of victory. During the campaign, it soon became apparent that English-speaking farmers, pleading the importance of their work and the scarcity of labour, were not going to have their sons drafted if they could help it. Recognizing some justice in what the farmers said and also keeping an eye on their votes, the Unionists promised not to draft farm labour. Perhaps they intended to keep their word but the fact remains that, shortly after being returned to power, Unionist politicians broke their promise. Farmers who had been quite willing to vote other men's sons into the army were furious with this breach of faith. They lost all confidence in Liberals and Conservatives alike and formed radical political parties of their own that played an important role in post-war Canadian politics.

It would be quite wrong to assume that the methods of the Liberal party in English-speaking Canada were one whit better than those of the Unionists. Disregarding the long-run effects of their words and actions, Liberal leaders were just as guilty of using any device to catch votes as were their opponents. Here, for instance, is the kind of appeal the Liberals made to the men overseas: 'Soldiers! While you with true British courage have faced appalling conditions, political vultures at home have been fattening upon public expenditures. Colossal fortunes have been amassed by Government pets through exorbitant profits, who have made no personal sacrifices. The political hangers-on at Ottawa have been raking in gold while you and your comrades were being raked by German shells.' Is it any wonder that many Canadian soldiers returned disillusioned from overseas?

But if the election campaign of 1917 was bad in English-speaking Canada it was far, far worse in Quebec. Anglo-Canadians, by their lack of understanding and their crude recruiting methods, may have asked for trouble in the first place, but in the two months preceding election day the French-Canadian extremists passed the bounds of all understanding. No words can possibly describe the tirades of utter hatred—against England, against the War and conscription, against the rest of Canada, against anything outside the cherished, selfish interests of Quebec— which poured out from the wild Nationalist orators and the incredibly violent Nationalist press. Their attacks on French-Canadian Unionists who dared to support Borden were the bitterest ever known even in Quebec's stormy politics.

So thoroughly organized was the Nationalist campaign that Unionist candidates were completely prevented from discussing their own platform. Unbelievable though it may seem, Unionists were howled down in every single meeting they tried to hold; revolver shots, stones and broken glass threatened their lives; police escorts were required wherever they travelled; and when their safety could no longer be guaranteed, their remaining meetings had to be cancelled! Nor did the Unionist newspapers in Quebec fare any better. Presses were smashed to pieces, editors were mobbed, their homes damaged and at least two of them were almost lynched by a murderous crowd. The situation became so serious that Borden's scheduled visit to Montreal was cancelled. A point had been reached where the Prime Minister of the Dominion of Canada could not safely speak in one of his own provinces!

A Divided Nation

When the ballots were counted it seemed, at first glance, that the Unionists, with 153 members elected, had won a sweeping victory. Laurier and the Liberals had carried 62 of the 65 Quebec seats but only 20 in all the other provinces. English Canada and French Canada were obviously ranged against each other more definitely, and with more bitterness and suspicion, than ever before in our history. However, the Liberals would have elected more candidates but for the soldiers' vote. Two hundred and sixteen thousand servicemen voted for the Unionists (only 18,500 for the Liberals) and these ballots were manipulated, according to plan, to give Borden's followers more seats in the House of Commons than they should have had. Also, it is important to notice, before condemning Quebec too strongly, that 504,000 English-speaking Canadians, or almost one in every two, voted against compulsory overseas service. This number would have been greatly increased had the farmers known beforehand that the Military Service Act would be applied to them. In other words, Canada was far more divided on the conscription issue than the parliamentary results revealed.

With almost fifty per cent of the civilian population opposed to conscription, it is not surprising that the authorities had great difficulty enforcing the Military Service Act. In the first draft call of 404,000 single men, 381,000 applied for exemption and well over two-thirds of these were allowed! Thousands of men refused to respond when called or deserted at the first opportunity; a military police force, formed for the purpose, worked with the Mounties to rout these men out from their hiding places; mines, lumber camps, farms and at least two Roman Catholic colleges were raided, sometimes under gunfire and with loss of life. In these and other drastic ways about 30,000 defaulters were apprehended and turned over to the Army, but as many more were said to be hiding in the bush country of Ontario and Quebec when the War ended. In Quebec City, rioting mobs destroyed the office and burnt the files of the Military Service Act registrar, the mayor refused to restore order or read the riot act, 1,800 soldiers were called out, civilians and servicemen opened fire on each other and for three days, according to reports submitted to the House of Commons, civil war did come to Canada.

In many ways, these conditions became worse during the remaining months of the War. In April 1918, when the second German offensive was at its height and the Channel ports were threatened, the Canadian government received an urgent appeal from Lloyd George to speed every possible man to the front. Despite the abuse heaped on him, Borden decided to cancel many of the previously granted exemptions, including those to farmers' sons. The farmers hid their sons, committed perjury, demonstrated and marched on Ottawa, and threatened to sue the government before the Privy Council of Great Britain for a breach of faith! Exasperated and angry, the federal authorities gave dictatorial powers to the Military Police, and the law courts began to hand down life imprisonment and even death sentences to defaulters.

Yet with all these difficulties—with farmers ranged against city-dwellers, Anglo-Canadians against French Canadians, Roman Catholics against Protestants, workers against employers, soldiers against civilians, with class divisions exaggerated and Canadian unity threatened—with all this, the Military Service Act dragged in only 60,000 recruits of dubious quality. Voluntary methods, intelligently applied, probably would have raised at least as many men. Whatever the reasons—exhaustion of manpower, too large an Army, indifference, hatred of war, isolation from Europe—conscription in Canada was a failure.

The Road to Independence

A New Source of National Pride
The first Canadian contingent arrived in England for advanced training at Salisbury Plain during October 1914, and were greeted with mixed feelings of pride and criticism. They were, it was said, a rough-and-ready-looking crew. More than one brawl had already broken out between them and the British troops stationed near Salisbury and people agreed that the Canadians—perhaps because they had too much money to spend—were the ones to blame. They were 'sloppy and undisciplined'; they did not snap to attention like the British Tommy

A Canadian battalion goes 'over the top', 1916.

when the National Anthem was played; and they saluted their officers, if at all, in a 'most casual and indifferent way'. In fact, Canadian privates did not seem to know their proper place; they frequented the same restaurants as did the officers and even dared, so it was reported, to call their superiors by first name! 'We must not expect the Canadians,' one newspaper cautioned the angry local residents, 'to behave as our men do. Anglo-Saxon though they are, they come to us from a rude frontier country where class and rank are unimportant.'

Time and good training revealed that the devil-may-care attitude and the extreme individualism of the Canadians were a final source of great strength on the Western Front. The Canadian Corps became not only a credit to the Empire but a source of tremendous and very justifiable pride to their own countrymen. This pride in the fighting record of our soldiers roused a stronger feeling of nationalism and a growing desire for the recognition of Canada as an independent country within the British Commonwealth of Nations.

Yet all this might not have happened if the War Office had had its way. Lord Kitchener did not plan to allow the Canadians to fight as one national unit. 'I have decided,' he told General Hughes, 'to divide your men up among the British regiments. They will be very little use to us as they are.' With an insolence which must have staggered the great Lord Kitchener, the Canadian Minister of Militia, when instructed to carry out this order, replied, 'I am damned if I will,' and stomped out of the War Office! Thereby, General Sir Sam Hughes did a great service for his country. Instead of losing its identity at the very beginning of the War, the Canadian Corps went on to become one of the finest fighting forces on any front.

We already know the appalling conditions which all men, English, French and German, friend and foe, had to endure in that utterly wasteful war of attrition. Nothing should be allowed ever to detract from the courage and stoic endurance of the soldiers from every country who went through the holocaust of the First World War. As for our own nation, successive generations of Canadians should always remember their countrymen who fought and died at Ypres, the Somme, Vimy Ridge and Passchendaele. Nor should the conscription controversy obscure the fact that the Canadian army was strong enough in the closing weeks of the War to spearhead the great offensive which, starting at Amiens, broke through the Hindenburg Line and carried them on to Mons. Many Canadians also served in the Royal Navy, the merchant marine or their own tiny navy, building up a small group of seasoned men who, in later years, helped to expand the Royal Canadian Navy into one of the largest and most skilful convoy fleets in the world. The many Canadians who joined the Royal Flying Corps took readily to the man-to-man combat of those days and among them were numbered some of the famous Allied aces of the War.

Sir Robert Borden Speaks His Mind

Canada's lack of military preparedness in 1914 was reflected in the fact that officers of the British regular army—first General A. H. Alderson and then General Sir Julien Byng—commanded the Canadian Corps during the early stages of the War. Also, almost every first-grade staff officer was a British regular and the Corps, although it fought as a unit, was under the absolute control of British Headquarters in France. In time, the Canadian government became more and more dissatisfied with this state of affairs and began to request not only a greater control over the destiny of its own forces but also some voice in the overall direction of the War. This desire for more recognition and power was due to increasing national pride in the achievements of our junior officers and men, to the development of strong differences of opinion with Great Britain over the conduct of the War, to the growing lack of confidence in the British High Command, and above all to the mounting casualty lists and the feeling that the Canadian Corps was used too frequently in the most dangerous places. (Of 420,000 Canadian soldiers sent overseas, 58,000 were killed and 175,000 were wounded.) As a result of all these factors and in deference to the rising wartime tide of nationalism, a Canadian soldier, General Sir Arthur Currie, was placed in command of the Canadian Corps in June 1917, after the battle of Vimy Ridge.

In his diary for June 1918, Sir Robert Borden, writing in England while the British and French were still trying to hold the final German offensive in check, had this to say about Sir Arthur Currie: 'I am convinced that the present depressing situation in which the British find themselves is due to lack of organization, lack of system, lack of preparation, lack of foresight and incompetent leadership. If the British Army had made the same preparations to meet the Germans as did General Currie and the officers and men of the Canadian forces, the German offensive could not possibly have succeeded as it did. To give you an example of what work will accomplish and what casual indifference and indolence will leave undone: last winter the Canadian Corps put out 375,000 yards of barbed wire entanglements by which every trench was thoroughly protected. On the other hand, the three nearby British Corps Commanders put out less than 100,000 yards between them and one had employed his men in building lawn tennis courts. . . . The Canadian Corps is probably the best organized unit of its size in the world today and this is due not only to the courage, resourcefulness and intelligence of the officers and men but also to Currie's great ability. I believe he is the ablest Corps Commander in the British Force.' Thus did Canada's Prime Minister pay tribute to this overweight, round-shouldered, unsoldierly-looking, former insurance executive from Victoria, B.C., who rose from the rank of private to command the whole Canadian Army Corps. The soldiers who served under General Sir Arthur Currie undoubtedly shared the Canadian Prime Minister's confidence in their commander and it is perhaps true that he revealed as much skill and certainly as much concern for the lives of his men as did any Allied general.

Although military control of our own forces and the appointment of Sir Arthur Currie received more public attention, questions relating to the general management of the War were to have much greater significance for Canada in the long run. During the first two and a half years, Prime Minister Asquith's government, inefficient and torn with personal jealousies, adhered to the principle, laid down by Lord Elgin at the 1907 Imperial Conference, that the responsibility for foreign policy could not be shared with their self-governing colonies. 'We recognize,' they tried to explain to the Canadian government, 'your right to have some share in a war in which Canada is playing so big a part. However, we do not see any way in which this can be done in actual practice. Since no scheme is practicable then it is very undesirable that the question should be raised.'

What Borden thought about this situation may be gathered from the reply he dispatched back across the Atlantic. 'The Canadian Government,' he wrote, 'has received just what information about the conduct of the War as could be gleaned from the newspapers and nothing more. Plans of campaigns have been made and unmade, vital steps have been taken, postponed or rejected without consulting our government in any way. . . . Indecision, inertia, doubt and hesitation have been altogether too conspicuous in the British cabinet. . . . One very able cabinet minister told me during my recent visit to England that the chief shortage there, in addition to shells, was of brains. . . . It can hardly be expected that we shall put 400,000 men in the field and receive no more consideration than if we were toy soldiers. Is this war being waged by the United Kingdom alone or is it a war waged by the whole Empire?'

The Imperial War Cabinet

Despite several other equally outspoken letters almost demanding some voice for Canada, Borden's protests received very little attention while the Asquith government remained in power. However, in December 1916, after several weeks of political manoeuvring, Asquith was ousted and a new coalition was formed under the aggressive leadership of Lloyd George. Although his cabinet had its full share of inefficient men appointed purely for political reasons, Lloyd George at least recognized that self-governing colonies were entitled to a share in helping to direct the Empire war. Also, he frankly admitted that some 'fresh blood and new ideas' were needed in England. Therefore, Lloyd George and his colleagues decided to create an administrative body to be called the Imperial War Cabinet. It was to consist of five specially selected ministers from the government of Great Britain sitting with the prime ministers of the overseas dominions. The Colonial Office immediately sent out invitations asking the dominion prime ministers to come to London as soon as possible and there, on March 20, 1917, the first true council for the Empire began its meetings.

These meetings of the Imperial War Cabinet were a great success. Its overseas members had access to all the information so long withheld from them; they freely discussed the most vital questions of Empire policy; they helped to make decisions dealing with the conduct of the War, the supply of men and munitions, war finance and certain peace proposals. As expected, statesmen like Borden, with his honest, down-to-earth ideas, and the brilliant General Jan Smuts, another great Boer imperialist from South Africa, brought a welcome fresh approach to all these Empire problems. The most colourful personality among them was a gnome-like little man described by his enemies as 'too stubborn to listen to reason, too loud to be ignored and too small to hit'. This was the amazing Billy Hughes, a former ship's cook, dock-hand and fish pedlar, the founder of Australia's Labour party. The Australian Premier may not have added much enlightenment to the discussions of the Imperial War Cabinet, but with his hot temper and lurid vocabulary, which 'could peel the bark off a gum tree', he certainly made sure that its sittings were seldom dull! The Imperial War Cabinet is important only because the dominion prime ministers met with their five British colleagues, not as colonial subordinates, but, for the first time, as absolute equals. In other words, it was another landmark on Canada's road towards independence within the British Commonwealth of Nations.

It may now be seen that the First World War, contrary to all expectations, did not check the growing desire for independence in the self-governing colonies. Instead, it hastened the further development of those nationalist feelings that had become apparent, especially in Canada, long before 1914. The War emphasized differences in outlook and customs among the colonies; it fostered a pride in the fighting record of their soldiers, strengthened their economic life and gave them a new sense of power and accomplishment. All this was recognized by the British government when Lloyd George, yielding to pressure from Canada, summoned the dominion prime ministers to meet as equals with the mother country in the Imperial War Cabinet. Once this principle of equality had been established there could be no return to colonialism. As a result of the War, each self-governing member of the British Empire was more firmly resolved than ever before to be master of its own destiny.

part 3
between two wars

10 VICTORY WITHOUT PEACE

In the Wake of War

On January 18, 1919, in the great hall of the Quai d'Orsay, Georges 'Tiger' Clemenceau, the hard-bitten old Premier of France, called to order the most important diplomatic gathering in the history of international relations. Paris was not the place to hold a peace conference; it was too full of bitter memories. Paris was the capital of a country that mourned a million and a quarter dead. Besides these terrible military casualties and the inevitable ruin of cities, factories and farms, the civilian population of enemy-occupied France had endured four years of looting and insult at the hands of the Hun. Not fifty years had passed since the Prussian Guards of Bismarck had marched in triumph down the Champs-Elysées after another war, sending up in flames a district of Paris under the eyes of its mayor. The mayor was a young man named Georges Clemenceau.

During the Paris Peace Conference, President Wilson asked: 'Pray, M. Clemenceau, have you ever been to Germany?'

'No, sir! But twice in my lifetime the Germans have been to France.'

More so than in any other Allied nation, hatred, vengeance and fear prevailed in France.

Continuing Violence in Europe

The Armistice had brought victory but not peace. The violent and brutal side of human nature, once released and encouraged in organized warfare, was not subdued by the mere stroke of a pen. Throughout Europe, thousands of wartime prisoners broke loose, pillaging and murdering their way towards home. Many Allied and enemy soldiers revolted against their officers and ransacked the towns where they were held awaiting discharge. Freed at last from Hapsburg rule, the races of the crumpled Austro-Hungarian Empire formed governments for non-existent countries and fought each other in a jumbled confusion of local battles, desperate in their cruelty, each designed to conquer land while the Peace Conference deliberated. Elsewhere, Greek and Turk, Italian and Serb, Pole and Lithuanian, Magyar and Romanian waged unrestrained warfare against one another, grabbing for the spoils before it was too late. Under the terms of the Armistice, the blockade of Germany still continued: starvation and disease stalked through the German streets. Those who could afford it shipped their children to Norway or Sweden, but the children of the poor died in droves. The entire social structure and national life of Germany threatened to collapse beneath the stress of hunger and malnutrition.

Chaos, poverty and misery among the masses, hatred and violence in the hearts of men—these were the inevitable results of war and the seeds of revolution. So

Karl Marx, the father of communism, had prophesied in his writings, and so Europe in 1919 seemed to prove. Kindled by the example of the Bolsheviks in Russia, discontent flamed up into communist revolution in Germany, Italy, Hungary and other parts of central Europe. The gigantic social upheaval going on in Russia itself was aggravated when the Western Powers sent military aid to the counter-revolutionary 'White Russian' armies and landed their own troops at Murmansk, Archangel and Vladivostok. The French fleet bombarded the Black Sea ports, a British army attacked from the south, the Baltic states revolted and in the Far East the Japanese poured thousands of soldiers into Siberia. As the statesmen debated in Paris, the worst civil war in all history raged on to claim over 10 million lives before the Red Army of Lenin, Trotsky and Stalin finally triumphed. In Hungary, the Magyar nobility crushed their communist opponents with almost unbelievable barbarism.

Elsewhere, other communist revolts were quelled but not before an ugly new form of tyranny and dictatorship, soon to be known as fascism, had made its first appearance. Even as the victorious powers planned the peace to end all wars, Benito Mussolini and his Black Shirt squads were clubbing the socialists and communists of Italy into submission. Thereby an evil force was released which would soon sweep democracy—the way of life for which the Allies had supposedly fought—from the face of Europe and reach its climax in the goose-stepping hordes of Hitler. In 1919, the year of peace, events in Europe were germinating a second world war and in its wake the prophecies of Karl Marx came much closer to fulfilment.

Unrest in the British Empire
Turbulent events beyond the borders of Europe also distracted the Peace Conference and spelled out trouble for the future. Southern Ireland, inflamed by the Sinn Fein party now demanding complete independence from English control, erupted into rebellion again early in 1919. The British government dispatched forty-three thousand troops across the Irish Sea. Winston Churchill, by this time reinstated in the British cabinet as Minister for War, claimed that these men were a hand-picked force of superior quality, but in truth they were a crude and at times a drunken lot. The methods of the Sinn Feiners were brutal, to say the least, but Churchill's 'Black and Tans' held their own as far as brutality was concerned. Conditions soon became so bad that Sir Herbert Samuel, one of the leaders of the Liberal party in England, was provoked to say: 'If what we are doing in Ireland today had occurred in Germany all Britain would be ringing with a denunciation of the tyranny of the Kaiser.'

Although the Irish tried in vain to get a hearing before the Peace Conference —most of their leaders were in British jails or had a price on their heads—they attracted much attention in the United States. Taking strange liberties with diplomacy and helping to strain relations between Lloyd George and President Wilson, both the American Senate and the House of Representatives passed resolutions favouring Irish independence. After a hair-raising escape from England, Eamon de Valera, the Sinn Fein leader, triumphantly toured the United

States seeking funds for the cause. He received a welcome such as only the Americans can stage and was hailed wherever he went as the 'President of the Irish Republic'. In due course, Southern Ireland, as Eire, did become an independent republic and de Valera was elected its president, but not before four years of murderous civil war had staggered the weary Titan with an added burden of debt and hatred.

While the Black and Tans were trying to subdue Ireland, another British army was being employed on a somewhat similar mission in Egypt. Despite repeated promises to the contrary, British troops remained there to protect the Suez Canal —the 'life line to India'—and the country became virtually a British protectorate. During the First World War, Great Britain took steps to strengthen her position, and increase her unpopularity, in Egypt. She deposed the Khedive and replaced him with a ruler more to her own liking; she compelled the natives to sell food at below-market prices, and promised to pay later; she drafted Egyptians against their will and contrary to her own assurances into the army and paid them one-fiftieth of the wage received by a British private; and under the pressure of war she used Egypt as a base for General Allenby's campaign against the Turks in Palestine.

It was not surprising, therefore, that the Egyptians, like the Irish, tried to send a delegation to the Peace Conference, hoping to rid themselves of the British and secure their independence. Great Britain, however, had no intention of yielding up her hard-won, strategic position in the land of the Nile. Zaghlul Pasha, the recognized leader of the Arab nationalist movement in Egypt, was arrested and deported to Malta where he cooled his heels until the Conference disbanded. When Zaghlul's followers rose in protest against such high-handed methods, General Allenby's army, still on the spot, was put to good use. Although faced with continuing riots and assassinations and the need to use martial law many times, although compelled to deport other nationalist leaders and to support, later on, the disgraceful Farouk as king, the British managed to hold Egypt as an unwilling vassal until after the Second World War. But the day of reckoning was only postponed and it may be said that the long shadow of Colonel Nasser and Egyptian independence fell across the British life line to India even in 1919.

On the very day Zaghlul Pasha was shipped off to Malta, a relatively unknown, wizened little man named Gandhi issued the first of his many anti-British orders to the Hindu masses of India. A strange mixture of saint and cunning politician, this mysterious, impractical leader—soon to be revered by millions of Hindus as the Mahatma, the 'Great Soul'—commanded his followers to celebrate a *hartal,* 'a day of quiet rest from all labour'. In less flowery western words, Gandhi ordered a one-day general strike against the British raj and, by some blind reasoning, convinced himself that it would be conducted without violence. A peaceful general strike in a country where the recognized nationalist leader, next to Gandhi himself, was G. K. Tilak, a terrible rabble-rouser who worshipped the blood-drinking goddess Kali and urged murdering the British to satisfy her thirst! *Swaraj*—Home Rule for India! Already this clarion call had roused the Punjab and Bengal to revolution, forcing the British government to execute over

Near Ahmedabad, India, in 1931, over a hundred thousand Hindus and Moslems gathered to hear Gandhi speak on independence for India.

sixty Hindu leaders and transport as many more to the remote Seychelles Islands for life. Gandhi, it is true, did not believe in violence and he cautioned his followers to use only passive resistance against the Europeans; 'soul force', he called it, instead of brute force. Even the Mahatma, however, preached his message in a language so passionate that the doctrine of non-violence, when it reached the hearts of his illiterate audience, became a flame of hatred and revolution.

It was almost to be expected, therefore, that Mahatma Gandhi's first day of passive resistance in India should become an orgy of bloodshed. During the second week of April, 1919, huge Hindu mobs rioted out of control, burning government buildings, tearing up telephone wires and railway tracks, wrecking trains, destroying any sign of western civilization they could lay their hands on and murdering scores of Europeans. The climax came at Amritsar, a city in the Punjab, where, in addition to massacre and destruction of property, two European bank managers were burned alive. When the excited mob gathered again next day in an enclosed public square, Brigadier General Reginald Dyer and a detachment of British soldiers fired on them time and again, killing over four hundred Hindus and wounding three times as many more. Possibly the British should not have been in India in the first place; perhaps the troops commanded by Dyer should not have fired without warning or continued their attack after the Hindus fled; perhaps they were justifiably provoked. At any rate, the 'massacre at Amritsar' on April 13 rang around the world and was entered as a black page in the annals of British history. And in this way, while the Peace Conference deliberated in Paris, the strange career of Mahatma Gandhi was launched in India.

In the years to come, Gandhi's doctrines of *Swaraj* and soul force, his imprisonments and long fasts, kept his country in a constant turmoil until the British withdrew from India after the Second World War. Then, by some strange twist of history, during the ensuing welter of civil war between the Moslems and the Hindus for control in India, the peace-loving little man whose years were so marred with violence met his own death from an assassin's bullet.

Civil War in China

To round out this part of our story, we should briefly note that brute force also ruled in the Far East. During the late stages of the War, the central government of China completely collapsed and ruthless local warlords seized power in all the provinces. Their ragged, undisciplined armies, forced to live off the land, plundered and killed the hapless peasants by the tens of thousands. In 1919, disease, starvation, murder and civil strife claimed more lives in China than did four years of warfare on the Western Front. Yet the statesmen in Paris, to their future sorrow, remained callous and indifferent. To the western world, sprawling, backward China was still an easy prey to be exploited; the more divided and torn she was internally, the easier it would be for the imperialist powers to keep the mining, railway, banking and other 'rights' that they had seized in earlier years. Unlike Ireland and Egypt, China did manage to have a delegation admitted to the Peace Conference—for the Allies had persuaded her to declare war on Germany—but the Chinese soon left for home, humiliated by the offhand, contemptuous treatment they received in Paris.

Under these circumstances, the local government at Canton—one of the many claiming to rule China—appealed to Russia for assistance. Preoccupied though they were with their own gigantic problems, the communists responded quickly and sent skilled organizers to help the Chinese. Thus, with the West in default, the doctrines of Karl Marx were first planted in the fertile soil of poverty-stricken China, and the way was opened for the civil war which broke out in 1928 between the Chinese communists and the nationalists of General Chiang Kai-shek. This struggle also provided the Japanese with an opportunity to attack China twice during the 1930s while the Western Powers were absorbed in the problems of the Great Depression. These Sino-Japanese wars blended eventually into World War Two and did not end until August 1945, when American aviators dropped their atom bombs on Hiroshima and Nagasaki. Perhaps, when the history of our turbulent century is finally written, the starting point for the Second World War will be placed, not in the heart of Europe with Hitler's attack on Poland, but in the tragically ignored Far East with Japanese aggression against a China torn by civil war.

Meeting after four years of devastating warfare, in a city of vengeance and hatred, with violence and tumult resounding all about them, desperately pressed for time before chaos, starvation and revolution spread any farther, with the fate of millions of people resting in their hands, the statesmen in Paris indeed faced a stupendous task. Never before in history was the need so great for wisdom, sympathy, unselfishness and forgiveness among the nations and the leaders of men.

The Big Three

Behind Closed Doors

During the critical last two months of the Peace Conference, no one in Paris knew for sure what was going on in the little library of the Place des Etats-Unis. Its great oak doors remained closed day after day and behind them a strange and somewhat disturbing drama was taking place. While Woodrow Wilson attended seriously to all the proceedings, Lloyd George and Clemenceau had already secured absolutely everything they wanted for Britain and France and were not interested in any more prolonged discussions, however much they might affect the welfare of other nations. Vittorio Orlando of Italy appeared to be somewhat ineffectual. Although relations between the four statesmen seemed cordial enough, visitors to the library sensed that beneath the surface things were not as they should be. Those who were admitted to that inner sanctum had no idea what transpired after they left it. They appeared as directed, gave their reports, answered a few cursory questions and were dismissed.

In this way, through 145 completely secret sessions, four men—three to be exact since Orlando hardly counted—drafted the peace treaties ending the First World War. While they met behind locked doors, the other delegates to the Conference idled away their time, serving on minor commissions, giving advice when asked for it but otherwise being absolutely powerless to influence any decision. During the entire Conference only six meetings were held with all the delegates present. These 'Plenary Sessions' brought the delegates together to approve, without discussion, a program decided in advance by the statesmen of the Big Powers. They were a farce, a mere sop to the pride of the smaller nations and to world opinion. If any speaker dared to criticize, Clemenceau could be relied upon to ride him into submission from his speaker's chair. The Big Three, having already made their decisions in secret conclave, were obviously bored.

In some ways, the dictatorial procedure was justifiable. The first Plenary Session, opening the Peace Conference on January 18, proved too large a meeting—and much too talkative—to be efficient. 'Peace by public clamour' was the way Lloyd George condemned not only the noisy meeting itself but also the newspaper publicity given to it. As we shall see shortly, the Big Three each had their own motives for wanting to exclude the press but it must be admitted that secrecy was desirable for other reasons. Working primarily in the interest of France, the Paris press also sold their independence to any with a case to present

(Left) Orlando, Lloyd George, Clemenceau and Wilson. (Right) Woodrow Wilson surrounded by an admiring and hopeful crowd in Paris.

and did their utmost to influence the delegates by a daily stream of purchased propaganda. Furthermore, it is true that as long as the smaller nations were allowed a voice in the proceedings, the Conference remained deadlocked, wasting precious time on a multitude of selfish, conflicting claims. For these reasons, the Big Powers—the ones possessing the military and naval strength and who felt from the beginning that they had the sole right to make the peace—gradually assumed more control. By the end of March three men, meeting privately within Wilson's library, had taken the fate of the world into their own hands and by their wills moulded the destiny of unborn generations. It may have been the only way, but it was a strange ending to a war for democracy.

The Prophet from the West
'Woodrow Wilson has come here with Fourteen Points while the good Lord himself only had ten.' This was the way the cynical, atheistic Premier of France referred to one of the most widely publicized speeches in all history and this was the offhand attitude which Clemenceau adopted towards Wilson's idealism all during the Peace Conference. On January 8, 1918, almost a year before the Armistice, the President of the United States had delivered his famous Fourteen Points address to Congress outlining with passionate conviction the principles for

which America was fighting—or thought she was fighting. Sixty million copies of this speech, translated into some twenty different languages, had been scattered all over the world; countless leaflets containing it were rained down on Germany and Austria from the sky; all the Allied Powers adopted it as a statement of their own war aims; and Germany laid down her arms on the definite promise that, with minor changes, the peace would be based on Wilson's Fourteen Points.

Thus the whole world seemed to know in advance the kind of peace Woodrow Wilson proposed. In everyone's eyes, the President stood for a just, openly-discussed, 'clean' peace—one in which all nations, friend or foe, great or small, would have a voice. The subjected peoples in Europe and in many of the colonial empires had their hopes for independence raised by his conviction that all racial groups had the right to decide for themselves how they should be ruled in the future. 'Self-determination', Wilson called it, and the slogan rang out to every corner of the globe. Small wonder that the Irish, Egyptians and Indians came surging towards Paris or that downtrodden Poles and Czechs clasped hands when they met and fervently uttered the one word, 'Wilson!' Above all, however, a torn and weary world looked to President Wilson for leadership because he believed in a League of Nations. Security for tomorrow! Freedom from fear! No more balance of power, secret diplomacy or dangerous alliances; no more armaments, oppressive taxation or compulsory military service! Instead, the nations would work together, keeping the peace by 'collective action'. That was it! No more war! Long before he reached Paris, Wilson was being hailed as a second Messiah and tens of thousands of devout people in Italy and central Europe were burning prayer candles beneath his picture.

No emperor or king ever received a more demonstrative welcome than did President Wilson when he arrived in Europe. Before the Conference began, in London, Rome and Paris, delirious throngs lined the streets to catch a glimpse of this Prophet from the West, this American Saviour who might rise above the tumult of passion and lead them to a new and peaceful world. Tragically, the American President trusted other statesmen to be guided, like himself, by unselfish idealism. History proved him wrong.

For some inexplicable reason, Wilson also failed to realize how fickle and basically selfish public opinion usually is. He fully expected that, with the people of the Allied Powers so unanimously behind him, their statesmen could not dare to oppose his Fourteen Points. Crafty old Clemenceau, with his long years of experience in unstable French politics and his realistic insight into the many weaknesses of human nature, knew better. To all Frenchmen and most Englishmen a 'just peace' meant grinding Germany to dust and dividing up the spoils. Popularity for Wilson would last only as long as he could satisfy both parties to every conflicting little dispute and this, of course, was humanly impossible. Having been placed on so high a pedestal, it was President Wilson's misfortune to be condemned for every unsatisfied nationalist ambition, however unreasonable it may have been.

Even more damaging to Wilson's influence at the Peace Conference was the fact that his own country turned against him. More accurately, we should say that the people of the United States were deliberately and wilfully led away from him. Wilson possibly should have included some Republicans in the American peace delegation instead of appointing only his own Democratic supporters. He was the only Democrat since Andrew Jackson to serve two consecutive terms as President. He pushed through Congress a number of domestic reforms which proved very distasteful to big business interests. These interests, mainly Republican, were determined to bring about less government interference in business and a return to the good old days of laissez faire. If the President were triumphantly to dictate a liberal peace to the world, his prestige would be so great that he might accept a third term or at least ensure the election of his successor.

Shortly after the Peace Conference opened, the Republican party, playing on the natural isolationist feelings of the nation, began to attack Wilson's most vulnerable point—the League of Nations. It was pictured as nothing more than an organization to protect the ill-gotten gains of the victors. Force was given to this argument by the rumours of dissension and grasping for spoils which came across the Atlantic despite the rigid censorship finally imposed by Wilson. Additional strength came from German and Irish Americans who echoed the growing dislike of their countrymen in Europe for the President. This Republican assault on the League of Nations was led by Henry Cabot Lodge of Massachusetts, chairman of the Senate Committee on Foreign Affairs, whom we have previously met as a tail-twister during the Alaskan boundary dispute. According to a critic,

Lodge's mind was 'like New England soil, very barren but highly cultivated'. Furthermore, he hated Wilson and there is little doubt that he attacked the League, not on principle, but purely for personal and party reasons. Ample campaign funds were placed at his disposal by Henry Frick and Andrew Mellon, two millionaires who had benefited from Republican high tariffs in the past.

This campaign reached its climax in 1920 and resulted in a Republican victory and the election of Warren Harding as President. For vile abuse and misrepresentation, it has few equals in American history. The Republican attack helped to kill not only the League of Nations and the peace treaties, which the Senate refused to ratify, but also Woodrow Wilson himself. Seven years as President of the United States, with the inferno of a World War and the madhouse of a Peace Conference thrown in, had taken their toll of his health. Thus the political fight he was forced to wage on his return from Paris proved too much for him. He was as much a victim of the War as the unknown soldier at Arlington.

According to many competent observers, the American people were prepared to accept the idea of a League of Nations before the Republican party started its campaign. Thus the real tragedy of Wilson's life lies in the fact that domestic party politics prevented the United States from joining the League of Nations.

The Old Tiger's Revenge
Different from Wilson in every respect, Clemenceau was a hard, calculating politician of the old school. He had no faith in the goodness of mankind. Selfishness, he said, was the supreme impulse with nations, as with individuals. Therefore wars were inevitable and France would seek security in alliances, balance of power, heavy armaments—and a Germany crushed to his complete satisfaction. Like most Frenchmen, Clemenceau had no real confidence in a League of Nations. The old secret methods of diplomacy suited him better. Lofty ideals were all very well to talk about, but to construct an international society on such a foundation was to ignore human nature. As for an open, negotiated peace, he would have none of it. Having won the War, he did not intend to let France lose the peace by submitting it for approval to 'quarrelsome little nations'. Discuss the terms with Germany? Never! How could Wilson think of such a thing! Germany was a defeated nation: she would be handed her punishment by the victors.

Whatever we may think of his politics and methods, it is important to remember that Clemenceau did no more than express the wishes of his countrymen. Had he not defended French interests exactly as he did, a vote of lack of confidence in the super-sensitive Chamber of Deputies would have quickly replaced him.

It is easy enough to understand this selfishness—or nationalism—of the French people. They suffered from a double and overwhelming fear. One fear was of renewed German aggression. Twice in fifty years France had been attacked by the same enemy. Frenchmen thought and spoke of those attacks as utterly unprovoked acts of violence by a nation steeped in militarism. Germany alone was guilty. Their own share in bringing on both the Franco-Prussian War and the First World War had been blotted out by years of propaganda and natural hatred. Their dread of Germany was intensified by the knowledge that, unlike their vigorous, virile rival, the population of France had levelled off and was threatening to decline. Churchill summed it up this way: 'The attitude of France is determined by the fact that, twenty years from now, she will have only half as many men of military age as Germany.' Other historians, less charitable, have said that France was a stagnant, decadent nation, living in past glory ,whose only hope for continued prestige and power in Europe was to crush defeated Germany beneath a harsh peace.

The other fear was economic. Already in a shaky position by 1914, France had failed hopelessly to face her financial difficulties during the War. By refusing to impose new taxes, by handling war contracts with lavish carelessness and tolerating extreme profiteering, by pouring out millions in paper money, she had piled up a prodigious debt. In addition, she now had to finance a staggering bill for property damage, pensions and widows' allowances. At the end of the War, therefore, France stood in grave danger of national bankruptcy unless she received a huge indemnity from Germany.

Cripple the military power of Germany so she could never wage war again; compel her to pay the costs of the one just ended. These were the aims of France at the Peace Conference. Thus we see that Georges Clemenceau represented a nation solely concerned with her own immediate perils. Nothing else mattered.

Lloyd George Does Well

Lloyd George, Winston Churchill and one or two other friends celebrated victory on Armistice Day with a quiet dinner at No. 10 Downing Street. Churchill has recalled the conversation they had with the British Prime Minister on that memorable evening. They spoke in wonderment of the mighty battle the Germans had waged for four years against such heavy odds; how you could not hope to rebuild Europe without them; how under the stress of defeat in the field and starvation at home Germany might collapse in communist revolution. They must not allow that to happen; a strong Germany was needed if only to serve as a buffer against the spread of Bolshevism from Russia. Germany, they also agreed, had been Great Britain's best European customer before the War and it would be folly indeed to let vengeance and hatred ruin her at the Peace Conference. Of course Germany must be made to pay reparations, but how? With gold, or goods or services? Germany certainly did not have the gold and if they paid in goods such as coal, steel or ships, they would simply put their competitors in Britain out of business. As for services, the only one they could provide would be free ocean transport and that would play havoc with the British Mercantile Marine. For these reasons, national interest and plain common sense indicated that the British delegation to Paris should hold out for a moderate peace with Germany.

The British Prime Minister, however, was a politician of the rough-and-tumble school rather than a real statesman; he tended to trim his sails to every whisper of public opinion. It was all very well to arrive at sane conclusions in the calm, after-dinner atmosphere of his residence in Downing Street, but what about the voters? What would they think? An election was coming up in December—the first in eight years, with 7 million new, highly unpredictable women voters—and the future of his coalition government was clouded with uncertainty. Lloyd George and his colleagues, therefore, took no chances during the 'Khaki Election'. Against what must have been their better judgement, they appealed to the base but popular instincts of hatred and revenge. Of course Germany was guilty. 'Hang the Kaiser!' And of course she must pay the costs. How about making England a fit place for heroes to live? Never mind the future—let's settle up the past. . . . Thus the British had their appetites whetted by the promise of a crushing indemnity even before their delegates left for Paris.

With this kind of election behind him, Lloyd George was in no better position to give moral leadership at the Peace Conference than was Clemenceau. Whenever he tried to wriggle out from under his election promises and follow a different course, the British public held him to strict account. They would not let him soften up on Germany or listen to 'that Moses from Washington with his new Tablets of Stone.'

The British Prime Minister went to Paris with yet another millstone round his neck. During the War the government of Great Britain, acting alone or some-times with France, made a number of secret treaties with its allies. There were, in blunt language, private bargains to divide up the booty when the Central Powers were defeated. The Italians, for instance, were promised parts of the Austro-Hungarian Empire and additions to their overseas possessions—provided Italy would join the Allied side. The Japanese were promised all the German islands in the Pacific north of the equator and German economic rights in the Chinese province of Shantung—provided Japan would send some destroyers to the Mediterranean while the U-boat menace was at its height. The Romanians were promised a large slice of Austria-Hungary called Transylvania, provided Romania would declare war on Germany. The Greeks, Jews, Arabs, Serbs and Poles were encouraged to aid the Allies by other secret deals often involving the same land—promised twice!

Most of the secret treaties were negotiated without consulting the wishes of the people who lived in the areas being bartered away. In other words, they were directly opposed to Wilson's principles of self-determination. Since the Allies had accepted the Fourteen Points as a basis for peace, the American President felt justified in refusing to recognize several of these wartime bargains, thereby causing some of the big disagreements at the Peace Conference. These disagree-ments, receiving wide publicity, helped to create the impression that the Conference was little more than a selfish contest for the spoils. Clemenceau, from the beginning, frankly admitted this, but the British cloaked their actions in more lofty phrases. In the face of the trouble caused by the secret treaties, it was difficult to claim, as Great Britain tried to do, that the Peace Conference was based on principles of abstract justice.

Wilson also tried to interfere with certain private ambitions shared by Great Britain with her overseas dominions. The extent of these plans may be judged from a statement made by the Colonial Secretary in 1917, shortly after the Imperial War Cabinet meetings: 'Let no man think that the struggle for Germany's colonies has been in vain. Let no man think that these colonies will ever return to German rule. It is impossible. Our Overseas Empire will not tolerate any suggestions of the kind.' Thus the British Empire delegation was agreed in advance that the Union of South Africa should keep German East and West Africa while Australia and New Zealand should have Samoa, New Guinea and the other German islands in the south Pacific. Only Sir Robert Borden, who claimed nothing whatsoever for his country, voiced a small objection to this arrangement. Both then and at the Peace Conference, he suggested that British prestige, especially in the United States, might be weakened if they appeared too grasping in their demands. As a concession to Wilson's point of view, the former German colonies were to be administered as 'mandates' under general supervision of the League, but in actual practice this reservation had little meaning.

Even Georges Clemenceau finally began to grumble about how much Great Britain and her dominions were gaining from the Peace Conference. 'The British,' he complained to a colleague as the Conference neared its end, 'have been rewarded with all the German colonies in the south Pacific and most of them in Africa, the destruction of the German fleet, the elimination of the German merchant marine as a serious rival and the exclusion of German competition from some of the markets of the world. . . . My friend Mr. Lloyd George has done well here in Paris.'

Lloyd George did very well indeed at Paris. He changed his mind about reparations, he shifted back and forth on German border questions and he did not even bother to study some of the most important problems of the peace. But when it came to the basically selfish aims of England and the Empire he was as stubborn as a mule. More so than any other statesman, the Prime Minister of Great Britain wrote the peace terms precisely to his own liking.

This does not mean that all the people in Britain agreed with Lloyd George's kind of peace. Far from it. The terms were too lenient or too harsh. The Empire was already big enough. Indeed it was cracking at the seams in Ireland, Egypt and India. Why add another million square miles of backward colonial lands to it? Reparations would ruin British trade. President Wilson was right—a punitive peace would not last. Great Britain had humiliated herself by joining in the scramble for spoils.

There was only one point on which there was almost universal agreement. This was the League of Nations. In 1919, the British people were much more taken up with the idea of a League than even the Americans were. They had endured much more of war, they dreaded a return to the constant anxieties and fears of power politics and fervently looked to this new institution to point the way towards peace. It is to Woodrow Wilson's eternal credit that the vengeance-thirsty victors even considered the League at Paris, but some of the British Empire delegation took just as much interest in it as he did. Sir Robert Borden, Sir Joseph Cook of Newfoundland, Louis Botha and especially Lord Robert Cecil and General Jan Smuts played an outstanding part in the Commission which drafted the Covenant of the League of Nations. With their faith and idealism, these statesmen brought a ray of hope to a world disillusioned by the spectacle of greed and national selfishness that was displayed at the Paris Peace Conference.

Signed in Sombre Black

By May 6, 1919, the fourth anniversary of the sinking of the *Lusitania*, the Big Three had finished their work. For the past week, six German statesmen had been waiting in a Parisian hotel, locked up behind barbed wire and under close guard. Now they were brought out to receive the Treaty. In one of the most dramatic moments in history, carefully staged by the French in the Trianon Palace, Clemenceau bitingly addressed the fallen foe: 'This is not the time or place for superfluous words. The day has come when we must settle our accounts. You have asked for peace. We are ready to give peace.' The Germans were told that they had three weeks in which to accept the two-hundred-page document thus presented to them on the point of a bayonet. There would be no oral discussion; only written comments would be acceptable. In a series of letters taking up twice as much space as the Treaty itself, the Germans made bitter but generally futile protests. In particular, they resented having been disarmed by a promise of the Fourteen Points and then having this 'peace of imperialism' handed out to them. And they denied from the beginning, as they were to do for all time to come, that their country was solely responsible for the War. But to no avail. Under the threat of renewed war, the German government reluctantly agreed to accept the peace.

On June 28, the fifth anniversary of the murder at Sarajevo, the drama came to an end in the famous, two-century-old Hall of Mirrors at Versailles. The stately gallery was eloquent with many memories, but among them all one must have stood out in the minds of the assembled delegates. Here in 1871 the German Empire had been proclaimed. And who could forget that when the German guns were thundering round Paris forty-nine years before, the Mayor of Montmartre had been a young doctor named Georges Clemenceau? This was his day! Yet strangely, it was not a gay and bright occasion. All the delegates were dressed in their dark morning suits and, apart from the rich paintings on the ceiling of the Hall of Mirrors, there were few touches of colour anywhere. As first the German and then the Allied representatives moved up in line to place their signatures on the Treaty, the prevailing colour reflected all around was sombre black—an omen, perhaps, of what this day would bring in the inscrutable future.

As the delegate from Uruguay signed his name and the ceremony ended, General Jan Smuts leaned over to his neighbour and whispered: 'You know, God has written a very different treaty from this.'

Blueprints for the Future

The Limited Interest of Canada

About halfway through the Peace Conference, the editor of the Toronto *Globe* expressed in these words the growing desire of the Canadian people that Sir Robert Borden should come back home: 'Is there any reason why the Prime Minister of this country should remain in Paris, in what is obviously a minor capacity, until the boundaries of Czechoslovakia and Poland are arranged, the

tangled mass of Balkan intrigue is sorted out and the last comma is inserted in the Peace Treaty? He has accomplished his mission and it's time he came home. Canada's work must be done on this continent and Sir Robert's place is in Ottawa, not Paris.'

True, Borden had accomplished his mission as Canadians saw it at the time. He had won the right, first of all, to have a separate Canadian delegation at the Conference. This had not been easy, despite the fact that our sacrifices had been far greater than those of a host of other, smaller nations who were accepted in Paris without question. The British Foreign Office was reluctant, as usual, to surrender its power. Furthermore, France, Italy and especially our neighbour to the south were not at all willing to see Great Britain and her dominions each have separate delegations. It would give the British Empire, so they protested, an unfair voting strength. However, with the support of Lloyd George and assistance from Jan Smuts and Billy Hughes, Sir Robert Borden carried his point. Canada and the other dominions were granted the right to send their own representatives to the Peace Conference. Status! Recognition in the eyes of the world as an independent country! This was what Canada wanted; indeed, it was her only real interest at Paris. Faithfully, the Canadian delegation pursued this question with determination, and success came at last with membership as an independent country in the new League of Nations.

Six weeks before the Conference ended, therefore, Sir Robert Borden returned to Canada. Not that he wanted to—he was serving on several commissions, enjoyed his work and felt, with justice, that his unbiased judgement was valuable —but the pressure of public opinion was too great to resist. Sir George Foster was left in Paris to sign his shaky signature, as head of the Canadian delegation, to the Treaty of Versailles. And Sir Robert Borden was acclaimed in Ottawa as the prime minister of a sovereign, independent power; prime minister, also, of a country which, having won recognition from the other nations, was not one whit interested in world affairs. As the editor of the *Globe* implied, what did we care about the boundaries of Czechoslovakia or Poland? Like the United States, we quickly slipped back into our isolated little niche across the Atlantic and let the world go by. We had earned the right to speak in international affairs but were too indifferent or timid to use it.

And yet, as we concentrated on our own affairs, war clouds gradually gathered over Europe, brewing up a storm which would inevitably suck both Canada and the United States into its vortex. Thus, within twenty years of the Paris Peace Conference, border difficulties in Czechoslovakia would bring the world to the brink of war. Within twenty years, the Luftwaffe of Nazi Germany would bomb Warsaw and Canadian soldiers would be fighting and dying again in a fiery conflict ignited by a boundary dispute—in Poland!

So we may see—although our countrymen at the time generally did not—that the decisions made at the Peace Conference were of utmost importance to Canada. World events which have shaped the whole course of our history—the

Outside the Palace of Versailles, June 28, 1919

Depression, the causes of the Second World War, that tremendous global struggle itself and a great deal of what has happened since—all had their immediate origins at the end of the First War. We simply cannot understand, therefore, the world in which we are living, an outside world becoming closer and more important to us every passing day, without some knowledge of the peace treaties.

Talking Points for the Nazis

The Treaty of Versailles was the number one talking point used by the Nazis to gain power in Germany—and from that moment the outbreak of the Second World War was just a matter of time. Adolf Hitler has described in his auto-biography how he used the Treaty to arouse the German people. 'I considered two lectures, namely, "The True Causes of the War" and "The Peace Treaty of Versailles", the most important ones so I repeated them over and over again. At first, the German people did not want to hear, did not want to understand, that Versailles was a disgrace, a shame, the cause of all their misery. . . . At each meeting I was met by hostile eyes but three hours later I had before me a surging crowd filled with the most sacred indignation and utter wrath. . . . Once more, I had torn a great lie from the brains and hearts of my audience.' Two lectures? Fiery, screeching, revengeful orations would be a better description! Hitler never delivered a rational lecture in his life but, year in and year out, he and the other Nazi leaders, at all their rabble-rousing meetings, drove home the message that Versailles was a dictated, harsh and unjust peace. It was based, they shouted, on broken Allied promises and the false assumption that Germany alone caused the War. Obey a treaty born in deceit and accepted under threat of invasion? Never! 'Rise up, Germany, cast off this piece of Allied treachery, be strong and proud once more!'

Although Hitler put far more lies into the minds of the German people than he ever tore out, there was, unfortunately, a foundation of truth in what he said about Versailles. It was a dictated peace. The Germans, by the Armistice Agreement, had been led to believe that the terms would be openly discussed. The Allies broke their promise, not only over this question of how the peace would be negotiated, but also on reparations. The victorious powers did not need to make promises; Germany was thoroughly defeated, but the fact remains that the Germans laid down their arms on a definite understanding about the bill they would receive. According to the Armistice Agreement, they could be made to pay 'for all damage done to the civilian population of the Allies and their property by the aggression of Germany by land, by sea and from the air'. Under the pressure of wartime hatred at the Peace Conference, item after item was added by the Allies—pensions and widows' allowances, the Belgian war debt, interest on Allied loans and so on—until the bill was much greater than the Germans had any reason to expect.

In fact, the wrangling over reparations lasted so many weeks that the Conference delegates were unable to total up the costs in time to include them in the Treaty. Germany was forced, therefore, to sign a 'blank cheque' promising to pay whatever sum a specially appointed Reparations Commission might decide in the future. Meanwhile, they were to pay on account, immediately, $5 billion in gold, ships, machinery, tools, chemicals and a long list of animal products, to be handed over by a starving nation just released from the Allied blockade! Over and above all this, the Treaty stated that Germany was to replace 'ton for ton and class for class all the merchant ships sunk or lost during the War' and to deliver 23 million tons of coal annually to France, Belgium and Italy for the next ten years. An Allied Army of Occupation was to be stationed in the Rhineland—at Germany's expense—until all these obligations were fulfilled. Then, in May 1921, the Reparations Commission brought down the final bill for damages. Thirty-two billion dollars—three times more than the economic experts had recommended —was to be paid in instalments of $500 million each year. The accumulated interest charges were greater than the annual payments so the bill would increase and last for ever! It could never be paid off! Small wonder that Germany accepted it only under the threat of renewed invasion. In 1929, when wartime passions had cooled down, this German debt to the Allies was reduced to the more reasonable figure of $8 billion—but not before Hitler and his friends had done a lot of heated talking.

In addition to this heavy-handed demand for reparations, the victors, as we know, parcelled out among themselves all the overseas possessions of Germany. The mandate system, requiring an annual report to the League of Nations on the administration of each colony, was little more than a smoke-screen thrown up to hide a plain division of the spoils. Also, the Allies confiscated all the foreign investments, amounting to some billions of dollars, which German businessmen had built up in South America, China and elsewhere in the world. The surrender of her colonial sources of oil, rubber and other raw materials, combined with the loss of three-quarters of her entire merchant fleet, almost ruined the export and shipping trade on which the pre-war prosperity of Germany was based. This fact, alone, made it very difficult for her to earn the money needed to pay reparations.

Furthermore, the European area of Germany was reduced by one-eighth through the loss of land to France, Belgium, Denmark, Poland and Czechoslovakia. What the maps do not show is that these ceded territories contained 6½ million former German subjects—another good talking and fighting point used by the Nazis—and well over half the German supplies of iron, coal, lead and zinc. Self-determination, it seems, was a minor consideration compared to the Allied desire to strike at the roots of German industrial power. Partly for this reason and partly to compensate for the destruction of her own mines, the rich coal fields of the Saar Valley were turned over to France. The region itself was to be administered by a League of Nations Commission on the understanding that, at the end of fifteen years, a plebiscite would be held to determine whether or not the inhabitants wished to return to German rule. This is an important point to keep in mind because Hitler, once in power, held his hand until January 1935, when the Saar voted overwhelmingly in favour of Germany. Then only, as we shall see later, did the Nazis feel free to destroy the last remnants of the Treaty of Versailles.

Strange as it may seem, the Nazis, once in power, were greatly aided in their bid for European domination by the fact that they took over an almost completely disarmed country. The Treaty of Versailles, of course, destroyed the military, naval and air power of Germany. Her army was limited to 100,000 men, her once-mighty navy was reduced to a handful of ships for coastal patrol duty and both services were hemmed in by a multitude of restrictions. Her air force was entirely eliminated. She could neither import nor manufacture poison gas, armoured cars, tanks or submarines. The fortifications on both banks of the Rhine River were demolished and the whole Rhineland area was demilitarized forever. All this was done, so the Germans were assured in the Treaty, as a preliminary step towards the limitation of armaments by the other countries. This agreement was reinforced in Article VIII of the Covenant of the League of Nations by which the member nations promised to reduce their arms 'to the lowest point consistent with national safety'. But in the post-war years national safety proved to be an elusive will-o'-the-wisp, the League did not provide security, and successive disarmament conferences ended in miserable failure. The statesmen tried in vain to control the weapons of war before removing its causes. As long as fear, poverty, economic rivalry and all the other causes of war remained in the world, large-scale armaments were thought to be the only source of security.

Protesting that Germany was surrounded by hostile neighbours armed to the teeth, the Nazis, therefore, proceeded to violate, one after another, all the disarmament provisions of the Treaty. Starting almost from scratch, unfettered by any outdated equipment or military doctrines, they were free to experiment with new strategic ideas and the very latest war materials. The victorious powers, on the other hand, not only allowed the Nazis to shatter Versailles, but also rested self-satisfied, smug and content in the thought that they had won the last war. The same old weapons and the same old-fashioned plans would do the job again! Thus Great Britain continued to stress the navy and ignored the potentialities of air power to such an extent that the Royal Air Force for a while was ranked seventh in the world. So, too, France built the Maginot Line, a super-trench that would hold the enemy out forever. Yet when the testing time came, the German blitz carried the Panzer divisions over, around and through the Maginot Line in less than five days!

As we shall see later, the significant fact about the first year of the Second World War was not so much that Germany took the offensive throughout, as that every novelty in strategy or tactics and every new military invention of any importance appeared on the German side. The airplane was a French, the tank a British, invention. Yet in the period between the two wars, it was the German army that developed and perfected the tactics of aerial and mechanized warfare. The parachutist landing behind enemy lines was a Russian device, studied and perfected by Germany and ignored by the satisfied powers. Indeed, it is difficult to exaggerate the advantage secured by Germany from the destruction of her whole military machine in 1919. It compelled her not only to modernize her equipment but also to think out again from the start every problem of strategy and organization while Great Britain and France clung to the glorious traditions of the past.

The New Map of Europe

The Peace Conference did not confine its treaty-making activities to Germany. Before Wilson and Lloyd George left Paris, the Big Three also had prepared a rough draft for the Treaty of St. Germain with Austria and the Treaty of Trianon with Hungary. These two treaties, by carefully applying the principle of national self-determination to the old Austro-Hungarian Empire, changed the map of central Europe almost beyond recognition. Four independent countries—Austria, Czechoslovakia, Poland and Hungary—were created or reinstated, partly or entirely, from the provinces of the former Dual Monarchy. Romania and Serbia (renamed Yugoslavia) both increased in size so much that, to all intents and purposes, they too may be regarded as new states.

Of these six main heirs to the Hapsburg estates, only Czechoslovakia had a reasonably decent record in the period between the two wars. All the others built up a shoddy history of political intrigue and corruption. The aristocratic ruling factions, especially in Romania and Hungary, ruthlessly exploited the peasants and workers, provoking revolution, counter-revolution and cruel reprisals by both sides. In the process, democracy was tossed overboard, scuttled by petty dictators aping Mussolini or Hitler. Purges, mass murders and assassinations sooner or later marred the record of every one of them. Endless boundary squabbles between them helped to keep Europe in a turmoil for twenty years. Even before the Second World War began, two of them—Austria and Czechoslovakia—had been swallowed up by the Nazis, despite the fact that the treaties of Versailles and St. Germain both prohibited any 'anschluss' or union between Germany and Austria. Three others—Hungary, Romania and to a lesser extent Yugoslavia—had become mere puppet states, dancing when Hitler pulled the strings. Something went wrong in central Europe and the Balkans when Woodrow Wilson's heralded principle of self-determination was applied to the lands once ruled by the Hapsburgs.

We must remember that the inhabitants of these new states had been living for a long time under an undemocratic system of government. (The same was true of the new Baltic states—Finland, Estonia, Latvia and Lithuania—which arose on Russia's borderlands during the Bolshevik Revolution.) It was too much to expect that all these different nations, once liberated, should suddenly prove capable of ruling themselves as skilfully as the older, more established democracies. Yet most of the new countries of Europe hopefully introduced complete self-government and extended the franchise to even the most uneducated of their citizens. Politically inexperienced, the problems they had to face were simply too much for them.

In the first place, none of these little countries, with the exception of Czechoslovakia, were economically strong. The principle of self-determination broke up the big, pre-war empires—which possessed a network of highways and railroads and a balance between industry and agriculture—and replaced them with many small, weak states. The new governments did not have the resources to satisfy the popular post-war demands for higher standards of living. Thus the poorer classes in each of these countries began to vote for socialist or communist parties, hoping that state control or ownership of the national wealth would bring them prosperity. In self-defence, the industrialists, the landlords and all others who stood to lose by the abolition of private property united—supported by the Church—to prevent the spread of socialism.

Democracy, they claimed, was a mere counting of heads, a silly device that allowed the ignorant, unpropertied classes, by the sheer weight of their numbers, to get into power and overthrow the established economic system. Democracy, therefore, must go. Scrap political freedom! Scrap the right to vote—the people did not really know what was good for them anyway—but save private property! Basically this was the argument—used also by both Mussolini and Hitler—which caused the social upheavals in all these small countries and led to the triumph of fascist dictatorships in the period between the two wars. The failure of democracy to find a satisfactory way of life for the masses created socialist and communist

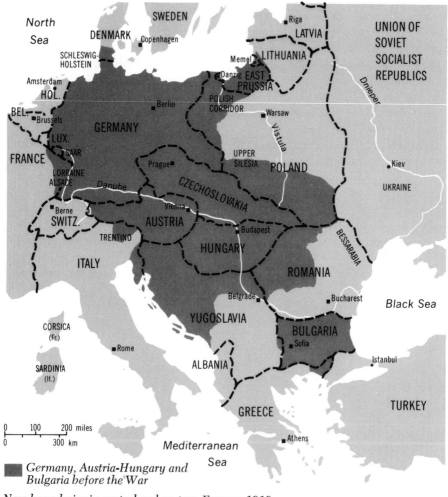

Germany, Austria-Hungary and Bulgaria before the War

New boundaries in central and eastern Europe, 1919

discontent and this, in turn, bred the anti-communist, anti-democratic movement known to history as fascism.

The new states were plagued with another series of problems arising from the fact that boundary lines in central Europe and the Balkans could not be laid out according to language and race. The racial groups living within the big European empires had moved back and forth and so mingled together that no border line, however carefully drawn, could separate one from another. The principle of self-determination, it is true, liberated millions of Poles, Czechs, Slovaks, Romanians, South Slavs and Italians from foreign rule, but in every single case a new minority problem was created.

These minorities—the Germans in Poland and Czechoslovakia, the Magyars in Romania, the Austrians in Italy, the Italians in Yugoslavia and so on—all nursed ancient hatreds for the very people who now ruled over them. Having once been in the driver's seat themselves, they feared and frequently received back some of their own rough treatment. Therefore, they kept up a constant agitation to break from their new masters and reunite with their nearby kinsmen. And their fiercely nationalistic kinsmen, as might be expected, shouted every encouragement back to them from across the border—which probably traced its tortuous path through open fields and woods, unmarked by mountains, rivers or other natural barriers, a completely artificial boundary, inviting trouble.

The delegates to the Conference foresaw this danger. As Woodrow Wilson himself said to them: 'Nothing is more likely to disturb the peace of the world than the treatment which might be meted out to minority racial groups.' The Big Powers did try to prevent trouble. All the smaller states were asked to sign special treaties guaranteeing racial, religious, linguistic and economic equality to the 30 million members of national minority groups living in Europe. Many of the countries concerned objected to signing on the grounds that the provisions interfered with their rights as independent nations, but the Big Powers insisted and the obligations were reluctantly assumed. Supervision of these minority treaties, as they were called, was given to the Council of the League of Nations and no guarantee could be changed without its consent. However, despite persistent efforts by the League to preserve harmony, the spirit of nationalism proved too strong and the racial hatreds too deep-seated to be controlled by law.

Perhaps the real root of the trouble lay in the fact that President Wilson's two main principles for peace—self-determination and a League of Nations— conflicted with each other at every turn. Self-determination stimulated intense national feelings in Europe and elsewhere in the world; it increased the number of fanatically patriotic little states and therefore made international co-operation more difficult than ever before. On the other hand, the League of Nations, to be successful, required all nations to make some sacrifices. The whole idea of collective security was based on co-operation, on common action to preserve the peace. If the Council of the League, for instance, unanimously decided that an act of aggression had been committed by one state against another, all the member nations promised, according to the Covenant, to apply 'economic sanctions' to the guilty country. This meant that, regardless of their own

particular interests, they would refuse to trade with the aggressor. They might
even be required to contribute money or armed forces to help fight a League war,
no matter how far away the conflict was. But all this, of course, demanded a spirit
of self-sacrifice and a willingness to recognize that all problems were world
problems, to be mutually shared and solved. It is a lesson we are only now
beginning to learn. It is a lesson the nations in the period between the two wars
did not learn.

During the 1920s, when world prosperity made an 'era of goodwill' easy to
achieve, the League enjoyed a flurry of success. Then the Great Depression
struck, the nations turned inwards to face their own gigantic difficulties and,
without support, the League was powerless to stem the rising tide of aggressive
nationalism.

The Denial of the Arabs

One of the most distinguished-looking delegates to the Peace Conference was a
tall, stately man named Amir Feisal. In his black, flowing robes and golden
turban, this swarthy Arab commanded attention wherever he went and yet, when
he first arrived in Paris, very little was known of the man himself or the mission
that brought him to the Conference. Only two members of the Canadian delegation, for instance, had ever heard his name before and they were only vaguely
aware that Feisal had been the leader of the 'Revolt of the Desert', the chieftain
who had persuaded the Arabs, with the help of T. E. Lawrence, his English
friend and adviser, to rise up against Turkey during the War. But Amir Feisal had
as proud a personal heritage as any delegate to the Conference and his purpose in
Paris was of utmost importance to the future peace of the world.

Feisal's family traced its ancestry back to Mohammed himself, who had founded
the Islamic religion early in the seventh century and whose successors had built by
conquest a great empire extending from the Arabian peninsula and Asia Minor,
across the whole of northern Africa and even into Spain. For five hundred years
this Arab or Muslim Empire, held together by a common language and a militant
religion, had been the cultural centre of the western world. Arab scholars
translated Greek and Roman writings, preserved ancient knowledge and made
outstanding contributions of their own in chemistry, physics, mathematics, music
and agriculture. The Arab Empire slowly decayed and was conquered, almost in
its entirety, by the Ottoman Turks at the beginning of the sixteenth century. As
we know, the Sultan, in turn, lost the North African parts of the former Arab
Empire to France, Italy and Britain but managed to retain control of Asia Minor
and the Arabian peninsula until the eve of the First World War. Although the
Turks thus ruled the very heartland of the Arab world for almost exactly four
centuries, they did not destroy the Arabic language or the Islamic religion. Arab
national spirit was still alive, ready to flare at a moment's notice if given a chance.
That chance came when Turkey joined the Central Powers and was defeated in
the War.

All this brought Feisal to Paris. The Turkish Empire was now to be carved up
and the leader of the Arab Revolt had come to plead for the independence of his

people. The President of the United States, he knew full well, had promised freedom for all the 'non-Turkish subjects of the Sultan'. Surely, above all, this must mean the Arabs! But Feisal had reason to hope for success even without the assurance of Wilson's Fourteen Points. Early in the War, his father, Ali Hussein, had refused to authorize an Arab uprising to aid the Allies until he made sure that it would lead to independence. As the influential ruler of the Hejaz and spokesman for the Arab nationalists, Hussein, therefore, wrote to Sir Henry McMahon, the British High Commissioner in Egypt, asking—demanding, perhaps, would be a better word—to know what guarantee Great Britain was prepared to make. Would His Majesty's Government recognize independent Arab states east of Suez, in the Arabian peninsula, Iraq and Syria? (Syria in those days included all

The Turkish Empire falls before the colonial and industrial powers. Britain and France control the oil fields, commercial outlets and strategic corners of the Middle East.

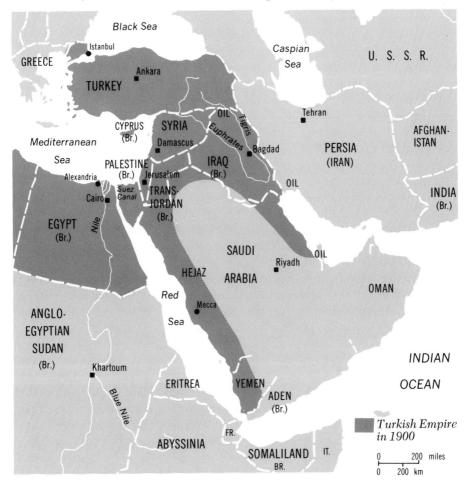

of modern Lebanon, Syria, Israel and Jordan.) A sharply-pointed question, touching many vital interests! This was but the first of a long series of letters exchanged between the two men—the famous 'Hussein-McMahon correspondence' from which so much trouble was to flow in the years ahead.

From the beginning of this correspondence, Sir Henry McMahon insisted there were two small areas in Asia Minor which the Arabs could not have. One of these was Lebanon where France held long-standing privileges and the other was southern Iraq in which Britain herself was interested. With these two minor exceptions, however, Great Britain finally agreed to accept the Arab proposals. This was confirmed by McMahon in a letter to Hussein, dated October 25, 1915. 'I am empowered,' he wrote, 'in the name of His Majesty's Government to assure you that Great Britain is prepared to recognize and support the independence of the Arabs in all the regions within the limits demanded by the Governor of the Hejaz.' Here was a definite promise by the British government to recognize Arab independence—it bears repetition—in the Arabian peninsula, most of Iraq and all of Syria, Israel and Jordan. It is important to notice that in none of McMahon's letters was there any mention of 'Palestine' (now divided into Jordan and Israel) as a reserved area; clearly it was to be a part of the new Arab world.

Within six short months of making this arrangement with Hussein, the British government turned right around and opened negotiations with France over exactly the same territory! The Foreign Office did not tell France that they already had reached an understanding with the Arabs; nor did they let the Arabs have any inkling of their dealings with France. The details of these Anglo-French negotiations were entrusted to Sir Mark Sykes and Georges Picot, the bargain they signed on April 26, 1916, being known as the Sykes-Picot Agreement. This bargain conflicted at almost every point with the promises given in the McMahon correspondence and made Arab unity and independence after the War completely impossible. Control of Lebanon and Syria was given to France, and Palestine and all of Iraq to Britain. Although one disturbing fact after another gradually leaked out about this Agreement, it was a long time before the Arabs could bring themselves to believe that the assurances given to them by Great Britain were valueless, if not downright deceitful.

This whole messy situation was made much worse when Allied politicians— especially Wilson, Lloyd George, Churchill and Smuts—yielded to the pleadings of a powerful group called the Zionists. Zionism was a world movement, financed by wealthy Jews, to promote the migration of their oppressed and poverty-stricken kinsmen back to the original Jewish homeland in Palestine. Back to the Bible lands! Here was an idea to catch the imagination of liberal-minded and religious people everywhere. During the War, this movement appealed to the Allied leaders not only for religious reasons but also because, if they publicly supported Zionism, the Jewish minorities in Germany and Austria-Hungary might revolt or at least cause trouble for the Central Powers. Also, when the United States entered the War, the large Jewish vote in that country had to be considered. In Great Britain, the Zionist cause was pressed with great vigour by the rich Jewish banker, Lord Rothschild; by Dr. Chaim Weizmann, a Russian-born Jew, whose chemical researches were helping the Allied war effort; and by Nahum Sokolow, a Russian journalist and a member of the Zionist executive, who had come to England in 1914 solely to win the interest of individual British cabinet ministers. Their efforts were finally rewarded when Arthur Balfour, the British Foreign Secretary, on November 2, 1917, wrote a most important open letter to Lord Rothschild.

This letter has become known as the 'Balfour Declaration' and stated: 'His Majesty's Government view with favour the establishment in Palestine of a national home for the Jewish people.' Yet the population of Palestine was, and had been for many centuries, over ninety per cent Arab! What would happen to all these people, in such a barren, crowded land, if the Jews came pouring in? This was a question to which Lloyd George and his colleagues gave very little thought. In fairness to them, however, it must be said that they had no intention of displacing the Arabs in Palestine to make room for the Jews. The British cabinet made this quite clear to the Zionists and also repeatedly assured the Arabs that they would not be uprooted from their homes. It is difficult to understand how the British government had allowed itself to be placed in such an impossible position. But if the British were thus careless or ignorant of the true facts in Palestine how much more so were the Americans! Their 'experts' at the Peace Conference—none of whom had ever been to the eastern Mediterranean—advocated that Palestine should become a Jewish state as soon as possible. Yet they were naive enough to believe that this could be done 'without sacrificing the rights of the Arabs'!

Returning to Amir Feisal, we may now see that he came to Paris on a hopeless mission. British, French and Jewish ambitions in the Near East blocked the road to Arab independence. The conflicts among all these selfish interests led to such a furious argument at the Peace Conference that Woodrow Wilson finally insisted that a special commission should be sent to prepare a report on the whole area. When neither Lloyd George nor Clemenceau would co-operate, Wilson went ahead on his own and dispatched two Americans, Henry King and Charles Crane, to the Near East. As a result of their findings, the King-Crane Commission strongly recommended that the Sykes-Picot Agreement should not be put into effect. Arab nationalism, now thoroughly aroused, would never submit to such a flagrant piece of old-fashioned colonialism. This was particularly true, they said, of Syria where Arab hatred and fear of France was intense; under no circumstances, therefore, should France have control of this area. As for Zionism, the Commission urged the serious modification of its entire program. Both King and Crane, on their own admission, favoured Zionism at first, but what they found in Palestine turned them against it. In the words of their Report: 'The fact came out repeatedly in our conference with Jewish spokesmen, that the Zionists looked forward to the complete displacement of the Arabs in Palestine. . . . Yet no one else, including the British officers consulted by the Commission, believed that the Zionist plan could be carried out without force of arms.'

Tragically, because its dire predictions all came true, the King-Crane Report was ignored by the Peace Conference. As even a casual glance at the map of the

Near East shows, the Conference decisions were based on the Sykes-Picot Agreement. The mandate system was introduced in a vain attempt to protect the Arabs to some extent, but in actual fact the mandatory European powers were free to do almost as they pleased. France took Syria and Lebanon, Great Britain received Palestine, Trans-Jordan and Iraq, and imperialism triumphed over the principle of self-determination, the Hussein-McMahon promises and the aspirations of the Arabs to control their own destiny. In the years to come, as the King-Crane Commission foresaw, Arab nationalism flared up in Syria, forcing the French to sack parts of Damascus and crush the Arabs with disgraceful cruelty. The clash between the inrushing Jews and the Arabs in Palestine tormented Great Britain for over twenty-five years until she was finally compelled to withdraw—leaving the two races to fight it out in the bitter Arab-Israeli conflict. And at the present time, 30 million people in the now independent Arab states have not forgotten the treatment handed out to them by the victorious powers at the end of the First World War. In the Arab world, as elsewhere, the Peace Conference sowed the seeds of future strife.

11   THE DAY BEFORE YESTERDAY

The Twenties Start to Roar

On April 28, 1919, a bomb big enough, it was said, to blow up the entire city hall, was found in Mayor Hanson's mail at Seattle, Washington. The following afternoon, a servant opened a parcel addressed to Senator Hardwick at his home in Georgia and a bomb in the parcel blew off her hands. Since the Armistice, Mayor Hanson and Senator Hardwick had been touring the country trying to arouse the American people to the danger of a communist revolution in the United States. Alien agents, Reds, Bolsheviks, so both men claimed, were fomenting trouble among the working class and the United States was on the verge of a revolutionary mass movement, similar to those that were playing havoc in Europe. Newspaper reporters, therefore, quickly assumed that the bombs had been sent by a foreigner, some Bolshevik or anarchist, as a warning to all those who dared to speak out against communism.

A few hours after the Hardwick bomb exploded, a clerk in the parcel post division of the New York Post Office found sixteen suspicious-looking brown packages lying on a shelf, ready for delivery. They were addressed to a number of prominent government officials and business leaders, including John D. Rockefeller, the president of Standard Oil, and J. P. Morgan, the internationally-known New York banker. Gingerly opened by the police, the packages were found to contain bombs and seemed to provide further evidence of a dangerous, radical conspiracy against American capitalism. Following this startling news came a series of homemade bomb explosions in other parts of the country, the most serious of which did no more than damage the front of Attorney General Palmer's house in Washington. The whole business might well have been attributed to a few maniacs, but the American public, reading the big headlines, became frightened and decided to strike back at the radical foreign agitators in their midst. Almost overnight, reports of the Paris Peace Conference and other international news disappeared from the front pages—pushed into the background by stories of violent strikes, anti-Bolshevist riots, bombings and lawlessness. Thousands of reasonable citizens, who should have known better, convinced themselves that a Red revolution, like the one in Russia, might begin at any moment in the United States. Fear and hatred of Bolshevism gripped the people, a wave of hysteria swept the country and by mid-June the 'Big Red Scare' was in full swing.

The Big Red Scare
Torn though the United States was by many prolonged, post-war strikes, the vast majority of the workers were loyal, peace-loving American citizens, seeking only to secure shorter hours and higher pay. Some unions, it is true, demanded

government ownership of the railroads, banks and mines and other socialist measures, but they did not advocate bloodshed to secure these aims. Revolutionary socialism—that is, true communism as taught by Marx and Lenin—was to be found mainly in a labour organization called the International Workers of the World and in the One Big Union which it sponsored. This group was led in the United States, as it was in many other countries, by extremists who took their gospel from Moscow and preached a ruthless doctrine of violence against capitalism. At the very most, however, this group of real communists numbered not more than forty thousand. To imagine that they could overthrow a nation of over 100 million people was almost ludicrous, yet the fear of Bolshevism provoked the United States, during the years 1919 to 1921, to embark on one of its periodic outbursts of extreme intolerance.

Shouting 'Down with Bolshevism, down with the Reds,' rioting mobs in many of the big industrial cities took the law into their own hands. Picket lines were stoned; union leaders were clubbed, 'roughed up' and threatened, their homes ransacked; trade union and socialist meeting places were invaded and frequently smashed to pieces. Joe Hill, a member of the International Workers of the World, was dragged out of jail and lynched by a mob who tied a rope round his neck and threw him off a bridge. Today a ballad celebrates his tragic career. This kind of public hysteria presented the American businessman with a golden opportunity to wield the whip hand over the working class. By picturing himself as a patriotic, hundred-per-cent American and pinning the Bolshevist label on all trade union leaders, he was able to destroy most of the gains secured by labour during the war years. The demand for the closed or unionized shop suddenly became an un-American activity, a goal desired only by 'long-haired foreigners and unwashed East-side Jews'; many perfectly legal strikes were declared by the courts to be illegal; union leaders were thrown into jail on flimsy pretexts; a boatload of suspected Reds was deported in the 'Soviet Ark' to Russia; and six thousand other suspects were rounded up in a one-day drive and herded, sometimes cruelly, into custody.

The school system was scoured from top to bottom for the slightest trace of socialism or liberal thinking of any kind. Ratepayers, the American Legion, the Rotary Club and the local Ladies' Aid Society formed self-appointed vigilante committees to ensure that all instruction was carried on in a spirit of uncritical reverence for the United States of America. Teachers and college professors were forced to sign oaths of allegiance and many of them were fired for teaching nothing more than the need for tolerance and understanding. The American Defense Society, the National Security League and a host of other witch-hunting organizations pored through textbooks, scanned magazines and newspapers, and pried into the theatre and the movies, hunting down people who dared to suggest that the United States was not well-nigh perfect. Intolerance seemed to become a virtue and anyone with liberal ideas soon learned to hold his tongue if he wished to hold his job. A great many organizations of one kind or another quickly discovered that they could defeat whatever they wanted to defeat by tarring it with the Bolshevist brush. Militarists, opponents of the League of Nations, Jew-

A modern rally of the Ku Klux Klan, showing the fiery cross, the white hoods and circus-like outfits of their leaders—Titans, Cyclops, Wizards, and other such ranks. Photographs of their operations in the twenties are very rare.

haters, Negro-haters, anti-Roman-Catholics, the proponents of every sort of cause, all wrapped themselves in the Stars and Stripes and proclaimed their enemies to be un-American Reds.

Under these circumstances, extreme racial and religious intolerance became part and parcel of the Big Red Scare. Along with the trade union leaders, the socialists, the radicals and the outright Bolsheviks, the most persecuted were the Negroes, the Jews and the Roman Catholics—minority groups within an over-wrought nation that was striving for a complete Americanism and undiluted Protestant white supremacy. Leading the pack along the trail of religious and racial persecution was the Ku Klux Klan. Originally formed to restore white supremacy in the days of the 'carpetbaggers' following the American Civil War, it claimed a national membership of over 5 million in the twenties and thirties. Cloaking its aims in lofty and idealistic phrases, this secret society—with its white robe and hood and its fiery cross—became an instrument of terror in many parts of the United States. Negroes were dragged off into the woods to be tarred and feathered or whipped into unconsciousness; five men kidnapped in Louisiana were bound with wire and drowned in a lake; a naturalized foreigner was flogged because he married an American woman; a Negro was lashed until he sold his land to a white man for a fraction of its cost. In these and countless other ways, the KKK contributed its full share to the post-war reign of terror.

Eventually the American people regained their sense of proportion. As the months passed by and wartime emotions subsided, the fear of Bolshevism faded into the background and the Big Red Scare became a thing of the past. For two years, however, this atmosphere of intolerance, repression and violence was the dominant feature of American life. It helped to defeat the League of Nations and revived the desire to be isolated from European affairs. In the minds of many neutral observers, it also raised serious doubts about the emotional stability of the United States in times of great stress.

A Prairie Plot

It is surprising—and very much to the credit of Canada—that a Big Red Scare did not develop in this country as it did in the United States. Some labour leaders certainly gave the Canadian people every reason to believe that they were plotting a socialist upheaval. Indeed, it is safe to conclude that there was as much revolutionary talk and planning in Canada as there was south of the border and that we would have been equally justified if a wave of anti-Bolshevist hysteria had swept through the country. Certainly, economic conditions—long hours, low wages that did not rise with the rising cost of living, and discontent among workers about the huge profits made during the War by the owners of industry—were favourable for socialist and Bolshevik agitators.

The first important signs of revolutionary activity appeared in March 1919, at a labour conference held in Calgary. Summoned to form a branch of the One Big Union in Canada, 237 delegates from the prairie provinces and British Columbia listened to speaker after speaker stand up and condemn capitalism, democracy and the basic foundations of our society in the most violent language. They heard E. T. Kingsley of the British Columbia Labour party, for instance, declaiming: 'I stand for the One Big Union—for the specific purpose of conquering the reins of power, by peaceable means if possible; and, if not, by some other means.' R. B. Russell from Winnipeg was more specific in his call to revolutionary action: 'A revolution is about to take place in Canada in which the workers will triumph and the capitalists will be in the same position as those in Russia.' Considering that at least 10 million property owners in Russia had been starved to death or shot since November 1917, when the communist revolution had begun, and that other unknown millions had been shipped off to prison camps in Siberia, Russell's meaning must have been abundantly clear. On the other hand, the Reverend William Ivens, a minister of the Methodist Church, did not think that force would be necessary provided the workers of North America supported the One Big Union. 'If we get rid of these mossbacked craft unions and organize by whole industries,' he said, 'labour will be so strong that all we have to do is walk into any factory, tell the owner we are going to take it over, and it is done.'

After listening to speeches of this kind, the Calgary Convention drew up a constitution for the One Big Union and passed a number of resolutions which clearly revealed the revolutionary mood and communist beliefs of the delegates.

The constitution of the O.B.U., for instance, began with the following words: 'Modern industrial society is divided into two classes, those who possess and do not produce, and those who produce and do not possess. Between these two classes a continual struggle takes place.' The idea that only the labouring class—those who supposedly do not possess anything but their skill—do any useful work and that the owners of industry are unproductive drones feeding off the labour of others, is taken directly from the writings of Karl Marx. The picture of society being a constant, inevitable struggle between two classes—completely ignoring the important middle class—is also a piece of straightforward communist doctrine suitable, perhaps, to certain backward areas of the world, but in no way applicable to a modern, industrialized country. Carried to its logical conclusion, as it was by Marx and other communist writers, the theory of the class struggle leads, not only to internal revolution, but also to a worldwide showdown between capitalist and communist countries. To the faithful followers of Marx there is no room for compromise and understanding either between workers and employers or between communist and non-communist nations.

The Calgary Convention also passed resolutions favouring the complete abolition of private property, condemned production for profits and recommended in its place 'production for use'—another communist catch-phrase bandied about freely in those days but defying any exact definition. Then again, the Canadian system of parliamentary government was no more than a 'capitalistic device to crush the legitimate aspirations of labour' and should be replaced by workers' committees or soviets, as in Russia. Finally, amid loud cheering and without discussion, the Convention sent fraternal greetings to the Soviet government, 'recognizing that they have won first place in the history of the class struggle'.

Just Plain Revolution

After the Calgary meeting adjourned, the western labour leaders swung into direct action. Big strikes, to take place more or less simultaneously, were planned for Brandon, Winnipeg, Saskatoon, Regina, Vancouver and other centres. Starting off like other labour disputes with a demand for shorter hours and higher wages in one or two obviously bad industries, these strikes, so the leaders hoped, would spread to all workers. Those who were satisfied or who already had contracts with their employers would be asked to stop work in 'sympathy' for the others. Thus, by means of the general sympathetic strike, whole cities could be tied up and the working class leaders would be in control. What these men had in mind was clearly stated by Ernest Robinson, a trade union official from Winnipeg: 'Geographically speaking, these strikes will continue until they extend from Halifax to Victoria. We will withdraw labour from all industry, and it will stay withdrawn until the bosses realize that they cannot stand up against the masses of labour. If we can control industrial production now, we can control it for all time to come and we can control the government of this country, too.'

These radical theories were first put to the test in Winnipeg, where a strike among the metal workers for a 44-hour week—in place of a 60-hour one—and an

Mounted police ride through the streets of Winnipeg among the crowds of strikers—a very inflammable situation.

85-cents-per-hour wage-scale broke out on May 1, 1919. Within two weeks, according to plan, this strike spread until some thirty thousand men had quit in sympathy for the metal workers and Winnipeg had become deeply involved in the only general strike in Canadian history. The attention of the entire nation was riveted on its progress, for Winnipeg during the next six weeks was virtually a besieged city. Not only were private businesses, factories, warehouses and retail stores closed but many essential public services were also cut off. Firemen, waterworks employees, electric light and power operators, street cleaners and garbage collectors, truck drivers, express company employees, telegraph and telephone operators, milkmen, bakers, millers, butchers and packing-house employees all were out on strike. Except for the railroads, whose employees refused to strike, Winnipeg was practically cut off from the outside world. A committee of labour leaders, headed by Russell, Robinson and Ivens, attempted to rule the city and even dared to call themselves the 'Winnipeg Soviet'. In the interests of public health and safety, these men allowed bakers, milkmen, electric power operators and a few others to resume their work, but they did so only 'by permission of the Strike Committee'. As one western newspaper said: 'This is not a strike; it is just plain, ugly revolution.'

With so many idle workmen, with several thousand returned soldiers on the verge of siding with the strikers and with tempers strained to the breaking point, it was almost a miracle that Winnipeg did not erupt into violence as did so many American cities. Towards the end of the strike, there was one serious riot which had to be quelled by the Mounted Police, the militia and the threatened use of machine guns, but with this exception the city remained comparatively quiet— although one boy was shot accidentally—during six weeks of extreme tension. The great majority of ordinary citizens—'white-collar' middle class—went about their daily lives as best they could and assisted the authorities in carrying on the essential services of the city. Their refusal to panic combined with the determination of government officials and industrialists not to yield before the threat of a general strike eventually convinced the workmen that further resistance was futile and many of them voluntarily began to drift back to work.

The strike, therefore, was to all intents and purposes over when, on June 17, the federal government stepped in, arrested the main leaders and rushed them away in the early morning hours to the Stoney Mountain Penitentiary. Considering all the trouble that these men had helped to cause, it is somewhat surprising that their arrest immediately provoked a storm of protest, not only by organized labour but also by many who had opposed the Winnipeg strike up to that moment. Telegrams poured in to Ottawa, other strikes were threatened, and many newspapers urged the government to adopt a more lenient policy. Some editors seemed to feel that long hours, low wages and the extremely high cost of living justified the action of the trade unions. Others went further and claimed that the owners of industry, by taking excessive profits during the War and by their apparent indifference towards labour, had themselves partly to blame for the feelings of bitter resentment that had helped to provoke the general strike.

Despite these pleas for leniency, however, ten labour leaders were eventually brought to trial, charged with sedition and conspiracy against the Dominion of Canada. Three of the accused men—J. S. Dixon, a member of the provincial parliament in Manitoba, A. A. Heaps, a Winnipeg alderman, and J. S. Woodsworth—put up such a brilliant defence that they were acquitted, but the other seven were sentenced to a year in jail. A more significant verdict, however, was given a short time later when the Reverend William Ivens, George Armstrong and John Queen—while still in prison—were elected to the Manitoba legislature. As one writer has pointed out, they walked, on their release, from one public institution to the other and took their seats. Alderman Heaps and J. S. Woodsworth were elected to represent Winnipeg constituencies in the federal legislature. Later on, Woodsworth helped to form a new political party in Canada and for many years was a very highly respected member of parliament, even among those who disagreed with his socialist ideas.

There is a tendency now to look back on the trial of the Winnipeg strike leaders as a gross miscarriage of justice. Labour conditions after the War were indeed bad and many of the workers' demands—including the right to organize trade unions by whole industries instead of by crafts—that were considered so radical in those days are now accepted as a matter of course. Many of the men involved in the Calgary Convention, the O.B.U. movement and the general strike have since proved that they were motivated by a genuine concern for the welfare of the working class and by a certain amount of Christian idealism. A number of them entered public life and were at least partly responsible for placing valuable social legislation on the statute books of Canada. On the other hand, it may still be argued that, as originally planned, the Winnipeg strike was a conspiracy designed by men who, for the moment, had fallen under the spell of the Russian revolution. Perhaps they did not really mean what they said, but the fact remains that the agitation that they started could have had very serious consequences. At the time, the Canadian people certainly believed that the whole situation was extremely dangerous, especially considering what was happening in Russia, in Europe and even in the United States. Under these circumstances, one of the important results of our only general strike was the fact that the country did not panic. This, in turn, seemed to be another encouraging sign that Canadians were developing an independent outlook, a certain national consciousness quite different from that of our influential neighbour to the south.

The Aspirin Age

Manners and Morals

The post-war decade has many nostalgic labels—'The Roaring Twenties', 'The Aspirin Age', 'The Era of Wonderful Nonsense', 'The Lost Generation'—phrases which suggest that the generation of the 1920s had a difficult time adjusting to the problems of living in the twentieth century. With few exceptions, U.S. social historians have pointed out how the American people, in their headlong rush towards greater and ever greater material progress, seemed to lose sight of their national ideals; how money-making, size and statistics of economic achievement became more important in their eyes than quality and spiritual values; how they considered good manners undemocratic and a cultivated mind a hindrance to success; how they turned their backs on Woodrow Wilson, the League of Nations and all other forms of idealism; how they refused, with unthinking optimism, to tolerate any suggestion that conditions in the United States could be improved; and above all how they accepted, with appalling uniformity, the customs and commonplace thoughts of the crowd. The sensational tabloid newspapers went a step farther and pictured American society as a three-ringed circus of sport, sex and crime.

The Big Red Scare set the pace for the entire post-war decade. It was only the first of many emotional sprees which sent the United States reeling through the Roaring Twenties in disorderly confusion. Disillusioned by the squabbles of the Peace Conference, frustrated by wartime regulations, bored by the high moral tone of Wilson's administration, and apparently feeling that life was futile and nothing much mattered, many people in the United States—and especially those living in the big cities—set out to forget it all and have a good time. As one of their historians has written: 'The country decided it might as well play—follow the crowd, take up the new toys that were amusing the crowd, go in for the new fads,

Contestants in the first Miss America contest, Atlantic City, New Jersey, 1921

savour the amusing scandals and trivialities of life.' This spirit, encouraged as it was for some by pay envelopes larger than ever, coincided with a number of important social and economic changes—the coming of the radio, the movies and the motor car; the rapid growth of cities; the new, war-born freedom for women; the appearance of confession magazines; the rise of high-pressure advertising; the attempt to prohibit the use of liquor—to produce a complete revolution in manners, behaviour and public taste.

Of these factors that helped to change the whole pattern of social behaviour during the 1920s, the most important was undoubtedly the tremendous increase in the use of the automobile. Quite aside from its use for business or ordinary family purposes, the motor car offered a readily available means of escaping from the watchful eye of parents and chaperons or from the restraining influence of neighbourhood opinion. American sociologists all agree that it did more than anything else to break down the pre-war moral codes and the older, more formalized relationships between the sexes.

Perhaps the most obvious sign of this revolution was the change in the appearance and social position of women. Up to this time, it had been considered unladylike for women and girls to work except in a very limited number of professions such as teaching and nursing. Now they came pouring out of the schools, the colleges and the sheltered existence of the home into all manner of new occupations. Smaller houses, apartments, the increased use of canned goods and packaged foods, shopping by telephone, the appearance of electric irons, washing machines, refrigerators, vacuum cleaners and a host of other appliances, ready-made clothes, eating out at restaurants, all served to cut down the former drudgeries of housekeeping and freed women, if not to work, then at least to enjoy much more leisure time. This, in turn, produced a phenomenal change in clothing styles. Silk and rayon began to replace cotton; sheer, flesh-coloured stockings were no longer luxuries for the rich; the voluminous petticoats of pre-war days were cast aside; and the hemline, which stood at a discreet ankle length in 1920, started to climb—despite all public protests and even State 'decency laws'—until it had reached the knee. Not content with short and skimpy clothes, women also sought the freedom of shorter hair and adjusted the size of their hats to suit their bobbed and mannish heads. The use of rouge and lipstick —both of which were considered almost immoral in pre-war days—became so popular that the female of the species spent over a billion dollars on paint and powder in this one short decade.

With equal determination and as another defiant sign of their quest for freedom, women took to smoking cigarettes. Even more significant, and certainly more disturbing to the nation, was the fact that men and women were drinking together. Describing this situation, one American observer has written: 'Among well-to-do people the serving of cocktails before dinner became almost socially obligatory. Mixed parties swarmed up to the curtained grills of speakeasies, uttered the mystic password, and girls along with men stood at the bar with one foot on the old brass rail. The late-afternoon cocktail party became a new American institution. . . . It was altogether probable that prohibition succeeded in reducing the total amount of drinking in the country as a whole and decidedly so among the working men of the industrial districts. Yet the fact remains that among the prosperous classes which set the standards of national social behaviour, alcohol flowed more freely than ever before and lubricated an unprecedented informality —to say the least—of manners.'

This informality of manners—this craving to be modern and smart and sophisticated—revealed itself in many other ways. Conversation in once polite circles became spicy, brutally frank and immodest. The discreet advertising of pre-war days gave way to bold, personal appeals for women to become more alluring and men more desirably masculine. The new movie industry produced many thoughtful and artistic films, but turned out many more productions full of vulgarity and cheap sensationalism. From the publishing houses came a whole series of novels which depicted in scarlet terms the supposedly immoral and degenerate life being led by the young people of the big cities. Risqué plays, which in pre-war days would have been banned even in New York, were produced for the benefit of capacity audiences. In many ways, the United States gave the surface impression of a nation that had lost some of its moral stamina.

Under these circumstances, it was almost inevitable that another wave of frenzied excitement should sweep over the country. The younger generation, so a shocked segment of America concluded, was going to the dogs—an attitude that was to appear again almost fifty years later. Many of these people agreed with the president of Florida University when he proclaimed: 'The low-cut gowns, the rolled hose and short skirts are born of the Devil and are carrying the present and future generations to chaos and destruction.' The Y.W.C.A., the churches and many women's organizations launched intensive campaigns against the new style of dancing which they condemned as 'impure, syncopated embracing to the barbaric wails of the saxophone'. Worried legislators in Utah,

Virginia and Ohio introduced bills designed to control the hemline by law and prevent the sale of any 'garment which unduly displays the lines of the female figure'. A vigorous but futile crusade was undertaken against the confession magazines and a vain attempt to control the motion picture industry was made through the establishment of a national censor's office. The Anti-Saloon League —which was largely responsible for the Eighteenth Amendment prohibiting the sale of liquor—continued its fight to keep America dry and tried to persuade indifferent state governments to spend more money on enforcement of the new laws. Fiery evangelists like the famous Billy Sunday and Mrs. Aimee Semple McPherson damned the twentieth century and all its work and drew huge crowds to hear them preach the impossible doctrine of salvation through a return to the simple, good old days. And finally, dozens of sociologists produced reams of statistics trying to prove whether or not conditions in the United States were really as bad as they seemed to be.

Despite the tremendous volume of evidence gathered by the sociologists, it is very difficult and dangerous to draw any general conclusion from their studies. No one has ever proved, for instance, that the people of the United States did more or less drinking during prohibition—if only for the simple reason that bootleggers did not keep any records. Nor has it been established that changing female fashions, the smoking habit, the free talk and rude manners were signs of a decay in national moral codes. It is, perhaps, safe to conclude that rural and small-town America—forming almost half the population of the country— changed very slowly and retained many of the simple virtues of family life and church. It took time for people to realize that the United States, like most other countries, was caught in a social upheaval that inevitably follows all major wars. Consequently, many of the changes were condemned simply because they were new and came so fast. Many features of the post-war revolution which seemed most shocking at the time are accepted today as a matter of course. However, the fact remains that, in the larger centres of population and among the social classes that set the pace, the Roaring Twenties produced a highly undesirable type of life. And this irresponsible, pleasure-seeking trend continued until the Great Depression compelled the entire country to re-assess its standards of value.

The Pursuit of Pleasure

Another feature of the post-war social revolution—one fully as important in its permanent results as those arising from the changing status of women—was the very large increase in all forms of entertainment. It is obvious, of course, that the rapid and almost simultaneous development of the automobile, the moving picture, and the radio offered pleasant new ways of killing time. These things, combined with the shorter working week, the abolition of laws prohibiting Sunday sport, the concentration of population in large centres, the new freedom for women and other factors, opened up a huge market for organized amusement. And the same high-pressure advertising that sold soap, face creams and electrical appliances was used with equal skill to 'ballyhoo' the athlete or the movie star. Millions of people went to see 'Babe' Ruth play baseball, 'Red' Grange play foot-

(Right) Babe Ruth
(Far right) Jack Dempsey

ball, Jack Dempsey box or Douglas Fairbanks perform his heroic feats on the screen, simply because they learned to know—and in many cases almost to worship—these stars in the columns of the press. This was the era when huge stadiums, expensive golf courses and thousands of movie theatres were built—the era when the American people began so fervently to idolize the stars of radio, screen and playing field and the era when these new demigods were elevated to a social position and received a financial return comparable to the top business or political executives in the country. Craving amusement and capable of paying for it to a greater extent than any other country, the people of the United States began to spend one-quarter of the national income each year on recreation and play.

Probably the most conspicuous sign of this new trend was the tremendous enthusiasm for spectator sports. College football—with altered rules to encourage the more frequent use of the forward pass and to make the game more spectacular —began to draw vast numbers of people who had never seen the inside of an institution of higher learning. The enormous popularity of football was at least partly responsible for the undesirable characteristics of American college athletics which have persisted to this day. It introduced a regrettable profes-sionalism not only in football but also—as they, too, became increasingly popular —in basketball, track and field, and swimming.

The limelight in professional sport during the 1920s was shared by baseball and boxing. The post-war attendance at league and World Series games increased by over three hundred per cent and baseball became a multi-million-dollar business. Boxing, on the other hand, achieved a popularity and respectability which it has not enjoyed under gangland control in recent years. Guided by a super-salesman named Tex Rickard and featuring for a full decade the fighting powers of Jack Dempsey and Gene Tunney, it reached a climax when the gates from their second bout exceeded $2½ million. Through football, baseball, boxing, through swim-ming, through golf and Davis Cup tennis, the United States became the most sports-conscious nation in the world.

Theda Bara, celebrated movie vamp, in a scene from Salome, *1918*

Competing with spectator sports for the interest of an amusement-hungry public were the radio and moving picture industries. In November 1920, KDKA, the first commercial broadcasting station, was opened by the Westinghouse Company in Pittsburg to broadcast the results of the presidential election and the Dempsey-Carpentier fight. The experiment was an immediate success. Soon everybody was talking, not about wireless telephony, as it was originally called, but about radio. Newspapers brought out pages of radio news, countless people set out to make their own crystal sets and loop aerials. In 1923 the crystal set, which transmitted sound only through earphones, gave way to the tube and loudspeaker set and immediately radio blossomed out as another new multi-million-dollar industry. Seven hundred broadcasting stations, correctly sensing large profits from advertising, quickly followed KDKA into business; annual sales of receiving sets jumped from $3 million to $650 million and by 1929 almost half the families in the United States had at least one radio.

The moving picture industry expanded with equal rapidity. Even before the invention of the 'talkie'—which did not come until 1927 and was not universal until the end of the decade—movie-goers were purchasing some 100 million tickets every week for admission to the nation's twenty thousand theatres. Silent movie audiences thrilled to the sweet innocence of Canadian-born Mary Pickford; the provocative charms of Clara Bow, the 'It' girl; the torrid love-making of Greta Garbo, John Gilbert and Rudolph Valentino; or the swashbuckling adventures of Douglas Fairbanks. Spectators of all ages were convulsed by the delightful foolishness of Charlie Chaplin and Harold Lloyd, while on Saturday afternoons Tom Mix shot up outlaws to the delight of his juvenile fans who invariably read all the captions out loud. Here, too, the cult of hero-worship was carried to extremes. Hollywood had a long way to go before reaching its present-day flamboyant and erratic position, but as the centre of the motion picture industry, even in the 1920s, it had already begun to attract an overwhelming amount of the nation's interest.

The Bandwagon of Prosperity

A number of circumstances combined to make this decade an exceedingly prosperous one. During most of these years, American exports found a ready market helping to repair the ravages of war in Europe. New industries—the movies, radio, rayon, cigarettes, chemicals, electrical appliances, telephones and above all the motor car—pumped rich blood into the whole economy. The automotive industry, employing either directly or indirectly over 4 million men, placed a car in two out of three homes well before the end of the decade. This in turn stimulated the building of highways—and of the garages, filling stations, bus terminals, hot-dog stands, restaurants and tourist homes that quickly ranged themselves along the main routes. The oil, iron and steel industries flourished to an even greater extent than in the pre-war railway-building era. The development of suburban areas outside the big cities, the resulting boom in real estate, the construction of theatres, stadiums, skyscrapers and power dams all helped to push the statistics of prosperity higher and higher. Henry Ford's doctrine of good wages, a low-priced product and production based on a minute division of labour by both men and machines was adopted on a country-wide basis. An ever-increasing number of salesmen and advertising agencies learned all the tricks of breaking down buyer resistance and helped to market the six-cylinder cars, the refrigerators, the radios and all the other consumer goods that came pouring out from the factories using these new mass-production techniques. Instalment buying increased to such an extent that, by 1929, twenty per cent of all retail sales were on credit and the public owed the storekeepers, the banks and the loan companies more than $6 billion.

The politicians also provided a hot-house environment for the rapid growth of business. The Republican party, under the leadership of presidents Warren Harding, Calvin Coolidge and Herbert Hoover, held office all during the first post-war decade. The more conservative members of this party set out to discredit Woodrow Wilson and the League of Nations mainly because the Democrats seemed to stand for social reform—and reform usually meant inter-ference in business. Any remaining zeal for government regulation of industry was quickly frightened into submission during the Big Red Scare. Consequently, the victorious Republicans, reflecting the fiercely nationalistic and reactionary spirit of the decade, gave unbridled freedom to the business community.

Under these circumstances, it is not surprising that a number of juicy scandals added to the excitement of the Roaring Twenties. During the early years especially, a series of charges—involving government building contracts, the leasing of publicly-owned timber and oil lands and the purchase of protection by the rum-runners—was climaxed, after the sudden death of Harding, by subsequent revelations about the President's shocking private life. Although the American people took a keen interest in these disclosures, the harshest condem-nation by the press and the public was reserved, not for those who had cheated the government, but for those who insisted on bringing the facts to light. 'Mistakes' might have been made, so the average businessman was inclined to believe, but it was unpatriotic to condemn them and discredit the government.

Reverence for the businessman and the worship of economic success appeared to be the most characteristic feature of life in the United States. According to one of the most astute economists of the day: 'The businessman has become the dictator of our destinies, ousting the statesman, the priest and the philosopher as the final authority on the conduct of American society. A great many people may have been disillusioned by some features of the Roaring Twenties, but of one thing, at least, they were certain. In the rich, booming United States, the band-wagon of prosperity would go rolling forward forever—and they might as well climb upon it. As early as 1922, there were over 14 million stockholders in American corporations—an increase of almost 4 million since the end of the war. This trend continued until it reached a frenzied climax during 1928 and the first nine months of 1929 in a wild splurge of sheer speculative gambling on the stock market. For days on end, the volume of trading broke all known records, the ticker-tapes ran far behind schedule, the price of common shares soared up and up, people bought on credit and hoped to repay the brokers out of paper profits and almost everyone was sure that the bonanza was just beginning. Few indeed were those who foresaw that the whole economic system of the United States was tottering on the brink of chaos; but, as someone said, it was fun while it lasted.

Rustic Echoes to the North

Small-town Tastes
Life in Canada during the 1920s did not roar quite as lustily as in the United States. Just as the Canadian people took the Big Red Scare more in their stride, so they also seemed to adjust to the problems of twentieth-century living with greater ease. They had their times of feverish excitement and national headaches, but not in large enough doses to justify calling this 'the Aspirin Age'; and no one could suggest that the first post-war decade produced a 'lost generation' of Canadians. All the factors that caused the social revolution of the Roaring Twenties were at work in this country and many of them originated in the United States, but their influence was modified as they moved northward across the border.

Why was this so? Why was the pace of life less hectic in this country than in the United States? Although it is difficult for an outside observer to be sympathetic with their viewpoint, American historians have suggested that their countrymen were disillusioned by the War and hoped to relax from its tensions in a gay round of sport, scandal, new fads and tremendous trifles. If this is true, the Canadian people, having been involved in the First World War for a longer time and to a far greater extent, had every excuse to indulge in the same restless, pleasure-seeking kind of life. The fact that they did not do so shows how thoroughly exhausted they were by the emotional strains of the War. With much better reason than the Americans, they also wanted to forget it all, but the majority of Canadians simply did not have enough nervous energy left to keep pace with their southern neighbours. By this time, also, they seemed to have developed a distinct national outlook capable of resisting American influences that did not fit the Canadian scene. Although generalities about the character of a nation are frequently unreliable, it is safe to conclude that a reserved and temperate attitude towards life had become apparent in Canada during the 1920s. Her long association with Great Britain, important differences in government and education, geographic location and especially the sacrifices demanded by the War combined to create an emotional maturity that was not always evident in the United States.

With or without this new national spirit, however, it was almost inevitable that social conditions in Canada should change more slowly than in the United States. When the War ended, exactly half the population of this country still lived on farms while another 20 per cent lived in centres of less than 15,000 inhabitants. Compared with the United States, where over 40 per cent of the people were concentrated in cities having *more* than 15,000 inhabitants, Canada was indeed a land of small towns and villages. Without any conscious effort on their part, therefore, Canadians escaped many of the big-city evils that caused so much concern in the United States. As in rural America, farmers and small-town residents across the whole of Canada clung to the moral codes and retained many of their pre-war customs. The real test of Canada's ability to maintain an independent national culture would come only when industrialization had created a much larger urban population.

Under these circumstances, with life in Canada changing gradually, the people had time to adjust to the new age without the worry and excitement that went on in the United States. Canadian women, for instance, adopted the new styles, shed pounds of clothing, raised their hemlines, bobbed or shingled their hair and had fewer children. After the War they besieged the offices of the trust and insurance companies, sold real estate, opened smart little shops, invaded the department stores, and deserted domestic service in favour of more interesting employment to such an extent that by 1929 the number of females engaged in trade and commerce had increased by over 1,000 per cent and one out of every five Canadian women had become a 'working girl'. They swam more, played golf and tennis, went in for physical culture and found more opportunities than ever before to be in the company of the opposite sex. The local golf club became the social centre of the smart set while almost every town had its more plebian 'summer pavilion' where the saxophone wailed out favourite hit tunes and couples did the Charleston, the strut, the butterfly or the bunny hop with as much gusto as in the United States.

Throughout all these changes, however, there was practically no undue alarm in Canada except for a brief flurry in Quebec at the beginning of the decade. Few people suggested that the younger generation was making mincemeat of the old moral codes or that manners and standards of conduct were in grave danger. Obviously, conservative small-town opinion had softened some of the more brazen features of this part of the social revolution. Although confession magazines made their appearance in Canada, they were not yet popular; the tone of the press and advertising was more subdued than in the United States; conversation was not so spicy; and the growing number of popular Canadian authors such as Charles G. D. Roberts, Ernest Thompson Seton, Stephen Leacock, Robert Service, Sir Gilbert Parker, Ralph Connor and Mazo de la Roche found their inspiration in the romance of the wilderness or in the simple virtues of rural life. The majority of Canadians continued to enjoy *Wild Animals I Have Known, The Kindred of the Wild, The Songs of a Sourdough, Sunshine Sketches,* the *Jalna* stories and *Anne of Green Gables* long after cosmopolitan Americans had taken to more sophisticated fare. Many Canadians undoubtedly read *This Side of Paradise, Dark Laughter, Lady Chatterley's Lover* and other novels published in the United States, but the best sellers in this country, as in rural America, were the wholesome western romances of Zane Grey and James Oliver Curwood or Gene Stratton Porter's nature stories.

Although most people seemed to abide by prohibition and were temperate when it was abolished, the Canadian government, the breweries and distilleries, and a large number of shady individuals in the border towns made things very difficult for American officials who were trying to keep the United States dry. 'Rum-running' into the United States was a characteristic of life in Canada all during the 1920s. It was a favourite topic of conversation, an almost constant source of friction and excitement along the border and a highly profitable, usually legal, business. The manufacture of liquor for export was not unlawful and the Canadian government adopted the attitude that if some individuals wanted to ship this particular product to the United States and take a chance with American revenue officers, it was their own affair. The result, as described by the Toronto *Globe,* was that: 'On the Canadian side of the Detroit River anyone can see, at almost any hour, liquor in cases and beer in barrels being unloaded from Canadian railways on Canadian docks and transferred to rum-running power boats. . . . Equal laxity is shown in the granting of official papers to vessels clearing for Cuba or Mexico. Small liquor-laden boats, incapable of a sea voyage, deliver their cargoes and return within a few days, even hours, to their point of departure. This farce is solemnly and regularly enacted under the very noses of Canadian customs officials.' Despite repeated requests from Washington, the Canadian government, concluding that it was up to the United States to enforce its own laws, refused to take action—a situation that provoked speculation in parliament and in the country as to just how much money the liquor interests were contributing to political-party campaign funds.

Canadian women not only passively resisted some of the less desirable features of this social revolution sweeping North America and western Europe, but also took vigorous steps to guide it in the right direction. This they did by using their new freedom and leisure time to organize clubs and welfare associations. With a zeal that stands out as one of the main features of this decade, they formed new associations or joined existing ones until, by 1929, there were over sixty important country-wide organizations, memberships had quadrupled and two women of every three in Canada belonged to a national society of some kind. In addition to encouraging child welfare, home-making, youth groups, missionary work, education, art, drama and a host of other civic projects, these women's organizations were partly responsible for maintaining interest in religion and church affairs. Despite the motor car and the growing popularity of Sunday sports, the church continued to be one of the great stabilizing influences in Canadian society during the 1920s.

Sporting Days

With only six cities of more than 100,000 inhabitants in the whole of Canada, it is not surprising that organized amusement of all kinds also developed at a slower pace than in the United States. Spectator sports, although increasing, were on a very modest scale. Until the end of the decade, there was not a stadium in the country capable of holding 14,000 people; professional football coaches were non-existent; none of the evils associated with college games in the United States appeared over here; and the Big Four and the Ontario Rugby Football Union were composed of purely amateur teams—although occasionally one heard of a star player 'finding' a ten-dollar bill in his boot. Since the western Canadian champions usually decided 'for financial reasons' that it was unhealthy to come east for a playoff, the Grey Cup was almost always a close contest between Ottawa 'Roughriders', Hamilton 'Tigers', Toronto 'Balmy Beach' or Queen's University.

Without imported American talent, the game of rugby retained many distinctive Canadian features. Instead of copying the standardized systems of play used in the United States, amateur coaches dreamed up their own concoctions. And although some of these were weird to behold, they were probably as interesting to watch as the one system in use throughout virtually all of North America today. With no forward passing until 1929–30 and running interference limited to one yard, the favourite ways of advancing the ball were by kicking or by spectacular three- or four-man end runs. Wonderful skill in this particular phase of the game brought nation-wide fame to the backfield combination of Evans to Batstone to Leadley and three consecutive Grey Cup championships to Queen's University.

Undoubtedly the most popular game in Canada was ice hockey. The professional National Hockey League, formed in 1917 and originally composed of Montreal 'Maroons', Montreal 'Canadiens', Ottawa 'Senators' and Toronto 'St. Pats', quickly expanded to ten teams by 1926. The Boston 'Bruins' were organized in 1924, the New York 'Rangers' introduced hockey to the new Madison Square Garden in 1925, teams were formed in Pittsburgh, Chicago, Detroit and Cleveland and for several years it was necessary to have two divisions in the N.H.L. with a play-off between the Canadian and American sections for the Stanley Cup. Partly because the farm-club system which now concentrates the star 'amateur' players in a comparatively few teams was in its infancy, every town in Canada worthy of the name had its own good hockey club. Although definite figures are not available, it is a reasonably good guess that there was more interest in local small-town hockey during the 1920s than there is today. The competition for the Memorial and Allan cups aroused just as much excitement and drew as many spectators as any professional game and raised the great teams from Port Arthur, the University of Toronto, Fort William, Trail and the University of Manitoba to positions of national prominence. Most famous of all, however, were the six regulars and two

The opening of Maple Leaf Gardens, Toronto, in 1931. (Photo, The Globe and Mail, Toronto.)

substitute players who formed the 'Varsity Grads'—Allan Cup winners and Olympic champions, by huge scores, in 1928.

On March 26, 1923, while radio listeners struggled with their earphones or placed them in glass bowls for better reception, a young man named Foster Hewitt, speaking from the old Mutual Street Arena in Toronto, made the first hockey broadcast in history over station CFCA. Although the game was an amateur playoff between Parkdale Canoe Club and Kitchener, this was the beginning of 'Hockey Night in Canada'. It might be added here that the Mutual Street Arena was one of the very few having artificial ice. Today in the province of Ontario alone there are over two hundred rinks, but during the 1920s there were fewer than a dozen in the whole of Canada. Many of the best-known teams played their league games on natural and sometimes open-air rinks; the hockey season started after Christmas and was always thrown off schedule by the 'January thaw'; practically every town had one or more outdoor rinks and although hockey for younger players was not as highly organized as it is today, it was at least not necessary for a boy to get up at six o'clock in the morning to enjoy the luxuries of artificial ice.

In additional to hockey and rugby, a great many other sports helped to satisfy the growing desire for recreation and amusement. Some of these enjoyed a brief spell of popularity and then declined while others became a permanent and important part of the national scene. Lacrosse, regarded by many as Canada's truly national game, had a brief fling as a professional spectator sport. With modified rules as 'box lacrosse' it captured the sports headlines until the domination of hockey relegated the game to contests of regional interest. During the 1920s, when highly specialized, expensive coaching had not yet become a determining factor, some of Canada's naturally gifted athletes often seemed to have a good chance in world competition. Interest in their endeavours and the publicity they rec· ived helped to arouse enthusiasm for their particular sport just as Nancy Greene's more recent triumphs raised hopes in the minds of thousands of young skiers. Perhaps for this reason rowing, paddling, tennis, speed skating and track and field played a more important role in the twenties than they do today. Stars such as Cyril Coaffee and Myrtle Cook in track, Charles Gorman and Gladys Robinson in speed skating and Joe Wright in rowing all held international reputations and some set world records. Three times during this decade Canada's Davis Cup team beat Cuba in the first round and then played exciting matches with Japan before losing the second round. The fact that the matches were played on native soil and that Willard Crocker, Jack Wright and Gilbert Nunns did so well helped to place tennis among the most popular of Canadian games.

It was also during the 1920s that golf and curling began to thrive. When the War ended, Canada possessed about a hundred golf courses, but interest in the game suddenly became so great that for a time new courses were built at the rate of over sixty each year. This pace slowed down after 1925 but by that time there were 292 golf courses in the country, an increase of almost three hundred per cent. Many of these new courses were publicly owned and among the thousands playing on them, some no doubt hoped to follow in the steps of Ada Mackenzie or Ross 'Sandy' Sommerville, the two best-known Canadian golfers of this decade. The growth of curling, now the most widely played game in Canada, was marked by the fact that the Macdonald Tankard, emblematic of the Dominion championship, was put up for competition for the first time in 1926–27.

And, finally, if only to show that Canadians also could become excited over tremendous trifles, a swimmer named George Young outlasted all others in a race from Catalina Island to the coast of California and won the $25,000 prize offered by William Wrigley, Jr. This feat aroused so much interest in 1927 that the directors of the Canadian National Exhibition were encouraged to stage a huge 'marathon swim' as part of their waterfront show. Attracted from all over the world by $50,000 in prize money, 289 greased contestants took the plunge, but only Ernest Vierkoetter and two other swimmers finished the twenty-one-mile course. For the next few years the marathon swim was a feature attraction at the C.N.E., but in time the crowds became tired of watching this gruelling endurance test and the race was abandoned.

Imported Entertainment

Again making allowance for difference in population, neither the radio nor the moving picture industry expanded as rapidly in Canada as in the United States. Both types of entertainment formed a very important part of the post-war social revolution in this country but, as in sports, purely Canadian conditions slowed down their rate of development. As we have already observed, about half the families in the United States owned at least one radio by the end of the Roaring Twenties and there was one motion picture theatre for every 7,300 people. In Canada, on the other hand, less than twenty per cent of all families possessed a radio while there was only one theatre for every 21,000 people. Despite these differences, however, it was through the radio and movies that American culture

Rudolph Valentino in a scene from The Four Horsemen of the Apocalypse, *1921.*

exerted its greatest influence on Canada. The domestic market here was much too small to justify the establishment of a native industry to manufacture movies and the British film industry experienced serious difficulties all during the 1920s. As a result, Hollywood productions completely monopolized our four hundred and fifty or so theatres and Canadian movie-goers flocked as eagerly as Americans to see Harold Lloyd in *Safety Last*, Charlie Chaplin and Jackie Coogan in *The Kid*, Rudolph Valentino in *The Sheik* and all the other great silent pictures. And with equal expectation, they waited to see and hear *The Jazz Singer*, starring Al Jolson—the first of the talkies.

Although there were seventy-nine commercial broadcasting companies in Canada by 1929, the majority of these were low-powered stations servicing a local area and relying to a large extent on programs provided by the American or Columbia Broadcasting Corporation. Consequently, the music of Paul Whiteman,

Radio Station CJOC, Lethbridge, in 1929

'The King of Jazz'; the theme songs of Ben Bernie, Guy Lombardo and the other great 'name bands' of this decade; and the voices of Rudy Vallee, Eddie Cantor and Amos 'n Andy were as familiar to Canadian listeners as they were to those in the United States. Due to radio, the same hit tunes were sung on both sides of the border; crazy, happy songs they were—'Yes, We Have No Bananas', 'Barney Google with the Goo-Goo-Googley Eyes', 'That Old Gang of Mine', 'Sunny Side Up', 'This Is My Lucky Day' and a host of others—all reflecting the prosperous, carefree spirit of the times.

Although most of these radio programs and movies were little more than harmless entertainment, some of them, by reflecting the irresponsible philosophy of the Roaring Twenties, tended to create an outlook on life which was not quite in keeping with Canadian standards. Many movies exaggerated the glories of American history, taught 'a hundred per cent Americanism', scoffed at European culture and—like their textbooks in this decade—contained a good deal of anti-British sentiment. This whole situation soon began to worry Canadian authorities. The moving picture industry presented an insoluble problem, but in 1928 a Royal Commission was appointed to investigate radio broadcasting. As a result of its labours, the Dominion government in 1933 created the Canadian Broadcasting Corporation to operate a network of publicly-owned radio stations. The main reasons behind this move were to foster Canadian ideals and culture, encourage native talent and limit the number of American programs coming into the country.

The North Atlantic Triangle

Testing the Ties of Empire

It is apparent that the post-war social revolution came to Canada primarily through the United States. American love for organized sports, American movies and radio programs, American magazines, American industrial designs and production techniques, American products and high-pressure advertising and business methods, American tourists, American trade unions and branch factories and investments in Canada—these and many other forces exerted greater pressure on this country during the 1920s than ever before. And as this pressure increased, as we became more definitely a North American nation, the influence of Great Britain in Canadian affairs inevitably declined. The distinct spirit of nationalism had been intensified during the War and had found concrete expression in the Imperial War Cabinet and membership in the League of Nations. The post-war social and economic changes in Canada still further strengthened this independent spirit and led our statesmen, along with those from the other dominions, to sever the remaining formal ties which bound the British Empire together.

In 1920, Canada was still technically a colony of Great Britain. The British parliament could pass laws applicable to the whole Empire; the Governor General, appointed by the party in power in Britain and acting under instructions from the Colonial Office, could reserve any bills for approval by London; the Canadian constitution was a British statute, which could be altered only by the parliament at Westminster; and the Privy Council was the final court of appeal for all legal cases. Foreign affairs were controlled by the British government on behalf of the whole Empire and the Dominion could not conclude its own treaties or establish diplomatic missions abroad. In actual practice many of these restrictions were seldom used, but in foreign affairs they were a real and very serious handicap to independent action. Starting from the new position secured at the Paris Peace Conference, the member states of the Commonwealth, therefore, set out during the 1920s to secure full freedom to conduct their own foreign relations.

The growing importance of Canada as a North American nation and the need to clarify her legal position within the British Empire was made abundantly clear by several events that occurred early in the new decade. The Peace Conference was no sooner over than serious rivalry between Japan and the United States began to develop in the Far East. As a result of Germany's defeat and the Russian revolution, Japan emerged from the War not only with the largest fleet in the Pacific but as the third naval power in the world. The United States, with many interests in the Far East and a long-standing but not always justifiable dislike for the Japanese, became alarmed by this new threat. Her alarm was intensified by the fact that Great Britain seemed anxious to renew the pre-war Anglo-Japanese Alliance for another ten-year period. Many Americans believed that this treaty

Arthur Meighen, 1920–21, 1926

William Lyon Mackenzie King, 1921–26, 1926–30, 1935–48

would be used by Japan to increase her power in the Far East and that it was a real threat to the United States. Anti-British feeling flared up in many parts of the country and remained strong as long as there was any prospect that the Japanese treaty might be renewed.

This was a serious matter for Canada, not only because she faced the Pacific and shared the American fear of Japan, but also because friendly relations between the United States and Britain were of the utmost importance to her. Influenced by the anti-Japanese propaganda in American newspapers, Canada decided to support the United States. Consequently, Arthur Meighen, who had become leader of the Conservative party and Prime Minister of Canada when Sir Robert Borden retired in 1920, went to the 1921 Imperial Conference determined to prevent the renewal of the Anglo-Japanese treaty. One American correspondent reporting the Conference from London stated that 'so nearly does Premier Meighen express the views of the United States that he must be credited with representing North American opinions rather than merely those of Canada. Despite the reluctance of Great Britain and the strong opposition of Australia and New Zealand, Meighen's mission was successful. In place of the exclusive Anglo-Japanese treaty, the Canadian government proposed a general meeting of all the countries having interests in the Far East. Partly as a result of this suggestion, the representatives of nine nations assembled at Washington in November 1921 to discuss Pacific and Far Eastern questions.

The Washington Conference resulted in the signing of three treaties, the most important of which provided for a certain amount of naval disarmament. Japan agreed to limit the number of her battleships to sixty per cent of the tonnage owned by either the United States or Great Britain, while Italy and France accepted a quota of thirty-five per cent. The participating nations also promised not to extend their military or naval bases in the Pacific and pledged themselves, in a document known as the Nine Power Pact, to respect the independence of China. Thus a costly naval race was averted for the time being and an uneasy balance of power was restored in the Far East. While the crisis lasted, however, Canada found herself in an uncomfortable situation which revealed once again the difficulties arising from her position as a close neighbour of the United States and, at the same time, a member of the British Empire.

Shortly after this, another equally revealing incident occurred at a place called Chanak on the European side of the Dardanelles. British troops were stationed there as part of an international force guarding the neutral zone that the Peace Conference had erected around the Straits. In September 1922, as a result of post-war troubles between Turkey and Greece, Turkey threatened to send a seasoned army of eighty thousand men across the Dardanelles into Europe. Other countries defending the neutral zone pulled out and left Great Britain to face the prospect of a war with Turkey. The British Mediterranean and Atlantic fleets steamed to the scene and several regiments were rushed out from England. At this point, the British government cabled to Ottawa asking whether Canada would send a force to help defend the neutral zone against the Turks. This request was supposed to be secret, but official sources in London gave it out to the Canadian press before the cablegram was received by the Dominion government. It seemed that the British cabinet was appealing directly to the Canadian people over the heads of their own government.

The publication of this British call to arms, as the press was disposed to regard it, created a great sensation in Canada and revived many old arguments. Henri Bourassa expressed the general viewpoint of Quebec with characteristic vigour in his newspaper. 'Chanak? Who in Canada has ever heard of Chanak until this moment? Canada has no interest in the region affected; she is in no way responsible for the situation which has caused the peril; why should Canada, with a new outpouring of blood, defend mistakes and obstinacy for which it is not responsible? Our duty in this matter is clear—to reply to England's request by a refusal.'

In English-speaking Canada, army officers came out of retirement, military headquarters were besieged with volunteers, most of the Protestant churches sent telegrams to Ottawa and on Sunday, September 17, with an enthusiasm which would have done justice to a mediaeval crusade against the infidel Turk, many pulpits rang out the call to arms. This time, however, there was a noticeable difference. Throughout English-speaking Canada, even in Ontario, there were many newspapers and a strong body of public opinion which agreed with the views of Quebec.

Correctly sensing this division within the country, W. L. Mackenzie King, the newly elected Prime Minister of Canada, played for time. The Dominion might send a contingent, so he advised London, but this would require approval by parliament. In the meantime he would 'welcome the fullest information possible before deciding to summon a special session of parliament'. Arthur Meighen, Conservative leader of the opposition, disagreed. In a speech which became famous and later boomeranged against him, he proclaimed: 'When Britain's message came, then Canada should have said, "Ready, aye ready; we stand by you."' Fortunately Turkey did not carry out her threat and the crisis blew over. However, the Chanak incident disclosed the serious lack of consultation between Great Britain and the dominions and strengthened the view that Canada should pursue an independent foreign policy.

An opportunity to express this determination was presented to Canada early in 1923 when Empire relationships were tested for the third time in as many years. For several months, Canadian and American fishery experts had been considering some way of establishing a closed season to protect the halibut while they were spawning off the coast of Alaska. Eventually the United States government submitted a draft treaty to Ottawa but worded it in such a way that it appeared to be a treaty with Great Britain. Ottawa officials claimed that this question did not in any way concern the mother country and insisted that the wording be changed. Another more serious snag arose when the British ambassador in Washington decided that he must sign the treaty, along with Canada's envoy, in order to make it legal. This had become the accepted practice in Laurier's day and the British government felt that the custom should be continued. Canada, however, maintained that the signature of her representative was quite sufficient. Great Britain finally yielded and allowed Ernest Lapointe, Canada's Minister of Fisheries, to sign the Halibut Treaty solely on behalf of the Dominion government. This new step towards independence in foreign affairs was accepted for future use by the Imperial Conference of 1923.

A Free and Equal Commonwealth
The difficulties associated with Canada's position as a North American nation were almost fully solved by the next Imperial Conference held in November 1926. This was probably the most important Conference since the first one, thirty-nine years earlier, at the time of Queen Victoria's Golden Jubilee. By the time it convened, status within the Empire had become an active political issue in two of the overseas dominions. General Hertzog, leader of the Boer Nationalists and the new Prime Minister of South Africa, had asserted in an election campaign that his country could secede from the Empire at any time it wished. The same sentiments were being openly expressed in the Irish Free State, while in Canada a federal election had just been fought on the question of restricting the powers of the Governor General. Thus the widespread belief that Imperial unity was at stake made this Conference the most momentous yet held.

The most important task facing the delegates was not to draw up a written constitution for the Empire but to clarify and define practices that had been in operation for many years. As Stanley Baldwin, the British Prime Minister, suggested in his opening address, a theoretical written constitution could no sooner be framed than 'it would have to be changed by the living growth in our midst'. The delegates must direct their efforts, so he said, towards interpreting the Empire to the world and 'clearing the ground of any political doubts as to its nature'. This the Conference did in the famous Balfour Report, a remarkable document so vaguely phrased that its meaning could be applied to almost any situation arising in the future. Recognizing that the Commonwealth 'defies classification and bears no real resemblance to any other political organization', the Report proceeded to describe it as a group of 'autonomous communities within the British Empire, equal in status, in no way subordinate one to another in any aspect of their domestic or internal affairs, though united by a common allegiance to the Crown, and freely associated as members of the British Commonwealth of Nations'.

Thus the Balfour Report, while introducing nothing new, redefined the Empire as a Commonwealth of free nations governed by a condition of independence and equality. Although it was accepted as a great imperial document and an inevitable milestone in the history of the English-speaking world, there were still many people who agreed with the viewpoint of the Toronto *Globe*: 'The Conference delegates have made no effort whatever to increase the bonds of union. Every clause in every article of the Report stresses the equality of the Dominions. Anything which savours of united effort is ignored.'

In keeping with the Balfour Report, the Imperial Conference also made important changes in the office of the Governor General. He was to serve no longer as the representative of the party in power in Great Britain but should be appointed by the Crown solely on the recommendation of the Canadian parliament. Since the Governor General, therefore, became the personal envoy of the King, the British government, in the future, would be represented at Ottawa by a new official called the High Commissioner. Also in line with the Balfour Report, Canada took another very important step towards independence when the government decided, with Great Britain's consent, to appoint a permanent minister to take charge of Canadian affairs in Washington. Two days after the 1926 Imperial Conference closed, it was announced from Ottawa that Vincent Massey, a man already prominent in the educational, business and public life of the country, had been selected as the first Canadian minister to the United States. Thus the day when 'etiquette forbade Miss Ottawa to speak to Mr. Washington except through Papa London' was ended; Canada assumed complete control of her own foreign relations and quickly established other ministries in France, Japan and elsewhere.

All that remained to be done after 1926 was to change several legal details that were not in accord with the principles of the Balfour Report. A special conference studied this problem in 1929; its report was adopted by the Imperial Conference of 1930, and its recommendations in turn were embodied in the Statute of Westminster. This Act, passed by the British parliament in 1931, concluded a long and important chapter in the history of Canada. It declared that in the future no imperial law was to apply to a dominion without its consent and also that no dominion law could be declared void by the British parliament. The last check on the legislative power of the dominions was removed. At the express wish of the Canadian government, amendments to the British North America Act were to be made as in the past by the British parliament and certain legal cases could still be appealed to the highest court in the Empire, the Judicial Committee of the Privy Council. These restrictions, however, could be removed whenever Canada wished and were retained simply because no satisfactory way to amend the constitution had been found up to that time. By 1931, therefore, through a century-long process of gradual change, the formal bonds of unity were broken and the British Commonwealth of Nations had been transformed from the old colonial type of empire into a league of independent states held together only by their common allegiance to the Crown.

A Nation in a Fireproof House

Once Canada had achieved her long-sought freedom she did not use it to any great advantage. Her pursuit of independence was based on the desire, not to advance a foreign policy of her own but to emphasize that her outlook on almost all international affairs was to make no promises, no commitments in advance, to wait and see. Perhaps she would act, but only if her own very limited national interests were obviously at stake. Explaining the reasons for this viewpoint, a distinguished Canadian once told the League of Nations Assembly that 'Canada lives in a fireproof house, far from inflammable materials'—the clear inference being that it did not matter, therefore, what happened to other people's houses.

Nowhere was this negative and defensive policy more apparent than in Canada's attitude towards the League of Nations. We are prone to criticize the United States for its extreme isolation in the post-war era. Considering how important American membership was to the success of the League and the bitter campaign waged against the Covenant in 1919–20, the criticism may be justified. But it should be kept in mind that there was a fairly strong movement in this country, possibly influenced by the United States, to withdraw Canada from the League of Nations. And this movement would have become much more influential but for the fact that League membership helped to establish Canada's independent status in the eyes of the world.

Canadian doubts about the new peace organization were clearly revealed at the very first meeting of the League when her delegates criticized the Covenant on three accounts. With some degree of justice, they joined with Australia in launching an attack against the Council because it was dominated by Big Powers who paid very little attention to the wishes of the smaller nations. They also claimed, again not without reason, that the League was a European and not a world organization. Speaking on this point N. W. Rowell, a man who had as much respect for the principles of collective security as any Canadian, said in the Assembly: 'You may say that we should have confidence in European statesmen. Perhaps we should. But it was European statesmen, European policies and European ambitions that drenched the world in blood, a tragedy for which the world is suffering and will suffer for generations; 50,000 Canadians under the soil of France is the price Canada has paid for European statesmanship.' This outburst, it might be added, provoked so much adverse comment that Rowell felt obliged later to apologize and to modify his remarks.

Canada's most persistent criticism, however, was directed against one of the key clauses in the entire Covenant. This was Article X which provided that members of the League would protect the territory and independence of all League members from external aggression and that if any such aggression threatened, the Council would decide what steps should be taken to check it. Acceptance of this obligation, of course, meant that Canada would be committing herself in advance to take part in settling disputes anywhere in the world, and this she was not prepared to do. Consequently, at each of the first four annual meetings of the League, the Canadian delegates made a determined effort to remove Article X from the Covenant. These efforts were not successful, but they helped to undermine confidence in the system of collective security almost before it started.

Led by France, another group of nations—ones that feared aggression and pinned their early hopes on the League—worked together not only to retain Article X but also to strengthen certain obvious weaknesses in the Covenant. Here again, the Commonwealth countries, including Canada, prevented any positive action. Indeed, it must be admitted that during the early formative years of the League, Great Britain and her dominions thought first of themselves, then of the Commonwealth and then, lastly, of the League of Nations. In this attitude they were neither better nor worse than any other group of countries, for all member states adopted towards the League a policy based on self-centred national interests. By 1925, therefore, it had become apparent that the League offered no real guarantee of security and many nations began to slip back into the old pre-war system of regional agreements, military alliances and heavy armaments.

Despite this dangerous trend, the remaining prosperous years of the 1920s were frequently called 'The Era of Goodwill'. The signing of the Locarno Pact by which eight European nations joined to guarantee the Versailles boundary line between Germany and France, the admission of Germany into the League, the scaling down of reparations payments, the removal of the Allied occupation army from the Rhineland and the fact that no serious international dispute arose to challenge the League, all combined to create a false sense of security. The climax to this era came in October 1928, when sixty-five countries, with unwarranted fanfare and optimism, signed the Paris Peace Pact, a vague, meaningless document providing that all nations should 'renounce war as an instrument of national policy'. Exactly one year later the economic system of the western world collapsed into depression, all international co-operation broke down and the nations began once more to travel the road towards war.

Neither Canada nor any other small nation could have done much to alter the tragic course of world events in the period between wars, but it may now be seen that the negative policies of this country during the 1920s helped to weaken the system of collective security. Of all the excuses or reasons that may be advanced to defend this policy, the most valid one certainly was Canada's continuing development as a distinct North American nation. With stronger conviction than any other country, she shared the universal belief that no league could be fully effective without the United States. All of Canada's efforts to whittle down the clauses in the Covenant were partly based on the hope that her powerful neighbour might be persuaded to join the League and, when these efforts failed, she too lapsed back into typical North American isolation.

12   FROM RICHES TO RAGS

The Boom Years

Once the halfway mark in the 1920s had been passed, the average middle-class Canadian began to think that life was good to him, very good indeed. A sudden depression had set in immediately after the War, but the country had recovered quickly. Around him, even in the home, were many signs of progress and prosperity. The new electric stove and refrigerator in the kitchen, the washing machine in the basement, the radio, even the electric lights themselves and the sturdy big telephone on the wall—all these and a great many other things showed how far the country had travelled in such a short time.

Canada on Wheels
The most obvious, but not necessarily the most important, sign of prosperity was the automobile. The phenomenal growth of the automotive industry and of all the others associated with it may be seen from the fact that in 1911, according to the census, there were only 21,000 cars and trucks in the whole country. This figure jumped to 275,000 in 1918 and soared in the next ten years to over a million, so that before the end of the decade there was one vehicle for every two Canadian families and, except for the United States, Canada owned more cars per head than any other nation in the world. Although twenty-nine different companies attempted to manufacture cars in this country, most of them could not stand up to the competition of Ford, General Motors and Chrysler, the familiar Big Three which began to dominate the automotive industry even as early as the1920s. Ford of Canada had been organized in 1904 by a group of far-sighted men in Windsor who acquired the rights to manufacture Ford cars about a year after the parent company had been established in the United States. Three years later, the McLaughlin family, carriage-makers in Oshawa, began to manufacture the Buick car in Canada. Later on, they secured the Canadian rights to Chevrolet, but in 1918 they decided to sell out to General Motors. Chrysler Corporation did not enter the Canadian market until 1925, but its growth was so sensational, both here and in the United States, that *Time* featured W. P. Chrysler as 'the man of the year' in 1929. Of all the cars on the road in those days—LaSalles, Durants, Maxwells, Pierce-Arrows, Gray-Dorts, Oldsmobiles and many others—the most popular by a long way was a seven-foot-high, twenty-horsepower monstrosity known the world over as the Model T Ford. Selling as low as $395—without a starter or other 'extras'—this was the average man's car, the farmer's car, the famous flivver, the puddle-jumper, the Tin Lizzie. It was the car that became a world institution, a personality, a member of the family. As Henry Ford's biographer has written: 'People loved it, laughed at it, swore at it, tussled with it,

Henry Ford said that he got the idea of the assembly line for the manufacture of cars from a visit to a watch factory. By 1923 his new methods had progressed to the extent pictured above—a complete body is lowered onto a completed chassis—and had begun to revolutionize American industry.

and lavished upon it an affection rarely accorded an inanimate thing. It was the central character in a million human dramas and the butt of countless jokes.' But until it was replaced in 1927 by the more expensive Model A, the 755,000 Model T's made by Ford of Canada did more than anything else to raise the automotive industry into fourth position in the nation's economy.

Associated with the increase in automotive manufacturing, the petroleum industry expanded so rapidly that by 1920 people were beginning to call the new decade 'the Oil Age'. With the demand for gasoline, diesel fuels and lubricating oils becoming so great and with the known supplies remaining limited, the major oil companies began to search the Near East, Africa, South America and India for new sources of petroleum. It might be mentioned here that this contest for oil produced probably the most interesting economic struggle in recent history between two vast industrial giants, the Standard Oil Company of the United States and the Anglo-Dutch Shell Company financed by the Rothschilds and other British and Dutch interests. This rivalry partly helps to account for American criticism of the peace treaties and for the spate of anti-British feeling that developed in the United States after the War. In a typical piece of tail-twisting, Warren Harding promised during the 1920 election campaign that he would throw the support of the United States government into the contest for oil. 'We have seen,' he told an audience in Oklahoma, 'Mesopotamia, the East Indies, Persia and Columbia all falling into the hands of British oil interests. Our own engineers and capitalists are in danger of being barred out of these areas—a process, I might add, which began with the lust for spoils at the Peace Conference.'

In a modest way, the Oil Age contributed to the prosperity of Canada. Before the War, there were only six oil refineries in the country and most of these were small 'stills' producing kerosene for lighting purposes. The first service station was built by Imperial Oil in 1908 at Vancouver, but service stations remained few and far between and hardy motorists continued for many years to buy most of their gasoline by the bucketful from grocery or hardware stores. So rapidly did the industry expand that by 1929 there were twenty-five modern oil refineries, producing over $100 million worth of petroleum products and possessing a great network of competing service stations along the main thoroughfares of Canada. Here again, familiar names dominated the scene, even in the 1920s, as Imperial Oil, McColl-Frontenac, British American and Shell secured a lion's share of the business. The first three of these had been formed many years before the War as Canadian concerns, but in due course they fell under the control of American interests. Imperial sold out to Standard Oil in 1898, McColl-Frontenac was taken over by Texaco during the 1930s, and British American is now controlled by Gulf Oil.

The petroleum industry would have been even more important but for the fact that Canada's sole native source of supply was an old and very small field located around Petrolia in southern Ontario. Although many parts of the country were probed in the search for 'black gold' the experts soon decided that their only real hope for success lay in Alberta. However, except for the blowing in of Imperial's famous Royalite natural gas well in Turner Valley, Alberta stubbornly refused to yield the secret of her riches. Thus, in the period between the wars, Canada was compelled to import, either by pipeline, railroad or tanker from distant ports, about ninety-five per cent of the crude oil used by her petroleum industry.

During most of the 1920s, the roads were so bad and the cars so uncertain that a fifty-mile drive was an adventure. When the War ended, four out of every five miles of road in Canada were classified as unimproved or improved dirt—which meant that, except for the blinding dust, they could be travelled with some degree of safety only in the summertime. In the spring and fall, the bottom tended to fall out of these roads so that the farmers, even along the Montreal-Toronto-Hamilton route, made an extra windfall pulling automobiles from the mud holes —a tow-rope was standard equipment for all motorists. The steep, ungraded hills were conquered with the help of passengers who dismounted and then panted along beside the car ready to push it over the last few critical yards to the top. A solitary driver usually played it safe and went up in reverse, if only to ensure

The first commercial paving with bituminous sand in Alberta, at Jasper, 1926

a steady flow of gas from the tank under the seat to the carburetor. With snow-clearing equipment almost non-existent, the majority of owners put their cars up on blocks for the winter while the daring few who persisted in driving used coal oil for anti-freeze, put electric light bulbs under the hood at night and resorted to hot water bottles to keep their feet warm. These exciting but somewhat primitive conditions gradually changed as provincial and municipal governments began to spend more and more money on highways. By the end of the decade, the country possessed 65,000 miles of gravel and almost 10,000 miles of hard-surface roads and the annual expenditures had risen to over $90 million. Compared with present-day highway costs of $1 billion each year this is a paltry sum, but in the 1920s it was a lot of money and formed one of the factors contributing to the prosperity of the times.

Better roads and more cars also stimulated the tourist trade. Until after the War, foreign visitors came to Canada mainly for business purposes and spent not more than $50 million annually while they were in the country. It was not long, however, before Canadian hotel owners, the railways, the tourist associations and the provincial governments undertook an intensive advertising campaign to attract the American tourist across the border with his car and his dollars. Speaking on this subject at the annual meeting of the Good Roads Association in 1920, Dr. P. E. Doolittle, the founder of the Ontario Motor League and the man

Off the road in Muskoka, Ontario, 1925

partly responsible for highway markers, the compulsory use of lights at night and
a speed limit of thirty-five miles per hour, made an interesting prediction:
'I am going to tell you that a transcontinental highway will be the biggest cash
asset of all the assets of Canada. There are in the United States 7½ million
automobiles in use, every owner of which is a possible visitor to Canada. If five
per cent of these cars entered Canada and stayed for thirty days they would
bring to this country over $200 million, for which you would not have to ship
anything out.' Although the Trans-Canada Highway was a long time coming,
Dr. Doolittle's estimate of the tourist trade fell far short of the mark. By 1929, over
4 million American visitors, lured by the 'scenic beauty of Canada's wilderness
wonderland' and the prospects of virgin hunting and fishing, were spending some
$320 million every year and the tourist trade had become a very important
business.

The New Industrialism
In much the same way as the automobile but not quite to the same extent, the
radio, the moving picture industry, electrical appliances, packaged and tinned
foods, industrial fabrics, chemicals, soap and drug preparations, cigarettes and a
multitude of other new or recently developed products all contributed their share
to the prosperity of the 1920s. They not only directly employed thousands of

workmen, paid out millions of dollars in wages and built costly factories and warehouses but also stimulated advertising, banking, insurance, sales and service agencies and fostered the growth of numerous companies to supply raw materials and parts. These industries possessed one feature in common which merits very special consideration. Almost without exception, they did not require large quantities of coal or iron. Instead, they relied on light metal alloys, used natural gas or petroleum for heat and, like the older aluminum and pulp-and-paper industries, needed a large amount of electricity. Thus the secondary manu-facturing of the 1920s placed a tremendous new premium on the non-ferrous mineral and hydro-electric power resources of the country.

Although Niagara Falls was first harnessed in 1895, the big development of hydro-electric power did not occur until the 1920s. During this ten-year period private companies and provincial governments, especially in Ontario and Quebec, invested over $600 million in generating equipment, the productive capacity of the power stations increased 300 per cent, and Canada's output of electric current became the second largest in the world, ranking next to the United States. In this same period, another 350,000 families installed electricity for the first time so that by 1930 seven of every ten homes in the nation enjoyed its benefits. As a result, therefore, of the continuing expansion of the pulp-and-paper industry, the rapid growth of secondary manufacturing and the extension of electricity into so many homes, the development of Canada's water-power resources was one of the main factors in causing the post-war boom.

Without the appearance of industries using electric power, Canada's chances of becoming an important manufacturing nation would have remained very slim indeed. Nineteenth-century methods of production required very great amounts of heat and power and these could be supplied, with the engineering knowledge then available, only by coal. The iron-and-steel industry that developed in Canada as a result of the pre-war railway boom did so, as we already know, mainly on imported coal and iron ore. This involved extra shipping charges and raised costs to such an extent that the industry probably could not have survived American competition but for tariff protection. Thus it was very fortunate for Canada that twentieth-century scientific knowledge revealed so many new industrial methods using hydro-electric power instead of coal. Many of these new methods, well under way in the 1920s, received a serious setback in the depression years, but during and after the Second World War they helped to place Canada sixth among the industrial nations of the world.

The Primary Exporting Industries

Despite the importance of these new developments, Canada's prosperity during the 1920s continued to rest on her great primary industries. And standing head and shoulders above all others as the nation's leading source of wealth was the pulp-and-paper industry. Well before the decade ended, the pulp-and-paper companies were paying more money in wages and salaries, had more capital invested, and were turning out products almost three times more valuable, than their closest rival. By 1929 Canadian companies controlled sixty-four per cent of

Ontario Hydro's Sir Adam Beck generating plant, on the Niagara River

the world's trade in pulp and paper and were exporting more than all other countries combined.

It is not surprising that this industry had such a field day during the 1920s. In the first place, Price Brothers, Howard Smith, Donnacona, Abitibi, Riordan and the other big Canadian producers enjoyed every conceivable natural advantage. For technical reasons, pulp-and-paper companies require large amounts of electricity, and good water-power sites were not only readily available throughout the entire Laurentian Shield but were situated close to some of the finest stands of softwood in existence anywhere. Generous provincial governments granted the rights to cut this timber, not for heavy payments made in advance, but for modest annual rentals and stumpage dues paid when the trees were removed. This combination of happy circumstances meant that the initial costs of setting up a paper mill were lower in Canada than in any other country. And right next door, in the United States, was the largest market in the world for the product. This American demand for pulp and paper was due partly to the depletion of timber tracts in the United States and mainly to the increase in advertising, the unprecedented growth in size and circulation of the daily newspapers, the appearance of a multitude of new magazines and the much greater use of paper products for packaging and building purposes.

By 1920 the price of newsprint soared from $65 to $120 per ton and Canadian producers shipped so much of their output across the border that the Dominion government had to force them to reserve some of the supply for our own newspapers. American pulp-and-paper companies did not relish the thought that so much of their market was being taken over by competitors from Canada. They tried, therefore, to persuade the provincial governments to remove the pre-war export restrictions on pulpwood so that the final processing could be done in the United States. When this failed, they put pressure on the American government to hit back at Canada with higher tariffs. But the advantages lay too heavily on the side of the Canadian pulp-and-paper industry. Despite all efforts to the contrary, over fifty per cent of the newsprint used in the United States during the 1920s was produced in Canada.

World conditions were also favourable to the continued expansion of another of Canada's great primary industries. The demand for foodstuffs in the industrialized countries of Europe, the resulting low duties on imports, the ravages of war and the temporary elimination of communist Russia as an exporting nation combined to raise the price of wheat to well over $1.50 per bushel during the last half of the 1920s. The low cost of ocean transportation arising from the wartime surplus of ships, the benefits to certain parts of the prairies resulting from the opening of the Panama Canal and the reduction of freight rates within the country, placed Canadian wheat farmers in a particularly good position to take advantage of these profitable prices. Equally important was the fact that the United States lent large sums of money to many of the war-torn countries of Europe and thus made dollars available for the import of foodstuffs.

This resulted in another wheat boom—the third and last one of the twentieth century—and helped to keep the nation's economy running at full throttle. Out West, the amount of land under cultivation climbed to almost 50 million acres; the prairie population increased by another three hundred thousand in the four years before 1930; and agricultural settlements extended far to the north in Alberta and Saskatchewan. The climax came in 1929 when a wheat crop of 567 million bushels broke all previous records and the income from wheat exports hit the $300 million mark. Canada's share of the international market, which stood at only 12 per cent in the period before the War, had risen to 50 per cent and the nation had become much the largest wheat-exporting country in the world. This new wheat boom stimulated many other industries and especially the building of railways. In a fresh burst of activity between 1924 and 1929, the Canadian Pacific and Canadian National invested $700 million in new branch lines and rolling stock, thereby bringing additional prosperity to the iron and steel industry and placing the manufacture of railroad equipment among the top five or six industries in the Dominion. By the end of this decade, however, the settlement of the western plains was virtually completed and the great original purposes of the National Policy seemed to have been fulfilled. Wheat had made its major contribution to Canada's growth and would never against exert such a decisive influence on the economic life of the country.

Although not so important as wheat or pulp and paper, Canada's other primary industries expanded with the times. The favourable export conditions which have been mentioned in connection with wheat, and the growing domestic market combined to keep slaughtering and meat packing, dairy products and lumbering among the top six industries of the nation all during this decade. The main developments in mining were not in silver and gold, as before the War, but in nickel, copper and other base metals required by the newer types of secondary manufacturing. In further explorations for new sources of mineral wealth the airplane began to play an important part. Of all the discoveries made in this period, the richest were the extensive copper deposits at Rouyn in northwestern Quebec and at Flin Flon in Manitoba. These discoveries brought two more famous mining companies into existence, the Hudson Bay Mining and Smelting Corporation to develop Flin Flon, and Noranda Mines, whose present-day industrial empire began at Rouyn in the 1920s.

It should be apparent that a great deal of Canada's prosperity in this decade depended upon the tremendous amount of money being invested in capital equipment. As distinct from consumer goods, which are used up quickly, capital equipment is the technical term to describe highways, factories, mines, flour mills, electric-power stations and other assets which not only last a long time but also increase the nation's productive capacity. During the 1920s, the amount invested in all such long-term assets was over $6 billion and produced a construction boom far exceeding anything witnessed in Canada up to that time. The development of the country in Laurier's day, it will be remembered, had been financed by British and American funds, but this post-war boom was financed mainly from Canadian savings. In other words, a large part of the nation's income was being used, through investment in stocks and bonds, to expand the productive capacity of Canadian industries. There was the possibility, of course, that the country some day might be able to produce far more than it could sell, but this was a danger which few people foresaw during the Roaring Twenties.

The Politics of Prosperity

As in the United States, the prevailing mood at Ottawa during the twenties was free enterprise, complete laissez faire—let the business life of the country roll along under its own power with as little government interference as possible. Although the contests for office were conducted with the usual fanfare and aroused the normal amount of partisan fervour, national politicians came up with no new ideas and introduced little new legislation of vital importance. Adjusting their thinking to the temper of the times, following, not leading, public opinion and as convinced as anyone else that life had never been better, they did very little to guide the nation's destiny. This complacent outlook, of course, suited the businessman down to the ground. With the trade union movement weakened as a result of the Red Scare and the government rarely interfering, he was free, within very broad limits, to do precisely as he pleased.

The Dominion government was in eclipse, not only because of its 'live-and-let-live' philosophy but also because its work, for the time being, seemed to be finished. During the first decades of the twentieth century the policies made in Ottawa were of utmost importance to the nation's welfare. But now the land was settled, the railways built, the tariff protected home industries and east-west trade, the War was over—and federal politicians, perhaps with some degree of justice, were content to rest on their oars.

And while they did so, almost all the social and economic developments of the 1920s combined to make the provincial governments more important than ever before. According to the division of legislative powers in the British North America Act, provincial authorities controlled the new highways and all the new schools, granted the mineral and timber rights, regulated the liquor traffic, supervised the growth of urban municipalities, taxed the theatres and the sale of gasoline and regulated the telephone and electric power systems. Consequently, the Canadian people began to look more and more for leadership to their provincial legislatures. The spirit of national unity, so strong in Laurier's day, tended to break down and was replaced by new provincial loyalties, especially in Ontario, Quebec and British Columbia. These three provinces grew fat during the 1920s. They owned the best water-power sites, the best stands of timber and the most extensive mineral deposits. They had more people, many more industries, more revenue from taxes, could build better roads and better schools, and generally could provide their inhabitants with a higher standard of living than any of the other provinces. Thus the new industrialism of the twentieth century, as it developed in Canada during the post-war decade, not only fostered 'sectionalism' but also made some provinces much richer than others.

Being relatively unimportant, federal policies may be passed over quickly. Only a few details are needed here, mainly to provide continuity between the end of the War and the time when Dominion government again becomes a dominant factor in the nation's life. After the death of Sir Wilfrid Laurier in 1919, Mackenzie King became the Liberal party leader, and in the following year Arthur Meighen succeeded Sir Robert Borden as prime minister and leader of the Conservatives. By that time, the coalition or Union government, formed to put through conscription, was beginning to break up and most of the Liberals had returned to their original party loyalties. In November 1921, the new political chieftains were first pitted against each other in a general election so unimaginative that the main issue, according to both parties, was still the tariff, despite the fact that the campaign took place with many post-war problems unsolved and in the midst of a sudden sharp depression! Only the traditional diehards of both parties managed to convince themselves that the outcome of the election was vital to the country.

Interest in this election, therefore, centred not on the old-time political parties but on the first new one to appear in Canadian history since Confederation. More so than most Canadians, the farmers were convinced that, although they might talk about it a great deal, neither the Liberals nor the Conservatives would do anything to lower the tariff. Both parties, so the farmers claimed, were hand in glove with the big eastern financial and industrial interests and did not really care about rural problems. Their discontent was aggravated by the sudden slump in the wheat market and the refusal of the government to introduce any corrective measures. And, of course, the farmers could not forget that a coalition of Conservatives and Liberals, despite promises to the contrary, had drafted their sons during the War. For these reasons, the United Farmers decided to go into politics on their own account. Their impact was politically important in three provinces, Alberta, Manitoba and Ontario. In Ontario, aided by Labour and independent members, they held sway from 1919–23 and then virtually disappeared from the scene with the Conservative victories of 1926 and 1929. In Alberta they dominated the provincial scene from 1921–35 and then vanished under a Social Credit landslide. In Manitoba they formed the government from 1922 to 1927, were then replaced by the Progressives, a federal wing of the party, and finally vanished in the Liberal victory of 1936.

Thus the first federal election of the 1920s was a three-way contest between the Liberals, the Conservatives and the new Progressive party with a program of low tariff appeal, under the leadership of T. A. Crerar. Apparently Mackenzie King was not taken seriously—a mistake that his political opponents would continue to make for the next thirty years—but when the ballots were counted it was found that the Liberals had won 117 seats. Meighen led a group of 50 Conservatives, while the Progressives numbered 64 including Agnes Macphail, the first woman member of parliament. J. S. Woodsworth and William Irvine, of Winnipeg strike fame, were elected as independent labour members. Under these circumstances, Mackenzie King became Prime Minister, but his administration was precarious without the support of the Progressives who held a balance of power.

This election set the pattern for the remaining years of the 1920s. The Liberals managed to secure enough seats to carry on, but only with the continued support of the Progressives. Arthur Meighen, discouraged by his failure to displace the Liberals after his brief tenure as Prime Minister during the Byng constitutional crisis in the summer of 1926, resigned in 1927 and was replaced as Conservative leader by R. B. Bennett, a millionaire lawyer and businessman from Calgary. The fact that Mackenzie King was forced to rely on the Progressives has led some observers to conclude that he remained in office only by introducing legislation favourable to the farmers. Except for a slight reduction in the duties on farm implements and a very modest Old Age Pension bill, the party in power made few concessions to the Progressives. It is perhaps safe to say that once the country rounded the corner and headed for prosperity, politicians of all shades forgot about reform and were content to let the bandwagon roll on its merry way. Only the critical voice of J. S. Woodsworth and a few other malcontents dared to suggest that anything could possibly be wrong in Canada during the last few years of the Roaring Twenties.

The Crash

Storm Signals

Beneath its glittering surface, the economic life of Canada during the last half of the 1920s was riddled with weaknesses. The most glaring and the most important of these was the fact that the nation's prosperity depended on a few great primary industries processing its agricultural, mineral and timber resources. Without exception, they were exporting industries, relying on world markets and exposed, therefore, to external influences beyond Canadian control. In most cases they were also highly specialized industries. During this decade, large areas of the country, where it was either wheat or nothing, pulp-and-paper or nothing, nickel or nothing, became committed to the export of a single commodity.

Furthermore, the income earned by exports brought prosperity to many other industries. The wheat trade, for instance, increased the manufacture of agricultural implements, gave business to the railroads, encouraged the construction of branch lines and rolling stock and stimulated the steel companies. The pulp-and-paper industry fostered the building of hydro-electric power dams and this, in turn, increased the demand for cement, structural steel, heavy machinery and miles of copper cable. The industrial expansion required to satisfy the demand for these and many other products caused a tremendous construction boom and the nation's whole economy became geared to a high rate of investment in fixed capital equipment.

It is also important to remember that the construction boom was financed by heavy borrowing through the sale of stocks and bonds and that the resulting interest payments to shareholders could be made only if the country continued to receive a large income from overseas trade. Indeed, Canadian corporations were far too confident of their ability to handle heavy capital debts and interest charges. This may be seen from the fresh crop of mergers and amalgamations that appeared in the 1920s. Some of these were straightforward business propositions, undertaken to eliminate duplication and waste. Bank mergers of this period, for instance, absorbed all the remaining small concerns and left the nation's banking business in the hands of ten very sound institutions. However, many mergers, especially in newsprint and in Nova Scotia's iron and coal industries, issued more securities to the public than the volume of their business justified. The interest charges on these excessively large debts were usually fixed or rigid—that is, they had to be paid regardless of whether economic conditions were good or bad. By 1929, Canada had her full share of big but financially weak, overcapitalized corporations that would crumble in bankruptcy if overseas trade began to slump.

In addition to its dangerous dependence on foreign markets, the economic life of Canada had many internal weaknesses. Perhaps the most disastrous of these was the fact that so much money was being invested in capital equipment. Because of this frenzied, overambitious industrial expansion, the nation's productive capacity, for both the foreign and domestic market, began to exceed the buying power of the people. Despite the record volume of business in 1929, stocks of newsprint, wheat, radios, shoes, textiles, building materials and a multitude of other products were piling up, unsold, in warehouses and the amount of freight moving back and forth across the country declined ominously. This did not mean, however, that Canadians had all the shoes and shirts they needed, that everyone who wanted a car or a radio or a home of his own had one. It did not mean that the people were satisfied and would buy no more. What the majority of Canadians lacked was not the desire to buy but the money. And they lacked the money because the prosperity of the 1920s was enjoyed by too few people.

Under a system of complete free enterprise such as Canada had during this decade, with no overall planning and practically no government control, it was inevitable that eighty-three per cent of the nation's business should fall into the hands of about one thousand big corporations and that they, in turn, should be owned by a comparatively small number of shareholders. The top salaried officials and shareholders of these corporations, along with some of the professional class, were among the few in Canada who could afford to save part of their income. Generally speaking, they were the ones who invested in stocks and bonds, reaped the rich dividends and hastened the unwise expansion of the nation's economy. The small size of this group may be gathered from the fact that in the whole of Canada by 1929 there were only 8,200 people earning more than $10,000 annually and, of these, 416 extremely wealthy men and women paid thirty-five per cent of all the income taxes collected by the federal government. In marked contrast to such wealth, the average income of a family of five was only $1,900 a year. Since this figure was a national average, including rich and poor, it is safe to conclude that many thousands of Canadian families lived on incomes considerably less than $1,900. And even this amount was $300 lower than the minimum calculated by the government to maintain properly a family of that size.

Furthermore, the cost of living was much higher than it needed to be. Businessmen liked to argue that all the money being spent on capital equipment increased the efficiency of industry and thus lowered costs of production. Competition between companies making the same kind of product, so they claimed, ensured that these savings would be passed on to the public in the form of lower prices. This perfectly good theory, however, did not work out in actual practice. New machinery and improved methods, it is true, increased industrial efficiency by some thirty per cent, but the consumer received few benefits and retail prices continued to rise slightly all during the 1920s. By 1929, therefore, it was clear that the savings achieved by scientific methods were being spent on increased advertising, larger dividends to shareholders and bigger salaries for company officials. Industrial leaders might have been wiser to lower prices, take a smaller profit for themselves and thereby make it possible for the buying public to absorb the nation's output over a longer period of time.

Even without such internal difficulties, Canada could do nothing to prevent the disaster that was about to strike. The economic life of our country was linked with the United States. Canadians may resent this dependency, politicians may vow time and again to do something about it, but the fact remains that, then as now, Canadian prosperity was completely and inevitably interwoven with the fortunes of her American neighbour. And by 1928–29 the United States, the great market where Canadians bought 65 per cent of their imports and sold over 40 per cent of their exports, the market that exceeded all others in importance, was tottering on the verge of chaos. The productive capacity of American industry was grossly overexpanded, excessive confidence in unbridled capitalism prevailed, the national income was concentrated in too few hands, unsold stockpiles were building up across the country and the bottom was about to fall out of the whole economy. Yet the American people were engaged in a final wild spree of stock market speculation, a giddy round of unwarranted gambling on the future, which sucked millions of dollars away from normal buying and hastened the inevitable crash.

While all this was happening, Canadian markets in Great Britain and Europe were being slowly strangled. Although large-scale scientific farming methods and cheap ocean transportation gave our exporters an advantage in Europe, most European countries were unwilling to sacrifice their own peasant population to cheaper food products from overseas. Just as soon as they recovered from the War, they began an understandable but dangerous drive for self-sufficiency not only in foodstuffs but also in almost everything else. Tariffs gradually climbed higher and higher, threatening to choke off international trade as one nation after another adopted the extremely nationalist and foolish idea that they could sell in foreign markets without buying from others. Although the climax to those developments did not come until after 1929, economic nationalism hung like a thundercloud over Europe during the last three or four years of this decade, and in the United States under the prodding of rampant, 'one hundred per cent' Americanism, the Republican administration also raised the tariff skyward.

Well before the final crash came, this growing network of restrictions on international trade began to weaken Canadian export markets. The volume of shipments from Canada to some of the smaller European countries and to the British Isles started to decline. The European and especially the American tariffs hit England's exporting industries hard and this, in turn, made it increasingly difficult for Great Britain, next to the United States our best customer, to buy from Canada. Germany, Czechoslovakia, Austria, Italy and several of the other European nations that continued to purchase Canadian products right up to the last moment only managed to do so by dangerously heavy borrowing in the United States. And by 1928–29 these precious American dollars on which so much of the post-war prosperity of Europe depended were being diverted away from international loans at modest interest rates and thrown into the surging New York stock exchanges. Furthermore, the drying up of these loans and the unwise American tariff policy combined to make it practically impossible for Great Britain and France to earn the dollars needed to pay their war debts to the United States. Complicating this tangled situation still further, France refused to meet any international obligation unless she could get reparations from Germany first —and the prosperity of Germany, more so than any other nation, relied on continuing loans from the United States. Thus, by 1929 the whole intricate fabric of international trade was beginning to crack wide open. And the Canadian people, despite their belief that they lived in a secure, insulated house, would be among the first to suffer from the impending crash.

A Pyramid of Billiard Balls

Few indeed were the people in Canada who saw it coming. The great majority, blind to the storm signals on every side, were just as confident as their American neighbours that the boom years of the 1920s would go rolling on and on. The financial pages of the newspapers far surpassed the sports pages for interest; month after month the Montreal and Toronto stock exchanges shattered all existing records. At first the forecasters predicted trouble ahead, but the soaring market proved them wrong so many times that even the most conservative financial men in the country were finally convinced that the Big Bull Market would last forever.

Brokerage houses like Solloway, Mills and Company and Stobie-Forlong-Matthews Limited, both of Toronto, or Mowat and MacGillivray with head-quarters in Ottawa—firms that later events proved to be shady operators—opened branch offices in dozens of smaller towns and cities. Their local agent might be a former grocer, a retired druggist, an insurance salesman, anybody—it did not seem to matter; ordinary small-town folk hung upon his every word. Let him but drop a hint of some new development in Canada Cement or Massey-Harris and the neighbours were off first thing next morning to buy a few shares. And it was more than likely that they would buy 'on margin', that is, they would put some money down as a deposit, hoping to pay the balance owing to the broker as the stock soared upward. If the stock fell, the buyer was required to cover the loss immediately, but no one worried about this remote prospect. It would also be a reasonably good guess that this speculator, wherever he lived, made his down payment with money borrowed from a bank or a finance company. Then, having purchased his shares on partial credit with borrowed money, he could turn right around and use them as security for further loans! And finally, raising this whole structure of credit still higher, many Canadian families bought cars, refrigerators, houses and a multitude of other things on the instalment plan, hoping that they could pay for them by gambling on margin in the stock market with borrowed funds!

With a keen eye on their own speculative fortunes and with no apparent foresight, Canadian businessmen took full advantage of the last golden days in 1929. In the final eight months before the crash, they poured almost $1 billion worth of new securities into the already saturated stock and bond market.

On September 3, 1929, the Big Bull Market on both the American and Canadian exchanges reached its glittering climax. That day Imperial Oil hit 41, McColl-Frontenac 45, Noranda 69, Ford of Canada 70, International Nickel 72, and almost without exception other leading Canadian securities established new record highs.

During September and the early part of October, however, the stock market began to slide. Thousands of speculators who had bought on margin were trapped. They sold their cars, mortgaged their homes, took desperate measures to meet the broker's call for more margin to cover the falling prices. And then when they could cover no longer, when their margin was exhausted, the brokers were forced to sell them out. The deluge came suddenly on Thursday, October 24, as thousands upon thousands of shares formerly held by marginal speculators were dumped onto the market. The entire structure of the Big Bull Market, honeycombed with unwise credit, now began to break under its own weight. Across the whole of North America, by telephone, telegraph and radio, word flashed out that the bottom was falling out of things; fear and panic gripped the people and selling orders poured in until the three o'clock bells rang to end the most disastrous day in the history of any stock exchange.

But the worst was still to come. On Tuesday, October 29, another avalanche of selling on the New York, Toronto and Montreal exchanges sent prices crashing down still further into the depths. Huge blocks of stocks were thrown onto the market for whatever they would bring. Not only the small traders but the big ones who a few weeks before had counted themselves millionaires were sold out, ruined in a matter of minutes, as one day's madness caused a record-breaking sale on Wall Street alone of over 16 million shares and the loss of billions of dollars. On the Toronto and Montreal exchanges, total sales reached the unprecedented figure of 950,000 shares with practically every stock falling ten or more points. During the next few days the panic subsided, but very heavy trading continued to drive prices down until at last on November 13 they reached rock bottom. By that time, Imperial Oil stood at 20½, with a resulting loss of equity to shareholders of $549 million; International Nickel at 25 had lost a staggering $646 million; Ford at 31 another $62 million; and altogether the major Canadian securities had been deflated in market values by almost $5 billion, a nose-dive of over fifty per cent from the peak of 1929.

The Big Bull Market was dead, and with it died the prosperity of the Roaring Twenties. At first, however, people simply could not believe that the crash would be followed by a serious general depression. Political and business leaders hastened to assure themselves and the country at large that there was no need for alarm. The collapse of the stock market was only an 'isolated event' which would help to bring 'speculators and brokers back to sanity'. General business conditions were far too good, so they said, to be upset by it. But the collapse of the Big Bull Market was just the beginning. The overexpansion of industry, the very unequal distribution of the national income, the overproduction of commodities under the stimulus of instalment buying and buying with stock market profits, the shaky condition of European trade, all these economic weaknesses killed the post-war boom. Not only in Canada and the United States but also in the British Isles and most of Europe, economic conditions gradually grew worse and worse as the entire western world sank into the depths of the greatest depression ever known. Thus the stock market crash of 1929 closed out the post-war decade and ushered in a new and tragic era, encouraging many nations to take the road to rearmament and war once again in their desperate attempt to find an escape from the evils of the Depression.

The Great Depression

Down and Down and Down

'Prosperity,' so almost everyone kept on saying throughout the year 1930, 'is just around the corner.' People still grinned at the flippant advertisements that asked, 'Wasn't the Depression Terrible?' and they laughed at the current joke about the fellow who registered at a hotel and the room clerk said, 'For sleeping or jumping, sir?' Of course, everyone knew that wheat had fallen during the year to ninety-six cents a bushel, that a huge unsold surplus was stored in the terminal elevators and that the farmers out West were beginning to squawk. But that seemed to be their habit and wheat at any time was an uncertain 'boom or bust' proposition. As for the faltering pulp-and-paper industry, even the president of its national association admitted that the big companies had only themselves to blame. They should have had enough common sense, so he said, not to expand their capacity by fifty per cent in the short space of the last two years.

People also knew, but were not too worried by the fact, that the sale of automobiles, radios, jewellery and other luxury items had slipped about ten per cent from the peak of 1929. Much less whisky was being drunk, but this was more than balanced by the heavier consumption of beer and cheap native wine. White-collar workers were taking small salary cuts and an increasing number of wage-earners in the industrial cities found discharge slips in their pay envelopes. Little groups of restless men could be seen any day clustered around the gates of the big factories, waiting for a job. The brand new Royal York Hotel in Toronto—'the largest hotel in the British Empire'—did not receive as many conventions or quite as many tourists as its C.P.R. management had expected. Office space in the equally new Canadian Bank of Commerce building—'the tallest in the British Empire'—remained ominously vacant. As the declining number of building permits revealed, industrial expansion was slowing down and families were postponing the construction of new homes. And this, in turn, began to affect the bricklayers, the carpenters and the plumbers and the cement, brick and lumber industries. The well-to-do closed their cottage in Muskoka, sold their second car and dispensed with some of their servants. And farther down the social scale, young couples gave up the struggle to make ends meet and moved in with their parents, mother did more mending, father's Sunday suit took on a shabby shine and the front porch went unpainted.

All these things, however, had occurred before. People consoled themselves with the thought that the business cycle—the rhythmic rise and fall of prosperity —was an unavoidable feature of capitalism. Had there not been a slump in 1907, and another in 1912 and a really severe one just after the War? But once they ended the whole nation had climbed to new heights of prosperity. Conditions were not as bad as they had been back in 1922. Just wait a while. Shoes would wear out, automobiles, radios and electrical appliances would break down, people would have to start buying again, factories would swing back into full production and pay cheques would grow fatter. Yes, it was easy enough in 1930 to argue that prosperity was just around the corner.

But as Canada and the other industrial nations rounded corner after corner, as the months ground on into 1931 and 1932, every figure by which human welfare is measured sank deeper and deeper into the quagmire of despair. No one joked or sang about the Depression now. The bravado and the optimism of earlier months died out and the world became grim and silent. Millions of men and women found life a stark struggle for survival. Serious people began to talk of the impending collapse of civilization. And all those who could remember the darkest days of 1914–18 said that, in terms of suffering and waste, mankind faced a greater catastrophe than war. By that time the tidal wave from the New York stock market crash had already swirled over Europe, rocking the weakened economic structure to its very foundations. American loans to European nations had ceased entirely and American markets were locked against all foreign trade by the highest import duties in the history of the United States. The Hawley-Smoot Act, by which Congress set these unprecedented tariff rates, was regarded abroad as a declaration of economic warfare. Partly to protect their own dwindling home industries and partly to strike back at the United States, twenty-five different governments representing most of the major nations of the western world also raised their tariffs to the highest levels ever known. Thus the trend towards economic nationalism that had begun during the Roaring Twenties reached its dismal goal in the depression years and prolonged the crisis.

As the Depression grew worse there had been one world conference after another—wheat conferences, tariff truce conferences, reparations and war debt conferences, disarmament conferences—but the nations stubbornly refused to admit the economic interdependence of the world. Each country clung to the doctrine of 'every man for himself'. As a result, Austria in 1931, then Germany, then Great Britain, Italy, France and the other nations of western Europe collapsed in financial chaos. Most of them were bankrupt or on the verge of bankruptcy and all of them, without exception, defaulted on their foreign debts. At the worst moment during the dreadful winter of 1932–33, two of every five factories in the capitalist world were closed, their machinery rusting in idleness, while most others worked far below full capacity. Forty-five million wage-earners, many of them heads of families with wives and children dependent upon them, searched in vain to find a job, never sure from one day to another where their next meal would come from. The high tariffs and a multitude of other restrictions imposed by bewildered governments combined with the tremendous fall in salaries and wages to cut world trade to the lowest point in half a century. Week after week, ocean freighters sat by the docks, their holds empty, their winches silent, while thousands upon thousands of stevedores idled endless hours away along the waterfronts of New York, London, Amsterdam and the other ports of North and South America and Europe.

The price of foodstuffs and raw materials, which form the bulk of international trade, had slumped by forty per cent from the levels of 1929. But despite the lowest prices within living memory, unsold surpluses of wool, cotton, sugar, wheat, rubber, nickel, newsprint and a great many other products continued to pile up around the world. By the end of 1932 the price of wheat, for instance, had fallen below forty cents per bushel yet the major exporting nations had a gigantic carry-over of almost 700 million bushels which they could not sell. In bitterness and anger, people learned that the United States, Brazil and some other countries had set out deliberately to destroy these unsold supplies. Governments paid farmers to cut down their wheat acreage, to slaughter their hogs and bury them rather than take them to market, to dump their milk down the drain. Thousands of bales of cotton and wool went up in smoke, coffee by the ton was poured into the Amazon River and insect pests were introduced into the rubber plantations to ruin the trees. The whole world was overflowing with riches, it had too much of everything, so some of the experts said. Cut down on production, destroy the surpluses, create artificial scarcities, use any expedient to drive the supply of goods down below the demand, and prices would have to rise again and all would be well.

But how could there possibly be too much of everything when so many millions were hungry, cold and destitute? How could there be too much food when men, women and children in Chicago, Montreal, London and elsewhere grovelled in the garbage at the city dumps, searching with their bare hands for some overlooked morsel to eat? How could there be too much wheat when, in every city everywhere, honest people stood day after day in the long 'breadlines' waiting for a handout, and food riots and hunger marches had become common occurrences? Looking down the perspective of years, to the days before the First World War, to the economic and military rivalry between the Big Powers, to the tragedy of the War itself, to the grabbing for spoils at the Peace Conference and to the more recent shortsighted, frenzied scramble for material wealth, many thoughtful observers concluded that the world was now paying for the selfishness and greed of the past.

Poverty in a Land of Plenty

The Great Depression was a particularly cruel blow to Canada. Thirty years of unbroken material progress, in which her natural resources found such ready markets and her people, next to the United States, enjoyed the highest living standard in the world, were now shattered in a few disastrous months. Before the full onslaught of the economic crisis, the volume of business done in this country —despite the fact that it contained less than one per cent of the world's population—placed Canada well up with nations many times her size. She ranked eighth among the industrial powers and sixth among the trading nations; her railways, her stock and bond market and the amount of shipping from her ports were fourth largest in the world; she borrowed more money abroad and had a greater tourist trade than any other nation; she was the world's leading exporter of wheat, newsprint and non-ferrous metals and one of the world's largest importers of coal, oil and steel products. It should be re-emphasized that all this

Breadlines such as this one in New York could be seen in most cities and towns in United States and Canada in 1930.

economic activity by a nation of less than 10 million people was made possible only because Canada gambled on continuing world prosperity and poured millions of borrowed dollars into the development of her natural resources. Producing far more than her own small domestic market could possibly absorb, her very existence depended on a high volume of international trade.

Now, however, as the Depression deepened, as world trade was sliced in half, Canada's vulnerable economic system completely collapsed. With her customers abroad facing financial ruin, with the highest tariffs ever known blocking her products from European and American markets, with the price of all her major exports and especially wheat sliding downhill, with world surpluses accumulating everywhere and with competition from Argentina, Australia, Russia and other overstocked countries, Canada's revenue from external trade dropped from almost $1,400 million in 1929 to less than $475 million in 1933—a calamitous fall of sixty-seven per cent in just three years. Companies directly or indirectly associated with foreign trade now had neither the money nor the incentive to invest in new factories or machinery and the entire investment and building boom crumpled rapidly. Once started, this landslide crushed the steel, coal, non-ferrous-metal mining, lumbering, cement and other branches of the vast construction industry. All these interrelated industries laid off so many men that by the winter of 1932–33 there were almost six hundred thousand unemployed in the country. The loss of earnings by this large group and the sixty per cent decline in all farm incomes helped to put the finishing touches to the market for automobiles, household appliances and a multitude of other consumer goods manufactured in Canada. Thus the whole business life of the nation, so delicately geared to world trade and capital expansion, spiralled downward.

When at last the Depression reached its worst during the winter months of 1932–33, Canada's whole economic system was travelling at little better than half speed, the national income, which measures the value of all the goods and services produced in the country, had fallen from $6 billion to less than $3½ billion, and some of the finest human and material resources to be found anywhere were wasting away in idleness.

Next-year Country
The resentment that all these depressed conditions aroused in Canada was greatly intensified by the fact that some economic groups and some parts of the country suffered much more severely than others. Those engaged in the primary exporting industries were caught in an apparently hopeless position. With the price of their products determined almost entirely by world conditions, the lumbering, fishing and mining industries of British Columbia, the prairie wheat farmers and the flour-milling industry, the base-metal mining and pulp-and-paper industries of northern Ontario and Quebec were absolutely powerless to shield themselves from the heaviest blows of the Depression. The heaviest burden, as might be expected, fell on the prairie provinces where dependence on a single cash crop proved disastrous when the bottom fell out of world wheat markets. In Alberta and Manitoba—and especially in the city of Winnipeg whose very existence

A destitute family on their way back to Saskatchewan from the Peace River area, 1934

depended on the eastward flow of grain—the situation was aggravated by widespread urban unemployment. The costs of providing not only fuel, food and clothing to all these destitute people but also seed, fodder and other supplies to tens of thousands of large-scale farmers who had staked everything on wheat, overwhelmed the financial resources of the three prairie provinces. For seven gloomy years, from 1930 to 1937, complete bankruptcy was avoided only by gifts and loans provided by the federal government.

The wheat farmers in Saskatchewan and in southeastern Alberta were dealt a doubly severe blow. Along with all others during the early years of the Depression, they had to sit back helplessly as the price of wheat fell from $1.60 a bushel in 1929 to only 38¢ by the end of 1932. In bewilderment and anger and then in dire fear, they saw the selling price of their only product slump below the costs of production and their sole source of income vanish almost overnight. They found themselves without the money to pay their taxes or the interest charges on the debts that they had piled up in good times. Many of them had their machinery, their crops and even their land and homes seized by creditors. The majority of families could not even afford to buy clothes. Bundles of castoff clothing sent from eastern Canada were all too frequently pilfered by other desperate people en route and even if they arrived safely were usually pitifully inadequate. Many prairie women dressed themselves and their children in clumsy garments made from old flour sacks or from burlap bags in which binder twine had once been wrapped. Families were forced to sacrifice their telephones, their daily or weekly newspapers, their radios and their cars and thus, through poverty, lost their access to neighbours and to the outside world.

And then in the spring of 1933, just as world conditions seemed to be improving a little, drought struck some sections of the prairies and especially the ill-fated dry belt of southern Alberta and Saskatchewan. This was the 40-million-acre area which had been unwisely opened for homesteading back in 1908. Now the country paid the penalty for letting the West just grow, like Topsy, without plan or

An abandoned farm near Cadillac, Saskatchewan. Huge dust storms removed the fine, light topsoil from farms in the 'dry belt' and left behind piles of drifting, useless sand.

foresight. During the next four years, a nation once accustomed to wonderful yields of 27 bushels per acre and annual crops of 350 million bushels or better watched in horror as the returns from some farms sank to 3 bushels an acre and the total production of the prairie provinces steadily declined until it reached 182 million bushels in 1937.

Not only the wheat crop but also the vegetable gardens shrivelled in the dry heat and thousands of cattle died of starvation and thirst. Families now faced not just loneliness and a drastic fall in living standards but outright starvation. Women who had once worried about their children being cold and miserably clad now struggled to keep them alive on a diet of bread, potatoes and 'gopher stew'. And yet, despite the pleading of governments and the urgent warnings of nature, the great majority of wheat farmers in the dust bowl continued to plant their fields always hoping that next year, or the year after, things would be better.

Unwanted Men

Southern Ontario and Quebec, which had enjoyed the greatest prosperity in the boom years, also suffered less than other regions during the Depression. In these two central provinces and to a certain extent in the Maritimes, the existence of mixed farming helped to cushion the heaviest blows. Although the average cash income of rural families in eastern Canada fell to well below $300 annually, the farmers at least could grow most of their own food and few of them faced actual starvation. Also, by resorting to a primitive system of barter with the local store-keepers—a sucking pig for a cheap coat, a pair of chickens and some eggs for a can of paint—they managed to keep their households going and retained their independence without relying on public charity.

Then, again, most of the domestic manufacturing companies were located in Ontario and Quebec and they were able to protect themselves in ways that the exporting industries could not use. Producing for the home market and being thoroughly shielded from all foreign competition by the high tariffs, these companies restricted their output and kept their prices as high as possible. Rightly or wrongly, company managers decided they would be better off selling less at higher prices than selling more at lower prices. They were able to do this not only because of the tariff but also because the mergers and amalgamations of the Roaring Twenties had centralized industry and finance in comparatively few hands. Thus the big corporations shifted some of the Depression's burden onto the consumers in the form of rigidly high prices. Some idea of the added resentment that this policy caused may be gathered from the fact that from 1929 to 1933 farm prices declined by almost exactly fifty per cent whereas the price of tariff-protected manufactured goods—boots, clothing, furniture, household appliances and many other items of everyday consumption—fell by only fourteen per cent.

Somewhat like the prairie wheat farmers, the industrial workers of Canada had only one thing, their labour, to sell and when society no longer required their services they, too, faced personal disaster. Never having earned enough to put away any savings, the receipt of a discharge slip immediately raised the terrifying prospect of trying to live in a modern society without money. Thousands upon thousands of Canadian families, struck down by unemployment through no fault of their own, were compelled to exist for weeks and months on public charity.

No words can describe the bitterness and anxiety of the men who stood 'flat broke', literally without a single cent in their pockets, before the factory gates for endless hours, hoping that a few new hands might be taken on. Although they must have known deep down in their hearts that there was no hope, the great majority kept on coming back, day after day, in all kinds of weather, to stand in line and wait. As the days wore on into weeks and the weeks into months, whole communities, and especially one-industry towns like Sydney, Oshawa, Sudbury or Windsor, took on a dirty, worn-out appearance. The shops were drab, unpainted and lifeless, the streets filled with restless, endlessly moving, idle, unwanted and shabby men. And behind these outward signs of stark poverty lay the tragedy of family life undermined by insecurity.

Adversity of this kind doubtless brought many families closer together, but they were united mainly in a grim struggle for survival. Wives and mothers toiled ceaselessly, skimping and saving in countless ways to make ends meet. Clothes were patched until they were threadbare; tables and chairs were held together with bits of rope or wire and when they could no longer be repaired were used for firewood; tea leaves and coffee grounds and soup bones were employed over and over again until there was no nourishment or flavour left; lard and watered-down canned milk replaced the fresh dairy products which, in other parts of the country, were going to waste, and very often families had nothing to eat for days on end but a dreary diet of oatmeal porridge and white beans. Many women went out to work, leaving their husbands to look after the home, for they could find jobs more easily than men. But the labour market was glutted and they were cruelly exploited. Subsequent government investigations revealed that thousands of Canadian women, especially in the textile, canning, confectionery and baking industries, worked sixty, sixty-five, even seventy hours a week to earn a meagre three or four dollars.

When they finally concluded that there was no work to be had in their community, a great many of the younger men, and some of the older ones as well, took to the road looking for employment. Hitch-hiking along the highways, walking miles between towns when they could not get a lift, stealing into empty boxcars or 'riding the rods' beneath the freight trains, they became the hobos, the tramps, the knights of the road who moved back and forth across the country during the depression years. Grotesquely dressed in pieces of castoff clothing, boots worn through and repaired with wads of cardboard, blistered or frostbitten feet frequently wrapped in burlap bags, weather-beaten and unshaven, begging for food and casual work from door to door, they were a tragically familiar sight in many parts of Canada. In the wintertime, they slept on the bare floors of the jails or the local town halls, sometimes with blankets supplied by compassionate citizens, more often without. In warmer weather, they gathered outside the towns, under the shelter of a clump of willow trees, usually beside the railroad tracks and there, in the hobo 'jungles', they shared their meagre food supplies and their burdens and slept on the ground beside an open fire.

The story of these countless drifting men would not be complete without some reference to the kindly, more fortunate Canadian families who helped them on their way. In every town from Montreal to Windsor or from Toronto to the north country, all during the worst years, volunteers devoted many hours each day to collecting clothing and organizing 'soup kitchens' for the transients. Housewives took them into their homes, allowed them to rest and warm themselves in the kitchen, gave them sandwiches and tea and often helped to restore their pride by letting them do a little gardening to earn their way. And more than one warm-hearted woman turned away to hide the tears in her eyes.

Groping for a Cure

The Politics of Adversity

The Great Depression caught most Canadian businessmen and politicians without any answers to the problems that plagued the country. After the stock market crash in 1929 the whole world was dazed and bewildered, and positive leadership was sadly lacking in almost all countries. As far as Canada was concerned, the causes of the economic crisis were mainly external and very few alternatives lay open to her statesmen. Furthermore, the country had been allowed to run along under its own steam, with less guidance and control than any other western nation, and the doctrines of pure capitalism were too deeply rooted to be changed overnight. Although the whole situation cried out for vigorous action by the federal government and many necessary steps have since been taken to cushion the blows of any future depression, the fact remains that Canada drifted more aimlessly during the 1930s than did most stricken countries.

The scarcity of constructive ideas was clearly revealed in the federal elections of July 1930. On public platforms across the country and on the radio—this was the first election in which campaigning over the airways was a decisive factor— the politicians promised to remove the scourge of unemployment and pledged themselves to revive world trade. Prime Minister King and the Liberal party tended to deny the very existence of any serious problems and adopted a timid, typical 'wait-a-while' policy. Conditions, they said, were bound to improve if

Unemployed men at Calgary, Alberta, in 1935, on their way to Ottawa to demand government action.

people would only be patient. But the man who had just lost his job or been cleaned out in the crash was in no mood to be patient. With or without justification, people always blame the party in power when things go wrong and Mackenzie King's popularity naturally sagged with prices. On the other hand, R. B. Bennett, the Conservative leader, was thundering across the country like a verbal tornado promising to retaliate against the Smoot-Hawley Act and to use the tariff to 'blast' his way into the markets of the world. Here was no ordinary politician, but a successful businessman, a millionaire in his own right. Surely he must know what he was talking about! Thus, on election day, the Conservatives were swept into office just in time to meet the full onslaught of the Depression with a platform no more constructive or unique than sky-high tariffs.

Making the most sweeping changes in the National Policy since its introduction in 1879, the new government granted increased protection to every industry of importance and raised the general rates by almost fifty per cent. These measures were supplemented later on, in 1932, by a series of preferential trade treaties signed in Ottawa with Great Britain and other Commonwealth countries. Although the Ottawa Agreements diverted some of Canada's importing and exporting business away from the United States and directed it into Empire channels, it may well be argued that, in the long run, the tariff policies of the government did more harm than good. Among other things, they made it easier for the sheltered domestic manufacturing industries to maintain high prices and thus, by increasing the costs of production for the primary producer, hampered the revival of our all-important external trade.

The federal government was also compelled to tackle the critical problems of wheat and unemployment. According to the British North America Act, the responsibility of caring for the unemployed was supposed to rest with the provincial and municipal governments. Previous depressions had not been long or severe enough to strain the limited resources of these governments, but this time the problem inevitably came to rest on Ottawa's doorstep. In order to save some provinces and a great many municipalities from outright bankruptcy, the Bennett administration had no choice but to advance very large subsidies for unemployment relief from the federal treasury. It also undertook a fairly extensive public works program and maintained several hastily built and very poorly administered relief camps for unattached men who had no families or homes. The Dominion government made further special grants to aid the three prairie provinces in their efforts to relieve distress among the wheat farmers. In addition to this, they paid a five-cents-per-bushel bonus on the 1931 crop and purchased some 200 million bushels which the farmers could not sell on the open market during the next three years. This wheat, stored at government expense, was not resold until world conditions began to improve in 1935. However, these measures failed to strike at any of the basic causes of the Depression; they were temporary, makeshift arrangements doing little more than tide the nation along on a day-to-day basis.

The Conservatives also conducted costly investigations into several particularly knotty problems arising from the Depression, but their findings produced very few concrete achievements. Royal commissions were appointed to study and make recommendations about the railroads, banking and finance, and the large spread between the prices received by producers and those finally paid by the consumers. The mounting deficits of the Canadian National Railway and the intense dislike in certain financial circles for Sir Henry Thornton, the hard-

R. B. Bennett,
1930–35

A soup kitchen in Port Arthur, Ontario

working and hard-living president of the government line, had revived the agitation to turn it over to the Canadian Pacific. A great many people, comparing the efficiency of the two, seemed to have quickly forgotten that the government-owned railroad was composed of several lines which had gone bankrupt in the first place under careless, overambitious private ownership. The Duff Report on railways put this question to rest by producing good evidence to show that the two systems should not be joined. As a result of its recommendation, however, the Canadian National and the Canadian Pacific eliminated a number of overlapping services and agreed to operate pool trains between Toronto, Ottawa and Montreal. Following the suggestions of the Macmillan Report on banking, the

Bennett administration in 1934 created the Bank of Canada, a central agency designed to control the private banks, to regulate the flow of currency and credit and to serve as an adviser to the federal government in financial matters.

The resentment caused by continuing high prices in certain sections of the country's economy was brought to a head by the startling revelations of the Royal Commission on price spreads. Appointed to investigate not only the gap in prices but also the effect of mass buying by chain and department stores, the commission unfolded a picture which suddenly became shocking in the midst of economic distress. Large retail stores using their immense buying power to beat down mercilessly the prices that they paid to primary producers and small manufacturers; starvation wages and sweatshop conditions in companies supplying the chain and department stores; the wholesale evasion of laws regulating hours and wages—these were but some of the features brought out in the evidence. It is safe to conclude that, as the commission dug deeply into the secrets of mercantile life in Canada, all those connected with it, except the small retailers and manufacturers, heartily wished the investigation had never started. However, their fears were groundless because the Stevens Report on price spreads, for reasons that have never been made clear, was quickly pigeonholed and forgotten.

Briefly, it may be seen that a dubious tariff policy, some hand-to-mouth relief measures, a central bank and a few minor economies in railway management were about all that the Bennett administration could show for its efforts. And meanwhile, the Liberal members of parliament placidly sat back on the opposition benches and offered practically no alternative program. They were content to let the Conservatives wallow aimlessly in the troughs of the Depression and to wait for the next election. Their noncommittal attitude may have been good political strategy but it was small consolation for a nation struggling to survive the worst economic crisis in modern history. Growing dissatisfaction with this lack of leadership on the part of both Liberals and Conservatives at Ottawa encouraged the wealthier provinces to embark on their own schemes and also led to the formation of several new political parties. During the depression years, for instance, the people of Alberta first yielded to the rosy promises of William Aberhart's Social Credit party; Quebec fell under the strongly clerical and somewhat dictatorial influence of Maurice Duplessis and his Union Nationale; and the voters in Ontario elected as premier the colourful 'Mitch' Hepburn, a Liberal politician with an extreme interest in the welfare of his own province and an intense dislike for Mackenzie King. The appearance of powerful provincial leaders like Aberhart, Duplessis and Hepburn naturally increased the trend towards sectionalism which we have already observed at work in the 1920s.

It was inevitable that the glaring injustice of so much poverty in a land of plenty should also stimulate the formation of a socialist party that advocated not just day-by-day emergency measures but a sweeping reorganization of the whole capitalist system. The impetus for this radical new movement came from J. S. Woodsworth, William Irvine and other Labour representatives who had continued to sit in parliament since the days of the Winnipeg strike and from a handful of Progressives, including Miss Agnes Macphail, who had refused to join either one of the old political parties as so many of their colleagues had done. Although all these leaders had long since lost any affection they might have had for Russia and revolutionary socialism, they continued to believe, even in good times, that society should be based on co-operation instead of competition and that a federation of farm, labour and other organizations representing 'exploited people' should be formed to bring this about. Now the collapse of capitalism and the obvious need for more government control seemed to present them with their long-awaited chance. Consequently, a series of meetings, culminating in a big convention at Regina in 1933, created the Co-operative Commonwealth Federation with J. S. Woodsworth as its national leader and a platform modelled on the British Labour party's doctrine of gradual socialism.

In a very vague and general sort of way, the C.C.F. advocated the establishment of a planned economic system in which the government would regulate the production and distribution of all goods and services. Believing that this could not be accomplished so long as the means of production lay in private hands, the new party also proposed the government ownership of certain 'key industries' such as the banks, the telephone and hydro-electric power companies, and the mineral, timber and other natural resources of the country. In addition to these outright socialist principles, the C.C.F. platform provided for unemployment insurance, old age pensions, family allowances, security of farm tenure against seizure by creditors, socialized health services, and many other measures designed to establish economic security and better living standards for the mass of the people. Since social legislation of this kind obviously would cost a lot of money, the C.C.F. made no bones about the fact that they intended to 'soak the rich' through increased income, business-profits, and inheritance taxes. In this way the government would be using its taxing power to redistribute the national income, taking some of it away from the wealthier classes and handing it out to the poor in the form of family allowances, free health services and other social benefits. The total effect of their program, so the C.C.F. supporters claimed, would be to eliminate the dangers of a future depression, to place far more purchasing power in the hands of the people and thus to raise the general standards of living and keep the nation's industrial life running at full capacity.

The C.C.F. platform was too rich a diet for most Canadians to stomach. In a country so accustomed to free enterprise, its socialist ideas of government ownership and control were greeted with a mixture of fear, horror and ridicule. Nevertheless, practically every piece of welfare legislation advocated by the C.C.F. has since been adopted in Canada. Thus this depression-born political party served the useful purpose of stimulating the old parties to do a little more progressive thinking and helped to pave the way for what is today called the 'welfare state'.

A New Deal for Americans

The ideas that were to have the most decisive influence on the future course of this country came, however, not from the C.C.F. or any other native political movement, but from the United States. As in Canada, the American people tended to blame the party in power for all their troubles and President Hoover's popularity, like Mackenzie King's, disappeared along with prosperity. Although this brilliant engineer and once highly respected President had given more positive leadership to his country than any other statesman in the western world, a 'smear campaign' soon pictured him as a cold, callous man, indifferent to the people's plight. Hard-working and sincere though he was, Hoover could not dramatize his battle with the Depression in a way to kindle popular imagination or revive the nation's morale. And he was no match for the dynamic personality who appeared as his rival for the presidency.

In accepting the Democratic party's nomination, Franklin Delano Roosevelt said: 'I pledge you, I pledge myself to a new deal for the American people.' From that moment on, throughout the summer and fall of 1932, his warm, reassuring voice began to restore confidence throughout the United States. 'Failure is not an American habit. It is common sense to take a method and try it.' Just what the Democratic candidate proposed to try was not quite clear at first. He spoke vaguely of social justice for the underprivileged, for 'the forgotten man at the bottom of the economic pyramid'. Getting out of the Depression was only a part of the problem. Lasting reforms in the whole economic system were needed as insurance against another collapse.

As he warmed to his task and election day grew closer, Roosevelt became more definite. He now spoke of *the* New Deal and promised that it would be brought about by old age pensions, unemployment insurance, control of crop surpluses, the easing of farm mortgage burdens, the regulation of wages and hours of work, the elimination of unfair competition, the raising of farm prices through government support, and the building of great power dams and other federal projects which would 'prime the pump' and create employment. He even dared to suggest that the Smoot-Hawley tariff was a blight on the good name of the United States and that world trade could be revived only by reciprocal agreements with other countries. And as the American people listened, they seemed to sense that these were no idle political promises but a hopeful set of blueprints for the future designed by an architect of great vision.

Commenting on the landslide that carried Roosevelt into the White House and the Democratic party into control of Congress, a veteran political observer wrote that it meant 'a new attitude in the United States . . . a firm desire by the American people to use their government as an agency for human welfare'. The new President extended the influence of the federal government into the whole economic life of the country, securing legislation which not only relieved immediate distress but also struck at the roots and causes of the Depression. Federal expenditures rose drastically, costly mistakes were made, the Supreme Court declared many laws unconstitutional and most business leaders waged war on the growing network of government regulations, but still Roosevelt and the group of experts known as his 'Brain Trust' kept on experimenting, discarding here and there, retaining what was good, until the New Deal became a reality.

While all this was being done, the vibrant, cheery voice of the President,

Franklin D. Roosevelt gives one of his fireside chats.

reaching out to the nation through his Sunday evening 'fireside chats' over the radio, helped to revive the spirit of the people. Gradually, the New Deal took hold. During 1933 and 1934, prices started to climb a little, factories reopened, pay envelopes grew fatter, people began to buy more and the United States, pulling itself up by the boot straps, slowly emerged from the depths of the Depression.

From his vantage point in Ottawa, Bennett watched the progress of the New Deal with growing interest, and in January 1935, in a series of fireside chats of his own, the Canadian Prime Minister went on the air and announced his conversion to the virtues of the welfare state in words which sounded very much like Roosevelt's. To the amazement of friend and foe alike, he proclaimed that the capitalist system must be overhauled from top to bottom. 'Canada on the dole is like a young and vigorous man in the poorhouse. The dole is a condemnation, final and complete, of our economic system. If we cannot abolish the dole, we should abolish the system.' And this, remember, came from a very successful businessman trained to believe in the benefits of unfettered individualism!

True to his word, the Prime Minister pushed through the next session of parliament a far-reaching program of reform, including minimum wage legislation, the forty-eight-hour week, a weekly day of rest, an unemployment insurance scheme, social security laws and the establishment of a central planning board called the National Economic Council. Although the majority of Canadians may have heartily agreed with the new laws, they could not help but wonder why Bennett had waited so long. With an election due in a few months, they were inclined to believe that his change of heart was little more than a last-minute effort to catch voters. And many of them knew, as both Bennett and King undoubtedly did, that much of this legislation dealt with 'property and civil rights' and would therefore be thrown out by the Privy Council on the grounds that it invaded provincial jurisdiction. Although the Liberal campaign was purely negative and critical, the voters, apparently concluding that Bennett had had his one and only chance, swept Mackenzie King back into office on election day with the greatest majority his party had ever had. Social Credit elected seventeen members, all from the West. The C.C.F. had seven including T. C. Douglas, who in 1944 was to head, as premier of Saskatchewan, the first socialist government in Canada and in 1961 would become federal leader of the New Democratic Party.

It may now be seen that the Liberals were extremely lucky. They had been kicked out of office just before the full impact of the Depression hit Canada and their return to power coincided with the revival of world prosperity. Thus they took the blame for an economic crisis that they were almost powerless to prevent and then, in the last half of the 1930s, gleefully claimed the credit for better conditions that they did very little to create. Canada gradually emerged from the depths of the Depression, but the continuing drought out West hung like a pall over the whole economy and any prosperity that the country enjoyed was due mainly to the revival of the United States and to the growing danger of a second world war. In due course, the Liberal party did introduce some extremely valuable reforms and became the ardent champions of the welfare state, but during the remaining years of the 1930s the attention of the Canadian people began to focus more and more on the black clouds gathering on international horizons.

13 THE GATHERING STORM

Collective Insecurity

Stretching across Manchuria from the Russian border to the Pacific Ocean, with a branch line extending southward through the Liao-tung peninsula to Port Arthur, is one of the most fascinating railroads in the world. As a source of international intrigue and periodic warfare, of true stories stranger than fiction, it has few, if any, rivals. Called the Chinese Eastern Railway, this line was built by Russia at the beginning of the twentieth century when the western powers were falling all over each other to secure land and economic privileges from hapless China. The Russians were just establishing themselves in Manchuria when Japan went on the warpath in 1904–5 and took from them the Liao-tung peninsula, Port Arthur and the southern spur of the Chinese Eastern Railway. For the next twenty-five years this branch line—renamed the South Manchuria Railway—was the main artery through which Japan pumped money and troops into Manchuria and transformed the whole region into a very valuable Japanese sphere of influence. The right to develop a rich but underpopulated province like Manchuria was doubly important to the Japanese because their own country was so small—about two-thirds the size of Manitoba—yet their population exceeded 60 million and babies were born at the rate of four per minute. It was with growing fear, therefore, that the Japanese leaders watched the revival of China during the 1920s. Before the end of the decade, the Nationalist armies of General Chiang Kai-shek had conquered most of the local warlords, a capital had been established at Nanking, many foreign privileges had been wiped out, and China seemed more united than she had been for many years. To the Japanese, the re-establishment of Chinese control over Manchuria seemed to be next on the list. Their anxiety was greatly intensified by the fact that the warlord of Manchuria—a man who had been content to let Japan exploit the country—was now showing unmistakable signs of co-operating with Chiang Kai-shek. Under these circumstances, with Manchuria drawing closer to China, the military leaders of Japan apparently decided that they had to strike very soon or never.

Japan Throws Down the Gauntlet

It is perhaps not surprising, therefore, that on the night of September 18, 1931, a section of the South Manchuria Railway was blown up 'by Chinese patriots'. According to Japanese reports, the culprits were caught red-handed and a fight took place between them and the Japanese railway guards. Some splintered ties and a bent rail were produced as evidence that there had indeed been an explosion, but no outside observer was allowed to visit the scene. The night train to Mukden arrived on time, a phenomenon which the Japanese explained by asserting that the heavy express had hurdled the broken rails without the slightest injury. No one on the train, however, heard any bump. And even more damaging was the fact that, before the incident occurred, Japanese troops, marching with smooth precision, were on the move throughout Manchuria. There have been many other incidents, real or imagined, along the South Manchuria Railway, but this explosion was different—for it killed the independence of Manchuria and its echoes were heard around the world.

The Japanese militarists could not have picked a better time for their attack on Manchuria. The economic crisis had cut Japan's vital foreign trade almost in half, the Smoot-Hawley tariff had blocked her textiles from American markets, unemployment was mounting and serious internal unrest threatened. A war would put the factories to work on military supplies, end unemployment and divert the people's attention from their own troubles towards patriotic events overseas. More important still, it would crush the Chinese threat to become the dominant power in the Far East. Although much stronger than before, China was still torn by civil war between the Nationalists and the Communists, and Chiang Kai-shek seemed to be more interested in defeating his own political opponents than he was in facing up to Japan. Thus the Japanese correctly assumed that Manchuria could be conquered without too much resistance from China.

The Japanese also correctly guessed that no other nation would lift a finger to stop them. The economic blizzard sweeping across the world had blinded western statesmen to all but their own very urgent problems. They could not be expected to see that the storm centre over Manchuria would some day engulf them in an even greater catastrophe. Just a month before the explosion on the South Manchuria Railway, Europe and especially Great Britain had passed through the worst financial crisis in recent history. In Britain, the Labour government had collapsed, a national coalition had been formed and the people were concentrating on another general election. Manchuria was far away, British trade with China was not important, and Chiang Kai-shek's Nationalist movement was anti-British. The United States, the one western country with great interests in the Far East, courageously announced that she would not recognize the Japanese conquest of Manchuria, but when it came right down to the critical test of giving full support to the League of Nations or refusing to supply Japan with oil and steel, she was no better than the rest.

Thus the League of Nations, facing its first serious challenge from a great power, was doomed to failure. The Council of the League confined its efforts to appointing committees, urging both sides to be moderate and engaging in long but futile discussions. Instead of attempting to name an aggressor as quickly as possible so definite action could be taken, the delegates studiously avoided the issue by insisting that, since neither country had made any formal declaration, there really wasn't any war! These delaying tactics were encouraged by Matsuoka, the Japanese delegate, who tactfully insisted that 'the League has no more loyal servant than Japan'. Of course his country had no intention of violating the Covenant or the Washington Treaty or the Paris Peace Pact. This was only 'police action' required to protect legitimate Japanese interests! These assertions were at first taken quite seriously, not only in Geneva but throughout most of Europe. The London *Times* was only expressing the accepted opinion—one that was uncriti-

Japanese occupation of Hailar, key city of far northwestern Manchuria, December 6, 1932

cally copied here in Canada—when it stated: 'The Japanese scheme is undoubtedly intended to provide Manchuria with an efficient government and an honest financial administration. . . . It would probably be erroneous to suppose that they deliberately plan to annex Manchuria.'

Although the fighting in Manchuria had practically ceased, an open admission of failure was postponed when the League appointed a commission, under the leadership of Lord Lytton, to conduct an investigation on the spot in the Far East. This commission did not report back to the League until September 1932, exactly one year after the trouble had started, and by that time Manchuria had disappeared from the map, being replaced by the Japanese puppet state of Manchukuo. Even so, the Lytton Report did not have the courage to name Japan as an aggressor and the application of economic or military sanctions was never discussed. All the League of Nations could manage was a resolution passed in February 1933, stating that the members could not recognize Manchukuo. When this happened, Matsuoka and his colleagues rose and left the Assembly with great dignity, never to return.

Fiasco at Geneva
In February 1932, during the Manchurian crisis, delegates assembled in another building for the long-awaited Disarmament Conference. Attended by politicians

and military experts from sixty-four countries, the conference was hailed as the greatest one the world had so far seen. Geneva hotels had made special arrangements to accommodate the delegates, the journalists, the representatives of the armament manufacturers with funds at their disposal to be used if necessary, and all others who were interested in the proceedings of the conference; and each official delegate was presented with a gold medal struck by the League in honour of the occasion. Thus for the next fourteen months, well on into 1933, Woodrow Wilson Avenue in Geneva was filled with talk—on the one side lengthy discussions about war in the Far East, on the other side even longer discussions about peace and disarmament.

The drastic disarmament of Germany after the War was intended to be only a preliminary step towards the limitation of armaments by other countries. This understanding was reinforced by Article VIII in the Covenant of the League by which all member nations promised to reduce their arms 'to the lowest point consistent with national safety'. Obviously, if the League really was a safeguard against war, national armed forces were hardly necessary. Governments that pledged themselves to abolish war and repeatedly stressed their allegiance to the League should have been able to carry out the obligations they had assumed at the Paris Peace Conference. During the 1920s, however, the League failed to provide security and most nations continued to rely on large-scale armaments. All were for peace, all were for disarmament, but none would give up any of the spoils from previous wars or reduce their armed forces. Since the nations failed to achieve any appreciable reduction in arms during good times, it was a foregone conclusion, therefore, that the World Disarmament Conference, meeting at the height of the economic and Far Eastern crises, would be a complete failure.

Yet the Disarmament Conference dragged on for more than three years. It became almost an institution, adjourning, reassembling and again adjourning. Altogether, twenty-seven different disarmament plans were laid before the Conference. The French suggested the creation of an international army under League control; the Russians, to everyone's amusement, proposed the total abolition of all weapons; while the British advocated the limitation of armaments which lent themselves to offensive rather than defensive warfare. It soon became apparent, however, that no distinction between offensive and defensive weapons would command general acceptance, and the Disarmament Conference adjourned for the last time in April 1935. Its failure, like the Manchurian fiasco, was another signpost marking the end of collective security and the return to power politics. Even more important, its lingering death overlapped by some months a dangerous new development, for in January 1933 Adolf Hitler seized the reins of power in Germany.

These two events stand in close relation to each other and jointly mark the transition from one period to the next. The failure of the Allied powers to carry out their promise to disarm justified, or at least gave Hitler the excuse for, the rearmament of Germany. Thus the vicious circle which the statesmen of 1919 had hoped to break was once more complete.

Heil Hitler!

The War and the peace settlement had left Germany crushed, spiritually and materially. A proud race like the Germans could not easily forget the humiliation of defeat or the 'dictate of Versailles'. And France, much more so than any other Allied power, set out during the immediate post-war years to make sure the Germans would never be able to forget that they were a conquered nation. Under the leadership of Poincaré, who had succeeded Georges Clemenceau as premier and whose intense hatred for the 'dirty Hun' was well known, France watched her neighbour like a hawk, waiting for the slightest excuse to pounce upon and weaken Germany still further. Poincaré's chance came at the end of 1922 when the Germans were forced to default on a shipment of telephone poles due on reparations account. Using this flimsy pretext and refusing to heed the warnings of Great Britain, French troops occupied the Ruhr Valley, thereby helping to cause the most disastrous period of inflation ever experienced by any nation.

The Ruhr was the industrial heart of Germany, producing over eighty per cent of the country's coal, iron and steel. Rather than surrender this vital region, the Germans resorted to passive resistance. Despite extremely harsh treatment by the occupying troops, they refused to carry out any orders given by their invaders, and the economic activity of the entire Ruhr area came to a standstill. In order to finance the patriotically idle inhabitants, the government in Berlin began to print more and more paper money, and as it did so prices climbed higher and higher until only a miracle could have saved the mark, and no miracle occurred. When inflation was at its height, the Reichsbank kept 1,783 printing presses busy making paper money. In pre-war days, the mark was worth about four to the dollar. Long before world opinion forced the French to get out of the Ruhr, it required 2½ trillion marks to buy a dollar! A dozen eggs sold for 250 billion marks and all other prices rose to equally astronomical levels.

This whole situation had a disastrous effect on Germany and helped to produce the conditions that allowed Hitler to seize power. Anyone in the country who had saved money—and this included most of the middle-class supporters of democracy—was wiped out. A nest egg of, say, 100,000 marks, a life savings once roughly equivalent to $25,000 in our money, literally would not buy a breakfast in 1923. People with satchels full of billion-mark notes struggled to buy bicycles, a suit of clothes, some grain, anything of real value, to replace paper currency which depreciated by the hour. Conversely, anyone in debt could practically find the money on the streets to pay off his creditors. The big industrialists especially were able to clear their companies of debt and secure complete control for themselves by buying out their shareholders with practically worthless money. Thus inflation forced the middle class down in poverty, raised a comparatively few businessmen to the pinnacle of power and created even greater extremes of rich and poor. During the depression years when communism threatened Germany, many of the industrialists who had profited from the debacle of 1923 helped to finance Hitler; at the same time, his popular mass following was drawn from the ranks of the disillusioned former members of the middle class.

The hopes of millions of desperate Germans that the mark would be restored to its former value were shattered when the Berlin government called in the old marks and issued new ones at a ratio of one to a trillion. Once the currency was stabilized, the German economic system gradually recovered and from 1925 to 1929, in common with other countries, Germany enjoyed a short period of prosperity. During this period Germany was admitted to the League of Nations, her relations with the Allied powers improved, the army of occupation was withdrawn from the Rhineland, reparations payments were modified and the German people began to carry their heads high once more.

Although German recovery was partly due to the organizing and scientific skill of her people, it was also based, as we know, on the shaky foundation of foreign loans. Once the New York stock market crashed and international lending ceased, the Great Depression hit Germany with particular severity. And as it did so, the feelings of defeat and shame, the loss of pride and confidence in their country's future, swept over the German people again. Some of them now began to listen to the communists but far, far more of them responded to the voice of Adolf Hitler and the other Nazi party chieftains. Under the direction of Dr. Goebbels, their propaganda expert, the Nazis became past masters in the art of appealing to the Germans with their traditional love for order and authority. Stirring oratory, posters, colourful banners, party songs and uniforms, torchlight parades, martial music, army discipline, the swastika which became their all-too-familiar insignia, theories of race superiority, emotional appeals rather than appeals to reason— these things attracted millions of Germans at a time when the only alternative seemed to be continued confusion and despair.

Hitler himself was a skilled orator, a real demagogue, in an age when broadcasting, microphones and amplifiers, and mass circulation newspapers enabled one man to address vast audiences. He was able to put into glowing words the groping, inarticulate feelings of the German people. And he promised them the moon—higher salaries, lower rents, cheaper food, higher prices, lower taxes, increased social services—all the earthly things desired by 'the little man in the little house with a little business who saw starvation staring himself and his family in the face'. More than this, he revived the racial pride and the confident, aggressive spirit of the German people. Communists and especially Jews were 'internationalists'. They had no love for Germany and they must be purged, driven out or into hiding, or exterminated. The Treaty of Versailles, the war guilt lie and reparations, all born in deceit, would enslave Germany no more. The land and the people torn from Imperial Germany in 1919 must be restored to the Fatherland. Democracy was weak and corrupt, an inefficient system forced upon them by the Allies. Only the elite, the gifted few, should rule. The Germans were a super-race to be governed in the future by supermen.

With twenty-seven different political parties competing for power in the Reichstag—far too many for the efficient functioning of democracy—no one group could possibly secure an overall majority. By January 1933, however, after a series of tumultuous general elections, the Nazis held more seats than any of their rivals. Thus the aging President Hindenburg, already in his dotage, had no

Hero-worship

choice but to invite Hitler to become the German Chancellor, a position that he accepted only on the understanding that he should have emergency dictatorial powers. The brown-shirted Nazi storm troopers, the Black Shirts, the dread Gestapo under the cruel direction of Heinrich Himmler, now quickly transformed Germany into a police state. The Reichstag building was burned to the ground, probably by the Nazis themselves, but the communists were blamed and persecuted as a result. Socialists, communists, Jews, democratic politicians, church leaders and professors, all who disagreed with the Nazi regime, were hunted down, thrown into concentration camps, driven into exile or cruelly shot to death. By the beginning of 1935, Hitler's grip on Germany was unchallenged; he had become *der Führer,* the idolized leader of millions who shouted 'Heil Hitler!' at the very thought of him.

During those early power-struggle years, however, Hitler was forced to stay his hand in foreign affairs until the plebiscite had been held in the Saar. This was the coal-mining region that had been taken from Germany after the War and placed under international control for a period of fifteen years. Afraid to take any chances with such a valuable asset, Hitler decided to wait until the Allies had given the people in the Saar an opportunity to vote themselves back into Germany. The only aggressive action he dared to take came towards the end of 1933 when Germany withdrew from the World Disarmament Conference and the League of Nations— two moves that were greeted with tremendous approval by the German people. Hitler also secretly encouraged the Nazi party in Austria to such an extent that in July 1934 they attempted to overthrow the government and join their country with Germany. This plot was foiled, but in the process of trying to capture the government buildings in Vienna the Nazis murdered Dr. Dollfuss, the anti-German dictator of Austria. Hostile world opinion compelled Germany to disclaim any connection with the Austrian Nazis, but the man who shot Dollfuss went to the gallows shouting 'Heil Hitler!' The time was rapidly approaching, however, when the Nazi leader of Germany would not back down, when he and the evil movement he represented would hurl defiance throughout the length and breadth of Europe.

The Return to Power Politics

Nazi Germany in Arms
On January 13, 1935, the inhabitants of the Saar Valley unshackled the Nazis. In a plebiscite supervised by the League, over ninety per cent of them voted in favour of returning to Germany. The formal transfer was made on March 1 and within three weeks Hitler undertook his first big move in foreign affairs. In a typical, rabble-rousing radio broadcast, pouring hatred for the Allies over the air waves, scoffing at their efforts to disarm, shouting that the Third Reich was ringed with hostile, heavily-armed nations, *der Führer* denounced the disarmament clauses of the Treaty of Versailles and proclaimed that from then on Germany recognized no limits to her military power. The whole country now plunged into an orgy of arms—men made and played with arms, capitalists drew profits from arms, youths were conscripted to use arms, and the Third Reich became a nation in arms. The entire educational system, from infancy onward, was directed towards producing a German who could with a minimum of additional training be turned into a soldier. This drunkenness quickly spread abroad until almost every factory in Europe was working night and day, piling up arms and munitions. And the people of Europe became prosperous once more by forging the weapons for their own ultimate destruction.

Following Hitler's declaration of March 16, 1935, France sent a strongly-worded protest to Germany, Great Britain dispatched a half-hearted one, and the League of Nations passed a resolution condemning the breaking of treaties. And the Germans went on about their business. Yet the outcome was not all gain for the Nazis. Hitler's aggressiveness immediately stimulated France and Czechoslovakia, who felt themselves particularly threatened by Nazi foreign

Rhinelanders greet Nazi troops riding into Dusseldorf as Hitler gambles on reviving Germany's dread Watch on the Rhine.

policy, to conclude defensive military alliances with the Soviet Union. Thus the Russian colossus was brought back into the European arena, and the German strategists were confronted with the familiar nightmare of preparing for a war on two fronts. Also, representatives from Italy, France and Great Britain met in April at the Italian town of Stresa and agreed that their countries would consult and co-operate with each other in their dealings with Nazi Germany. Considering that all these countries were reasonably well armed, their precautions tipped the balance of power decisively against Germany. For this reason, Hitler was compelled to be more conciliatory until Germany had time to build up her armaments or something happened to break the combination of powers ranged against him.

It was not long before signs appeared that Germany's opponents were not as united as they should have been. Within a month of joining the Stresa Front against Hitler, Great Britain turned right round and began to negotiate with him. In June, to the utter surprise and anger of France and Italy, these negotiations led to the signing of an Anglo-German treaty by which Great Britain recognized Germany's right to increase her navy to thirty-five per cent of the British strength. Thus the British government, having recently condemned Hitler for violating Versailles, now gave Germany permission to ignore some of its provisions and to possess certain kinds of ships, including submarines, altogether prohibited by the treaty.

This sudden shift in British policy was based on sound reasoning. A growing body of opinion had swung over to the view that the only effect of the French understanding with Czechoslovakia, Russia and Italy was to isolate and encircle Germany and to perpetuate the inequalities of the Versailles Treaty—in short, to maintain the very conditions that had been largely responsible for the Nazi revolution. Those who held this opinion, while not denying that Germany might be a danger to peace, believed that French, Italian and Soviet policy merely aggravated the danger and that the first aim of the British government should be to break the ring round Germany and to engage in friendly discussions of her grievances. The trouble with this 'policy of appeasement', as it came to be called, was that a man like Hitler interpreted it merely as a sign of weakness and not as a decent attempt to co-operate with him. Later on, appeasement may have seemed a product of weakness, but in its initial stages it was based partly on a sense of fair play and partly on the old British policy of maintaining a balance of power in Europe.

There was another and perhaps even more important reason behind Great Britain's sympathy for Germany. Hitler's dictatorship, unlike the communist one in Russia, had not destroyed capitalism. Indeed, the big industrialists seemed to be thriving as never before and one of the loudest boasts of the Nazis was that they were anti-Bolshevik and that they alone were responsible for crushing communism in Germany. In Great Britain, the majority of middle- and upper-class people were inclined to believe, therefore, that the fascist type of dictatorship in Germany and Italy, when compared with communism, was the lesser of two evils. They also feared that, if anything happened to undermine Hitler's prestige, Germany might crumble again in chaos, thus giving the communists a second chance to get into power.

Opposed to this view, a minority of very outspoken people in the British Isles—mainly intellectuals—looked upon the Soviet Union with great admiration. After all, complete free enterprise had proved itself to be a miserable failure, state control was the obvious answer and surely Russia, with her wonderful Five Year Plans and her complete freedom from any of the evils of the world Depression, pointed the way towards Utopia. People like George Bernard Shaw, Julian Huxley, Walter Duranty, Maurice Hindus and a host of others made pilgrimages to Moscow. Blind to the inevitable evils of any police state, they accepted as gospel everything they were shown or told; at home, they broadcast, lectured, wrote bestselling books and helped to arouse a great deal of sympathy for the Soviet Union.

With public opinion in the western democracies so divided, with the majority leaning towards fascism, indeed with black-shirted fascists openly parading in Great Britain and especially in France, Hitler was reasonably sure that strong action would not be taken against him. And if there was any doubt left in his mind, it was about to be removed by the actions of Benito Mussolini. By the spring of 1935, the Sawdust Caesar of fascist Italy was resolved that his strutting time had come.

A New Caesar

Signor Mussolini found or manufactured the excuse for which he was looking in the ancient African kingdom of Abyssinia. This country was the only independent native state of any importance left in Africa and it lay, most conveniently, between the existing Italian colonies of Somaliland and Eritrea. Being three times the size of Italy itself, it would make a very useful addition to Mussolini's empire and greatly increase his waning prestige. At one time, *il Duce* did not have to worry too much about such things as prestige. In the 1920s, he seemed to give his people a much more efficient and prosperous administration than the corrupt democratic politicians whom he had displaced immediately after the War. Foreign observers used to say that Mussolini was a 'benevolent dictator' and that, since over fifty per cent of the population could not read or write, his regime was probably better for the country than democracy. With the coming of the world Depression, however, Mussolini lost his popularity and, with unrest spreading throughout Italy, decided to follow the same obvious and easy way out as the Japanese militarists had taken in Manchuria.

Like Japan, Italy also was a poor country, a 'have-not' nation, devoid of oil, rubber, cotton and many other essential industrial raw materials. Her prosperity depended on imports and exports, on the tourist trade, and on the large sums of money sent back home by Italian emigrants—sources of wealth that left the country at the mercy of world conditions. But instead of realizing that Italy needed peace and a revival of world trade, as indeed did Canada, Denmark, Sweden and a great many other equally exposed nations, Mussolini followed the all-too-popular argument that he had to have more colonies. He also stressed the fact that his country was badly overcrowded and that the United States, Canada and Australia had made matters much worse by closing their doors during the depression years to all Italian immigrants. Mussolini did not explain why, if Italy was so overcrowded, he had imposed fines on bachelors, paid bonuses for early marriages and large families, offered state-financed honeymoons, prohibited birth control and done everything in his power to encourage an increase in population. Nor could he get around the well-known fact that Italian emigrants preferred the comforts and higher wages of modern industrial nations and that the last place in the world to attract them would be wild, backward Abyssinia.

Despite these considerations, which might have deterred more intelligent men, Mussolini and his advisers resolved to conquer Abyssinia. A border skirmish in which some Italian soldiers were killed near the Abyssinian village of Walwal provided Mussolini with the pretext to demand an apology and a large indemnity from Emperor Haile Selassie. All during the spring and summer months of 1935, while the responsibility for this incident was being debated and the usual committees investigated, Mussolini poured troops into Somaliland and Eritrea. By September, it was apparent that these lengthy discussions were only a smoke screen to hide Italian military preparations in Africa and that hostilities might break out at any moment.

Having carefully observed the League's failure to check Japan, the Italian fascists were equally sure that they, too, could carry out their imperial designs without being seriously challenged. They also knew that France would make almost any colonial concession to retain Italian friendship against the growing menace of Nazi Germany. Indeed, all the evidence seems to indicate that, during the Stresa Front negotiations, the French government had given Mussolini a completely free hand to pursue his plans regardless of what might happen to Haile Selassie and his tribesmen.

However, the fascists underestimated their other Stresa Front partner. Failing to see the significance of the Anglo-German naval treaty, they assumed that Great Britain, like France, would be too worried about Hitler to bother with a minor war in a remote corner of Africa. But the more Mussolini built up his forces around Abyssinia, the more British public opinion, correctly sensing that this was the last chance for collective security and peace, became determined to stand up for the League of Nations. In August, in a widely publicized straw vote known as the Peace Ballot, over 10 million Englishmen voted in favour of applying economic sanctions against any nation—meaning Italy—that was declared to be an aggressor by the League. This tide of pacifist sentiment, this demand that the Manchurian failure should not be repeated, was too strong for any British government to ignore and politicians of every persuasion quickly proclaimed a new-found faith in the Covenant of the League.

The most vigorous and undoubtedly the most sincere of these statesmen was Anthony Eden, who had recently been appointed Minister for League Affairs in the British government. In Eden, admirers of the League found their perfect champion. He was young, he was handsome, he was brilliant and enthusiastic, and above all, he believed in collective security. Until brute force eventually triumphed over everything he stood for, millions of people throughout Europe and the Commonwealth fixed their hopes in him with almost pathetic fervour.

In addition to the influence of Eden, there was another reason why the British government decided to resist Mussolini. Unlike the Manchurian crisis in 1931, Great Britain's overseas interests were directly involved. Many Englishmen, and especially the Conservative members of the national coalition, regarded Italy's aggressiveness as a threat to the timeworn problem of the Suez Canal and the route through the Red Sea to India. Even more important in their eyes was the fact that the Blue Nile and the Atbara, two tributaries of the Nile River rising in the highlands of Abyssinia, provided over eighty per cent of the summer and fall flood waters on which the fertility of both the Sudan and Egypt depended. The prospect of Italy in control of Abyssinia, threatening the route to India and the water supply of Egypt, presented a challenge which the British government had to accept. Thus by September 1935 it was apparent not only that Mussolini was going to attack Abyssinia but that when he did, his main opponent would be Great Britain. And among those who watched this growing Anglo-Italian rivalry with the greatest interest was Adolf Hitler.

On October 2, the long-expected telegram from Haile Selassie was received at Geneva announcing that Italian troops had crossed the Abyssinian border. The cumbersome machinery of the League now went into action with surprising rapidity. Under Eden's guidance, the Council declared Italy an aggressor and within three weeks, limited economic sanctions, for the first time in history, had been applied by most of the member nations. But why limited sanctions—why, when world opinion was so strongly behind the League, did the nations not sever trade with Italy entirely? Why were coal, iron and steel and above all oil omitted from the embargo list? Why was the Suez Canal left open, when closing it to Italian shipping would have brought Mussolini to his knees faster than anything else? Perhaps it was because *il Duce*, from the very beginning, shouted defiance from his Roman balcony, proclaiming that the application of complete sanctions or the closing of Suez meant a full-scale war in the Mediterranean. He may have been bluffing but no one, not even those who voted for the Peace Ballot, was willing to risk calling his bluff. The French government, especially, did not want to cause an open break with Italy, and the British, despite their interest in Abyssinia, apparently concluded that it was not worth an all-out war effort.

At this critical testing time when the course of history might have been changed, the nations were afraid to apply full economic sanctions. 'Peace at any price!' And for this reason, all during the Abyssinian war, Italian merchantmen threaded their way past British warships guarding the eastern Mediterranean, cleared the Suez Canal, steamed on past other British ships in the Red Sea and reached Eritrea in safety. While the inhabitants of Abyssinia defended themselves with spears, the Italians were able to conquer the country by the use of machine guns, tanks and poison gas poured down on unprotected tribesmen from the air. And, back in Rome, Mussolini hailed the victory as the greatest in the long and illustrious history of that city; the triumphs of Caesar were but trifles compared with the Italian conquest of Abyssinia.

The Watch on the Rhine

Complete sanctions might have been applied against Italy but for an event of utmost importance. By December 1935 a committee of the League was actually giving serious consideration to oil, coal and steel sanctions. But while this committee met and Mussolini hurled defiance at the League and war in the Mediterranean threatened, the foreign ministers of Britain and France were in secret session trying to find a way to appease *il Duce*. Behind closed doors, Sir Samuel Hoare and Pierre Laval agreed on a proposal to hand over most of Abyssinia to Italy—provided, of course, that the waters of the Atbara and the Blue Nile were not included in the bargain. And this, remember, came from a British government recently re-elected on the solemn promise that it would support the League of Nations! News of this apparently shoddy agreement leaked out before the public could be prepared to accept it and an outburst of indignation in Britain quickly killed the Hoare-Laval scheme. Sir Samuel was forced to resign, being replaced as foreign secretary by Eden—an appointment which was greeted throughout the British Isles as 'the best Christmas present the government could have given to the nation'.

During the winter months of 1936, Eden renewed the League's attempt to apply oil sanctions against Italy. Whether or not his efforts would have succeeded it is impossible to say because at this critical time Adolf Hitler decided to make his second big move in foreign affairs. On the morning of Saturday, March 6, the world awoke to hear the news that German troops, at that very moment, were marching across the bridges into the Rhineland. In defiance of Versailles and many other treaty obligations, the Germans were re-occupying the zone that was meant to be demilitarized forever. More than this, as Hitler assured the Reichstag on the previous evening, they were going to rebuild the fortifications along the border between France and Germany. Once more, 'the watch on the Rhine'! No longer would French troops be able to enter the Rhineland at will. The West Wall, when completed, would hold them out and the German army would be free for adventures elsewhere.

For the next forty-eight hours, while the world held its breath, the French cabinet met in continuous session trying to decide whether or not to mobilize against Germany. The fate of Europe depended upon their decision. According to Sir Winston Churchill and many other competent observers, it was at this point, more than any other, that the Second World War might have been averted. France alone was still strong enough to drive the fledgling German army out of the Rhineland. If she and her allies in central Europe had mobilized, there is little doubt that the mere threat of force would have compelled the Germans to back down. And if Hitler had been humiliated, if his bluff had been called at a time when he still depended on bluff, he might have been torn from his seat of power by ambitious successors, and, in the ruthless Germany which he had created, might have lost his life. France, however, decided not to mobilize until she knew what the British policy would be. Accordingly, the French ministers went to London hoping to secure support from Baldwin's government. But as new dark clouds gathered over Europe, memories of the ghastly slaughter of the First World War had been revived, filling the British people with a longing for peace at any price. This was the period of appeasement, of the sustained British attempt to buy off the dictators by giving them what they wanted. There were notes and protests to the League of Nations, but once more the German bluff succeeded.

The Berlin-Rome-Tokyo Axis

It was now clear to both Italy and Germany how useful they had been to each other. During the next few weeks, therefore, while the Italian air force was mopping up the remnants of the Abyssinian cavalry, Mussolini and Hitler publicly professed their newly found friendship. An opportunity to test this partnership, soon to be called the 'Rome-Berlin Axis', appeared almost immediately.

In July 1936, less than two months after Emperor Haile Selassie sailed for refuge on a British cruiser, one of the bloodiest civil wars in history broke out in Spain. To prevent it spreading into a European conflict, twenty-seven nations agreed not to intervene but to stand aside while the Spanish army, backed up by the Roman Catholic Church, the big landowners and the industrialists, fought it out under the leadership of General Franco against the socialist government that the poverty-stricken people had recently elected to office. Italy and Germany saw in General Franco a possible new addition to the ranks of fascism, a useful man for strengthening their own position and weakening that of the democracies. Consequently, in defiance of the non-intervention agreement that they had signed, Mussolini and Hitler openly, boastfully, flagrantly poured men and military supplies into Spain to aid Franco. And this went on for three terrible years while the democratic nations closed their eyes or looked the other way.

Volunteer Canadian participation in the Spanish Civil War was extremely high on a per capita basis. There were over 1,200 enlistments on the Loyalist

Republican side in comparison to the American involvement of about twice that number. The Canadians, sincere in their belief that this was the war to stop fascist aggression, paid their own way to Spain or received token allowances for travel from the Committee to Aid Spanish Democracy. Despite the Foreign Enlistment Act of 1937 which provided severe penalties for accepting service with foreign armies and which certainly aided the non-intervention policy farce, Canadian volunteers grew in numbers and in 1937 were organized into the Mackenzie-Papineau Battalion of the 15th International Brigade of the Spanish Republic.

The Canadian unit fought with distinction at Belchite, Teruel, on the Aragon Front and, near the final days of the Spanish Republic, in the Battle of the Ebro. Following the Munich Conference, the international brigades were disbanded in the fall of 1938 and the grim process of repatriation began, slowed by a government which had disapproved of this involvement from the beginning.

Thus the Spanish Civil War still further revealed the weakness of the democracies, cemented the Rome-Berlin Axis and tipped the balance of power in favour of the fascist states.

Yet another crisis affected Britain at this time. In January 1936, before Hitler reoccupied the Rhineland, George V, who had seen the British Empire through the First World War, died and was succeeded by his eldest son as Edward VIII. During the final stages of the Abyssinian crisis and the first months of the Spanish Civil War, the new King became involved in a lengthy dispute with the British cabinet, arising from his desire to marry an American woman who was about to secure a second divorce. The fear that this marriage might divide his people or endanger the position of the monarchy compelled Edward to abdicate in December 1936. The Duke of York now became king as George VI and was crowned amid impressive ceremonies in May 1937.

The abdication crisis took its toll of the ailing Stanley Baldwin and he resigned shortly after the coronation of George VI. He was succeeded as prime minister by Neville Chamberlain, an opinionated and overconfident man whose 'all-pervading hope was to go down in history as the Great Peace-maker'. Thus, as European politics moved into a critical new phase, the government of Great Britain was in the hands of a prime minister who believed that he, personally, could come to friendly terms with Hitler and Mussolini.

Nazi Germany, however, could not feel secure as long as the Soviet Union stood unchallenged on her eastern frontiers. During the year 1936, therefore, the Germans negotiated a loosely worded agreement with Japan to work together against communist Russia. In 1937, Italy joined this anti-communist pact, thus forming the Rome-Berlin-Tokyo Axis, a partnership that gave much comfort and encouragement to Japan.

Since the Manchurian crisis, the Japanese had been shipping opium into northern China, softening up the people, placing pro-Japanese officials in responsible positions, strengthening their own fortifications on the mainland and

Benito Mussolini and Adolf Hitler

doing everything in their power to prepare for a renewed attack on Chiang Kai-shek. With the Spanish Civil War occupying the minds of European states-men and with the friendship of Germany and Italy assured, the Japanese militarists decided that their hour to strike again had come.

In July 1937, once more Japanese soldiers swarmed into the northern provinces of China, the Japanese navy shelled the coast, Japanese airmen dropped bombs 'by accident' on British and American ships, reckless pilots shot up the inter-national quarters of the cities, killing Europeans, and Japanese officials when reprimanded by the West said they were very sorry. A committee of the League of Nations met in Brussels, issued a report condemning Japan and passed a resolution expressing moral support for China. And the conflict in the Far East continued.

By the end of the year 1937, Adolf Hitler no longer needed to rely on bluff. The German army, air force and navy, equipped with the very latest weapons, were growing stronger by the hour; the West Wall was nearing completion, an impregnable fortress against the advance of France; the democracies were weak, divided and confused; and the Rome-Berlin-Tokyo Axis obviously had the ruth-less determination and the power to do as it pleased. With a civil, almost an international, war raging in Spain, with the conflict in the Far East spreading like wildfire, the dictator of Nazi Germany was now ready to take over completely the centre of the world stage.

Hitler over Europe

Not a Finger for Austria
On February 21, 1938, a hushed House of Commons listened while Eden explained why he had just resigned as Britain's foreign secretary. His reasons, however, did not satisfy the House; the members seemed to feel that he was hiding something that he could not or would not say. To those in the inner circle of the government, Eden's resignation came as no surprise. They had known for some months that the Foreign Secretary's relationship with Prime Minister Chamberlain was not what it should have been. No two men could have been more opposed in their views—Chamberlain, with his desire to interfere in foreign affairs and his determination to appease the dictators; Eden, the champion of collective security, of increased armaments and a strong stand against the fascists; a clash between them was inevitable sooner or later. But why had Eden resigned so suddenly at this particular time?

We know now that Eden had one and probably two reasons for his resignation which circumstances compelled him to keep secret. During the previous month, President Roosevelt, having become deeply worried about the international situation, had proposed to invite Britain, France, Germany and Italy to a conference in Washington. Before doing so, however, he sought the views of the British government. Since his own country was so violently opposed to any entanglement in European affairs and there was the danger that isolationist sentiment might be aroused against him needlessly, Roosevelt requested that these preliminary discussions be held in the strictest confidence. Only if his suggestion met with 'the cordial approval and wholehearted support of His Majesty's Government' would he then run the risk of American disapproval and invite the other countries to send representatives to Washington. But Chamberlain, acting on his own initiative and against the wishes of the Foreign Office, turned a deaf ear to Roosevelt's proposal. The conference, he said, would offend the dictators and imperil the friendship he was developing with them!

This was one reason for Eden's resignation. Commenting upon it, Churchill—in those days a great admirer of Eden and a bitter foe of appeasement—has written: 'No event would have been more likely to stave off, or even prevent, war than the arrival of the United States in the circle of European hates and fears. . . . To Britain it was almost a matter of life and death. . . . We must regard its rejection—for such it was—as the loss of the last frail chance to save the world from tyranny otherwise than by war. That Chamberlain, with his limited outlook and inexperience of the European scene, should have possessed the self-sufficiency to wave away the proffered hand stretched out across the Atlantic leaves one breathless with amazement.'

Eden also guessed—there is strong evidence to indicate that he and the British government actually were informed in advance—that Adolf Hitler was about to seize Austria. And he resigned as foreign secretary partly because he knew that when the time came, his government would pursue a policy which he simply could not condone. By mid-February there was every reason to suspect that Hitler's next move would be Austria. On the twelfth of the month, just a few days before Eden's resignation, *der Führer* had summoned Kurt Schuschnigg, who had succeeded the murdered Dollfuss as Austrian chancellor, to his private hideaway at Berchtesgaden. Here they met in secret session—only the results of their discussions were made public—but Schuschnigg has left a description of what actually happened. In his memoirs, he describes how he sat opposite Hitler, hands gripping his chair, perspiration streaming from his forehead, listening to an ultimatum that meant death for his country. The Austrian Nazis were now so strong, so Hitler said, that they must be taken into the government; their leader, Seyss-Inquart, must be given the all-important Ministry of the Interior, controlling the police; and cabinet positions must be opened to other Nazis. And if Schuschnigg refused, the German army had a long-standing, detailed plan to invade Austria!

Schuschnigg had no choice but to return to Vienna and carry out the instructions given to him by Hitler virtually at pistol point. However, no sooner had he admitted some Nazis into his government than he began to regret it. Confident that the people of Austria were still behind him, Schuschnigg, therefore, announced over the radio that a plebiscite would be held on Sunday, March 13. A democratic test of strength was the last thing Hitler wanted because it would reveal that the Austrian Nazi party was a minority movement composed mainly of young men who were not old enough to vote. Consequently, two days before

the plebiscite was to be held, Schuschnigg received another ultimatum, this time by telephone from Berlin, demanding his resignation as chancellor, the appointment within two hours of Seyss-Inquart as his successor, and the immediate cancellation of the proposed appeal to the Austrian people.

Schuschnigg resigned, but desperate, last-minute opposition to Hitler now came from another quarter. The aging Austrian president absolutely refused to appoint any Nazi as chancellor. He was apparently determined to expose the Germans to the world in their true colours, to make them use force so they could not pretend, as they had hoped to do, that the Austrian people really wanted Hitler. Thus the German army was compelled to use the invasion plan Hitler had ordered his generals to prepare secretly back in 1936, at a time when he was publicly proclaiming that he had no desire to annex Austria. And although the Austrians were incapable of any military resistance, everyone knew that the German occupation was in fact a real invasion.

Surrounded by army officers, Hitler proclaims to the huge crowd in Vienna's Heldenplatz (Heroes' Square) that Austria is now part of the German Reich.

On March 12, 1938, therefore, *der Führer* announced from Vienna that Austria had ceased to exist and was to be incorporated into Germany. Neither Great Britain nor France lifted a finger for Austria. Just as Eden had suspected, the Chamberlain government received the news of Austria's conquest with almost complete indifference, as if they had been expecting it to happen. Only Russia, speaking through her Foreign Minister, Litvinov, a Jew with many good reasons for hating Hitler, dared to suggest that action should be taken against Germany. This proposal, however, was so coldly received in both London and Paris that it was quickly dropped. Thus, for the second time in less than three months, Chamberlain turned away an offer of assistance from a powerful nation whose mighty help Great Britain soon would need so desperately. And Adolf Hitler, by the easy conquest of Austria, added over 7 million subjects to the Third Reich and established a common frontier with his Axis partner in Italy. More important still, Greater Germany was beginning to close in around Czechoslovakia.

A far-from-innocent activity sponsored by the Nazi government in Austria after its occupation. These boys are merrily consigning to the bonfire all the books condemned by the Nazis as Jewish or Marxist and thereby liable to corrupt young minds.

The War of Nerves in Czechoslovakia

On April 24, 1938, a man named Konrad Henlein made a speech at Carlsbad in which he demanded that the residents of the Sudetenland should be given greater political freedom by the government of Czechoslovakia. The Sudetenland was a mountainous district in northwestern Czechoslovakia where some 3½ million German-speaking people formed one of the largest minority groups anywhere in Europe and provided Hitler with all the excuse he needed to cast covetous eyes on this rich, highly industrialized area. And Henlein was Hitler's henchman in Czechoslovakia, the Nazi leader of the most fanatic elements among the Sudeten Germans. As may be guessed, his Carlsbad speech, delivered under orders from Berlin, was designed to ignite a new phase in the Nazi war of nerves.

After April 24, Dr. Goebbels, the ruthlessly skilful Nazi expert on propaganda, turned his machine loose on Czechoslovakia. The controlled newspapers and radio of Germany now proclaimed their support for the 'lost Germans' in the Sudetenland, praised the 'courageous' Henlein, and hurled abuse across the border at the government of Czechoslovakia. President Eduard Benes, one of the finest democratic statesmen to appear in Europe between the two wars and an ardent anti-Nazi, became their prime target in a bitter campaign of flagrant falsehood. Henlein was instructed to step up his acts of violence, thus forcing Benes to impose martial law and provoking the shootings and bombings that Goebbels had to have for his propaganda mill. Out came the big headlines, the Big Lies. Czech troops fire on peaceful crowd! Benes in league with Jews and Bolsheviks! German rights denied! While all this was going on, the military and air forces of the Third Reich conducted 'routine manoeuvres' along the border in an attempt to intimidate the government of Czechoslovakia. Within three months of the conquest of Austria, therefore, the Nazis had revealed that Czechoslovakia stood next on Hitler's list.

Although this first crisis subsided and the world breathed easier for a while, on May 28 Hitler called a secret meeting of his military advisers and instructed them to prepare plans for the invasion of Czechoslovakia. If we can believe the evidence given by them to the Allies after the Second World War, Hitler's generals were aghast at his audacity. Although he had re-armed Germany, occupied the Rhineland and seized Austria, they could not believe that his bluff would succeed a fourth time. According to all these military experts, only the air force was up to standard. The West Wall, or the Siegfried Line as they were now beginning to call it, was far from completed; the four-year-old army lacked training and needed several thousand more officers, and they could muster only thirty-five divisions, whereas France alone had more than one hundred; the navy was pitifully small and the submarine-building program still had a long way to go. Germany was not ready for war. Czechoslovakia alone, with her excellent army, her strong border fortifications and her world-famous Skoda munitions works, could stave off the military power of the Third Reich for many months. And if Czechoslovakia stood firm, France would have to come to her aid. During that very month, Daladier, the new Premier of France, had renewed his country's long-standing pledge to support Czechoslovakia in event of war. Great Britain's position was uncertain, but if France mobilized she would be morally obliged to do likewise. This was a combination of powers, so Hitler's generals insisted, that Germany simply could not handle.

Even more disturbing to the German High Command, however, was the threat of Russia. Alone among the nations, the Soviet Union had dared to challenge the Nazi conquest of Austria and now Litvinov was making it abundantly clear that his country intended to honour its friendship with Czechoslovakia. No one, least of all the German strategists, doubted Russia's sincerity. Not only was she bound to Czechoslovakia by the defensive alliance of 1935 but her dictator, Joseph Stalin, and his colleagues had every reason to hate the Nazis for their intensive crusade against communism. Furthermore, Stalin and Benes were firm friends. It was a well-known fact in those days that back in 1937 the President of Czechoslovakia had helped to uncover a plot within the Russian army to overthrow Stalin and introduce a pro-German regime. As a result, some five or six thousand top-ranking Russian officers had been shot and the Red Army thoroughly purged of any German sympathizers. Thus, it was almost a foregone conclusion that the Soviet Union would join France and possibly Great Britain in resisting any Nazi aggression against Czechoslovakia.

Hitler, however, refused to listen to reason. Relying on his own intuition, scoffing at his generals' fears, he continued his war of nerves against Czechoslovakia with varying degrees of intensity all during the summer months. Meanwhile, the German High Command, with grave misgivings, prepared its plans for invasion. The time to strike was set for sometime in September. On September 12, 1938, therefore, at the huge annual Nazi party rally in Nuremburg, Hitler unleashed against Czechoslovakia one of the most violent verbal attacks of his career. This was Henlein's signal for a fresh outburst of violence in the Sudetenland. Once more Benes was forced to introduce martial law, and Henlein had to flee across the border with a price on his head. From the safety of Germany he now demanded, not simply greater political freedom for the Sudeten Germans, but the outright surrender of the whole region to the Third Reich.

Betrayal at Munich

At this moment, with martial law in the Sudetenland, with Henlein demanding secession and the German dictator urging him on, the Prime Minister of Great Britain—without consulting his cabinet, without advising either the French or Russian governments—invited himself to visit Hitler. At this very moment also, if we can believe their own evidence, some of the highest-ranking officers in the German army planned to overthrow Hitler and the Nazi party regime. As the German Chief of Staff who was in on the plot has described it: 'We did not intend to kill the Nazi leaders—merely to arrest them, establish a military government, and issue a proclamation to the people that we had taken this action only because we were convinced they were being led to certain disaster.' But on the day of the plot, the conspirators heard the news that Chamberlain was coming to Germany and decided to wait. Perhaps—they did not really think so, but perhaps—Hitler might carry it off after all without a war.

Chamberlain flew to Germany on September 16 and, following in Schuschnigg's footsteps, proceeded to Berchtesgaden for his meeting with Hitler. There he learned that the Nazi leader wanted the Sudetenland, nothing more; this was his last territorial claim in Europe. 'In spite of the hardness and ruthlessness I thought I saw in his face, I got the impression that here was a man who could be relied upon when he had given his word.' Chamberlain, therefore, came away from Germany seriously convinced that the peace of Europe depended upon yielding graciously to Hitler's demands. When informed of this view, Daladier's government in France, meekly and in complete disregard for their oft-repeated promises to Czechoslovakia, decided to follow Great Britain. A joint Anglo-French proposal was drawn up which involved turning over to Germany all areas in the Sudetenland containing more than fifty per cent of German inhabitants. The transfer was to be made without the use of the German army—nothing must be done to indicate to the world that Britain and France were yielding to the threat of force. This was to be a peacefully negotiated agreement based on 'the right of self-determination for the Sudeten Germans'.

At first, the government of Czechoslovakia was determined to fight rather than give up the Sudetenland. But at two o'clock on the morning of September 21, the

Gathered at Berchtesgaden, Hitler's mountain retreat, to sign the Munich Peace Treaty in 1938, are (left to right) Neville Chamberlain, Edouard Daladier, Adolf Hitler, Benito Mussolini, and Count Ciano.

British and French ambassadors in Prague called on Benes and told him that there was no hope left. When news of this heavy-handed pressure leaked out, both the French and British governments officially denied that any such thing had happened. Now, however, it is a firmly established fact that Czechoslovakia was compelled by her own friends to accept the Anglo-French proposal. Having thus secured Benes' reluctant consent, Chamberlain flew to Germany again to tell Hitler of his success and to work out the details of the transfer. At Godesberg, where the two men met, Chamberlain found a very different Hitler—a ranting, arm-waving Hitler who shouted and orated at him as if he were addressing a Nazi party rally. To Chamberlain's amazement and horror, the dictator of Germany now demanded that his army should occupy the Sudetenland with no fixed limit to their advance and no guarantees for the safety of the remaining parts of Czechoslovakia. Hitler was compelling Chamberlain to take a strong hand.

The day after Chamberlain returned from Germany, the British and French governments rejected Hitler's Godesberg ultimatum. Behind the strongest fortress line in Europe, the Czechs now began to mobilize their army of 1½ million men. Daladier's cabinet agreed to honour their obligations and ordered the partial mobilization of the French army. Litvinov—despite the fact that up to this moment Britain and France had been negotiating with Hitler as if the Soviet

Union were non-existent—repeated his country's determination to stand by Czechoslovakia if France did likewise. Word flashed out from the Admiralty to mobilize the British fleet. The whole world watched with growing anxiety as Europe moved rapidly towards the brink of war. But behind the scenes President Roosevelt, Prime Minister Chamberlain and Benito Mussolini were making frantic, last-minute appeals to Hitler. Even more important, his military and naval advisers repeatedly urged him not to run the risks of war. Thus, at the eleventh hour, at the very height of the worst international crisis since 1914, Hitler agreed to meet Chamberlain, Daladier and Mussolini at Munich for one more conference. Czechoslovakia and Russia were not invited to attend. On September 29, therefore, for the third time in as many weeks, the Prime Minister of Great Britain flew to Germany.

The conference at Munich witnessed the climax to the policy of appeasement and the crowning achievement in Hitler's game of bluff. The 'Big Four' agreed that, commencing on October 1, the German army could occupy practically the whole of the Sudetenland within ten days. To all intents and purposes this was invasion. The Czechs were to withdraw immediately, leaving everything—the border forts, the Skoda munitions factories, the hydro-electric installations— intact behind them. The remaining parts of Czechoslovakia would be guaranteed 'later'—another broken promise which helped to litter the paths of diplomacy between the two wars. Thus the Munich Conference did little more than place a stamp of approval on the demands which the German dictator had made at Godesberg. Under the cloak of being an international agreement, it allowed Hitler to do almost everything he had intended to do anyway. And no one was more surprised than his own generals. Once again, *der Führer* had been right! Surely, they now said, here was a gifted leader to be followed without question. His success at Munich, therefore, helped Hitler to become the undisputed master of Germany.

Chamberlain returned to England convinced that he had snatched peace out of the very jaws of war. To the cheering throng who greeted him at the airport he said: 'I believe it is peace in our time.' In London, he told the huge crowds outside the prime minister's office: 'This is the second time there has come back from Germany to Downing Street peace with honour. I believe it is peace in our time.' And throughout the entire civilized world, the vast majority of people, having faced the immediate prospect of war only to have it miraculously withdrawn, hailed Chamberlain as a saviour. It has been said that, at Munich, Chamberlain knew war was coming and that he sacrificed Czechoslovakia in order to give Great Britain and France a few more precious months to get ready. But Chamberlain did not act from weakness. With the best of motives, he and all who agreed with him sincerely believed that war could be averted by discussion round a conference table. Only after the outbreak of war had proved how tragically wrong they were did the advocates of appeasement claim that they were playing for time at Munich. We know now, however, that even if this were so, the German High Command also welcomed the breathing spell and used it more effectively than did either Great Britain or France. And when the war did come, it was far more devastating and much harder to win because, at Munich, the Allies sacrificed not only the friendship of Czechoslovakia but also the military power of the Soviet Union.

Peace Indeed, but Freedom Even More

The illusion of 'peace in our time', the hope that Nazi Germany was satisfied, lasted less than six months. On March 14, 1939, the confidence inspired by Munich was shattered completely when the German army closed in and seized what was left of Czechoslovakia. Having been so cruelly deserted by their allies at Munich, the 11 million Czechs and Slovaks passively yielded to the inevitable. Neither the government, which by this time had fallen under the control of Nazi sympathizers, nor the dispirited people made any attempt to resist. The Nazi occupation of Czechoslovakia marked a new and more deadly phase in the history of European diplomacy between the two wars. By seizing control over so many millions of Czechs and Slovaks, people of an entirely different race upon whom he had no claim whatsoever, Hitler now revealed in cold, clear light the true nature of his ruthlessness.

Up to this moment, both Hitler and all those who tried to appease him had been able to find some slight justification for his aggressive actions. Thus the rearmament of Germany had been accepted abroad because other nations, despite their promises to do so, had refused to disarm. And the seizure of Austria and the Sudetenland had been defended on the grounds that the inhabitants were German-speaking people who would sooner or later make good citizens within the Third Reich. Now, however, Adolf Hitler had taken a step that was absolutely inexcusable—and no one realized this more fully than the Prime Minister of Great Britain.

Three days after the German army had seized Czechoslovakia, therefore, Chamberlain made a long, widely publicized speech, defending the policies he had attempted to carry out and concluding with these words: 'I do not believe there is anyone who will question my sincerity when I say there is hardly anything I would not sacrifice for peace. But there is one thing I must except, and that is the liberty that we have enjoyed for hundreds of years and which we will never surrender. . . . No greater mistake could be made than to suppose that, because it believes war to be a senseless and cruel thing, this nation has so lost its fibre that it will not take part to the utmost of its power in resisting such a challenge if it is ever made.' The long years of appeasement that had witnessed the rearmament of Germany, the occupation of the Rhineland and the building of the Siegfried Line, the Nazi intervention in the Spanish Civil War, the formation of the Rome-Berlin-Tokyo Axis, and the seizure of Austria, the Sudetenland and finally Czechoslovakia, were now ended.

The new British policy was quickly put to the test. Nazi Germany had no sooner swallowed Czechoslovakia than a series of events, whose pattern had become all too tragically familiar, revealed that Poland was to be Hitler's next victim. The German minority in Poland and the predominantly German population living in the international city of Danzig, acting under orders from Berlin, now fomented riots and strikes, disobeyed Polish officials, smuggled in arms and did everything in their power to harass the government in Warsaw. From across the border, the strident voice of Hitler, backed up by the entire Nazi press, accused Poland of maltreating her German-speaking subjects and demanded the immediate return of Danzig to the Third Reich. Chamberlain decided to meet the new challenge with vigorous action. On March 31 he announced that the British government had joined with the French to guarantee Poland against aggression. Now at last the two western democracies were determined to stake their lives upon protecting the next small country on Hitler's list. And they would soon have to do so because on April 3, less than a week after the Anglo-French pact was signed, the dictator of Germany issued a secret order to his Chief of Staff directing him to prepare plans for the invasion of Poland.

During the spring of 1939, therefore, with the tension over Poland mounting and the battle-lines more sharply drawn, both sides stepped up their military preparations to fever pitch. In Great Britain, the territorial army was doubled in size, conscription was introduced and the factories began to work round the clock turning out war materials of all kinds, but especially the anti-aircraft guns and the famous Spitfires and Hurricanes that were soon to save England by the narrowest of margins. The military experts of Great Britain and France joined in continuous consultation and their diplomats worked together to secure a closer understanding with Romania, the Baltic states and some of the other smaller European countries. To all these preparations Hitler replied by denouncing the Anglo-German naval agreement and, more ominously, his treaty of friendship with Poland. Then, in a series of angry tirades, he accused Britain and France of deliberately fostering hatred for Germany, strangling her trade and encircling her with a ring of hostile powers. In vain, by letter and by personal interviews in Berlin, members of the British government tried to show Hitler that Germany, by her aggressive actions and her broken promises, had only herself to blame for the alliances that were being built up around her. But Hitler was in no mood to listen. The hour for revenge was almost at hand. His oratory now reached a pinnacle of power—boasting, threatening, hurling defiance at the democracies and drawing the German people with him towards war.

'Germans of Wilhelmshaven! Volksgenossen and Volksgenossinen! Remember the past! . . . When the Fourteen Points of President Wilson were announced, Germany believed these assurances and laid down her weapons. And then a breach of faith began such as the world had never seen. . . . The German colonies were stolen from us, German foreign securities were simply confiscated, and our merchant marine was taken away. Then came financial pillage such as the world has never up to this day seen. Reparations of astronomical figures were imposed on the German people and about which even English statesmen said that they could be paid only if the whole German nation reduced its standard of living and worked fourteen hours a day. What German spirit and German diligence had created and saved in decades was now lost in a few years. Millions of Germans were torn away from the Reich. . . . The League of Nations was made not an instrument of understanding but a guarantor of the meanest dictate that human beings have ever thought out. . . . Germany has borne this fate patiently. I also tried at the beginning to solve every problem by discussion. At every problem I made offers, and they were every one refused!

'The German soldiers, more than two million in number, who died in the Great War, did not die in vain. From their sacrifice a new, strong Great German Reich has arisen. . . . Twenty years ago the Party was founded, at that time a very small structure. Recall the distance covered from that time until today. Recall the extent of the miracle that has been worked upon us. And have faith, therefore, in the future road of the German people in the coming great future! Germany: Sieg Heil! sɪᴇɢ ʜᴇɪʟ! SIEG HEIL!'

The Die is Cast

Beneath all the feverish preparations for war, however, there was one unanswered question of vital interest to both sides. What would be the position of the Soviet Union? For Germany, the prospect of a war on two fronts any time in 1939 was dreadful to contemplate and if Hitler did not fully realize this, his generals and his diplomats certainly did. As for Great Britain and France, their guarantees to distant, isolated Poland were practically useless without a military agreement with Russia. Hoping to secure some kind of definite understanding, the British ambassador in Moscow, therefore, was instructed to open discussions with Litvinov. In view of how they had been so shabbily ignored at Munich, it is somewhat surprising that the Soviet government, on April 16, made a formal offer to join in a mutual assistance pact with Britain and France against Nazi Germany. But one day later, secretly in Berlin, the Russian ambassador had a long talk with officials of the German Foreign Office during the course of which he dropped the very broad hint: 'There exists for Russia no reason why she should not live with Germany on a normal footing. And from normal, relations might become better and better.' Apparently, Joseph Stalin had decided to play both sides off against each other!

The British and French governments made practically no effort to accept the Russian offer. Held back by their inherent distrust of communism, blind to the urgency of securing Soviet aid, the leaders of the two democracies considered the Russian proposal at a leisurely pace, questioned whether or not it would alienate the smaller states of eastern Europe, pondered on the weaknesses of the Red Army and wondered if Stalin really meant what he said. As Winston Churchill has written: 'If, for instance, Chamberlain on receipt of the Russian offer had replied: "Yes. Let us three band together and break Hitler's neck," or words to that effect, Parliament would have approved, Stalin would have understood, and history might have taken a different course.' But Daladier and Chamberlain hesitated and while they did so, signs appeared on every side that Germany and Russia were drawing closer together. Top-ranking diplomats with bulging brief cases moved back and forth between the two countries; Russian newspapers for the first time in fifteen years dropped their anti-German tone; and the Nazi press no longer harped on Bolshevism but stressed the evils of the two democracies. And in May, Litvinov, the Russian diplomat who believed so strongly in supporting the West, the Russian Jew whom Hitler detested, was removed from office and replaced as foreign commissar by Molotov, a hard, calculating and very different type of man.

Eventually these symptoms became so obvious that the British government sent a special mission to Moscow to accept the Russian offer for an alliance. But it was too late. Tired of waiting for the democracies to make up their minds, Stalin and Molotov had decided to throw in their lot with Nazi Germany. During June and July, therefore, while the British mission cooled its heels in Moscow and received evasive answers to all its questions, Russian and German diplomats were ironing out the final details of an agreement between their two countries. On August 22, the Russian ambassador to France gave a warning of what was about to happen. 'The question of military collaboration with France,' he said, 'has been in the air for several years but has never been settled. Last year, when Czecho-slovakia was perishing, we waited for a signal from France, but none was given. . . . The French and British governments have now dragged out the military and political discussions too long. For this reason, the possibility is not to be excluded that certain other political events may now take place.'

Next day, August 23, the news broke. Throughout the western world, in Canada and the United States, in Britain and France, the newspapers carried the biggest headlines since November 11, 1918. NAZI-SOVIET PACT SIGNED! REDS JOIN HITLER! Surely, people asked, these two arch-enemies, fascist Germany and communist Russia, could not so suddenly become friends? It was, of course, all too true. The two countries had signed a non-aggression pact, a promise not to fight each other, and a secret agreement, known later, to share in the spoils of Poland. At last, Adolf Hitler was really free. A weak, isolated Poland to the east and then on to France and Great Britain and a war in the west only. The nightmare of the German strategists was over.

That day, also, Chamberlain telegraphed a message to Hitler: 'Whatever may prove to be the nature of the German-Soviet Agreement, it cannot alter Great Britain's obligation to Poland which His Majesty's Government have stated in public repeatedly and plainly, and which they are determined to fulfil. It has been alleged that, if His Majesty's Government had made their position more clear in 1914, the great catastrophe would have been avoided. Whether or not there is any force in that allegation, His Majesty's Government are resolved on this occasion there shall be no such tragic misunderstanding. If the case should arise, they are resolved, and prepared, to employ without delay all the forces at their command.' Hitler, however, could not be delayed or intimidated by this eleventh-hour warning. Danzig and the Polish corridor must be his! The Polish government must send an envoy to Berlin immediately with full powers to make a settlement, once and for all! Frantically, the British ambassador in Berlin strove to hold Hitler back. And equally frantically, the British ambassador in Warsaw urged the Polish government to hurry and get an envoy over to talk with Hitler. But the Poles, remembering Austria and Czechoslovakia, hesitated and were afraid. Five times in as many days the British government, by telegraph and

Hitler declares war on Poland.

personal message, pressed the Poles to hurry, until finally, on August 31, an envoy
was sent to Berlin. By this time, however, the die was fully cast. The invasion plans
for Poland were now ready and Hitler was no longer bluffing.

On September 1, German aircraft roared eastward into the rising sun, heading
for their first mission over Warsaw, and at the same time German tanks rolled
across the border into Poland. Later in the day, the British government, without
setting any definite time limit, demanded a firm promise from Germany that this
action against Poland would be stopped. It also sent a curt warning to its
ambassador in Berlin: 'If the German reply is unsatisfactory the next stage will
be either an ultimatum with time limit or immediate declaration of war.' During
the next forty hours, the German invasion of Poland proceeded on schedule and
the French and British made their final preparations. The governments in London
and Paris waited—but no reply came from Germany. At nine o'clock on the
morning of September 3, therefore, a second ultimatum was sent to Berlin
demanding an answer within two hours. Two hours and twenty minutes later, the
British ambassador in Berlin received a message: 'The German Government and
the German people refuse to receive, accept, let alone to fulfil, demands in the
nature of an ultimatum made by the British Government.' By that time, however,
Chamberlain and Daladier already had broadcast to their countrymen that
Britain and France were at war with Germany.

part 4
through the valley of armageddon

14 THE YEARS OF ENDURANCE

The Lull before the Storm

Very early in the War one of England's most gifted soldiers wrote in his diary: 'A lovely, mild day which makes it harder to realize that humanity can be so mad as to be at war again. It is all too ghastly even to be a nightmare. . . . I suppose it is only through such punishments that we shall learn to love our neighbour as ourselves.'

Humanity Gone Mad Again

This time, there would be no period of monotonous siege warfare in France, no war of attrition, aimlessly attempting to grind human resources down to the last surviving platoon. This was a real world war, a complex global struggle extending from the steaming jungles of Burma and the hot sands of the Pacific islands to the far northern wastes of the Arctic. Men fought and suffered under the burning sun of the African desert, stifled in the humid heat of the tropics, shivered and froze in the winter vastness of Russia or perished in the icy waters of the north Atlantic. At one extreme, in the cold darkness of the seven seas submarines stalked their prey, and at the other, man's latest engines of war penetrated the stratosphere, fulfilling their dire missions in every remote corner of the earth.

This was a scientists' war. The finest minds in the world tragically directed their knowledge for six long years to invent new, ever more deadly weapons of destruction. The tank and the airplane now reached maturity; gigantic tank battles opened the War and continued all through it; aircraft swooped hawklike on any movement by land or on the narrowed seas. From the air, armies were pinned down by day, daring to move only under cover of darkness; armed men were suddenly dropped from the sky and as quickly picked up and deposited elsewhere. Submarines and huge battleships, once regarded as impregnable floating fortresses, were chased and bombed or torpedoed from the air. Great naval battles were fought by fleets—invisible to each other over the curve of the horizon—which sent out their carrier-based aircraft. And from the air, the full, terrifying effects of modern warfare were carried home to the civilians. Night after night, tons of high explosives and incendiary bombs were hurled down on cities until some of them were pulverized, their industries shattered, their historic monuments destroyed and their populations driven underground.

The delicate, almost instantaneous control of armoured vehicles and aircraft and their close co-operation with both the infantry and artillery was made possible only through the perfection of radio. Radio also enabled the master strategists to conduct vast, intricate military operations on a truly global scale. Radar was developed to detect hostile aircraft, distant ships or lurking sub-

One of a number of groups of radar towers already operating in Britain in 1939. This 'Chain Home' system was the eyes and ears of Fighter Command, the defence arm of the Royal Air Force.

marines; eventually radar guided bombers to their targets and sighted the guns of fighter planes. Scientists produced the pilotless airplane, the rocket and the guided missile—weapons that not so many months before had existed only in the imagination of science-fiction writers. Finally, urged on by this desperate race for survival, the genius of man unfolded the secrets of the atom. Two small atomic bombs—small by today's standards—were dropped on the Japanese cities of Hiroshima and Nagasaki, bringing the Second World War to a sudden and unexpected end. Hiroshima and Nagasaki: these were the doomed cities whose names will stand recorded in history forever, marking the beginning of the Atomic Age. The full consequences of their fate still lie far in the future. One thing only seems certain. With the development of nuclear weapons during the eleventh hour of the Second World War, men took into their hands the power to annihilate themselves.

No doubt you have seen movies and telecasts of the War or read about it; already more books have been written about the Second World War than about any other event in the whole of history. *The Dam Busters, Reach for the Sky, The Cockleshell Heroes, The Wooden Horse, The Great Escape, The Cruel Sea, One of Our Submarines*—these and a host of other stories are familiar to most students. They are indeed breath-taking tales, full of adventure, heroism, and almost unbelievable endurance. Each one describes only a microscopic part of the great global conflict and a great many of them must be read to obtain a complete view of the War. Even so, there is a danger in reading such books. Most of them are success stories; they tend to dramatize war, picturing it not as a deadly struggle for survival but as an exciting, dangerous adventure. They seldom reveal the full, massive horrors of war. They do not picture the waste of human and material resources—resources which, if directed with the same tremendous energy and the same staggering sums of money as mankind used during those six years of destruction, could have accomplished so much positive good in the world. In other words, a great deal of the literature about the Second World War does not convey the urgent need for all of us to learn to love our neighbour as ourselves.

The history of this War is far too complex to be told in a few chapters of any one book. It is, in its overall global pattern and in all its countless details, a gigantic story that will continue to be unfolded for many years to come. Here we can do no more than barely skim the surface of the most dramatic story in the whole long history of man. But as you read this it might be well to keep one thing in mind. You are reading about the tragic failure of a civilization. True, our side won this war, as we did the first one; but we have not yet achieved peace and security. Triumph and tragedy: two world wars within living memory, but the goal seems today as far away as ever. Throughout all time, men of good will have searched for some way to resolve their differences without recourse to war. It has been called the 'Quest of Ages'. So far in the twentieth century, we have not succeeded in that quest. Twenty years of uneasy peace was all that we could manage. By September 1939, humanity was at war again.

Blitzkrieg in the East
From the very moment, on September 1, 1939, when the Luftwaffe thundered eastward towards the rising sun, a dread new word entered into the vocabularies of the world. This was the *blitzkrieg*—the lightning war—a violent, ruthless, overwhelming demonstration of the power of mechanized warfare. Squadron after squadron of Stuka dive bombers screamed down to rooftop level, dropping their bombs on the unprotected Polish towns and raking their streets with machine-gun fire. Communications were destroyed, the army was shattered by dive-bombing and demoralized by paratroopers. There was little defence because the antiquated Polish air force had been knocked out on its airfields before it ever left the ground. A tremendous cavalcade of tanks, armoured cars and motorized artillery, moving like clockwork, without apparent hurry, closed in on Poland from three sides. Advancing under a protecting cloud of over two thousand airplanes, this mighty German army struck terror not only in Poland but in the hearts of countless people elsewhere.

Polish resistance was brave but vain. Their old-fashioned army, with its cavalry brigades and nineteenth-century methods, was no match for the foe. Within two weeks Poland's army of over 2 million ceased to exist as an organized force although isolated groups of valiant soldiers fought on. The citizens of Warsaw, their city surrounded and battered day and night by heavy artillery and bombers, held out until their food, water and ammunition supplies were gone. On September 28, Radio Warsaw ceased to play the national anthem and Hitler entered the ruined city. Poland might have lasted longer but for Russia. On September 17, with German consent, the Russian army had swarmed across the defenceless eastern frontier of Poland. Confronted with the Wehrmacht in the west and the Red Army in the east, resistance collapsed and Poland, divided between Germany and Russia, once more disappeared from the map of Europe.

Sitzkrieg in the West

While this almost mechanical destruction of Poland was taking place, Great Britain girded herself for war. Silver barrage balloons, straining on their leashes like watchdogs, floated up into sky above London. Truckloads of sandbags appeared as if by magic and volunteers began to barricade the doorways of important buildings as protection from flying bomb-splinters. A blackout was enforced, and city dwellers soon learned to move about at night like cats, guided only by the white lines painted on tree trunks, curbs and gateposts. A brilliant galaxy of searchlights, competing with the stars, pierced the sky like luminous pencils crossing and recrossing one another. Young and old lined up for gas masks, for it was thought that the Germans would drop bombs of poison gas. Two hundred thousand extra beds were squeezed into the hospitals in expectation of dreadful casualties. Schoolchildren, labelled with their destination, were collected in the railway stations, herded into overcrowded trains and hurried away from the dangers of the big cities. They seemed too dazed to cry and they were not frightened because they did not yet know the real meaning of fear. Many mothers and fathers, however, wept openly for they were old enough to have haunting memories of a hot August night in 1914 or of London crowds celebrating an Armistice won for them by a lost generation of other men who died in a war to end war.

One after another, the ships of the merchant marine came into port to be equipped with submarine detectors and old guns saved from the First World War. Glistening white liners took on a drab new coat of grey and looked more like battleships than luxury steamships. The day war was declared, a brief but inspiring message was flashed to the fleet: 'Winston is back.' After an absence of almost exactly a quarter of a century, Winston Churchill had been reappointed to his old post, First Lord of the Admiralty. So far as could be foreseen at the time, the Royal Navy was ready.

As in 1914, a British expeditionary force was rushed across the Channel in support of France. Despite the Luftwaffe and the U-boats, 160,000 soldiers and 24,000 vehicles were landed secretly, without the loss of a man or a weapon. They were a hastily collected, undertrained, poorly equipped force—a territorial army, utterly incapable of waging a blitzkrieg or resisting one. Many of them had been recently drafted from England's unemployed. Pale, lacking in stamina, never quite sure of three square meals a day until they had joined the army, these men —brave and determined though they were—had received no training to compare with that lavished on the B.E.F. before the First World War. Yet the avalanche of fire and steel soon to descend upon them would far exceed what the Old Contemptibles had to face during the First Battle of Ypres.

This inexperienced British army immediately moved up to a front-line position along the Belgian frontier. Here, on the same battle-scarred fields of Flanders, they dug trenches and laid out barbed wire entanglements just as others had done twenty-five years before. Here they could see how dry rot had eaten away the fighting spirit of once-proud France. With grave misgivings, they noticed that the territorial French troops on either side of them were slovenly, unshaven and listless. 'What shook me most,' one of the British corps commanders wrote, 'was the disgruntled, insubordinate look on the faces of these men.' This same observer went on to say—and his judgement is supported by many of his fellow officers— that he had no faith in the French High Command. He saw that General Gamelin, the Supreme Commander, the one-time brilliant officer who planned the miracle of the Marne, was now old and tired; that his lieutenants, indulging daily in enormous champagne lunches, were 'more interested in eating than in fighting'; and that the aging French generals, in their colourful capes and immaculate breeches, 'were living on the glories of the past and ignoring the present'.

Knowing what we do now, it is safe to conclude that the French army—a huge force with eighty-four active divisions and more tanks than any other nation— was beaten before it started. Any confidence its officers may have had vanished the day the Russians signed their non-aggression pact with Hitler. For this meant that the Poles were doomed and that Germany, instead of having to fight on two fronts, could concentrate all her power in the West. Even with Russian help during the First World War, France had been bled white and her generals were determined that this should never happen again. This time, France would remain strictly on the defensive, letting the Germans batter themselves to pieces against the great border fortifications known as the Maginot Line. This new super-trench of steel and concrete would keep the enemy out forever. When the testing time came, however, the Maginot Line proved to be little more than a trap for thousands of helpless French soldiers and France was overwhelmed as easily and quickly as was Poland.

It was not only the army and the French generals who were weighed in the balance and found wanting. The French nation as a whole had no heart for this war. They felt that the British, with their persistent policy of appeasement, had prevented France from striking down Hitler when she was strong enough to do so. Now, against a powerful, rearmed Germany, it was too late. Thus the French people, like their army, accepted defeat before it came. Indeed, many of the intellectual, business and political leaders of the country openly admired the better elements in the Nazi movement. These men and women were not traitors —only a few of them actively worked with the Germans—but they despised their ever-changing, perpetually squabbling government and favoured some form of stronger rule such as the Nazis had established over Germany.

This dispirited lack of confidence in their country was not entirely caused by its weak form of government or the simple inefficiency of its politicians. The leaders of the Third French Republic must also take responsibility for their personal failings. Few governments have existed in a shabbier moral atmosphere than in the last days of the Third Republic. Describing this situation, an American businessman, long resident in Paris, has written: 'In talking to Frenchmen I sensed in them more than disillusionment with their political leaders. I was deeply impressed with the disgust and shame which many Frenchmen felt over the private lives of the men who were to lead France to disaster.' Bribery, favouritism, corruption and a general attitude that the government was fair game to be cheated or exploited for personal gain had become almost a daily part of the French political scene. Cruel though it is to say so, it seemed that modern France needed a purging period of great humiliation before she could ever regain her former glory.

Thus the British Expeditionary Force and the dispirited army of a weak, divided France remained inactive behind the Maginot Line while the Germans overran Poland. Answering the hail of bombs on Polish cities were peace pamphlets dropped by the Royal Air Force on Berlin, as they waited for the Germans to turn on them. But war did not come to France and Britain right away. Fortunately, Germany also had her share of old-fashioned generals and by the time Hitler had persuaded them that the blitz could rip through Belgium and France as easily as through Poland, it was too late. One of the most severe winters in many years, with dense fogs, rain and snow, grounded the Luftwaffe and forced the Nazi leader to postpone his offensive in the West until the following spring. But for this the Germans might have reached the English Channel nine months earlier, at a time when the Fighter Command of the Royal Air Force was still twenty squadrons short of the force that was barely to win the Battle of Britain in 1940.

In western Europe and England, therefore, months of waiting followed the declarations of war. A horrible sense of impending doom hung over everyone. There was bitter fighting in far-off Finland, but except at sea Britain and France had no part in it. Men called it the 'phoney' war or the sitzkrieg. It was the lull before the storm.

Juggernaut over Europe

Invasions in the North
On the evening of April 5, 1940, the German consul in Norway invited a number of distinguished visitors, including many government officials, to see a film called *The Baptism of Fire*. It showed the whole story of Germany's conquest of Poland and ended in a series of dreadful scenes taken during the bombing of Warsaw. The audience sat transfixed with horror and dismay. This was, of course, precisely what the Nazis intended because innocent-looking freighters, their holds laden with invasion troops waiting for the signal to pounce, were already

moored in the four main Norwegian ports, and units of the German fleet were under way to lend them support. The Nazis wanted to make sure that the Norwegian leaders saw what happened to people who dared to oppose Hitler.

Four evenings later the Germans struck, bringing war to innocent Norway for the first time in many centuries. By land, sea and air, without any warning or declaration of war, they tried to extinguish another neutral nation in one dark night. At the same moment, German armies also rolled across the unfortified frontier into Denmark. Faced with tremendous odds, the Danes had no choice but to surrender almost without a fight. Soon, however, the usual process of exploitation and looting began and soon the Danish underground movement began its courageous campaign of sabotage against the invader. In Norway the people, their staunch Viking spirit roused once more, flamed into furious resistance as soon as they realized what was happening. But within forty-eight hours, all the principal Norwegian ports were in German hands.

The Allies, knowing how desperately they themselves needed Norway, dispatched troops from France—at the very moment when every man was needed there—in a vain attempt to dislodge the enemy from Narvik and Trondheim. In the far north, near Narvik, the British navy, even without adequate air protection, won two naval battles which, if properly followed up, might have changed the course of the Norwegian campaign. But this isolated victory was not enough. The military and naval authorities failed to co-operate and were soon completely outwitted by the precision movements of the highly trained German forces. By the end of April the Allied troops, except for a small detachment at Narvik who managed to hold on for another month, were forced to withdraw. Too little and too late: the phrase was to be repeated many times before the power of Hitler's Germany was finally crushed.

In less than two months, the Germans had conquered Denmark and Norway and isolated Sweden. From Denmark, they obtained bacon, butter, oils and control of the Baltic Sea—and, what was more important, denied these things to Britain. From Norway, they obtained timber, pulpwood, fish and the vital supply of Swedish iron ore which for many years had been shipped through Norway to the ice-free port of Narvik. And from the deep Norwegian fjords, German submarines and warships could slip out to destroy British shipping along the route to Murmansk, soon to become so very important. Out of the wreckage and confusion in Norway, the Allies could find only one consoling fact. Although both sides had suffered about equally in the naval fighting off the coast, the Germans could ill afford the ships that they had lost. When the critical time arrived, Hitler did not have the sea power to invade the British Isles.

Blitzkrieg in the West

The 'phoney' phase of the War ended with the German attack on Norway. Now it exploded in the most overwhelming military onslaught ever seen by man. On May 10, while mopping-up operations were still going on at Narvik, Hitler released the blitzkrieg against Holland, Belgium, Luxemburg and France. On May 10, also, Winston Churchill became Prime Minister of England.

The British people were ashamed of the defeat in Norway and indignation had swept through the country. In parliament, one of Chamberlain's closest friends, quoting from the speech used by Oliver Cromwell against the Long Parliament many years before, had condemned the government in these terrible words: 'You have sat here too long for any good you have been doing. Depart, I say, and let us be done with you. In the name of God, go!' Chamberlain fell before the storm, being replaced by Churchill at the head of a national coalition government. It was perhaps fitting that on the very day Hitler attacked in the west, he should be confronted by that amazing and valiant man who, more than any other, was to defeat all his wicked designs.

The new Prime Minister could offer nothing but 'blood, toil, tears and sweat'. . . . 'You ask, what is our aim? I can answer in one word: Victory—victory at all costs, victory in spite of all terror, victory however hard and long the road may be.' In their hour of destiny, the British people had found a leader.

'The fight which begins today will decide the future of Germany for a thousand

The German attacks of May and June 1940. Hitler, remembering how the German attack of 1914 over this same ground had slowed down into the futile war of attrition, drove on to Paris rather than slow down to mop up the armies encircled at Dunkirk.

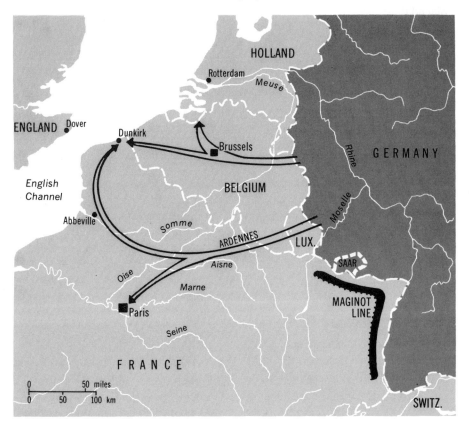

years. Now do your duty.' Thus Hitler addressed his army just before the battle for control of western Europe. Commencing at dawn on May 10, the army's duty was to overrun Holland, Belgium and Luxemburg, conquer France and so bring Britain to her knees. The Dutch, hoping they would be by-passed as in the First World War, were totally unprepared. The Belgians, striving to maintain a strict neutrality and terrified of giving the Germans an excuse to attack, had forbidden any Anglo-French forces to enter their country in time to prepare a joint system of defence. Therefore, the armies of Britain, France and the Low Countries, although numerically about equal to the Wehrmacht, could not work together until after the first blows fell. Once more, it was too late. The German plan of attack was one of the most skilfully organized and efficiently conducted campaigns in military history. Surprise, treachery and ruthlessness increased the advantage which the Nazis already possessed in superior equipment.

Within four days, most of Holland was in German hands. To make doubly sure of a quick victory, the Luftwaffe wantonly subjected Rotterdam—which was an open city—to a hideous bombardment, killing thousands of civilians. Under the threat to give other cities similar treatment, Dutch resistance ceased. Two weeks later, Belgium suddenly capitulated and in doing so, as we shall see later, placed the entire British Expeditionary Force in deadly peril. Then France, giving up even more easily than the rest, left Great Britain to fight on alone.

Softened by Nazi and communist propaganda, riddled with inefficiency in military and political circles, lacking faith in their government and its leader, the French people had no will to win. Furthermore, the military experts of France now failed to foresee, just as they did in 1914, where the Germans would strike their heaviest blows. Expecting a repetition of the Schlieffen Plan, they prepared to meet the full weight of the Wehrmacht along the Franco-Belgian border. Hence, the best French troops and the whole British Expeditionary Force were concentrated along this front. Between these northern armies and the end of the Maginot Line, seventy-five miles farther south, lay the Ardennes Forest— a rugged, hilly piece of country, crisscrossed by swift rivers and claimed by the French to be an impregnable natural fortress. Convinced that the Nazis could never come through it with their armoured divisions, General Gamelin decided to guard this section with a thin line of second-rate colonial troops, a few very light tanks and some horse-drawn artillery. Yet it was here, in this very sector, that the mechanized might of the enemy descended on France.

Two days after the fighting began, it became apparent, even in the utter confusion at French Headquarters, that the Allied defensive plans were all wrong. A German army of twenty-eight divisions was in Belgium, another much smaller one faced the Maginot Line, but hurtling through the Ardennes under the skilful command of General von Rundstedt was a gigantic army of over half a million men. Led by seven of the dread Panzer divisions and protected by clouds of screaming Stuka dive bombers, they churned over the rough countryside with relentless ease, brushing the terror-stricken French troops aside in wild disorder. Once through the weak front lines and out into the open, the Germans raced straight westward across France at a pace never before known in warfare. Making upward of thirty miles each day, meeting practically no resistance, riding along the main roads with the cupolas of their tanks wide open and waving to the French villagers as they went along, the invaders reached the English Channel at Abbeville in just ten days. Thus the Allied armies were cut in two with no hope of reforming their lines.

The Panzer divisions then curled up the coast, capturing all but one of the Channel ports in quick succession and threatening to encircle the northern group of Allied armies. It was under these very critical conditions that Leopold, King of the Belgians, surrendered his country to Hitler. This step—taken so quickly on May 27 that the British and French were caught completely off guard—exposed the Allies to the other German army now coming at them, unimpeded, through Belgium. The British Expeditionary Force and the French troops along the Channel—a total of some 400,000 men—seemed doomed. Winston Churchill feared that within a week it would be his 'hard lot to announce the greatest military disaster in our long history'. But the little port of Dunkirk was still in Allied hands, the sea was open and Britain still ruled the waves. Lord Gort, commanding the B.E.F., was instructed, therefore, to form a bridgehead at Dunkirk and the Admiralty Office signalled the Royal Navy to carry out Operation *Dynamo*.

Dunkirk

Between May 27 and June 4 occurred what was probably the greatest miracle of the Second World War. Pressing on Dunkirk from three sides and from the air, the Germans pounded the docks, the oil-storage tanks and the town itself until the whole area was a seething mass of towering orange flames and billowing black smoke. Yet the B.E.F. and their French comrades heroically fought their way back into this raging inferno and then through it to the beaches beyond. Then, standing exposed to the incessant deluge of bombs and shells rained down on them by the enemy, they waited in line for boats to pick them up.

The Royal Navy, knowing for a week that this crisis was approaching, had collected every available fighting ship, but the number that could be spared from duty elsewhere was pitifully small. At this moment, the seafaring people of England rose in a spirit of ancient defiance and brought to the rescue every vessel that would float. The most fantastic armada in history, numbering 665 civilian craft and 222 naval units, assembled in the British ports nearest Dunkirk—ships of every size and shape but all sharing the same stubborn purpose. There was the old *Brighton Belle* that carried holiday crowds in the days before the Boer War, and the Thames fireboat *Massey Shaw*, armed only with her fire pumps. Ferry-boats from all the Channel ports, dockyard tugs towing mud scows, gay little fishing boats with jaunty names, mine sweepers, trawlers and destroyers, weekend pleasure yachts and open speedboats wholly unsuited to the Channel chop, all were there. Never before had such a fleet gone to war!

One of these amateur sailors has described what he saw at Dunkirk in these words: 'Lines of men wearily staggering across the beach from the dunes to the shallows, falling into the little boats, great columns of men thrust out like human

(Above) British and French troops on the beach at Dunkirk awaiting their turn for evacuation. (Right) German cavalry enter Paris in June 1940, beginning four long years of occupation.

piers into the water among the bomb and shell splashes. . . . As the front ranks were dragged aboard the boats, the rear ranks moved up, from ankle-deep to knee-deep, from knee-deep to waist-deep, until they, too, came to shoulder depth and their turn. The little boats that ferried from the beach to the big ships in the deep water listed drunkenly with the weight of men. The big ships slowly took on lists of their own with the enormous numbers crowded aboard. And always down the dunes and across the beach came new hordes of men, new columns, new lines. . . . We muddled, we quarrelled, everybody swore and was bad-tempered; boats were poorly handled and broke down, arrangements went wrong. And yet out of all that mess we beat the experts, we defied the law and the prophets, and where the Government had hoped to bring away 30,000 men, we brought away 350,000. If that was not a miracle, there are no miracles left.'

Germany's defeat began at Dunkirk. On May 27, 1940, Hitler's plans for the destruction of the Allied armies in the West were on the point of fulfilment. Yet in nine hectic, wonderful days, Britain had turned a disastrous defeat into a great moral victory. The seamen of England had rescued the Allied forces from what seemed like certain death or captivity and the bulk of the B.E.F. lived to fight again.

The Fall of France

As silence settled over the beaches at Dunkirk, the Germans began the final campaign in the Battle of France. Turning southward, they crossed the Somme and by June 10 reached the banks of the Marne, where, in the war before, a more determined generation of Frenchmen had so staunchly held their ground. On this day, with France reeling before knock-out blows, Mussolini decided it was safe to join the fight and launched his fascist forces against the French Mediterranean front. This was, in President Roosevelt's biting condemnation, 'a stab in the back' dealt by Sawdust Caesar to win his share of the glory and the spoils.

By this time, France was in a state of panic. The government fled from Paris; the armies, though still large, were in headlong retreat; an unbroken, sweating, swearing, terror-stricken stream of humanity flowed south along all the highways and byways. Taxicabs, Paris buses, bread vans, ice trucks, sports cars—anything with four wheels and an engine—all packed with human beings, crawled along the jammed-up roads, groaning, backfiring, boiling over under the merciless glare of the hot June sun. As one foreign observer has written: 'In that world of terror and confusion, it was difficult to believe that these were the citizens of France, citizens whose forefathers had fought for their freedom like tigers and stormed the Bastille with their bare hands.'

The French government, reorganized under the dubious leadership of Marshal Pétain, Admiral Darlan and Pierre Laval, threw in the sponge on June 21. Just as the French had arranged the Paris Peace Conference to remind the Germans of the Franco-Prussian War, so, now, Hitler staged a dramatic setting for his revenge. The Nazi terms were handed out to France in the same railway carriage, brought from the Paris Museum and placed on the identical siding in the Compiègne Forest where the Allies had dictated their armistice to the Germans in November 1918. The northern half of France was to be completely occupied and put to work for Germany. Southern France was to remain 'unoccupied' but under the control of a puppet government set up in the town of Vichy by Pétain and his friends.

Not all Frenchmen, however, followed old Marshal Pétain along the road to Vichy and collaboration with the Nazis. General Charles de Gaulle made his way to London where he started the Free French Resistance Movement. In a stirring radio appeal he asked 'all Frenchmen, wherever they may be, to unite with me in action, in sacrifice and in hope. Our country is in danger of death. Let us fight to save it.' And under the red cross of Lorraine—the banner flown by Joan of Arc— the Free French fought on.

If Necessary, Alone

The Battle of Britain
For many weeks after Dunkirk, as Britain and the Commonwealth stood alone, waiting for Germany to attack, Prime Minister Churchill repeatedly warned the House of Commons in secret session that 'an invading force of 150,000 picked men might create mortal havoc in our midst.' During those weeks, time was the most precious thing in all Britain: time to refit an army which had left its equipment at Dunkirk; time to mine the beaches, build tank traps and lay flame throwers out into the sea; time to train a volunteer Home Guard to defend its native countryside; time to destroy the signposts which might help German paratroopers find their way; above all, time to rebuild the Hurricane and Spitfire fighter squadrons lost to the R.A.F. during the Battle of France.

And Hitler—making one of the greatest mistakes in his career—gave the British time. Although he seemed to be at the pinnacle of his power, with western Europe lying at his feet, Hitler hesitated to challenge England's world-wide maritime power. Aside from the fact that he had neither the surface fleet nor the U-boats to tackle such a formidable foe, he was already beginning to distrust his Russian ally. During the preceding winter and spring, while Germany was busy elsewhere, the Russians had seized parts of Finland, all of Latvia, Estonia and Lithuania, the province of Bessarabia from Romania and other territories that they had lost after the First World War. These defensive steps, obviously directed against the Nazis, brought the Red Army uncomfortably close to German soil.

Anti-aircraft units roll through Red Square, Moscow, on the twenty-third anniversary of the Bolshevik revolution, November 7, 1940.

(Above) Pilots scramble to Hurricanes during the Battle of Britain. (Right) The tumult in the skies over Britain could not easily be photographed, but this painting by Roy Knockold gives a good idea of the action during the first great decisive air battle in history.

Hitler, therefore, instead of concentrating on England, began to toy with the idea of invading Russia. Just as he wanted a pact with Moscow in 1939 to cover his rear while he attacked in the West, so now, in the summer of 1940, he needed a pact with London to free his hand against the Soviets. Thus he waited, making overtures of peace, hoping against hope that Great Britain would yield without a fight.

Across the Channel, Churchill's stirring words rang out in the House of Commons, rallying Englishmen everywhere and giving Hitler his answer. Great Britain, the Prime Minister said, would fight on, 'if necessary for years, if necessary alone. . . . The whole fury and might of the enemy must very soon be turned against us. Hitler knows that he will have to break us on this island or lose the war. . . . Let us brace ourselves therefore to our duties and so bear ourselves that, if the British Empire and Commonwealth last for a thousand years, men will say, "This was their finest hour." ' The voice that spoke for England hurled scorn upon all the German peace proposals.

Hitler and his advisers finally began to plan for the invasion of the British Isles; Operation *Sea Lion*, they called it. The German High Command agreed

that the Royal Air Force would have to be knocked from the skies before a Channel crossing could be attempted. Reichsmarshal Goering was supremely confident of success. By midsummer, his air force outnumbered the British three to one. Even so, the odds were not as great as they would have been if Hitler had attacked immediately after the fall of France. The British strength in Spitfires and Hurricanes, down to 330 after Dunkirk, had risen again to over 700. And the aircraft factories, working round the clock, were now turning out almost 500 single-engine fighters a month. The firepower and manoeuverability of these planes was legendary. Pilots, not planes, were the problem. In all England, only 1,400 trained men were available for duty. Flying sortie after sortie, sometimes six or seven a day, these were the famous few—recruited not only from Britain but also from Canada, Poland and the United States—who outmatched the Luftwaffe in skill and daring. No tribute was ever more deserved than that which Churchill paid to these courageous men: 'Never in the field of human conflict was so much owed by so many to so few.'

With the launching of *Sea Lion* fixed for the third week in September, the Germans had to hurry, yet it was not until August 10 that the Luftwaffe set out to destroy the R.A.F. Striking at the radar stations so vital to England's defence, bombing the airfields closest to London, and engaging the British fighters in furious individual combat, the Germans released the kind of attack that the R.A.F. most feared. Although their own losses were heavier, the Luftwaffe, which could better stand the strain, began to knock out the Hurricanes and Spitfires of

Fighter Command faster than they could be replaced. Had the policy been continued, the Luftwaffe might have emerged victorious. But on August 25—more by accident than design—the first German bombs fell on London. The next day Churchill ordered British bombers to hit Berlin. Hitler was furious. 'If they attack our cities,' he screamed into the radio, 'we will rub out their cities from the map.' So the Germans switched their tactics and began to make mass daylight raids on London. This proved to be another one of their great mistakes—a turning point in the Battle of Britain—for the change in German strategy gave Fighter Command a much better chance. Alerted by radar stations that the Germans had neglected to destroy, guided by excellent ground-to-air communications, dog-fighting against a foe without such communications and still further handicapped by Goering's order to remain in rigid massed formations, the R.A.F. now began to inflict staggering losses on the Luftwaffe. In desperation, the German High Command decided that they could afford to make only one more supreme attempt to clear the R.A.F. from the skies.

On September 15, 1940, hoping to draw the R.A.F. into mortal combat, the Luftwaffe staged their famous—and last—massive daylight attack on London. This was the fiercest fight of all. Wave after wave of bombers—each plane escorted by five Messerschmidt 109's—thundered in over the southeast coast of England. The drone of aircraft and the roar of bursting bombs continued all through the day. High up, almost out of sight, the fighters hunted the enemy and shot them down. The clear blue sky was etched by vapour trails and stained with the dark flames of falling planes. Three of every four that fell were German. By nightfall, the critical phase in the Battle of Britain was over, for when the Germans totalled up their losses they were forced to admit defeat. In two weeks of daylight fighting over London, they had lost 435 aircraft at a cost to the British of only 165. This was a price Germany could not pay. The Luftwaffe had failed in its mission; Hitler shelved Operation *Sea Lion* and ordered his grand invasion fleet to be dispersed.

The Blitz

But the Luftwaffe was not finished with London—the real blitz was yet to come. Since they could not conquer the R.A.F. in daylight, the Germans resolved to pound the civilian population into submission by gigantic night bombings. For the next three months, without respite, the Luftwaffe battered the great city at the heart of the British Empire. First, their target for the night was saturated with incendiary bombs until the whole area was a sea of leaping flames, standing out brighter than at noon. Then came squadron after squadron loaded with high explosives. Forty-seven times in a row, the 'All Clear' sounded only with the dawn as weary, red-eyed Londoners emerged from their shelters and trudged off to work through the desolate scenes of new destruction. The Germans inflicted deep scars on almost every part of the capital. Buckingham Palace, Westminster Abbey and the House of Commons, factories, schools, churches, office buildings and above all the homes of the people came under fire. But the East End suffered most severely. Here, in the great slums of London, the Nazis hit the undernourished

Dawn comes to the blitzed city of Southampton.

and very poor, the ones least able to stand the appalling physical strain had it not been for the courage in their stout Cockney hearts.

The full story of the blitz is an epic of the ordinary people—the policeman who carried away an unexploded bomb in his bare hands; the sorrow-stricken men and women who kept on with their jobs; the firemen who fought as many as seven hundred fires a night; the routine work of the Civil Defence, the doctors and ambulance drivers, the air-raid wardens and the night fighters of the Royal Air Force, all of whom took their lives in their hands almost every night. By mid-November, London had robbed the Luftwaffe of its expected triumph and proved that she could take it.

In a final bid for victory, Goering now directed his bombers to the industrial cities of the Midlands and the North. Coventry, Birmingham, Manchester, Liverpool and Sheffield, one after another were subjected to murderous, night-long raids and each, in turn, rose heroically to the test. Far from destroying civilian morale, the high explosives that rained death and destruction on England only served to harden the determination of her people. During the ensuing winter months the raids became less frequent and finally petered out, leaving the British cities to enjoy a long period of quiet. Thus Great Britain survived the blitz—survived and grew miraculously stronger.

The Battle of the Atlantic

The blitz was only a part of the titanic contest which Great Britain had to wage, alone, throughout the world. An overpopulated, highly industrialized little island, incapable of producing enough for 50 million people to live on, let alone fight with, it was essential for Britain's survival to keep the Atlantic and Mediterranean life lines open. Upon the Royal Navy and its air arm, therefore, was placed the almost intolerable burden of patrolling the sea-lanes of the world, tracking down

A convoy makes its way slowly over the cold, grey waters of the Atlantic. A bomb from a German raider just misses a destroyer.

marauding cruisers and pocket battleships, protecting convoys against the U-boats, sweeping mines from the harbours, running the precious cargoes not only through the gauntlet to the British Isles but also from the mother country to Egypt, India and the Far East.

As never before in history, England's sea communications were at the enemy's mercy. Controlling the entire coast from Narvik in the north to the Pyrenees, the Germans set out from every harbour and every airfield in western Europe to destroy the life lines to Britain. Surface raiders such as the *Graf Spee*, the *Admiral Scheer*, the *Scharnhorst* or the newly completed *Tirpitz* and *Bismarck*—battleships possessing exceptional speed and firepower—stole away under cover of darkness before R.A.F. reconnaissance planes could spot their movements. U-boat wolf packs, in ever-increasing numbers, glided from their dens to hunt in the grey, cold seas, and long-range Condors took off, loaded with magnetic mines and aerial torpedoes. Day after day—even when the Battle of Britain was at its height—the Royal Navy, the Merchant Navy and the Royal Air Force fought through gales, mine-infested waters and hostile skies so that England could carry on.

The Battle of the Atlantic is a story which may never be fully told. A part of it was written into the logbook of every ship, great or small, that ploughed back and forth across the Atlantic—each little part being, in itself, an epic tale of great hardships, stoic endurance, continuous peril and eventual triumph or sorrow. What piece of fiction, for instance, could be more deeply stirring than the way the *Jervis Bay* steamed to death and immortality? Trapped by the *Admiral Scheer* while escorting a convoy of thirty-nine ships from Halifax to Liverpool, this lone, poorly armed merchantman did not stand a chance. Yet Captain Fogarty Fegen and his crew headed straight for their giant adversary, holding their fire until the

Admiral Scheer was within their own short range. With her bridge blown away, ablaze from stem to stern and sinking fast, the *Jervis Bay* held the German raider at bay long enough for her convoy to escape.

The details of this and a multitude of other equally dramatic events in the Battle of the Atlantic must be omitted here. We should briefly note, however, that the Royal Navy soon asserted its superiority over the German surface fleet. Early in the War, three cruisers ran down the *Graf Spee*—but not before she had wrought havoc with British shipping—and drove her into the harbour of Montevideo where she was scuttled. Later on, in May 1941, the super-dreadnought *Bismarck*—a 45,000-ton, thick, squat giant of a ship—was chased through the ice floes off Greenland and sunk by aerial torpedoes and sixteen-inch naval guns. Although the British lost the *Hood* and let the *Scharnhorst, Prince Eugen* and *Gneisenau* slip through their fingers, the Royal Navy held command of the surface seas from this time on.

They were also able to take the sting from Hitler's first secret weapon, and one of his most dangerous. In November 1940, while the blitz was at its worst, naval engineers found and dissected an unexploded magnetic mine. Within a week its mysteries had been solved, but while the secret lasted Germany's magnetic mines blew up many ships. There seemed to be no answer, however, to the U-boat menace. No matter what the British did, more and more new German submarines glided down the ways and joined the packs hunting at sea. By the spring of 1941, they were sinking merchant ships three times faster than Great Britain and America together could replace them. Despite the fact that she had beaten off the Luftwaffe, frustrated invasion and gained control of the high seas, England's Atlantic life line was being frayed to pieces and her people—with every item severely rationed—had to take in their belts another hungry notch.

War in the Mediterranean

The entry of Italy into the War, combined with the fall of France, created an equally dangerous situation along England's Mediterranean life line. Ever since his rise to power Mussolini had dreamed of building a great Italian Empire in Africa and making the Mediterranean into his own private sea. In the autumn of 1940, with Great Britain facing the full fury of the blitz, the Italian dictator decided that the riches of Egypt and control of the Suez Canal were now his for the taking. And indeed, every advantage seemed to be with Mussolini. He had developed the Italian navy into a first-class battle fleet; he boasted over one hundred submarines and an elite corps of underwater demolition experts known as 'frogmen'. His planes, taking off from airfields in southern Italy or Sicily, could easily cut Britain's perilously long communications with Egypt. In Libya, his largest African colony, an Italian army of 225,000 men was poised to strike at Egypt from the west while another force, almost as large, stood along the border in Ethiopia and Eritrea, ready to attack from the southeast. Thus the time had come, so Mussolini thought, to smash Britain's global power at the Nile delta and at Suez. The vital link between Africa and Asia—on which, more than any other spot on earth except England herself, the defence of the free world depended—

would be severed and the way opened to the oil fields of the Middle East and the wealth of India. The Roman Empire would be revived with *il Duce*, the demigod, as its modern Caesar.

On September 13, 1940, with visions such as these dancing before him, Mussolini released his double attack on Egypt. A month later, the flames of war also licked across the Adriatic from Italy to the Balkan peninsula as Mussolini—hoping to win outposts for his assault on Egypt—launched an utterly unprovoked attack on the Greeks. Here too he expected an easy victory, but in the mountains of Greece, as in the deserts and jungles of Africa, his forces met nothing but defeat and humiliation. By midwinter, the Italian armies, whose perfumed officers lived in the lap of luxury like ancient kings and whose soldiers possessed no real heart for fighting, had been reduced on all fronts to a fleeing, disorganized rabble. In the Libyan campaign alone, Field Marshal Wavell's meagre force, brilliantly led in actual battle by General Richard O'Connor, drove the Italians five hundred miles back from the Egyptian border, capturing 130,000 prisoners and 400 tanks at a cost of less than 2,000 British casualties.

Although outnumbered and constantly subjected to attack from land-based planes, Britain's Mediterranean fleet soon mastered the Italian surface fleet. On November 11, in one of the first torpedo plane attacks of the war, British pilots from the Fleet Air Arm sank almost half the Italian navy in Taranto harbour. A few months later, Admiral Cunningham's Eastern Mediterranean Fleet inflicted crushing defeat on an Italian naval force off Cape Matapan. After these two defeats, the Italians had had enough. They failed also to capture the little island fortress of Malta, although it was probably the most vulnerable of all Britain's outposts. If Malta had fallen, the Mediterranean life line almost certainly would have been cut, thus forcing England into the impossible task of convoying supplies for Egypt round the southern tip of Africa. But Malta did not fall. Despite the fact that she had to fight off 3,200 air raids during the first two years of war and that, at one time, the small garrison there had only three old aircraft, which were nicknamed 'Faith', 'Hope' and 'Charity', Malta never ceased to serve as a British bastion against the Axis.

We may now see that, just as long as Hitler was content to leave the fighting in Africa and the Mediterranean to his Italian friends, Great Britain was more than able to hold her own. By March 1941, however, the German High Command had managed to persuade Hitler that he must bolster the faltering efforts of his Axis partner. Thus the Afrika Korps, under the very skilful leadership of Field Marshal Erwin Rommel, was sent to Libya and crack troops moved in to rescue the Italians from their predicament in the Balkans.

To meet this new double-barrelled German threat, Great Britain took an immense gamble and lost. At the very moment Rommel was gathering his strength to attack in the desert, almost half of Wavell's forces were shifted from North Africa to support the Greeks in the Balkan peninsula. These British troops, equipped with little else but courage, had no hope of stemming the Nazi advance. Three mechanized German armies poured into Yugoslavia—cutting this country to pieces and reducing Belgrade to a smouldering tomb where seventeen thousand civilians perished in a matter of hours—and then raced on through Greece. Within a month it was all over. As the German swastikas were raised over Athens, the British were being evacuated from Greece in what was another smaller but no less heroic Dunkirk.

From the Greek mainland, they crossed over and tried to hold the strategically important island of Crete. Here, the Germans, using fanatical Nazis picked for their passionate devotion to Hitler, launched the first airborne invasion in history. Their losses were enormous, but for ten days the supply of new paratroopers kept on coming, wave after wave, without letup. In the end, the Royal Navy, lacking any air support whatsoever and exposed to the ferocity of the Luftwaffe, limped off to Egypt carrying about half the British troops away from Crete. And while these disasters were taking place in the Balkans and Crete, Rommel released his first great offensive, driving the British back once more to the borders of Egypt and recapturing everything the Italians had lost except the town of Tobruk. In this barren, hot little Mediterranean port, a division of Australians—the 'rats of Tobruk' as they proudly called themselves—endured the sandstorms and the bombings, the eternally salty drinking water, the bad food, the monotony and the clouds of flies, and served, like Malta, as another British outpost against the Axis.

Despite the reverses inflicted upon her during the spring of 1941, the end of

The Mediterranean theatre of war

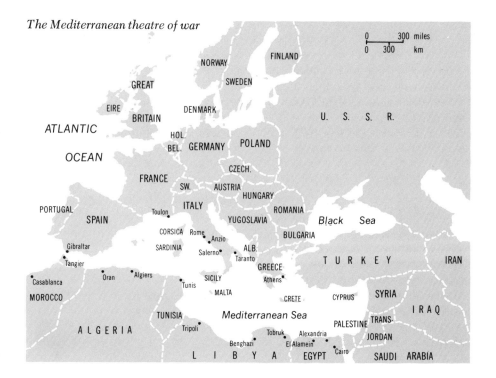

Britain's desperate year alone found her still in control of the Mediterranean life line. By the thinnest of margins, she had maintained a ring of salt water and desert round the forces that had conquered Europe. The outstretched arm of British sea power held on, forcing the impatient dictator of Germany to strike eastward, like Napoleon, across the boundless plains of Russia.

It is easy enough for us now, looking back on these events, to see what Hitler should have done once he realized that the British Isles could not be invaded. He should have bargained his way into fascist Spain, seized Gibraltar and Malta and immediately combined with the Italians to drive the British out of Egypt. This was what the German High Command urged him to do and this was precisely what the British, under the decisive influence of Churchill, took such immense risks to prevent. But Hitler, refusing to listen to any advice, ignored the Mediterranean until it was too late and then, 'like an enraged bull, maddened by a skilful toreador, charged blindly at the great mass of Russia'.

The Grand Alliance

Operation Barbarossa

On June 22, 1941, one day later in the year than Napoleon, Hitler invaded Russia. This was Operation *Barbarossa*—the greatest and most brutal assault ever hurled by any nation against another. One hundred and sixty-four divisions, numbering more than 2 million men, with thousands of tanks and airplanes in support, were unleashed against the Soviet Union. One offensive drove through the Baltic states towards Leningrad; the second, the major offensive, headed straight east towards Moscow; while the third, under the skilful von Rundstedt, smashed through southern Poland towards the Ukraine. Thus three huge armies struck along a battlefront over twelve hundred miles in length, extending from the Arctic Circle to the Black Sea. With them, death and devastation stalked into the tundra, the forests and the steppes of Russia.

'When *Barbarossa* begins,' Hitler told his generals, 'the world will hold its breath and make no comment.' But on that fateful Sunday in June, Prime Minister Churchill held neither his breath nor his tongue. Broadcasting from London, he said: 'No one has been a more consistent opponent of Communism than I have for the last twenty-five years. I will unsay no word that I have spoken about it. . . . But can you doubt what our policy will be? Any man or state who fights on against Nazidom will have our aid. . . . It follows, therefore, that we shall give whatever help we can to Russia and the Russian people.'

Mixed though his feelings were about his new involuntary ally, Churchill thus made clear the position of his government. Hitler was the only enemy; Russia and Great Britain were partners against a common foe; the Grand Alliance was beginning to take form. Behind the scenes, however, Churchill and Stalin viewed each other with suspicion and their respective countries failed to develop the mutual trust necessary for a permanent partnership and a lasting peace. Far from being truly grand, their alliance, like so many others, was held together only by the necessities of war.

The Russians seemed to have no inkling that for six months Hitler had been preparing to destroy them. More than once, British agents warned them—and they could see for themselves—that German armies were mobilizing along their borders, but as Churchill reports: 'Nothing any of us could do pierced the prejudice and fixed ideas which Stalin had raised between himself and the terrible truth. . . . Moreover, the Soviet government, at once haughty and blind, regarded every warning we gave as a mere attempt by beaten men to drag others into the ruins.' Thus the German invasion, despite the alarms and rumours which filtered through Europe during the spring, caught the Soviets completely by surprise. As in Poland, the Luftwaffe, flying in with the first dawn, bombed unsuspecting cities and destroyed hundreds of Russian planes on the airfields before they ever left the ground. On the frontier there was pandemonium. In the dust and noise and confusion, no one—least of all the Soviet Supreme Command—knew which way the Wehrmacht was travelling. In actual fact, it was moving eastward on every highway, road and country lane across the border, swarming into Russia. Behind the frontier, loudspeakers blared out frantic commands—mobilization orders, anti-gas and air-raid precautions, a state of siege throughout the land. And that night, as in all the other countries of Europe, the lights of Russia were blacked out.

Caught so completely off guard, Russia suffered one disastrous defeat after another during the first three months of *Barbarossa*. The Russian people—men, women and children alike—fought for their villages and towns with utmost courage; the peasants defended every inch of the fields that their forefathers had tilled for generations; everything was destroyed or burnt, so as to leave nothing but scorched earth in the hands of the victors; and ruthless guerrilla warfare, breaking out behind the Germans, took its dreadful toll. Despite all this, the Red Army, even with the best of leadership, was driven back four or five hundred miles all along the huge front from Leningrad to the Black Sea.

Faced with defeat on this scale, Stalin immediately appealed for all possible aid from Great Britain and the Commonwealth—yet, not so long before, during the Battle of Britain, he had been prepared to barter with Hitler for their destruction. First, he wanted war materials— especially aluminum, tanks and aircraft. Hard pressed though she was, Britain not only gave these and other vital materials to Russia, either from her own factories or from American supplies designed originally for herself, but also undertook the enormous additional burden of convoying them through the dangerous Arctic passage to Murmansk. More than this, Stalin clamoured for a 'second front'—for British landings, regardless of risk or cost, in western Europe in order to divert some of Hitler's hordes away from Russia. But Great Britain had neither the strength nor the highly specialized landing equipment necessary for an amphibious attack on a heavily defended, hostile coast. A second front was out of the question yet the Russians urged their case so vigorously—claiming they were bearing the brunt of the German onslaught virtually alone—that Churchill was forced to indulge in some more blunt talk.

'Remember,' he cautioned the Soviet ambassador in London, 'that only four months ago we in this Island did not know whether you were coming in against us on the German side. Indeed, we thought it quite likely that you would. . . . Whatever happens, and whatever you do, you of all people have no right to make reproaches to us.'

Once started, this argument over a second front continued to strain the Grand Alliance for the next three years. Neither the Russians nor the Americans seemed to understand fully the peculiar position Great Britain occupied as an insular and maritime power. It would have been the height of folly for her to compete with the massive armies of the continental nations. Indeed, it may be said in this connection that Dunkirk was a blessing in disguise for it rescued England from another disastrous war of attrition on the Western Front and released her from the land-bound policies of the French. Thus England was free to employ her sea power anywhere in the world and produce results out of all proportion to her size. Only in this way had she been to able to survive her year alone.

Predicting a short war in Russia, Hitler had once said: 'We have only to kick in the door and the whole rotten structure will come tumbling down.' Soviet Russia, however, was much more powerful than Hitler ever realized, her people were tough and hard, the Red Army fought with an unparalleled mixture of hatred and fanatical zeal, and eventually the very vastness of the country—which Stalin's generals used to great advantage—began to cushion the German blows. By the beginning of October, therefore, all three German armies, despite the spectacular initial victories, had failed to reach their objectives. Although the enemy was hammering at their gates, both Leningrad and Moscow miraculously held out and von Rundstedt was still hundreds of miles away from the Caucasian oil fields. The three months set aside by Hitler for conquest of Russia had slipped away and victory was far beyond his grasp. Once the fall rains were over and the ground was hard with frost, the Germans made one more supreme attempt to knock the Russians out, not by headlong assaults on the big cities, but by destroying the Red armies one after another in a series of 'annihilation battles'. Instead of the speedy victories that he had promised, Hitler had to drive the youth of Nazi Germany into the fearful slaughter of a conflict in which neither side asked or gave any quarter—into what one writer has described as the 'bloodiest front in history'. And in this new war of attrition the Red Army could outlast the Wehrmacht.

It now became apparent, also, that Hitler, like the would-be conqueror who had taken the same road to Moscow over a century before, had begun his attack one month too late to beat the Russian winter. The blizzards which had swept Napoleon's armies to disaster now brought snow and bitter cold to halt the Germans in their tracks. At this very moment, in December 1941, as the Red Army began its first winter offensive, world-shaking events, far away in the Pacific Ocean, were bringing war to the United States and making this a truly global conflict. The time had come when 'only the stars are neutral'.

General Winter was always an ally to the Russians. Here his weapon of rain and mud bogs down German trucks.

Arsenal of Democracy

From the very beginning of this War, unlike the first one, neither the President nor the vast majority of the American people were really neutral. Having followed the day-by-day downward course of European events on the radio and in the press, they had learned to distrust Nazi Germany and hate Hitler long before the invasion of Poland. After the fall of France, they realized to an ever-increasing degree that Great Britain's fight was their fight and were prepared to offer her almost every kind of help short of war itself. Their first important contribution was made on the eve of the blitz in September 1940, when the United States transferred fifty over-age destroyers to Britain in exchange for military bases in Newfoundland, Bermuda and elsewhere in the New World. This famous destroyers-for-bases deal was, of course, a completely un-neutral act, but the American people had concluded that it would be fatuous to sit on the sidelines with folded hands while England went under. They might be next. So the old ideas of strict neutrality gave way to self-interest—and the United States became a 'nonbelligerent neutral', though such a phrase was unknown in international law.

Valuable as these American destroyers were in the Battle of the Atlantic, they were not enough. British funds were running low—up to this time England had 'to lay hard cash on the barrelhead' for everything she received from the United

States—and some way had to be found, as Roosevelt said, 'to eliminate the dollar sign' from Anglo-American business dealings. During the fall of 1940, however, he could take no action. While Londoners fought off the blitz, the United States was fighting a presidential election and foreign affairs, as usual, were paralysed during the campaign. Once it was over and Roosevelt had been re-elected for his record-breaking third term, the historic Lend-Lease Bill was introduced into Congress in January 1941. Great Britain, or any other nation resisting Nazi aggression, would be allowed to place orders in America for weapons and supplies which they could never pay for in cash. In a vague and very generous sort of way it was assumed that these arms, or replacements for them, would be returned when the war was over. The 'America First' group and others who clung blindly to the old nineteenth-century doctrines of isolation attacked the Bill bitterly. Despite this opposition, Congress passed the Bill by an overwhelming majority and thereby made what amounted to an unofficial declaration of war on the Axis.

In glowing terms, President Roosevelt hailed the passage of Lend-Lease. 'Our country is going to be what our people have proclaimed it must be—the arsenal of democracy.'

Quickly, the vast industrial power of the United States was geared for war. A trickle, a stream and then a flood of supplies flowed across the Atlantic towards the British Isles. They did not, however, always reach their destination, for the wolf-pack toll of shipping was at its very height. It was not long, therefore, before President Roosevelt authorized the U.S. Navy to convoy Lend-Lease materials on their way to Britain. This step, taken in July 1941, shortly after Hitler invaded Russia, once more brought the periscope to bear on American merchant vessels and warships. Although no serious damage was done during the summer months, a number of nasty scuffles with German submarines finally provoked Roosevelt to make his famous 'shoot-on-sight' speech. In it, he told American naval officers to shoot first at 'these rattlesnakes of the Atlantic' and ask questions later. With a zeal that stands in marked contrast to its indifferent attitude during the first three years of the First World War, the navy of the United States obeyed its orders. Thus, in the fall of 1941, a real 'shooting war' started although neither side had made any formal declaration of hostility.

Volcanic Isle

But it was in the Far East that the darkest clouds were gathering. Here, the Japanese warlords—the leaders of the navy and army who exerted such a tremendous influence on the political life of Japan—held long-cherished ambitions to establish a 'New Order' in Asia. A small, barren country, lacking in resources, highly industrialized and desperately overcrowded, Japan had always been forced to buy most of her food and raw materials from other countries. In an age of tariffs and economic warfare, she lay exposed to the whims of her competitors. Japan yearned for colonial expansion and greater economic security. When Hitler conquered the Low Countries and France and threatened to destroy Britain, the Japanese looked with longing eyes to the rice fields of French Indo-China, the spices and especially the oil of the Dutch East Indies, the rubber and tin of British Malaya and even the fabulous treasures of India. With the rest of the world concentrating on Hitler, only the United States barred her way to these dazzling riches.

At first, the Japanese proceeded cautiously. Emperor Hirohito, Prime Minister Konoye, many of the politicians and even some of the naval chiefs, who had a wholesome respect for British and American sea power, did not want to risk war. Under pressure from the extremists in September 1940, this group somewhat reluctantly put the screws on the hapless Vichy government and extorted military bases in the northern part of French Indo-China. At the end of the same month, more or less in reply to the destroyers-for-bases deal and as a warning to the United States, they also signed a definite military alliance with Germany and Italy. Otherwise, however, the moderates were able to keep control until Hitler invaded Russia. Then the warlords, led by Foreign Minister Matsuoka and the hard-bitten General Tojo, took over. Freed from any worry about Russia, they landed troops in southern Indo-China and quickly turned this whole region into a bristling Japanese base from which they could pounce on the coveted Dutch East Indies and Malaya. The United States countered this move by sending greatly increased aid to Chiang Kai-shek—we should remember that China and Japan had been fighting each other since 1937—and by placing a rigid embargo on all trade with Japan. Not to lose face, Tokyo retaliated with her own embargo and thereby brought economic intercourse between the two countries to a stand-still. Thus, by the fall of 1941, the United States was waging a bitter trade war with Japan and a shooting (though undeclared) war with Japan's ally, Germany.

Even at this late date, the moderates in Japan still hoped to settle their differences with the United States. They expressed a willingness—how serious we cannot say—to pull out of Indo-China entirely provided they were guaranteed supplies of oil and other essential materials. Such a bargain, of course, would have enabled the Japanese to continue their war with China. While this offer was under consideration in Washington, Winston Churchill—who was kept fully informed about all these developments by his friend Roosevelt—advised the United States that Chiang Kai-shek was about ready to throw in the sponge and would certainly do so if American shipments to Japan were renewed. For this reason, perhaps more than any other, the Roosevelt administration refused to compromise and, on November 26, 1941, told the Japanese to get out of China and Indo-China lock, stock and barrel. This was the high point—and the breaking point—in the long-drawn-out negotiations between Japan and the United States. On this day, Cordell Hull, the American Secretary of State, warned his naval and military colleagues that matters in the Pacific now rested in their hands. And on this same day, large units of the Japanese fleet secretly set sail southward on the paths to war and ultimate destruction.

Pearl Harbor after the Japanese attack. In the foreground is the capsized minelayer, U.S.S. Oglala. To the left appears the 10,000-ton cruiser, Helena, which was struck by a bomb, and beyond are U.S.S. Pennsylvania, Maryland *and* Shaw, *ablaze.*

Pearl Harbor

No one knew just where in the Pacific the first blows would fall. The awful danger, which Churchill and the British cabinet feared more than anything else, was that the Japanese would attack Dutch or British colonies and have the common sense to leave the United States alone. If this happened, there was the tragic possibility that the United States would maintain her neutrality. Strangely enough, President Roosevelt and his trusted friends shared Churchill's fears. Even more than the British, they knew that, unless the Japanese struck at some American possession in the Pacific, it would be difficult to get Congress to declare war. Being far ahead of public opinion and Congress, these men understood what might happen to their own country if it remained neutral very much longer.

On December 7, 1941, the Japanese made one of the most colossal blunders in recent history and hurled their carrier-based planes against the American naval base at Pearl Harbor. Democrats and Republicans, isolationists and interventionists, labour and capital now joined ranks in a solid phalanx and the United States moved from peace to war with a unity she might never have achieved but for the folly of Japan. Thus the aerial torpedoes that sank the battleships in Pearl Harbor also sank American isolation—perhaps forever.

The attack on Pearl Harbor caught its American defenders, quite literally, half-asleep. This probably should not have been so. Cordell Hull and others in Washington had issued warnings to be on the alert; British naval intelligence had advised that the Japanese were already on the move elsewhere in the Pacific; the Americans themselves had cracked Japan's secret code and had copies of all her telegrams to Germany; and Admiral Nagumo's gigantic task force, its six aircraft carriers loaded with planes and high explosives, had been under way from Japan for fully a week. Yet the enemy swooped in over Hawaii undetected until their bombs rained down on Pearl Harbor. All they met on the way in was a tiny private plane out for an early Sunday morning spin. One hour and fifty minutes later, two-thirds of the United States Pacific Fleet was in ruins, a twisted mass of black and sunken steel. Thus by ten o'clock on the morning of December 7—'the date that will live forever in infamy'—mastery of the Pacific Ocean had passed from American to Japanese hands. But part of the Pacific Fleet, including the mighty carrier force that eventually wrought such vengeance on Japan, was not at Pearl Harbor that morning. And of the ships sunk, all but one were salvaged and placed back in active service within a year.

Churchill greeted the news of Pearl Harbor with a sigh of relief. His Grand Alliance was now complete. 'At this very moment,' he wrote, 'I knew the United States was in the war, up to the neck and in to the death. So we had won after all! . . . The British Empire, the Soviet Union, and now the United States, bound together with every scrap of their life and strength were twice or even thrice the force of their antagonists. . . . Many disasters, immeasurable cost and tribulation lay ahead but there was no more doubt about the end.' For six terrible months following Pearl Harbor, one defeat after another rocked the Grand Alliance on all fronts. Far from being settled, the outcome of this titanic global struggle hung in the balance until halfway through the year 1942. Only then did the tide begin to turn.

15   THE YEARS OF VICTORY

The Turn of the Tide

Admiral Nagumo's sneak assault on the Hawaiian Islands was only a part of
Japan's cunning plan to conquer the Far East in one fell swoop. Within a few
hours of the disaster at Pearl Harbor, every other American possession in the
Pacific—the Philippines, Guam, Wake and Midway—had been attacked from the
air as a prelude to outright invasion. At the same time, the Japanese struck at
British bases in the Orient, bombing Hong Kong and Singapore and landing
specially trained jungle fighters on the Malayan coast. Warned of these landings,
the battle cruiser *Repulse* and the giant new battleship *Prince of Wales* set out to
smash the invaders before they could attack the great fortress-city of Singapore
by land. Travelling without air protection of any kind, these valuable ships
presented the Japanese with too good a chance to miss. By noon next day, they
were at the bottom of the sea, blown to pieces by torpedo bombers. Their loss
dashed all British hope in the Far East and gave Japan command of both the
Indian Ocean and the Pacific. Among a proud, seafaring people, Churchill was
not the only one who 'turned over and twisted in bed as the full horror of the news
sank in upon me'.

Before the end of this tragic month, December 1941, the Japanese had landed
on the Philippines, seized Guam and Wake, captured Hong Kong, crossed the
borders from Thailand and Indo-China into Burma, sent 200,000 jungle fighters
swarming down Malaya towards Singapore and jumped the South China Sea into
all the important islands of the Dutch East Indies. This combined land, sea and
air blitz was faster, more complex and on a far greater scale than anything ever
attempted by Hitler.

The Lowest Ebb

But all this was only the beginning. The sturdy Japanese—whose superb fighting
qualities were underestimated at first by their 'superior' western antagonists—
proved to be a formidable foe. Skilfully directed by a ruthless High Command,
conditioned by centuries-old tradition to choose death rather than surrender, the
'little yellow men' swept from one victory to another during the first six months of
1942. By February 1, they had slashed their way through the supposedly impenetrable jungles of Malaya and were besieging Singapore. Unwisely designed only to
resist attacks from the sea, this great fortress—the Gibraltar of the East— with its
garrison of sixty thousand Australian and British troops collapsed in less than two
weeks. In March, following several severe naval defeats, the Dutch East Indies
surrendered and were incorporated, with all their riches, into the Empire of the
Rising Sun. While these events were taking place, General Douglas MacArthur
and a gaunt band of Americans were hanging on in the Philippines by the skin of

their teeth. Everyone knew the end was in sight when General MacArthur, on orders from the President of the United States, was flown out to safety in Australia. In April, worn down by hunger and disease, the American garrison in the Philippines yielded to General Homma's swarming hordes. And in the following month, to climax it all, the Japanese completed their conquest of Burma and severed the only road by which the Allies could send aid to China. By the early summer of 1942, they had isolated China, were massed along the borders of India and were threatening Australia from their newly conquered island bases in the north.

Black as this picture was, the Allies were no better off elsewhere. After Rommel took over in North Africa the desert battle had swayed back and forth with first the British, then the Germans in retreat. Early in 1942, as events in the Far East were going from bad to worse, the Desert Fox hurled his Afrika Korps at the British Eighth Army with greater intensity and more rapid success than ever before. The British retreated in confusion, hoping to reorganize at Tobruk, but on June 21 this important port—a symbol of Allied strength in Africa—was forced to surrender with all its accumulated supplies and thirty-three thousand men. The Eighth Army managed to dig in for a last-ditch stand along the El Alamein Line, barely one hundred miles from Cairo, but by midsummer it seemed that Rommel would sweep right on through. Mussolini certainly thought so, for he came to Africa, complete with horse and bright new uniforms, ready for a triumphal entry into the capital of Egypt.

At this time the Russian front also seemed to be on the verge of collapse. During the Wehrmacht's first winter in Russia the poorly clothed and underfed German soldiers had endured the cold and the Red Army's counterattacks with a grim courage. On the coming of spring in May—as the Japanese were overrunning Burma and Rommel was gathering momentum in Africa—Hitler launched his second offensive against the Soviet Union. This time he did not make the mistake of attacking along the entire length of the Eastern Front. Concentrating their forces in the south, the Germans aimed to capture the rest of the Ukraine and then drive forward to the Volga River, the Caspian Sea and the oil fields of the Caucasus. For three months the Nazi war machine rolled relentlessly towards its objectives, swarming over the Ukraine and finally reaching the outskirts of the all-important city of Stalingrad on the banks of the Volga. Here the Russians had decided to make their final stand. If they failed the Soviet Union would face disaster and the way would be wide open for the Wehrmacht to cross the Caucasian Mountains into Turkey and Iran. If this happened and if Rommel cracked El Alamein, the two German armies, joining hands in a giant pincer movement, could quickly grasp the Middle East and reach the frontiers of India. While this dread possibility threatened, the Japanese were poised to attack both Australia and India.

Thus in the summer and early fall of the year 1942, the fate of the world seemed to depend on the outcome of the battles raging at El Alamein and Stalingrad. It was at this supremely critical time, with Allied fortunes at their lowest ebb, that the tide began to turn.

Stalingrad

Stalingrad held. The Luftwaffe, flying as many as two thousand sorties a day, poured over a million bombs into it; heavy German artillery shelled it ceaselessly from such close quarters that 'the streets seemed to sway and the Volga trembled in its banks'; the hardened soldiers of General von Paulus' Sixth Army hemmed it in from three sides; the only open passage across the river was combed with machine-gun fire; yet Stalingrad did not fall. Its defenders turned every factory, every house into a fortress, fighting for it floor by floor and room by room. Each Russian soldier became a 'stone of the city'—and a city cannot retreat, it can only be smashed to pieces. The enemy crawled in so close that movement by day was out of the question. At night, Germans and Russians alike crept through the rubble with tommy guns, grenades and knives, groping for enemy flesh in the darkness. Stalingrad had become a symbol of victory or defeat in this gigantic clash of iron wills, and neither side would yield.

On November 19, a freezing rain fell on the ruined city, turning it into a

The Lowest Ebb. The strategic centre for the Allies is in the oil-rich Middle East. British and Russian troops occupied Iran in 1941.

German & Italian occupation before Sept. 1, 1939, and Japanese occupation before her attack on China and Manchuria in the 1930s

Axis conquest to late 1942

quagmire and forecasting the return of the dread Russian winter. On this day, General Chuykov ordered his soldiers to summon every last ounce of remaining energy for a counterattack. At the same time, another Russian army, coming up from the outside, cut the enemy supply lines and trapped the Sixth Army. A ring of death now closed in on the Germans. With their ammunition running out, with nothing to drink but foul water from the half-frozen mud holes, reduced to eating sewer rats, dogs and shell-shattered horsemeat, riddled with typhus and bitterly cold, the Wehrmacht—in blind obedience to Hitler's mad orders—fought on for another terrible sixty days. Finally, on January 31, 1943, von Paulus and ninety thousand men surrendered—the only survivors of the great army which had once swept through the Low Countries and helped to drive the British into the sea at Dunkirk. Thus ended one of the most brutal and certainly one of the most decisive battles in history. Stalingrad was the turning point in the Second World War. From then on, the Red Army kept the offensive and Hitler never won another victory.

Victory in Africa

El Alamein also held and grew stronger. A few weeks after the fall of Tobruk, when everything looked so black, Churchill and his brilliant Chief of Staff, Field Marshal Lord Alanbrooke, flew to Egypt to see for themselves what was wrong. Finding a weary and dispirited army they decided to make some changes. The command of the Middle East, therefore, was entrusted to General Sir Harold Alexander and that of the Eighth Army in the field to his devoted friend, General Bernard Montgomery. In these three men—Alanbrooke, Alexander and Montgomery, all of whom had fought together on the beaches of Dunkirk—Great Britain found a winning combination. As one famous war correspondent reported: 'Within forty-eight hours of Monty's arrival, every man in Egypt knew that a fresh new wind was blowing, that their new commander was something quite different, something unique. He instilled in them, magically, his own magnificent super-confidence.'

Having formed the top-level team to trap the Desert Fox, Great Britain and the United States strained every nerve to give them the weapons for the job. Hundreds of tanks, as well as jeeps, trucks, self-propelled guns and aircraft began to reach Egypt at the very time when Rommel's own supply lines were extended to the utmost limit and his men exhausted. By mid-October 1942, Montgomery had built up definite superiority over his adversary and was ready to unleash the Eighth Army in all its new-found might.

(Left) The city that became a fortress. Defenders of Stalingrad march through the shells of buildings, every room of which became a strong-point until reduced to rubble.
(Above) House-to-house fighting in Stalingrad.

At the same moment, the Allies were putting the finishing touches to a far more daring and dangerous scheme. This was Operation *Torch*, the highly secret plan to invade the French colonies in Africa and thus land behind Rommel's lines. *Torch* was a tricky proposition because all these colonies—Morocco, Algeria and Tunisia—were owned by Unoccupied France and the local military governors and naval officers were loyal servants of the German-controlled Vichy government. Most of them were also violently anti-British. There was the grave danger, therefore, that the French force stationed in the colonies would resist the invasion and give Hitler time to send in reinforcements. Hoping to prevent this, it was agreed that the United States, whose relationships with Vichy had been more cordial than the British, should take charge of *Torch* and try to persuade some of the French officers in the colonies to allow the Allies to land without a fight. Mainly for this reason, also, a comparatively little-known American, General Eisenhower, was placed in command of *Torch*. Admiral Cunningham and other British officers with long experience in the Mediterranean were sure the invasion fleet could reach Tunisia safely and land very close behind Rommel. The American experts, however, were unwilling to accept British advice or run the

One member of a German tank crew surrenders to British infantry, October 1942.

risks involved. Hence it was decided that the landings should be made at Casablanca, far away on the Atlantic coast of Morocco, and at the ports of Algiers and Oran in Algeria. By mid-October *Torch* was ready to be lit and the Allied strategists waited in breathless anxiety lest the secret should fall at the last minute into German hands.

On October 23, 1942, the roar of eight hundred guns broke the moonlit silence of the Egyptian night and in twenty minutes of flashing, deafening chaos opened the battle of El Alamein. Like Stalingrad, this was to be one of the decisive battles of the War—and of history. After great initial difficulty—involving a head-on clash, reminiscent of the campaigns in the First World War—Monty's army broke through Rommel's skilful defence and by November 8 the Afrika Korps was in confused retreat across the desert. The same day, right on schedule, a great armada of eighty-five troop- and warships converged on their objectives at the other end of the Mediterranean. Miraculously, the secret of *Torch* had been kept and the invasion, setting out from widely separated ports in America and England, had safely beaten the U-boats and the watchdogs of the Luftwaffe.

Despite the careful preparations made by the United States, however, the Allies encountered stiff resistance from the French, especially at Casablanca and Oran. This might have imperilled the success of the entire expedition but for Admiral Darlan, the one Frenchman who seemed to have any control in Africa. For some mysterious reason, this notorious agent of the Vichy government suddenly deserted to the Allies and ordered all resistance to cease. Furthermore, he attempted to persuade the remnants of the French fleet stationed at Toulon to sail across the Mediterranean and join him. In a towering rage over this piece of treachery, Hitler drove his troops into Unoccupied France towards Toulon, but the French naval officers scuttled seventy-three of their ships before the Germans got there. Although they would not fight with the British, these naval officers, apparently, were equally determined not to let the French fleet fall into Nazi hands. Hitler also seized Tunisia, thus beating the Allies to an extremely valuable base, which they might have had from the beginning if Admiral Cunningham's advice had been followed.

The details of the campaign waged by Eisenhower in the west, and Alexander and Montgomery in the east of Africa, need not concern us here. It is sufficient to notice that their death blows were delayed by a combination of Rommel's brilliant defence, the African rainy season and the tough terrain in Tunisia where the Germans made their last stand. Strangely enough, when the end did come, in May 1943, there was no fight to the finish, no Dunkirk—an evacuation was not even attempted. Rommel and other top-ranking officers were flown out to safety but 266,000 Italian and German soldiers, in a state of muddled collapse, were left to surrender ingloriously. Thus the Nazis were cleaned out of Africa; Egypt, the Suez and the Near East were secure at last.

The Invasion of Italy

In January 1943, with the North African victory in sight, Churchill, Roosevelt and their Chiefs of Staff met at Casablanca to plan the future course of the War. Everyone agreed that, sooner or later, they must assault the Atlantic Wall of Europe and establish a second front, to satisfy Stalin and to carry them right into the heart of Germany. When the time came, this would be Operation *Overlord*— probably the most difficult military undertaking in all history. At this point, however, the first serious differences of opinion arose between the American and British strategists.

In the war against Germany the Americans now set their sights exclusively on *Overlord*. They would not admit that an attack on any other part of Europe might help to defeat Hitler directly or even make the Channel crossing easier by keeping some of his strength pinned down elsewhere. The American Chiefs of Staff were also gravely worried about the Far East. In a recent effort to recapture the island of Guadalcanal, they had found the Japanese willing to fight in defence 'with a tenacity unto death surpassing anything in modern experience'. If an enemy like this were given time to store up stocks of food and ammunition throughout the vast area which they controlled, 'the bloody process of extermination would have to be carried from island to island and might take years.' Thus, beginning with an attack on Burma and an attempt to reopen the road to Chiang Kai-shek, the Americans wanted to mount a full-scale offensive in the Pacific as soon as possible.

Against this view, Churchill and his advisers argued that, during the months it would take to get ready for *Overlord*, they should keep the Germans fighting hard in the Mediterranean. Therefore, they proposed an Allied invasion of Sicily as a stepping stone to an all-out assault on the Italian mainland. This, they said, would draw Hitler into a major campaign in southern Europe and weaken him in the West. At the same time, it might cause Mussolini's downfall and provide bases in Italy for the Allied air forces to attack German targets which were at present beyond the reach of long-range bombers. Furthermore, the British were afraid that, due to American enthusiasm, *Overlord* might be launched too soon without adequate preparation, and the Allies would find themselves in another war of attrition. Fresh in memory also was the exceedingly costly, experimental raid on Dieppe which had clearly revealed the strength of Hitler's western defences. Thus the British reasoned that there were other ways to beat Hitler in addition to a headlong assault on his strongest fortifications. And they believed that the Japanese would not be so tough once the Nazis collapsed in Europe.

The Combined Chiefs of Staff at Casablanca finally worked out a compromise. In keeping with British opinion, it was agreed that General Eisenhower should use all his forces, once they were finished in Africa, for an invasion of Sicily (Operation *Husky*). But in deference to American wishes, the question of Italy was left unsettled and no long-range plans were made for an offensive on the mainland. Furthermore, it was understood that, following *Husky*, some of Eisenhower's naval and air forces would be transferred to England to train for *Overlord* while many of his landing craft would be sent to Burma. Therefore, even if the Allies did decide at the last minute to invade the Italian peninsula, they would not have enough strength left in the Mediterranean to conquer it quickly.

In the course of events this is exactly what happened. Commencing on July 10, 1943, the invasion of Sicily progressed so well—it required only 38 days to capture the island and 100,000 prisoners—that the Combined Chiefs of Staff suddenly did decide to attack Italy. The Americans, however, still insisted that the men and equipment earmarked for *Overlord* and Burma should be taken from Eisenhower as originally planned. Their British colleagues were shocked at this policy for it seemed to them that a great victory was within reach but the Allies were not using their power to grasp it. Indeed, a quick victory seemed all the more certain when the fascist regime collapsed on July 25 while the Allies were still fighting in Sicily. After twenty-two years of dictatorship, the Italian people—who did not want the war in the first place and who were now afraid of Allied reprisals— deposed Mussolini and threw him in jail. The report that the new government was prepared to surrender as soon as the Allies landed on the mainland reached Roosevelt and Churchill in August while they were holding a top-level meeting at Quebec. However, it was now too late to take full advantage of the Italian situation. The Allied strategists should have been prepared to occupy southern and central Italy the moment the fascist government fell, but their lack of a long-range plan gave Hitler time to rush in reserves from the north. Before Eisenhower was ready to attack the mainland, German troops were in control.

On September 8, the Allies began their invasion with landings on the open, shell-swept beaches at Salerno. And on the same day, it was announced to a jubilant western world that the Italian government had signed an armistice

A tank of the Three Rivers Regiment in action north of Ortona, Italy, in January 1944

calling for unconditional surrender. But for the soldiers in General Mark
Clark's Fifth Army and General Montgomery's British Eighth Army the surrender
of Italy was no cause for celebration. For them, nothing but months of dreary,
dangerous fighting lay ahead. The Germans, the land and the weather, as well as
their own delayed start, were all against them. It rained and rained until the
fertile black valleys were knee-deep in mud, the rivers flowed in torrential flood and
the hills were too greasy to climb. Yet they had to be climbed, yard by yard, one
after another against murderous fire, for the Germans by this time were in control
along the rocky ridges of the Apennines. And on each one of these rugged hills
a handful of enemy snipers could hold out for a long time against tremendous
odds. Throughout that fall, therefore, the Allies made painfully slow progress,
'crawling up the leg of Italy like a sow bug', and failing to crack the Gustav Line
that protected Rome.

The people back home were disappointed and began to wonder if the tide had
really turned after all. This pessimism provoked Ernie Pyle, one of the War's
greatest reporters, to write: 'No one who has not seen that mud, those dark skies,
those forbidding ridges and ghostlike clouds that unveiled and then quickly hid
the enemy, has the right to be impatient with the progress along the road to
Rome.' And unknown to all but a few top Allied leaders, the global strategy
that had weakened Eisenhower's hand in Italy was almost ready for fulfilment in
France, Burma and the Pacific.

Overture to *Overlord*

Failure of the New Order

Not only on the battlefields was the tide beginning to run against the Nazis. By the winter of 1943–44, Germany was losing another equally important and most interesting part of the War. From the very beginning, Hitler made one tremendous mistake in his grandiose plans to dominate Europe. He knew that, alone, his country was no match for all the rest of the continent, but in his scheme of things Germany would devour her victims one after another, seize their wealth and resources—oil from Romania, grain and coal from Poland, dairy products from Denmark, steel mills from Czechoslovakia and so on—and thus grow steadily more powerful while her opponents were being weakened. By extending the benefits of his New Order to the people in each conquered country, Hitler had to have at least their passive co-operation. Slave-labour gangs, concentration camps or, if they were Jews, simple extermination would take care of those who refused to see the light.

On paper this plan was logical enough, but as one historian has written: 'It merely left out of account such irrational things as love of country and hatred for tyranny.' Contrary to Nazi expectations, therefore, all the conquered nations immediately set up 'governments-in-exile' and continued the fight from foreign soil as best they could. Tens of thousands of their soldiers, sailors and airmen escaped from Europe to train and fight with the Allies. And hundreds of thousands who could not get away waged a relentless, underground warfare against the dark invader. They blew up railways, ammunition dumps and bridges and they sent vital factories and precious oil storage tanks up in flames; they tipped off British agents to every German secret they could lay their hands on; they sheltered fugitives from the terror of the Gestapo and helped Allied prisoners of war escape to freedom: they did all this and ten thousand other things, at risk of torture and death, in an all-out effort to sabotage the Nazi war effort.

In blind fury, the Gestapo and other German secret agencies struck back at the Resistance Movement. The western world in those days heard a great deal about the wholesale massacres, the deportations and the slave-labour camps. And most of what they heard was true. Nothing can wipe from the pages of German history the almost unbelievable punishment handed out to the Czech village of Lidice for the murder of one Nazi official, or the dark stains of the concentration camps at Auschwitz, Belsen, Buchenwald or Dachau where, among thousands of others, countless Jews were killed, often for no other crime than belonging to the Jewish race. At Auschwitz, for instance, an extermination camp of appalling efficiency, it was possible for the Gestapo to gas 2,000 persons in a quarter of an hour and repeat the operation three or four times a day. At this camp alone, it was reported by the Nazi commandant himself that 2½ million persons were gassed and that half a million died of starvation and disease. Our western world, however, seldom heard about the brute savagery of the underground which provoked the Germans into some of their worst reprisals. Helpful though they were to the

A burial pit at Belsen

Allies, it must be admitted that the Maquis in France, General Tito's Partisans in Yugoslavia, the patriots of Czechoslovakia, Norway, Greece and Belgium and above all the Polish Underground, with its intense racial hatreds, fought this silent, deadly war with a primitive savagery that sometimes knew no bounds.

This underground rebellion against the Nazis, combined with their losses in Russia and Africa and the Allied bombings of their industrial cities, eventually placed an intolerable burden on Germany's capacity to produce war materials. By the beginning of the year 1944, the German economic system had reached its utmost limit—even the genius of Albert Speer, Hitler's Minister of Production, could expand it no further—and it was apparent that the New Order in Europe had failed to achieve its purpose. By this time, the factories of Britain, Russia and especially the United States—far from getting weaker as Hitler seemed to expect —were rolling out an ever-increasing number of tanks, trucks, guns, ammunition and, above all, bombs, aircraft and ships. Their combined production was now five times greater than the German and still gathering momentum. The Allies already had won the critical battle of supply and time was fighting on their side.

Furthermore, the great convoys carrying supplies and troops to Britain in preparation for *Overlord* could now cross the ocean in almost complete safety. Allied scientists, already well on the way towards winning their own 'secret war' against the enemy, had driven the U-boats from the North Atlantic. Their first step in this direction had been the development of very long-range aircraft capable of covering 'the Gap' in mid-Atlantic—a favourite rendezvous of the wolf packs. These aircraft were equipped with a miraculous new type of radar that enabled them to locate submarines with great accuracy and without revealing their own approach. This invention transformed the Battle of the Atlantic overnight and compelled Admiral Doenitz, whose experts never did figure out the secret device being used against them, to withdraw his U-boats to safety. Hitler drove them out to sea again, but they suffered severe losses and did very little damage to Allied shipping for the duration of the War.

The same device that sealed the fate of the U-boats, known in secret code as H2S, was also installed in the Allied bombers flying into Germany. H2S was a small radar set that threw on a screen in the cockpit an instantaneous picture of the ground below. Since it could 'see' in the dark it was particularly valuable to the R.A.F., which conducted most of their sorties over Germany at night. Before its adoption in 1943, the British bombers had been flying blind and their raids— even the highly publicized 'saturation' ones on the Ruhr and Hamburg—had failed to cripple German industry. Now, H2S improved their accuracy and eliminated some of their indiscriminate bombings which, like the blitz, had served only to arouse greater determination in the civilian population of the enemy.

About the same time, the Research Committee of the R.A.F. also learned how to jam the radar system which Germany had built across western Europe. They found that bundles of tinfoil—called 'windows' in code—gave off a loud 'echo' when dropped and looked like aircraft on the enemy screen. Confused by this apparently simple device, the radar stations were no longer able to guide the night fighters of the Luftwaffe with such deadly accuracy.

Meanwhile, the American air force in Britain—which did all its bombing in daylight—was facing a different but even more critical problem. For many months, its bombers had to fly 'naked' for the very simple reason that no fighter aircraft was capable of escorting them all the way into Germany and back again. Swift German planes wrought havoc with them until the scientists and engineers perfected the Mustang—one of the finest long-range fighters developed by either side during the War and a major factor in defeating the Luftwaffe. Finally, adding further to these triumphs on the home front, the aircraft industry developed the huge, four-engined B-29 and Lancaster bombers, each one of which was equipped to carry ten thousand pounds of high explosives.

Aided by all these scientific advantages, the Allied air forces, by the beginning of the year 1944, had established definite superiority over the Luftwaffe in western Europe. With the British flying at night and the Americans by day, they were now ready to 'bomb round the clock' and bring utter ruin and retribution to the cities of Germany.

Plans for a Second Front

Late in 1943, with all these signs of victory in view, Roosevelt and Churchill—
who by this time were old hands at long-distance flying—arranged to meet in
Cairo and from there go on to Tehran, in Iran, for strategic talks with Stalin. They
also planned to invite General Chiang Kai-shek to come to Cairo for 'two or three
days at the end of the Conference' to discuss the Far East. The Prime Minister,
therefore, was surprised to find when he arrived in Egypt that Chiang was already
there and fully prepared—as a result of his private correspondence with
Roosevelt—to dominate the proceedings. As Churchill has written: 'The talks of
the British and American Staffs were sadly distracted by the Chinese story, which
was lengthy, complicated and minor. . . . All hope of persuading Chiang and his
wife to go and see the Pyramids and enjoy themselves fell to the ground, with the
result that Chinese business occupied first instead of last place at Cairo.'

The British delegation was also deeply disturbed by the fact that Roosevelt
and Chiang Kai-shek held long, completely private conversations during which
the President promised to open a full-scale amphibious assault on Burma before
the summer of 1944. This promise again raised the question of providing enough
landing craft for *Overlord* and also reopened the Anglo-American argument over
the relative importance of the Mediterranean and Pacific theatres of war.

At Cairo the American tendency to distrust British colonialism made its first—
but unfortunately not its last—wartime appearance. Roosevelt simply would not
trust such an outspoken imperialist as Churchill to deal fairly with the Chinese.
Partly for this reason and partly because the United States was so deeply involved
in the Pacific, the President supported the Chinese cause with great zeal.

The unexpected emphasis on Chinese affairs at the Cairo Conference did not
give the American and British strategists time enough to settle their differences
before going to Tehran. Beyond the broad understanding that the invasion of
France was their prime objective for 1944 and that it would start sometime in
May, therefore, they were unable to present a united front when they met with
Stalin. Churchill still argued that American plans in the Pacific were weakening
the preparations for *Overlord*. With this in mind, he urged another Mediterranean
offensive in the spring, hoping to draw more German troops from France before
the invasion began. This was the same stand he had taken at Casablanca prior to
the invasion of Italy. By this time, however, Churchill had another and very
important reason for his interest in the Mediterranean. He was now beginning to
worry about Russia's post-war ambitions. There was the danger that the Russians
might drive the Germans out of central and southern Europe and then refuse to
leave when the War was over. If the Anglo-American forces in Italy could be
reinforced and break through the Gustav Line, they might reach Austria,
Czechoslovakia and possibly Hungary before the Red Army. If, in addition,
troops could be spared to secure a toehold in Greece or Yugoslavia, so much the
better. The British Prime Minister was trying to plan the final battles with post-
war political aims in mind.

The sole objective of the American Chiefs of Staff was to win the War in a
hurry: 'get the boys back home' and never mind the peacetime consequences.

And the fastest way to do this, they reasoned, was to invade France and throw the rest of their might at the Japanese in the Pacific. Any other campaigns would fritter away their resources and do no good. Therefore, even before they left Cairo, the American Chiefs of Staff were resolved to 'gang up' with the Russians against Churchill and his advisers.

Thus the Americans played right into the hands of Stalin. He vigorously supported *Overlord*, which he genuinely wanted and had been urging for many months, and joined with the Americans to kill any British plans for an extensive campaign in the Mediterranean. By doing so, he not only ensured a second front but also turned his allies away from central and southern Europe and directed their attention exclusively to the Atlantic Wall. When the War ended, therefore, it was inevitable that the Red armies would be in control of central Europe and most of the Balkans. Perhaps this would have happened anyway—there is no guarantee that Churchill's Mediterranean schemes would have succeeded—but the Tehran Conference certainly clinched the matter. It not only determined Anglo-American strategy for the year 1944, but also tipped the post-war scales in favour of the Soviet Union.

Hitler's Secret Weapons

Strangely enough, Hitler was relieved when his secret agents, shortly after the Tehran Conference, advised him that the Allies were planning to invade western Europe somewhere, sometime in 1944. He knew that Germany's chances of decisively beating Russia were not so good as long as one-third of the Wehrmacht and two-thirds of the Luftwaffe were forced to remain in the West watching Britain and the United States. But if an invasion were attempted and repulsed— as he was certain it would be—he would be free to concentrate all his forces in the East and bring Russia to her knees. And the sooner this happened the better, for time was running out and the Nazis had to win in a hurry before the economic power of their enemies overwhelmed them.

Hitler also realized that neither Britain nor the United States would give up simply because their attempted invasion of Europe was defeated. It would take more than this to knock them out and Hitler believed that his scientists had found the answers. They had come up with four inventions which the Nazis were convinced would win the War. The electrosubmarine, which did not have to surface to recharge its batteries and could, therefore, stay under water for long periods of time, was already past the blueprint stage by the beginning of 1944. It would beat that secret radar device being used by enemy air patrols and win the final round in the Battle of the Atlantic. Jet-propelled planes, still experimental but definite in the near future, would regain mastery of the air for the Luftwaffe. And above all, well into production, were Hitler's two terrifying 'vengeance weapons'—the flying bomb (V-1) and the deadly, faster-than-sound rocket (V-2). From their launching sites across the Channel, they would blast the British Isles to pieces. Originally, the Nazis planned to release the V-1 and V-2 early in 1944 and thus break up the invasion before it started. But tips from the Polish Under-ground had enabled the R.A.F. to destroy the experimental station on Peenemunde

Island and delay the whole program by several months. Later on, guided this time by maps from the Belgian Underground and using the new H2S radar, Allied bombers had knocked out most of the launching sites. Even so, by tightening up on security regulations and building a small new type of perfectly camouflaged launching base, Hitler was confident that he could begin his second blitz on Britain not later than June or July.

And finally, Hitler pinned some of his hope for victory on the chance that Professor Fleischmann and his colleagues at Strasbourg University would solve the particular problem that had been assigned to them. If they did, even at the eleventh hour, there could be no possible doubt whatsoever about the outcome of the War. But his was a forlorn hope. Another team of scientists at Los Alamos, in faraway New Mexico, were already much closer than the Germans to discovering how to make an atomic bomb.

This Is It

The Time Had Come
Overlord was no secret. The preparations for it during the winter and spring of 1944 were far too gigantic to be hidden, even from the enemy. Everyone, friend and foe alike, knew that it was coming and coming soon. The men in the Allied air forces, for instance, knew that their round-the-clock bombing of German industrial centres had a far deeper purpose than before. Their huge raids, reaching a pitch of intensity which made the blitz on London look like child's play, were clearly designed to smash Hitler's economic power before the invasion began. Then, late in March, their targets had been changed to the railway lines, the locomotive sheds, the repair depots, the sidings and the bridges in France. D-day, they said, must be close now, for they were obviously cutting to ribbons all German communications with France, thus isolating the Nazi forces in the west and, at the same time, making it almost impossible to move reinforcements from one part of the Atlantic Wall to another. Likewise, the reconnaissance squadrons could not help but know the reasons for their work. Day after day, flying in at wave-top level, they were taking photographs of every square inch of the Atlantic Wall, showing each detail of the enemy's obstructions on the beaches and even the individual soldiers guarding the concrete pillboxes along the coast.

The two million soldiers in Britain fully realized that they, too, were getting ready for the invasion—if not on D-day, then at least as part of the follow-up. And there was no doubt which it would be in the minds of those men who practised landing on the beaches of the Moray Firth amid the live ammunition of their comrades; or of the paratroopers who dropped on the pleasant English countryside with their heavy loads of demolition equipment. Then again, the sailors in every one of the fifty-three hundred ships that rode at anchor in all the ports along the coast, knew what they were waiting for. Around Portsmouth,

Southampton and the Isle of Wight especially, where the harbours overflowed with ships, it was apparent that such a vast, assorted fleet could have but one purpose.

Not only in Great Britain but also in the United States and Canada tens of thousands of skilled workers sensed that what they were making had something to do with the invasion of Europe. Take the new amphibious tanks that could swim ashore under their own power and then keep right on going over dry land. Why were so many American factories building these at such a feverish pace? Or the amazing new ones called 'bobbins' that could lay a carpet of matting on the ground as they went along and leave it there as a roadway for others to follow. Would these not be for use on treacherous clay beaches? Or the 'flail' tanks. What else could they be for but to beat a path through the minefields on D-day and open a way for the infantry? Or this sudden drive to manufacture landing craft. Surely they were not all for use against the Japanese? And besides, as every railway man, every stevedore and every merchant seaman knew full well, they were heading eastward, across the Atlantic and into the British Isles.

The civilian population along the coast and in all the southern counties of England lived with the invasion plans from day to day and watched them grow. They saw the harbours and the fleet, the merchant ships steaming in and out and the trucks rumbling to and from the docks. They watched along the roadsides as endless miles of armoured equipment rolled by. They saw the laneways piled high with ammunition and the fields lined with tanks and trucks. They knew the units stationed in their villages and the soldiers by name. Day and night, they heard the planes, the restless noises of men and machinery in ceaseless preparation, and there was no doubt in their minds.

But what all these millions of people—airmen, soldiers, sailors and civilians alike—did not know was the exact date of D-day or where, along the eighteen-hundred-mile coast of western Europe, the invasion would strike. These were among the most important and closely-guarded secrets in all history; everything depended on keeping them from the enemy and only a few top Allied leaders knew the answers. Straightforward military calculations—distance from English ports and airfields, the nature of the beaches, the German defences and the French countryside beyond—narrowed their choice for the landings to one of two areas. They could be either in the Calais District or on the coast of Normandy. As we already know, D-day had been originally set for sometime in May and Stalin had been promised this at the Tehran Conference. However, the reluctance of certain American naval officers to part with any of their landing craft from their vast operations in the Pacific made it necessary to postpone the whole invasion plan— an almost fatal delay, for the weather conditions were perfect in May. The exact day had to be carefully decided by the Allied leaders. They wanted to approach the enemy under cover of darkness, but both the navy and the air force needed at least an hour of daylight for one last devastating bombardment of the coast defences. They decided to touch down at low tide so the engineers could demolish the German obstacles exposed on the beaches and the landings could continue, with less danger, as the tide came in. And the airborne attack required a moonlit night.

By combining all these considerations, D-day had to be set for a time when there was a low tide on the beaches about an hour after dawn following a night with a full moon! There wasn't much choice or margin for error.

Then again, only the top Allied leaders were in a position to see the overall pattern of this whole gigantic organization. They alone knew, for instance, that the Germans had 63 divisions in western Europe whereas they could muster, even after D-day, only 37. If this enemy weight could be brought to bear quickly against the landing beaches, *Overlord* was doomed. Although the pilots who carried out the mission did not know it at the time, this was the reason why French communications had to be smashed to pieces. Allied Headquarters also realized, from their studies of the Dieppe Raid, that the first assaults of the infantry had to be supported by close-in, drenching firepower and that the preliminary attacks by ships and planes could not knock out the enemy positions. And so they ordered 'floating artillery which the infantry could take in with them', and this, of course, was the reason for the queer assortment of armoured vehicles and specialized tanks which aroused the curiosity of all who saw them. Public curiosity had also been stirred by the great floating piers and miles of tubing stored at certain places along the coast. But the planners knew, again from the Dieppe Raid, that the Germans would demolish any port they tried to capture. Thus, two prefabricated, complete harbours, soon to be world-famous by their code name, 'Mulberry', would be towed across the Channel and assembled in France. As for the tubing, it was for 'Pluto'—pipelines under the ocean to feed the twenty-five thousand vehicles which were to be a part of Operation *Overlord.*

While all these intense preparations were being made in England, the Germans steeled themselves to meet the invasion they knew was coming. By the same reasoning as the Allies, they also had narrowed down the point of attack to one of two places: it had to be either the District of Calais or the coast of Normandy. Von Rundstedt, the German commander in the west, was certain it would be Calais. Both Hitler and Rommel, who had been appointed in January to the special task of strengthening the Atlantic Wall, were almost equally sure the landings would be in Normandy. Far from agreeing on this critical point, the German High Command also could not decide how to meet the invasion and von Rundstedt, Hitler, Rommel and others argued over strategy right up to the last moment. And while they wrangled and hesitated, the Allies did their utmost to confuse them still further. Dummy fleets and dummy army camps, complete with inflated rubber tanks and stacks of plywood gliders, were built along the coast opposite the point which the Allies had no intention of attacking. For every bombing raid or reconnaissance flight into the critical area, two or three were flown elsewhere in France to mislead the Germans. British secret agents befuddled Himmler's Gestapo with over one hundred false reports and the French Underground, relishing this deadly war of nerves, spread rumours until the Germans did not know which way to turn. When the month of May passed by, with the weather perfect and the Channel like a millpond, some of them began to say that an Allied invasion was not coming after all.

But in England by this time, the training grounds were empty and quiet, for the men had been moved into the big camps along the coast and their final briefing had begun. In the closely guarded huts, each man was shown maps and models of his own objective on D-day and aerial photographs gave him an exact picture of the shore as he would first see it. Once the briefing officers had unfolded the details of the plan, there was nothing left to do but wait. An eerie silence settled along the coast and over the harbours. There was little movement, for the whole area had been sealed off and no one could go in or out. The only way out now was in a landing craft going to France. Beyond the coastal strip, travel anywhere in England was restricted, the ports were closed, foreign visitors could not enter or leave the country, and the mail, already strictly censored, now did not move at all. The silence drifted up from the coast and extended over England; people seemed to talk in whispers, tense with excitement, for they knew the time had come.

At four o'clock in the morning of Monday, June 5, in a house near Portsmouth, a small group of men were holding a fateful meeting. Foremost among them was General Eisenhower who had been appointed, shortly after the Tehran Conference, the Supreme Commander of the Allied Expeditionary Force that was to invade Europe. With him were his deputy-commanders, Air Chief Marshal Tedder and General Montgomery, Admiral Ramsay and Air Chief Marshal Leigh-Mallory, his Commanders in Chief of the army, navy and air forces. Their names are worth remembering because these were the men who planned the most complex, the most carefully organized and one of the most brilliantly executed military undertakings in the annals of history. Now, with everything ready, they had one final duty to perform.

Outside, there was a drizzling rain, low clouds scudded across the sky and the wind howled, swaying the pines and churning the Channel. In weather like this, an invasion was out of the question. Twenty-four hours earlier, the whole vast mechanism of *Overlord* had been swung into action and some of the ships had put out to sea, only to be recalled because of the storm. But now it was reported there was a fifty-fifty chance that conditions might improve slightly. The choice facing Eisenhower, therefore, was between launching the invasion in weather which would make it nothing but a gamble or postponing it for another two weeks until the tides were right again. But could it be postponed? The invasion forces were already cooped up in ships and other units had moved into the camps on shore; not only had the men been briefed but they now knew exactly where they were going in France. If all these men were brought ashore again, even assuming there was room for them, it was too much to hope that the secret would not leak out. The real choice seemed to be now or never and Eisenhower, deciding the chance must be taken, cast the die with the words: 'O.K. We'll go.'

Later on that morning, June 5, the invasion fleet flowed out to sea, out into the stormy Channel, heading for France and the long-awaited second front. Four years earlier, almost to the day, the Royal Navy under the command of Vice-

On the way to Normandy

Admiral Ramsay had rescued the British Expeditionary Force from the beaches of Dunkirk and General Montgomery had been among those saved. This was the fulfilment of destiny, for these same two men were now part of the team that was directing the Allied forces back into Europe. Along the coast, at Plymouth, Dartmouth, Southampton and the other ports, people proudly watched them go —the greatest armada ever to leave that historic shore. For weeks, these people had been waiting, expecting it to happen anytime. Now they said to themselves or to each other: 'This is it.'

All day long, the fleet steamed slowly towards the coast of France, aiming at a point about halfway between the District of Calais and Normandy. Even if enemy planes had spotted them—and they did not—it would have been impossible to tell where the ships were going to strike. They could turn north towards Calais or south towards the beaches of Normandy. That night, under cover of darkness, the great fleet turned, at the appointed place, and headed south. And that same night, many hours later, the Allied bombers began to fly across London, winging their way over to support the landings. In a city almost immune to the noise of aircraft, the people woke up and listened. This was something different. They had never heard anything like it before—the steady drone of bombers flying over them for two and a half hours without a single pause! All across the great city, people looked out from their windows, up into the dark sky, and whispered in awe: 'This is it'.

D-day

As Eisenhower himself has explained, once he made his decision there was nothing more he or anyone else at Allied Headquarters could do. Their work was done and D-day, June 6, 1944, became solely a 'soldiers' battle'. The beaches were assaulted, the Atlantic Wall destroyed and the Allied armies led back into Europe by officers and men mainly below the rank of brigadier. All these men had been so thoroughly briefed and fulfilled their dangerous assignments with such courage that Operation *Overlord* was a complete success. How could it be otherwise when it had been so carefully planned, when no detail, however small, was left to chance and when the Germans were so completely fooled that von Rundstedt was convinced for several days after June 6 that the Normandy landings were only a diversion and not the real invasion? As a tribute to Allied co-operation, which seemed to reach its peak of efficiency in organizing and carrying out *Overlord*, it could be recorded here that the beach-heads were established with far fewer casualties than anyone expected. The total did not exceed 11,000 and of these not more than 2,500 lost their lives—figures which will always stand in marked contrast to the Somme, Passchendaele and the other wasteful battles of the First World War.

The initial credit for the small losses on D-day seems to belong to Churchill and some of his advisers. With bitter memories of the previous war in mind, the British vigorously maintained, especially at Cairo and Tehran, that the original plans for *Overlord* were not powerful enough to ensure success. Some of their American colleagues, on the other hand, did not seem to appreciate the difficulties in a sea-borne attack against the Atlantic Wall. They were too impatient to get going and, as one military historian has written, 'supremely confident of their ability to out-produce and overpower Hitler, if not out-manoeuvre him'. Thus D-day might have been a much more costly operation had it not been for the Anglo-American disagreements which we have already discussed. Once General Eisenhower was appointed Supreme Commander, however, all argument ceased. He agreed with Churchill that *Overlord* had to be strengthened and by his drive, his ability to work with others and the complete confidence he inspired in all his colleagues, Eisenhower found the men and materials to do the job. Even Admiral King, who more than any other was determined to hang on to all American equipment in the Pacific, yielded to Eisenhower's persuasion.

For the Western Powers, D-day was the supreme event of the Second World War. In comparison to it, everything that followed seemed anti-climactic and, although everyone knew it would not be easy, there was little doubt in the minds of the people or their leaders that victory now was just a matter of time.

The Second Front

Before the Allies could break out of Normandy, the Americans had to clear the enemy from the Cotentin peninsula and capture Cherbourg while the British and Canadians, experiencing some of the hardest fighting imaginable against Panzer divisions personally directed by Rommel, had to seize the city of Caen. Once these objectives were accomplished, however, their armies shot across France like thunderbolts. Travelling faster than any Panzer division ever did on the way into France, one American army swept southward across Brittany to the mouth of the river Loire; another raced eastward towards the Seine and Paris; and the British and Canadians, after Caen fell on July 19, turned eastward and also headed for the river Seine. With Allied forces pressing in on the suburbs, the Paris Underground burst out against the German garrison and compelled it to surrender. On July 25—a landmark in the recent history of France—a Free French army marched proudly back into the capital and Paris went wild with joy. The celebrations continued for three days, reaching a delirious climax when General Eisenhower reviewed French, British and American troops marching through the Arc de Triomphe. By this time all France, south of the Seine, had been liberated from Nazi tyranny.

By this time, also, the first serious signs of strain were beginning to show inside Germany. A group of army officers, knowing they were beaten and hoping to negotiate a separate peace with the Western Powers, tried to get rid of Hitler before he dragged the nation down to utter ruin. As the Nazi leader presided at a conference, a brief case containing a time bomb was slipped against the table-leg where he sat. A few minutes later the bomb exploded, but although several officers were killed Hitler miraculously escaped with minor injuries. Among the hundreds who were implicated in the plot, one of the Allies' most skilful opponents, Rommel, chose suicide rather than torture and public execution. Partly because of this attempt on his life, Hitler followed the advice of his staff and decided to pull out of northern France. During August, therefore, four Allied

(Above) Canadians street-fighting in the Dutch town of Arnhem in April 1945. Notice the V for Victory daubed on the wall in the right foreground. (Right) Allied tanks and Bren gun carriers advancing in Normandy, August 14, 1944.

armies, two American, one British and one Canadian, swept forward almost unopposed from the Seine to the Franco-German border.

The Canadian Army's assignment was to clean the Germans from the coast, seize the Channel ports and free northern Belgium. This assignment was completed just in the nick of time for Hitler had already released his first vengeance weapon—the V-1 flying bombs or, as they were nicknamed, the 'buzz bombs'. Thus the city of London was enduring a second blitz almost as destructive of human life as the first one. Anti-aircraft guns, barrage balloons and fighter planes accounted for some of the bombs. Daring pilots, flying at four hundred miles per hour—a terrific speed for those days—'nudged' many more into the sea or drove them down with the force of their slipstream. But over thirty per cent of those fired reached London and it was only when the Canadians, on their way up the coast, captured the main launching sites near Calais that the people in Britain could begin to relax. Even then, they had to contend with the far more deadly V-2 rockets which were fired from mobile bases. Only by hounding the V-2 launching units all over western Europe did the Allies prevent these terrifying weapons—for which there was no known defence—from doing more damage than they did.

By September, just three months after the Normandy landings, a vast Allied army, now numbering well over 2 million men, was poised along a 250-mile front from Ostend to the Swiss border, ready for the invasion of Germany. So quickly had they travelled through France that there were many confident predictions that the War would be over by Christmas. But facing them now was the famous Siegfried Line, manned by a determined Nazi army fully as large if not as well equipped as Eisenhower's. Rather than risk the costs of a frontal assault, the Allied High Command decided to make a bold attempt to outflank the Siegfried Line by airborne landings in the north, on the German side of the Meuse and Rhine rivers. On September 17, therefore, in an operation which far exceeded the airborne assaults on D-day, one British and two American paratroop divisions were dropped behind the German lines. The Americans secured the vital bridges assigned to them, but near the Dutch town of Arnhem the British First Airborne Division was surrounded and overwhelmed. Eight thousand specially trained and very brave men were dropped across the Rhine; fewer than two thousand came out alive. With fatal casualties over twice as large as on D-day, Arnhem was a major Allied tragedy.

After the failure of this attempt to turn the Siegfried Line, the Allies had no choice but to storm it with frontal assaults. Before this could be done, however, they had to improve their supply lines which were still based on the Mulberry harbours in distant Normandy. The only captured port which the Germans had not destroyed was Antwerp, but this could not be used because the Nazis still controlled both banks of the river Scheldt between it and the sea. Consequently, during October and part of November, Canadian and British forces were occupied in the costly Battle of the Scheldt, clearing the Germans out of the mud-flats and islands at the mouth of the river and opening a way into the largest port in north-west Europe. Once this was done, the Allies began to build up for an attack which

The Allied invasion of Europe

••••• *Front line, Dec. 15, 1944*

–– *Front line, Mar. 28, 1945*

▲▲▲▲ *Front line, Sept. 15, 1944*

ııııııı *Front line, April 21, 1945*

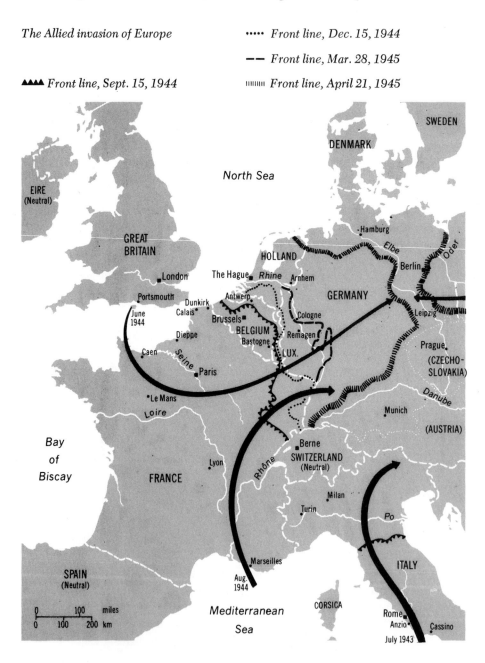

it was confidently expected would carry them across the Rhine. By this time, however, it was too late. The fall months had given the Nazis time to build up strength in the West so that, in December, to the complete surprise of the Allies, Hitler launched a gigantic and almost successful counter-offensive.

This German attack was almost an exact repetition of the one used in 1940 to overthrow France. Crashing into the rugged forests of the Ardennes where the Allies, once again, were weakest and directed by the same skilful General von Rundstedt, the Nazis planned to split the Western Powers in the centre and perhaps roll them back into the sea as they had done at Dunkirk. In 1940, in a similar situation, the French armies had fled. The Americans, confronted with an offensive of equal magnitude, fought back and held the Germans at both ends of their powerful thrust. In the centre, however, the Nazis advanced almost to the river Meuse before they were stopped at Bastogne. Thus a large dint, soon to be famous in G.I. terminology as 'the Bulge', was created in the Allied lines, and all prospect of invading Germany before the year's end had disappeared. Far from winning the War by Christmas, several months of extremely bitter fighting faced the Western Powers before they could straighten out the Bulge, crack the Siegfried Line and cross the Rhine into the heartland of Nazi Germany. And this delay, as we shall see shortly, played a very important part in causing the failure of the Grand Alliance in peace.

In this connection, it is also important to record here the outcome of the fighting in Italy during the year 1944. In the winter and early spring, while the Allies were preparing for *Overlord*, their armies in Italy were building up for a supreme effort to break the Gustav Line and reach Rome. Daring and costly landings were made at Anzio, behind this Line on the Mediterranean coast, but it was not until June—after the famous battle at Cassino—that the Allies finally broke through into the Holy City. In fact, the joyous news that Rome had fallen was announced to the western world on June 5, the very day the invasion fleet set out for Normandy. President Roosevelt said: 'The first of the Axis capitals is now in our hands. One up and two to go!' The capture of Rome, however, was not the end in Italy. Fighting hard over the rough terrain we have already described, the Germans retreated from one defensive position across the peninsula to another. After each hard-won advance, the Allies found their way barred by another mountain range, or a new river, and incessant machine-gun fire. During the fall, in the mud and freezing rain, their advance once more slowed down and finally ground to a halt south of the Po River, a long, long way from German soil.

Thus, at the beginning of the year 1945, the armies of the Western Powers both in France and Italy were being held in check by the Germans. Meanwhile, the vast forces of the Soviet Union had been rolling forward without defeat for almost twelve full months. Under these circumstances, with the Russians winning in the East and a stalemate in the West, Britain and the United States were in no position to bargain successfully about the future of Europe. Yet bargain with Russia was precisely what they now had to do, for it was at this critical point that Churchill, Roosevelt and Stalin met at Yalta for the most important conference of the War.

The Disputed Road to Victory

Stalin in the Driver's Seat

By the time the Big Three met at Yalta in February 1945, the Red Army had driven the Nazis out of every square foot of the million square miles which the Wehrmacht had conquered in the earlier years of the War. In the greatest counter-offensive in military history, they had regained an area almost five times the size of modern France. They had knocked Romania, Bulgaria and Finland out of the War; they had crossed the Polish frontiers and were driving well into Germany; and, farther south, they were rolling on their mighty way towards Czechoslovakia and Hungary. It was very difficult for the people of the Western Powers, with their attention focused on the fortunes of their own armies, to imagine the magnitude of the fighting by which their Russian ally had accomplished this amazing task. To them, the Russian front, with its queer place names and vast distances, seemed confused and far away, almost another conflict altogether. Yet it was here on the Eastern Front that the greatest campaigns of the War were fought. During the Red Army's surge towards Germany there were battles which far exceeded Stalingrad in the number of men employed, in casualties, in tanks, guns and aircraft. And the fighting was equally brutal, for the ancient hatreds between the Teuton and the Slav produced a barbaric savagery unknown in the West.

Behind these advancing armies of the Soviet Union lay an utterly devastated country. Its earth had been scorched first by the Russians themselves as they retreated and then by the Germans; great tank battles had churned over its villages and the rival air forces had finished off what was left. When he flew to Russia late in the War, General Eisenhower reported that he did not see a farmhouse or a building of any kind, still intact, anywhere between the Polish border and Moscow. In addition to this appalling physical damage, the civilian and military population of the Soviet Union had suffered over sixteen times more deaths, as a direct result of the War, than Great Britain and the United States put together. Fifteen million people had lost their lives and another 25 million had been made homeless and destitute.

With all this in mind, Premier Stalin came to Yalta knowing that his country would require many years to repair the ravages of war. He also knew that part of the trouble had been caused by the little states lying along the western borders of the Soviet Union. By their connivance with the Nazis, as in the case of Romania, Hungary, Bulgaria and Finland, or by their natural weakness as in Poland and the Baltic countries, they had made it easier for Hitler's hordes to pour into Russia. Large Hungarian, Bulgarian and Finnish forces had fought with the Nazis all through the War and Romania, especially, had sent twenty-two full divisions to aid the Wehrmacht in its attempt to conquer Russia. Nor could Stalin forget that Poland and Romania, taking advantage of Soviet weakness after the First World War, had wantonly, and in defiance of the League of Nations, invaded Russia and seized large pieces of her territory. Under all these circumstances, the

Russian dictator was determined that never again would the western borders of his country be so vulnerable. By establishing puppet governments that would dance to Russia's tune, he would build a system of buffer states, or 'satellites', thus giving the Soviet Union security in the west. Stalin was resolved to hang on to the countries in eastern and central Europe where the Red armies were already in control. Indeed, Russian campaigns against Germany were designed from the beginning to place Stalin in position to drive a hard bargain with his western allies.

Roosevelt Plays for Friendship

President Roosevelt arrived at Yalta deeply concerned about the war in the Pacific. In order to understand his position and his apparent willingness to deal with Stalin almost too freely, it is necessary to consider some of the events in the Far East that had given him cause for worry. In the months following Pearl Harbor, the Japanese, it will be remembered, had driven the Allies into the extreme southeastern tip of New Guinea and from there were threatening to invade Australia. At this critical point, however, their offensive had been stopped by a combined Australian and American force under the command of General Douglas MacArthur. Immediately, and long before they were adequately prepared, the Allies began a series of limited counterattacks designed to contain the Japanese in New Guinea and force them from their bases in the nearby Solomon Islands. During 1943, as in Russia, Africa and Sicily, the tide also began to flow with the Allies in the Pacific. General MacArthur's ragged forces, in one of the most punishing campaigns of the entire war, cleared the Japanese from the eastern half of New Guinea while American victories at Guadalcanal and Bougainville freed the Solomons. Thus the threat to Australia was removed and the Allies were ready for a full-scale offensive.

Two possible routes across the Pacific pointed the way back to Japan and ultimate victory. Following one of these, the Allies could drive the Japanese from the rest of New Guinea, cross over at its western end into the island of Halmahera and there build bases for an invasion of the Philippines. If these steps were successful, they would be within striking distance of Formosa, then the Ryukyus and finally the home islands of Japan. With so many big islands to capture, it was the infantry, supported by naval and air forces, that would have to travel this road. The other choice for the Allies lay through the multitude of tiny coral islands which stretch, by groups, in a great curve across the mid-Pacific from Australia to Japan. By capturing widely scattered naval and air bases—say one or two in each group of islands—they could control vast areas and eventually work their way up close enough to assault the Japanese mainland. Clearing and protecting this road would be mainly a task for the navy.

In the two years after Pearl Harbor, the fighting strength of the United States had grown to such prodigious proportions that the Americans were able to take both roads at the same time. Spending $9 billion a month on war account, the United States had become a military colossus. Eight million men and women already had joined one of the three services—there would be 12 million before the War's end—so that nearly every family in America had some relative in uniform. The U.S. Navy, with over 4,000 ships and 80,000 landing craft, was not only the largest and most powerful in the world but greater than the combined fleets of all the belligerent powers. In the Pacific alone, the Americans had one hundred aircraft carriers, bigger and faster than any pre-war battleships, and equipped with thousands of planes. One of these carrier fleet units—the famous Task Force 59—was by itself more powerful than the entire Japanese navy.

With power like this, it was not surprising that, during the year 1944, the Americans swept from one victory to another over the Japanese. General Douglas MacArthur, taking the road from New Guinea and directing one of the cleverest campaigns of the War, reached Leyte Island in the Philippines by October, two months ahead of schedule. Some idea of the magnitude of his operations may be gathered from the fact that more men—about 290,000—went ashore on the first day of the Leyte invasion than landed in Normandy on D-day. In a supreme effort to repel this invasion, the Japanese committed every available warship to battle, but units of the American navy under Admirals Kinkaid and Halsey trapped them in Leyte Gulf and sank twenty-seven ships. With this victory, the Americans regained complete mastery of the Pacific Ocean and ensured the conquest of the Philippines. By the time the Yalta Conference opened, MacArthur's forces were besieging Manila, the capital city on the island of Luzon. Meanwhile, as the army thus moved up from New Guinea, the United States Navy, under the control of Admiral Nimitz, was fulfilling its mission among the tiny islands of the mid-Pacific. Commencing with the bitter fighting for Tarawa in the Gilbert Islands, they cleared the Marshalls, destroyed the great Japanese air base on Truk and captured Saipan and Guam in the Marianas. As General MacArthur's forces closed in on Manila, the navy and its air arm began to pulverize the island fortress of Iwo Jima, north of the Marianas and only eight hundred miles from Tokyo. Okinawa in the Ryukyus would be next—and then Japan.

Victorious though the American forces were, this gradual destruction of the Japanese Empire was being achieved at a dreadful cost. Using the time after Pearl Harbor to great advantage, the Japanese army had placed detachments of their finest soldiers all through the vast Pacific archipelago. Entrenched behind great walls of concrete, steel, coral, sand and coconut logs, these garrisons could not be destroyed by even the heaviest naval or air bombardment. Refusing to surrender no matter what the odds against them—as the very low number of prisoners testifies—they had to be dug out by the infantry and exterminated, almost one by one. When the end was in sight, desperate Japanese tied bombs round their waists and hurled themselves into the opposing trenches or flew their loaded suicide planes onto the decks of American battleships.

By the time of Yalta, this determined foe still controlled innumerable islands which the Americans had bypassed in the Pacific, as well as the coastal provinces of China and their own homeland. Some of President Roosevelt's military advisers had assured him, therefore, that it would require at least another eighteen months to defeat the Japanese. Faced with this discouraging and costly prospect, the President was determined to persuade Stalin to throw the full weight of the Soviet Union against Japan just as soon as the war in Europe was over. In order to save American lives in the Pacific, Roosevelt was quite prepared to deal with Russia—and Stalin was in a bargaining mood.

President Roosevelt also hoped that Russian intervention would enable the United States to defeat Japan before Great Britain, France or Holland could regain their former colonies in the Far East. If American forces got there first, the President and his advisers would be in a position to dictate the form of government these colonies should have before any of them were returned to their former imperialist owners. This was the old American distrust for colonialism— which we have observed at work in the Cairo Conference—showing up again. With this in mind, Roosevelt already had persuaded Queen Wilhelmina of Holland to promise self-government for the Dutch East Indies once they were liberated from Japanese control. Likewise, he had also indicated to France that

American offensives in the Pacific

—— *Limits of Japanese expansion, 1942*

➡ *American thrusts towards Japan*

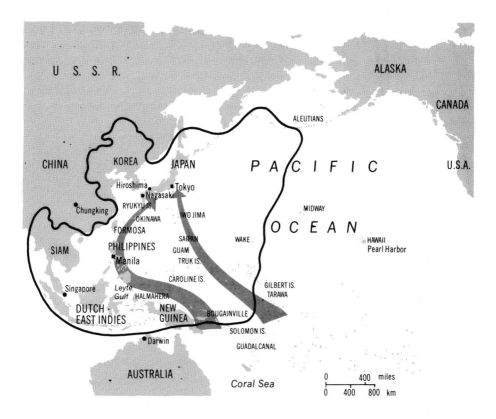

U.S. Marines landing on Iwo Jima. They try to hide in the hollows of the sand among the bodies of their comrades. From the cliffs the Japanese pour a murderous rain of bullets onto the beach below.

the re-establishment of her rule over Indo-China would not be tolerated. And from the beginning, he had made it clear to Churchill—although it was public knowledge at the time—that the United States was not in the War to help Great Britain 'hang on to her archaic, mediaeval Empire ideas'. This source of Anglo-American disagreement had arisen back in August 1940, when Roosevelt and Churchill held the first of their many conferences. Meeting in Newfoundland to define their war aims, the two statesmen had pledged to the world at large, in the famous Atlantic Charter, their united faith in the 'four freedoms'. To Churchill this meant only destroying Nazi tyranny in Europe, but Roosevelt had a much broader interpretation. 'I can't believe,' he said privately to the British, 'that we can fight a war against fascist slavery and at the same time not work to free people all over the world from a backward colonial policy.' Although ready to admit that British colonial administration was more progressive than most, President Roosevelt, like many of his countrymen, believed colonialism was so evil that 'even good empires must be bad.'

It was partly for this reason that the United States Chiefs of Staff would not allow the British to have any voice in the conduct of the Pacific war. Nor were they willing, at any time, to have British forces play a major role in defeating

Japan lest Great Britain should not only regain her former empire in the Far East but also expand it. In fact, they were so suspicious of their ally's post-war ambitions—and Churchill, as we shall see, had given them some additional cause for concern—that many competent historians claim the American delegation arrived at Yalta more willing to trust Stalin than they were the British Prime Minister. Many of them would have agreed with Eisenhower when he wrote that one of the reasons the United States and Russia could get along together was that 'both were free from the stigma of colonial empire-building by force.' How any man could reach such a conclusion in the face of Russian intrigue before the First World War or the record of American imperialism in the Philippines, Cuba, Panama and elsewhere, is beside the point. The fact is that American leaders who should have known their history better came to Yalta holding such beliefs.

Mingled with this attitude, however, was a genuine and very commendable desire to deal with the Russians on a friendly, man-to-man basis and to win their confidence. President Roosevelt, motivated mainly by the highest form of idealism, wanted to be fair so that the Soviet Union would willingly join any post-war organization to maintain peace. During the preceding fall, steps in this direction had already been taken at an Allied meeting held in Dumbarton Oaks, near Washington. There it had been decided to create a world organization, to be known as the United Nations, with a Security Council, a Secretariat and a General Assembly, similar in most respects to the old League of Nations. At Dumbarton Oaks, the Russian delegate had expressed strong fears that the little nations, by sheer weight of numbers, would have too much power unless the big ones had some control or veto over their decisions. He also startled the other representatives by demanding that each one of the sixteen states in the Soviet Union should have separate membership. Thus, knowing that Russia was luke-warm but that the new organization would be meaningless without her, President Roosevelt went to Yalta resolved to get Stalin's whole-hearted support for the United Nations.

Churchill's Deep Distrust

The Prime Minister of Great Britain, as we know, was a long-standing, extremely bitter foe of communism. It is fair to say that he regarded the alliance with Russia mainly as a 'wartime marriage of convenience' which was most unlikely to survive after Hitler had been defeated. Indeed, Churchill seriously entertained the idea that, once the Nazis were driven from Germany, the Wehrmacht should not be too quickly disarmed in case it had to be used against the Soviet Union. So much for the Grand Alliance! Some of Churchill's critics claim that the Prime Minister hastened the end of the western world's partnership with Russia because he assumed, from the beginning, that Stalin was a dangerous man. Distrust bred distrust and grew in a vicious circle. It might have been different, they say, if the Americans had been free to negotiate with Stalin, unfettered by Churchill's intense dislike for communism. On the other hand, it may well be argued, in the light of what has happened since, that the Prime Minister, with his deep knowledge of history and his long experience in European politics, was one of the leaders smart enough to see the handwriting on the wall. Certainly, as far as Churchill and his advisers were concerned, the Soviet Union had provided ample grounds for their suspicions long before the Yalta Conference.

The governments-in-exile of three unruly little countries—Greece, Poland and Yugoslavia—were the immediate cause of the Anglo-Russian discords which helped to break up the Grand Alliance. In the period between the two wars, these countries, like all others in central and eastern Europe except Czechoslovakia, had failed miserably to make a success of democracy. Torn by incessant squabbling among a multitude of political parties and settling their internal differences by riots, rough-house strikes, political assassinations and other forms of violence, all three had given way to some kind of dictatorship. Their wartime governments-in-exile, therefore, were far from being truly democratic and did not necessarily command popular support among the people back home in Europe. The bitter pre-war feuding dragged on and the resistance movement against the Nazis in all these countries was badly split between those who favoured the governments-in-exile and those who cordially detested them. Among those who put up the strongest resistance to the German invaders were the communist elements in the Underground. And they were also the group who most violently opposed their governments-in-exile.

Having very little choice at the beginning of the War, Great Britain extended diplomatic recognition to all refugee governments in London and, as time went on, became deeply committed to support them. Thus she found herself tangled in their quarrels and ranged with them against their communist and other opponents in the Underground. Once the Red armies started to roll, the Soviet Union, of course, backed up the other side and so, well before the Yalta Conference, Churchill and Stalin were supporting opposing forces in the contest for power in eastern Europe.

In Yugoslavia, Churchill was able to beat Stalin to the punch quite easily. By 1943, while the Wehrmacht was still deep in Russia, it became apparent that King Peter's refugee government in London did not merit British confidence. The king's supporters in Yugoslavia were openly intriguing with the Nazis while another group, the Partisans, under the communist leadership of a man who called himself Tito, were fiercely fighting against the Germans. Under these circumstances, the British eventually dropped King Peter, flew military missions and aid to Tito's forces and after the War recognized him as the legal ruler of the country. Partly for this reason, Marshal Tito, the present communist dictator of Yugoslavia, has never been fully under the influence of the Soviet Union.

In Greece and Poland, however, the situation was much more complex and dangerous, and no solution satisfactory to the British had been found by the time the Russian armies began to enter eastern Europe. Consequently, the Prime Minister, deciding that he should make a direct bargain with Stalin before it was too late, flew to Moscow in October 1944 for a meeting with him. Roosevelt wanted to be there, and would have been but for the fact that he was busy campaigning for his fourth term as President of the United States. As Roosevelt suspected, Churchill made a bargain with the Soviet dictator that virtually divided the Balkan peninsula into two spheres of influence. By it, Great Britain was given a 'controlling interest' in Greece, Russia was to have a free hand in Hungary, Bulgaria and Romania, while Yugoslavia was to be shared, fifty-fifty. There were no modifying conditions of any kind to this blunt bargain. When the Americans protested that it was a direct violation of the Atlantic Charter, Churchill was quick to point out that, as far as he was concerned, it was only a 'temporary wartime agreement'. However, he completely neglected to give this interpretation to Stalin and there is no doubt that the Russians came to Yalta believing that, with British permission, they had a free hand in the affairs of Hungary, Romania and Bulgaria.

Churchill also tried to solve the tangled problems of Poland when he met with Stalin at Moscow. By that time, there were two governments claiming to speak for the whole country—the one in London, supported by Great Britain, and a new one called the Lublin Committee, set up by Russia and composed of communist members from the Polish Underground. The Prime Minister knew that, with the Red Army moving in so quickly, the London Poles to whom he was particularly committed were in danger of being squeezed out. He hoped to end the bitter rivalry between these two factions by blending them into a joint government formed by representatives from both sides. Premier Stalin was willing to accept this suggestion on one condition which requires, at this point, a word or two of background explanation. At the end of the First World War an impartial committee headed by Lord Curzon had drawn the boundary line between the newly revived Polish nation and Russia. It was a fair line, carefully attempting to separate the two racial groups, but the Poles refused to accept it. They attacked Russia and forcefully extended their frontiers eastward, about one hundred and seventy-five miles beyond the Curzon Line. Stalin now wanted this land back and was prepared to deal with some of the London Poles provided they would agree to the Curzon Line as their new boundary. Stalin was also willing to compensate Poland for this loss with territory in the west at Germany's expense. Much to Churchill's dismay, the Polish leaders in London refused to consider this proposal. By their stubbornness towards the Lublin Committee and the Soviet Union, the London Poles incurred the unbending opposition of the Russian dictator. And this, as we shall see, played a vital part in the sorry story of Yalta.

In December 1944, a few weeks after their Moscow meeting, the Churchill-Stalin bargain in the Balkans was put to the test. By this time, the Germans were beginning to pull out of Greece and a British force had been landed with a would-be Greek government composed of monarchists, who supported King George VI, and representatives from the various resistance groups, including some communists. This coalition had been formed abroad and was to be set up in Athens once the Nazis had been driven out. No sooner had the British troops been hailed as liberators, than strong Greek communist forces began to attack the city, hoping to seize control. Despite their promises to the contrary, the communist members of the government could not or would not keep their comrades in order. Under these circumstances, Prime Minister Churchill sent a secret telegram to the British commander in Greece telling him to shoot down the communists and 'act as if you were in a conquered country where a local rebellion is in progress.' After several weeks of bitter, hand-to-hand fighting, the communist uprising was crushed.

While all this was going on, there was no criticism from Russia and no aid of any kind was sent to the rebels in Greece. As Churchill has written: 'Stalin adhered strictly and faithfully to our agreement in October, and during all the long weeks of fighting the communists in the streets of Athens not one word of reproach came from *Pravda* or *Isvestia*.' Now, however, Stalin could expect, when the time came for him to act in Hungary, Bulgaria and Romania, that the British would carry out their part of the bargain and stand aside. An equally important result of British intervention in Greece was the violent reaction it provoked in the United States. The use of British forces against the Greek communists, who so recently had been fighting the Germans, raised a storm of protest in Washington and Churchill came under the fiercest criticism of his whole wartime career. All this was greatly intensified when the strongly-worded secret telegram, which he had sent at the beginning of the rebellion, fell into the hands of an American journalist and was spread in ugly headlines across the country. As a result, the relationships between Great Britain and the United States were more strained than they had been at any other time during the War. It was most tragic that such suspicion and discord should have developed on the eve of Yalta for, as one historian has written, 'it seems to have led Roosevelt and some of his intimates to presume that the future threat to world peace would not come from Russia but from the old colonial powers, and particularly Britain.'

16   TRIUMPH AND TRAGEDY

The Iron Curtain Falls

The Yalta Bargain
When the outcome of the Yalta Conference was broadcast on February 11, 1945, all the Allied nations, and especially the United States, hailed it as one of the most important steps ever taken to promote peace and happiness in the world. And indeed, in the published text of the decisions made by the Big Three there was just cause for joy. First of all, Great Britain, the United States and Russia pledged themselves 'to build a world order under law, dedicated to peace, security, freedom and the general well-being of mankind' and to work together 'in assisting the peoples liberated from Nazi tyranny to create democratic institutions of their own choice'. This pledge, known as the Declaration on Liberated Europe, seemed to guarantee that the Soviet Union would not abuse its gigantic power in the countries already occupied by the Red armies. Then again, raising up the hope for a world peace organization which had been dashed down at Dumbarton Oaks, the Big Three invited all the nations, great or small, to attend a conference at San Francisco in April, to draw up a charter for the United Nations.

Even the tangled problems of Poland seemed to have been settled at Yalta. It was agreed that Russia's border would be extended to the Curzon Line while the Poles would receive their promised compensation from German territories in the west. As for the two rival governments, the Lublin Committee set up by the Soviet Union would be 'reorganized on a broader democratic basis with the inclusion of democratic leaders from Poland itself and from Poles abroad'. Stalin also accepted the Anglo-American doctrine that the Nazis must be forced to 'surrender unconditionally'—thus removing any chance for Hitler to try any last-minute separate bargaining with either Russia or the Western Powers. Once defeated, Germany was to be divided in four occupation zones, one each for France, Great Britain, the United States and the Soviet Union. Some said that France did not deserve a zone but this was a minor matter arousing little public discussion. Other decisions regarding reparations, the trial and punishment of Nazi war criminals, and dismantling of heavy German industry were all questions on which the people of the western world readily could agree. However, it was the Declaration on Liberated Europe, the promise to create a United Nations peace organization and the settlement of the Polish question which caused the deepest satisfaction and held out the greatest hope for the future.

But what did all these fine, lofty phrases really mean? Did the Declaration on Liberated Europe, for instance, apply to Hungary, Romania and Bulgaria or were those countries still private hunting grounds for the Soviet Union? Who was to supervise the 'free elections' these turbulent countries were meant to have—

Churchill, Roosevelt and Stalin at Yalta

only Russia or all the Great Powers? What kind of 'democratic leaders' from the Polish government-in-exile would the Lublin Committee accept and, while this was being decided, what would the communists be doing to their political enemies in Poland? Could the United States and Great Britain send observers into Russian-occupied territory to see that everything was up and above board or would this be an insult to their eastern ally? What concessions had been made to secure Stalin's support for the United Nations, and did his interpretation of 'freedom' and 'democracy' coincide with that of Churchill and Roosevelt or did he have something else in mind? These and a great many other dangerous questions remained unanswered in the Yalta Declaration. The people of the western world failed to see that the decisions of the Big Three were so broad and vague that they 'could be stretched by either side all the way from Yalta to Washington'.

The general public did not realize, of course, that the broad generalities of the Declaration were designed to conceal the fact that behind the closed doors of the Levadia Palace at Yalta the Big Three had bargained and wrangled for a whole week. Almost every issue found Churchill pitted against Stalin while Roosevelt attempted to play the role of arbitrator and judge. With very little true agreement, the best they could do, therefore, was to issue a general Declaration which each statesman could interpret to his own liking. Despite all this, Roosevelt came away from Yalta believing that it had been the most encouraging conference of all! As one of his closest advisers said: 'We were absolutely certain that we had won the first great victory of the peace. The Russians had proved they could be reasonable and far-seeing and there wasn't any doubt in the minds of the President or any of us that we could live with them peacefully for as far into the future as any of us could imagine.'

Furthermore, the public did not know that several of the Yalta decisions had been withheld from the published Declarations. The most important of these secret agreements—necessarily so because it involved highly confidential military information—was the Russian promise to enter the war against Japan within three months of Germany's surrender. In a series of completely private talks with Stalin, President Roosevelt purchased this promise of Soviet aid by agreeing to restore all the privileges and territories that Russia had lost to the Japanese in the war of 1904–5. These included the right to operate the main railways in Manchuria, the use of Port Arthur as a naval base and the ownership of the southern half of Sakhalin Island. The fact that Russia had stolen these territories from China in the first place and that, according to the Cairo Conference, Chiang Kai-shek expected them to be returned to him, did not seem to bother anyone. The President also agreed that Russia should be given some Japanese islands off the coast and recognized Soviet control of Outer Mongolia.

This whole bargain was made, as we know, because the American Chiefs of Staff felt that the Pacific war 'might last until 1946 and cost another million lives' unless the Red Army was employed on the Chinese mainland against Japan. However valid his reasons, there is no doubt that President Roosevelt sacrificed some of his most cherished principles, for he had always fought against secret territorial changes and insisted that he would recognize no spheres of influence. Yet in much the same way as Churchill and Stalin had divided the Balkans, he now gave what amounted to a Russian sphere of influence in both Outer Mongolia and Manchuria. While remaining so critical of French, Dutch and British colonialism in the Pacific—indeed, he even tried at Yalta to persuade Churchill to forfeit Hong Kong as a gesture of friendship to China—the President yielded almost without a question to the Far Eastern ambitions of the Soviet Union. And by doing so, he presented Stalin with the power, as we shall see later, to help the Chinese communists drive Chiang Kai-shek out of the country.

In the post-war period, when the ambitions of Russia in both Europe and the Far East had been all too clearly revealed, the Yalta Conference was denounced in the United States as a sell-out to the communists. Frustrated by the feeling that they had been sold a gold brick by Stalin, Roosevelt's political opponents embarked on a witch hunt to weed out the communists, the fellow travellers, who, they said, had riddled the President's administration with disloyalty. While men like Alger Hiss, an American adviser at Yalta who was suspected of spying and convicted on a charge of perjury, seemed to prove their case, the outside observer is inclined to believe that this anti-communist crusade was carried too far. Not only has the United States been unreasonable at times in her dealings with Russia but in the early 1950s, when Joseph McCarthy was head of the Senate Govern-ment Operations Committee, good citizens were afraid to say or write publicly what they believed. Until common sense regained control, this raucous demagogue seemed to challenge the foundations of democracy and certainly led to a violent attack on the memory of President Roosevelt. The more charitable of his critics inferred from the President's death shortly after Yalta that he was a sick man, not quite in control of all his faculties. The rest accused him of deliberately trying to strengthen Russia. Neither of these assertions is in keeping with the facts. Roosevelt made an honest, a desperate attempt to win Soviet friendship at Yalta and the broad, general promises made by Stalin convinced all the American delegation that these efforts had been successful, that Soviet good faith was indeed assured.

There is no doubt, however, that the American negotiators made some tragic errors in judgement at the Yalta Conference. They should have foreseen that the Lublin Committee was unreliable—that both it and the Polish government in London should have been disbanded and a fresh start made, as the British tried to insist. They should have realized, as the British did, that if Germany was too thoroughly crushed after the War, no combination of western European nations would be strong enough to stand up to Russia—unless the Americans themselves left large armies on the continent and this they were not prepared to do. They should have known—and therefore supported Churchill's Mediterranean plans —what would happen to the central European countries if the Red armies reached them first. Perhaps above all, they should have understood, as any study of history reveals, that whoever controlled northern China would be in a position to dominate all that vast country. President Roosevelt and his advisers failed to realize that they were dealing, not just with Russia, but with the dynamic force of international communism striving for world power through violence and revolution. Thus the President of the United States had convinced himself somehow or other that he could trust Stalin as much as, if not more than, Churchill—and he should have known better.

The Ring of Death
The Yalta Conference lasted exactly one week. In those same seven February days, the Allied air forces hurled down on Germany two times more high explosives than the Luftwaffe dropped during the whole course of its blitz on Britain. And this was just the beginning of a stepped-up air offensive calculated to reduce every German city to rubble and burn the last remnants of Nazi tyranny out of Europe. By this time, also, a ring of death had closed in on the Wehrmacht and the Allied armies were ready for the kill. In the east, the forces of the Soviet Union had reached the Oder River along its entire length from the Baltic Sea to the borders of Czechoslovakia. In the south, the combined British, American and Canadian forces of General Alexander were prepared to pour through the Gothic Line and down into the Po Valley with a momentum that no longer could be stopped. In the west, the Bulge had been pounded out of existence and General Eisenhower's seven great Allied armies—one Canadian, one British, four American and one French—were back again facing the Siegfried Line along the German border.

Loading a Stirling bomber

On February 8, the day Roosevelt made his Far East bargain with Stalin, the Allies opened the second-to-last campaign of the war in the West. Commencing with a Canadian attack in the north, Eisenhower's armies, one after another, pierced the frontier fortifications and began to drive the Wehrmacht back towards the Rhine River—towards the one remaining water barrier blocking their way into the heart of Germany. And one after another, they reached the flood-swollen Rhine only to find that the fleeing Germans had blown up all the bridges behind them. More than a dozen times the Allies arrived just in time to see the great bridges go crashing down. By the beginning of March, the Wehrmacht had been cleaned out of the Rhineland, but every attempt to seize a crossing over the river had been foiled. Then, on March 7, an American division moving along the hills above Remagen saw to their amazement that the famous Ludendorff railway bridge was still intact. A motorized platoon dashed through the town and reached the river with only ten minutes to spare. While engineers tore up every demolition cable they could find, infantry raced across the standing span to the other side. Two small charges went off and the whole structure shuddered dangerously, but the main fuse failed to fire and before another could be set the defenders were overpowered. In an attempt to stem the American flood which began to pour through at Remagen, the Germans weakened their defences so badly that other Allied forces were able to build pontoon bridges elsewhere over the river without too much opposition. Before the end of March, therefore, Eisenhower's armies were across the Rhine and the Allies had hurdled the last great barrier in the West.

Now only two hundred and fifty miles separated the armies of the Western Powers from the Red Army in the East. Savage fighting lay ahead on both fronts but there was only one full-scale battle left. This was for the Ruhr Valley, the greatest industrial region in Europe and the major prize in western Germany. Canadian, British and American forces quickly encircled this area—or what was left of it, for the Allied air forces had been pounding the Ruhr without mercy —and systematically began to cut the trapped German armies to pieces. After eighteen days of hopeless resistance, a quarter of a million enemy soldiers capitulated and their commanding officer, General Model, committed suicide— the first of many Nazi leaders who took the easy way out once the end was in sight. Seeing himself doomed, Hitler issued a decree that 'the battle must be continued without consideration for our own people.' To him the end of his own life meant the end of everything and therefore all that was left of Germany must be destroyed: 'all industrial plants, all electrical facilities, waterworks, gasworks . . . all food and clothing stores . . . all bridges, all railway installations, the postal system . . . also the waterways, all ships, all freight cars and all locomotives'. Thus the German people would be annihilated and their country transformed into a ghastly desert.

But this was the command of a broken, nerve-wracked and lonely man—a desperate command which even Hitler himself could no longer enforce. Few among the Nazi leaders now believed that the V-2 rockets, the jet-propelled airplane, the electric submarine or any of the other miracles promised by Hitler could save them. After their crushing defeat in the Rhineland and the Ruhr, the whole Western Front had collapsed in chaos and the road to Berlin lay open to the Anglo-American armies. Indeed, if the German people had one final wish it was that the Western Powers would reach Berlin before the armies of the Soviet Union. One and all, they were terrified by the very thought of Russian vengeance once the Red Army entered their capital city. With this in mind, the remaining strength of the Wehrmacht had been concentrated during the final weeks of the War along the Eastern Front. Thus the Russians did not even get across the Oder River until one of Eisenhower's rapidly moving armies was within fifty miles of Berlin. Farther south, Allied forces were also rolling into Czechoslovakia with comparative ease, heading for Prague—the only other capital city anywhere in eastern or central Europe that was not already in Russian hands. Then, at this critical moment, for reasons which the western world could not understand, Eisenhower's great offensive slowed down and waited—deliberately waited for Stalin's soldiers to take both Berlin and Prague.

The Communists Show their Hand

While the Allied armies were winning the final battles of the War, a bitter quarrel developed between the Western Powers and the Soviet Union over the meaning of the Yalta Declaration. Almost before the ink was dry on the agreements signed by the Big Three, the communsts had shown their hand in Bulgaria and Romania.

Although he did not say so, Stalin clearly revealed that he regarded these two countries as his private preserve and that as far as he was concerned, the Declaration on Liberated Europe did not apply to either of them. In February, Soviet agents moved in, demanding the establishment of completely communist governments. With the Red Army displaying its power in the streets of Sofia and Bucharest, Bulgaria and Romania unwillingly became the first Soviet satellites. Likewise, when the Red Army reached Vienna in March, Stalin set up a provisional government to his own liking and prohibited American or British observers from entering the country. Later on, the Western Powers were able to checkmate Soviet ambitions in Austria, but not before this hapless country had been exploited by a decade of partial Russian occupation.

It was over Poland, however, that the Big Three quarrelled most violently. As Churchill has written: 'This was the test case between us and the Russians of the meaning of such terms as democracy, sovereignty, independence, representative government and free and unfettered elections.' Despite almost endless meetings, the Lublin Committee was not enlarged to include other Polish leaders. All these men, so Foreign Secretary Molotov insisted in harsh and unyielding terms, were anti-communists and anti-Russians and therefore completely unacceptable to the Soviet Union. Russia had to have security on her western borders and she simply could not take a chance on a hostile government being established in Poland. Although admitting the weaknesses of the Polish government in London, Churchill and to a lesser extent Roosevelt tried in vain during these final months of the War to persuade Stalin to allow free elections in Poland. Making matters much worse, the Soviet Union claimed that the Lublin Committee should represent Poland at the forthcoming San Francisco Conference. When Great Britain and the United States refused pointblank to accept this suggestion, the Russians threatened to boycott the Conference and for a while it seemed that this important part of the Yalta Declaration was also going to be violated.

Nor would the Soviet Union allow British and American missions into Poland to observe what was going on behind the advancing Red Army. Dark stories came out of Poland in those days—stories of revenge against the conquered Germans, of Polish 'democrats' assassinating Russian army officers and of Soviet reprisals among the enemies of the Lublin government. There seems to be very little doubt, however, that things were done by both sides in Poland to make the western world shudder with horror. It should be noted here that the Polish people were given no chance to express themselves until two years after the War and by that time it was too late. In an election that was neither free nor unfettered, the Lublin government was upheld by a great majority of the voters.

It may be seen that Churchill's worst fears of communist Russia seemed to be confirmed in the weeks following the Yalta Conference. Under these circumstances, he suggested time and again to both Roosevelt and Eisenhower that the final Allied offensive should be directed towards Berlin and Prague. With Germany practically defeated anyway, nothing else mattered but securing these two political prizes. 'We must,' he said, 'shake hands with the Russians as far to the East as possible.' Only in this way could Great Britain and the United States regain the bargaining power they had lost and perhaps force Stalin to respect his pledges. The American leaders, however, turned a deaf ear to all of Churchill's pleadings. For reasons that were not in keeping with the facts, they stuck to their original narrow military plans and refused to race the Red Army into either Berlin or Prague. When President Roosevelt died on April 12, the British Prime Minister—after pausing to pay tribute to 'the greatest American friend we ever had'—addressed his case to the inexperienced Harry Truman. The new President, however, had no choice but to follow the advice of his Chiefs of Staff and they persisted in opposing Churchill's plans. Thus the Allied armies were halted, or diverted to mopping up almost non-existent Nazi forces, at the very moment when they could easily have captured the capital cities of both Germany and Czechoslovakia.

The clash between the communist and non-communist world would have occurred, of course, regardless of how the western Allies had fought the final stages of the War. However, the lack of a far-sighted policy in Washington and the indifference of the American High Command to Churchill's warnings gave the Soviet Union a headstart in the post-war struggle for power in Europe. By the time hostilities ceased in Europe, the territories under Russian control included parts of Finland, the three Baltic states, all of Germany east of the Elbe River, all of Poland and Czechoslovakia, a large part of Austria and the whole of Hungary, Romania and Bulgaria. All the great capitals of central Europe—Warsaw, Berlin, Prague, Vienna, Budapest, Bucharest and Sofia—were in the grasp of the Red Army. Around this vast area, an iron curtain of secrecy and suspicion was drawn down by the Soviet Union, dividing East from West even before the guns were silenced. And so, this chapter is called 'Triumph and Tragedy': triumph because the Grand Alliance won the battles; tragedy because it failed in peace.

The Quest of Ages

Victory in Europe
On the night of April 26, 1945, Benito Mussolini and a handful of faithful fascist followers tried to escape across the Alps into Switzerland. Disguised in German uniforms, they joined one of the many Nazi convoys fleeing before the advancing armies of General Alexander. But the party was stopped by border patrols, and *il Duce* was recognized and taken away to prison. Others in the group, including his mistress, Clara Petacci, were also placed in custody. The next morning she and Mussolini were dragged out and brutally shot by Italian partisans who had decided to take the law into their own hands. That same morning an American lieutenant crawled out to the middle of a wrecked bridge across the Elbe River and shook hands with a Russian officer who had wriggled his way out from the other side. Thus the armies of the Western Powers and the Soviet Union met and the ring of death closed round Nazi Germany. Two days later, in an underground

shelter amid the ruins of what was once Berlin, Adolf Hitler shot himself through the mouth and his mistress, Eva Braun, poisoned herself beside him. According to instruction, the two bodies were burnt in the courtyard and 'Hitler's funeral pyre, with the din of Russian guns growing ever louder, made a lurid end of the Third Reich.'

Now even the most fanatical knew that further resistance was hopeless. Commencing on the Italian front, local Nazi commanders threw in the sponge one after another until finally, on May 8, Hitler's successor, Admiral Doenitz, unconditionally surrendered the remaining land, sea and air forces of Germany to General Eisenhower. Some parts of the world burst out into tumultuous rejoicing, but in the United States V-E day celebrations were tempered by the thought of Japan, while millions of destitute, hungry and homeless people in ravaged Europe had no room in their heart for any real joy. There was also the deeply disturbing prospect—becoming more apparent every day—that the freedom-loving people of the world might have sacrificed in vain. Having helped to defeat the evil forces of Hitlerism, would justice and law prevail in Europe or was some new form of tyranny threatening to replace the German invader? A wonderful spirit of fellowship and co-operation had been achieved by the Great Powers during the war years. Would this unity last or was the Grand Alliance going to fall to pieces now that all the battles had been won and the common foe defeated?

The Charter of the United Nations

All the battles had not been won. The greatest enemies of mankind—ignorance, poverty, intolerance, racial distrust, injustice, national selfishness and insecurity—the basic causes for war had yet to be conquered. Here, then, was a tremendous challenge for the nations to unite in combating the material and spiritual foes of human welfare. If this call to battle aroused their enthusiasm and if they devoted their best abilities to waging it successfully, the people of the United Nations, co-operating in peace as in war, might win the most important victory of all. Facing up to this challenge, the Big Three, as we know, had arranged at Yalta to hold an international conference to draft a charter for the new world peace organization.

On April 25, 1945, therefore, with Nazi Germany on the verge of collapse and with flags flying at half-mast in honour of Franklin Roosevelt, delegates from the forty-six United Nations held their first meeting in San Francisco's Memorial Opera House. Among the two hundred statesmen from every race and clime were such distinguished figures as Britain's Foreign Secretary Anthony Eden; Edward Stettinius, the recently appointed American Secretary of State; Field Marshal Smuts, South Africa's white-haired veteran of the Paris Peace Conference; and Russia's Foreign Commissar Molotov—whom Stalin had sent as a tribute to the memory of President Roosevelt even though the Western Powers refused to accept representatives from the satellite state of Poland. After listening to several addresses of welcome, including an extremely thoughtful one from President Truman, the delegates set about their difficult task deeply conscious that civilization must not fumble its second chance.

The United Nations General Assembly, New York

Unfortunately, the San Francisco Conference only served to widen the breach that had been growing between Russia and the Western Powers. All the most heated discussions that took place during the two months it was in session seemed to find the Soviet Union ranged against her wartime partners although she was not always to blame. The American newspapers, looking for sensational copy, invariably exaggerated and distorted the Russian point of view and thereby made matters worse than they really were. Thus Molotov and his colleagues were unjustly charged with delaying the work of the other delegates and with preventing the formation of a strong world organization. For instance, when Molotov fought against the admission of Argentina, he was accused in the press of doing nothing more than snarl back at the West because they had refused Poland's application. In actual fact, Argentina was a fascist dictatorship which had openly aided Germany all during the War and the Western Powers were probably wrong in securing membership for this turncoat Latin American republic. Likewise, the press thoughtlessly raised a rumpus when Molotov demanded seats in the new organization for the Ukraine and White Russia. Yet both Churchill and Roosevelt had accepted this request, almost without question, at the Yalta Conference. Aside from the fact that Russia had such a gigantic population, Churchill frankly agreed that, if two of the Soviet Union's sixteen states were given seats, all the members of the British Commonwealth of Nations might also be admitted without opposition.

The main source of disagreement at San Francisco, however, developed over the question of how much influence the smaller states should have in the United Nations. Here, too, Russia was accused of wanting to rule the roost although Great Britain and the United States were equally determined to concentrate power in the hands of the major wartime allies. As Churchill said at Yalta, he did not want 'the fumbling fingers of forty nations prying into the affairs of the British Empire'. Roosevelt and later Truman were also fully aware that, if the United Nations Charter gave the smaller states the right to interfere in any way with American authority, the Senate would toss it out as unceremoniously as they had the Covenant of the League of Nations. Vigorously opposing this attitude, the small nations proposed numerous amendments, resorted to delaying tactics and doggedly fought against being dominated by the Big Powers.

The charter that finally emerged represented a solid victory for the Great-Power viewpoint. Following the familiar pattern of the old League of Nations, it provided for a democratic General Assembly composed of all member states, a Security Council in which the five Great Powers had permanent seats (Great Britain, the United States, Russia, France and China) and six other states were chosen for two-year terms, and a Secretariat to carry on the daily work of administration. The General Assembly, meeting once a year, could discuss and make recommendations to the Security Council on any matter within the jurisdiction of the United Nations Organization but it had absolutely no power to compel the Council to take action. Thus it was nothing more than an international debating forum where the small powers might air their grievances. Observers seemed to believe, however, that the General Assembly, by serving as a 'town meeting of the world' would focus public opinion as an effective force and bring about greater harmony.

The Security Council, on the other hand, was given a great deal of power over all questions involving the maintenance of peace. It could employ economic or military sanctions against an aggressor or step in and enforce a settlement before any dispute reached the stage of an armed clash. However, no action could be taken to ensure peace unless all five of the permanent members were in agreement. This, of course, was the famous 'veto' provision which served notice on the world that the Big Powers would obey international authority only when it suited their interests. Events soon demonstrated their willingness to use the veto. As it turned out, the Russians employed it most often, because nations belonging to the American power bloc constituted a majority and controlled the U.N. machinery. Had the situation been reversed, the United States undoubtedly would have wielded the veto to thwart the designs of Russia and her satellites.

The United Nations Organization created at San Francisco lacked power in yet another very important way. Having no body of international law behind it, steps to settle any dispute could only be taken after prolonged debate. The Charter did not even contain a definition of what an 'aggressor' was. Therefore, no act of violence, however flagrant, automatically enabled the member states to go into action immediately. Every case had to be handled individually by the Security Council where there was the perpetual threat of the veto and the danger of Big

Power domination. Furthermore, the United Nations in the future could not correct this situation by making laws to govern the conduct of its members. Obviously, neither the Assembly nor the Security Council was qualified to be a legislating body. The voting procedure in both was so artificial that it could not be relied upon to reflect accurately the wishes of the world community. In the Assembly, where each state had one vote regardless of size, a small minority of the world's people could impose their will on the majority. In the Security Council, a single great nation, using the veto, could block any action desired by all the others. At San Francisco, much was said about the injustice of a big power like the United States or Russia having the right to veto. Very little was said about Liberia and Luxemburg, for example, having equal voting power in the Assembly with the United States and Russia.

In actual fact, neither the small powers nor the big ones were yet prepared to surrender any real authority to the United Nations. Some observers believe that things might have been different if the Conference had been held after the first atomic explosion. This, they say, might have frightened the nations into creating a much stronger organization. As is was, however, the United Nations entered the difficult post-war period possessing very little real power and relying for its success almost entirely on the voluntary co-operation of the member states. Failing this, the nations would have no choice but to fall back, once again, to the old, dangerous and costly system of seeking security through heavy armaments, alliances and the ever-present threat of a third world war.

The Fate of Germany

On July 17, about three weeks after the San Francisco Conference adjourned, the Big Three arrived in Potsdam, just outside Berlin, for their final meeting of the War. Ten troubled years were to elapse before the top leaders of Great Britain, the United States and Russia—the members of the once Grand Alliance—were to meet again. By that time Stalin was dead, memories of wartime co-operation between the three powers had faded into the past and the Cold War between the West and East was at its height. Signs that the old order was already beginning to change were apparent at Potsdam not only by the presence of the new American President replacing Roosevelt but also by the fact that the British Prime Minister brought with him Clement Attlee, the leader of the Labour party.

Shortly after Germany's surrender in May, the coalition government that had guided Britain all during the War ended when the Labour party members of it resigned. Under these circumstances Churchill had been compelled to call a general election. This election had been held on July 5, well before the Potsdam Conference, but no one knew the results. Millions of ballots were locked up in England waiting for the soldiers' vote to be gathered in from all over the world. Adding, therefore, to the suspense and uncertainty of the times was the thought that the ballot boxes would be opened and the results made known while the Potsdam Conference was in session. Although most outside observers took it for granted that the British people would reward their great leader with re-election, Prime Minister Churchill brought Attlee to Potsdam just in case.

At Potsdam the Big Three decided to retain exclusive control over what should be done with the defeated enemy states in Europe. There would not be even a pretence at holding a general peace conference of all the nations. Instead, it was agreed that a Council of Foreign Ministers representing the five Big Powers should draw up all the details of the so-called 'minor peace treaties'—meaning the ones with Italy, Hungary, Romania, Bulgaria and Finland. As for Germany, it had already been decided at Yalta that Great Britain, the United States, Russia and France should occupy and control it for an indefinite length of time. For this purpose, four occupation zones had been marked out not only for the country as a whole but also for the city of Berlin which stood entirely within the Soviet zone.

Following the general plans laid down at Yalta, the Big Three now drew up a detailed blueprint for the future administration of Germany. Germany was to be ruled by an Allied Control Council made up of the Commanders in Chief of the four powers. Each general in the Allied Control Council was to govern his country's specific zone and share in decisions concerning Germany as a whole. Unfortunately, the Big Three failed to explain what they meant by 'matters affecting Germany as a whole'. It was generally understood, however, that the people in each zone would be treated alike and that the country would be handled as one economic unit even though no central government was to be established for the time being. It was also agreed that each country could secure reparations by dismantling some of the heavy German industry in its own zone. Since the territory occupied by the Soviet Union was mainly agricultural, the Russians were authorized to take a certain amount of industrial equipment from the other three zones. As will be seen later, the attempt to govern a divided Germany according to the rules laid down at Potsdam eventually became the major source of friction between the East and West in the Cold War.

The Potsdam Conference was still in session when the time arrived to open the ballot boxes in England. Therefore, while Truman and Stalin went sightseeing among the ruins of Nazi Germany, the Prime Minister and his political rival set off home to hear the results. They were not what the outside world expected. Once the War ended the British voters apparently had begun to think in terms of secure jobs, higher wages, better housing and daily bread—things far removed from Churchill's busy and preoccupied mind. Undoubtedly more concerned with world affairs than domestic conditions, the Prime Minister had concluded a listless, uninspiring campaign. In marked contrast, the Labour party, hammering home the need for social reform, had promised the electorate a great deal of welfare legislation including government ownership or control of certain key industries. Then again, there seemed to be the feeling that Great Britain had very little chance of co-operating successfully with communist Russia as long as a man like Churchill stayed in power. And finally, faced with the constant worldwide criticism of colonialism many Englishmen began to question Churchill's faith in the continuing glories of the British Empire.

Whatever the reasons, it was Prime Minister Clement Attlee who returned to Germany for the final few days of the Potsdam Conference. The election had swept the Conservatives out of power and given the Labour party, for the first time in British history, a clear-cut majority in the House of Commons. Thus Great Britain would be governed for the next five years by a left-wing socialist party with an overwhelming mandate from the people to introduce its radical program. And Winston Churchill, frankly admitting that he neither expected nor relished the role, would have to be content to be the leader of the opposition.

The End of a Familiar Era

During the Potsdam Conference a cablegram arrived for President Truman containing the words, 'Babies satisfactorily born.' This meant that the American team of scientists, headed by Dr. Robert Oppenheimer, had won the race against time, the experiment in the New Mexican desert had been successful, and the atomic bomb was a reality. Man had taken the first big step towards harnessing the basic power of the universe and invented a weapon that would not only revolutionize warfare but could alter the course of history and civilization. This meant also that the United States now had the power to end the War in one or two gigantic blows instead of conquering Japan yard by yard as everyone had feared they might have to do. Without any hesitation, therefore, the Big Three sent an ultimatum, known as the Potsdam Declaration, demanding that Japan should surrender unconditionally. The Declaration did not mention the atomic bomb but its last sentence warned: 'The alternative for Japan is prompt and utter destruction.'

The fanatic Japanese militarists, apparently prepared to commit their nation to mass suicide rather than accept unconditional surrender, publicly announced they would 'ignore' the Potsdam Declaration. On the sixth of August, therefore, a lone B-29 flew over Hiroshima, a city of 343,000 people, and dropped a small bomb with the destructive force of 20,000 tons of TNT. The bomb descended on a little parachute and exploded before it landed. Hiroshima was instantly obscured by a great rolling cloud of dust and smoke. When it settled, sixty per cent of the city was gone and 173,000 people were dead or dying. President Truman now issued another surrender ultimatum to the dazed Japanese. This, too, was ignored and on the ninth of August, a second, more powerful atomic bomb was dropped on the city of Nagasaki. The same day the Soviet Union, fulfilling its long-standing Yalta promise, declared war on Japan and thereby earned an easy seat at any Far Eastern peace conference. Faced now with destruction such as the world had never known, the Japanese agreed to accept the Potsdam Declaration and on Tuesday, August 14, simultaneous announcements from Washington, London and Moscow proclaimed that the Second World War was over.

Within minutes of President Truman's announcement, the American people, no longer restrained, burst out from their homes to celebrate V-J day. Across the whole nation, all the traditional signs of victory—church bells, factory whistles, fire sirens and skyrockets—flared and rang and shrieked. Delirious paraders snake-danced through the streets, played leapfrog up and down the boulevards, commandeered streetcars and buses and hung Hirohito from dozens of lamp-

General Douglas MacArthur and Admiral Chester Nimitz board the U.S.S. Missouri *to accept the unconditional surrender of Japan.*

posts. New York City, hardly unaccustomed to noise and furor, surpassed itself. As one reported described it: 'With the first flash of V-J, up went the windows and down came the torn telephone books, the hats, bottle, bolts of silk, books, waste-baskets and shoes—more than five thousand tons of jubilant litter. Whole families made their way to Times Square until two million people were milling about, breaking into snatches of songs, hugging and kissing anybody in sight, greeting each twinkle of news on the *Times* electric sign with a cheer that roared from the East River to the Hudson. The celebrations swirled on into the dawn, died down, broke out again next afternoon and finally subsided only with another midnight.'

And yet, in a way, this jubilant carnival mood did not ring quite true. The crowds were almost too gay—as if they were trying to forget what had happened just a few days earlier to Hiroshima and Nagasaki. Indeed, over all the victory celebrations, according to observers both in the United States and elsewhere, the fact of the atomic bomb 'hung like some eerie haze from another world'. People seemed to sense, even in their joy, that this was the end not only of the War but also of a familiar era, and the beginning of the new, uncertain Atomic Age.

The most devastating of all conflicts had concluded in a holocaust so terrifying that men and women everywhere realized humanity could not survive another war.

Fire in the Ashes

Russia Spurns the West

If ever a statesman threw away golden opportunities to advance the interests of his own country, it was Joseph Stalin during the last eight years of his life. At V-J day, the Russian dictator stood victorious in Europe and Asia, allied in friendship with the only other powerful nation left in the world. Due to the Soviet Union's magnificent fight against Nazi Germany, he possessed the gratitude and respect of the United Nations. In eastern Europe, his armies occupied poverty-stricken agricultural countries where the simple logic of communism held a magic appeal for millions of downtrodden, ignorant peasants. Throughout the rest of torn and weary Europe, other millions of bombed-out, uprooted industrial workers were also ripe for communism. Yugoslavia had already yielded to its attractions without external pressure, Czechoslovakia was tottering, while in France, Italy and Greece at least one-third of the population—as free elections were later to show —now believed that democracy would never bring their children good food, good schools and sunlit homes. Combined with the ravages of war, the long-standing social decay of these three countries with their endless party squabbles, their inefficiency, their miserable wages and squalid slums—made uglier in each case by the extravagance and luxury of the rich—had created a class of men who had lost all faith in the western way of life. Thus, if Stalin had played his cards correctly, all these dissatisfied and disillusioned elements in Europe might have turned willingly to the Soviet Union for leadership and help.

But years of dictatorial authority in a harsh totalitarian state had closed Stalin's mind to any possibility of working co-operatively with the people of other nations. As soon as the War was over, therefore, he or Molotov or whoever wielded power within the mystery-shrouded Kremlin, ruthlessly completed the Soviet domination of eastern Europe which had begun at Yalta. The timetable varied from state to state but by the end of 1946 all vestige of freedom had been stamped out in Poland, Romania, Hungary and Bulgaria; scores of political opponents had been imprisoned or liquidated; and the goodwill which Russia might have retained had given way to festering hatred. In turn, the sad fate of these countries began to disturb many thousands of would-be communists in France, Italy and Czechoslovakia.

More alarming than Stalin's aggression in Europe, however, was the behaviour of his representatives in the United Nations and the Council of Foreign Ministers. In the U.N., Russian spokesmen used the veto incessantly to choke off investigation into communist activities in various parts of the world; they obstructed the formation of an international police force; sabotaged all efforts to set up controls over atomic energy; staged stormy walkouts and used the platforms of the world peace organizations to denounce 'capitalist, imperialist, warmongering' United

States in violent and abusive language. Although justice occasionally lay on her side, the Soviet Union clearly revealed a deep-seated distrust of the western world and a haughty contempt for the United Nations. Likewise, Molotov dragged his colleagues in the Council of Foreign Ministers through seemingly endless hours of nagging, futile debate about the treaties to be signed with Italy, Romania, Bulgaria, Hungary and Finland. Eventually, after many months of wrangling, the five minor treaties were drafted and approved and 'peace' was officially restored to most of Europe. As might be expected and as Churchill foresaw during the war years, the Western Powers achieved their aims only in North Africa and Italy—that is, in the areas liberated by their armies—while Soviet ambitions were legally confirmed throughout all of eastern Europe.

America Becomes Alert

For about a year and a half after V-J day, President Truman and his advisers, following the Roosevelt tradition, were reluctant to admit that they had made a mistake about Russia. Furthermore, with wartime savings bulging their bank accounts, the American people were far too busy having a glorious spending spree to pay very much attention to the Soviet Union. The big football weekends roared back, television sets sold like hotcakes, and any night was likely to burst into a New Year's Eve. Regardless of controls, prices skyrocketed and black market, under-the-table deals in cars, apartments, houses, meat, whisky, sugar and many other scarce items flourished—as they did also in Canada. Despite this mounting inflation, the great mass of American citizens were living at a higher material standard than they had ever known.

According to most American observers, a large part of this boom was due, not so much to special post-war conditions as to the New Deal laws passed during the depression years. Welfare legislation helped to fill the weekly pay envelopes; state control gave the trade unions their new-found power to bargain with the big corporations and secure better wages and working conditions; federal subsidies to agriculture allowed the farmer to buy more machinery and send his sons to college. In these and many other ways, the New Deal seemed to be fulfilling the dreams of a bygone era. But could all this welfare legislation be carried too far? Was there a danger that the American people might lose their drive and initiative and adopt the attitude that the world owed them a living? Would they expect, like some of the British under the Labour party, that the government should protect them 'from the cradle to the grave'? A great many Americans, disgusted with the incessant levelling tendencies of democracy and resenting the high taxes and government controls required by the welfare state, were beginning to think so. Speaking out for this group, Republican Senator Robert Taft said: 'We have got to break with the corrupting idea that we can legislate prosperity, legislate equality, legislate opportunity. All these good things came in the past from free Americans freely working out their own destiny.' To conservative men like Taft, New Deal legislation, with all its handouts and controls, was simply creeping socialism—and from socialism to communism was only a step.

Consequently, when President Truman, calling his program the Fair Deal, began to introduce even more social benefits for the masses—such as old age pensions and unemployment insurance—his political opponents, led by the 'Old Guard' in the Republican party, set out to beat him at all costs. New Dealers, Fair Dealers, supporters of Roosevelt or Truman, liberals who advocated almost any kind of reform were denounced as socialists, pinks, reds, fellow travellers, communists and even traitors. This witch hunt was partly a genuine attempt to weed out communist agents from the American government and partly a frustrated reaction to the feeling that Stalin had hoodwinked them at Yalta. In addition, the crusade against communist Russia was also an indirect attack on the whole reform movement in the United States. Whether or not this attack was justified, the fact remains that domestic party politics led the American government to be more intolerant of Soviet behaviour than they should have been at certain critical times.

However, even without these internal quarrels, it was inevitable, once the Grand Alliance broke up, that capitalistic United States and communist Russia should become the giants in the post-war struggle for power. Gradually, therefore, amid all the excitement of their spending spree, the American people became more and more conscious of the Soviet Union. Always the Russians pushed their way into every discussion. In and out of Washington, people now spoke not only of Churchill's 'Iron Curtain' but also, more ominously, of the 'East-West clash'. And then, Bernard Baruch, whose plan for the control of atomic energy had been disdained by Russia, said in the course of a public address: 'Let us not be deceived —today we are in the midst of a cold war.' Overnight, this phrase, so aptly describing the situation, caught on with the American people and the 'Cold War' became a commonplace in their language. By the beginning of the year 1947, they were ready to believe that the United States faced not simply the threat of war with another country but a vast conflict involving their entire way of life.

The Crusade against Communism
America's fear of Russia and her determination to prevent the further spread of communism first became apparent in faraway Greece and Turkey. Since before V-E day British troops had been stationed in those two countries to bolster up the existing governments and keep the native communist movement under control. This task had been especially difficult in Greece where large bands of communist guerrillas received a steady flow of supplies from Russia's satellite states in the Balkans. In February 1947, Great Britain, deciding she could no longer carry this burden, advised the United States that she was pulling her troops out of both Greece and Turkey. At this time, she was not only garrisoning her zone in Germany and feeding starving Germans but also had troops in North Africa, in turbulent Egypt and Palestine, in Burma, Malaya and Hong Kong. Furthermore, violent winter storms had disrupted her already strained economy, paralysing her business life, causing her people to shiver in their homes like mediaeval peasants, and forcing Attlee's government to face the fact that the Empire now overtaxed Britain's strength. As will be seen later, the decision to leave Greece and Turkey

was but the first in a series of events which compelled Great Britain to abandon her long-standing imperial position in Burma, India, Palestine and Egypt.

Without British support, it was almost certain that Greece would fall under Soviet influence, the independence of Turkey would be undermined and the whole eastern Mediterranean might be sucked in behind the Iron Curtain. Faced with this prospect, President Truman went before Congress and, in a speech which his advisers had deliberately designed 'to scare hell out of the nation', demanded $400 million for economic and military aid to Greece and Turkey. Using words which immediately became known as the Truman Doctrine, he stressed that the time had come for the United States to support any country resisting the advance of communism.

The Truman Doctrine, however, backfired in some parts of the world and in the United States. Since the government of Greece at the time had a reputation for corruption and oppression, it appeared that the Americans were pouring money down the drain. Because American officials tried to supervise how the dollars were spent, it seemed that the United States was trying to secure economic control of other countries. Above all, it seemed to many critics that the United States was simply using small, troubled nations as pawns in a gigantic contest with the Soviet Union. What kind of foreign policy would avoid these difficulties and at the same time halt communist expansion? Perhaps wisely, Truman's policy planners did not see the problem primarily as a military one. It seemed to them that worldwide disturbances were being caused, not by communist activity but by poverty, wartime devastation and other conditions which would be exploited by some kind of dictatorship even if no Reds existed. The sensible program for the United States, therefore, was to use her vast wealth, without any strings attached, to repair the ravages of war, end unemployment and misery and bring prosperity back to western Europe.

This new proposal was announced in June 1947 by General George Marshall, who had been Roosevelt's highly esteemed Chief of Staff during the War and was at this time the American Secretary of State. The Marshall Plan offered financial help to all European countries, including Russia and her satellites, provided they would get together, make arrangements for mutual assistance and send a detailed statement of their joint needs to Washington. The Soviet Union—suspecting that this was another American attempt to crack open the Iron Curtain and wreck Russian power in eastern Europe—scoffed at the Marshall Plan and refused to let any of her satellites take part in it. Led by France and Britain, however, the other European nations eagerly accepted the offer, arranged to meet in Paris during the summer and eventually presented a list of requirements amounting to over $22 billion. Staggered by this figure, Senator Taft and other American politicians protested that the nation would go bankrupt and grumbled loudly about 'Global New Deals' and huge handouts to countries that would not lift a finger to help themselves. For a time, the Marshall Plan was in danger, but early in 1948 a communist upheaval destroyed the remnants of freedom in Czechoslovakia and this, combined with the growing menace of communism in Italy, frightened Congress into passing the necessary legislation. From then on, with American dollar aid pouring across the Atlantic, the nations of western Europe began their long and successful uphill struggle towards post-war prosperity.

By its very threat to revive prosperity, the Marshall Plan destroyed the basic Russian assumption that communism would spread naturally and inevitably throughout the ruins of wartorn Europe. All their delaying tactics had been designed to prevent recovery and now wealthy, capitalistic America had frustrated them. Feared and hated by the men in the Kremlin, the Marshall Plan therefore completed the rupture between Russia and the United States. When it became law, the genial, beaming face of Stalin that westerners had come to know during and immediately after the War took on its former grim and steely lines. The once-voluble Molotov became rigidly silent. The countries receiving American dollars did less and less business with eastern Europe until eventually all trade ceased. Behind the Iron Curtain, now more impenetrable than ever before, the number of arrests and executions increased as the Soviet Union bound the satellites more closely to herself. Russian aid to the communists in China, negligible up to this point, began to pour across the border and the Comintern, an international organization to promote world communism, was revived. Perhaps above all in importance was the fact that the Council of Foreign Ministers gave up trying to make a peace settlement for divided Germany. As General Marshall warned the Russians, the period of talk was over and the time for action had come.

Action, not Words

While Congress was debating the wisdom of the Marshall Plan, it became apparent that the most difficult and probably the most dangerous issue separating Russia from the West was the question of Germany. Regarding the Third Reich as a conquered nation to be looted without mercy, the Soviet Union had refused from the beginning to co-operate with the other three occupying Powers. In direct violation of the Potsdam agreement, the Russians sealed off the Eastern Zone with a wall of secrecy and terror, they savagely pumped out reparations without telling the Allies what they were taking, and they throttled the food supplies that normally feed West German cities. Under these circumstances, the United States and Great Britain felt justified in refusing to let the Soviet Union have her promised share of reparations from the Western Zones. And once this happened, any further hope for a settlement was out of the question.

Since all attempts to manage Germany as a single economic unit thus failed, the whole country remained in an appalling condition, doomed, it seemed, to be a charity case for Great Britain and the United States. The forlorn people who lived in the ruins of Hitler's Germany could feel little beyond hunger. Unhealthy children, bloated with starvation, roamed the streets clad in the cut-down Wehrmacht jackets of their fathers. White-faced men and women collapsed at their jobs for lack of food. As late as 1947, even the conquerors' statistics showed that the daily German ration was thirty-three per cent below the minimum necessary to sustain life. The search for shelter was a nightmare; almost half the homes in Germany had been destroyed yet the country was being forced to absorb 8 million refugees thrust into it from behind the Iron Curtain. Here and there across Germany lay little pockets of unscarred land, but the highways that ran from town to town were torn and ruptured by the passage of war, tanks had disembowelled the roadbeds, artillery and planes had shattered the bridges. The major cities were little more than heaps of stone and brick, rank with the smell of sewage and filth. Eighty-two per cent of all industry stood idle and in ruins. Money was meaningless; cigarettes, candy bars and other simple American products were currency. While the British and American military governors viewed this whole situation with deep sympathy and tried to do something about it, the Soviet Union played for time, hoping that the German people in their despair, might turn to communism.

As long as this state of affairs continued, the Marshall Plan had very little chance for success. Great Britain, the United States and even France realized that a western Europe strong enough to resist Soviet aggression was impossible unless Germany became prosperous and united. Consequently in the spring of 1948, shortly after the Marshall Plan was put into operation, the Western Powers agreed to unite their zones completely and invited German politicians to form a central government for the whole area. This was, of course, another violation of the Potsdam agreement but, as Marshall had said, it was time for action, not words. The Russians, also realizing how important German recovery was to all of western Europe, retaliated by blockading the roads and railways running from the West into Berlin. Their objective was not to make the Allies leave the former capital city but, by threatening to starve its 2½ million people, to prevent the formation of a united Western Germany.

Under these trying and very dangerous circumstances—with the world holding its breath lest some 'incident' should touch off a full-scale war—the British and American air forces began the famous airlift into Berlin. Day and night for almost exactly a year, landing one a minute on the runways, Allied planes fed the people of Berlin until the Russians, recognizing defeat, finally called off the blockade. Because the airlift involved so many human beings and was clothed in such vivid drama, most observers regard it as the turning point in the history of post-war Germany. As one historian has written: 'It was not simply that the American pilots enjoyed the thought of dumping bags of candy for Berlin's children over the roofs as they came in to land. It was that in Berlin, Americans and Germans stood together, both facing a common enemy. Emotionally, they were allies.'

Having won the airlift, the Allies proceeded to set up the Federal Republic of Germany, with its capital at Bonn, and the German people elected Konrad Adenauer as their chancellor. In return, the Russians organized their zone into the satellite German Democratic Republic and the division of Germany that we know today was complete. Strange as it may seem, western Germany at present is the strongest and healthiest of European states and her former conquerors now court her friendship. Although the Allies vowed at Potsdam never to allow German rearmament, the Bonn government possesses a strong army and Heinkel, Messerschmidt, Krupp and others are back in the munitions business with the Western Powers' support and blessing.

A Balance of Power in Europe

As a result of the breakdown in negotiations over Germany and the increasing tension arising from the Berlin airlift, the non-communist world became increasingly aware of the twenty-two combat divisions that the Russians had stationed in East Germany. During the troubled months of 1948, there seemed to be the danger that the Soviet army might surge westward to take by force what the Russians were losing by purely economic warfare. There was no military power capable of halting such an advance once it started. 'All the Russians need to reach the English Channel,' one American spokesman observed, 'is shoes.' Realizing that

The boundaries of Europe are changed again as Russian influence spreads westward.

■ NATO *countries*
■ Soviet *satellites*
▨ Yugoslavia — Communist State but neutral

the Marshall Plan was not enough, the Western Powers therefore decided to create a definite military alliance which would restore the balance of power. The first step in this direction was taken in March 1948, when Great Britain, France and the Benelux countries (Belgium, the Netherlands and Luxemburg), acting under the guidance of Ernest Bevin, Britain's Foreign Secretary, signed a fifty-year mutual assistance pact. Known as the Brussels Treaty, the agreement committed these five countries to aid each other if any one of them was attacked. Although the Americans were elated with this development and immediately made plans to support and extend it, no real action could be taken during the remaining part of the year because the United States was involved in another presidential election. Once this was over—and President Truman, to almost everyone's complete surprise, had been elected for another four-year term—the Western Powers acted quickly.

On April 4, 1949, after a series of preliminary conferences, the Brussels Pact countries plus Norway, Denmark, Iceland, Portugal, Italy, Canada and the United States met in Washington to sign the North Atlantic Treaty. Later on, the alliance was still further extended to include Greece, Turkey and the Federal Republic of Germany. While the preliminary clauses contained some eloquent references to economic and political co-operation and paid lip service to the continuing value of the United Nations, the treaty was primarily a military agreement binding fifteen nations to support each other in case of war. As a result, the signatory powers created the North Atlantic Treaty Organization with a European command under General Eisenhower and a permanent secretariat, located in Paris, to co-ordinate the military efforts of 365 million people. Although continually hampered by differences of opinion among the member states, the North Atlantic Treaty Organization, urged on and financed mainly by the United States, gradually built up its land, sea and air forces and became another bulwark against the spread of communism.

Thus the NATO countries, under relentless pressure from the Soviet Union, were forced into relying once more on alliances, balance of power, heavy armaments and the constant threat of war to protect their way of life. Within four short years of V-J day, co-operative diplomacy through the United Nations had failed and the age-old search for peace had been turned back along the old familiar paths—paths which in the past have led inevitably to war. It is impossible, of course, to predict whether the genius and goodwill of man, combined with the fear of modern thermonuclear weapons, will solve the problem this time or whether the old methods will produce the same old fatal consequences. All that may be said with certainty is that the North Atlantic Treaty Organization, along with the Truman Doctrine, the Marshall Plan, the unification of Western Germany and other measures served their immediate purpose and checked the power of the Soviet Union in Europe. But while these policies were being successfully applied against Russia, dangerous pressures were building up in other areas. At the mid-century mark, these pent-up forces burst out in a series of turbulent events that almost completely obscured Europe and focused world attention on the Near and Far East.

The Explosive East

Zionist Victory in the Near East

During the winter months of 1946, boatloads of Jewish refugees, uprooted in Europe and unwanted elsewhere, were prevented by the British navy from landing in Palestine. All the entry visas, so the British government said, had been used up, but an angry and sympathetic world, remembering the frightful wartime suffering endured by the Jews, refused to accept such a simple explanation. Dramatic newspaper stories headlined the tragedy of barring these people from their traditional homeland. Photographs of sleek destroyers challenging little overcrowded transport vessels covered the front pages and helped to arouse public opinion, especially in the United States, against Great Britain. And yet, cruel and heartless though this action seemed to be, there was a good reason for it. The British now realized, after years of bitter experience, that Zionist ambitions to create an independent Jewish state in Palestine—where the Arabs still out-numbered the Jews by three to one—would upset the Near East and possibly turn the whole Arab world, with its 40 million people, against the Western Powers. British officials also knew that no native communist movement existed anywhere in the Near East and that the Arabs had a basic, mainly religious, distrust for the teachings of Lenin and Marx. Consequently, it seemed to them that Russian influence could be kept out of this vital region as long as the West remained on friendly terms with the Arab leaders. With all this in mind, Great Britain not only hoped to prevent Jewish refugees from flooding into her mandate in Palestine but also resisted the efforts of France to regain control over Syria and Lebanon. Thus, in time, the long-cherished Arab plan for a united nation composed of Syria, Lebanon and Palestine might have been fulfilled.

This prospect for a reasonably stable Arab world was thrown away when American political leaders, Republican and Democrat alike, demanded that 100,000 Jewish refugees should be admitted into Palestine without delay. Prompted though they may have been by sincere compassion for the refugees, there is little doubt that the political power of the Zionists and the large number of Jewish voters in New York State and Illinois also provided this somewhat unwarranted interference. Faced with irritating criticism from the United States and compelled to carry out a distasteful policy, the British finally decided to get rid of their responsibilities in Palestine. In April 1947, about two months after withdrawing her troops from Greece and Turkey, Great Britain, therefore, tossed the complex Arab-Jewish quarrel into the lap of the United Nations and announced that her mandate would be terminated in twelve months' time. After many weeks of discussion, during which the American government advanced no less than seven different solutions, the United Nations proposed to divide Palestine into two microscopic little countries. A United Nations Commission was to define the exact boundaries and supervise the area for a year. The detailed partition terms were so unfair to the Arab majority that a good deal of American pressure was necessary before the Security Council approved the plan and even then, as the *Times* said, 'the scheme would have been carried in no other city but New York.'

In May 1948, the Jews in Palestine beat the gun and proclaimed the independent state of Israel before the United Nations Commission had even left Lake Success. And President Truman, with a national election coming up in the near future, clinched matters and ended all discussion by recognizing the new state almost before it was born. However, a league of Arab countries, led by Egypt, Syria and Jordan, refused to accept this situation and immediately declared war on the Israelis. Crippled by internal rivalries and poor organization, the Arab League proved no match for the small but highly trained Israeli forces. Early in 1949, therefore, despite their vast superiority in numbers, the Arabs admitted defeat and allowed the United Nations to arrange an uneasy ceasefire by which they recognized, in fact if not in theory, the Jewish conquest of most of Palestine. During the fighting, six or seven hundred thousand Arabs fled the country or were driven out into Jordan, Syria and Egypt. Here, even to this day, these homeless victims of war and guerrilla violence exist in squalid tent camps on whatever care the United Nations can afford to give them.

The Arab League apparently had no intention of maintaining peace with Israel. Bound more closely together by their common hatred for the Jews, they soon began to build up their strength and plot revenge. Their ambitions led them to seek military help from Russia and this, in turn, sparked a whole series of events which electrified the western world and greatly weakened its influence through the Near and Middle East. Meanwhile, during the five years following the Arab-Israeli truce in 1949, international attention was diverted away from the Mediterranean to China and the Far East.

The Red Yellow Peril

In 1948, while tension over the Berlin airlift and the Arab-Israeli war was at its height, the American people became increasingly aware that news reports from the Far East were getting more and more ominous. The Chinese communists, having conquered Manchuria, were pushing farther and farther southward; General Chiang Kai-shek's armies were in chaotic retreat; Chiang himself had fled to Formosa and a squat, peasant-faced man named Mao Tse-tung seemed to be rising to prominence. And then suddenly, on August 5, 1949, every newspaper, every radio and television station confirmed the Americans' worst fears. The government had issued a 'White Paper' officially admitting that vast China with its 600 or so million people and the greatest potential market on earth, had fallen to the communists.

Chiang and his advisers, so the White Paper said, had only themselves to blame, but a thoroughly alarmed and frustrated America refused to accept this explanation. Somewhere, somehow along the line, the government of the United States, so everyone seemed to feel, had made a tragic mistake. Americans had always regarded China as their special overseas mission. As with the British in Africa and

Soldiers of the Communist People's Liberation Army on guard against renewed Japanese invasion, on a stretch of the Great Wall of China.

India, a mixture of hard-headed business reasons and a certain amount of genuine idealism had persuaded them that it was their duty to help feed the Chinese, to educate them, to convert them and nudge them along to an American democratic way of life. Their interest in China had led them step by step towards Pearl Harbor. To drive the Japanese out of China, they had expended untold treasure and given the lives of thousands of their sons. And yet now, just four years after the War, all their tremendous efforts seemed to have been in vain. General Chiang Kai-shek, their man, the leader from whom Americans expected so much, was beaten and Mao's communist party, hostile to everything the United States stood for, controlled the entire country.

In the minds of most Americans, there was now the grave danger that the communist leaders of China and Russia, working hand-in-glove, would form an anti-western Asiatic alliance dominating one-quarter of the earth's surface and more than a quarter of its people. The old 'yellow peril' that had haunted the United States in the days before the Second World War was revived in a new and more terrifying form. Very few people in the United States foresaw the possibility that some day the clash between Soviet and Chinese ambitions in the Far East would split these two giants apart. American fears were greatly intensified less than two months after the fall of China, when President Truman announced to his daily press conference: 'We have evidence that in recent weeks an atomic explosion occurred in the Soviet Union.' Ever since Hiroshima, western scientists had been predicting that Russia could not possibly discover the secrets of the atomic bomb until at least 1952. Yet here it was, three years ahead of schedule, stripping the American people of whatever security they felt behind their atomic stockpile.

The opponents of the Roosevelt-Truman administration now got busy. The New Dealers, pinks and pro-communists in the government, so these critics claimed, had overemphasized the evils of Chiang's regime and had pictured Mao, not as a dangerous communist, but as a simple, honest reformer trying to help the Chinese people. Being sympathetic to Mao, officials in the State Department had closed their eyes to the fact that he was nothing more than a tool in the hands of the Soviet Union. But above all, it was the 'Great Betrayal' at Yalta which had assured Mao's final victory. The Red Army of the Soviet Union, occupying Manchuria with Roosevelt's consent, had turned over vast quantities of captured Japanese weapons to their Chinese comrades and had established flourishing communist communities before withdrawing in 1946. This, more than anything else, had given Mao the strength he never should have had and allowed him to sweep the Nationalist armies into the sea.

The people in the United States have spilt more ink and expended more oratory trying to settle these questions than on any other event in the entire history of American foreign policy, and the arguments between them are far from settled even yet. From the welter of conflicting evidence, however, certain tentative conclusions seem to emerge. First of all, Chiang Kai-shek never lost a battle for lack of military supplies which the United States might have provided. Any advantage the Chinese Reds secured from Japanese weapons turned over to them by Russia was more than balanced by some $4 billion of American aid which reached Chiang between V-J day and 1949. By the time the Soviet Union, angered by the Marshall Plan, began to support Mao openly the Nationalists were already in full flight. It seems likely that the Chinese Reds would have won the Civil War without Russian help and even if there had never been a Yalta Conference.

The Nationalists had completely lost the confidence of the Chinese people. Chiang's government was riddled with inefficiency and corruption, torn by international dissension, and apparently not interested in the welfare of the masses. Chiang himself was extremely dictatorial and his officials used the cruellest of police measures to ferret out and crush their opponents. Yet they failed to suppress the gangsters, the food hoarders or the speculators and, in many cases, were actually in alliance with them. The communist party, on the other hand, was carefully recruited, highly trained and led by men of fanatical zeal. Their armies were well fed and well disciplined and their treatment of the populace stood in striking and favourable contrast to that of the hordes who served the Nationalists. Mao's officials, unlike most of Chiang's, ate and lived simply, were hard-working and devoted to what they believed to be the welfare of the people. Although the Chinese Reds received encouragement from the Soviet Union, they won the Civil War in China because they secured, and to a large measure deserved, popular support among the masses.

The Korean War

A People's Republic of China, modelled after the Soviet Union, was established at Peking, countless photographs of Mao and Stalin tacked up across the country proclaimed their friendship for Russia, foreigners were driven out, their property confiscated, and a frenzied nationalistic crusade was launched against all western influences. Then in February 1950, just as so many people feared, the new allies formalized their partnership by signing a thirty-year mutual assistance pact. Thus strengthened, Russia and China were encouraged to embark on a series of adventures, starting in Korea, which strained the United Nations to the limit of its endurance and brought the Great Powers to the brink of a third world war.

The United States and her friends had long known that Korea was a troubled spot. By mutual consent at the end of the War, the Russians had occupied North Korea while the Americans took over control in South Korea. The 38th parallel, which divided the two zones, was simply an arbitrary line hastily drawn to define areas where Japanese commanders would surrender to American or Soviet forces. Neither the United States nor Russia had the vaguest idea what to do about Korea although it was assumed that their occupation was temporary and that a unified, independent country would be formed. Unfortunately, as the Cold War developed in other parts of the world, the 38th parallel gradually hardened into a permanent boundary. In the North, the Russians set up another one of their puppet regimes which they proceeded to arm with the usual ruthless efficiency. In the South, the United States imposed democratic institutions on an unprepared populace and co-operated with the U.N. in setting up a fire-eating old nationalist named Syngman Rhee as leader of a native government favourable to the Western Powers. When the occupying armies of Russia and the United States finally withdrew in 1949, therefore, they left behind them an artificially divided and torn Korea with two rival governments, both claiming the right to rule the whole country.

No one, least of all the Koreans, regarded this division as permanent. North and South alike planned conquest but the communists, being much better prepared, beat Syngman Rhee to the punch. On June 25, 1950, the North Korean army surged across the 38th parallel, flagrantly challenging the Western Powers to try and stop them. 'It is now time,' a European diplomat cabled home from Washington, 'for Uncle Sam to put up or shut up and my guess is that he will do neither.' But the diplomat guessed incorrectly. Before the end of June, President Harry Truman, with the whole nation solidly behind him, had ordered American occupation troops to move across from Japan into Korea, had placed General Douglas MacArthur in command, and had pledged the armed might of his country to support the government of Syngman Rhee.

At the same time the American delegate to the United Nations rushed a resolution through the Security Council, condemning the communists and calling on all member nations to send aid to South Korea. This remarkable resolution was not vetoed by Russia for the simple reason that her delegate was boycotting the United Nations because it would not recognize Mao's regime in China. The fact that her delegate could have taken his seat again at any time but did not do so, leads to the conclusion that the Soviet Union was delighted to see the United States become involved in a costly war, far away from home. That American forces would bear the brunt of the fighting was quickly made clear when only sixteen of the sixty members in the United Nations accepted the invitation to assist the South Koreans. To many people living in the colonial areas of the world, the desire to be free of any foreign yoke, to be rulers of their own destiny, was a far more important issue than any fight between the West and the Soviet Union. Thus most of the Afro-Asian countries—remembering that all of their former colonial masters were included among the Western Powers—remained neutral, refusing to commit their 1½ billion people to either side. Under these circumstances, the Korean War must be regarded, not as a United Nations effort to stop aggression, but as a conflict between South Korea supported mainly by the United States, and North Korea assisted by communist China and Russia. Even so, Truman's leadership at this time was another indication of how far the American people had travelled along the road away from isolation. By rising so quickly to the challenge in Korea and by attempting to rally world opinion against aggression, the United States increased the prestige of the United Nations and may have saved it from going the way of the old League.

The original and only objective of the United Nations was to drive the communists out of Korea—a feat that General MacArthur, using the brilliant tactics for which he was already famous, accomplished after three months of savage fighting. At this point, most of the countries that had supported collective action wanted to call a halt but the United States, rightly or wrongly, was now determined to prolong the war and unite Korea by force. A very reluctant United Nations finally sanctioned the invasion of North Korea and early in October their forces crossed the 38th parallel. General MacArthur, completely misunderstanding the political situation in the Far East, assured his government that this action would not bring either Russia or China into the war. The Soviet Union was content to sit on the sidelines sending in tanks and planes, but on November 26, on the eve of western success, thirty-three Chinese divisions, screaming and shouting in warlike frenzy, swarmed all over the U.N. lines. Up and down the wild Korean gorges, in sub-zero weather and violent snowstorms, MacArthur's troops had to fight their way back to the 38th parallel. Here, despite the yellow hordes pouring into North Korea from the 'bottomless well of Chinese manpower', the United Nations managed to hold their ground and a grim stalemate settled in along the border.

To a soldier's mind, however, a stalemate is not a very good way to end a war. In direct defiance of his government, General MacArthur, therefore, openly began to advocate that the American air force should bomb Chinese bases and supply lines running into Korea and that Chiang Kai-shek's forces should be unleashed from Formosa to attack the Chinese mainland. He was not alone in his thinking, and some men still argue that the United States should have bombed China and plunged, then and there, into a full-scale war not only with Mao but also with the Soviet Union—for there is little doubt that this would have been the outcome. Perhaps they should have risked the moral

A Canadian soldier gives some food to Korean children.

judgement of the future and used the atomic bomb to blast their two gigantic oriental opponents while America still held a long lead in nuclear weapons. Many of those who supported MacArthur, who believed in a 'get really tough' policy, knew that these were the possibilities and apparently were prepared to take the chance. The American Chiefs of Staff, however, refused to accept MacArthur's plan because it would involve the United States 'in the wrong war, at the wrong time and in the wrong place'. We may go farther and say that if MacArthur had had his way, the United States might have started the first atomic war in history. This danger was not entirely eliminated until April 1951, when President Truman, justifiably incensed by MacArthur's outspoken criticism, removed the General from all his commands.

Unwilling to pull out and admit defeat, equally unwilling to take a tough course and risk a war with Russia, the Truman administration let the conflict in Korea drag on. It soon assumed a meaningless quality—the killing of a few hundred communists here when there were thousands farther north, the taking of some nameless hill only to lose it, still unnamed, a few days later. Eventually, in June 1951, peace talks were started but these, like the war itself, drifted on and on through weeks of endless, seemingly futile debate. Over a period of two years—during which men died, misery flourished in Korea, Stalin passed from the scene and the American people, tired of the Democrats, elected General Eisenhower as President of the United States—the deadlocked discussions continued in the forlorn Korean town of Panmunjom. Finally, in July 1953, a ceasefire restored peace, but since then all efforts to unite Korea have failed, and it seems that the division of this unhappy country will continue in the foreseeable future.

The Suez Crisis

Just as the war of nerves began to ease off a little in Asia, the Arab population of Egypt flared up against the Western Powers and directed the spotlight back to the Near East. We have seen how Great Britain forced her way into Egypt and then refused to leave despite repeated promises to do so. It will also be remembered that, although the Suez Canal was operated by an international company, the British regarded it more or less as their private preserve and took upon themselves the right to police it with imperial troops. As Prime Minister Ramsay MacDonald once frankly said in the House of Commons: 'The security of the British Empire in Egypt remains a vital *British* interest and the absolute certainty that the Suez Canal will remain open for the free passage of *British* ships is the foundation on which rests the entire defence strategy of the British Empire.' With a policy such as this, it is not surprising, therefore, that the end of the Second World War found British troops still stationed in Egypt and the British government as determined as ever to keep them there.

However, after the Arab-Israeli conflict had aroused such strong feelings against the West, Egypt's desire to throw out the British reached a fever pitch. Mobs attacked the troops in Cairo and Alexandria, guerrilla warfare broke out, Cairo was sacked, foreign property was destroyed and finally, in 1952, the incompetent King Farouk was deposed in favour of a fiercely nationalistic military dictatorship. This sort of thing had happened often enough in the past, but now the British government, weakened by the Second World War, could not strike back as in the good old days. Hoping to regain the popularity she had lost by encouraging the Jews, the United States gave her support to the demands of Colonel Nasser, the Egyptian dictator. Under these circumstances, even though Winston Churchill, the ardent champion of the Empire, was Prime Minister once more, the British government had no other choice but to give in. Consequently, in 1954 the British forces were withdrawn and their seventy-four-year-old occupation of Egypt came to an end. They left, however, on the definite understanding that, if Egypt were attacked by another country, they could come back in again to defend the Canal Zone.

Having accomplished this objective, Nasser felt free to step up the undeclared, hit-and-run war which had been going on with the Israelis ever since the 'truce' was signed in 1949. According to the terms of this agreement, neither side was meant to increase its military power, but the Jews, with their worldwide contacts, usually managed to obtain all the arms they needed. Although equally willing to violate the United Nations truce terms, the Arabs had no such source of strength and Nasser's frequent requests for arms were turned down by both the United States and Great Britain. Up to this moment in the long history of the Arab world, the Western Powers had held a virtual monopoly of the munitions trade into the

Near East. Now, however, to their dismay, the Egyptians appealed to the Soviet Union and through it made a deal with the satellite state of Czechoslovakia. And this, in turn, sparked an explosion which blew the Near East wide open for communist intervention.

Although the bargain to buy arms from Czechoslovakia might not have drawn Egypt towards the communist camp, the United States and Great Britain certainly clinched matters by their reaction to it. Alarmed by what they thought to be the pro-Soviet trend in Nasser's policy and justifiably annoyed at his willingness to mortgage his country's future to pay for communist munitions, the two powers decided to apply strong economic pressure against Egypt. Therefore, on July 19, 1956, they took the stern step of withdrawing their promised financial aid from the huge Aswan dam project on the Nile River. Not to be outdone, Nasser retaliated within a week by seizing control of the Suez Canal! With or without western money and regardless of all international obligations, the tolls from this rich enterprise, so he claimed, would be used to finance the Aswan dam. Now the fat was really in the fire—not so much for the United States as for Great Britain and France. In a divided and insecure world, both those Western Powers recoiled from the prospect of a hostile Egypt standing astride the Suez Canal. Consequently, when a number of international conferences revealed that Nasser would not back down, France and Britain, now under the premiership of Anthony Eden, caused what will long be known in history as the 'Suez Crisis'.

The crisis started on October 26 when Israel—possibly deciding to strike before the Arab League became too strong—suddenly launched a full-scale attack on Egypt. The Canal Zone was threatened by invasion! Now according to the agreement made in 1954, British troops legally could go back into the country again. Taking full advantage of this situation and moving with reckless speed, Great Britain and France dispatched a combined force to Port Said early in November. Its sole purpose, so they said, was to protect the Canal and keep the Jews and Arabs apart.

Was all this a mere coincidence, as the British and French claimed? How was it, a suspicious world wanted to know, that the two Western Powers were so fully prepared to step in the very moment Israeli troops crossed the Egyptian border? Why did British planes bomb Cairo only? Why was all the military action against the Egyptians while the Israelis were left free to overrun large slices of Arab land? Confronted with questions like these, a great many people in the West quickly concluded that the whole crisis had been pre-arranged by Britain, France and Israel—the timing, so it seemed, was far too good to be anything but a deliberately planned, joint invasion. An angry, buzzing, disillusioned world denounced the Anglo-French move as outright aggression and clamoured for an immediate ceasefire. The government of the United States, having helped to cause the trouble in the first place, refused to support its NATO partners, while the American people joined the critical chorus protesting against Great Britain. The Soviet Union stepped up her delivery of arms to the Near East, offered to send volunteers to help Nasser and threatened to start a shooting war with guided missiles.

During the Hungarian revolt in 1956, a huge statue of Stalin was demolished and the bronze head dragged through the streets of Budapest. A traffic sign is fastened to the head.

While the Suez crisis was reaching its peak, the people of Hungary rose in armed revolt against their communist officials. Even as the British were moving in on Egypt, Russian tanks rolled across the border into Budapest, bringing support to Hungary's puppet government. In a babel of voices, the communists and non-communists hurled charges of aggression at each other—the one in Egypt, the other in Hungary. The neutral, uncommitted world found both sides, East and West alike, equally guilty. In their minds, there was little to choose between British and French action in Egypt and what the Russians were doing in Hungary. A world of difference, however, soon became apparent—even the Afro-Asians saw it and paused to think. Defying world opinion and refusing to allow the United Nations to intervene, the Soviet Union cruelly crushed the Hungarian revolt. On the other hand, Britain and France very quickly yielded to the United Nations. Although the threat of Russia and her disgraceful conduct in Hungary may have influenced this decision, the two Western Powers were prepared to recognize the wishes of the majority. As a result, Great Britain and France withdrew from Egypt in December and their troops were replaced in the Canal Zone by a United Nations Expeditionary Force, to guard the uneasy border between the Arab states and Israel. Unfortunately the situation could not be completely restored in favour of the Western Powers. As a result of the Suez crisis, the Soviet Union had penetrated the Near East.

part 5
the divided world

17   TUMULT AND TERROR

Land of Silks and Spices

No conflict since World War Two has had as much effect on the world in general and the United States in particular as the civil struggle in Viet Nam which began in 1945. The trinity of superpowers—the United States, the U.S.S.R. and the People's Republic of China—have been involved in this conflict from the very beginning.

Saigon—Holiday Capital of the East
By the opening years of the twentieth century French empire-builders in the East controlled Indo-China, the area which included the present countries of Viet Nam, Laos and Cambodia. Siam (now Thailand) remained technically an independent kingdom divided into French and British spheres of influence. French colonial rule followed the typical European techniques of that time. Western material, educational and religious values replaced the traditional culture of the Vietnamese. The aristocratic, scholar-administrator hierarchy of the former Annamite Empire was replaced by those Vietnamese willing to accept the changes and a new ruling elite was formed, naturally dominated by the French. The youth of this group were frequently educated in France and, just as the British used Eton and Oxford to indoctrinate the sons of their colonial ruling class, St. Cyr and the Sorbonne emphasized to the Vietnamese the virtues of *la belle France*. Within a few years Saigon became the Paris of the Orient.

While this new class enjoyed high living standards and prestige, resentment of foreign control increased. All senior administrative posts were in French hands, and most of the economic rewards from agricultural development and industrial exploitation went back to France. Despite French restrictions, Vietnamese political activity grew and revolutionary nationalist groups became increasingly influential. During the years 1930-31 a series of nationalist uprisings occurred. Though the French suppressed this activity severely, the Vietnamese Communist party which had been founded in that year survived. It was the only Vietnamese group linked to an international political movement and it used this contact to rebuild and consolidate its position.

During the Second World War, when Japanese authorities occupied Indo-China, many refugees and resistance fighters, some of them members of anti-French groups, fled to southern China where they were welcomed by Allied troops who used their intelligence units to obtain information regarding the Japanese occupation. The Vietnamese patriots were joined by Ho Chi Minh, a Moscow-trained professional revolutionary who had worked in Asia for the Far Eastern Bureau of the Comintern. Ho was unique among Vietnamese revolutionaries because of his knowledge of guerrilla tactics and his experience of international politics. In 1941 he formed the Viet Minh, a 'United Front' move-

ment ostensibly including all shades of political opinion and having as its goal
the independence of Viet Nam. From the very first it was organized and controlled
by communist elements and designed to set up a communist regime. The Viet
Minh's well-armed guerrilla forces in North Viet Nam were able to seize power
following the Japanese surrender and, despite opposition from rival nationalist
groups in the South, Ho Chi Minh proclaimed the Independent Democratic
Republic of Viet Nam on September 2, 1945.

British occupation forces quickly turned over South Viet Nam to the returning
French, who under General de Gaulle were determined to restore their colonial
sovereignty. Negotiations with the Vietnamese communists broke down and on
December 19, 1946, Ho Chi Minh attacked the French in Hanoi, and the war
began.

The Domino Theory

Recognition of the Viet Minh by the People's Republic of China and the U.S.S.R.
in 1950 changed United States policy towards the war. The French campaign
hitherto had been looked upon with disfavour as an attempt to restore colonialism, but now the forces of Ho Chi Minh were seen as part of a communist drive
to control the East, and U.S. aid was accelerated. In May 1953, President
Eisenhower announced that he had given France a special grant of $60 million to
support her campaign against the Viet Minh rebels, and a report to the French
National Assembly in 1954 stated that the United States to date had paid seventy-
eight per cent of the cost of the anti-communist fighting in the Indo-China area.

In 1954 nineteen nations, including the U.S.S.R., Red China, North Korea and
the sixteen allies in the Korean War, met at Geneva in an attempt to formulate
peace settlements for Korea and Indo-China. At the end of July a settlement
called for an armistice in the civil war, division of Viet Nam into North and South
at the 17th parallel, elections by 1956 to determine future rulers and structure
of the country, and recognition of Laos and Cambodia as sovereign states. An
International Control Commission was set up to police the armistice, on which
Canada served along with Poland, under the chairmanship of India. Neither the
United States nor South Viet Nam signed the final declaration of the Geneva
Conference although Under Secretary of State Walter B. Smith declared the U.S.
would 'refrain from the threat or use of force to disturb the Agreement'. The
Geneva Agreement ended the fighting and enabled France to extricate her armed
forces with some remnant of dignity, but it left a divided Viet Nam ruled by two
governments bitterly opposed to one another.

The South Vietnamese adopted a republican government with Ngo Dinh Diem
as its first president, and French influence ended. Diem was remarkably successful in rebuilding South Viet Nam, but he did it at the cost of making many
personal enemies, of alienating the powerful Buddhist group and of creating a
strong autocracy governed to a great extent by military men. Hanoi's reaction
to the success of the new government in South Viet Nam was one of infiltration
and preparation for a new offensive when the time was ripe. Viet Minh members
were ordered to cache their arms in caves and tunnels and to reintegrate into

(Above) Camouflaged troops of the Viet Cong race into battle against American and South Vietnamese forces. (Right) A Buddhist monk burns himself to death in Saigon, to protest government persecution of Buddhists.

South Vietnamese life, prepared for that day when as a guerrilla army they would be ready for renewed activity.

For almost five years rebuilding and reorganization continued on both sides. 'Viet Cong', the name given to the communist guerrillas in the South, became a headline word in 1960. In December the Hanoi government announced the formation of the National Liberation Front—a new name for the Viet Minh— and activity against the government of the South was intensified. To combat Viet Cong successes and at the same time to strengthen his ruling clique, President Diem introduced stricter security measures, carried out with ruthless efficiency by his brother, Ngo Dinh Nhu, head of the secret police. Emergency decrees stifled opposition parties in the alleged parliament and all candidates running for office had to have presidential approval. Diem's assumption of further dictatorial powers alienated many of his erstwhile supporters, including some American officials.

In spite of this alarming totalitarian trend, however, containment of communism in accordance with the 'domino theory'—if Viet Nam falls all Southeast Asia becomes communist—was the keynote of American foreign policy, and U.S. economic and military aid poured into South Viet Nam in ever-increasing amounts. By now violations of the Geneva Convention had become commonplace and the function of the International Control Commission grew negligible as

escalation of the war on both sides continued.

The corruption and inefficiency of the Diem regime in dealing with the Viet Cong and the National Liberation Front became increasingly apparent and eventually, with certain American foreknowledge and possible connivance, army elements plotted a coup. On November 1, 1963, Diem was assassinated and the military men took over. For the next three years, internal power struggles marred any effective government operation against the Viet Cong, and more and more American involvement in this kind of action became necessary. The Viet Cong responded with intensive attacks against U.S. installations.

Between August 2 and 7, 1964, two American destroyers, the *Maddox* and the *C. Turner Joy*, were attacked by North Vietnamese patrol transport boats in the Gulf of Tonkin. In reprisal, U.S. aircraft bombed North Vietnamese bases. When President Johnson appealed to Congress for vindication of this action, the House of Representatives resolved 'to take all necessary measures to repel any armed attacks against the forces of the United States and to prevent future aggression.' Now massive aid from the U.S. poured in and the Viet Cong, reinforced by North Vietnamese regular troops, intensified their operations south of the 17th parallel. Air strikes by the U.S. were stepped up, and ground troops officially went into action on combat missions.

In 1965, the undeclared war in Viet Nam assumed full-scale proportions. American diplomats pressured members of SEATO for troop assistance; South Korea responded with 30,000 men and Australia and New Zealand sent small

Front-line schoolchildren in North Viet Nam. When enemy aircraft are overhead lessons have to stop while the children seek safety in the shelter they have made.

contingents. The U.S. Air Force intensified its bombing and mined the rivers in North Viet Nam; the navy shelled shore installations. New weapons came into use: napalm—liquid fire to smoke the Viet Cong out of their underground warrens; defoliation bombs to destroy vegetation and reveal guerrilla hideouts; and 'smart' bombs guided to their targets by laser beams. 'Search and destroy' missions to capture communist undercover agents and destroy their enclaves culminated in the infamy of the My Lai massacres.

By January 1, 1968, there were 475,000 U.S. servicemen in Viet Nam—more than the peak strength of American forces during the Korean War. This vast commitment achieved some success. By February the North Vietnamese action had slowed down, defections from the Viet Cong were increasing, strategic areas had been recaptured and morale in the South Vietnamese army was improving.

It was at this time that the North unleashed the great Tet Offensive. Coming on the first day of the Lunar New Year at the time of a mutually declared truce, it took the form of attacks on nearly every city and town throughout South Viet Nam. While its declared intention of provoking a popular uprising against the government failed and the communists sustained huge losses, its propaganda impact was effective. The cost in money and lives was so great that there arose a tremendous flow of American public opinion against continuing U.S. involvement.

In March 1968 President Johnson reacted to this surge of protest by ordering the

cessation of all bombing of North Viet Nam beyond the 20th parallel in return
for a North Vietnamese agreement to hold talks at ambassadorial levels, but the
North Vietnamese demanded a total, unconditional end to American bombing.
On November 1 Johnson yielded to this demand and agreed that the Paris talks
would include delegations both from the government of South Viet Nam and from
the National Liberation Front. The initial optimism generated by these steps was
soon dispelled, however, as the Paris peace talks degenerated into propaganda
utterances by Hanoi and mutual accusations of armistice and neutrality zone
violations. By April 1969 U.S. troop strength had reached its peak of 549,000.

The Nixon Doctrine

Shortly after Richard Nixon's election to the presidency in 1969, the so-called
'Nixon Doctrine' began to appear. The objective of this doctrine was disengagement of the United States from her military role in Asia—though certainly not
disengagement from Asia. Nixon stressed three specific points: Asian countries
must become increasingly self-reliant in accepting the responsibility for their
own defence; existing treaty commitments would be honoured, but the U.S.
would not enter into new defence agreements; and the U.S. would continue to
provide a shield against nuclear attack.

In the early summer of 1969, Nixon undertook publicly to withdraw American
soldiers from Viet Nam, instructed that the most modern equipment be given to
the South Vietnamese army and encouraged South Viet Nam's president, Nguyen
Van Thieu, to replace the departing American units with Vietnamese. 'Viet-
namization' of the war had begun. The first American withdrawal of troops took
place on July 7, 1969, when 814 soldiers were flown home. This token withdrawal
was followed by massive ones, until at a televised news conference on June 29,
1972, the President could announce that U.S. ground forces had been reduced to
a mere 40,000. Half a million men had been moved out of Viet Nam in three years.

N.L.F. response to this 'winding down' of U.S. participation was not encouraging. In April 1972 the North opened their biggest attack since the Tet Offensive
of 1968. Twenty-five thousand 'regulars', equipped with Soviet-supplied armour
and artillery, burst out of the demilitarized zone and swarmed into the northern
provinces, scoring early successes. To check this new threat President Nixon had
few options. The use of American ground troops was unthinkable with the withdrawal program in effect. Air power was the answer. Within a week air strength
in Indo-China was doubled, aircraft carriers were in operation and the unconditional bombing of the North was resumed for the first time in four years. In a
further step to assist the South Vietnamese, Nixon ordered mining of the harbours
of North Viet Nam, especially Haiphong, and initiated a naval blockade. As the
chief supplier of Hanoi is the U.S.S.R., this action raised terrifying possibilities,
but though ritual denunciations came from Moscow and Peking no specific
retaliatory measures were taken. This strong action was successful in slowing the
momentum of the Northern offensive, but the war dragged on.

Resumption of the Paris peace talks in the summer of 1972 raised hopes for an
end to the war, but by December they had broken down once more. The United

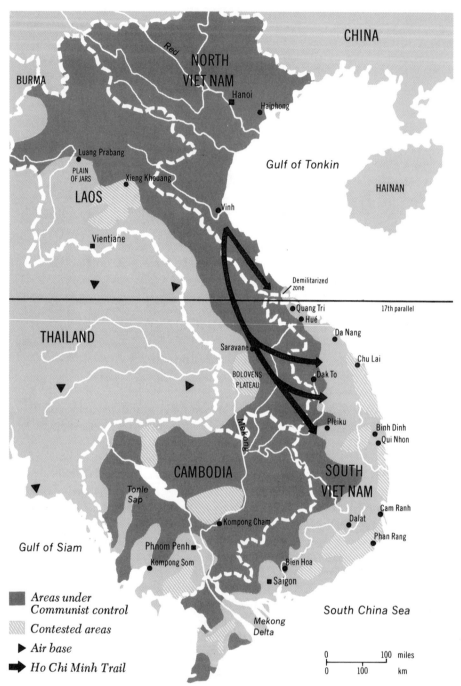

The Indo-Chinese peninsula at the close of the Viet Nam War in January 1973.
The Ho Chi Minh Trail was a supply network linking North Viet Nam with Viet Cong
bases in the South.

States reacted to this with the heaviest aerial blitz in history, centring on the
Hanoi and Haiphong area. In all, more than 7 million tons of bombs were dropped,
and 29 U.S. planes were lost. The raids were called off on December 30, and on
January 8 peace negotiations were resumed. Finally, on January 23, 1973,
President Nixon was able to announce, on an internationally televised broadcast,
that a peace agreement had been reached.

The formal signing of the peace took place in Paris on January 27 and all
parties involved in the war—the United States, South Viet Nam, North Viet Nam
and the Viet Cong—were signatories to the pact. The agreement included the
return of all U.S. prisoners of war within sixty days and the withdrawal of the
remaining 23,000 U.S. troops in Viet Nam during the same period. Arrangements
for a political settlement in Viet Nam were left vague and most observers felt that
a period of continued guerrilla warfare between the Viet Cong and the South
Viet Nam government was inevitable. To see that the peace terms were adhered
to, a new international commission was set up consisting of representatives from
Canada, Hungary, Poland and Indonesia.

It seemed that the war had finally ended—an undeclared war that had bitterly
divided the States and had cost that country at least $200 billion. Nearly 46,000
U.S. servicemen had lost their lives and over 305,000 were wounded or missing.
It was reported that South Vietnamese casualties were some 575,000 and those
of the enemy nearly a million. Untold thousands of civilians had been killed,
wounded, or rendered homeless, and a generation had grown up in Indo-China
amid violence, suspicion and death. There was little elation over the settlement,
merely relief that at long last it was over. And there was the haunting fear that the
peace might not be permanent and that the tragic struggle might have been in
vain.

Middle East Ferment

The Arab League
The Middle East countries have continued to be points of friction and potential
confrontation between the U.S.S.R. and the West. Three factors dominate events
in this area: the growth of Arab nationalism, the desire of the people for better
living standards, and the presence of vast oil resources, vital to the great industrial
powers of the West. Israel challenges their dreams of a new Islam. The abject
poverty of their masses invites the growth of communism with its promises of a
better life. Oil enriches their leaders and enables them to bargain with both the
East and the West. Yet their nationalism is hampered by internal conflicts, their
political and economic reforms by power intrigues between military leaders and
civilian politicians, and their oil negotiations by lack of technical knowledge and,
at times, by corrupt officials.

After World War Two the Arab nations formed a league designed to draft policies of general Arab interest and to take united action to carry out these policies. Its positive achievements have been in the revival of Islamic culture and in the economic field. An Arab Postal Union has been set up, an Arab Development Bank established, and an attempt made to organize an Arab Common Market. But despite the aggressive guidance of Egypt's dynamic Colonel Nasser, rivalries for the leadership of the Pan-Arab world have limited the success of the organization even in united action against the common enemy, Israel. Now, since Nasser's death, there seems to be no leader capable of unifying the Middle East.

Intrigue, violence, revolution, war and highjacking marked the fermenting Arab world as it went through the tumultuous sixties and into the seventies. Civil war racked Jordan as tough, diminutive King Hussein crushed risings against his regime. Hussein withstood his most serious threat during the autumn of 1970. Believing that he was determined to reach a political compromise with Israel, the relatively moderate *Al Fatah* group combined with the militant Popular Front for the Liberation of Palestine (P.F.L.P.) to challenge the King's authority. During the first week of September the guerrillas highjacked three airliners of British, Swiss and U.S. registry and held them at a Jordanian airstrip. They threatened to blow up the aircraft and 300 passengers unless certain Arab commandos imprisoned in Israel and Europe were freed. Britain, Switzerland and Israel acceded to the guerrilla demands; the passengers were released and the aircraft destroyed. But a week later Hussein launched a full-scale campaign against the guerrilla forces and triumphed after a bloody ten-day civil war. The aftermath of this incident was the formation of the 'Black September' terrorist group whose activities included the kidnapping and murder of several Israeli athletes at the Olympic Games in Munich in 1972 and the assassination of Israeli diplomats by 'explosive letters'.

Algeria, an independent republic since 1962 following a bitter struggle with France, has become a powerful force in the Arab world. The techniques of its guerrilla fighters, the famed National Liberation Front, have been copied by 'liberation armies' all over the world, including the I.R.A. and, in Canada, the F.L.Q. President Houari Boumédienne, former army chief, seized power in 1965. Virulently anti-western, he seems determined to wear the mantle of leadership for the Arab world. But, confronted by serious economic problems and a continuing power struggle, he may well remain the successful revolutionary unable to rule.

Syria and Iraq, dominated by socialistic military juntas, provide refuge and assistance to the guerrilla groups but are constantly embroiled in territorial disputes with neighbouring Jordan. Libya and Tunisia remain relatively stable, while Lebanon maintains an uneasy balance between a population that is half Christian and half Moslem, and the influence of its explosive neighbours. Morocco, most westerly of the Arab states, dutifully pays lip service to the policies of the Arab League, but in 1969 signed a pact of association with the European Economic Community.

The Garden of Allah

Ringed by the Red and Arabian seas and the Persian Gulf lies the legendary Arabian Peninsula. Here nomadic tribes still roam with their flocks, searching for the sparse grasslands and green oases as their forefathers have done for countless generations. Here, too, is located Mecca, Holy City of the Moslem world. Four-fifths—a million square miles—of this forbidding land is Saudi Arabia, greatest oil-producing country of the Middle East, whose crude oil production for 1971 was 5 million barrels a day.

King Faisal dominates the land, a hawk-nosed patriarch, son of the famed desert warrior, Ibn Saud, who along with Lawrence of Arabia freed the Arab lands from Turkish oppression during World War One. Some idea of the backwardness of the kingdom may be gained from the fact that when Faisal took over the throne in 1964 one of his first acts was to abolish slavery. Faisal is ultra-

The Middle East after 1967. Inset, the Six-Day War.

⟶   *Israeli air strikes*
▶▶▶▶   *Israeli naval attacks*
┄┄┄▶   *Principal Israeli advances*
▓▓▓   *Territories gained by Israel*

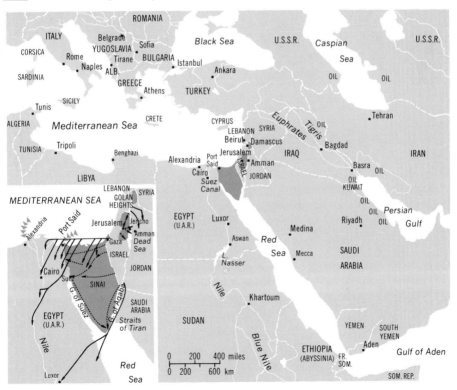

conservative, maintaining the strict traditions of Moslem law. He has no sympathy for the revolutionary socialism of many of the Arab League countries. Though he gave financial assistance to Egypt and Jordan following the Six-Day War with Israel in 1967, he quarrelled bitterly with Nasser and his relationships with Syria and Iraq are icily diplomatic. In 1969 his brother, Prince Fahd, visited Washington in an apparently successful attempt to improve relationships which had become strained during the Six-Day War.

Oil accounts for ninety per cent of the country's revenue. The government-controlled General Petroleum and Mineral Organization attempts to co-ordinate oil production and mineral-related industries with the national interest. Today most operations are carried out by the Arabian-American Oil Company, a consortium whose members include Texaco, Mobil, Standard Oil and the Getty Oil Company. Recently Japanese interests have secured government concessions for offshore drilling.

In 1970 there were sporadic outbursts of violence and protest against the absolute rule of the desert king. These demonstrations, primarily student-oriented, lacked coherence and leadership and were quickly quelled. However, there are continuing signs of dissatisfaction. The winds of change may yet ruffle the sands of Saudi Arabia.

Kuwait, a tiny Arab sheikdom on the northeastern coast of the Persian Gulf, literally floats on a sea of oil. It is estimated that one-quarter of the world's reserves lie beneath its arid surface. With a gross national product of $1.2 billion, Kuwait boasts of one millionaire for every 230 citizens. Under the benign rule of Amir Sheik Sabah-as-Salim, the country is a capitalist welfare state without any poverty. It has contributed over a billion dollars to the Arab Economic Development Fund since 1961. While financially encouraging the Arab League, Kuwait's relationship with the West, particularly Britain, France and the United States, is a friendly one. But increasing Soviet influence among the revolutionary movements along the Persian Gulf and territorial demands from left-wing Iraq are causes for concern in the only state in the world where the telephone service is free.

Iran, once the seat of the ancient Persian empire, is a constitutional monarchy in theory, ruled for the past thirty-two years by the iron-willed Shah, Reza Pahlavi, whose father, an army officer, seized the throne in 1921. During the sixties the Shah launched the so-called 'White Revolution', a series of reforms including the abolition of serfdom, the breaking up of vast feudal estates to give the peasant population their own land, and the building of many schools. While some of these reforms alienated the more conservative elements, they succeeded in creating a strong bond of affection between the predominantly rural population and the Shah, and immensely strengthened his power. For example, student unrest in the early seventies which featured protest against the monarchy brought immediate and angry reaction from peasant and workers' groups in favour of the Shah's rule.

In foreign affairs the Shah has been able to maintain a delicate balance between his socialist neighbour, the U.S.S.R., and the capitalist western nations. Iran

In March 1967 the American-owned tanker, Torrey Canyon, carrying 120,000 tons of oil, split in two when she went aground off Land's End, England. The stinking, black oil slick polluted 200 miles of Cornwall coastline, killing untold thousands of sea-birds and costing an estimated $5.6 million to clean up.

recognizes the People's Republic of China and maintains diplomatic relations with South Africa. Its chief difficulties are with Iraq and the U.A.R. over the sovereignty of the sheikdoms of the Persian Gulf.

Much of the success of the Shah's government lies in the oil resources of the country. Iran is the fourth largest oil-producing country in the world and this commodity accounts for eighty-nine per cent of its export trade. The industry is run by an international consortium headed by British, U.S., Dutch and French companies. The revenues collected from the oil industry have been used freely to carry out the government's reform program.

Oil, then, is the name of the game in the Middle East. And it is an international game. Around the derricks in the blazing heat can be heard the slow Texan drawl, the clipped English consonant, the ponderous Russian guttural, the excited twang of the French, the staccato chatter of the Japanese. Tankers owned by the great companies fill their compartments with the viscous black brew of power for the industries of the world and plough through the oceans to the refineries. Sometimes bunkers crack and corruption oozes out to kill the birds and the fish, to foul the beaches, and to poison the very sea itself. But the search and the rewards continue.

In the embassies and the consulates, the intrigue for drilling and export rights is a never-ending game of influence and chance. Smiles and toasts greet the negotiated successes; in failure lies the threat of mobs in the streets, of burning refineries and smashed equipment, the tramp of soldiers' boots and the gleam of steel. Oil is the lifeblood of the industrial world and the Middle East is the pumping heart.

As Nasser visits an Egyptian village, peasants reach out to touch their idol.

Gamal, the Beloved

Nasser's death on September 28, 1970, was a tremendous blow to the Arab cause in the Middle East. Gamal Abd-al Nasser had been the first Egyptian to rule Egypt since the days of the Pharaohs. With his creation of the United Arab Republic, he almost single-handedly brought Egypt into the twentieth century. For nearly twenty years he dominated the Arab world with his dynamic leadership and was a leading figure on the world's political stage.

His ambitious program was to modernize Egypt, to improve the living standard of the people, to share the limited arable land with the peasants who had tilled it since time immemorial and to increase its food productivity, to solve the illiteracy problem and raise the standard of education, and above all to inspire the people with national pride and a sense of purpose. In a country hidebound by Moslem tradition and with a population cowed by years of exploitation, his domestic reforms were difficult to achieve. He was faced with basic problems that have no instant solution. A population of 35 million with a three per cent annual increase —one of the world's highest rates—and conservative religious leaders doggedly opposed to family planning in a country of limited resources was, and is, of major concern. The Aswan High Dam, the most magnificent engineering achievement since the Pyramids, has proved of dubious benefit, preventing the annual spring inundation of the Nile Valley so that artificial fertilizers are now required for the once lush farm lands. The reclaimed desert land, over a million acres, watered by the Aswan project has not achieved the expected food production, chiefly because of the salt content of the soil. Illiteracy remains as high as eighty per cent. There is a chronic shortage of teachers and educational materials, and the traditional Moslem educators are firmly opposed to modern teaching programs.

Despite the limited success of Nasser's reforms, the personal loyalty he attracted was tremendous. The national sorrow shown at his death was unprecedented and millions of grief-stricken people accompanied his funeral cortege. To the ruling and middle classes he had given a national purpose and the idea of a destiny of leadership in the Arab world. Under him the U.A.R. became a nation to be reckoned with in the councils of the world. And to the millions of peasants exploited for centuries by alien rulers and condemned to brutal servitude he was the man who had recognized their misery and done something to improve their desperate way of life.

The Six-Day War

Continuing Arab-Israeli hostility during the sixties flared up into the Six-Day War of June 5 to 11, 1967, which ended in a shattering Arab defeat with the United Arab Republic, Jordan and Syria suffering the most.

Following the Suez crisis of 1956, U.N. Secretary General Dag Hammarskjold persuaded Israel to withdraw her forces to the 1948-49 boundaries and to agree to a United Nations Emergency Force (U.N.E.F.) patrolling this ceasefire line. The initiation of this U.N. force was the work of Lester Pearson, then Canada's Minister of External Affairs. For the next ten years U.N.E.F. troops maintained a fragile and often-violated barrier between the Arab and Israeli armies. Canadian forces assisted in this operation, which extended from the Gaza Strip through the Sinai Peninsula to the entrance of the Straits of Tiran. It was an uneasy armistice, a waiting period to negotiate a peace that was not to be achieved.

The continuing changes in the Arab world altered the situation drastically. Egypt's Nasser, whose short-lived United Arab Republic had dissolved in 1962 (though Egypt retained the name), was now faced with the problem of leading and attempting to control the actions of three aggressively nationalistic states— Algeria, Iraq and Syria. Two main factors would determine the common policy and action these countries would take during the next five years: a dedicated desire to eradicate Israel as a sovereign state and the need to demonstrate to the other Arab states that Nasser and the nations that followed him were the undoubted leaders of the new Islam.

Between 1964 and 1966 Arab guerrillas stepped up their raids against Israel. Many of these hit-and-run attacks were launched from Jordan by well-established terrorist groups. From the Golan Heights, Syrian artillery shelled Israeli *kibbutzim* in the farmlands of Upper Galilee. U.A.R. commandos slipped through U.N.E.F. patrol lines to raid Israeli posts in the Sinai desert and east of the Gaza Strip. For the Israelis it was a time of sudden death, in the fields from sniper bullets, and from bombs and machine-gun bursts in the market places. Retaliation grew in intensity and Israeli counterattacks were particularly effective against the Jordanian and Syrian raiders.

Israeli soldiers in the Old City of Jerusalem. They have erected a cairn to their comrades who died in the wrecked tank shown. The Garden of Gethsemane is in the background.

At this time Nasser was continually pressured and criticized by his Arab allies. What effect were his raiders having? Was he hiding behind the U.N. lines and letting his friends bear the brunt of Israeli reprisal? Where was the leadership of the great Gamal, the idol of Islam? Units of the Jordanian army were now openly clashing with Israeli forces, and in April 1967 a violent artillery bombardment sent Israeli jets into Syrian skies and more than half a dozen Syrian MIG fighters were shot down. In early May the Russians informed Syria and the U.A.R. that Israel was massing troops on the Syrian border to attack and overthrow the government of that country. There is no evidence to prove that this Soviet report was true, but it forced Nasser's hand. U.A.R. forces moved eastward in the Sinai desert and demanded passage through the U.N. ceasefire lines. The request was relayed to U.N. headquarters in New York, and Secretary General U Thant acceded to the demand. U.A.R. troops moved across the Sinai and were face to face with the Israelis once again after ten years.

There is every reason to believe that Nasser would have been content to stop at this point; the threat—if there had been one—against the government of Syria was now neutralized, with U.A.R. forces close at hand to give assistance if needed. But the militant Arab states, possibly encouraged by the ease with which the U.N.E.F. had been thrust aside, called for additional action—stop Israel's access to the Red Sea—even though the Israeli government had consistently warned that such an action would mean war. On May 24, 1967, Nasser's forces blockaded the Straits of Tiran, and Israeli shipping could no longer move out into the Red Sea and the southern oceans of the world. A week later the U.A.R., Jordan and Iraq signed a mutual defence pact and Iraqi troops moved into Jordan to support King Hussein's army. The lights blazed bright and long in the U.N. building by the Hudson River as the tension mounted. But the special sessions merely provided opportunities for Arab propaganda speeches. Israeli Foreign Minister Abba Eban proposed that an international committee headed by Britain and the U.S. should ensure the freedom of shipping in the Gulf of Aqaba and the Straits of Tiran. Though such an action would have removed one of Israel's chief reasons for war, the suggestion was ignored.

Both the U.S. and the U.S.S.R. seemed to feel that war was inevitable and their attempts to moderate the attitudes of the countries over which they had some influence were of no avail. Units of the Soviet, British and U.S. Mediterranean fleets moved into dangerous proximity in the eastern Mediterranean. Inflammatory speeches from all Arab nations denounced Israel. Fanatical Arab nationalists called for the *Jehad*, the Holy War, to avenge the defeats of 1948 and 1956 and to wipe out the infidel nation that had dared to transgress on the sacred soil of Islam.

On June 5, 1967, with a clear dawn, the jets zoomed in from the desert and from the brilliant blue Mediterranean. Within three hours 300 U.A.R. aircraft smouldered in ruins on nineteen airfields; the Israelis were at war. Refuelling quickly after their first strike, the aircraft screamed eastward to destroy the Jordanian air force. Back to base again and then into the northwestern sky to destroy and cripple the Russian-supplied airplanes of Syria and Iraq. It was over in brief hours and the Star of David ruled the Mid-Eastern skies.

At the same time Israeli armoured brigades smashed into the Gaza Strip and went west into the forbidding desert of the Sinai where they encountered and destroyed the crack tank and mobile forces of the U.A.R. in the hardest-fought engagement of the war. Now the battle became a rout as Israeli aircraft strafed and bombed the retreating armies, and Israeli ground forces led by their one-eyed hero, Moshe Dayan, who had been born in Palestine's first *kibbutz*, chased the demoralized U.A.R. armies to the banks of the Suez. By June 7 the entire Sinai Peninsula was in Israeli hands and Nasser's forces were in full retreat.

On the eastern front it was the same story. Jordanian artillery shelled Jerusalem on June 5, but after two days of heavy fighting with Hussein's troops the Old City with its Wailing Wall was in Israeli hands and by June 8 the invading forces had been driven eastward across the Jordan River. A U.N. ceasefire appeal was violated by Syrian artillery firing from the Golan Heights and the Israeli army went into action again. What was supposed to be an impregnable fortified chain of hills was captured after a brief battle. The plain of Damascus stretched out before the forces of Israel and the Syrian guns were silent. The Six-Day War was over, and military experts credited Israel with winning the most decisive war of the twentieth century.

The Aftermath

For the first time in a short, troubled history, Israel now had well-defined borders, easy to defend against her Arab enemies. The Israeli victors stood on the west bank of the Jordan and on the Golan Heights; they controlled the life line of the Straits of Tiran and were firmly entrenched on the east bank of the Suez Canal. But it was a victory that brought no peace. Defeat was a massive blow to the military pride of the Arabs and merely increased their hostility. They had lost lands and people; over a million Arabs now lived under Israeli rule, many of them amid conditions of incredible squalor, in refugee camps and in barbed-wire desert enclosures. More desperate than the Arab minority in Israel were the thousands who had fled to Jordan, Syria, Lebanon and the United Arab Republic. They were the dispossessed who lived only for revenge.

Arab reaction to the conduct of the western countries during the war was confusing and inconsistent. Much of this, of course, was due to the divisions and national jealousies within the Middle Eastern nations themselves. The United States, the main object of Arab hatred, was accused of assisting, protecting and even inspiring the Israelis to launch the Six-Day War. Having been regarded as pro-Israel since her role in the Suez crisis, Great Britain too was subject to Arab criticism. However, when British Foreign Secretary George Brown, a diplomat not noted for his diplomatic language, demanded in the General Assembly that Israel should withdraw immediately from all the conquered territory, the Arabs toned down their verbal attacks, much to the relief of the stripe-suited entrepreneurs of the British oil interests.

France was the popular western nation in Arab public opinion. De Gaulle, seeing a chance to restore fading French influence in the Moslem world, remained ostentatiously neutral during the war and bitterly condemned the Israelis for attacking first and then daring to seize Arab territory. The General did not point out—and the Arabs seemed to forget—that most of Israel's military equipment and particularly the aircraft so essential to the victory had been purchased in France.

When the war ended in disaster for the Arab countries involved, there was a great display of praise for the diplomatic, economic and military aid given by Russia. There was also disillusionment and disappointment. Why had the U.S.S.R. not come to the aid of its allies and risked a clash with the U.S.A.? Why had the U.S.S.R. voted for a ceasefire at the U.N.? Why after the war had ended did the U.S.S.R. continue to press hard for a peace settlement with the hated Israelis? The Arab revolutionaries and nationalists found the actions of Russia impossible to understand and faith in Russian effectiveness dwindled.

This disillusionment with the Soviets reached a low point in July 1972 when some twenty thousand advisers left the U.A.R. at the request of President Aswar Sadat, who had succeeded to the presidency following Nasser's death. Russian military personnel remained, some of them as pilots of the MIG's that kept a watchful eye on the Israeli aircraft, and some as missile experts manning the ground-to-air defences of the Suez.

This hands-off attitude was not directed only at Russia. In a four-hour speech

Eight children died and twenty were wounded when Arab terrorists ambushed and destroyed this school bus near the Israeli-Lebanese border in March 1970.

in Cairo on July 25, Sadat accused both the Soviet Union and the United States of misleading the Arab states—one power in failing to deliver arms and the other in failing to achieve a just peace.

Little progress has been made in settling the Middle East question. The return of the conquered Arab territory is one of the main problems. While Israel might agree to certain areas going back to their former owners—Syria, Jordan and the U.A.R.—she will consent to this only on the basis of direct negotiations with the Arab countries concerned, and only if positive guarantees of her borders are part of these negotiations. Israel considers specific areas as essential to her defence—the Golan Heights, Jerusalem and certain areas in the Gaza Strip and Sinai desert—and there is no evidence that she will agree to restore these areas to their former owners. A strong element in Israel led by Moshe Dayan, Minister of Defence, opposes returning any of the captured territory. To deal directly with Israel regarding any land disposal or reallotment would seem to recognize Israel's claim as a sovereign state, which the Arabs seem determined not to do. The Arab states would prefer any negotiations to be handled by the U.N. or by a Great Power Conference, but Israel shows little inclination for this type of talk.

The growing power of the Arab guerrilla movement is having a disturbing effect on the political structure and stability of the Middle East. The increasing number of these underground fighters, easily recruited from the teeming refugee camps, is becoming a menace to the rulers of even those countries that openly encourage their operations. The chief guerrilla groups, *Al Fatah* (The Conquest) and the Popular Front for the Liberation of Palestine, seem unwilling to compromise. They want Israel as an Arab state.

The major tragedy of the raid and counter-raid tactics between Israel and the guerrillas is the killing and wounding of innocent people. An Israeli air raid on April 8, 1970, at the village of Bahr-al-Daqar in the United Arab Republic resulted in 46 deaths, 45 of them children, and the wounding of 30. In July 1972 the United Nations Security Council condemned Israel's bombing of the town of Hasbaya in southern Lebanon. In both these incidents, Arab guerrillas were using the locations for training purposes and as bases for raids on Israeli territory. One of the bloodiest and most senseless terrorist attacks occurred in June 1972 when a Japanese terrorist trio recruited by the P.F.L.P. fired machine-gun bullets and threw grenades into the crowd at Lod International Airport, killing 24 people. Most of the Arab nations shared the horror and revulsion of the world at these indiscriminate killings. Such acts of violence make any solution to the Middle East problem complex and difficult.

Apart from some political agreement and a highly unlikely change in terrorist tactics, the one million Arabs now living in Israeli-held territory may provide the key to any permanent change in the situation. If Israeli treatment of this large minority—almost a third of the population—can provide a workable compromise and include equality of opportunity, the entire situation could change for the better—but it is a very big 'if'.

Despite the political inflexibility of both sides and the terrorist attacks, there are signs that the impasse in the Middle East may yet be solved. Nasser, just before his death, accepted certain U.S. peace proposals as a basis for discussion and indicated a willingness to at least establish contact with Israeli representatives. Yet recent developments in the U.A.R., particularly the removal of Russian influence which favoured Israel, might seriously affect a compromise. Jordan and Israel are close to an agreement that would permit Jordan to use the harbour facilities of the port of Gaza, occupied by Israel since 1967. Reports in July 1972 from Libya and Kuwait seemed to indicate that certain Arab countries were ready to resume closer contact with the western nations, particularly with the United States.

In the meantime, raids and counter-raids continue to make tragic headlines in the world's newspapers. The naval bases of the U.A.R. shelter the ships of the Soviet Mediterranean Fleet and in those same waters cruise the watchful navies of the United States and Great Britain.

Confrontations in the West

Berlin Crisis—To Build a Wall
To Vienna in the summer of 1961 came the handsome, youthful President Kennedy who, since his election the year before, had infused the American people and indeed the whole western world with a new sense of purpose and achieve-

ment. He came to meet squat, fiery-tempered Nikita Khrushchev, Premier of the Soviet Union. From shepherd boy to metal worker to front line Bolshevik in 1918, Khrushchev had survived the power infighting of the Soviet establishment during the troubled thirties and forties and had fought as a tough guerrilla leader in the bitterest struggles of World War Two. After Stalin's death he had led the campaign against the power excesses of the Stalinist regime. The only Russian leader since the revolution to visit the United States, he had had top level discussions with Dwight D. Eisenhower in 1959. And now he was ready to talk again to a President of the United States.

The talks concerned Berlin, chief European confrontation spot in the Cold War. As we have seen, after World War Two Germany was divided into four zones of occupation administered by Great Britain, France, the United States and the U.S.S.R. From 1948 on, the Allies agreed on a central government for the western zones and on September 21, 1949, the Federal Republic of Germany was formed. By 1951 the U.S., France and Britain terminated their state of war with Germany and in 1955 the Soviet Union somewhat tardily followed suit. On May 5 of that same year, the Federal Republic of Germany became a fully sovereign, independent country with its capital at Bonn. The Eastern Zone became the Soviet-dominated German Democratic Republic on October 7, 1949, but has been recognized as a sovereign state by none of the major Western Powers and by only a few non-communist governments.

The great city of Berlin lies ninety miles within the German Democratic Republic, linked to the Federal Republic of Germany by road, rail and air corridors. West Berlin, with its population of almost 2¾ million, worked and shared in the tremendous economic revival of the Federal Republic from 1955 on. This section of the city became again a dynamic and exciting metropolis whose very appearance illustrated the success of the new Germany. The slower development of the Eastern Sector under orthodox Marxist Walter Ulbricht was disturbing and discouraging to many East Germans. The contrast was visible for all to see. Why was the decadent capitalist system so successful? Why were there no queues for food in West Berlin? Why were the shops full of consumer goods? Why were the wages higher?

The answers, of course, were many—a natural resource lack, Soviet reparations seizure of heavy machinery and manufacturing equipment, Allied bombings that had smashed the industrial complexes, and the iron determination of Ulbricht to build a socialist Germany at whatever cost. But these answers were neither understood nor accepted by many East Germans and through West Berlin moved a new refugee stream. By the early summer of 1961 more than three million East Germans had fled. Ulbricht appealed to Moscow for assistance. The Russians had the solution: turn over the access routes to West Berlin to the German Democratic Republic (G.D.R.). To the Western Powers this could only mean another confrontation of greater magnitude than the Berlin blockade of 1948. It was to attempt to defuse this situation that Kennedy and Khrushchev met in Vienna.

The Russian Premier's attitude seemed deliberately provocative. It was the intention of the Soviet Union, he declared, to sign a separate treaty with the

German Democratic Republic to make West Berlin a 'demilitarized free city', and naturally the access routes to that city would be controlled by the G.D.R. The U.S. President replied that such a decision was quite unacceptable and might lead to military action by both countries, with unpredictable results. During the conference Khrushchev remained stubbornly insistent. He may well have thought he could outwit and intimidate the young man whose administration had been seriously embarrassed six weeks previously by the Bay of Pigs incident in Cuba. But the Russian Premier was dealing with a man whose easy-going charm cloaked an iron will and determination—a Kennedy characteristic that Khrushchev did not appreciate or understand until it was too late. Shortly after the Vienna meeting U.S. Secretary of State Dean Rusk announced to a NATO Council meeting that the Soviet Premier's proposals regarding Berlin were unacceptable.

As the crisis heightened, the exodus from East Berlin increased; a thousand refugees per day poured into the Western Sector during the early days of July 1961. Check points were strengthened and border controls tightened, but to no avail. These measures merely encouraged the ingenuity of those fleeing from the East. They came hidden inside bales of hay, crouched beneath the hollowed-out seats of automobiles, squatting inside empty beer kegs. The manufacture of false identity papers, border crossing cards, exit visas and work permits became the prime industry of the black market and the underground press. And they kept coming, despite the long years of imprisonment if detected and the rifle fire of the border guards. Among them were professional men and women, skilled technicians, experienced workers—men and women needed by the G.D.R. for its great socialist experiment. By the end of July, fifteen thousand people had crossed the forbidden border.

Then the German Democratic Republic, aided by the Soviet Union, moved decisively. On August 1, East Berliners working in West Berlin had their identity cards confiscated; on August 13, the borders were closed and the building of the Berlin Wall began—five feet of concrete topped with broken glass and barbed wire; and by August 22 all crossing points but one were closed to foreigners. The Western Powers protested, but the wall grew higher and along the twenty-five-mile frontier a three-hundred-foot zone was bulldozed, a grey, flat no man's land between coercion and freedom.

On October 25, following a series of incidents between Soviet guards and American military convoy personnel, U.S. tanks and British and French troops appeared in ever-increasing numbers at the check points. Two days later, red-starred tanks of the Soviet Union rumbled in and for nearly twenty-four hours the turret guns of the superpowers pointed in silent menace at each other. The Russian tanks move away first, and shortly afterwards the American tanks headed back to their bases. Ten years went by with continued, annoying incidents as the grim wall remained.

On September 3, 1971, after thirty-three working sessions over a seventeen-month period, the ambassadors of Britain, France, the U.S.S.R. and the U.S.A. signed the first stage of a three-part Berlin treaty—the first agreement concerning Berlin signed by these four powers since 1949. Basically the agreement meant that the Soviet Union now formally accepted the close economic and political

The Berlin Wall, looking into East Berlin

relationship between West Germany and West Berlin. The U.S.S.R. again accepted its responsibility for the access routes to Berlin. The treaty included the easing of restrictions on visits by West Berliners to the Eastern Sector and arrangements concerning the transit of goods between the two areas. It was definitely stated that West Berlin would be represented by West Germany in all international organizations but that West Berlin was not part of the Federal Republic of Germany.

After prolonged conferences between representatives of East and West Germany, this treaty was approved on December 11 by the West Berlin Senate. The delay in signing was caused by East German insistence that some limit be placed on the number of West Berliners entering the eastern part of the city. A compromise arrangement was reached whereby West Berliners could obtain entry permits for periodic visits of up to thirty days but their use of transportation to and from the East was strictly regulated.

The final clause in the treaty, which was a breakthrough in German-Soviet relations and a triumph for Chancellor Willy Brandt, was the need for the Bundestag's ratification of the agreements made by West Germany and Poland in 1970. The Bundestag—the German Federal Diet—corresponds in many ways to our House of Commons, and has the task of introducing and passing all legislation. These German-Polish agreements included stronger economic ties with eastern Europe and particularly the Soviet Union, a present acceptance of German national boundaries (although further negotiations for adjusting these boundaries would be considered), and the tacit admission that the Soviet Union could speak and make agreements for its eastern satellites—in this case Poland and East Germany—despite the fact that they were sovereign states. It took months of careful and adroit political maneouvring by Brandt to achieve the necessary ratification. It came at Bonn in May 1972—248 of the 496 members

voting for ratification and 10 against, with 298 members of the Christian Democratic Union abstaining. Chancellor Brandt had won and he could announce
'a new phase in the history of the Federal Republic'. And indeed, his partially
successful attempt to enhance the relationship between the German Federal
Republic and eastern Europe was a further achievement in lessening the gap
between the Soviet Union and the West.

Cuban Crisis—Week on the Brink

It was the autumn of 1962 and the weather had been warm yet cool with that
particular fall tingle that most Canadians enjoy. But there was an uneasiness
about in the land. A year ago the Berlin Wall had gone up. The Cold War kept
the world in disturbing fear. And now it was Cuba.

Dr. Fidel Castro, communist dictator since 1959, had freed his land from the
economic domination of the United States and from the military clique which had
ruled by club and prison and death. He had nationalized the industries, socialized
the land, but the cost had been great. The sugar cane would have rotted in the
fields had it not been for the Soviet Union, motherland of the communist world.
But Russian friendship had a high price and in the autumn of 1962 the Cubans
were presented with the bill.

From September 2 on, the U.S.S.R. had been supplying Cuba with defensive
weapons, including short-range anti-aircraft missiles, radar installations and
torpedo boats with ship-to-ship guided missile equipment. Some thirty-five
hundred military technicians accompanied the weapons. The Soviet Union
justified this arms supply on the grounds that the Castro regime was threatened
by other Latin American states and that an attempt to invade Cuba was imminent.
The United States watched the arms build-up with growing concern and alarm.
Certain military advisers in the Pentagon urged unilateral action to stop the
flow of weapons. President Kennedy uttered repeated warnings to Cuba and the
U.S.S.R. concerning the establishing of offensive weapon bases on the island, but
the build-up continued.

On Monday evening, October 22, the President of the United States, appearing
on TV, spoke to the world. The familiar Kennedy smile was gone, the eyes were
serious and weary-looking. In chilling detail he announced that new missile sites
had been installed in Cuba by the Soviets. Several of them were of medium range,
capable of delivering nuclear warheads for a distance of more than a thousand
miles. Other sites being installed would be able to send nuclear warheads as far
north as Hudson Bay and as far south as Lima, Peru. Cuba had been transformed
into a strategic offensive base pointed at North and South America.

The proposals to combat the build-up were logical and frightening. They were,
in part, (1) 'All ships of any kind bound for Cuba from whatever nation or port
will, if found to contain cargoes of offensive weapons, be turned back,' and (2) 'It
shall be the policy of this nation to regard any nuclear missile launched from Cuba
against any nation in the western hemisphere as an attack by the Soviet Union on
the United States, requiring a full retaliatory response upon the Soviet Union.'

Kennedy then announced that the resolution to be submitted by the United

Fidel Castro speaking at an outdoor rally in Havana

States to an emergency meeting of the U.N. Security Council would call for
dismantling and withdrawal of all offensive weapons in Cuba, under the supervision of U.N. observers, before the naval blockade would be lifted. There was an
impassioned appeal to Chairman Khrushchev 'to move the world back from the
abyss of destruction', an offer to continue negotiations for a nuclear disarmament
treaty, and a solid recommitment of support for 'the brave people of West Berlin'.

Millions of people slept uneasily that night and for other nights to come. The
world knew that cargo ships from the Union of Soviet Socialist Republics,
carrying the missiles of death, were moving steadily towards Cuba, and that the
warships of the United States of America were taking up positions around the
island, and waiting.

On Tuesday morning, October 23, the Security Council at the United Nations
met in emergency debate. U.S. Ambassador Adlai Stevenson outlined his country's
position and emphasized the need for the blockade and U.N. inspection of the
missile sites. He ended with this challenge: 'Let it be remembered, not as the day
when the world came to the edge of nuclear war, but as the day when men resolved
to let nothing thereafter stop them in their quest for peace.' Both the Cuban
ambassador to the U.N. and Valerian A. Zorin of the Soviet Union denounced the
American resolution and accused the United States of a series of aggressive acts
against Cuba. The Organization of American States approved the U.S. quarantine
plan unanimously. Tension grew at the U.N.

On October 24, U.N. Secretary General U Thant sent identical letters to President Kennedy and Premier Khrushchev asking for voluntary suspension of all arms shipments to Cuba and of the quarantine measures involving search at sea for a three-week period to enable 'the parties concerned to meet and discuss with a view to finding a peaceful solution to the problem'. Both leaders accepted the offer, and the following day Thant appealed to the Soviet Premier to avoid a clash between Russian ships on their way to Cuba and American forces determined to enforce the blockade. On October 26 Thant received this answer: 'We have ordered the masters of Soviet vessels bound for Cuba but not yet within the area of the American warships' piratical activities to stay out of the interception area as you recommend.' And on the same day, Premier Khrushchev sent a message to President Kennedy—the text of which still remains in the secret files —agreeing to withdraw offensive weapons from Cuba. Another note from the Soviet Premier arrived on October 27 suggesting that the U.S. abandon its missile bases in Turkey in return for the dismantling of the Cuban bases. This same note also outlined a program for renewal of nuclear disarmament talks and limitation of nuclear testing. Kennedy chose to ignore its 'trade missile bases' offer, but accepted the other terms. The tense situation was defused, and by Sunday, October 28, the confrontation stage had passed. Khrushchev agreed to withdraw missile bases from Cuba, Kennedy agreed not to invade, and the world sighed with relief.

The Russian cargo ships turned back to their ports; the sleek warships of the U.S. Navy leisurely completed their observations in the Caribbean; the missile sites were dutifully dismantled and packaged for shipment back to the U.S.S.R. On January 7, 1963, in a joint note to Secretary General U Thant, the U.S.A. and the U.S.S.R. declared the crisis over.

In the late fifties, Castro, the lawyer revolutionary, had appealed to the American people as the underdog fighter against the repressive, brutal dictatorship of Fulgencio Batista, a tough army officer who had seized power in Cuba in 1952. Castro's first attempt at upsetting the Batista regime was an attack on the army barracks at Santiago de Cuba in 1953. It was a disastrous failure and two-thirds of his 150 followers were killed or captured. Castro fled to the U.S. to raise money for the cause, and returned the following year to lead his followers from their hideouts in the Sierra Maestra mountains of Oriente province. In the meantime, Castro's second-in-command, Ernesto 'Che' Guevara, a superb revolutionary fighter who later became a legendary figure to the 'New Left', had recruited and trained guerrilla groups, and in October 1958 Che led successful uprisings. The Batista forces became dispersed as the revolutionary strikes took place in many areas. Castro moved down from the mountains. A November rising in Havana showed Batista that he had lost his urban supporters, and quarrels among his own army leaders further affected his ability to cope with the unrest. In January of 1959 Batista fled from the island and in February Castro became premier.

The leader of the revolution moved quickly to set up a communist state. Laws breaking up the vast estates and turning over the running of the huge sugar plantations to the peasants affected U.S. interests in the sugar industry. American oil refineries were nationalized without compensation to their owners, and by the end of 1960, all major industries in Cuba had been taken over by the state. In an effort to force compensation the American government placed an embargo on the purchase of sugar, Cuba's largest crop, the export sale of which is essential to the country's economy. The Soviet Union, in turn, moved quickly to defend a socialist state and announced the purchase of Cuba's sugar crop at a fixed world market price; Czechoslovakia and the People's Republic of China followed suit.

Early in 1961, following a military threat to their naval base at Guantanamo, the United States broke off diplomatic relations with Cuba. In April of that year Cuban exiles, trained and equipped by the C.I.A., attempted to topple the Castro regime by a futile invasion at the Bay of Pigs, but were completely defeated. In 1962, Cuba was expelled from the Organization of American States and a complete trade blockade was imposed.

Despite vast loans from the U.S.S.R.—reportedly as high as $500 million per year—and a total debt in the last decade of nearly $6 billion, the Cuban economy remains stagnant. For the past six years the sugar crop has failed to reach its target quota. Salt is the only unrationed foodstuff, consumer goods are non-existent, and the service industries have practically disappeared.

There is growing concern in the U.S.S.R. about Cuba's economic policies. The director of the Soviet State Planning Commission, Nikolai Babakov, spent two months in Cuba in 1971 attempting to solve the problems of agricultural productivity. An incentive program was begun, to provide rationed consumer goods to those workers who raised their output, and workers were conscripted to harvest the sugar crop. In spite of these measures, only 6 of the desired 7 million tons of sugar were produced. The only encouraging government claim was an estimated twenty per cent increase in industrial productivity—a benefit to the sixty per cent of workers who comprise the urban population.

In 1972 there were some indications that Cuba was moving back to more normal relationships with the non-communist world. Chile resumed diplomatic relations with Cuba and a lengthy visit to that country by Castro in 1971—his first visit to a Latin American country since the revolution—was an outstanding success. Peru and Ecuador were stopping-off places for the Cuban Premier on his way back to Havana. O.A.S. members put considerable pressure on the United States to end the diplomatic and economic isolation imposed on Cuba in 1962, and certainly President Nixon's policy of rapprochement with China and increasing friendliness with the Soviet Union made the stiff-lipped attitude towards Cuba difficult to maintain. Sweden and Spain signed Cuban trade pacts, and in July 1972 Canadian and Cuban diplomats were working out the details of an air highjacking treaty between the two countries—the first such arrangement made at an international level.

The hard economic facts of life seem to have tempered the evangelical zeal of socialist Cuba. Though still a harbour for revolutionaries in exile, like the F.L.Q. kidnappers of James Cross and Pierre Laporte, the old fervour seems to have abated. Cuba may well be seeking a way back.

18 VIVE LE CANADA!

Canada at Britain's Side

Hitler's invasion of Poland. What a long time ago that seems to us now—a distant day, half forgotten in the momentous events that have swirled the world into all the uncertainties of the nuclear age. Now it is necessary in this final chapter to retrace our steps and look at the war and post-war years from a purely Canadian viewpoint.

On Friday, September 1, 1939, in Canada the Labour Day weekend was coming up, school was due to re-open in five days and many families were preparing for the last holiday of the summer season. For many other families, however, the holiday had no meaning. Four hundred thousand wage-earners were unemployed, the scars of the drought lay upon the prairie provinces and the country as a whole was still smarting from the effects of the depression years. At six o'clock on that fateful morning, the Deputy Minister of External Affairs in Ottawa telephoned the Prime Minister, getting him out of bed to tell him that, according to persistent radio reports, the Wehrmacht was crossing the borders into Poland. Mackenzie King, it was said, listened to the news and hung up without saying a word. Perhaps he was still half-asleep, but more likely the Prime Minister was too stunned to speak because he, along with the great majority of his countrymen, had believed that the policy of appeasement would bring 'peace in our time'. Now that vision was shattered. Hitler had crossed his Rubicon and the Canadian people once again faced the prospect of a major war.

This time, however, Canada would have to make her own declaration of war as an independent country within the British Commonwealth of Nations. Later on that first day, therefore, the telephone calls and telegrams went out from Ottawa summoning the members back to the capital for an emergency session of parliament. The issue was never in doubt. On September 7, four days after Great Britain and France had opened hostilities against Nazi Germany, the Prime Minister of Canada met a parliament whose mind was fully made up. The Speech from the Throne, one of the shortest on record, was read by the Governor General and quickly moved and seconded by two Liberal backbenchers. Dr. Robert S. Manion, the pleasant but ineffectual politician who had succeeded Bennett as Conservative leader, then pledged his party's full co-operation. According to custom, he was followed by the Prime Minister who took three rambling hours to review the whole international situation and to assure the members that acceptance of the Throne speech would be followed by a declaration of war. There was, he said, only one reservation. In the interests of national unity and with the bitter memories of 1917 in mind, his administration would never introduce conscription of men for overseas service.

The Prime Minister's words and fears were powerfully underlined by Ernest Lapointe, the Minister of Justice and one of the most respected French-Canadian statesmen of our time. 'Sons of one country, brothers in one family, for the future of Canada is it not imperative that no section of Canada, no race, no creed, should inflict upon the other sections, the other races or the other creeds incurable wounds which might destroy our country forever?' The province of Quebec, he explained, was just as anxious to see this thing through to the end as any other part of the country, but French Canada would never accept conscription and neither he nor any other Quebec member would remain in a government that attempted to introduce compulsory military service overseas. Then he glowered across at the opposition benches and asked: 'Is that clear enough?' And it was clear enough. At that early moment, every political party in Canada agreed that conscription would split the country and was an issue to be avoided at almost any cost.

With this understanding in mind, and partly because of it, the entire House of Commons, English- and French-speaking members alike, voted almost unanimously in favour of going to war. There were only three dissenters—two French-Canadian members and J. S. Woodsworth, the respected leader of the C.C.F. and a deeply sincere Christian pacifist who sacrificed himself and his political career at this time by refusing to change his convictions. Thus, on September 10, His Majesty King George VI, acting on behalf of his ministers in Ottawa, proclaimed Canada's declaration of war against Nazi Germany.

Unity on the Home Front

Canada had no sooner gone to war than some of the extremists in Quebec tried to squirm out of it. Editorials show that if the French Canadians had been in a position to do so, they would have gladly followed the example of the United States and remained neutral. Knowing this, Premier Maurice Duplessis dissolved the provincial legislature, called a new election with war as the main campaign issue and undertook to challenge the right of the federal government to speak for the people. Quebec, he said, wished to have 'autonomy within Canada'. Thus, for selfish political purposes, the leader of the Union Nationale was prepared to disrupt the national war effort, isolate Quebec, ignite the hatred of English-speaking Canada and damage his own race for years to come. With only a small degree of exaggeration one Canadian historian has written: 'In retrospect this may be considered the most important election in modern Canadian history. A nation frantically attempting to prepare for war was required overnight to confront the oldest problem of its life and prove to itself and the world whether it was a nation or not.'

This was a challenge the federal government simply could not ignore. Duplessis had to be defeated. Thus Ernest Lapointe and other French-speaking members of the Liberal administration in Ottawa were sent into Quebec to fight the Union Nationale and to urge the people, with passionate oratory, to support Adelard Godbout, the Liberal leader. These men put their own political careers on the line by warning that if Duplessis were returned to office they would resign from the cabinet and thus leave the province without any voice in federal affairs. Even more important than this, however, was the fact that Lapointe and his colleagues repeated their promise to Quebec that they would never serve in a government which adopted conscription for overseas service. Mainly as a result of this high-powered campaign, the French-Canadian voters, on October 26, declared against autonomy and swept Duplessis into the discard where, at this particular time in our history, he undoubtedly belonged. And perhaps the rest of Canada should have noted more carefully the promise that had been given to ensure this victory.

While Canada slumbered through the 'phoney' phase of the war, another attack, this time from the extremists in Ontario, also threatened to destroy national unity. The War was not very many months old before Mitchell Hepburn, the wisecracking, ambitious Liberal Premier of Ontario, began to listen to the siren song of all those who believed that an effective war effort was measured only by masses of troops marching off to faraway battlefields. In an apparent attempt to smash the power of his own party in Ottawa and perhaps elevate himself to a position of national prominence, he launched a bitter campaign against Mackenzie King and the federal government for their 'gross misconduct of the war'. George Drew, the up-and-coming leader of the Conservatives in Ontario, and his friend, George McCullagh, the publisher of Toronto's *Globe and Mail*, gleefully and quite naturally rallied to support a Liberal premier who was undertaking to wreck his own party in federal politics. In time, Hepburn's attack became so violent that many moderate people quickly forgot the good work he had accomplished as premier of Ontario during the depression years. By distorting facts and undermining confidence, his campaign, in its own way, threatened the national war effort just as much as did the extremists from Quebec.

The final verdict about Hepburn and the efficiency or otherwise of the federal government was made by the people of Canada. The last election for the House of Commons had been the one in 1935 which resulted in the defeat of Bennett. Therefore, with the five-year time limit nearly up, King dissolved parliament and called for a general election on March 26, 1940.

In the ensuing campaign, Dr. Manion and the Conservatives demanded the establishment of a national government formed by all political parties. There is much to be said for a coalition government in wartime if only because it lessens the necessity for party politics when a nation's life is at stake. But King, like Woodrow Wilson at the Paris Peace Conference, was so confident of his own ability that he scoffed at the thought of joining with other political parties. He insisted that the Liberal party was deep in good manpower, that it represented all parts of the country and, although he did not say so in as many words, he clearly implied that the Conservatives had nothing to offer. And apparently the country agreed with him because on election day the Hepburn-Drew combination was shattered, Dr. Manion himself was defeated and the government of

Mackenzie King was returned to office with the largest majority in Canadian history. Perhaps the only real loser was Premier Hepburn for he was soon to be ousted by the Conservatives led by George Drew.

The Federal Octopus

The 'phoney' war, the lull before the storm, gave Canada a necessary breathing spell to put her house in order. By the end of March, 1940, as a result of the political developments described above, the most serious internal strains had been put to rest, at least temporarily, and the country was more united in spirit than it had been for many years. And just in the nick of time, because within the next three months, as we know, the blitzkrieg struck down Norway, Denmark and the Low Countries, drove the British from the beaches of Dunkirk, knocked France out of the War and left the British Commonwealth of Nations standing alone against the might of Germany. Suddenly Canada found herself thrust into the role of a major belligerent, the second strongest country left in the war against Hitler. At a time when no one could foresee that either Russia or the United States would join the conflict, the resources and manpower of this country formed the thin margin between victory and defeat.

Almost overnight, therefore, Canada was forced to discard her previous, limited outlook and plunge into a total, all-out war effort. 'Total war'—a new phrase meaning that in order to provide all the equipment required by modern, mechanized warfare, the nation must direct its entire productive capacity and resources towards one single purpose. And this could be accomplished, of course, only by giving unlimited authority to the government in Ottawa to regulate and control the whole economic life of the country. Up to this time the federal government had been somewhat overshadowed by the provinces but now, after Dunkirk, it grew until its power and influence were felt as never before. The right to do this was provided by the War Measures Act which set aside any constitutional limit to the power of the federal government and gave the cabinet authority to issue emergency decrees, by orders in council, without reference to the House of Commons.

During the remaining years of the War, thousands of these orders in council as well as many special acts of parliament extended the sway of the central government to a degree undreamed of at any previous time in our history. In addition to all the regulations governing the three armed services and the raising of billions of dollars through taxes and loans, the manpower resources of the country were diverted by the National Selective Service Act away from non-essential jobs and into war work. Beginning with restrictions on the use of wool, leather, lumber, steel and oil, almost every article entering into war production or civilian consumption eventually was brought under official control. A strict system of quotas limited the production of automobiles, electrical appliances and many other civilian commodities; a price ceiling was imposed on practically all goods and services, including rents; wages were frozen at existing levels and regulations were introduced to control strikes and lockouts; gasoline, sugar, butter and meat were carefully rationed and every citizen had a ration book containing coupons to be used whenever purchases were made. However, no one suffered any real hardship and those who ran short usually managed to trade coupons with more provident neighbours. The basic purpose of all these and a multitude of other regulations was to cut down on non-essential goods and services, direct materials and manpower into war production and prevent any serious increase in the cost of living such as the country had experienced during the First World War. Although in an undertaking of such magnitude many mistakes were inevitable, it is generally conceded that these three objectives were achieved and that, with the exception of Great Britain, Canada managed her wartime economy as well as any country in the world.

This could never have been accomplished without a gigantic increase in the number of highly trained, permanent officials employed by the government. In response to the need for expert help, some of the finest minds in Canada, a veritable brain trust, migrated to Ottawa to join the civil service and to act as advisers to the cabinet ministers. At all times, the civil service has been more influential than the public imagine, but during the war years it attained a new level of power and responsibility. The tremendous burdens assumed by the federal government, the centralization of authority in the hands of the cabinet, the deluge of orders in council that no cabinet could begin to read, the countless regulations that only the experts who wrote them fully understood, all combined to make the civil service more powerful than ever before. Ideas and policies no longer came through the cumbersome machinery of the House of Commons but from the permanent officials, operating quickly and quietly behind the scenes. This decline in the importance of parliament was the price democracy had to pay for efficiency in wartime. This powerful, war-born civil service has persisted in the continuing decades of crisis and, in the opinion of some observers, threatens to undermine the proper functioning of parliamentary democracy. If this is true, then wartime Ottawa, with the cabinet and the permanent officials in charge of everything, set a pattern for a new kind of political life in Canada.

Total War
Of all the federal agencies that reached out from Ottawa during the war years, the most important was the Department of Munitions and Supply under the skilled and dynamic leadership of C. D. Howe. This was the department charged with the sole responsibility of making all defence purchases and of mobilizing the industrial resources of Canada to meet the needs of war. It possessed almost unlimited authority to control raw materials, to issue contracts to private industry, and to purchase, expropriate or manufacture directly any of the infinitely varied supplies required by the armed forces of Canada and her allies. The department was unique among the Allied nations. No similar body existed in any other country and nowhere else was all the purchasing done by one central agency possessing so much power. Like many men in positions of great authority, Howe and his expert staff made their share of bad friends, but nothing should be allowed to detract from the phenomenal results achieved by Canadian industry under their general management.

From a small organization with only a handful of staff, the Department grew
into a commercial and industrial giant providing employment, either directly or
indirectly, for over a million men and women—more than three times the number
engaged in war work during the 1914–18 period. As the largest business organization in the history of this country, it made or bought during the height of its
activity $65 million worth of munitions each week and by the end of the War its
total purchases exceeded $10½ billion! The significance of this figure may be
gathered from the fact that it is as much money as the Dominion government
spent in its entire history from Confederation up to and including the year 1932.

The industrial activity stimulated by this department was much greater in
range as well as in magnitude than similar developments during the First World
War. Although the arsenals and small-arms factories turned out far more shells
and light guns than they did in the 1914–18 period, Canadian production was no
longer confined mainly to these two items. In addition to many hundreds of
smaller craft, Canadian shipyards produced more than 1,000 naval and cargo
vessels; the aircraft factories contributed nearly 15,000 planes; the automotive
industry turned out 700,000 transport trucks and almost 50,000 armoured fighting
vehicles; the armament companies manufactured 1.5 million machine guns,
100,000 heavy guns, 110 million shells and bombs and more than 4 billion rounds
of small-arms ammunition. Important new industries such as synthetic rubber,
optical glass, petrochemicals and plastics were brought into existence; some
$450 million worth of radar and signals equipment was produced; many millions
of dollars were spent on military establishments and many millions more on
personal equipment for service men and women. And all this was accomplished
while Canada's basic agricultural industry expanded by over forty per cent and
provided the Allies with more than twice as much food as in 1914–18. Less than
one-third of Canada's total war production was used by our own forces at home
and abroad. The remainder went to Britain, Africa, India, Russia, China and the
south Pacific. And because Great Britain and some of the other United Nations
did not have the dollars to pay for these supplies, Canada introduced her own
version of Lend-Lease aid, advancing almost $4 billion to her allies before the
end of hostilities. All this was a truly remarkable achievement for a nation of less
than 12 million people—an achievement also of great value in the post-war
years because it greatly increased Canada's manufacturing capacity and left her
with a better balanced and more mature industrial structure than she had ever
had before.

Although price controls and other strict regulations prevented wartime
profiteering from running rampant as it did during the First World War, a great
many people were critical of the way Howe's department handled its contracts
with private industry. The government usually agreed to pay a company's full
costs of production plus ten per cent above these costs as profit. These 'cost plus'
contracts obviously put a premium on inefficiency because the higher the costs
the greater was the profit. Ten per cent of $50,000 is a lot less than ten per cent
of $100,000. Despite the fact that government inspectors tried to prevent abuses,
there was a great deal of waste and duplication, serious enough at times to make

one suspect that it was deliberate and to justify the conclusion that Canadian industry could have accomplished even more than it did. The leaders of the C.C.F. and others with socialist views went a step farther and argued that easy cash on the barrelhead and not patriotism was the main motive behind our war effort. They also maintained that if the government could draft a man into the army at $1.50 a day, it should also use its power to conscript industry and wealth. Although these opinions were widely circulated and the popularity of the C.C.F. increased during the War, the majority of Canadians seemed to be satisfied that there was no other way to get the job done and that, generally speaking, patriotism kept the Canadian economy running at a high level of efficiency.

Financing Canada's war effort was almost as challenging a task as that faced by the Department of Munitions and Supply. Averaging about $12 million per day, the Dominion's war expenditures finally reached the staggering total of $20 billion. Recalling the mistakes made during the First World War, J. L. Ilsley, the Minister of Finance, and his advisers attempted to raise as much of this as possible by taxation rather than by borrowing. Customs and excise duties, sales taxes and other forms of raising revenue were drastically increased; the provinces were persuaded to give up their right to tax the incomes of individuals and corporations for the duration of the War, and the income and corporation taxes were then increased to finance this gigantic war effort. As a result of these and other measures, the federal government paid over 50 per cent of the costs of the War on a day-to-day basis out of taxes. This stands in marked contrast to the 1914–18 period when only 15 per cent of the costs were financed by taxation. Thus, Ilsley's department kept the burden of debt as low as possible and at the same time, by restricting the amount an individual had to spend, helped to prevent inflation.

The remainder of the war costs that could not be paid out of current revenue had to be met, of course, by borrowing through the sale of Victory bonds. During the First World War, as we have observed elsewhere, four of every five Victory bonds were purchased by the insurance and trust companies, the banks and other commercial concerns. As a result, peacetime taxes were used to transfer wealth, in the form of interest payments, into the hands of a comparatively few wartime bond holders. And this in turn was one of the many causes for the inequality of income that weakened the Canadian economy during the boom period in the 1920s. During the Second World War, however, over half of the $10 billion raised by Victory loans was subscribed by private individuals, many of whom were people of average means. After 1945, therefore, the payment of interest charges on the public debt transferred wealth back into the hands of many thousands of Canadian citizens, thereby helping to maintain the purchasing power of the country.

Canada's Fighting Men

The record of achievement described in the preceding pages is made all the more remarkable by the fact that the armed forces of Canada enlisted over a million

Tiger Moth planes at an R.C.A.F. training school, 1941

men and women during the course of the Second World War, five-sixths of them by voluntary methods. In 1939, the Royal Canadian Navy consisted of fifteen ships and a tiny establishment of about 1,700 men. Well before the end of hostilities, this pocket navy had been expanded to over 900 vessels, of which some 350 were classified as fighting ships; its manpower had risen to 90,000 officers and men; and there were over 5,000 'Wrens' in the Women's Royal Canadian Naval Service. By the spring of 1944, the Royal Canadian Navy was the third largest in the Allied world, strong enough not only to provide a hundred per cent of the close escort for all North American convoys to Britain but also to contribute more than 100 ships and 10,000 men for the sea-borne invasion of Normandy.

The growth of the Royal Canadian Air Force was even more striking. From a peacetime establishment of 4,500 officers and men, the R.C.A.F. expanded to more than 200,000, including 16,500 in the Women's Division. By the end of the War, with 45 squadrons overseas, Canada had become the fourth strongest air power among the United Nations, ranking next to such giants as the United States, Great Britain and Russia. Canadian fliers saw action in North Africa, Malta, Sicily, over the beachheads of Anzio and Salerno in Italy, in Burma, Ceylon and India; they played a major part in softening up western Europe before D-day and formed one-quarter of the air crews engaging in the final assault on Nazi Germany. In addition to all this, the Dominion government managed, and to a large extent financed, the British Commonwealth Air Training Plan under which some 130,000 airmen from all parts of the Commonwealth, and free forces from Norway and Poland, were trained on Canadian soil.

Commencing with one hastily trained division that was sent to the British Isles during the 'phoney' war, the ground forces were rapidly expanded until Canada had more than five full divisions overseas and the total number of men and women, at home and abroad, had climbed to well over 650,000. This force was so much larger than the one raised during the First World War that in April 1942 the three infantry and two armoured divisions in Britain were organized into a

(Above) On the beach at Dieppe after the disastrous raid of August 19, 1941. Of five thousand Canadians who were landed, only two thousand returned. (Right) Canadians on the march in Italy, 1944.

fullfledged Canadian Army under the command of General McNaughton. For the next fifteen months, however, these troops were held in Great Britain and, except for the large-scale raid on Dieppe, saw no action. It was originally intended that the Canadian Army would be trained to the peak of efficiency and then used as a spearhead—in General McNaughton's words, 'as a dagger pointed at the heart of Berlin'—in the eventual invasion of Europe. This plan to keep the army intact was upset by a persistent and increasing clamour in Canada, demanding that the Canadian troops should be sent into battle.

As one historian has written: 'Apparently there were groups who needed the emotional satisfaction that they derived from casualty lists in order to feel that Canada was bearing her proper share in the War. Repeated assertions by government spokesmen that the army was being kept in Britain by the desire of British authorities did little to diminish the criticism directed at Ottawa.' The predominant role of the Canadians at Dieppe failed to satisfy these emotions and when Canadians were excluded from the forces that invaded North Africa in October 1942, the public pressure on the government became too strong to resist.

In July 1943, therefore, over the protests and the eventual resignation of General McNaughton, the Canadian Army was broken up and the 1st Division was dispatched to take part in the invasion of Sicily. After the landings on the Italian mainland, it was joined by the 5th Armoured Division and for most

of the remaining months of the War these two Canadian divisions, as part of the British Eighth Army, played an important role in the liberation of Italy. Then on D-day, June 6, 1944, two days after the Canadian troops in Italy had helped to capture Rome, the 3rd Canadian Division was one of the five Allied divisions that led the assault on the beaches of Normandy. On their heels, superbly trained Canadian soldiers by the tens of thousands poured across the Channel until by July 26 every unit of the Canadian Army overseas was in action. From then on, fighting some of the toughest, least spectacular yet most vital assignments, the Canadian Army, having helped to take Caen and liberate Normandy, swept the Germans from the Channel ports, opened Antwerp by clearing the approaches of the river Scheldt, launched the first offensive for the Rhineland and participated with all its strength in the final drive across the Rhine.

The Conscription Issue Once Again

In view of all that has been recorded in the preceding pages, it is most unfortunate that the fine achievements of this country, both on the home front and overseas, should have been marred by the old argument about conscription. We have already observed that all political parties promised that conscription for overseas service would not be introduced and these pledges were repeated vigorously by both Manion and King during the 1940 election. The military authorities also assured the government that Canada could maintain her army overseas without conscription. However, in unofficial circles across English-speaking Canada, there was an undertone of discontented voices that demanded compulsory overseas service from the very outset of the War. In order to meet this criticism, the government introduced a system of compulsory training for home defence only. The training period, originally set at thirty days, was gradually extended until finally, in 1941, it was announced that the draftees would remain in service for home defence indefinitely. The government probably expected that once the men were in uniform many of them would enlist for overseas service and to some extent this did happen. The majority, however, showed a surprising ability to resist all the pressures and all the inducements held out to make them 'go active'. Thus, at a time when Canada was in no danger of invasion and when manpower was badly needed for industry, the country found itself in possession of a conscript force derisively nicknamed the 'zombie army'.

About the time that this 'zombie army' came into existence, the question of compulsory service overseas was brought into the open by a change of leadership in the Conservative party. After his defeat, Dr. Manion resigned and the Conservatives, somewhat in desperation, turned again to Arthur Meighen, who finally agreed to accept their leadership on the explosive platform of 'compulsory selective service over the whole field of war'. In February 1942, on the strength of his platform, the new Conservative leader attempted to win a seat in the House of Commons by means of a by-election in South York. The contest, a two-way affair between Meighen and a C.C.F. candidate named Joseph Noseworthy— with Hepburn and some Liberals throwing all their weight behind Meighen and with other Liberals supporting the C.C.F. candidate—developed into one of the most highly publicized and expensive by-elections in Canadian history. On election day, the voters in South York ruined Meighen's political comeback and sank the hopes of the Conservative party, but the damage had been done. During a period when there was no real crisis in manpower, when voluntary enlistments for all three services were being maintained at a satisfactory rate, the old controversy over conscription had been tossed fully into the political arena.

Partly to meet this Conservative challenge and partly to satisfy the 'conscriptionists' within his own party, Mackenzie King decided to ask the people to release the Liberals from their no-conscription pledge. On April 27, 1942, therefore, a plebiscite was held in which the country voted yes or no to the question: 'Are you in favour of releasing the government from any obligation arising out of any past commitments restricting the methods of raising men for overseas service?' This technique, if it was meant to reveal a united national feeling, was a sad failure. Sixty-four per cent of the voters favoured giving the government a free hand, but while the percentage of 'yes' votes was over 80 per cent in Ontario, Manitoba and British Columbia, it was a bare 28 per cent in Quebec. Thus the plebiscite did no more than reveal and sharpen the division between Quebec and the rest of Canada. And yet a great many people now claimed that the government, with this popular vote to back it up, should introduce compulsory overseas service immediately. It is true, of course, that democracy is based on majority rule, but it is equally true that the majority are not entitled to ride roughshod over the opposition. Democracy must proceed by compromise, and, although compromises are usually weak and seldom satisfy either side, students of government generally agree that this is the only way to ensure national unity. And this reasoning applies with special force to a country like Canada that has inherited such a complex racial problem. Instead of being heralded as a go-ahead signal, therefore, the plebiscite was regarded by King and the majority of his cabinet as yet another warning to be cautious.

It was easy enough, of course, for the government to pursue a cautious policy and to avoid conscription as long as the Canadian Army remained in Great Britain. But after D-day the severe fighting in Europe produced such heavy battle casualities that by October 1944 the supply of reinforcements for Canadian infantry divisions was completely exhausted. A shortage did not exist in the navy, in the air force or in the armoured divisions of the army. According to the official history of the Canadian Army, the root of this problem lay in the fact that our military experts, in common with those from many other countries, completely underestimated the number of casualties among the infantry and that 'too many men were trained for the armoured forces and the artillery, too few by far for the infantry.' Despite the fact that they had compulsory overseas service, both the United States and Great Britain also faced this problem and the British War Office was forced to disband two infantry divisions in order to provide reinforcements for other formations. Canada might have followed some such course, but Colonel Ralston, the Minister of National Defence, and his military advisers maintained that the army should be kept intact and that this could be done only by compulsory overseas service. The conscription problem of 1914–18 was to be repeated.

During the last two weeks of October, the Liberal administration— with some of its members supporting Ralston and others following Mackenzie King in his last-minute attempts to evade conscription—seemed to be on the verge of collapse. Rumour had it that a coalition government, perhaps with Ralston as prime minister, was about to be formed. Colonel Ralston, however, was not a self-seeking man. On November 1, solely to emphasize what he believed to be the proper course, the Minister of National Defence resigned—some say he was simply fired—and from then on was content to remain in the background while General McNaughton, his successor, attempted to raise the necessary reinforcements by voluntary methods. When it became obvious that McNaughton was not going to succeed, the government finally, on November 23, agreed to send overseas 16,000 of the draftees who had been trained for home defence. As later events proved, this number was sufficient to provide reinforcements for the duration of the War. Even this limited departure from voluntary methods, however, was enough to provoke the resignation of C. G. 'Chubby' Power, the Minister of National Defence for Air, while in English-speaking Canada the use of the home defence army instead of outright conscription brought coals of fire down on Mackenzie King's head.

Attempting to take political advantage of this situation, 'Honest John' Bracken, the new Conservative leader, publicly stated that many of the draftees had thrown their equipment overboard just as soon as they marched up the gangplank of the

Sir John A. Macdonald's unhappy predicament in 1885 is one that all Canadian prime ministers since then have had to face at some time during their career.

A RIEL UGLY POSITION.

troopships. Although in fact only one demented soldier had done anything like this, Bracken's statement received widespread publicity, both at home and abroad, and many people felt that it did a great deal of damage to the good name of Canada. Their resentment is regarded as one of the factors that led to the defeat of the Conservatives in the general election held shortly after V-E day. John Bracken's indiscretion, however, only serves to illustrate an unfortunate weakness of party politics. Mainly for political purposes, Mackenzie King has been fiercely assailed and almost as fiercely defended for his actions during the last few months of the War. According to his opponents, the Prime Minister was motivated solely by a desire to stay in office while his supporters maintain that his main concern was national unity. But whatever the verdict of history on Mackenzie King may be, it should not obscure the fact that this country remained reasonably united during five and a half trying years of war and that the Canadian people have every reason to be proud of their achievements.

The Decades That Roared

The Boom in Foreign Trade
Even before V-J day, almost every Canadian who paused to think about the future had become convinced that history was going to repeat itself. 'We're in for it, for sure,' they said. 'It will be 1921 all over again.' With wartime savings bulging their bank accounts, people would now go on a spending spree, buying all the things they could not get during the War, prices would shoot upward, the lid would be blown off all government controls and then, after a brief but hectic period of prosperity, everything would come crashing down. How could the country possibly absorb back into peacetime occupation the million men and women from the armed forces or the other million who had been engaged in war work? How could a nation whose population had increased by not more than eight per cent but whose industrial equipment had almost doubled even begin to consume the products of her factories? Surely, people said, Canada faced years of difficult readjustment from war to peace and in the process would be lucky to avoid another prolonged depression.

But history did not repeat itself. The post-war buying spree, it is true, did develop just as everyone predicted it would. Government controls were removed and with everything from automobiles and washing machines to nylons and good red beef in scarce supply, prices did soar upward—but they, along with every-thing else, kept right on going. Almost without a ripple of disturbance, the wartime boom rolled forward through the fifties, on into the sixties, establishing new records of achievement with each passing year until every figure by which the material progress of a nation is measured was shattered beyond recognition.

What all those who predicted a depression apparently overlooked was the fact that Canada's prosperity is rooted in her primary industries and in international trade. And in the post-war period, just as in the Laurier era or the years leading up to 1929, world conditions were particularly favourable to the products of our fields, forests and mines. Ready markets overseas existed to help rebuild a war-torn world and to feed millions of its starving people. About the time this period of reconstruction ended, mounting world tensions, with the resulting billions of dollars in defence expenditures, raised world trade to new levels. In 1954 following the Korean War, and again in the early sixties, the United States and to a lesser extent Canada experienced a mild slump—a 'recession' was the new word coined to described it. But each time the world trade boom was soon in full swing again. By 1970 Canada was fourth among the exporting nations of the world.

As in all previous periods of prosperity, it was—and still is— the American market, far more than any other, that determined the volume of our external trade. With its huge industrial complex thriving as never before, the purchasing power of our giant neighbour was at its highest level in history. With welfare legislation helping to maintain this power, with defence and defence-related expenditures exceeding $85 billion per year, including the involvement in Viet Nam and the vastly expensive National Aeronautics Space Administration (N.A.S.A.) project,

Looking up the St. Lawrence Seaway near Cornwall, Ontario. The Seaway was completed in 1959 after nine years of construction and an expenditure of $1 billion.

the U.S. continued to be our best customer, taking over seventy per cent of our $17 billion export total in 1970.

As Cold War tensions have lessened vast new markets have been opened up. Our wheat sales to the U.S.S.R. led to closer economic relationships in the sixties, and our initiative in extending diplomatic recognition to China in 1970— a move which was followed two years later by the U.S.—has resulted in developing trade with this huge country.

Since the days of the sodbusters and the men in sheepskin coats, wheat has held a special place in our economy; indeed, wheat and Canada are almost synonymous in many parts of the world. During the fifties the world wheat market held up very well. In 1953 the Canadian crop reached an all-time high of 701,973,000 bushels and the Wheat Board sold most of it at an average price of $1.80 per bushel. By 1964 the value of Canadian agricultural exports reached a total of $1,702,017,000 and grain products made up two-thirds of this amount. This is a far cry from the beginning of our story when the 1901 crop was only 60 million bushels and the value of wheat exports was less than $7 million.

But the old problems of world surpluses, faltering markets and domestic overproduction continue to plague this uncertain industry. Despite new markets in the U.S.S.R., China, Japan and the European Economic Community and the federal government's policy of encouraging wheat growers to diversify their crops, the selling of this vast yearly wheat production remains a major problem and by the end of the sixties wheat had declined to seventh place in Canada's export commodities. There are two major reasons for this situation—world oversupply and increased competition from other wheat-growing countries, particularly the U.S.

As the wheat surpluses continue to pile up in the storage elevators of the West, spiralling costs for labour, machinery and interest on loans have caused a decrease in the farmer's net income. In 1969 total cash receipts from farm operations declined 20% in Saskatchewan, 9% in Alberta and 4% in Manitoba. In Laurier's day, or even in the 1920s, such a decline would have set back the whole economy, but the export value of other products has risen so greatly that the effect today is primarily a regional one. It is nonetheless important in our national life because it contributes to the economic and political sectionalism that is a major problem of present-day Canada. Not since the 'hungry thirties' has the western farmer felt so isolated in the economic framework of the country.

El Dorado and Then Some

There were other new developments of utmost importance to Canada's prosperity that the pessimists of 1945 could not possibly foresee. Up to the end of the Second World War, our progress as an industrial power had been hampered by our almost complete lack of iron ore and oil. Most of our iron ore had to be imported from Newfoundland or the United States. Likewise, with the coming of the automobile Canada was forced to import ninety-five per cent of her oil requirements. Although the country found consolation in its hydro-electric power resources and in the resulting development of the pulp-and-paper, aluminum and light secondary manufacturing industries, a great many Canadians no doubt wished that nature had been even more bountiful.

Now these wishes have been more than fulfilled. The post-war decades have revealed spectacular wealth in oil and iron. In February 1947, after years of exploration and the expenditure of millions of dollars by the leading oil companies, Imperial Oil discovered the great Leduc field a few miles southwest of Edmonton. Recognizing that the oil from this field lay in a similar geological formation to those in Texas and New Mexico, the U.S. oil giants—McColl-Frontenac, British American, Gulf—and the great multinational corporation of Shell, joined Home Oil, the Hudson's Bay Company and the Canadian Pacific Railway in an intensified search for petroleum that still continues. Spending billions of dollars in exploration and development ($1 billion in 1965 alone) the petroleum and natural gas industry has become one of the largest contributors to the Canadian economy. New fields larger than Leduc have been discovered at Redwater, Pembina, Swan Hills and Rainbow Lake. In 1969 Panartic Oils Limited, an industry-government syndicate, was rewarded with initial success in drilling on Melville Island in the high Arctic. The existence of huge oil reserves has been verified, not only in Alberta but in Saskatchewan, Manitoba, British Columbia, the Mackenzie River delta and the Great Bear and Great Slave Lake areas. Near Fort McMurray, in the Athabaska tar sands field, the American-owned Syncrude

(Above) Lowering 30-inch pipe into a ditch dredged in a river during construction of Canada's first major natural gas pipeline. The 650-mile line, completed in 1957, starts in the Peace River country and ends at the international border southeast of Vancouver. (Right) First oil in the Canadian Arctic was struck in January 1970 at Atkinson Point, more than a mile deep.

Canada Limited has been granted permission to construct an extraction plant costing $190 million, and the wild horses of Sable Island may soon be another memory as offshore drilling has indicated the presence of oil in the Atlantic shelf close to the coast of Nova Scotia.

Canada's production of crude petroleum in 1969 was over 408 million barrels, nearly three times the amount produced in 1960—an all-time record. Most of it was purchased by the United States. The continuing and developing presence of foreign firms in the petroleum and natural gas industry is a matter of concern for the National Energy Board and for all Canadians; it is estimated that 72% of the petroleum refineries and 65% of Canada's oil and gas wells are U.S. owned.

According to the experts, it is almost impossible to tell just how large Canada's oil reserves really are. As of January 1, 1971, liquid hydrocarbon reserves were estimated at 10,439 million barrels and the potential crude oil in the Athabaska tar sands area was forecast at between 300 and 600 billion barrels. It is claimed that these sands alone could meet U.S. requirements at the 1969 rate for sixty years. But estimates are no sooner made than they have to be scrapped for higher ones. The day may well come when Canada is one of the world's leading exporters of 'black gold'.

The development of the western oil fields—like the opening of the prairie wheat lands at the beginning of this century or the coming of the automobile in the 1920s—brought new life to many other parts of the Canadian economy. The search for oil, for instance, led to the discovery of large additional supplies of natural gas. Separate pipelines were built to carry oil and natural gas to markets in central Canada, the Pacific coast and several points on the American border. The mileage of this network has tripled within the last ten years. The world's longest natural gas transmission line, 2,300 miles in length, stretching from the Alberta border to Montreal, and with branch lines to U.S. markets near Cornwall, Ontario, and Emerson, Manitoba, was built by Trans-Canada Pipelines. The initial financing of this project by the government, introduced by C. D. Howe, then Minister of Trade and Commerce, caused 'The Great Pipeline Debate' of 1956 and contributed to the defeat of the Liberal government in the following year. It should be noted, however, that Trans-Canada Pipelines repaid the $80 million debt to the federal government well ahead of schedule and by 1970 was 95% Canadian owned.

At the present time the natural gas industry has investments in Canada of over $4 billion and the export value of this commodity in 1970 was $206 million. The most recent estimate of natural gas reserves is a record 53.3 trillion cubic feet, but like the projection of oil reserves this figure is constantly increasing.

As a result of the great oil and gas discoveries, costly new refineries have been built and the petrochemical industry, in its infancy during the war years, has surged to a position of national, and often controversial, prominence. New uses for petroleum and natural gas are being discovered every year and the industry already manufactures a wide range of products including synthetic rubber, plastics and synthetic fibres, bringing new prosperity to such companies as Canadian Industries Limited, the Canadian Chemical and Cellulose Company, and the Dow Chemical and Polymer plants in Sarnia, Ontario.

Although almost all parts of Canada have felt the influence of the oil boom, the greatest changes have taken place in the province of Alberta. Taking a royalty from every barrel of oil and every cubic foot of gas, this province has cleared itself of debt and in accordance with its Social Credit principles has paid its citizens an annual 'social dividend', at first in cash but more recently in the form of civic auditoriums, hospitals and other public works. Although the Social Credit regime was defeated by the Conservatives under Peter Lougheed in 1971 after being in office for thirty-six years, the economic policies of Alberta have remained relatively unchanged. And this is the province, remember, that during the dust-bowl years was on the verge of bankruptcy.

Equally as spectacular and fully as important as the oil boom has been the discovery and development of vast iron ore deposits. Despite the rapid growth of our own steel industry, Canada has become one of the world's leading exporters of iron ore. The main driving force behind this remarkable development has been the prospect of an expanding market for Canadian iron ore in the United States. The American steel industry has grown so rapidly that its domestic reserves of easily workable high-grade iron ore from Minnesota's Mesabi range are virtually exhausted. The remaining ores in the United States are very extensive but of low grade and American steel companies expect in the future to rely more and more on imports. Only Canada and Venezuela are in a favourable position to supply this huge market. As in the case of oil, therefore, American companies, hoping to secure a long-term source of supply, have played a predominant part in the development of the iron-mining industry in Canada, and today 86% of the industry is U.S. controlled.

The first ore body to be discovered and brought into production lay at the bottom of Steep Rock Lake, 150 miles west of Lake Superior and directly north of the Mesabi range. Before mining operations could begin, the lake had to be drained, a river had to be diverted from its course and tons of silt had to be dredged up from the lake bed. The completion of this formidable engineering task in 1944 by the Steep Rock Iron Mining Company disclosed the existence of what is probably one of the largest remaining deposits of high-grade iron ore in the western hemisphere, with reserves estimated to last for many decades.

Perhaps more important in the long run than Steep Rock has been the development at Knob Lake, along the Quebec-Labrador border. The existence of iron throughout this whole region had been known for many years, but the costs of bringing ore out from such a remote and completely undeveloped terrain were prohibitive. After the War, however, with the end in sight on the Mesabi range, the project became economically feasible and the Iron Ore Company of Canada

Open-pit iron mine at Steep Rock, Ontario

was formed to provide the capital and skill necessary to develop these vast resources. Representing a merger of the Hollinger Mining Corporation of Canada, the Hanna Coal and Ore Corporation of Cleveland and five leading American steel companies, this huge organization quickly completed all the preliminary work and in the summer of 1954 the first iron ore from Labrador moved down to the St. Lawrence.

The Quebec-Labrador Railway was built to iron ore fields at Schefferville and then extended to Labrador City to serve the projects of Wabush Mines and Carol Lake. The north shore St. Lawrence ports of Sept Iles, Pointe Noir and Port Cartier were built and developed into the most efficient loading harbour facilities for iron ore in the world. International companies moved into the Ungava-Labrador territory, particularly the Krupp organization from the highly industrial Federal Republic of Germany. Japanese developers indicated their willingness to finance the new iron bonanza and, as we have seen, the Americans were always present. The investment of these multinational corporations was huge, and Canadian production almost doubled from 21 million tons of ore in 1960 to over 40 million tons, valued at $432 million, by 1970. Iron ore moved to tenth place in the list of Canadian exports and was on the way up.

The discovery and exploitation of uranium since 1945 has added its share to the excitement, the speculative fever and the general prosperity of Canada. Although Canadian-produced uranium played a part in the development of the atomic bomb during the war years, it was not until after V-J day, with the atomic age literally mushrooming into existence, that Canada was thoroughly scoured for this precious mineral. For a time, professional geologists and rank amateurs alike had their geiger counters, and more than one novice thought he had struck it rich at his summer cottage or even in his backyard.

As a result of this intensive search, important discoveries were made and developed at widely different points in Canada. The Elliot Lake area, fifteen miles north of Lake Huron, was estimated to contain 93% of Canada's uranium resources, compared to the 6% estimate for the area around Beaverlodge in northern Saskatchewan—site of the ambitiously named Uranium City. Smaller deposits were found at Bancroft, Ontario, and more recently in northeastern Quebec and Labrador. Eldorado Mining and Refining Limited was purchased and organized as a Crown corporation in 1945. The company controlled all uranium mining by government licence and their refining plant in Port Hope, Ontario, was among the first in the world. Canada became the world's largest uranium producer and a leader in post-war development of atomic energy.

This boom, however, was short-lived. Many countries, particularly the United States, soon found that they had too much uranium; other countries encountered technological difficulties in nuclear plant construction, and there were delays in reactor and fuel design. As a result, Canadian uranium production came almost to a halt by the mid-sixties. Elliot Lake nearly became the youngest ghost town on record and Uranium City took on the appearance of a deserted village. The federal government came to the rescue by stockpiling ore and limiting production. By 1969 Denison Mines at Elliot Lake produced at approximately two-thirds its capacity and Eldorado Nuclear Limited was operating on a fifty per cent basis. New techniques were perfected to produce a complete range of refined uranium products for world markets, but attempts at long-term sales were limited. Production declined from 25.5 million pounds of unrefined uranium in 1960 to 7.7 million in 1969, and the value from $270 million to slightly less than $50 million. While uranium producers look forward to a growing market in the seventies as present stockpiles are exhausted and new capabilities for atomic fuel are discovered, the uranium quest proves once again that mining, even at its best, is a boom-or-bust proposition.

In spite of setbacks such as those encountered in the uranium field, Canadian mining in general is undoubtedly a success story. When our story began in 1900 the value of mineral production in Canada was $65 million; by 1970 it was $5.5 billion—double the amount it had been in 1960. Today Canada is the top world producer in asbestos, nickel, platinum and platinum metals, silver and zinc; second in bismuth, cadmium, gold, gypsum, potash, sulphur and uranium; and third in aluminum, iron ore, lead and natural gas. Canada produces about sixty different minerals and leads the world in diversified mineral exports. Canadian mining has come a long way indeed since Fred La Rose staked out his Cobalt claim in the early years of the twentieth century.

The Population Boom

Even with the developments described in the preceding pages, the prosperity of Canada in the fifties and sixties would never have been so great but for a tremendous increase in our domestic trade. Of all the factors causing this home market to boom, the increase in population was certainly the most obvious and one of the most important.

After the War, immigrants poured into the country almost as fast as during the

Laurier era. In 1957 over a quarter of a million people came to Canada, led by an exodus of 118,000 from the austerity and economic distress of post-war Britain; from Germany, Austria and the Balkans came 70,000 and 30,000 Italians left their crowded cities and worn-out farms for a new life in Canada. While the influx was considerably reduced in the next three years, during the fifties 1.5 million immigrants arrived in this country.

During the next ten years the number of immigrants fluctuated considerably. During the years 1960-63, the average annual immigration figure was considerably less than 100,000 and in 1961 it dipped to 71,000, the lowest point in fifteen years. Canada's need for skilled immigrant workers rose in 1963 and resulted in a series of government regulations designed to secure this type of new citizen. Advertising in Europe took on the aspects it had had in the days of Clifford Sifton. Immigration officers were stationed in key cities in Europe to service applications —Madrid, Marseilles, Bordeaux, Milan, all had their Canadian representatives. Today the Canadian government has 38 of these centres in twenty-two countries. Area offices were established so that adjacent countries could be visited by teams of officials who outlined the advantages of Canada, explained the requirements and cut through the 'red tape' of the application process. In all this the key phrase was 'the skilled worker' and officials emphasized the need for immigrants whose professional or technical knowledge would enable them to establish themselves quickly in the fast-developing Canadian society.

The 'new look' in Canada's immigration methods has had outstanding success. The year 1967 provides a good example. During that twelve-month period, of 222,887 immigrants 119,539 were workers, and of that group 87% belonged to the skilled category while those in the managerial or professional ranks numbered 30,853.

Social unrest in America and opportunities in the Canadian professional field more than doubled the U.S. complement arriving in Canada during the sixties. Immigrants from Great Britain maintained first place on the immigrant ladder until 1970. Then the pattern changed. Immigration figures for 1971 showed a total of 121,900 new arrivals. In keeping with an increase first evident in 1968, India contributed 5,131 of the immigrant total and China 5,000. But the greatest surprise was the emergence of the United States for the first time in history as the major source of immigrants to Canada. No less than 24,368 Americans arrived here in 1971. In second place were the British, followed by the Portuguese and the Italians.

With the continuous influx of immigrants, with one of the highest birth rates in the world, with a healthy race living to a ripe old age and with the entrance of Newfoundland as a tenth province in 1949 adding some 350,000 people, the population of Canada surged upward from less than 12 million in 1945 to 18 million at the start of the sixties.

Canadians, since the 'good old days' of 1911 when the 'missing million' played havoc with the population estimates, have always liked to play guessing games with the census figures. In the mid-fifties they were enthusiastically predicting a population of over 25 million for Canada by 1980. They based their prophecy on

Prime Minister Louis St. Laurent welcomes Newfoundland into Confederation at the official ceremonies in April 1949. Seated at right are Joseph Smallwood, first premier of the new province, and former Prime Minister Mackenzie King.

two traditional factors that changed rapidly and upset their calculations. First, they believed that European recovery following World War Two would take generations to achieve and that the downcast and downtrodden peoples of the Old World would continue to flock to these lands 'flowing with milk and honey' across the Atlantic. But West European recovery was swift and the dynamic enterprise and ability of the people of that continent, aided and abetted by American capital, had by the 1960s turned Europe into a successful community which its inhabitants were loath to leave.

And secondly, the self-appointed prophets did not foresee the phenomenal change that was to occur in the structure of society in the sixties. Basing their forecasts on the record birth rate of 28.9 per thousand in 1947, they did not anticipate the economic and philosophic changes that would profoundly affect the family unit. Emphasis on continuing education and increasing costs of living caused most young married couples both to become members of the work force. This precluded early and large families. Concern for the world's population explosion on the part of the better educated and more socially conscious generation was another factor in limiting the size of families. And public, religious and medical opinion finally adopted a more realistic attitude towards birth control. By 1968 the birth rate had fallen to 17.6 per thousand, the lowest on record.

The changing status of women, subject of a Royal Commission in the early seventies, had much to do with the declining birth rate. Between 1964 and 1969, the number of women employed rose from 1,911,000 to 2,508,000 and by the end of the decade one out of every three women in Canada was a member of the labour force. Over 50% of this group were under thirty-five years of age and 56% were married. Along with this female employment increase came demands for equality with male workers—equal pay for equal work, equal opportunities in job progression and, above all, equal recognition for equivalent capabilities. Various women's groups were formed to achieve these objectives and the Women's Liberation Movement became a force to be reckoned with by employers, politicians, and husbands. While the movement at no time advocated the abolition of the family unit, its philosophic influence brought the role of the family under critical observation.

In 1961 Canada's population was 18,238,000 and by 1971 it had risen to 21,681,000—an increase of only 3,400,000. During the fifties, the increase had been 4,300,000. More than anything else, the change in the status of women in the last decade has altered the entire family picture as we once knew it. And this has been a world-wide transformation. The present heads of state in India, Ceylon and Israel are women and so is the chief negotiator for the Viet Cong. New estimators of population growth may have to change the old tribute to the ladies and say, 'The hand that doesn't rock as many cradles rules the world.'

Urban Sprawl
The seventy-five per cent increase in population since the end of World War Two has been confined almost exclusively to our larger towns and cities. Since the closing of the agricultural frontier at the end of the 1920s and with the mechanization of farming methods, migration from the rural areas to the cities has continued.

If we use the census definition of 'urban'—communities having a population of 1,000 or more—then 75% of all Canadians in 1971 belonged to this category. Between 1961 and 1971 the number of cities of over 50,000 increased from nineteen to twenty-seven, and 11 million people—more than half the population—were city dwellers. It is estimated that 90% of the Canadian population will be urban dwellers by the year 2000.

These figures stand in sharp contrast to the rustic twenties when 70% of all Canadians lived on farms or in centres of less than 15,000 people. Since 1945 the birth of suburbs sprawling out here, there and everywhere—with their miles of new and treeless streets, their sewers, gas- and water-mains and resulting mud, their thousands of homes 'all alike and all in a row', and their dozens upon dozens of streamlined schools built to educate the products of the post-war population explosion, with their motels, their supermarkets, their shopping centres and their sleek, low industrial buildings, have completely obliterated once familiar town or city limits and stimulated an unprecedented boom in construction of all kinds.

The construction industry has five major divisions: residential, commercial, institutional, industrial and engineering. The total expenditure for these varied types of construction shot up from $6 billion in 1961 to an estimated $15 billion ten years later. At the present time the industry directly employs 700,000 workers, and the production, selling and transport of building materials provides a weekly

A huge shopping plaza and highway complex near Toronto. (Photo, The Globe and Mail, Toronto.)

wage for another 325,000. During the past fifteen years over $30 billion has been spent on housing, reaching a record high in 1969 when over 200,000 residential units were started and other units repaired at an estimated cost of $4,228,000. Approximately 30% of the yearly construction expenditure in Canada goes into this section of the industry. Commercial, institutional and industrial building accounts for another 30%, and engineering construction, which includes highways, docks, waterworks, sewage plants, dams, electric power stations, park establishments and communications, comprises the remaining percentage.

As the population has moved into the cities and as the new life style has developed, apartment living has increased tremendously. The condominium has become the darling of the realtor. Basically a condominium is an apartment dwelling where the units are individually owned but shared facilities such as hallways, elevators, heating system and grounds are financed jointly. In every urban area, too, high-rise apartments point skyward. Another fashion in the building trade is the town house. Many builders restore and refurbish homes in the inner city cores; others construct row housing, copying the architectural styles of a hundred years ago. The number of single dwellings, duplexes and semi-detached houses built in 1970 was 81,500, but row housing and apartments totalled nearly 109,000.

On the surface the housing section of the construction industry presents a progressive picture—but it is a deceptive one. We have seen how the population of the urban areas has grown in the past decades. Naturally this growth has resulted in an accelerated demand for housing, particularly among low-income groups. Like most fast developing countries, Canada has always had a housing shortage. The country entered the sixties, when population growth was at its height, without a backlog of housing units; few dwellings were built during the depression years and scarcely any (except very temporary ones) during World War Two. In the sixties, the cost of building single-unit dwellings skyrocketed; property, material and labour costs rose astronomically and mortgage rates followed suit. In a seller's market, the cost of purchasing older homes was prohibitive for average income groups. From the viewpoint of the builder, it became economically more advantageous to build multiple dwelling units. There was an annual loss of houses owing to disrepair, unfavourable locations or because they were torn down to make way for commercial and industrial development or expressways, and these factors contributed to our perennial housing shortage.

Housing for low-income families, then, has become a major Canadian problem and one of the greatest political footballs of the decade. At the federal level of government, the National Housing Act, with the Central Mortgage and Housing Corporation as administrator and co-ordinator, works 'to promote the construction of new houses, the repair and modernization of existing houses and the improvement of housing and living conditions'. Since 1967 much of the effort of this agency has been directed to housing for low-income groups and two-thirds of the federal housing budget in 1970—$854 million—was allocated to housing for low-income families, elderly people, students and handicapped individuals. It is expected that this amount will provide 35,000 units.

But thousands of families still live in overcrowded, substandard dwellings. Experimental attempts to set up 'court type' multiple dwellings in rundown areas have met with little success and much opposition. There is an increasing trend on the part of government agencies towards renovating old neighbourhoods without destroying the single-unit dwellings, and maintaining the community spirit of the area. While this is an admirable concept, the costs involved in repairing older houses may well be too high for it to continue. The demand is so great and the cost of subsidized building and rental so high that any present solution to low-income housing seems inadequate. Governments at all levels are still searching for an answer to Canada's serious housing problem.

The benefits of urban growth are obvious. They include increased opportunities for skilled workers, an interesting variety of job selection for the young, and added rewards and opportunities for professional men and women. A vast selection of goods and services are readily available. There is an increased potential for investment and the possibility of greater profits. And most important to the younger generation is the availability of enriched educational, cultural and entertainment activities and the excitement of the 'big town'. But the dangers and drawbacks of highly concentrated numbers of people in a relatively small area have become increasingly and frighteningly apparent in the social, political and economic disturbances that afflict the older American cities. This malaise has spread to Canada and will almost certainly continue.

Having yielded too quickly to the promoters in their midst, many communities have failed to maintain a proper balance between residential and industrial development and are already finding that the cost of their schools and roads and other urban needs is placing an increasingly heavy tax burden on the home owner. In the headlong rush of progress—which sometimes means no more than an opportunity for a limited number of people to make a fast dollar—natural beauty spots, parks and farmlands and historic sites have been swept aside and some of our summer resort areas lying closest to the big centres of population have been opened up so fast that they now provide about as little privacy as a backyard in the city.

One concept of urban planners may be a step forward in solving the problems of rapid urban growth. 'Satellite cities' of between 100,000 and 200,000 population are envisaged, where planned industrial development and housing, and controlled environment, will create the new Edens of the urban era. But until that or some other solution becomes a reality, pollution, urban decay, and the bleak and lonely impersonality of city living will remain with us. From the concern of governments at all levels, from citizen groups, and from the interest and new ideas of the younger generation, the dilemma of the big city may some day be solved.

Trade Union Giants

Not only is the population of Canada larger and more concentrated, it is also very much richer than ever before. This remarkable improvement is partly due to the ability of industry to stand the strain of higher wages and salaries and partly to the new-found strength of the trade-union movement. Although trade unions began to exert some influence in Canada during the first decade of the twentieth century, their progress was slow and in the period between the two wars the percentage of wage-earners belonging to trade unions actually declined. In the course of the Second World War, however, the federal government, purely as a temporary measure, put through a number of orders in council, including one to compel collective bargaining between employees and their employers, that greatly encouraged the growth of trade unions. By 1945 their membership had risen to 700,000, an increase of over one hundred per cent since the beginning of the War.

In the months following V-J day, with the trade-union leaders attempting to make labour's wartime gains permanent and the employers equally determined to resist them, Canada experienced a large number of serious, and at times illegal, strikes in almost every phase of her economy. Coming at the beginning of the post-war spending spree when factory managers were most anxious to keep their plants operating, these strikes ended in a series of resounding trade-union victories. Higher wages, holidays with pay, the closed shop, the 'check-off' system compelling employers to collect union dues from their workers' pay cheques, compulsory collective bargaining and other benefits secured by these victories gave the working class a greater share of the national income and made trade unions more popular than ever.

For several years, however, the labour movement weakened itself to some extent by the fierce rivalry for new members between the Trades and Labour

Congress, representing the traditional craft unions, and the Canadian Congress of Labour, speaking for the more recently formed industrial unions. At this point it should be recalled that these two Canadian federations were affiliated respectively with the American Federation of Labor (A.F. of L.) and the Congress of Industrial Organizations (C.I.O.) and that the same rivalry existed in the United States as over here. In 1955, the entire labour movement in North America was greatly strengthened when the A.F. of L. and the C.I.O. agreed to unite into one huge federation while their affiliates in this country joined to form a new central governing body called the Canadian Labour Congress (C.L.C.). More recently, there has been a decided increase in the number of national and regional unions, from 52 in 1965 to 64 in 1970. Membership in Canadian unions jumped from 1,459,000 in 1960 to today's over 2 million—about 27% of Canada's labour force.

In 1961 the Canadian Labour Congress, which represents about 75% of organized labour, entered the political arena. Unlike its British counterpart, labour in Canada had lacked united political action, but in that year, led by the dynamic Claude Jodoin, they attended the Cooperative Commonwealth Federation (C.C.F.) convention and assisted at the birth of the New Democratic Party (N.D.P.). Jodoin was an active supporter of Tommy Douglas, a long-time socialist who became the new party's leader. Douglas' Bible-belt oratory, debating skill and self-righteous assurance made him an able parliamentarian and he led the N.D.P. until 1970, when he retired. Only 22 N.D.P. members were elected to the House of Commons in 1968, and Douglas himself lost his seat. However, in the 1972 election David Lewis led the party to a 31-seat peak and a strategic bargaining position in the Liberal minority government. While the C.L.C. supported the New Democratic Party with contributions and funds from its membership, the rank and file rarely voted as a block for any one political party. Although this state of affairs may alter in the seventies, it is safe to say that the C.L.C.'s political impact during the last decade was less than had been hoped for.

Possibly the most significant change in the union scene during the sixties occurred in Quebec. The labour situation in Quebec had long been one of low wages, long hours, poor working conditions and few fringe benefits. In the late fifties the Canadian and Catholic Confederation of Labour (C.C.C.L.) was dominant. Nearly all of its members were French speaking and Roman Catholic. However, as the political and economic atmosphere of Quebec changed radically in the sixties so did the C.C.C.L. Renamed and reorganized as the Confederation of National Trade Unions (C.N.T.U.), it soon became the most militant and aggressive union in Canada. The C.N.T.U. has allied itself with the growing nationalism in Quebec and has had amazing success in organizing professions, particularly teachers, nurses and engineers. It has been fortunate in having effective leaders—Jean Marchand, who entered the political field in the mid-sixties and later became a cabinet minister in the Trudeau government, and Marcel Pepin, its present leader. Critics of the C.N.T.U. point out that its apparent overwillingness to use the strike technique may seriously affect its public image. However, radical, militant and media-conscious as the C.N.T.U. may be, it is probably the most vital labour organization in Canada today.

Strikes and lockouts in the sixties were many and varied. In 1965 they involved 172,000 workers and their duration in man-days was 2,350,000; in 1969, 307,000 workers took part in strike activity costing 8 million man-days. While the manufacturing, mining and construction industries had their perennial share of labour disputes, it was in the service industries that strikes created the most problems. With the tremendous increase in urbanization, the service industries have multiplied and now employ over half of Canada's labour force. Because service industries are non-productive in terms of goods they have long been areas of low pay, long working hours and poor working conditions. Apart from the railways, they have lacked union organization, and consequently in the last few years they have been major targets for union membership drives.

From the mid-sixties on, a wave of service industries strikes hit the major urban areas. TV technicians, garbage collectors, airline mechanics, dockhands, teachers —much to the delight of their students—hydro workers, and even police, created or threatened havoc in the tightly organized urban centres. One could rarely visit any major city in Canada without observing a parade of picketers marching determinedly up and down some strike-bound area. New work stoppage techniques came into being. There was the 'rotating strike', where postal workers went off their jobs on certain days in selected areas. The 'work to rule' ploy was used, where the absolute minimum amount of labour was expended in a job and no extra effort put forth or overtime considered. Then, too, there was the deliberate 'slowdown'. Management responded to these techniques by locking out employees, outright dismissing of those involved in strike action, or using non-union strikebreakers or administrative employees to carry on their operations. Naturally strike actions by the unions and reprisals by management have caused bitterness, ill feeling and, on occasion, violence. While generally the public has been sympathetic to strikers, the recent large number of strikes in the service industries have alienated many people. As work stoppage in some service industries can become a danger to the community at large, legislation has been passed at both provincial and federal levels aimed at making strikes in essential services unlawful and insisting on compulsory arbitration.

The federal Department of Labour, established in 1900, dealt with industrial relations and manpower. Since January 1, 1966, the Department of Manpower and Immigration has attended to all manpower activities and the Department of Labour has concerned itself with industrial relations in the federal field, for example, shipping, interprovincial railways, air transportation, and radio and TV broadcasting. Some important federal legislation has been carried out in the post-war years. The Industrial Relations and Disputes Investigation Act of September 1, 1948, gave employers and employees the right to organize and bargain collectively and permitted trade unions to be certified as bargaining agents for employee groups. The Canada Fair Employment Practices Act of 1953 prohibited any discrimination in hiring individuals based on race, colour, religion or national origin. The Canada Labour (Standards) Code, an act of 1965, was a most important one, defining, among other things, the forty-hour week, two weeks' vacation with pay as well as eight statutory holidays, and a minimum wage of

Garbage bags piled high during a strike of public employees in Toronto in 1972

$1.65 per hour for persons 17 years of age and over. And on January 1, 1968, the Canada Labour (Safety) Code, the first general safety legislation, was passed by the Canadian parliament.

Provincial governments are empowered by the B.N.A. Act to enact labour legislation and basically it is a provincial undertaking. In general the provinces have followed the federal pattern, but there are some interesting exceptions. Farm labour and domestic service are excepted from minimum wage regulations. Minimum wages vary in Saskatchewan between urban and rural areas. Nova Scotia and Prince Edward Island do not have the same minimum wage for both sexes—it is twenty per cent lower for female workers in most categories. Public holidays vary across the provinces from five to eight per year. All provinces forbid discrimination in hiring according to federal definition, but Newfoundland added political opinion and social origin to the list in 1969 when the province set up its first anti-discrimination legislation. Prince Edward Island excluded tips from its definition of wages. And Newfoundland, not to be outdone in labour amenities, passed the Weekly Day of Rest Act—every employee to be granted 'a rest period of at least twenty-four hours in every seven days, wherever possible on Sunday'!

The growth of the Canadian labour movement since World War Two has been phenomenal. Achievements have been in the fields of increased pay, shorter hours and union security. Fringe benefits varying from pension plans to subsidized meals in company cafeterias have been obtained. The guaranteed annual wage has become a reality in some industries. Automation, wage rate inequality among industries, wage parity with U.S. employees in the same job, residual rights (the claim of management to change matters not specifically covered in the contract agreement) and inflation—all these remain as controversial issues in the labour-management field. But whatever the outcome of these disputes may be, the workers of Canada should be determined to elect trade-union officials capable of wielding their power with a sense of responsibility to society in general as well as for the benefit of their own members.

The Welfare State

Through a multitude of new or greatly extended social welfare laws, the federal and provincial governments also have helped to make the Canadian people richer than ever before. According to the terms of the British North America Act, most legislation dealing with such things as mothers' allowances, child welfare, hospital care, compensation for industrial accidents, widows' pensions and many others, falls under the jurisdiction of the provinces and they, in turn, have delegated some of their responsibility to the municipalities and to voluntary agencies like the United Appeal. Varying from province to province, the whole system has become extremely complex and must lie outside the scope of this book, but some idea of how important it is may be gathered from the fact that at the present time more than thirty per cent of all provincial revenues are spent on welfare benefits. Even more important, however, is the vast program of social security legislation of all kinds introduced by the federal government since the depression years. By the end of the first post-war decade 5,225,000 Canadian children were receiving almost $400 million in 'baby bonuses' and 755,000 people were drawing $360 million in old-age pensions, while the unemployed claimed benefits of over $200 million. And it is obvious, of course, that these sums, totalling almost $1 billion annually, added greatly to the purchasing power of the people and helped to cause the boom in Canada's domestic trade.

Yet these welfare costs were to be a mere drop in the bucket compared to the skyrocketing expenditures of the sixties. In 1965 the Canada Pension Plan came into being. It provided retirement, disability and survivor benefits for all Canadians, with equal contributions being made by employee and employer. The plan is administered by the Department of National Health and Welfare. Benefits paid out by this fund in 1970 amounted to about $773 million. The Canada Assistance Plan, put into operation in 1966, brought the federal government further into the welfare field by guaranteeing to the provinces that it would pay fifty per cent of the cost of 'assisting persons in need'. This particular plan, highly regarded by authorities on social legislation, covers a wide range of needs from help for the blind to child care in welfare agencies. It also makes it possible for the provincial governments to increase and improve their existing welfare services. The estimated cost of this program in 1972 was $437 million. The Medical Care Act of 1968, a state-operated compulsory medical insurance financed by federal and provincial authorities, cost an estimated $1,360 million in 1972.

In addition to these major welfare measures many others have been started and increased. A guaranteed income supplement has been added to the old-age pension plan. Family and youth allowances have been increased. To assist Canadians in their pursuit of physical fitness and to enable amateur athletes to develop in their chosen fields and complete creditably in international competitions, the Fitness and Amateur Sport Program appeared in 1961. Special retraining programs enable low-income persons and welfare recipients to upgrade their skills, and opportunities for disabled persons to combat their physical handicaps are continually being devised and implemented. The list of welfare programs is a seemingly endless one and it continues to grow. Between 1962 and 1972 the cost to all levels of government of health and welfare schemes rose from $3.7 million to over $8 billion! Of this staggering amount the federal government pays 61%, the provinces 37%, and the municipalities 2%.

It should also be recalled, from what has already been written about Canada during the Great Depression, that welfare legislation serves a double purpose. Through taxation, it takes money away from individuals and corporations who otherwise might invest too much of their savings in Canadian industry, and thus lessens the danger of overproduction. At the same time, it helps to maintain the purchasing power of the country by giving money to those who will spend it for their daily needs. Unemployment insurance payments have the added advantage of helping to prevent seasonal unemployment from spreading through the whole community. For these reasons, therefore, it is generally conceded that welfare legislation not only improves the general standard of living but also provides a vital safeguard against the impact of another serious depression.

On the other hand, welfare legislation, once started, tends to snowball. Promises to increase old-age pensions or family allowances, hospital care or unemployment benefits are among the most popular of all modern vote-catching methods. Just as, in the old days, communities were promised a railway, a well-surfaced road, a higher tariff or a lower one, so in every election political leaders now vie with each other in assuring the public that their party will hand out more and more social benefits. And all this, so they usually say, can be accomplished without increasing taxes! But we can not have our cake and eat it too. The welfare state costs money.

In the Shadow of a Giant

Foreign Investment
During the early stages of the post-war boom, Canadians were able to provide most of the money needed for expansion from their own savings, but in recent years the country has been forced to rely more and more on funds from the United States. Even by the end of the first post-war decade, American companies had established over three hundred new branches in Canada and American investors owned $12 billion worth of the country's fixed assets. Between 1955 and 1965 this investment almost doubled and at the present time United States capital investment in Canada totals over $30 billion. More than three-quarters of the industries involved in motor vehicles and parts, industrial electrical equipment, iron mining and rubber products, and more than half of the industries connected with petroleum refining, gas and oil wells, textiles, pharmaceuticals, soap and cleaning compounds, and industrial chemicals are controlled by U.S. corporations.

The United Kingdom has a total of $3.5 billion invested in Canada, and other countries about $3 billion. While these amounts seem relatively unimportant in the overall total, it should be noted that capital investment from Japan and from the European Economic Community, particularly West Germany, has shown a higher rate of increase than that from the U.S. in the past five years. This may indicate a new trend in the Canadian economic scene.

It is frequently overlooked, also, that our own investments in other countries are extremely high for a country of our size. In 1970 Canadian companies and companies under Canadian control had $9 billion invested abroad. This figure represented a fifty per cent increase since 1960 and investment development abroad continues to grow to the tune of over a billion dollars per year.

A glance at the headlines in almost any Canadian newspaper today, however, makes it clear that foreign ownership has become a major concern. A brief outline of three topics that are of particular interest at this time may help to explain some of the problems involved.

The Auto Pact

We have already observed that manufacturing is the most important of our industries. It provides two-thirds of our commodity exports and with a 1970 payroll totalling over $700 million is the direct support of one-third of our population. One of the most important industries in Canada today, the manufacture of motor vehicles and parts, is essentially a product of foreign investment.

By 1964 the Canadian auto industry was in poor shape. Production was down, European models were cutting into the market, car prices were almost a third higher than in the U.S., and Canadian branch plants, faced with a limited market, were unable to expand and increase their efficiency. Tariff regulations at that time forced each plant to produce a full line of models and limited the sales to Canada. Canada was faced with the necessity of expanding the industry to provide jobs for an ever-increasing labour force, and U.S. manufacturers needed to streamline their continental operation to compete with foreign imports and increase their North American sales.

It was in this atmosphere that the Agreement on Automotive Products—the Auto Pact—was signed by Prime Minister Lester Pearson and President Johnson on January 16, 1965. Briefly, the pact stated that import duties on cars and parts moving between U.S. manufacturers and their Canadian plants would be removed. Three safeguards were written into the pact to assist the Canadian industry: there was to be a minimum level of Canadian content in car production; as sales in Canada increased the production of cars and parts in Canada was to increase; and major U.S. auto companies agreed to expand their Canadian operations by $240 million within the next three years.

The pact was greeted with jubilation by its supporters. By 1968 U.S. auto makers had poured $400 million into their Canadian plants and some 80,000 people were employed in the industry. However, there were disadvantages. Many Canadian auto parts manufacturers were bought out by the American giants; plant conversions and more automated production techniques forced many workers to move to other factories and in some cases to retrain for new jobs. Downward change in the prices of Canadian automobiles was not as great as had been expected, and critics of the pact were quick to point out that it was another 'sell-out' to American big business. There were Americans, as well, who criticized the agreement, and in December 1971 the Canadian government announced that the U.S. wanted a complete duty-free movement of all cars and parts between Canada and the United States.

There are some Canadians who believe that this suggestion would provide the consumer with a cheaper model—and possibly it would. But others believe that this would flood the country with American-made cars and seriously affect the entire industry. Economic nationalists—and there are many today—believe the safeguards should be strengthened to further protect the industry. Yet another suggestion is for the government to establish a Crown Corporation and set up a distinctively Canadian automobile industry under public ownership. Whatever way the Auto Pact is revised, changed, or even scrapped, it remains as one of the prime examples of an extended industry created by foreign investment.

Publish and Perish

The Canadian publishing industry, plagued by high production costs, limited advertising revenue and a small market, has nearly succumbed to the financial blandishments of American ownership during the past decade. The few Canadian magazines still surviving struggle along gamely, but the O'Leary Commission Report, which recommended that advertising in Canadian editions of U.S. magazines should not be claimed as a tax-deductible expense, gathers dust in the Parliamentary Library in Ottawa and American magazines of every description fill the magazine racks and the waiting rooms of Canada.

Book publishers face similar problems, which reached a climax in 1970. In the fall of that year W. J. Gage Limited announced that it had sold its textbook division to an American firm, Scott, Foresman and Company of Illinois. At that time Gage was one of the four remaining large publishers that was Canadian-owned. Shortly afterwards the Ryerson Press, the oldest publishing house in Canada, announced its intention to sell out to the American-owned McGraw-Hill Publishing Company. The sale of these two firms became a matter of serious concern to many Canadians. Both were deeply involved in the publication of school textbooks and there was the nagging fear—probably unjustified—in the minds of Canadians that these would in future contain more than their share of American attitudes and subject matter. It was also feared that Canadian authors would find even less opportunity to publish their work, when already the number of Canadians who actually lived by their pen could almost be counted on the fingers of one hand.

In the following year Jack McClelland, owner of McClelland & Stewart Limited and a dedicated member of the Committee for an Independent Canada, announced that if additional capital were not forthcoming his publishing house would have no alternative but to seek a buyer. He stressed the fact that the buyers, or at least the providers of additional funds, must be Canadian. However, the weeks went by and there seemed to be little evidence that Canadian investors were interested in the book publishing business. Finally, the Ontario government,

(Above) This surrealistic scene was photographed near Lethbridge during building of the Alberta-California natural gas pipeline in the winter of 1960–61. Cold air has condensed moisture rising from the freshly-turned earth of a creek bed. (Right) Ontario Hydro's nuclear generating station at Pickering, under construction. The huge plant was opened in July 1971. (Photo, The Globe and Mail, Toronto.)

which had established a Royal Commission on Book Publishing following the Gage-Ryerson sell-outs, came to the rescue and a million-dollar loan was made available to McClelland & Stewart under the administration of the Ontario Development Corporation. The Canadian taxpayer discovered that to publish Canadian was going to cost him money.

Energy for Sale

By 1980 or even sooner the United States will be facing a critical shortage of energy resources. John G. McLean, chairman of the National Petroleum Council's Committee on U.S. Energy Outlook, has this to say: 'The nation's requirements for energy will about double between now and 1985. In this period, we shall have to rely upon oil, gas, coal and nuclear energy for at least ninety-five per cent of our needs. If present trends continue, our indigenous resources of these materials will not be developed fast enough to meet our growing requirements.' We in Canada have energy resources in great quantity. Our third problem in the foreign ownership area is, how do we handle this vast supply of oil and natural gas, of

potential nuclear energy, of hydro-electric power and of that most precious of
natural resources—water?

We have already seen that increasing demand for our oil and natural gas sends
these exhaustible resources pouring south of the border in ever-increasing
quantities. Our nuclear energy industry still stagnates under U.S. import
restrictions, but that new fuel will in future drive the industrial wheels of our great
neighbour. Our power dams, led by the new giant complex at Churchill Falls in
Labrador, will soon produce the kilowatt hours of electrical energy that will light
up the eastern seaboard of the United States. Our fresh water under the terms of
the Columbia River Treaty of 1961 will make fertile the low-rainfall areas of the
northwestern states. But where does that leave us? As the Arctic pipelines creep
through the delicate wilderness, as smokestacks foul the sky, as dams block our
swift-flowing streams and turn them into concrete-lined ponds—what will be
left to us?

Already our energy-sharing projects with the United States indicate that for
short-term cash payments we may have suffered permanent long-range effects in
ecological damage and loss of control of our own energy resources. Critics of the
Columbia River Treaty point out that the Canadian dams on this river have
flooded some of the richest farmland in British Columbia and have seriously
disturbed the wildlife environment, and that they prevent the use of Columbia
River water in irrigation projects for the dry belt of Alberta and Saskatchewan.
The plan for the Churchill-Nelson rivers complex in Manitoba involves damming

the Churchill 250 miles from its Hudson Bay mouth and backing up its surplus
water into the Nelson system to provide additional hydro power. This billion-
dollar-plus investment, sending surplus electrical power to the United States, will
not only destroy the habitat for whales and seals and for thousands of waterfowl,
but will displace an Indian community of over two thousand people which at
present is one of the most successful and self-reliant in the country. In Quebec,
the enormously expensive James Bay river system realignment will involve the
relocation of some six thousand native people, environmental upsets that cannot
be estimated owing to the lack of intensive studies on the possible results of the
scheme, and a huge influx of foreign capital to finance the necessary construction.
The proposed Mackenzie valley pipeline and highway, over a thousand miles
in length, linking northern Alberta to the high Arctic and passing through some of
the most fragile environment in the world, has encountered much opposition both
from conservationists and from economists who worry about the effect of such a
large outside investment on the sovereignty of Canada.

The control of our energy resources may well be the most important single issue
in Canada in the very near future. Government agencies like the National Energy
Board may become the only guarantors of our existence as a country and, in the
long run, our existence as human beings. As with most of our problems, there is a
wide division of opinion; in keeping with the traditional Canadian attitude a
middle way may seem to be the most advantageous to us. Critics of a continental
energy scheme in North America, a proposal to set up a 'free market' in energy
resources, see it as the final step in relegating Canada permanently to the role of
hewer of wood and drawer of water. To them it means continued economic
underdevelopment, a further erosion of Canadian sovereignty, and a permanent
state of high unemployment because resource extraction does not require a large
labour force. Advocates of the scheme see in it the only way that Canada can
further develop its resources and create an economic structure that will provide
employment for the nation's fast-growing labour force. In spite of these divergent
points of view, a new and impelling awareness on both sides that no natural
resource in the world is inexhaustible gives us hope that a workable and beneficial
solution can be reached while there is still time—and while there are some areas
of our great natural wilderness still unspoiled.

We Stand on Guard

From 1967 to the present no less than three federal government committees have
examined in depth the problem of increasing American ownership of Canadian
industries. In 1967, Finance Minister Walter Gordon set up a task force to
investigate the structure of Canadian industry. An ardent economic nationalist,
Gordon chose his investigating team from the university cloisters and selected
Professor Melville Watkins as chairman. During its investigations and public
hearings the committee was hailed as the forerunner of a new and enlightened
group that would produce a unique economic policy for the Canada of the sixties.
But when the report came out in March of 1968, the Toronto *Globe and Mail*
remarked, 'A potential bomb has fluttered to earth with a gentle plop.' Other

newspapers were kinder, but there was no wild outburst of enthusiasm for its recommendations. The main theme of the report indicated that while Canada had benefited from foreign ownership and the influx of foreign capital, outside influences had limited economic growth in certain areas, threatened Canadian native industry and, most important of all, had a tendency to impinge upon Canadian sovereignty. At a time when the memories of Expo '67 and Centennial Year celebrations still warmed the hearts of Canadians, this last observation probably had the most impact. Among its numerous suggestions, the report advocated a government agency to regulate the expansion of the multinational firms and to encourage them to develop autonomous firms in Canada. It strongly advised that U.S. parent companies should be forbidden to hinder their Canadian subsidiaries from trading with communist countries that were on the U.S. 'black list' at that particular time. The formation of a Canada Development Corporation was outlined, the chief functions of which were to be the promotion of Canadian ownership and the providing of funds for company expansion and formation when capital was in short supply and there was danger that foreign interests might take control. Three years later, on November 18, 1971, the Canada Development Corporation came into being.

In 1970 the Committee on External Affairs and National Defence, under the leadership of Ian Wahn, moved into the 'Keep Canada for Canadians' field. The Wahn report was similar to that produced by the Gordon Commission but it added a Canadian Ownership and Control Bureau to supervise foreign takeovers of the country's firms, proposed a fifty-one per cent ownership by Canadians in vital sections of the economy, and further suggested that investment limitations be imposed upon foreign companies. The Committee issued definite warnings that U.S. decisions on the problems of the American economy might have a detrimental effect on the Canadian industrial structure.

These predictions became harsh reality in August of 1971. In the early weeks of this pleasant summer month when many Canadians were enjoying their annual vacation, President Richard Nixon announced the imposition of a ten per cent surcharge on manufactured goods being imported into the United States. As we have seen, Canada's export trade to the United States is the life blood of our economy and, despite the fact that automobiles and parts, due to the Auto Pact, and most resource materials were exempt from this additional tax, the downward push of the surcharge was felt throughout our economy.

The latest federal investigation was the Gray Report, issued in December 1971. In addition to confirming the work of Watkins and Wahn, this report strongly supported the setting up of a federal government screening agency, to consider future foreign investment in Canada from all angles—research, ecological significance, financing, employment capability, trade potential—before it would be permitted.

While the government of Canada and the Canadian people waited for some standard policy in the control of foreign takeovers, a situation arose that forced immediate action. The Roman Corporation announced the proposed sale of the controlling interest in Denison Mines to a British-American firm. As Denison

Mines was one of Canada's major uranium-producing companies the federal government took immediate steps to prevent the sale. On March 19, 1970, J. J. Greene, Minister of Energy, Mines and Resources, announced a new policy of limiting foreign participation in the uranium industry. The sale was blocked and the government accepted the financial responsibility of stockpiling uranium until 1974 in order to keep production going at the Denison Mine at Elliot Lake.

A week prior to this incident the outspoken Mr. Greene had outlined the new attitude that Canada was adopting towards her southern neighbour, in an address at Denver, Colorado. He said: 'Canadians have come to the conclusion that they want to build something of their own. Those Canadians who are candid will admit that we were, until recently, quite satisfied to be but a small microcosm of America. Our only complaint was that we were not more so. You had more money, higher wages and incomes than we did. This was the only beef, and the remedy of this defect was our chief aim. But now the scene has clearly changed. Canadians are determined that they will build something which is clearly their own, and not the pale and small image of the great and powerful civilization to our south.'

The advantages and disadvantages of foreign ownership have been the subject of so much discussion recently that we must certainly be reminded of the Reciprocity argument and the famous election of 1911 that we discussed earlier in our story. But the cry of loyalty to the Empire has been replaced by the cry of loyalty to Canada. The problem of foreign ownership of our resources and our industries is one of the most important challenges that we shall have to meet in the seventies, if we are to survive as a sovereign nation. It will be no simple task.

My Country 'Tis of Thee

In April 1960, an award-winning American journalist from Minneapolis was given an assignment to travel across Canada and prepare a study of the country. After touring from coast to coast, this experienced newspaperman reported: 'We Americans are involved in the strangest "war" in our history. We are the passive participants in a cultural cold war with Canada, whose citizens spend millions of dollars to repulse a "cultural invasion" Americans don't know they are making. . . . I found Canadians airing an endless array of grievances against the United States and a general tendency to make us the whipping boy for most of their troubles.'

There is no doubt that a great deal of critical feeling towards the United States had arisen in this country. As we have seen, American financial assistance, such as the Marshall Plan, supplied to the western European countries after 1945 was a major factor in controlling the expansion of totalitarian regimes during that period of chaos and rebuilding after the defeat of Nazi Germany and its allies. Similarly, following the defeat of Japan, aid of the same type not only restored the Japanese economy but helped it to develop into one of the world's most important trading powers today. Substantial economic aid was also made available to the United Kingdom, Canada, and indeed any country outside the communist bloc. However, many foreign aid programs seemed to reflect the shoring up of the status quo, in direct opposition to all the 'brave new world' promises that America had announced in her war aims. Aid given to such countries as Nationalist China and pre-Castro Cuba certainly did not reflect the 'democratic way of life' that has been such a source of pride to the American people since their beginning as a nation.

Much of the American aid program was military in concept and designed to surround the Soviet Union with a ring of nuclear missile bases. In 1963 bitter political controversy flared up in Canada over the proposed arming of the Bomarc missiles with nuclear warheads at Canadian missile sites. Debate on this proposal resulted in a lack of confidence motion in the House of Commons against the Progressive Conservative government of John Diefenbaker and the resignation of the government. Critics of the American aid program at this time also point out that the post-war economic situation gave unbridled opportunities to the big U.S. companies to invest cheaply in western Europe and Japan and that this period saw the establishment of many of the vast multinational corporations whose activities are causing increasing concern. While all these things are true, and resentment against the program was great, it should be equally remembered that this aid provided the markets which were the basis for our post-war prosperity, and may well have prevented the emergence of a totalitarian Europe.

The decade following the war revealed many symptoms of the weaknesses of American civilization and the media, eager to exploit the sensational aspects of society, displayed these weaknesses glaringly to the world. The 'payola' scandals in telecasting, the rampant prejudices of Governor Orval Faubus towards the Negroes at Little Rock in Arkansas, the wild crusade of Senator Joe McCarthy against everything he regarded as un-American, the gangster-like corruption of David Beck, James Hoffa and other labour leaders, the highly emotional appeals for popularity by General Douglas MacArthur when he returned from the Korean War, and the dangerous 'brinkmanship' diplomacy of John Foster Dulles with his theories of massive retaliation and his threats to carry the world to the very verge of war found many Canadians assailing the United States and assuring themselves that such things simply could not happen over here.

The image of the United States in Canada and throughout the world underwent a change for the better with the election in 1960 of forty-three-year-old John Fitzgerald Kennedy as the youngest president in American history. His unforgettable inaugural address of January 20, 1961, called for a new approach and reflected a vigour and reasonable determination that promised to lift the cynical tensions that had been so much a part of the post-war world.

'So let us begin anew—remembering on both sides that civility is not a sign of weakness, and sincerity is always subject to proof. Let us never negotiate out of fear. But let us never fear to negotiate.

'Now the trumpet summons us again—not as a call to bear arms, though arms we need—not as a call to battle, though embattled we are—but a call to bear the burden of a long, twilight struggle year in and year out, rejoicing in hope, patient in tribulation—a struggle against the common enemies of man: tyranny, poverty, disease, and war itself. . . . And so, my fellow Americans, ask not what your country can do for you—ask what you can do for your country.'

The Kennedy speech seemed not so much aimed at home consumption as offered to a world-wide audience. The Kennedy image had an immediate appeal to young

Demonstrators outside the United States Embassy in Ottawa in May 1972

people and if ever a time was the time of youth, this was the time.

On Friday, November 22, 1963, Kennedy was assassinated, and a few hours later Lyndon B. Johnson became President of the United States. The Johnson years, lasting as they did until 1968 when Richard Nixon became President, were years of unparalleled domestic turmoil and bitter controversy in the United States, and, as usual, American events had a great impact on our Canadian way of life. As we have seen previously, the Johnson administration accelerated the American involvement in Viet Nam, and this conflict, believed by many people to be immoral (was there ever a war that was moral?) and unjustified, divided the United States more than any other event since the Civil War. The young people desperately took to the streets, attempting to bring their disapproval and moral indignation to the attention of their older rulers who could not, or would not, understand their attitude of protest. It was a time of police clubs and mace, of smashed and occupied campuses, of riots in the streets, and as the decade drew to an end there was the poignant tragedy of Kent State. The campus revolution had its repercussions in Canada at Simon Fraser University, McGill, and particularly Sir George Williams in Montreal where the computer wing was occupied and destroyed.

The desperate struggle for civil rights by the American Negro—the marches on Washington, the long, hot summers that erupted in the burning of Watts, the frustrated violence of the Black Panthers, and the tragedy of the Soledad brothers—was part of a crying need for change that came too slowly for a generation who saw little hope for a world where power was based on nuclear holocaust and 'progress' meant ecological destruction. In Canada the young marched too, against the wars, against the destroyers of the last great wilderness, against the concrete jungles. They marched for their native peoples, for the dignity and way of life of the Indian and the Eskimo who for so long had been relegated to the position of second-class citizens in a nation that smugly proclaimed against apartheid. They objected to the placid acceptance of the 'permanent poor' as an inevitable fact in our society. And all shared in the agony of murder when Martin Luther King and Robert Kennedy were gunned down.

We have always been inclined to blame the United States for most of our difficulties, and our growing national pride intensifies this attitude today. When our divorce rate or our use of drugs or our criminal statistics jump up another notch or two, when our trade unions become unruly or graft is found in high places, when the discipline in our schools is not what it should be, when we cannot sell our wheat or uranium, when our defence installations become obsolete almost before they are completed, or when our young people adopt queer haircuts and take part in protest marches, it is the United States, the American way of life, American television or American periodicals that are so frequently blamed by distraught Canadians.

Our touring American journalist, therefore, undoubtedly did find many signs of a 'cultural cold war' between this country and the United States, but he should not have been surprised by this fact. The present-day chorus of criticism and resentment is all part and parcel of a constant struggle by a young and sparsely settled country to maintain a distinct nationality while lying in the shadow of such a mighty neighbour. And in recent years, with American interests penetrating every nook and cranny of our economy, with American trade unions influencing our labour force, with the United States buying most of our exports and supplying most of our imports, with American weapons guarding our frontiers, with American tourists flocking across the border every year, with American magazines far outselling our own, with American publishers taking over our struggling textbook industries, with American movies and radio and television, the struggle has become more difficult than ever before.

It is natural for Canadians to resent and fight against the cultural and economic influence of the United States in their country. Relations between our two nations might be improved if American leaders were more sensitive to our feelings and tried to understand the difficulties Canadians have had to face in their struggle to build a united country from coast to coast, from east to west, in defiance of the economic and geographic forces constantly pulling at them from the south. We might also attempt to understand their problems without the self-righteous attitude we frequently adopt. Our American journalist found that a fervid nationalism has fired us up, but what is the basis of the patriotism he discovered? Is it not primarily pride in our material progress, in the new riches and prosperity we have achieved since the War? What other deep feelings do we share to bind us together as Canadians? We may take great pride as a nation in the wonderful development at Kitimat in British Columbia—where engineers diverted a river into a great tunnel in the Rockies to drive electric turbines located deep in the mountainside —but what else do the people in central Canada or the Maritimes have in common with those in British Columbia? We followed the exciting discoveries at Knob Lake on the Labrador-Quebec border, but is the understanding between Quebec and the rest of Canada greater than it used to be?

(Far left) Louis S. St. Laurent, 1948–57. (Left) John George Diefenbaker, 1957–63.

No nation ever achieved unity and true greatness solely on the basis of material wealth or a negative attitude towards its neighbours. Greatness demands a spiritual and intellectual growth, an inner sense of unity shared to some extent by every citizen in the country. And the way in which we Canadians may reach this higher goal was clearly revealed at the beginning of the 1950s when the federal government appointed a Royal Commission to study the intellectual, non-economic side of Canadian life. Under the direction of the Rt. Hon. Vincent Massey, this Commission reported that Canada was a country with very little cultural development. In accordance with the recommendations of this report the federal government began to give grants to the universities and in 1957 created the Canada Council to encourage writers, painters, musicians and others who contribute to the intellectual life of Canada. The grant total of the Canada Council in 1970 was $30 million.

There is no doubt that the Canada Council marks the path which Canadians must strive to follow with greater vigour in the future. We need exciting musicians and poets to sing about Canada, vigorous painters to catch her grandeur and beauty, inspired novelists and playwrights to dramatize her way of life, historians to reveal the heroes and the romance too long buried in her past and gifted teachers to preserve and interpret her traditions in glowing words. And above all, we need people who appreciate such things and understand their value. Only when Canadians from coast to coast and enjoy national intellectual achievements shall we be able to resist the cultural influence of the United States. And only then shall we become a truly great nation.

The Politics of Change

While it is not the function of this book to discuss the merits of present-day political controversy, we should at least briefly note the changes in leadership since 1945. Perhaps in recognition of their efficient management of the country in the war years, their welfare legislation and the general prosperity of the times, the voters of Canada maintained the Liberal Party in power all during the first post-war decade. As a result, Mackenzie King was able to retire in 1948 while still in power, having served as prime minister for a longer time than any democratically elected leader in modern history. He was replaced by Louis St. Laurent, a successful corporation lawyer from Quebec. Meanwhile the Conservatives, hoping to find some formula to end the long Liberal sway, selected George Drew as their leader instead of John Bracken. But despite his outstanding achievements as Premier of Ontario, Drew was unable to lead his party to victory in either the 1949 or 1952 federal elections. Finally, when ill health forced his retirement in 1956, an enthusiastic Conservative convention selected John Diefenbaker to be their sixth party chieftain in less than twenty years.

By this time the opinion was growing that the Liberals, having been in office so long, had become extravagant and indifferent to the wishes of the people and that the country needed a change. This general feeling of discontent, combined with the bitter controversy over the Suez crisis, the closure forced by the Liberals on the Trans-Canada Pipeline debate in the House of Commons, and the dynamic oratory of their new leader, carried the Conservatives in 1957 to their first election victory in twenty-two years, though they did not have a majority. Hoping to get a more decisive verdict, Diefenbaker soon dissolved parliament and called for another general election. This time the voters left no doubt whatsoever. On March 31, 1958, they returned the Diefenbaker government to Ottawa with 208 seats and the largest majority in Canada's political history. Between these two elections St. Laurent retired, leaving a crumpled Liberal Party to the leadership of Lester B. Pearson. As the Liberal Minister for External Affairs and Canada's spokesman at the United Nations, 'Mike' Pearson had established a brilliant international reputation.

For almost the next ten years, the story of Canadian politics centred around these two men. Indeed, the sixties brought to Canada a period of political turmoil unparalleled since the early days of Confederation. In the decade following the Diefenbaker triumph of 1958 there were four elections and three of them resulted in minority governments. In 1962 the Progressive Conservatives secured a slim margin of victory but with their 116 seats were dependent on support from an N.D.P. group of 19 and 30 Social Credit members. In the elections of 1963 and 1965 the Liberals secured the largest party standings in the House, 129 and 131 respectively, but that magic majority number of 133 continued to elude both parties.

Prior to the 1968 election, the Progressive Conservative and Liberal parties chose new leaders. The Conservatives selected Robert Stanfield, a successful provincial politician who had brought Nova Scotia into the Conservative fold in 1956. The decision to replace Diefenbaker by Stanfield seriously split the convention delegates and adversely affected the party's chances in the upcoming election. In place of Mike Pearson, who wished to retire, the Liberals chose Pierre Elliott Trudeau, a wealthy intellectual and Minister of Justice in the Pearson cabinet. Trudeau's particular political style, his personality and relatively 'mod' appearance fitted the mood of the sixties and the Liberal Party swept into power in the 1968 election. However, in the election of October 1972, the Conservatives won 107 seats and Liberals only 109; the N.D.P., led by David Lewis, marshalled their

(Far left) Lester B. Pearson, 1963–68. (Left) Pierre Elliott Trudeau, 1968–

biggest-ever group of 31 members, and the Creditiste Party in Quebec, headed by Réal Caouette, elected 15. Trudeau entered a precarious period of minority rule.

Any final assessment of this decade which brought Canada into the seventies must await the objectivity of future observers. It was a time of high statesmanship and low political intrigue, a time of power struggles within the parties themselves, a time when the politicians were regarded by the Canadian people with cynicism and almost despair. Yet there were triumphant achievements like the Canadian Bill of Rights, the Indian Franchise Act, progressive welfare legislation, the Canadian flag, the glory of Expo, and many others, but above all, by the time the decade ended there was a new spirit of political awareness among the people of Canada that augurs well for the future.

Divided We Stand

Terror in the Streets

'It has now been demonstrated to us by a few misguided persons just how fragile a democratic society can be, if democracy is not prepared to defend itself, and just how vulnerable to blackmail are tolerant, compassionate people.' With these words Prime Minister Pierre Trudeau explained to the Canadian people the passing of the War Measures Act on October 16, 1970. The act, which suspended all civil liberties in Canada, had never before been used in peacetime. This step had been requested by the Quebec authorities, including Premier Robert Bourassa. The reasons given for this emergency measure were the kidnapping of James Cross, British Trade Commissioner in Montreal, on October 5, the kidnapping and murder of Pierre Laporte, Quebec Minister of Labour and Immigration, on October 10, and 'a state of apprehended insurrection' in the province occasioned by the activities of Le Front de Libération du Québec (F.L.Q.).

On Saturday evening, October 17, the F.L.Q. called Radio Station CKAC in

(Right) A Canadian soldier in combat uniform stands in front of Montreal city hall in October 1970 after Premier Bourassa requested assistance from the federal government to protect public buildings during the Cross–Laporte kidnapping crisis.

Montreal and instructed a reporter to pick up a message at Place des Arts. It read: 'In the face of the arrogance of the Federal Government, and of its valet Bourassa, the F.L.Q. has decided to act. Pierre Laporte, Minister of Unemployment and Assimilation, has been executed at 6.18 tonight by the Dieppe Cell (Royal 22nd).' A crudely drawn map was included to show where Laporte's body was to be found. Minutes later, police, reporters, and soldiers converged on a parking lot in St. Hubert. The kidnap car was there. Cautiously a demolition squad opened the trunk and found the body of Pierre Laporte.

'As long as we live in Canada, where anybody can express his thoughts freely, then we should rid our system of those who use bombs in attempts to achieve their goals. We should all be ready to fight the clique trying to reform things with terror and terrorism.' Thus had spoken Pierre Laporte, a leader in the reform movement in Quebec and a journalist for *Le Devoir*, where he had exposed corruption in the Union Nationale government of Maurice Duplessis. In 1962 he had become municipal affairs minister in the Lesage government. A confirmed believer in the federal system of government, he had alienated the radical nationalists in Quebec by bluntly declaring against 'a national state which would be a myth and on whose altar the safety and well-being of its citizens would have to be sacrificed'. The discovery of his body sent through every Canadian a wave of revulsion and horror and brought the sombre realization that assassination was now part of our political scene.

For two long months the ordeal of James Cross continued and the nation held its breath in expectation of additional disaster. At last the kidnappers' hideout was discovered, and on December 3 James Cross was freed. His abductors were given safe-conduct to fly to Cuba in exchange for his release. Two days before, the House of Commons had approved a Public Order Bill to replace the controversial War Measures Act. Canadians breathed easier, but we all knew now that it could happen here; the days of innocence were over.

The Quiet Revolution

Before World War Two, Quebec had dwelt in self-imposed isolation. This isolation had been a sincere attempt by the conservative rural population of Quebec and the church hierarchy to preserve the language and culture of the province from any threat of assimilation by English-speaking Canada. But Quebec had suffered. The economic scene had been dominated by interests, mostly English-speaking, whose objectives were exploitation of resources and cheap labour supply, the social structure had suffered from a rigid class structure almost unknown in the rest of Canada, and the provincial government had seemed determined to preserve a paternalistic status quo.

Late in the fifties and during the sixties a new trend, sometimes called the Quiet Revolution, became apparent in Quebec. Certain major factors contributed to this

(Left) The government's invocation of the War Measures Act in October 1970 aroused strong and conflicting emotions in the Canadian people. The flag atop the Peace Tower flies at half mast for Quebec's Labour Minister Pierre Laporte.

change: the growth of urban population and industrial development accompanied by an increase in radical trade union movements; a trend away from the old, classical educational system towards technological and social science training; the increased role of the government in social service; the growing belief that the provincial authority had to be the protector of the native culture; and the waning power of the Church. Prominent in the Quiet Revolution were Father Georges-Henri Levesque, former Dean of the Faculty of Social Sciences at Laval University, Pierre Trudeau and Gérard Pelletier, co-founders and co-editors of *Cité Libre*, 'the magazine which helped to change a society', Claude Ryan, editor of the powerful Montreal newspaper *Le Devoir*, and many other concerned writers and politicians.

Political events moved quickly in Quebec during the sixties. Maurice Duplessis, ultra-conservative leader of the Union Nationale Party, died in 1959, and in the election of June 1960 the Liberal Party, led by Jean Lesage, came into power. The following six years saw sweeping reforms. The educational system was modernized; the vast power corporations were formed into the Quebec Hydro and administered by the province; and the General Investment Corporation was set up to develop and own the secondary industry of the province. The limited success of the Lesage government reforms slowed down in 1966, and with the return to power in the same year of the tradition-bound Union Nationale under the leadership of Daniel Johnson, the Quiet Revolution became for a time a tranquil revolution.

In 1970 the Liberals returned to power under the youthful Robert Bourassa with a clear majority of 72 seats. Few provincial elections have ever been watched with greater interest than this one. From 1960 on there had been a revival of the demand for special status for Quebec within the framework of Canada. Indeed, many well-intentioned and sincere Quebecois felt that Quebec should become an independent state and yet maintain economic ties with Canada. There was a meteoric increase in the number of radical separatist groups in the province and to many of these, change was too slow in coming. The proposed changes of the older parties were unacceptable to many Quebecois because they implied a continued dominance by the English-speaking establishment. Admission by Donald Gordon, president of the C.N.R., that French Canadians were not proportionately represented in senior positions in that organization, Prime Minister Diefenbaker's apparent unwillingness to set up a study on biculturalism and bilingualism, and a lack of knowledge in the rest of Canada of the transformation that was taking place in *la belle province*, alienated the Quebecois. In 1962 Dr. Marcel Chaput announced the formation of the Republican Party of Quebec, and a new organization, the F.L.Q., came into being. Dedicated to establishing a Marxist independent country of Quebec, and allegedly linked to militant left-wing groups in Algeria and Cuba and to the Black Panthers in the United States, this group used all the techniques of terrorism—bombings, thefts, kidnappings, and the ultimate weapon of assassination. Their activities have aroused hostility and distrust in the rest of Canada towards even the more moderate supporters of the Quiet Revolution.

The most important separatist party to emerge from the nationalistic revival in

Quebec was the Parti Quebecois, led by the articulate René Levesque, a former member of the Lesage cabinet. In the election of 1970 the party won only seven seats but—and this is a most important statistic—they captured 23% of the popular vote as compared to 42% for the victorious Liberals. Well organized, with a dynamic leader, this group may well be the force to reckon with in any solution to the Quebec problem.

Despite federal attempts to conciliate and adapt to the new wave of political thinking in Quebec, the problem of keeping the province within the confederation of Canada is an extremely crucial and important one today. The Official Languages Act, the Royal Commission on Bilingualism and Biculturalism, the large number of Quebeckers who hold important posts in the federal cabinet, the triumph of Expo '67, are all positive contributions to the unity of our land. But there is widespread resentment in the other provinces by those who feel that a dual language system is unnecessary, unsuccessful and wasteful; in the West by those who are convinced that their interests are being neglected while Quebec's aspirations are being encouraged; by economic critics who believe that Quebec's share of the regional disparity program is too great; by political critics who feel that Quebec's representation in the federal cabinet is out of all proportion. All these attitudes contribute to a dangerous dichotomy in Canadian life. On the other hand, the refusal of the extreme nationalists to accept any solution but complete independence for Quebec merely adds fuel to the divisive fire that threatens our nation today. The bombs are silent at the moment, but most of the problems still remain. And until men of common sense and unbigoted sincerity work out a realistic compromise our land may soon be divided.

Separatism in the West

Although the situation in Quebec is the all-important one, there have been other manifestations of separatist feeling throughout the nation that deserve brief mention. From the viewpoint of the prairie provinces the federal government at Ottawa has done little to solve the problems that plague the grain farmer and have caused a consistent decline in his income over the past few years. Markets are uncertain, freight rates remain high, labour problems slow down grain deliveries, the International Grains Agreement Association has not settled a cost structure for wheat. All these factors have given the West the idea that Ottawa has lost interest in the wheat farmer—yet earlier in our story we remember him as the bulwark of the Canadian economy.

The mood of disenchantment has been intensified by the Official Languages Act. French-speaking Canadians are outnumbered by German- and Ukrainian-speaking Canadians in every prairie province, and in British Columbia there are more Chinese-speaking Canadians than French. Consequently, westerners see little reality in the two-language concept, believing that it is just another sop to Quebec nationalism and fearing that senior government positions will only be given to those from eastern Canada who are bilingual.

The result of this dissension has been the formation of western separatist parties —the British Columbia Separatist Association of Vancouver, the Western Canada

Separatist Movement, with headquarters in Edmonton, and the Dominion of
Canada Party, a Calgary-based group not truly separatist in philosophy but
dedicated to amending the Official Languages Act and seeing that the West gets a
better representation from those who wield the power in Ottawa.

Goin' Down the Road

One of the most highly acclaimed Canadian movies of the sixties was *Goin'
Down the Road*, the story of two young Maritimers and their venture into the
big-city jungles of mid-Canada. The theme of the film is repeated with increasing
frequency every day, for during the past decade migration from Newfoundland,
Prince Edward Island, New Brunswick and Nova Scotia has steadily accelerated;
an estimated 200,000 people have left the eastern seacoast during this time. This
exodus is not surprising when we consider the perennial economic problems facing
the Maritimes.

Forty-five per cent of the low-income earners of Canada live in the East and the
unemployment rate is the highest in the country—10.5% in August 1972. The
traditional primary industries no longer provide enough employment opportunities. Fishing, although the overall catch value continues to increase, has suffered
from the impact of automation in fishing techniques and in the increase of 'floating
fish factories'. From 1961 to 1971 the number of fishermen in Canada declined from
80,000 to 65,000 and this drop has been particularly significant in the Maritimes.
The lumbering industry, already characterized by seasonal unemployment, has
been affected similarly by modern technological advances. The coal mines of Cape
Breton, some of them stretching for three miles under the ocean, are being phased
out because of high production costs.

In an attempt to solve their economic problems the provincial governments are
trying to encourage the increase of secondary industry. Their relationships with
the federal government, and particularly with the Department of Economic
Expansion which was set up in 1968, are extremely close. Financial incentives of
all kinds—forgivable loans, tax-free property inducements, participation of Crown
agencies in running industries that private enterprise has abandoned—have been
used to encourage industrial development. These efforts have had varied success.

Maritimers resent the fact that they are labelled the 'have-nots' of Canada. In
many cases they feel that the federal aid program and grant system lacks understanding and imagination in dealing with their problems, and with their rich
heritage of autonomy and pride in their early history they find unacceptable what
they consider to be condescending paternalism—a 'hand-out' system that acts not
as a permanent cure but rather as a soothing salve. Concern for their economic,
social and language problems has, to some extent, polarized their feelings against
the provinces of mid-Canada. It has particularly influenced the thinking of many
of them against a federal system which they believe relegates the Atlantic
Provinces to a source of cheap labour, exploitable resources, and quaint, neglected
historical sites. This attitude on the part of the rest of Canada may be typified by
the suggestion once made by the *Calgary Herald* that 'tiny P.E.I. should be made
into a national park, if and when amalgamation takes place'!

The *Herald's* scornful suggestion referred, nevertheless, to a possibility that has been considered at various times, that a union between Nova Scotia, Prince Edward Island and New Brunswick would be beneficial. The question was raised again in 1970 when the report of the two-year Maritime Union Study under the chairmanship of Dr. John Deutsch, principal of Queen's University, was presented to the three premiers in Charlottetown's Confederation Chambers. In brief, the report advocated a union of the three provinces following a ten-year period which was to be spent in settling the economic and administrative machinery of the proposed amalgamation. The premiers somewhat cautiously agreed in principle to the submission, but decided that further study of the report was necessary. When these studies are completed, it may well be found that a union would enable the Maritimes by their combined strength to influence the federal government to find permanent remedies for their economic woes and restore their dignity as the birthplace of Canadian Confederation.

Middle Power

Canada in the Space Age
There was a day when a glance at the map was a source of comfort to Canadians. Two great oceans separating us from Europe and Asia, the frozen north, and the friendly strength of the United States to the south seemed to prove that we did indeed live in a fireproof house. Canadian troops might be required from time to time to fight overseas, but no one seriously believed that the ravages of war would ever come directly to our own shores. Now all this has changed. Intercontinental missiles can span the oceans or cross the Pole in a matter of minutes and Canada lies in the direct line of fire between the two greatest military powers the world has ever known. If a third world war does come, Canada will be turned into a modern Belgium with every village in the country standing in the front lines. Never again shall we have to face conscription in its familiar form because the next time everyone, rich and poor, old and young, French- and English-speaking, will be in it together. Underlying every other consideration today must be the thought that the quest of ages has failed to attain its goals; we live in the ever-present danger of war, and civilization possesses the power to destroy itself.

Even before the bomb was dropped on Hiroshima and the world entered the atomic age, Canadian statesmen realized that the old days of isolation and complacency were gone forever. Starting with the San Francisco Conference and the role of our delegates in helping to write the charter of the United Nations, Canada began to take an active and positive part in international affairs—not because she wanted status and recognition, as in 1919, nor to satisfy any selfish national ambitions, but solely because her stake in world peace was obviously so great. Since 1945, therefore, through vigorous membership in the United Nations and a willingness to assume all the obligations of its charter, Canada's international commitments have been carried far afield

Within the limits of her powers as a medium-sized nation, Canada's achieve-

This radar station is a link in our far northern chain of defence installations.

ment in foreign affairs since 1945 stands in favourable contrast to the years when we shut our eyes to the storm clouds gathering in Manchuria, Abyssinia or elsewhere in the world. Representatives from this country took part skilfully in all the early work of the United Nations and when faith in collective security was undermined by the growing tension between East and West, Mackenzie King and St. Laurent were among the first to suggest the North Atlantic Treaty Organization. As a full-fledged member of NATO, Canada provided twelve air squadrons, an infantry brigade and part of her fleet for the defence of the North Atlantic community; she contributed to the building of bases in western Europe and assumed obligations to give military support to NATO countries as far away as Greece and Turkey. When the Korean War broke out, Canada immediately accepted her full responsibilities as a member of the United Nations and eventually made a military contribution that was exceeded only by the United States and Great Britain. Her share in the Korean War and in NATO raised Canada's defence expenditures so high that by the early 1950s some $2 billion, about half the total national budget, were being spent annually for this one purpose.

Canada's post-war interest in foreign affairs reached a fever pitch when British, French and Israeli forces invaded Egypt and brought the Suez crisis to a climax in October 1956. With many Canadians passionately supporting Britain and many others condemning her actions as a return to old-fashioned, high-handed imperialism, public opinion in this country was more seriously divided than at any previous time in recent history. But while the Canadian people debated this question with anger—though frequently with little logic or knowledge—and while the United Nations censured Britain, France and Israel as aggressors, Lester Pearson took the lead in bringing the hostilities to an end. And as we have seen, a United Nations Emergency Force, composed largely of Canadian soldiers, was established to supervise the withdrawal of the invading troops from Egypt and to police the Arab-Israeli borders. Although Pearson received wide overseas acclaim and a Nobel Peace Prize for his efforts, his failure to give unquestioning support to Great Britain at the time of the Suez crisis undoubtedly helped to defeat the Liberal Party in the Canadian general election of 1957.

In the opinion of many observers, the Canadian outlook on foreign affairs slipped badly and became confused and uncertain during the remaining years of the 1950s. If this is true, the change was entirely due to failure of the Canadian people to adjust their thinking to startling new developments that began to rock world opinion within a year of the Suez crisis. In October 1957 the first Russian satellite was launched into orbit around the earth. Sputnik marked man's first faltering step towards conquering outer space. But more than this, Sputnik also began a terrifying new phase in the Cold War because the rockets that put the satellites into orbit could be used to drop hydrogen bombs on almost any city in the world. Thus, by one stroke of science, the fastest bombers, the best fighter planes and interceptors, the most sensitive radar screens seemed to be made obsolete and the world suddenly faced the prospect of a push-button war.

The gigantic, costly race to master outer space left many countries, including Canada, breathless and far behind and underlined once again the awesome power of the United States and Russia. Confronted with forces of such magnitude, it was perhaps understandable that many Canadians should throw up their hands in frustration and say, 'What's the use? What can I do, what can a small nation like Canada do, in a world like this?' And finding no satisfactory answer, no acceptable national foreign policy, the average Canadian was driven to the conclusion that the fate of the world lay in other hands and that he might as well pursue his own daily interests, hoping for the best. Perhaps we let ourselves become too confused by the tumult of the times. Perhaps we were not thinking far enough into the future—or far enough back to the lessons of the past. We were worrying too much about our own immediate security, concentrating too closely on Mutniks, Luniks, Arrow interceptors and Bomarc missiles, and on what to do if war did come. While in the past wars have never been averted by preparing for them, it may well be one of the great ironies of twentieth century history that man's perfection of the ultimate means of destruction has brought him to understand that the use of these doomsday weapons would be unthinkable.

In 1964, attempting to define Canada's role in foreign affairs, the Secretary of State for Foreign Affairs declared: 'Canada's position in the world is that of a middle power. This involves some limitations upon the conduct of Canada's foreign policy but it also provides Canada with opportunities for action.' Indeed Canadians, either military or civilian, have been involved in every peacekeeping operation that the United Nations has initiated, from the Middle East to Kashmir,

(Above) A teacher in Brazil prepares to distribute sandwiches made of Canadian codfish to the children of her school. (Right) A team of Canadian experts who are running Zambia's railways while training Zambians in management techniques.

from Cyprus to the Congo. Following the Geneva Convention of 1954, Canadians took part in the International Control Commission for Laos, Cambodia, and Viet Nam, and at the conclusion of the Viet Nam War were asked to participate in the new peacekeeping force.

In keeping with the relaxation of international tensions, particularly in Europe, and in an attempt to divert defence spending from military equipment to more constructive foreign aid programs, the Canadian government began in 1969, and continues, a reduction of its military contributions to NATO. While this action drew some criticism from NATO members it should be pointed out that since 1950 Canada has contributed over $2 billion to this organization. It should be noted, too, that Canada continues to maintain an army brigade and an air division in Europe and naval forces in the North Atlantic, and participates with the United States in the defence plans for North America.

During the last twenty-five years, Canada has contributed over $6 billion in financial assistance to more than 70 different countries. The Canadian International Development Agency has operated and administered this plan since 1960. In addition, voluntary agencies like the Canadian University Service Overseas (C.U.S.O.) and CARE provide qualified professional and technical manpower, food, educational aids and health services to many of the under-

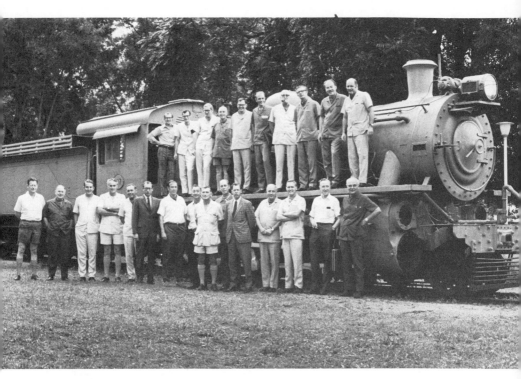

developed nations of the world. Canadians may be proud that our country has contributed so much to the less fortunate nations of the world.

Two major achievements in foreign affairs are due in no small part to Canadian influence during the past few years. They are the improved relationship between the Soviet Union and the West, and the long-delayed acceptance of the People's Republic of China into the United Nations. Despite critical accusations of a do-nothing policy in foreign affairs, the overall policy of Canada—nebulous though it may have seemed—was not merely to be against communism but to seek some sensible method of coexistence. While the political cynics may scoff and declare that it was merely our way of selling our wheat surpluses and maintaining our essential export trade, our economic relationships with the communist countries from the mid-sixties on showed a sense of reality and an awareness of the need for responsible compromise rather than a balance of terror. It should be remembered, too, that during this period in history we did not accept the bullying of communist threats, but welcomed refugees from Czechoslovakia, from Hungary, from Tibet, and from all countries where political repression threatened freedom-loving people.

As our trade relationships with Russia increased, our cultural exchanges expanded, travel between the two countries increased, our heads of state exchanged visits; and all these events gave us a new outlook on a nation that had been isolated from us for such a long time. This did not mean agreement with either the policies or the political philosophy of the Soviet Union. It did mean a better understanding of the leaders and people making up one of the most

important nations in the world. Much the same pattern followed our diplomatic recognition of the People's Republic of China. It may well be that by our dealings with these countries we showed the way towards a lessening of tensions between United States and the two great Asian powers and pointed to some common ground on which to discuss their differences. Middle-power diplomacy may have achieved what brinkmanship never could.

The Invisible Bond

Through her membership in the British Commonwealth of Nations, Canada is associated with some of the least developed countries in the world. Since 1945 the British government has granted independence or self-rule to most of her former colonies in Africa and Asia, but in each case has encouraged them to remain associated with Great Britain in the Commonwealth. The first important step in this direction was taken in 1947 when the British withdrew from India and Gandhi's long crusade for *swaraj*, which we observed in its infancy after the First World War, came to an end. The two main religious groups then decided to go their own separate ways with the Moslems forming the state of Pakistan and the Hindus creating the much larger state of India. These two newly independent republics chose to retain their Commonwealth connections under the leadership of their prime ministers, Liaquat Ali Khan of Pakistan and Jawaharlal Nehru of India. Ceylon, Malaya (later Malaysia) and Ghana (formerly the Gold Coast) early became independent nations within the Commonwealth.

During the sixties several members of the Commonwealth withdrew from the organization—Somali in 1960, the Southern Cameroons in 1961, South Africa in the same year, and the Maldive Islands in 1965. Southern Rhodesia declared its independence in 1965, a fact not recognized by the United Kingdom. In 1964 Tanganyika and Zanzibar united to form the Republic of Tanzania but remained

Statesmen attending the British Commonwealth Conference in London in May 1960. The countries represented are (left to right) Malaya, Ceylon, India, New Zealand, Canada, the United Kingdom, Australia, South Africa, Pakistan, Ghana, and the Federation of Rhodesia and Nyasaland.

within the Commonwealth framework.

Today the Commonwealth numbers twenty-eight nations, with a population of close to 850 million and an area that covers almost one-quarter of the earth's land surface, and includes some of the most important of the emerging African, Asian and Caribbean countries. The entire relationship is quite voluntary and there is no specific political structure. While the Queen is regarded as the symbol and head of the Commonwealth, her actual powers are non-existent. Yet despite its nebulous nature it has achieved much and continues to be an important grouping of nations.

Like all underdeveloped nations, our inexperienced partners in the Commonwealth face gigantic problems in their long, uphill climb towards a new way of life. Distrusting anything that smacks of colonialism, reluctant to take sides in the Cold War, confronted with appalling poverty, illiteracy, overcrowding and disease, yet aspiring to build democratic governments based on principles of liberty and justice, the Afro-Asian countries need encouragement, sympathetic understanding and financial assistance given without any strings attached. Canada has already done a great deal in this direction. Through the Colombo Plan, the federal government between 1950 and 1969 contributed $1.2 billion for capital and technical assistance in Asia and brought over 6,000 people to this country for educational training of all kinds so that they might give more enlightened leadership and service to their respective countries. Since 1958, the year of the formation of the Federation of the West Indies, Canada has contributed over $82 million, in the form of interest-free loans or outright grants, to the Commonwealth Caribbean Program. Following the Commonwealth Prime Ministers' meeting in 1960, a special Commonwealth Africa Assistance Plan was inaugurated. Canada's initial contribution to this plan, which was in essence a Colombo Plan for Africa, was $10 million; by 1969 this annual contribution had risen to more than $25 million. One of the major projects of this plan has been the building, staffing and equipping of the Trades Training Centre at Accra in Ghana. Other groups too numerous to mention are benefiting from our foreign aid program.

Even so, critics frequently remark on the paltriness of our giving to the under-developed nations. And possibly our assistance does add up to a miserly sum, coming as it does from such a richly endowed country whose ordinary citizens enjoy a standard of living far beyond the dreams of the Afro-Asian peoples. In hard, practical terms, every dollar spent on their behalf is a sound investment because it tends to create goodwill and to expand Canadian markets overseas. But this is not the test. Every dollar spent on the fight against world poverty and ignorance may be an investment for democracy and a step towards lasting peace.

Even with much greater financial assistance from the western world, the Afro-Asian countries may not develop according to our wishes. They may fight among themselves, yield to corrupt or dictatorial governments or fall under the influence of communism. We have already witnessed this happening in many parts of the Commonwealth: the power struggle in Ghana that ousted Kwame Nkrumah; the tragedy of Nigeria when the Biafrans attempted to gain their independence; the black-white confrontations in South Africa and Rhodesia; the clash between India and Pakistan in 1971 resulting in the formation of Bangladesh; and the expulsion from Uganda of many of its Asian people even though most were Ugandan-born. Tragic though these events may be, they should come as no surprise. Emerging states beset by tribalism, illiteracy and poverty, where the democratic philosophy is completely alien, will inevitably be faced with trials and agonies. Nevertheless, the risks must be taken because, in the years ahead, the rise to prominence of the Afro-Asian countries may prove to be one of the most important developments of the twentieth century.

The type of problem Canada is likely to face in the future as a member of the Commonwealth was clearly revealed in the spring of 1960 when the black people of South Africa rose in protest against the segregation or 'apartheid' policies of their white government. Justifiably outraged by the brutal consequences of segregation, many Canadians demanded that South Africa should be thrown out of the Commonwealth. Many others, however, argued that expulsion would merely harden Prime Minister Verwoerd's viewpoint and that South Africa should be kept in the Commonwealth where other members might persuade her to modify her policies.

The door was kept ajar but to no avail and South Africa formally withdrew from the Commonwealth in 1961. However, the South African issue within the frame-work of Black Africa tended to become more and more explosive. Following the assassination of Prime Minister Verwoerd in 1966 and U.N. condemnation of the South African refusal to give up the mandated territory that had been assigned to its administration by the League of Nations, the South African government led by Prime Minister Vorster embarked on an arms build-up to protect itself from guerrilla raids and strengthen internal security. Shortly before the Commonwealth Conference at Singapore in January 1972 the United Kingdom was negotiating an arms sale to South Africa. Such an action, it was felt in many quarters, would

The Queen shares a happy moment with Prime Minister L. B. Pearson and Mrs. Pearson during her visit to Canada in 1967. (Photo, The Globe and Mail, Toronto.)

result in the African states leaving the conference and possibly dissolution of the Commonwealth itself. However, the Canadian delegation headed by Prime Minister Trudeau averted possible disaster at the conference by persuading the African delegates that the arms issue should be considered in the context of the entire African community and that Britain would consult with the Commonwealth nations prior to any arms sale. The Canadian diplomats also were influential in drafting a declaration of principles which, in effect, emphasized the continuing diversity of the organization and rejected the use of force or economic pressure in implementing Commonwealth decisions.

Differences of opinion like this are an inevitable and, within reasonable limits, a highly desirable feature of democracy. But when these internal divisions become too sharp, as at the time of the Suez crisis, or when they are based on passion and prejudice, they serve only to undermine the efficiency of our government. It should be apparent that a constructive foreign policy—which is much more difficult to pursue than a purely negative and defensive one—must be founded on enlightened public opinion. And this depends to a very large extent upon our educational system, using the word 'education' in its widest sense to include not only the schools, but the press, radio, television and all other means of mass instruction. As Marshall McLuhan has said, 'The medium is the message.' The future of civilization has become a race between education and catastrophe.

Science can be applied to win wars, but the application of science alone can never bring enduring peace. The successful pursuit of this quest of ages depends more on the existence of a large body of thoughtful, informed citizens, capable of making independent, sound and unprejudiced judgements upon domestic and world affairs. A citizen who ceases to be thoughtful is no longer a good citizen. A civilization that is no longer a thoughtful one will surely die. For peace will not come through weapons of destruction; it will come from the minds and hearts of the thoughtful and informed men and women of our time.

INDEX

ACKNOWLEDGEMENTS

Quotations

F. L. Allen, *Only Yesterday* (New York: Harper & Row), 230
Robert Laird Borden, *Robert Laird Borden: His Memoirs* (Westport, Conn.:
  Greenwood Press, Inc.), 189–90
Winston Churchill, *The Gathering Storm* (Boston: Houghton Mifflin Co.), 311, 338,
  339, 340, 345, 359, 380
A. A. Divine, *Miracle at Dunkirk* (Pleasantville, N.Y.: Reader's Digest), 325–6
Eric Goldman, The Crucial Decade (New York: Alfred A. Knopf Inc.), 395
A. R. M. Lower, *The North American Assault on the Canadian Forest* (Toronto:
  Ryerson Press), 57
E. W. McInnis, *Canada: A Political and Social History* (New York: Holt, Rinehart
  & Winston), 450
Carl Rowan, article (Toronto Star Limited and *Minneapolis Tribune*), 480
R. E. Sherwood, *Roosevelt and Hopkins* (New York: Harper & Row), 383

Photographs and cartoons

Canadian Pacific, 10–11
Canadian Press, 414–5, 458, 471, 476, 482, 487, 488
Eaton's of Canada Archives, 78, 79
Ford Motor Company (by courtesy), 251
Glenbow-Alberta Institute, 59, 192–3, 242, 271
Imperial War Museum, London, 130, 145, 147, 157, 158–9, 317, 331, 352, 385
Information Canada Photothèque, 456, 461, 497
Manitoba Archives, 69, 226
Miller Services, Toronto, 201, 208, 254, 307, 313, 326, 333, 334, 390, 406, 410, 418,
  420, 427, 430, 433, 437, 439
Notman Photographic Archives, 54
Ontario Archives, 61, 66, 74, 77, 126, 185
Ontario Hydro (by courtesy), 256
Public Archives of Canada, 17, 19, 24, 27, 29, 34–5, 38, 45, 49, 51, 52, 53, 82–3,
  119, 129, 132, 155, 160, 166–7, 169, 173 (top), 177, 188, 244, 253, 277, 330, 355,
  365, 369, 449, 450, 451, 454, 464, 484, 486
Saskatchewan Archives, 272–3, 276
Sovfoto, 350, 351
Toronto Star Syndicate, 85, 173 (bottom), 179, 223, 278, 298, 382, 494
United Press International, 135, 290, 302–3
Vancouver Archives, 44
Wide World Photos, 100, 111, 113, 197, 200, 229, 232, 233, 241, 269, 282, 286, 292,
  304, 314–5, 326, 329, 341, 344, 357, 368, 376, 395, 413, 419, 428, 459, 487, 496,
  498–9